AF693399

AN ECONOMIC BACK
TO MUNICH

Soviet and East European Studies

Editorial Board

A. BROWN R. W. DAVIES P. HANSON D. LANE MARY MCAULEY
R. W. PETHYBRIDGE LEONARD SCHAPIRO
G. H. N. SETON-WATSON F. B. SINGLETON

The National Association for Soviet and East European Studies exists for the purpose of promoting study and research on the social sciences as they relate to the Soviet Union and the countries of Eastern Europe. The Monograph Series is intended to promote the publication of works presenting substantial and original research in the economics, politics, sociology and modern history of the USSR and Eastern Europe.

Soviet and East European Studies

FIRST BOOKS IN THE SERIES

A. Boltho, *Foreign Trade Criteria in Socialist Economies*
Sheila Fitzpatrick, *The Commissariat of Enlightenment*
Donald Male, *Russian Peasant Organisation before Collectivisation*
P. Wiles, *The Prediction of Communist Economic Performance*
Vladimir V. Kusin, *The Intellectual Origins of the Prague Spring*
Galia Golan, *The Czechoslovak Reform Movement*
Naum Jasny, *Soviet Economists of the Twenties. Names to be Remembered*
Asha L. Datar, *India's Economic Relations with the USSR and Eastern Europe, 1953–1969*
T. M. Podolski, *Socialist Banking and Monetary Control: The Experience of Poland*
Rudolf Bicanic, *Economic Policy in Socialist Yugoslavia*
S. Galai, *Liberation in Russia*
Richard B. Day, *Leon Trotsky and the politics of economic isolation*
G. Hosking, *The Russian Constitutional Experiment: Government and Duma 1907–14*
A. Teichova, *An Economic Background to Munich*
J. Ciechanowski, *The Warsaw Rising of 1944*

AN ECONOMIC BACKGROUND TO MUNICH

INTERNATIONAL BUSINESS AND CZECHOSLOVAKIA 1918–1938

ALICE TEICHOVA

Reader in Economic History
University of East Anglia

CAMBRIDGE UNIVERSITY PRESS

CAMBRIDGE UNIVERSITY PRESS
Cambridge, New York, Melbourne, Madrid, Cape Town, Singapore, São Paulo

Cambridge University Press
The Edinburgh Building, Cambridge CB2 8RU, UK

Published in the United States of America by Cambridge University Press, New York

www.cambridge.org
Information on this title: www.cambridge.org/9780521200653

© Cambridge University Press 1974

This publication is in copyright. Subject to statutory exception
and to the provisions of relevant collective licensing agreements,
no reproduction of any part may take place without the written
permission of Cambridge University Press.

First published 1974
This digitally printed version 2008

A catalogue record for this publication is available from the British Library

Library of Congress Catalogue Card Number: 72–89811

ISBN 978-0-521-20065-3 hardback
ISBN 978-0-521-07396-7 paperback

Contents

List of tables *page* vii

Acknowledgements xv

Introduction xix

1 The distribution of international investment 1

Creditors and debtors 1

Direct foreign investment in Poland and the countries of the Little Entente 14

2 Foreign investment and international cartels in the economy of Czechoslovakia 30

1 Estimates of direct foreign investment in industry and banking of Czechoslovakia at the end of 1937 30

2 International cartels in the Czechoslovak economy 1929–38 54

3 Mining and metallurgy 62

1 Direct foreign investment in the mining and metallurgy industry in Czechoslovakia 62

2 The participation of the Czechoslovak iron and steel industry in international cartels, 1926–38 137

4 Mechanical and electrical engineering 189

1 Longterm direct investments of foreign industrial combines and banks in the engineering and electrical industry in Czechoslovakia 189

2 International cartels in the mechanical engineering and electrical industries in the Czechoslovak Republic 221

5 The chemical industry 277

1 Chemical products, mineral and vegetable oils 279

2 The influence of international cartels on the Czechoslovak chemical industry 312

6 Banking and longterm foreign loans 336

1 Foreign investment in Czechoslovak banking before Munich 336

2 Foreign longterm loans in Czechoslovakia before Munich 367

Conclusion 377

Sources consulted 383

I List of abbreviations for archives used in this work 383

II List of official publications 385

III List of periodicals 386

IV List of directories and business publications 388

Bibliography 389

Index 405

List of tables

1 1 Longterm investments of the three creditor states (1930) (excluding state loans and short-term investments) *p. 2*

2 Longterm investments of the U.S.A. (excluding war loans) in million $ *p. 4*

3 Distribution of British foreign investments, 1913–30 (%) *p. 5*

4 French longterm investments abroad in 1933 *p. 6*

5 Foreign capital employed in certain countries, 1930 *p. 8*

6 British companies operating abroad. Capital outstanding: dividends and interest received (£m.) *p. 10*

7 Companies registered abroad: nominal amounts of British capital outstanding: dividends and interest received (£m.) *p. 10*

8 Balances of international payments of the United States of America, 1927–37 (in millions of old U.S. gold $) *p. 12*

9 Balances of international payments of France and overseas territories, 1927–37 (in millions of old U.S. gold $) *p. 13*

10 Comparative estimates of longterm foreign investment in Poland and the states of the Little Entente, 1936–9 *p. 16*

11 Foreign capital in the Polish private economy, 1929–35 *p. 18*

12 Transfers of profits, interest, dividends, royalties and other sums from Poland abroad and Poland's income from foreign trade, 1929–35 (in million zlotys) *p. 19*

13 Balance of payments of Yugoslavia, 1926–36 (in million dinars) *p. 22*

14 Transfers of interest, dividends and profits from Czechoslovakia abroad, according to current items of the balance of payments, 1929–37 (in million Kč) *p. 26*

15 Transfers of interest, dividends and profits from abroad into Czechoslovakia, according to current items of the balances of payments, 1929–37 (in million Kč) *p. 26*

16 Balance of payments of Czechoslovakia, 1929–37, merchandise and transfers of interest, dividends and profits (in million Kč) *p. 28*

2 (1) I Distribution according to industries of Czechoslovak industrial, commercial and transport companies, joint-stock banks and insurance companies with foreign capital participation – 31 December 1937 (in 1,000 Kč) *p. 38*

II Distribution by industry of Czechloslovak joint-stock companies with foreign capital participation – 31 December 1937 (in 1,000 Kč) *p. 42*

III Share of direct foreign capital investment in the basic nominal capital of joint-stock companies by branch of industry in Czechoslovakia – 31 December 1937 *p. 46*

IV Direct foreign capital investment in Czechoslovak enterprises – 31 December 1937 *p. 48*

V Joint-stock and basic capital of domestic and foreign companies in the ČSR in 1935 (in million Kč) *p. 52*

VI Territorial distribution of foreign joint-stock companies actively operating in the ČSR in 1935 *p. 53*

2 (2) 1 Survey of cartel agreements of Czechoslovak industrial and commercial companies with foreign firms (1926–September 1938) *p. 56*

2 Survey of cartel agreements between Czechoslovak industrial and commercial companies and foreign firms (1926–September 1938) *p. 60*

3 (1) 1 Territorial distribution of direct foreign capital investment in the mining and metallurgy industry of Czechoslovakia (31 December 1937) *p. 63*

2 Output and employment in mining in Czechoslovakia, 1937 *p. 64*

3 The value of mining output in Czechoslovakia, 1936 *p. 64*

4 Distribution of world steel production, 1929–36 (%) *p. 66*

5 Distribution of pig iron production, including compounds of iron, 1929–36 (%) *p. 66*

6 Steel production in the main European countries, 1929–37 (in 1,000 tons) *p. 68*

7 Pig iron production (including compounds of iron) in the main European countries, 1929–37 (in 1,000 tons) *p. 69*

8 Share of the cartelized and non-cartelized metallurgy industry in Czechoslovak production of crude steel, 1921–36 *p. 73*

9 Share of the Big Three in Czechoslovak crude steel production, 1921–36 *p. 74*

10 Changes of ownership relations in the Vítkovice Mining and Foundry Works (1918–38) *p. 78*

11 Combine of the Vítkovice Mining and Foundry Works, 31 December 1937 *pp. 84–5*

12 Combine of the Mining and Metallurgic Company, 31 December 1937 *pp. 94–5*

13 Eugène Schneider's most important directorships, 1921–1937 *p. 104*

14 Directorships of Aimée Lepercq, representative of Schneider et Cie., 1922–38 *p. 108*

15 Position of the Prague Iron Company in the Mannesmann combine, 31 December 1937 *p. 126*

3 (2) 1 Quotas in the International Steel Agreement of 30 September 1926 *p. 142*

2 Actual balance sheet of the EIA, October 1926–March 1927 *p. 143*

3 Quotas in the International Steel Agreement of November 1926 *p. 144*

4 Percentage shares in export quotas of heavy rails in IRMA, February 1937 *p. 155*

5 Percentage shares in the export of wire products within IWECO *p. 157*

5*a* The participation of Czechoslovak steel industry in the International Steel Cartel, 1938 *p. 161*

6 Quota scheme agreed by members of the ESC on 25 April and 5 May 1933 *p. 162*

7 Export quotas of the Central European Group in Southeast Europe from 1 January 1930 to 30 June 1934 *p. 163*

8 Exports of steel products from Czechoslovakia to Austria, 1926–37 (in metre centners) *p. 165*

9 Export of steel products from Czechoslovakia to Hungary, 1926–37 (in metre centners) *p. 169*

10 Total direct exports of steel and rolled products from Czechoslovakia (all deliveries) *p. 173*

11 Trade in steel products between Czechoslovakia and Poland (1926–37) (in metre centners) *p. 174*

12 Exports of the ISC and Czechoslovak Group (deliveries abroad in tons) *p. 177*

13 Calculations of export quotas for merchant bars according to a communication from ISC of 22 January 1937 *p. 178*

14 Quota shares in the ISC in percentages of total exports (1937–8) *p. 179*

15 Distribution of export quotas among members of the Big Three (10 June 1936) *p. 180*

16 Distribution of import quotas in 'organized' markets for merchant bars among members of the ISC, December 1937 *p. 182*

17 Distribution of import quotas in 'organized' markets for structural shapes among members of the ISC, December 1937 *p. 182*

18 Distribution of import quotas in 'organized' markets for thick plates among members of the ISC, December 1937 *p. 183*

19 World price movements of some steel products from June 1926 to December 1937 with special reference to the effectiveness of international cartels (prices in gold £ f.o.b. Antwerp) *p. 185*

4 (1) 1 Territorial distribution of direct longterm foreign investment in the engineering industry of Czechoslovakia, 31 December 1937 *p. 194*

2 Comparative state of the Škoda-Works (ŠZ) and the Českomoravská-Kolben-Danek (ČKD) on 31 December 1937 (in millions Kč) *p. 195*

3 Škoda-Works combine, 29 January 1937–30 September 1938 *pp. 200–1*

4 Czechoslovak–French division of the board of directors of the Škoda-Works between 1919 and 1937 *p. 210*

5 Territorial distribution of direct longterm foreign investments in the electrical industry of Czechoslovakia, 31 December 1937 *p. 218*

4 (2) 1 Participation of the Czechoslovak engineering industry in international cartels, before 1938 *p. 223*

2 Cartel agreement between the Czechoslovak and Austrian manufacturers of wheels, wheelsets, axles and tyres for locomotives, tenders and wagons, concluded 8 December 1920 (valid from 1 January 1920 to 31 December 1922) *p. 227*

3 Changes in export quotas within the Czechoslovak–Austrian cartel concerning wheelsets, tyres and axles for locomotives, wagons and tenders *p. 233*

4 Czechoslovak foreign trade in railway wheels and wheelsets (diameter 36 cm and over), 1926–37 *pp. 234–5*

5 Czechoslovak foreign trade in iron parts of wheels, tyres, wheel disks, wheel spokes, 1926–37 *pp. 236–7*

6 Czechoslovak foreign trade in railway axles, 1926–37 *pp. 240–1*

7 Export quotas in the cartel for forged pieces (1932) *p. 246*

8 Export quotas of rolled zinc products according to cartel agreement of 19 January 1929 *p. 254*

9 Export quotas of rolled zinc products according to cartel agreement of 1 January 1934 *p. 256*

10 Wholesale prices in the Czechoslovak Republic *p. 260*

11 Representation of member groups in the International Cable Development Corporation, Vaduz *p. 267*

5 (1) 1 Territorial distribution of direct foreign investment in the chemical industry of Czechoslovakia (excluding mineral and vegetable oils), 31 December 1937 *p. 279*

2 Association for Chemical and Metallurgical Production (Spolek), 31 December 1937 *pp. 280–1*

3 Territorial distribution of direct foreign investment in the mineral oil and vegetable fat industries in Czechoslovakia, 31 December 1937 *p. 295*

4 Lever Bros. & Unilever combine in Central and Southeast Europe, 31 December 1937 *pp. 300–1*

5 Changes of ownership relations in the Schicht combine, 1918–38 *pp. 304–5*

6 Average earnings in several European factories of the Schicht combine, 1928 *p. 311*

5 (2) 1 The International Nitrogen Cartel *pp. 318–19*

2 Chemical products in international cartels with Czechoslovak participation *pp. 324–5*

3 Foreign trade of the Czechoslovak Republic in hydrogen peroxide 1925–37: cartel no. KR 180 concluded in 1930 *p. 327*

4 Foreign trade of the Czechoslovak Republic in ammonium sulphate 1925–37: cartel no. KR 246 concluded in 1932 *pp. 328–9*

5 Foreign trade of the Czechoslovak Republic in potassium hydrogen sulphate, 1925–37: cartel no. KR 349 concluded in 1933 *p. 330*

6 Foreign trade of the Czechoslovak Republic in potassium sulphate (fertilizer), 1925–37: cartel no. KR 349 concluded in 1933 *pp. 332–3*

7 Foreign trade of the Czechoslovak Republic in sodium hydrogen sulphate, 1925–37: cartel no. KR 349 concluded in 1933 *p. 334*

6 (1) 1 Czechoslovak joint-stock banks with nominal capital exceeding Kč 100 million, 31 December 1927 *pp. 338–9*

2 Territorial distribution of direct foreign investment in Czechoslovak joint-stock banks, 31 December 1937 *p. 343*

3 Czechoslovak joint-stock banks with nominal capital exceeding Kč 100 million, 31 December 1937 *p. 344*

4 Bank for Commerce and Industry, formerly Länderbank, 31 December 1937 *pp. 346–7*

5 Anglo-Czechoslovak and Prague Credit Bank, 31 December 1937 *pp. 352–3*

6 The Czech Bank Union, 31 December 1937 *pp. 354–5*

7 Czech Escompte Bank and Credit Institute, 31 December 1937 *pp. 358–61*

8 Živnostenská Bank, 31 December 1937 *pp. 362–5*

6 (2) 1 Statement of government debts of the Czechoslovak Republic, 31 December 1927 *pp. 368–9*

2 U.S. foreign loans at interest of 8¾ per cent or more annually, in terms of the rate to maturity (based on nominal rate, price to bankers, and length of life of each issue) (in $1,000) *p. 372*

3 Statement of government debts of the Czechoslovak Republic, 1 January 1938 (from the Budget for 1938) *p. 374*

4 Longterm foreign loans in Czechoslovakia, 31 December 1937 *p. 375*

Key to symbols used in tables

→ Direction of investment

- - - Foreign investor in Czechoslovak company

—— Czechoslovak company

═══ Foreign company with Czechoslovak investment

Abbreviations used in tables

C. / Cap.	Capital
Cz.	Czechoslovak
ČSR	Czechoslovak Republic
Kč	Czechoslovak Crowns

Acknowledgements

Over the long years of research for this book and in the writing of it I am indebted to my family, my friends and colleagues and to my students in Czechoslovakia and Britain, and also in the German Democratic Republic, the Federal Republic of Germany and the United States of America. My formal expression of thanks is wholly inadequate but I welcome this opportunity to record how much I benefited from my family's understanding and patience, my students' enthusiasm and my colleagues' interest, the debates with them, as well as their advice, concern and sympathy in difficult and turbulent times.

It gives me great pleasure to offer public gratitude to those who have helped in different ways towards the publication of this book. I am especially grateful to Professor Peter Mathias without whose interest in my work and sustained support this book might not have seen the light of day. To him my warm thanks are due for reading the manuscript. I have also profited from the comments of those colleagues who read the manuscript at various stages in its Czech version: Dr Gerhard Fuchs, Professor K. Gajan, Docent K. Kašík, Professor A. Klíma, Dr O. Kružík, Dr B. Levčík, Professor R. Olšovský, Dr P. Reiman. I must thank my referees appointed by the Cambridge University Press for their incisive reports and I have been guided by their suggestions. The views expressed, however, are my own and for any errors and omissions I must take personal responsibility.

My warmest thanks go to Professor Muriel C. Bradbrook, the Mistress of Girton College, Cambridge and to the Fellows of Girton College, who have given me refuge and made me welcome in their midst as a Bye-Fellow. Thus they created favourable conditions for me to continue my research, and revise and prepare my English manuscript for publication in this country.

At the same time I gratefully acknowledge the hospitality of the President and Fellows of University College, Cambridge, where I was a Visiting Fellow during the academic year 1969–70. My personal thanks are due to Professor Lord Kahn, Miss Esther Simpson, O.B.E., and Dr R. M. Young for their support at that time.

I owe a great debt of gratitude to the institutions which have provided financial aid to further my research. As a member of the teaching community of Charles University in Prague I received aid to travel in search of records in libraries and works archives scattered all over Bohemia, Moravia and Slovakia. I am also grateful for the support of the Social Science Research Council which enabled me – through a research project headed by Mr M. M. Kaser and based at St Antony's College, Oxford – to complete the English version of my book. I am very grateful to Mr Kaser, who also read chapters of my work, for the assistance he has extended to me.

I should like to express my appreciation to all the directors and staff of the archives and libraries in which I conducted my research for their kind and willing cooperation. The list of archives and sources indicates the extent of my indebtedness. I would like to mention Ing. Ivo Kruliš for particularly valuable advice on technological matters during my work in the archives of the National Technical Museum in Prague, and for providing expert service and making me exceptionally welcome. I should like to thank the staff of the works archives of the Škoda-Works in Plzeň and Prague, of the chemical works in Ústí nad Labem and Pardubice, and of the German Central Archives in Potsdam.

The typing and secretarial work has been competently executed and I must gratefully acknowledge the help of Mrs F. Dorcey and Mrs M. Thompson of Girton College and of Mrs E. Hitchborn and Mrs D. Roberts of the University of East Anglia. To my son Peter I extend my heart-felt thanks for his expert draughtsmanship in preparing my graphs for the press.

The greatest debt of all I owe to my husband, Dr Mikuláš Teich, without whose constant encouragement, untiring support, patient advice and helpful comment this book would never have been written, and to him this publication is dedicated.

May 1972 ALICE TEICHOVA

Girton College, Cambridge
and the University of East Anglia, Norwich

Introduction

Munich is regarded as a landmark in modern history. Many authors have enquired critically into the political and diplomatic events which led to the dismemberment of Czechoslovakia in 1938, and in rapid succession to her occupation by Germany and the outbreak of the Second World War. But in none of the published work so far has the economic background to Munich received the attention it deserves. This book helps to redress the imbalance by studying direct foreign investment, foreign longterm loans and the activities of international cartels in Czechoslovakia in the interwar period.

From her foundation on 28 October 1918 to her dismemberment after the Munich Agreement of 30 September 1938 the Czechoslovak Republic remained an independent state, neither owning colonies nor a colony herself. At the same time, her political and economic system was influenced by complex financial and diplomatic relations. The question which then arises and which is discussed in this book, is how the economy of a formally independent and industrially relatively advanced country not under the direct rule of the Great Powers found itself dependent not only on them but also on powerful business and financial groups operating in Central and Southeast Europe.

The book contains a detailed factual study of the presence of foreign capital and its business connections in the interwar economy of Czechoslovakia, which played a key role in Central and Southeast Europe. The extent of the financial links and the intricate relationships with foreign interests are traced far beyond Czechoslovakia and thus a considerable part of the international business network in Europe is revealed. The most important international cartels are studied and analysed and their influence on output, prices and the home and foreign trade of the Central and Southeast European countries is shown. In the process of this undertaking evidence is presented of the increasing severity of competitive struggles in this region, above all, between West European and German financial and business interests in the 1930s.

The book is divided into six chapters, with an introduction and a conclusion. The first chapter surveys the distribution of foreign investment in the inter-war world generally and pays particular attention to France's allies – Poland and the countries of the Little Entente. Thus Czechoslovakia's place in the chain of international investments is established. This is followed by a chapter surveying the presence of foreign capital in the Czechoslovak economy between the wars, and giving an outline of international cartels associated with Czechoslovak industry. It also contains a discussion of the sources and literature used in my research for the book. Separate chapters deal with foreign capital participation and business organization in the main growth sectors of the Czechoslovak economy – mining and metallurgy (chapter 3), mechanical and electrical engineering (chapter 4), the chemical industry (chapter 5). Chapter 6 is devoted to foreign participation in banking and to an assessment of foreign longterm loans.

The results of the study are summarized in the conclusion, where it clearly emerges that the operations of large economic units, such as Schneider–Creusot, Solvay, Imperial Chemical Industries and Unilever, as well as international cartels, have a history. In time their course of action led to the movement of considerable areas of production from a free market situation to an ever more administered production-, marketing- and price system. A substantial part of their international activities in Central and Southeastern Europe was based on and radiated from Czechoslovakia. In this area international political developments before Munich influenced and in turn were affected by economic factors and these relationships are analysed in this book.

I

The distribution of international investment

Creditors and debtors

Just as the First World War resulted in a new division of territories between victors and vanquished, it also led to significant transfers in foreign longterm investment throughout the world.

Until 1914 Great Britain, France and Germany had been the main investors of capital, drawing interest and profits from the majority of nations in the world. After her defeat in the First World War Germany ceased to be a creditor country and became one of the most indebted states, not only in Europe but in the world as a whole. Great Britain still held first place in the world statistics of foreign investment, but the United States of America – a debtor nation before 1914 – took second place, closely following Great Britain. It was clear that she would shortly become the principal exporter of capital and the principal creditor nation. With a much smaller amount of capital investment abroad, France became the third largest creditor in the world. Although other countries also exported capital, on balance their indebtedness was greater than their credits and they were in one way or another tied to the creditor states. Between the two world wars almost all countries were debtors, principally of the United States of America and Great Britain, but to a lesser extent of France: at the same time Britain and France became major debtors of the U.S.A. The countries of Central and Southeast Europe formed a link in the chain of international financial and capital investment relations. Their place in the investment and credit system arose out of the redistribution of territory, spheres of interest and economic forces after the First World War.

Table 1. *Longterm investments of the three creditor states (1930) (excluding state loans and short-term investments)*

	Global (in millions)			In Europe (in millions)		
Countries	Own currencies	Czecho-slovak crowns	%	Own currencies	Czecho-slovak crowns	Percentage of total investments
Great Britain	£3,726	611,064	100	£0.300	49,200	8
U.S.A.	$15,675	517,275	100	$4,282	141,406	30
France	Frs. 72,000	100,800	100	Frs. 40,000	56,000	60

Average value of Czechoslovak crowns in 1930: £1 = Kč 164; $3 = Kč 100; Frs. 76 = Kč 100.

Source: computed from *The Problem of International Investment.*

During the inter-war period, capital investment reached its greatest height in 1930, when the longterm investment of the three main creditor states in all parts of the world amounted to more than £7,000 million.[1] State loans and short-term credits are excluded from this sum, as are investments by Great Britain, the U.S.A. and France in each other's economies (Table 1).

British investment in Europe amounted to only 8 % of total British foreign investment; American investment accounted for 30 % and French investment for as much as 60 % of their respective total investment abroad. On the other hand, British investment in Europe, if we take the sum involved as shown in Table 1, was not significantly smaller than French investment in Europe. The largest proportion of total longterm investment was absorbed by Germany – RM 18,000 million in 1930. Short-term investment in Germany was almost as high as longterm – RM 16,000 million. Of the total foreign investment in Germany, the American share was about 50 %, the British 10–12 % and the French about 5 %. The remainder was held by Holland, Switzerland and Sweden, although a large part of this also came ultimately from the U.S.A., Great Britain or France.[2] After the war, Central and Southeast Europe, formerly

[1] Royal Institute of International Affairs, *The Problem of International Investment* (London, New York, Toronto, 1937), p. 16.

[2] Compiled from data in *The Problem of International Investment*, p. 17.

the main area of German and Austrian economic influence, was drawn into the financial and capital orbit of the Entente Powers and into their mutually competitive struggles.

In all areas towards which the Great Powers directed their capital exports they also became competitors. Investment flowed into the British Dominions and Colonies and into the South American Republics, as well as towards Europe. These three were therefore the most important world markets for capital investment in the inter-war period.

American investors saw favourable opportunities to invest their capital in territories of the British Empire. In spite of the British government policy of preferential tariffs within the Empire and various safeguards directing investment to the Empire, American capital investment penetrated into the Dominions, whose population commanded a far greater purchasing power than that of the rest of the British Empire.[1]

Longterm U.S. investment in the British Empire, mainly in Canada, totalled \$221 million in 1914;[2] by 1930 it had increased to \$4,600 million.[3] British investment was still paramount in the Empire – £2,187 million in 1930, 60% of all British overseas investment.[4] However, Britain's position was seriously threatened by American investors who were often financially much stronger. French capital exports to the British Empire were relatively small.

The Latin American Republics were the third group of countries absorbing capital from leading industrial nations. In 1930 British investment there amounted to £830 million and American investment to about \$5,150 million.[5] Again French investment was relatively small.

Changes in the amount and direction of capital exports can be judged by comparative statistics based on the official figures of the American and British governments. Although these figures cannot be regarded as completely accurate they do show the general tendency of capital exports from the main creditor countries and confirm the outline given here.

[1] *Final Report of the Committee on Industry and Trade*, March 1929 (Cmd. 3282), p. 23.

[2] Cleona Lewis, *America's Stake in International Investments* (Washington, 1938), pp. 652–4.

[3] *The Problem of International Investment*, p. 17.

[4] Ibid.

[5] Ibid.

Table 2. *Longterm investments of the U.S.A. (excluding war loans) in millions $*

Areas of the world	1913	1930	1935
Canada	750	3,942	3,764
Central America	50	276	897 (Central America and Mexico)
Mexico	1,050	695	
South America	100	3,042	2,937
Europe	350	4,929	3,543
West Indies	100	1,233	1,107
Africa	—	118	132
Asia	205	1,023	820
Oceania	—	419	405
Total	2,607	15,677	13,605

Source: The Problem of International Investment, p. 166.

From a glance at Table 2 it is evident that the direction of American capital exports after the First World War, when the United States changed from a debtor to a creditor nation, is not accidental. American capital supported the shaken foundations of the European capitalist states with a variety of longterm investments and credits, while investing large amounts in Canada, South Africa, Australia and other British dependencies. In accordance with their economic Pan-americanism investors in the United States changed the balance of their longterm investments in favour of the Latin American Republics. A group of British economists investigating the problems of international investment in 1937 recognized 'the fact that economic and political interests can never be completely separated'.[1] As evidence they quoted the public announcement made by the Department of State on 3 March 1922, asking American bankers and concerns to inform the State Department of their intended foreign investments and to obtain advice on the desirability of such investments, in view of the national interests involved.[2] After that date almost every foreign loan had the approval of the United States government, which therefore assumed the power to direct foreign investment from the economic as well as the political point of view.

Statistics from Great Britain also show the relative position of

[1] Ibid., p. 180. [2] Ibid., p. 181.

Table 3. *Distribution of British foreign investments, 1913–30* (%)

Areas of the world	1913 (%)	1930 (%)
British Empire	47	59
USA	20	5
South America	20	21
Europe	6	8
Rest of the world	7	7
Total	100	100
Total in million £	(4,000)	(3,726)

Computed from Robert Kindersley, 'British Overseas Investments', *Economic Journal*, 1933.

longterm foreign investment before 1914 and between the two world wars (Table 3). Although it tended to decline, the total of British investments abroad did not change spectacularly between 1913 and 1938. However, significant shifts took place in the composition of foreign investment, thus proving the predominantly defensive character of British investment policy. British investors tried to compensate for the decline in their assets on the American continent by concentrating more on investment in the British Empire. Their interest in Europe increased somewhat after the victory of the Entente over the Central Powers. Western capital then flowed into Central and Eastern Europe and British, American and French interests often clashed.

A similar situation developed in post-war exports of capital from France. There is not enough reliable statistical material for a thorough comparison of the data of all three creditor nations. It is, however, a historic fact that the Quai d'Orsay was closely connected with the high finance of France and that capital exports were strongly influenced – as to a large extent in every country – not only by profit motives but also by French colonial and power-political interests. In accordance with these, French capital investment was directed towards Europe, above all to Poland and the states of the Little Entente. Later, in the 1930s, however, new French investments were almost entirely

Table 4. *French longterm investments abroad in 1933*

Nature of investment	Frs. (in milliards)*	Kč (in milliards)*
Pre-war investments evaluated in 1928	35	49
Capital invested in new colonial and foreign issues 1919–28	5	7
Capital in direct longterm foreign investments 1919–28	10	14
Purchases of direct foreign investments and new issues in the colonies and abroad (1928–33)	22	31
Total	72	101
Sale of foreign investments 1930–3	−12	−17
Total in 1933	60	84

* Average value of Stock Exchange rates in 1933: Frs. 76 = Kč 100.
Computed from *The Problem of International Investment* and Robert Kindersley, *Economic Journal*, 1933.

directed towards her own colonies. Because French finance was hit by the world crisis later than others, French foreign investments, unlike those of other countries, reached their peak in 1933 (Table 4).

Longterm French investment abroad increased between 1928 and 1931 and only in this period was this item in France's balance of payments of the same importance as before 1914.[1] At the beginning of the world economic crisis French foreign investment did not suffer the same fall as British and American; on the contrary, it increased somewhat. However, the following years of crisis did limit French investment considerably.

The salutary state of official statistics and the valuable results obtained from government and semi-official economic and social commissions of enquiry in Great Britain and the United States have made it possible for us to outline, at least approximately, the respective positions of the main capital exporting countries and trends in their investment policies. With French data we come up against a lack of official information about longterm investments abroad and only a very few unofficial guesses exist. Of these the estimates of Pierre Meynial in *La*

[1] *Statistical Year-Book of the League of Nations 1937/38* (Geneva, 1938).

Revue d'économie politique are most acceptable and are usually quoted.[1] The state of information in other countries is far less satisfactory. Reliable statistics on longterm direct foreign investment in European countries are very rare indeed, mainly because official data, even on total direct foreign participation in the economy of individual countries, is practically non-existent. This is especially true concerning the distribution of foreign capital holdings within industries and financial institutions. Precise statistics are available only about foreign government loans. One of the few serious efforts to gain an insight into the overall distribution of foreign capital holdings in various countries was made by the League of Nations in 1930, using information chiefly of a commercial character and data from the balance of payments of the countries under investigation. As a result of this a survey of the distribution of foreign capital investment excluding government loans was produced in 1930. A team of experts from the Royal Institute of International Affairs made some corrections to it and it is reproduced here in Table 5.

Although the numerical data in Table 5 are only approximate, the order of the capital-importing countries corresponds, on the whole, to the actual tendencies in the inter-war period. The place occupied by Czechoslovakia confirms that capital was exported by her, but that on balance more foreign capital was invested in Czechoslovakia than Czechoslovak capital abroad, while other Southeastern European countries were only receivers of investments and did not export capital at all.

The underlying motive for exporting capital is to maximize profits and open up new profitable markets. No capital holding is gained and no credit is provided disinterestedly, however varied the considerations leading to the decision to place foreign investments: e.g. the control and exploitation of sources of raw material; the desire to create an international monopoly in certain products; participation in another country's industrial production, in order to evade tariffs which would be imposed were the goods imported; to take advantage of lower wages than in the creditor nation; or, in extending longterm

[1] Cf. *The Problem of International Investment*, p. 199; also TNEC, *Regulations of Economic Activities in Foreign Countries*, Monograph 40 (Washington, 1941).

Table 5. *Foreign capital employed in certain countries, 1930*[a]

Country	Foreign capital employed: Gross	Foreign capital employed: Net[b]	Interest and dividend payments: Gross	Interest and dividend payments: Net[b]	Foreign capital employed per head
	(£ millions)				(£)
Germany	1,350[c]	925	68	49	20
Canada	1,330	955	56	38	127
Australia	817[d]	753	36	34	122
China	660	580	20	20	1.5
Argentina	640	635	32	32	55
India	575	565	26	25	2
Brazil	520	520	16[e]	16[e]	13
Dutch East Indies	320	320	22	22	5
Cuba	295	295	(1)	(1)	74
South Africa	260	260	15	15	34
Japan	260	50	12	2	4
Chile	250	250	11[f]	11[f]	64
Poland	234[g]	205	11	10	7
Romania	200	200	8	8	11
New Zealand	197[h]	189	9	9	128
Hungary	143[i]	143	7	7	11
Norway	126[j]	94	5	4	45
Austria	120	80	5	3	18
Peru	115	115	(1)	(1)	17
Greece	115	115	6	6	18
Denmark	94[k]	53	5	3	27
Czechoslovakia	88	46	7	3	6
Colombia	85	85	(1)	(1)	9
Venezuela	80	80	(1)	(1)	25
Uruguay	60	60	4	4	3
Yugoslavia	60	60	5	5	5

[a] *Major sources:* League of Nations, Balances of Payments; Corporation of Foreign Bondholders, Reports; Statistical Yearbooks of Canada, Australia, New Zealand, India, and South Africa; Statistical Yearbooks of League of Nations; Staley, *War and the Private Investor*, App. 1; *South American Journal*; *Moody's Manual of Investments*; *Klimber's Record of Government Debts.*

[b] I.e. after deductions on account of each country's investments abroad.

[c] Of which about £575 million consisted of short-term capital.

[d] Of which short-term capital = £34 million.

[e] These figures refer to 1932.

[f] These figures refer to only six months of 1930.

[g], [h], [i], [j], [k] Of which short-term capital: [g] £71 million; [h] £25 million; [i] £49 million; [j] £40 million; [k] £23 million

[1] No accurate estimate can be made because a large part of the foreign capital consists of 'direct' investments.

Source: The Problem of International Investment, p. 223.

loans, to provide purchasing power for products in the lender's country and to profit both from interest on the loans and from the export of goods, etc. to the borrowing country. The increasing importance of capital exports tends to accompany a high degree of concentration and the growth of multinational combines. And in the wake of this development, international economic and political interests become more and more integrated. The powerful financial and industrial groups of creditor states essentially had a monopoly of the world's capital exports between the two wars. They participated in production and trade and drew profits from the countries of all continents in which they had invested their capital. Thus they shared in the domestic economies of all debtor nations.

With the growing importance of international investment after the First World War profits from foreign investment became distinctly more important than profits from foreign trade, although, especially during the boom years of the inter-war period, the volume of industrial output increased absolutely and relatively and the volume of foreign trade expanded. These tendencies had already appeared in Great Britain before 1914, but between the two wars in particular income from foreign investments emphasized the negative balance of trade figures. While the volume of imports into Britain rose by 18 % between 1913 and 1930, exports fell by 32 %.[1] Thus a deficit in the balance of trade arose, which in 1930 amounted to about £392 million,[2] but which was compensated for by profits from overseas investments, as well as income from commissions and payments for services. From a total of about £4,000 million longterm investments overseas, Great Britain received annually about £270 million in profits; the income from shipping services and financial transactions was estimated at £195 million.[3] In the 1930s invisible exports were not always able to compensate entirely for the negative balance of trade,[4] but they became comparatively far more significant in the balance of payments. In this context capital participation by British banks and businesses in industrial enterprises and banks overseas

[1] *Committee on Finance and Industry Report*, Cmd. 3897 (London, 1931), p. 46.
[2] Ibid., p. 305. [3] Ibid., p. 46.
[4] Cf. *Statistical Year-Book of the League of Nations*, Balances of International Payments (Geneva, 1938).

Table 6. *British companies operating abroad. Capital outstanding: dividends and interest received (£ million)*

	Share capital			Loan capital			Total dividends and interest
Year	Nominal amount	Dividends	% of capital	Nominal amount	Interest	% of capital	
1929	802	67.7	8.4	385	18.3	4.7	86.0
1930	815	59.0	7.1	390	17.5	4.5	76.5
1931	813	33.3	4.1	397	15.5	3.9	48.8
1932	816	29.0	3.6	389	13.5	3.5	42.5
1933	823	29.5	3.6	387	12.5	3.2	42.0
1934	840	32.4	3.9	388	13.1	3.4	45.5
1935	849	37.8	4.5	388	14.0	3.6	51.8
1936	840	43.4	5.2	379	13.6	3.6	57.0
1937	847	57.9	6.8	363	13.5	3.7	71.4
	Average dividend 5.3%			Average interest 3.8%			

Table 7. *Companies registered abroad: nominal amounts of British capital outstanding: dividends and interest received (£ million)*

	Share capital			Loan capital			Total dividends and interest
Year	Nominal amount	Dividends	% of capital	Nominal amount	Dividends	% of capital	
1929	436	42.0	9.6	403	19.7	4.9	61.7
1930	391	31.7	8.1	391	19.3	4.9	51.0
1931	376	22.7	6.0	384	18.2	4.7	40.9
1932	344	22.1	6.4	375	17.1	4.6	39.2
1933	345	20.5	5.9	350	14.7	4.2	35.2
1934	352	26.0	7.4	335	13.8	4.1	39.8
1935	370	29.7	8.0	328	13.7	4.2	43.4
1936	377	35.1	9.3	326	13.4	4.1	48.5
1937	390	37.8	9.7	328	12.8	3.9	50.6
1937*	400	21.1	5.2				
	Average dividend 7.56%			Average interest 4.4%			

* Estimate of private and unquoted investments to be added to statistically more reliable estimates for quoted securities.

became particularly important, compared with the provision of credits abroad. This is borne out by Tables 6 and 7.[1]

A comparative analysis of the figures in Tables 6 and 7 shows that the highest rate of profit was obtained from British capital participation in companies which were registered abroad, with an annual average of 7.56 % dividends between 1929 and 1937; even in the years of the Great Depression the average annual rate of dividends never fell below 6 %. The rate of profit was not as high in companies registered in Great Britain and operating overseas. Their dividends averaged 5.3 % during the same period, and fell to 3.6 % in the worst crisis years. The return from credits was much lower than that from direct capital holdings; the average rate of interest from loans to foreign companies with British investments amounted to 4.4 % and from loans to British companies overseas to 3.8 %. Income from credits provided by Great Britain to territories of the British Empire and to other states remained almost unchanged, with a rate of interest of between 3.8 % and 4.3 %.[2] British investments overseas, in particular credits, sustained severe losses during the world economic crisis. Some debtor countries stopped paying interest on their loans and others, like Greece or Germany, absolutely refused to discharge their obligations as debtors. The drop in the volume of British capital holdings in overseas firms in the crisis years was, however, somewhat less severe and picked up more quickly (Table 7). Investment of capital in British companies operating overseas even rose steadily (Table 6), in comparison with the changing volume of British credits.

If we compare the effect of the 1929–33 crisis on the volume of and income from British trade and credits, on the one hand, with its effects on the volume of capital holdings and dividends received from them, on the other, we find that profits from foreign longterm capital holdings show the greatest stability. There can be little doubt that British financial and business circles willingly held on to their direct capital holdings, which provided them with a regular and comparatively safe income at a relatively high rate of profit.

[1] R. M. Kindersley, 'British Overseas Investments 1937', *Economic Journal* (1938), pp. 621, 626 and 630.

[2] Ibid., p. 613.

Table 8. *Balances of international payments of the United States of America, 1927–37 (in millions of old U.S. gold $)*

Year	Merchandise	Interest and dividends	Other services	Total goods and services	Gold	Total
1927	417	679	−572	524	154	678
1928	738	680	−684	734	272	1006
1929	382	699	−681	400	−120	280
1930	386	769	−580	575	−278	297
1931	17	621	−493	145	176	321
1932	150	455	−504	101	−11	90
1933	67	325	−218	174	139	313
1934	−173	220	−169	224	−726	−502
1935	−118	207	−179	−90	−1027	−1117
1936	−155	195	−235	−195	−608	−803
1937	.	.	.	−78	−818	−896

	Capital items			
Year	Longterm	Short-term	Total	Balance due to errors and omissions
1927	−740	845	105	783
1928	−671	−228	−899	107
1929	−90	−95	−185	95
1930	−213	−465	−678	−381
1931	234	−719	−485	−164
1932	247	−489	−242	−152
1933	39	−383	−344	−31
1934	121	94	215	−287
1935	272	635	907	−210
1936	446	244	690	−113
1937	302	174	476	−420

Source: *Statistical Year-Book of the League of Nations 1937/38* (Geneva, 1938).

In the United States, too, income from foreign investment played an increasingly significant role in the inter-war years, compared with income from foreign trade. Between 1923 and 1929 the total income from American capital investment in other countries was three times as great as the estimated profits from foreign trade (i.e. export and import balances, payments

Table 9. *Balances of international payments of France and overseas territories, 1927–37 (in millions of old U.S. gold $)*

Year	Merchandise	Interest and dividends	Other services	Total goods and services	Gold	Total
1927	4.2	479.1		483.3	20.6	503.9
1928	−129.3	619.5		490.2	−253.7	236.5
1929	−435.4	752.4		317.0	−336.7	−19.7
1930	−506.2	708.5		202.3	−459.8	−257.5
1931	−519.1	454.3		−65.8	−725.0	−790.8
1932	−395.3	45.6	156.7	−193.0	−724.4	−917.4
1933	−352.6	72.5	168.5	−111.6	81.1	−30.5
1934	−264.0	98.0	121.4	−44.6	−57.6	−102.2
1935	−232.9	141.0	62.7	−29.2	587.7	555.5
1936	−325.4	149.8	64.3	−111.3	808.7	697.4
1937	−418.2	147.0	125.0	−146.2	.	.

Source: Statistical Year-Book of the League of Nations 1937/38 (Geneva, 1938).

for shipping and other services).[1] This trend continued and was very pronounced during the world economic crisis, when income from private capital invested abroad far exceeded profits from the reduced volume of foreign trade. This is shown in Table 8.[2] The data in this table are not fully comparable with British data, but even so the statistics give a convincing picture of the relationship between income from investment and foreign trade. The enormous growth of American investment abroad made an important contribution to the expanding economic and political power of the United States.

Unfortunately, the quality of French statistics does not permit a similar analysis, or a more thorough comparison with Great Britain and the United States. It is, however, known that the total income from French foreign investment rose between 1920 and 1930 from Frs. 2,000 million to Frs. 4,700 million.[3] In the French balance of payments before 1934, profits from foreign investment constitute the second highest item of income after receipts from the tourist trade; from 1935 onwards income from foreign investments becomes substantially larger than total

[1] *Statistical Year-Book of the League of Nations 1937/8* and *Balances of Payments* (Geneva).

[2] Ibid.

[3] *The Problem of International Investment*, p. 216.

receipts from tourism and takes the first place[1] (Table 9). If we take into account the fact that the French foreign trade balance, just like the British, was strongly negative during these years, then the exceptional significance of regular profits from foreign investments becomes quite apparent.

Direct foreign investment in Poland and the countries of the Little Entente

Economically and politically foreign investment became one of the crucial factors in international relations, and created various patterns of dependency upon the Great Powers among capital importing countries. After the war Central and Southeast Europe – though not physically divided up among the victors of the First World War – became one of the three most important world markets for capital exports from the Great Powers of the Entente.[2]

The shift of interest towards Central and Southeast Europe was doubtless also connected with the loss of the Russian market after the October Revolution in 1917 and the consequent nationalization and confiscation of foreign investment by the Soviet government. In this situation the United States of America took advantage of any opportunity to place longterm credits in Central and Southeast European countries and British and French investors also hoped to find there a substitute for their losses in Russia. Before 1914 the majority of French long-term investment in Europe had been in Tsarist Russia. A leading figure of Polish banking circles, Leopold Wellisz, emphasizing the guarantee given by the Polish state to foreign investors, reminds his readers that of the many thousands of millions of francs invested by France in the territory of the former Russian Empire the only part to be saved was that which had been invested in Poland.[3] Half of British investment in Europe before 1914 was also understood to have been in Russia.[4] It is therefore easy to understand why other European areas attracted the interest of investors in London and Paris.

[1] *Statistical Year-Book of the League of Nations 1937/8.*

[2] The role of foreign capital in the Balkan countries is discussed in an article by L. Berov, 'Le capital financier occidental et les pays balkaniques dans les années vingt', *Études balkaniques*, T. II–III (Separatum) (Sofia, 1965).

[3] L. Wellisz, *Foreign Capital in Poland* (London, 1938), p. 152.

[4] *The Problem of International Investment*, p. 145.

In addition France, Britain and the United States wanted, where possible, to take over from their defeated German and Austrian competitors in Central and Southeast Europe. The new states in this territory, although politically and formally independent, were in reality encompassed by a net of financial and diplomatic relations reducing them to various degrees of dependency: the world's largest combines and the great banks increasingly asserted their influence on their economies; their politics were, in effect, subordinated to the political power systems of the Great Powers. Governments and influential business circles in Central and Southeastern European countries put these policies actively into effect by leaning heavily – financially and politically – on their stronger allies in domestic and foreign policy. Thus, the states of Central and Southeastern Europe became increasingly dependent upon the financial resources of France, Great Britain and the U.S.A. The degree of dependence varied in the different countries but usually more or less corresponded to the proportionate strength of foreign capital in their economies.

Foreign investors turned their attention not only to the defeated states (Germany, Austria, Hungary, Bulgaria, etc.) but also to Poland and the states of the Little Entente. The factors common to these countries were: considerable foreign indebtedness, a great deal of direct foreign investment in their economies, significant foreign participation in their armament industries[1] and, last but not least, the vital interests of foreign banks and industrial combines who had invested capital for profitable returns.[2] At the same time the differences between the countries of Central and Southeast Europe in which foreign capital was invested were not negligible. The impact of foreign capital on these countries depended on their own economic strength, on their social structure and on their state of development. Czechoslovakia had features in common with other states in the area and also differed from them in some important respects. These differences are shown by comparing statistical estimates of the amount of foreign longterm investment in Czechoslovakia with the amount of foreign investment in Poland, Yugoslavia and Romania. In the absence of reliable Polish, Yugoslav or Romanian source material, information is taken from con-

[1] Ibid., p. 21.

[2] Cf. TNEC–Monograph 40, p. 46.

Table 10. *Comparative estimates of longterm foreign investment in Poland and the states of the Little Entente, 1936–9*

Country	Foreign debt as % of total public indebtedness	Industrial enterprises: Direct capital investment in joint-stock companies as % of total share capital	Industrial enterprises: Direct capital investment in limited companies as % of their total capital	Direct capital investment in banks (as % of their total capital)	Direct capital investment in insurance companies (as % of their total capital)
Poland (1936)	63	44.2	89.7	29*	—
Yugoslavia (1937)	85†	61	—	75	—
Romania (1939)	90	83	—	73–5	70
Czechoslovakia‡ (1937)	17.5	29	3	15	26

* Data refer to 1931. † Data refer to 1932.
‡ Only Czechoslovakia also exported capital.
Source: L. Wellisz, *Foreign Capital in Poland*; B. Jurković, *Auslandskapital in Jugoslawien.* Figures for Romania were estimated from *Anuarul Statistic al Romăniei* (1938, 1939), *Statistisches Taschenbuch von Rumänien* (1941) and *Statistica Soc. An.* xx (1938).

temporary semi-official publications and, where possible, from estimates made on the eve of the Second World War. Neither official nor semi-official statistics exist for Czechoslovakia; the estimates and their evaluation which form the major part of this book are my own. Table 10 provides a basis for comparing approximate magnitudes. It does not claim numerical precision but does aim to show the relative position of Czechoslovakia in the distribution of foreign investment between the Central and Southeastern European countries.

Poland

Poland occupied the fourth place in Europe (excluding the Soviet Union) in population (33.4 million) and the fifth place in area (388.000 km²).[1] More than 60 % of Poland's population

[1] *Statistická ročenka Republiky československé* (Statistical Yearbook of the Czechoslovak Republic) (Praha, 1937), p. 303; further data concerning Poland are taken from L. Wellisz if not otherwise stated.

were involved in agriculture. As a predominantly agricultural country with comparatively little developed industry, considerable natural wealth and a low wage level, Poland attracted foreign capital. She herself did not export capital and the rather insignificant amount of Polish investment abroad[1] mainly represented selling agencies and branches of Polish companies in which foreign capital participated. In the inter-war years a stream of government loans from the Entente Powers flowed into the country, together with private capital investments in Polish banking and industry. According to estimates, on 1 January 1936, the total amount of foreign investment in Polish banking and industry somewhat exceeded the sum total of government and municipal loans to Poland from abroad. Direct foreign investments and all forms of foreign credit – except public loans – extended by foreign investors to Poland up to 1 January 1936 were estimated at 3,800 million zlotys and the foreign debt of the Polish state and municipalities amounted to 3,600 million zlotys. On 1 October 1936 the foreign debt of the Polish Government amounted to 63 % of Poland's total public indebtedness.

Direct foreign capital participation in Polish industry was at a similarly high level. According to official estimates, on 31 December 1935 foreign holdings amounted to 44.2 % (i.e. 1,714.5 million zlotys) of the total capital of all joint-stock companies in Poland. Foreign capital participation in limited companies, which still played a very important role in the structure of the Polish economy compared with the Czechoslovak, was 89.7 % (i.e. 226.4 million zlotys) of the total. Foreign capital predominated in the leading branches of industry; in mining and metallurgy foreign capital participation came to 71 % in joint-stock companies and 93.1 % in limited companies; in the electric power industry to 81 % in joint-stock companies and 99.7 % in limited companies; in the chemical industry to 60 % in joint-stock companies and 87 % in limited companies. The largest foreign investor in Polish industry was France and the second the U.S.A. The Germans took the third place, although their investments fell considerably on the eve of the Second World War, while those of British investors rose.

[1] *The Problem of International Investment*, p. 223.

Table 11. *Foreign capital in the Polish private economy, 1929–35 (in million zlotys)*

Year (31 December)	Short-term bank credits	Cash credits to industrial enterprises	Goods credits	Share in Polish enterprises	Capital and credits of branches of foreign enterprises	Long-term bond credits*	Total
1929	676	1,828	1,116	1,474	366	194	5,654
1930	643	1,829	525	1,654	371	189	2,211
1931	401	1,884	244	1,685	340	317	4,871
1932	292	1,689	138	1,751	326	312	4,508
1933	248	1,540	122	1,754	323	310	4,297
1934	259	1,262	110	1,737	312	284	3,964
1935	276	1,154	95	1,692	301	273	3,791

* Private longterm mortgage credit institution loans and longterm debenture bond-issues of private enterprises.

Direct foreign participation in Polish banks was calculated at 29 % (76 million zlotys) in the 1931 statistics. The largest number of shares was held by French and British banks. Foreign credits to Polish private enterprise, although falling off between 1929 and 1935, continuously exceeded the sum total of foreign direct capital investment. This emphasizes even more the decisive significance of foreign capital in Poland before the Second World War.

Table 11 confirms the greater stability of direct longterm capital investment (cf. the column 'Share in Polish enterprises' and the column 'Longterm bond credits to Polish industry') compared with short-term credits.[1] Short-term bank credits fell steeply in the crisis years and did not show any marked tendency to revive in the period of recovery. Direct longterm capital investments and credits, on the other hand, showed an overall expansive trend.

It is difficult to establish a precise measure of profits from

[1] Compiled by L. Wellisz from official statistics and from private business and banking information given exclusively to the author, cf. p. 131.

Table 12. *Transfers of profits, interest, dividends, royalties and other sums from Poland abroad and Poland's income from foreign trade, 1929–35 (in million zlotys)*

Year	Transfers in respect of cash credits	Transfer in respect of company profits and other sums	Total remittances from investments	Remitted* by government and local government boards and state-owned banks	Total transfers	Income from foreign trade
1929	113.2	172.4	285.6	137.5	423.1	−298
1930	130.0	163.1	293.1	190.9	484.0	187
1931	103.6	157.2	260.8	198.0	458.8	411
1932	72.1	98.0	170.1	130.0	300.1	222
1933	43.7	73.6	117.3	109.1	226.4	133
1934	41.3	66.8	108.1	69.1	177.2	176
1935	31.3	58.2	89.5	63.5	153.0	65.5
Total 1929–35	535.2	789.3	1,324.5	898.1	2,222.6	896.5

* Interest and commissions on the government, local government and state-bank indebtedness.

capital directly invested in private enterprise, as there are various ways of transmitting profits from country to country, in addition to the straightforward international transfers which have become part of inter-company relations in multinational combines. Also, part of the sums earned by foreign investment might remain in the country for further investment or be ploughed back into the concerns which generated them. The only statistically discernible transfers are those which appear in the balance of payments. Thus for Poland these transfers of profits, dividends, interest and other sums are shown in Table 12 and are compared with Poland's income from foreign trade.[1]

The structure of the balance of payments of a capital importing country is, of course, the complete reverse of that of a leading creditor nation. Although the exact data for total transfers of profits from foreign investments out of Poland are

[1] Ibid., pp. 39, 185–6, and data from *Bilans Płaticzny Polski* and *Concise Statistical Yearbook of Poland.*

held to be much higher, it appears quite clearly from Table 12 that income for foreign trade with Poland between 1929 and 1935 was not at any time sufficient to cover the total outflow from the country in the form of dividends, interests and payments. In the relatively short period recorded in Table 12 total profits of all kinds remitted abroad were almost three times as great as the income to Poland from foreign trade. As Poland's economy was relatively underdeveloped and as there were great financial demands on her, her obligations abroad could have been met only 'by adapting the whole domestic economy of the country to the necessity of securing sufficient means for effecting transfers to other lands'.[1]

Yugoslavia and Romania

Foreign capital obviously had a very strong hold over the economy of Poland. Its hold over Yugoslavia and Romania was even stronger. Austrian, and to a lesser extent Hungarian, capital lost its pre-eminence in the economy of the Succession States, and the intermediary functions of the Viennese banks between Western European finance and the Balkan countries diminished considerably. Germany's capital exports had been mainly directed into East and Southeastern Europe before the First World War,[2] but between the two world wars Germany's previous favourable conditions for economic penetration into the industry and banking of this area practically ceased to exist. On the other hand, capital investment by the Western Powers flowed vigorously and effectively into Central and Southeastern Europe. The most important contributions were made by France, Great Britain and the U.S.A., and, additionally, by investment from Czechoslovakia.

Before the First World War Czech capital was already being invested in industrial enterprises and banks in the territory of the Austro-Hungarian Empire; in the inter-war period further capital investment by Czechoslovak banks and enterprises took place. Much of the Czechoslovak capital export to South-

[1] L. Wellisz, pp. 187–8.

[2] Zd. Jindra, 'K otázce pronikání německého imperialismu na jihovýchod v období před rokem 1918' (The Problem of the Penetration of German Imperialism into the Southeast in the Period before 1918), *Acta Universitatis Carolinae*, Philosophica et historica 2 (Praha, 1961).

eastern Europe was included under the special conditions operating at the time in French and British capital exports. Although the significance of German capital was not negligible, German industrial combines and banks were unable to dislodge France, Great Britain, the U.S.A. and Czechoslovakia from their leading positions in the Yugoslav and Romanian economies, even in the decade when Germany regained her strength, i.e. between 1929 and the outbreak of the Second World War. Only the violent intervention of Germany after 1939 changed the balance of power between Western and German capital investment in this area.[1]

The foreign indebtedness of the state of Yugoslavia amounted to 85% of her total public debt. In the period 1933–7 the external state debt increased further compared with the internal, as a result of additional loans which the Yugoslav Government was obliged to contract in France, Britain and the U.S.A. in order to cover interest, commissions and other payments arising out of previous loans.[2] Taken in order of magnitude French interests were the strongest, with Britain following closely. Capital from France and Britain was predominant in the Yugoslav mining and ship-building industries. Austrian and Czechoslovak investors were principally involved in Yugoslavia's wood, sugar and textile industry and also in banking, while Swiss, American and Belgian capital was invested in the electrical, oil and chemical industry. The weakest group of foreign investors in Yugoslavia were German businessmen and bankers, who could not participate in the capital exports of the financially stronger nations and had to relinquish some of their pre-war positions in Yugoslavia's mining and electrical industries.[3]

The share of foreign investment in the total nominal capital of all Yugoslav joint-stock companies on 31 December 1937 was estimated by B. Jurković at about 61%, and in the 14 most

[1] Germany did not even become the most important foreign investor in Yugoslavia after the occupation of Austria in 1938 and of Czechoslovakia in 1939, as V. Král erroneously maintains (cf. II, p. 19). She remained behind France, Britain and the U.S. until the outbreak of war, although she moved forward somewhat in relation to other countries. Cf. B. Jurković, *Das ausländische Kapital in Jugoslawien* (Berlin, 1941), p. 441.

[2] B. Jurković, pp. 232–40.

[3] Cf. M. Lamer, *Weltwirtschaftliche Verflechtungen Südslawiens* (Zagreb, 1933), p. 57.

Table 13. *Balance of payments of Yugoslavia, 1926–36 (in million dinars)*

Year	Goods, services and gold					Capital items			
	Merchandise	Interest and dividends	Other services	Gold	Total	Longterm	Short-term	Total	All[a] items
1926	−744	−902	1,201	−8	−453	298	210	508	55
1927	−1,776	−1,137	1,621	−8	−1,320	1,437	−287	1,150	−170
1928	−2,180	−1,164	1,797	−4	−1,551	1,086	402	1,488	−63
1929	−531	−1,267	2,527	−5	724	828	−1,290	−462	262
1930[b]	−524	−1,763	268	9	−2,010	.	.	.	.
1931[b]	−620	−1,687	488	4	−1,815	.	.	.	.
1932[b]	−70	−640	255	.	−455	.	.	.	.
1933[b]	124	−296	252	.	80	.	.	.	.
1934[b]	−112	−413	263	2	−260	.	.	.	.
1935[b]	294	−1,092	646	−97	−249	579	−511	68	−181
1936[b]	367	−860	623	−9	121	.	.	.	.

[a] The balances in this column are due to errors and omissions.

[b] In the years 1930–6 amortization payments in respect of public debt are included in debit figures entered under 'Interest and dividends' (instead of 'Longterm capital items'). The amount involved was 85 million dinars in 1935.

Source: S. D. Obradović, *La politique commerciale de la Yugoslavie* (Institut de recherches économiques de l'École des hautes études économiques et commerciales, Belgrade 1939) in *United Nations Balances of Payments 1939–1945* (Geneva, 1948), p. 206.

important banks of the country at about 64% of their total nominal capital. The same author, deriving his results from official data, estimated total participation of foreign capital in Yugoslav banking at approximately 75% in 1937. These figures, however much of an approximation, indicate the predominance of foreign capital in the economic life of Yugoslavia. This is also borne out by the large transfers of payments abroad, leaving Yugoslavia with a mostly negative balance of payments (Table 13).

Similarly, until 1939 the greater part of industry and banking in Romania was in the hands of French, British and American capital. Unfortunately no contemporary statistics are available but it seems that the external debt of the Romanian state amounted to about 90% of Romania's total public indebtedness.[1] In his outline of Romanian history M. Roller estimates – admittedly very roughly – foreign investment in Romanian industrial enterprises at about 50% and in insurance companies at about 70% of their total nominal joint-stock capital.[2] Foreign participation was especially large in Romanian banking, with investments from Britain and the U.S.A. leading: there the ratio between domestic and foreign capital was estimated at 25–27:75–73 between 1934 and 1939; in the five leading banks foreign participation amounted to 83.8%.[3] Neither Yugoslavia nor Romania exported capital.

The burden of remittances of interest, dividends and other forms of profits abroad both on Yugoslavia and Romania was substantial and the governments of these countries, as well as private enterprises and banks, had to call on further foreign capital to enable them to fulfil their financial obligations, thus increasing their foreign indebtedness and dependence on the powerful creditor nations.

Foreign capital therefore found favourable conditions for investment in Yugoslavia and Romania; raw material wealth, cheap labour and outlets for industrialization which were, quite logically, subordinated to the interests of the exporters of capital. The creditor states linked their loans to trade agreements securing a market for their industrial products in these pre-

[1] *The Problem of International Investment*, p. 225.

[2] M. Roller, *Dějiny Rumunska* (History of Romania) (Praha, 1957), p. 467.

[3] B. Spiru, *Freiheit, die sie meinen* (Berlin, 1957), p. 210.

dominantly agrarian countries. At the same time the creditors' economic influence, especially in the case of France, was enhanced by a system of political and military treaties, by which Poland and the countries of the Little Entente were tied to their powerful allies.

Czechoslovakia

Within the network of international capital relations in the inter-war period the pre-Munich Czechoslovak Republic occupied a key position in Central and Southeastern Europe, geographically, economically, politically and strategically. Although Czechoslovakia belonged in area and population to the medium-sized states of Europe (her area of 140,508 km² was the thirteenth largest and her population of 14,729,536 the ninth)[1] in volume of industrial production she was counted among the world's ten leading nations.[2] About half the employed population was occupied in industry, transport and commerce, with a relatively small percentage (38 %) in agriculture. According to the 1930 world population statistics, Czechoslovakia ranked sixth in terms of industrial employment.[3] The productive capacity of Czechoslovakia's industry considerably exceeded her domestic demand. Even though the new state comprised only 21 % of the territory and 26 % of the population of the former Habsburg Empire,[4] she retained about 70 % of the total industrial capacity of the empire,[5] which had provided a convenient outlet for Czech industry and until 1918 had been its home market.

After 1918 Czechoslovak industry, which was comparatively highly developed, was faced with an immensely diminished home market, unable to absorb its products. The problem of foreign trade, of finding export markets, was therefore one of the most pressing questions facing the Czechoslovak economy; the country had to export at least 30 % of its industrial output in

[1] *Statistická ročenka Protektorátu Čechy a Morava*, 1941, p. 143.

[2] R. Wagner, *Panství kapitalistických monopolů v ČSR* (The Rule of Capitalist Monopolies in the ČSR) (Praha, 1958), p. 27.

[3] *Compass*, Čechoslovakei (1939), 2007.

[4] R. Olšovský *et al.*, *Přehled hospodářského vývoje Československa v letech 1918–1945* (Survey of Economic Development in Czechoslovakia 1918–1945) (Praha, 1963), 2nd ed., p. 24.

[5] Ibid., p. 19. The Czech Lands traditionally supplied the other parts of the Habsburg Monarchy with manufactured goods.

order to survive.[1] This continual marketing problem, arising out of a shrinking demand on the domestic market and diminishing export opportunities on the world market, called forth increasing competition on a national and international scale and accelerated changes in the structure of the main branches of industry as well as in agriculture. Tendencies towards concentration in the Czech Lands had appeared quite distinctly before the break-up of the Monarchy, and they intensified rapidly between 1920 and 1929. Further impetus was given to this process by an influx of longterm capital investment by foreign financial groups, which joined forces with the most influential domestic industrial and banking enterprises.

The high degree of concentration and the strong movement towards the formation of monopolistic combines in banking and industry attracted foreign capital investment, as the pyramidal structure which resulted provided opportunities for extensive connections in the economy of Czechoslovakia itself, and favourable conditions for further capital expansion, through subsidiaries of Czechoslovak banks and industrial combines, into the economies of Southeast European countries. During the inter-war period Czechoslovak joint-stock banks and industrial enterprises, either themselves subsidiaries of foreign concerns or closely linked with them, continued to export capital to other Eastern and Southeastern European countries, especially to Czechoslovakia's partners in the Little Entente. In this way 'mixed' Western and Czechoslovak capital found its way into the Southeastern European area. Other structural factors in the economy of Czechoslovakia contributed to the interest taken by investors; a fairly cheap labour force, the comparatively stable political conditions of a bourgeois-democratic system of government, the strategic and geographical position of the country, and the fact that Czechoslovakia was one of the seven largest armament suppliers at that time.[2] Last, but not least, the inflow of foreign capital investment together with increased concentration was deliberately supported by the Czechoslovak government as part of its policy of cultivating the

[1] *Hospodářská politika čs. průmyslu v letech 1918–1929* (Economic Policy of Czechoslovak Industry 1918–1928) (Praha, 1928), p. xli.

[2] *Compass*, Čechoslovakei (1939), Internationale statistische Übersichten, p. 2005.

Table 14. *Transfers of interest, dividends and profits from Czechoslovakia abroad, according to current items of the balance of payments, 1929–37 (in million Kč)*

Year	Interest on state and municipal loans	Interest on credits to industry and banks	Profits from bonds (coupons)	Profits from the film monopoly	Patents	Dividends and profits from property, enterprises and services	Total transfers
1929	330	93	215	65	55	330	1,088
1930	469	118	180	90	60	330	1,247
1931	317	110	177	110	65	300	1,079
1932	263	88	100	52	60	280	843
1933	215	77	100	40	60	280	772
1934	166	87	80	15	80	280	808
1935	225	81	145	21	78	280	830
1936	218	97	136	20	90	271	832
1937	226	109	173	19	97	190	814
Total	2,429	860	1,306	432	645	2,541	8,313

Table 15. *Transfers of interest, dividends and profits from abroad into Czechoslovakia, according to current items of the balances of payments, 1929–37 (in million Kč)*

Year	Interest on state loans	Interest from loans to industry and banks	Profits from bonds (coupons)	Profits from the film monopoly	Patents	Profits from property, enterprises and services	Total transfers
1929	41	65	417	6	20	—	549
1930	39	56	341	5	22	—	463
1931	38	57	383	4	25	—	507
1932	35	47	336	3	25	—	446
1933	33	41	250	7	30	—	361
1934	27	39	200	6	30	—	302
1935	25	39	176	4	30	—	274
1936	25	17	126	6	33	—	207
1937	25	20	134	6	37	—	222
Total	288	381	2,363	47	252	—	3,331

Entente Powers, particularly France. At the same time the Czechoslovak government, actively supported by Czech bankers and industrialists, tried to achieve political and economic consolidation with the assistance of Entente investments and by complicated capital transfers, in order to dislodge German and Austrian economic influence from key positions.

In these complex relationships inter-war Czechoslovakia emerges as both a capital-importing and a capital-exporting country. On balance, however, she remained a debtor country.[1] Official statistics of her indebtedness present a somewhat more favourable picture than data on the indebtedness of Poland, Yugoslavia and Romania. The essential fact, however, of the similarity between these economies of Central and Southeast Europe remains: after the First World War, in spite of substantial changes in the structure of her economy, Czechoslovakia was also an area which attracted longterm Western investment and specifically served as a jumping-off point for further capital expansion in the Southeastern European region.

No official statistical material exists about the volume, distribution or influence of foreign capital in the economy of pre-Munich Czechoslovakia. Figures about the indebtedness of the Czechoslovak state alone are available in the annual 'Statements of State Debts of the Republic of Czechoslovakia', which show that between 1927 and 1937 the average external debt amounted to 20 % of total public indebtedness.[2] Thus, compared with the foreign indebtedness of the Polish, Yugoslav and Romanian states, the Czechoslovak external debt was substantially smaller, in relation to its internal debt. But, in addition to interest payments on state loans, which show substantial transfers of profits, dividends and other sums abroad, other remittances in Czechoslovakia's balance of payments indicate the existence of a significant amount of direct capital investment in the country's economy. Tables 14 and 15 show the relationship between transfers of interest, dividends and profits from Czechoslovakia abroad and from abroad into Czechoslovakia between 1929 and 1937.[3] Czechoslovakia was able to balance

[1] See also conclusion reached by authors of *International Capital Movements during the Inter-War Period*, United Nations (Lake Success, 1949), p. 8.

[2] *Statistická ročenka* (1928–38).

[3] Compiled from *Statistická ročenka* (1929–38) and *Statistická ročenka Protektorátu* (1941).

Table 16. *Balance of payments of Czechoslovakia, 1929–37, merchandise and transfers of interest, dividends and profits (in million Kč)*

Year	Balance of transfers of interest, dividends and profits*	Balance of trade merchandise
1929	−539	534
1930	−784	1.759
1931	−572	1.354
1932	−397	−144
1933	−411	23
1934	−506	898
1935	−556	679
1936	−625	99
1937	−592	992

* Balance of total transfers from Tables 5 and 6.

the constant deficit on this account with her income from foreign trade until the thirties (Table 16).[1]

It is impossible to draw conclusions about the magnitude of foreign investment in Czechoslovak banking and industry simply from the amounts of – and changes in – transfers of profits, dividends, royalties and interest. Nor can the total profits from direct and indirect investment be precisely ascertained, for items in the balance of payments register only sums which were actually transferred from country to country. In the sophisticated interrelations of combines and banks reaching across national borders, innumerable commercial and financial transactions take place which do not appear in official statistics. Remittances in the balance of payments, as shown in Tables 14 and 15, should therefore be regarded merely as showing certain trends which are a helpful indication in an enquiry into the influence of direct foreign capital investment. It is this type of investment which provides the greatest opportunity for the exporter of capital to influence production, the

[1] Ibid. and *Zahraniční obchod Republiky československé* (Foreign Trade of the Czechoslovak Republic) (1929–38).

domestic market and exports of the capital-importing country[1] – and often also its politics.

There can be little doubt that income from foreign investments played a very important part in the economies of Great Britain, the United States and France, which, as creditor countries, drew on a considerable part of the national income of the majority of nations. This situation created tensions between the creditor and debtor nations, especially during the Great Depression of 1929–33, when all differences became more acute and the most indebted states endeavoured to shake off their obligations, if necessary by force.

Although the volume of international investment reached its peak in 1930, a sharp fall occurred in 1931–2 and after that it remained essentially stable until the outbreak of the Second World War. Most conspicuous was the fall in incomes from loans to Europe and Latin America, where a large number of countries repudiated their contractual obligations and ceased to repay their debts. In Europe this was done first by Germany and then by Bulgaria, Greece, Hungary, Romania, Yugoslavia and Sweden. Czechoslovakia continued to meet all financial obligations throughout her independent existence.

Thus on the eve of the Second World War exporters of capital came to think of international investment as a problem arising from the extremely uneven economic development of the various countries, accelerated and worsened by the world economic crisis.[2] However, of all forms of international investment, direct capital holdings appeared to retain the greatest stability and to guarantee investors comparatively high returns.[3] Direct long-term capital holding therefore played an increasingly significant part in international relations. In a general sense, it was in the interest of investors to protect and hold on to their foreign possessions, especially direct longterm capital investments, and in the following chapters evidence is presented to show that no voluntary withdrawal of such investments had taken place before 1938.

1 Cf. TNEC, *Direct Foreign Investments in American Industry 1937*, Monograph 6 (Washington, 1941), p. 100.

2 *International Capital Movements during the Inter-War Period*, pp. 6, 70.

3 '...direct investments came through the depression reasonably well and even increased in value...', J. H. Dunning, *Studies in International Investment* (London, 1970), p. 3.

2

Foreign investment and international cartels in the economy of Czechoslovakia

I Estimates of direct foreign investment in industry and banking of Czechoslovakia at the end of 1937

One of the reasons why no monograph has so far been published on the significance of foreign investment in the Czechoslovak economy during the inter-war period is probably the difficulty of obtaining reliable data. In the pre-Munich period Czechoslovak banks and industrial firms – as indeed those of other countries – did not publicize information about foreign participation in their enterprises. Books on aspects of the economy of Czechoslovakia do not provide figures for the amount or distribution of foreign capital directly invested in the country,[1] nor do the official statistics of the Czechoslovak Republic. A more serious attempt at providing an estimate was made by the League of Nations but even that is rather incidental.[2]

A more reliable measure of foreign capital investment in a country's economy can be obtained in cases where an official or semi-official enquiry has been conducted into investment, concentration or monopoly, as for instance in Great Britain in the 1930s,[3] in Germany in 1928,[4] and in the United States in

[1] Cf. M. Weirich, *Staré a nové Československo* (Old and New Czechoslovakia) (Praha, 1938); V. Klimecký, *Strukturní změny v hospodářství světovém a československém* (Structural Changes in the World Economy and the Czechoslovak Economy) (Praha, 1936).

[2] This applies to the general problem of getting reliable data about the amount of direct capital investment by one country in the economy of another. Cf. *The Problem of International Investment*, p. 16.

[3] Especially data in *The Problem of International Investment*.

[4] *Enqueteausschuß–Ausschuß zur Untersuchung der Erzeugungs–und Absatzbedingungen der deutschen Wirtschaft* (Berlin, 1928–31).

1938.[1] No such enquiry was initiated by the Czechoslovak government before the *Anschluss* of Austria and Munich, but the German occupation authorities in the so-called Protectorate of Bohemia and Moravia ordered the Central Statistical Office in Prague to undertake an investigation of all financial, commercial and industrial enterprises during 1940 and 1941 and at the same time to ascertain foreign participation in them.[2] In this way the German occupation authorities tried to obtain an estimate of the investment gains to the German economy resulting from the dismemberment of Czechoslovakia. Valuable material was collected in the archives of the Central Statistical Office, and was further enriched by a Czechoslovak government enquiry in 1945 into direct foreign investments, in connection with the nationalization of industry and banking in post-war Czechoslovakia.[3] The aggregate results of the German enquiry into the state of combines and foreign investment in 1940–1 and of the 1945 Czechoslovak enquiry were published in Czech economic journals in 1946.[4] However, neither of these enquiries was directed towards ascertaining the state of foreign investment up to 31 December 1937 or 30 September 1938, except for a special comparative investigation into the capital participation of enemy states (Germany, Austria, Italy, Hungary and Romania) in the economy of Czechoslovakia in 1938 and up to 1 May 1945. Thus an estimate was obtained of the spoliation of the Fascist states in the field of capital holdings.[5] In the case of Austria, however, the Czechoslovak State

[1] *Investigation of Concentration of Economic Power*, Temporary National Economics Committee (TNEC), Descriptions of Hearings and Monographs of the Temporary National Economics Committee, 31 vols + 6 supplementary vols, 42 monographs (Washington D.C., 1941).

[2] ASÚS–*Koncernové šetření* (Enquiry into Combines).

[3] ASÚS–cizí účasti–Šetření Statního úřadu statistického o cizích účastech (Enquiry of the State Statistical Office into Foreign Participation).

[4] *Statistický zpravodaj* (Statistical Reporter) v, 479–82, 588–91; vi, 360–4, 393–7; vii, 197–8; *Statistický obzor* (Statistical Horizon) xxiv, 59–84; xxv, 45–65; *Statistický zpravodaj* viii, 149–50; ii, 196–9; *Statistický obzor* xxvi, 56–60; *Československý průmysl* (Czechoslovak Industry) (1946) ii, 46–8. K. Maleček used these publications in his book *Hospodářská diktatura koncernů* (Economic Dictatorship of Concerns) (Praha, 1948) but does not refer to them as his source.

[5] ASÚS, Dobrozdání (Reports on Combines). Cf. Table 5 in A. Teichová, 'Příspěvek k poznání zahraničních spojů finančního kapitálu v Československu' (Foreign Links of Finance Capital in Czechoslovakia), *Sborník Vysoké školy pedagogické*, Filosofie–historie 1 (Collected Studies of the University of Education, Praha, 1957).

Central Statistical Office commented that no precision could be attached to their figures for Austrian capital holdings in 1938.[1]

From the relatively complete and reliable information about foreign investment in German-occupied Czechoslovakia a fairly credible measure of foreign participation in the Czech economy as a whole between 1939 and 1945 can be obtained; in particular, the increase in German direct investment between 1938 and 1945 is measurable;[2] this is not so for the inter-war period. However, in the sources collected in the course of the German and later Czechoslovak investigations there is a comparatively large, although scattered, amount of direct and indirect evidence on the immediately preceding period of the thirties.[3] I have therefore made these official investigations my starting-point in reconstructing foreign capital participation in the economy of

[1] ASÚS, Rakouské kapitálové účasti na podnicích v ČSR dle stavu z roku 1938 (Austrian capital participation in enterprises of the ČSR in 1938); the following note was added to the material: 'The total value of the foreign participation in firms in which Austrian capital was invested cannot be precisely ascertained because data from the ceded frontier districts are not available. On the territory of the so-called Protectorate no exact data could be found. It is very probable that these figures cannot be taken into consideration.' V. Král used these figures in volume I of his *Otázky hospodářského a sociálního vývoje v čs. zemích 1938–1945* (Questions of the Economic and Social Development of the Czech Lands 1938–1945) (Praha, 1957), p. 55, without referring to the reservations of the State Statistical Office regarding the reliability of their statistical results.

[2] Cf. ASÚS–cizí účasti. Setření Státního úřadu statistického o cizích účastech, Německé kapitálové účasti v podnicích Československa dle stavu z roku 1938 (German capital participation in enterprises of the ČSR in 1938) and Německé kapitálové účasti v podnicích Československa dle stavu k 1. v. 1945 (German capital participation in enterprises of the ČSR as to 1 May 1945); cf. A. Teichová, 'Foreign Links etc.'; V. Král, I, p. 55, II detailed analysis of German capital participation during the war 1939–45.

[3] The Enquiry into Combines conducted by the so-called Central Statistical Office of the Protectorate of Bohemia and Moravia, referring to 21 December 1940, consists of questionnaires to all firms and the statistical processing of the resulting data from a number of aspects, including from the point of view of foreign direct investment in the Protectorate. The enquiry continued to gather additional information throughout the period of occupation. After the war the State Statistical Office carried out an enquiry into foreign capital participation in Czechoslovak enterprises, down to 1 May 1945, which comprises questionnaires to individual firms. Some of the information goes back to 1938, but rather inconsistently and not in all cases. Of special value were expert reports submitted by managements of the most important Czechoslovak banks and industrial enterprises, in which foreign investment is often discussed in detail, particularly the mechanism of the German take-over from 1938 to 1945. These materials are now deposited in the Central State Archives in Prague (SÚA).

the country before Munich. Further valuable facts and information were obtained from the main and subsequent Trials of War Criminals at Nuremberg in published[1] and unpublished sources.[2] Of particular importance for ascertaining the property relationships of banks and concerns in Czechoslovakia with foreign financial institutions and combines are materials gathered in evidence for proceedings against Flick, the Minister for the Reich's Economy in the Hitler government, against Kehrl of the same ministry and against Rasche, director of the Dresdner Bank, who with a group of collaborators prepared, planned, and after Munich implemented, the integration of the most important Czechoslovak banks and concerns into the economy of the German Reich.

Company archives were also tapped, especially those of the chemical and metallurgical industries, which are deposited in the State Central Archives in Prague and had not as yet been used for research, nor for the greater part sorted or registered. The study of these materials was extremely helpful in clarifying relations between domestic and foreign holders of capital in Czechoslovak enterprises.[3] At the same time, the unique sources of the Cartel Register, which are deposited in the State Central Archives in Prague, containing over a thousand agreements valid in Czechoslovakia between 1933 and 1945, give in many instances reliable, if dispersed, data about the controlling influence of foreign companies in Czechoslovak industrial enterprises.[4] In the economic section of the Archives of the Czechoslovak Ministry of Foreign Affairs I was able to find and verify data, mainly for the 1930s, in correspondence between the Ministry of Finance and the Ministry of Foreign Affairs. But the bulk of the material in the economic section of the Foreign Ministry's Archives was not sorted or registered and therefore was not accessible to scholars.

[1] Internationales Militär Tribunal, Fall XI, Grüne Serie.

[2] DZAP–Dokumentenbücher, Protokolle, etc.–Nachfolgeprozesse (NID). The material consists of verbal protocols of the trials, testimony of witnesses, submissions of leading politicians, generals, industrialists and bankers, and a large number of documents presented as evidence by the plaintiffs and defendants.

[3] These works archives contained details of the funds of management in the chemical and iron and steel industries, accounts, syndicate agreements between foreign and Cezchoslovak shareholders, reports on investments and trade (see list of archives, pp. 383–5).

[4] The Cartel Register will be referred to as SÚA–KR.

However, the most valuable evidence for the amount and actual influence of foreign capital holdings was found in the works archives of the largest industrial concerns in Czechoslovakia.[1] Certain data about the links between Czechoslovak and foreign capital were collected from reports and correspondence in the Archives of the Central and Regional Czechoslovak Chambers of Commerce and Trade, while a wealth of information on this subject concerning the iron and steel industry was obtained from the archival material of the Selling Agency of the United Czechoslovak Iron Works (Prodejna sdružených československých železáren), which is deposited in the Archives of the National Technical Museum and in the Central Liquidating Office of the Ministry of Foundries and Mines (Archiv Ústřední likvidační správy ministerstva hutí a dolů) in Prague.

The problem of foreign investment in pre-Munich Czechoslovakia should, of course, also be studied in the archives of banks and concerns in the countries which made the investments. Such a course is, however, impossible, as these sources are not open to scholars. Those relevant company histories which have been written, such as those of Unilever, Vickers, Royal Dutch Shell and Imperial Chemical Industries, have been taken into account here. As the archives of the German Democratic Republic have been made available to historians, conditions for studying German inter-war economic interests in Czechoslovakia are now somewhat more favourable. Most relevant in this respect are the *Deutsches Zentralarchiv* in Potsdam and the *Sächsisches Landesarchiv* in Dresden for the period 1919–23, but the archives for the 1930s are more fragmentary. The material of the *Auswärtiges Amt*, the *Reichsinnenministerium* and the *Reichswirtschaftsministerium* provide information especially about Germany's attempts to retain her capital holdings in Czechoslovakia against the pressure of Czechoslovakia's nationalization drive, at the same time documenting the stubborn efforts of German economic and political institutions to penetrate the Czechoslovak economy. From correspondence of German Consulates and the German Embassy with the Czechoslovak government and of the *Auswärtiges Amt* with the German Embassy in Prague a much more precise picture of Czecho-

[1] See list of archives, pp. 383–5.

slovak–German capital relations was obtained. Studies were then extended to the material of the *Deutsche Wirtschafts-Institut* in Berlin, where part of the archives of the Deutsche Bank was deposited. It emerges clearly from this material that the leading German financial institutions regarded Germany's stake in Czechoslovakia as insufficient and kept transfers in property relations, reports and accounts from Czechoslovakia's banks and large enterprises in heavy industries under close observation.

In my first short article on 'Foreign Links of Finance Capital in Czechoslovakia'[1] I outlined some problems connected with direct investment by foreign financial groups in Czechoslovakia before 1938. This evoked a sharp polemical exchange – one of the first of its kind in Czechoslovak historiography of the 1950s – between V. Král and myself[2] in the pages of the *Czechoslovak Journal of History* (Československý časopis historický – *ČSČH*). In his subsequently published book on the aggressive take-over of Czechoslovak banks and industrial combines by German banking and business in post-Munich and occupied Czechoslovakia,[3] V. Král does not solve the problem of the relationship between domestic and foreign capital in the pre-Munich Czechoslovak economy. However, he does interpret the changes in the structure of capital holdings in the Second Republic (30 September 1938–15 March 1939) and in the so-called Protectorate of Bohemia and Moravia as resulting from the decision of the West in the years before Munich to retreat voluntarily from Central and Southeastern Europe, which was to become an exclusive sphere of influence of German imperialism.[4] This concept of 'an economic Munich before the political Munich' had been generally accepted in Czechoslovak historiography and had found its way into almost all outlines of inter-war history published in the 1950s and 1960s.[5] While

[1] A. Teichová, 'Foreign Links etc.' (1957).

[2] *ČSČH* (1958), VI, 3, 542–4; (1959) VII, 1, 114–21; (1959), VII, 3, 473–8.

[3] V. Král, *Otázky hospodářského a sociálního vývoje v českých zemích 1938–1945*, II (Praha, 1958).

[4] Ibid., p. 10.

[5] Cf. e.g. *Na obranu republiky proti fašismu a válce* (Defence of the Republic against Fascism and War) (Praha, 1955); R. Olšovský, *Pronikání německého imperialismu do jihovýchodní Evropy* (The Penetration of German Imperialism into Southeast Europe) (Praha, 1961); R. Olšovský *et al.*, *Přehled hospodářského vývoje Československa v letech 1918–1945* (Survey of Economic Development in Czechoslovakia 1918–1945), 2nd ed. (Praha, 1963) and others.

there certainly was a tendency to avoid further longterm investment in Czechoslovakia, especially after Hitler's rise to power, the concept of a voluntary withdrawal of Western capital holdings to make room for German penetration is untenable.

Using the data and information collected during my research, an attempt was made to reconstruct the history of each significant capital holding by a foreign bank, concern or person in the Czechoslovak economy between the two wars; to ascertain its nominal value, its influence on economic units in the country and the conditions of its origin, its development and its termination, so far as evidence permitted. In this way my further analysis also contributes to the elucidation of the economic roots of the events which led to Munich and to the Second World War.

For a statistical evaluation of total direct longterm foreign investment in the economy of Czechoslovakia the end of the last complete year in the independent existence of the inter-war Czechoslovak Republic was chosen, i.e. 31 December 1937. During 1938 the repercussions of the *Anschluss* of Austria in the spring began to make themselves felt and the events of Munich in the autumn, with the implementation of the Munich Agreement, disrupted the economic life of Czechoslovakia, preparing the ground for her full subordination and integration into Germany.

For statistical purposes the year 1937 offers some further advantages, especially in making comparisons possible. A relatively large number of statistical surveys was published all over the world and statistical series concerning the development of the national economy of Czechoslovakia until 1937 were compiled retrospectively by the Central Statistical Office in Prague.[1] In economic literature generally, on the one hand, 1937 is regarded as still being a 'normal' pre-war year[2] and, on the other hand, a special significance is attributed to it because a recession began to set in about mid-1937 with certain similarities to 1929. Last but not least, comparatively normal international relations were still held to exist.[3]

In the context of the following statistical tables direct foreign

[1] *Statistická ročenka Protektorátu Čechy a Morava, Doplněk za bývalou Československou republiku* (Addition concerning the former Czechoslovak Republic) (Praha, 1941).

[2] For this reason 31 December 1937 was chosen for the enquiry of the U.S. Senate Committee on foreign capital in the American economy. TNEC, Monograph 6.

[3] Cf. R. M. Kindersley, *Economic Journal* (1938), 610.

longterm investment was defined as participation in the nominal basic capital of a bank, industrial enterprise, transport or commercial company. This follows the practice of most statistical investigations into direct foreign capital investments and provides a viable measure for calculations as well as a basis for comparing investments in companies of different legal status. The intention was not to ascertain the exact money value of foreign investment in the economy of Czechoslovakia, but rather to arrive as nearly as possible at an estimate of the magnitude of foreign direct capital participation in relation to domestic capital, and to measure the proportionate shares of the various national groups of foreign investors. For this purpose nominal basic capital served best as a common denominator.

Table I, 'Distribution according to industries of Czechoslovak industrial, commercial and transport companies, joint-stock banks and insurance companies with foreign capital participation – 31 December 1937', shows the number and basic nominal capital of all companies and also of those with foreign participation; the amount of the foreign capital holdings in relation to totals of nominal basic capital of joint-stock and limited companies in the various industries, sectors, and in the economy as a whole. For the total numbers of joint-stock and limited companies, Central Statistical Office data were taken as a basis,[1] but in the column 'Mining and metallurgy' the number of joint-stock companies was increased by one important enterprise, the Vítkovice Mining and Foundry Works, with a basic nominal capital of 599 million Kč. Therefore the total basic nominal joint-stock capital in Table I differs by that amount from the official statistics. In this case it would have been misleading to ignore one of the most significant concerns in the Czechoslovak mining and metallurgic industry and one in which foreign capital participated fully, merely because it could not be legally defined as a joint-stock, or as a limited company. In the 1930s the Vítkovice Mining and Foundry Works had all the main characteristics of a joint-stock company, but, for reasons which are discussed later (p. 81), the owners decided not to carry through the legal change from a mining company to a joint-stock company.[2]

[1] *Statistická ročenka* (1941), 174–5.
[2] PA–VŽKG, Ostrava–VHHT vedení 50, Zisky a ztráty (Profits and losses), 12.

Table I. *Distribution according to industries of Czechoslovak industrial, commercial and transport companies, joint-stock banks and insurance companies with foreign capital participation – 31 December 1937 (in 1,000 Kč)*

Industrial, transport and commercial companies, and banks and insurance companies	Total no. of companies: Joint-stock	Total no. of companies: Limited	Number of companies with foreign participation: Joint-stock No.	Joint-stock in %	Limited No.	Limited in %	Basic nominal capital of all companies: Joint-stock	Basic nominal capital of all companies: Limited	Basic nominal capital of companies with foreign participation: Joint-stock Capital	Joint-stock in %	Limited Capital	Limited in %	Share of foreign participation in nominal capital of all companies: Joint-stock Capital	Joint-stock in %	Limited Capital	Limited in %
Mining and metallurgy	45[1]	25	37[1]	82	8	30	1,807,400[1]	24,300	1,786,690[1]	98	17,000	68	1,145,637[1]	64	15,221	63
Metalworking industry (engineering, power and electrical)	181	248	55	30	6	5	2,040,200	285,600	793,253	39	4,640	2	353,606	17	2,704	1
Chemical industry (also mineral and vegetable oils)	121	127	59	48	5	4	1,306,000	44,000	1,149,122	88	14,020	32	710,581	55	13,000	29
Textile industry	96	64	38	40	—	—	794,800	43,000	451,300	57	—	—	227,937	29	—	—
Glass, porcelain and ceramics industry	125	158	23	18	—	—	684,200	92,500	232,161	34	—	—	74,008	18	—	—
Paper industry	30	24	9	30	—	—	217,100	13,300	135,000	62	—	—	35,510	16	—	—
Food industry	278	159	20	7	—	—	1,465,600	103,200	120,950	8	—	—	58,395	4	—	—
Wood industry	53	61	7	13	—	—	119,400	24,100	34,400	29	—	—	26,859	23	—	—
Building industry	32	89	8	25	3	3	84,400	28,500	77,700	92	2,500	9	18,434	22	2,500	9
Musical instruments	3	4	1	33	—	—	2,400	2,600	1,000	41	—	—	1,000	41	—	—
Leather industry	15	11	—	—	1	9	57,500	3,800	—	—	150	4	—	—	130	3
Sugar refining (119 factories)[2]	—[3]	—[3]	22	—	—	—	—[3]	—[3]	310,956	—	—	—	176,149	—	—	—
Distilling (53 factories)[2]	—[3]	—[3]	7	—	—	—	—[3]	—[3]	48,700	—	—	—	13,678	—	—	—
Other branches of industry	84	148	—	—	—	—	420,500	57,900	—	—	—	—	—	—	—	—
Industrial enterprises total	1,063	1,118	286	30	23	2	8,999,500	722,800	5,141,232	57	38,310	5	2,841,794	32	33,555	4
Commercial companies	122	500	6	5	1	—	362,600	187,900	45,332	13	200	—	33,571	9	50	—
Transport	76	19	7	9	—	—	509,200	9,500	115,361	23	—	—	25,307	5	—	—
Miscellaneous (hotels, pawnshops, theatres, hygienic stores)	94	275	—	—	—	—	256,500	100,300	—	—	—	—	—	—	—	—
Industrial, commercial and transport total	1,355[1]	1,912	299	22	24	1	10,127,800[1]	1,020,500	5,301,925[1]	52	38,510	4	2,900,672	29	33,605	3
Banks (joint-stock)	78	—	7	9	—	—	1,526,900	—	537,750	35	—	—	224,817	15	—	—
Insurance companies	48	—	23	48	—	—	126,447	—	81,150	64	—	—	32,810	26	—	—
Domestic companies total (industry, commerce, transport, banks, insurance)	1,481	1,912	329	22	24	1	11,781,147	1,020,500	5,920,825	50	38,510	4	3,158,299	27	33,605	3
Total of all companies	3,393		353 (10%)				12,801,647		5,959,335 (48%)				3,191,904 (25%)			

Explanations: percentages are always given in relation to the basic nominal capital of all joint-stock companies or all limited companies.

[1] including basic capital of the Vítkovice Mining and Foundry Works;

[2] number of industrial enterprises according to data in *Statistická ročenka* (1941);

[3] number of joint-stock companies and total nominal capital not known.

The branches of industry in Table I are quoted in accordance with the nomenclature of the Statistical Yearbook of the Czechoslovak Republic and the distribution of foreign capital holdings in Czechoslovak industry, commerce and banking has been adjusted as far as possible to official statistics, although a certain lumping together of industries has resulted from this. This, however, has been rectified in the detailed Table IV, 'Direct foreign capital investment in Czechoslovak enterprises – 31 December 1937', in which industries are separated and are easier to survey. However, mining and metallurgy is cited as one industry throughout, as these two branches are inseparably interlocked in all respects. The concept of 'Metalworking industry' in the official statistics is, moreoever, unsuitable for our purposes, because it includes parts of the metallurgical as well as the mechanical and electrical engineering industries.[1] To avoid mistakes in the calculation of foreign participation the official concept of the 'Metalworking industry' had to be extended in Table I to include engineering, the electrical industry and electrical power industry, as these were so closely integrated in the field of foreign investment. Also in the official statistics[2] the chemical industry includes the mineral- and vegetable-oil industry and the numbers of companies with foreign participation and the amounts of basic nominal capital were, therefore, adjusted to accord with this concept in Table I. Similarly, it was necessary to put together into one column the 'Glass, porcelain and ceramics industries' because many of the larger enterprises in which foreign capital was invested produced goods of all three kinds. The vertical and horizontal overlapping of various industries causes statistical problems which had to be solved case by case in order to arrive at tolerably acceptable results.

A further problem is presented by sugar refineries and distilleries, which in official statistics are not specified as branches of industry, but are included in the number of joint-stock companies under the heading of 'Food industry'. In my results, however, there is a clearly definable number of joint-stock sugar refineries and distilleries with foreign capital participation and a clearly definable amount of basic nominal capital involved,

[1] Cf. *Statistická ročenka* (1941), 176 and notes on p. 179.
[2] Ibid., p. 176.

which I included in Table I. The Statistical Yearbook of Czechoslovakia gives the numbers of sugar refining plants[1] and distilleries,[2] which are included in Table I, but they do not coincide with the numbers of joint-stock companies in these industries, and therefore no figure could be arrived at for the total joint-stock capital in sugar refining and distilling. The total number of joint-stock banks and insurance companies and the amount of their nominal capital were calculated from the official Statistical Yearbooks and *Compass, Čechoslovakei.*[3]

The advanced stage of concentration in the structure of Czechoslovak industry and banking emerges perceptibly from Table I. In this connection the decisive position in the economy of joint-stock as against limited companies is significant. While the number of limited companies was more than a third greater than that of joint-stock companies, the total basic nominal capital of limited companies amounted to barely one-tenth of that of joint-stock companies in Czechoslovakia at the end of 1937. Foreign capital was obviously more interested in investment opportunities in joint-stock companies and actually participated only in 1–2 % of the total number of limited companies, with a relatively insignificant 3 % share in their total basic nominal capital. While foreign participation in the basic nominal capital of limited companies came to 63 % in the mining and metallurgy industry, to 29 % in the chemical industry and to 9 % in the building industry, there was no foreign capital invested in limited companies in any of the other branches of industry, where the number of firms was large but the total basic capital relatively unimportant. In spite of this I have summarized in Table I not only the number of all joint-stock companies, banks and insurance companies, and the amount of their nominal capital, but also the same information for all limited companies, in order to present as full a picture as possible. Thus at the close of 1937 there existed a total of 3,393 companies in Czechoslovakia and in 353 of them direct foreign capital investment was ascertained, i.e. foreign capital participated in about 10 % of all enterprises. The total basic nominal capital of all 3,393 companies was Kč 12,801,647,000, of which Kč 5,959,335,000, or 48 %, formed the capital of

[1] Ibid., p. 173. [2] Ibid., p. 183.
[3] Ibid., pp. 223; *Compass, Čechoslavakei* (1939), 246, 1371.

the 353 companies with foreign investment. This means that only 10 % of the total number of companies were directly involved with foreign investment, but their aggregate capital amounted to 48 % of the total basic nominal capital of all Czechoslovak enterprises in industry, trade, transport and banking. This is evidence of a significant degree of concentration and is, at the same time, an indication that foreign capital was invested mainly in the economically stronger enterprises.

The last figure in the last column of Table I shows that, at 31 December 1937, foreign participation accounted for about 25 % of the total nominal capital of all companies. The total basic nominal capital of the 353 companies with foreign investment amounted to Kč 5,959,335,000, of which the share of foreign participation was calculated as Kč 3,191,904,000, i.e. 53 %.

This foreign investment – speaking in mere numerical terms – was able to exert a direct influence on about half the basic nominal capital (i.e. 48 %) of the Czechoslovak economy. On the other hand, this leaves 52 % of the total basic nominal capital in the hands of domestic enterprise.

As joint-stock companies were of decisive significance in the economic structure, Table II, 'Distribution by industry of Czechoslovak joint-stock companies with foreign capital participation – 31 December 1937' calculates the participation of direct foreign investment in them and the proportion of domestic to foreign capital in 'mixed' companies, i.e. in Czechoslovak joint-stock companies containing foreign investment. Table II shows that foreign capital participated in 329, i.e. 22 %, of the 1,481 joint-stock companies.[1] The aggregate nominal capital of all 1,481 companies amounted to Kč 11,781,147,000, of which 50 %, i.e. Kč 5,920,825,000, was directly interlocked with foreign capital. The concentration of the Czechoslovak economy emerges here, when it is seen that 22 % of the companies own 50 % of the capital of all joint-stock companies in industry, trade, transport, banking and insurance. Foreign capital participation in the 329 companies in which foreign investment was found amounted to Kč 3,158,299,000, i.e. 27 % of the total nominal capital of all joint-stock com-

[1] Inclusive of the Vítkovice Mining and Foundry Works – viz. footnote 2, p. 37.

Table II. *Distribution by industry of Czechoslovak joint-stock companies with foreign capital participation – 31 December 1937 (in 1,000 Kč)*

Industrial, transport and commercial companies, banks and insurance companies	Number of joint-stock companies			Nominal basic joint-stock capital			Share of foreign participation in nominal basic capital of joint-stock companies		
	Total	With foreign participation							
		No.	in %	Total of all companies	Companies with foreign participation	In % of all companies	Amount of foreign participation	In % of all companies	Proportion of domestic to foreign capital in 'mixed' companies*
Mining and metallurgy	45[1]	37[1]	82	1,807,400[1]	1,786,690[1]	98	1,145,637[1]	64	36:64
Metalworking industry (engineering, electrical and power industry)	181	55	30	2,040,200	793,253	39	353,606	17	56:44
Chemical industry (also mineral and vegetable oils)	121	58	48	1,306,000	1,149,122	88	710,581	55	38:62
Textile industry	96	38	40	794,800	451,300	57	227,937	29	49:51
Glass, porcelain and ceramics industry	125	23	18	684,200	232,161	34	74,008	18	68:32
Paper industry	30	9	30	217,100	135,000	62	35,510	16	74:26
Food industry	278	20	7	1,465,600	120,950	8	58,395	4	52:48
Wood industry	53	7	13	119,400	34,400	29	26,859	23	22:78
Building industry	32	8	25	84,400	77,700	92	18,434	22	76:24
Musical instruments	3	1	33	2,400	1,000	41	1,000	41	—:100
Leather industry	15	—	—	57,500	—	—	—	—	—
Sugar refining (119 factories)[2]	—[3]	22	—	—	310,956	—	176,149	—	43:57
Distilling (53 factories)[2]	—[3]	7	—	—	48,700	—	13,678	—	71:29
Other branches of industry	84	—	—	420,500	—	—	—	—	—
Industrial enterprises total	1,063	286	30	8,999,500	5,141,232	57	2,841,794	32	45:55
Commercial companies	122	6	9	362,600	45,332	13	33,571	9	26:74
Transport	76	7	9	509,200	115,361	23	25,307	5	88:22
Miscellaneous (hotels, pawnshops, theatres, hygienic stores)	94	—	—	256,500	—	—	—	—	—
Industrial, commercial and transport total	1,355[1]	299	22	10,127,800[1]	5,301,925[1]	52	2,900,672[1]	29	46:54
Banks (joint-stock)	78	7	9	1,526,900	537,750	35	224,817	15	58:42
Insurance companies	48	23	48	126,447	81,150	64	32,810	26	60:40
Total (industry, commerce, transport, banks and insurance)	1,481	329	22	11,781,147	5,920,825	50	3,158,299	27	47:53

See notes to Table I for [1], [2] and [3].
* 'Mixed' companies are Czechoslovak firms with direct foreign investment.

panies. The ratio of foreign to domestic capital in these companies appeared as 53:47.

Foreign capital participation was greater in industrial enterprises than in banking, commerce and transport. Foreign investment was directly associated with 30 % of the industrial enterprises shown in Table II, influencing 57 % of the total nominal joint-stock capital of all companies in industry. The absolute amount of foreign participation in the nominal joint-stock capital of Czechoslovak industrial enterprises as a whole was calculated as 32 %, and the proportion of foreign to domestic capital in industrial enterprises containing foreign investment was 55:45.

In commercial and transport companies foreign investment was found to be relatively small on the whole; on the other hand, the proportion of foreign to domestic capital was strikingly high in those commercial companies in which foreign investment was present, i.e. 74:26.

Out of a total of 78 joint-stock banks, foreign capital was invested in 7, in which the relationship between foreign and domestic capital was calculated as 42:58. Foreign capital participation in Czechoslovak banking as a whole was estimated at 15 %. Insurance also attracted foreign investment and at the end of 1937 48 % of all joint-stock insurance companies were found to contain foreign capital, and these companies together held 64 % of the total capital in Czechoslovak insurance. The amount of foreign capital invested was calculated at 26 % of the aggregate nominal joint-stock capital of all insurance companies; and the proportion of foreign to domestic capital in 'mixed' companies stood at 40:60.

It is evident from Table II that foreign direct investment was not distributed evenly over all branches of industry in Czechoslovakia. The greatest participation of foreign capital was observed in the basic branches of modern industry, which had attained a relatively high degree of concentration.[1] In mining

[1] The high degree of concentration and monopoly is discussed in R. Olšovský *et al.*, and also in A. Dobrý, *Kdo vládl v předmnichovské republice* (Who ruled the pre-Munich Republic, Praha, 1958), P. Eisler, *Monopoly v hutnictví kapitalistického Československa* (Monopoly in the Metallurgical Industry of Capitalist Czechoslovakia, Praha, 1955), *Monopoly v hornictví kapitalistického Československa* (Monopoly in the Mining Industry of Capitalist Czechoslovakia, Praha, 1956), *Monopoly v chemickém průmyslu kapitalistického Československa* (Monopoly in the Chemical Industry of Capitalist Czechoslovakia, Praha, 1959), R. Wagner.

and metallurgy foreign capital participated in 82 % of all companies and owned 64 % of the total joint-stock. Directly, and in an obviously decisive way, it could influence 98 % of the basic capital in this branch of industry. It would serve no useful purpose, nor would it be easy, to separate mining from metallurgy, as foundries and iron and steel works owned coal and iron mines and, as a rule, mines and iron and steel works were controlled by one or the other of the three biggest concerns in the country. The case with enterprises falling under the heading of 'Metalworking industries' in Table II is somewhat different, because this column expresses the sum of several more independent branches of industry, i.e. the engineering, electrical and electric power industries, which were not as closely interwoven as mining and metallurgy. Altogether foreign direct investment amounted to 17 % of their aggregate nominal joint-stock capital and the proportion of foreign to domestic capital in companies containing foreign investment came to 44:56. However, if we separate engineering from the electrical industry we obtain a more precise numerical picture.[1] In the Czechoslovak engineering industry foreign capital held about 16 % of the total joint-stock, but its share rises steeply to 40 % if we take account only of the companies in which it participated directly. Similar figures were arrived at for the electrical industry – including power works – where foreign capital participation was estimated at 26 %: in 'mixed' companies the share of foreign capital was 52 %. The figures for the chemical industry also include mineral and vegetable oils, in accordance with the definition of the Central Statistical Office in Prague (Table II), and thus a 55 % share of foreign capital holdings was obtained, with the proportion of foreign to domestic capital in the companies with foreign investment amounting to 62:38. By separating these two branches of industry a clearer insight can be obtained. In the chemical industry, excluding mineral and vegetable oils, 33 % of the total nominal capital was found to be in foreign direct investment,[2] and in the 'mixed' companies the relation of foreign to domestic capital was 46:54. On the other hand, an absolute predominance of foreign capital emerges in the

[1] *Compass, Čechoslovakei* (1939), statistical data for 1937 on pp. 774 and 1053.
[2] Total joint-stock capital in the chemical industry, according to *Compass, Čechoslovakei* (1939), amounted to *c.* Kč 968 million in 1937, cf. p. 939.

Czechoslovak mineral and vegetable oil industry, where foreign participation reached 97 % of the total basic nominal capital.[1]

The percentage of foreign participation in the Czechoslovak textile industry was relatively large, amounting to 29 % of the total nominal joint-stock capital. In textile enterprises containing foreign investment, the average proportion of foreign to domestic capital was 51:49. Considered in terms of the traditional belief in the purely Czech character of the food industry, the amount of foreign participation in sugar refining and distilling is remarkable. Foreign capital holdings were found in 22 sugar refineries, where the relation of foreign to domestic capital was found to be 57:43. In 7 distilleries foreign participation amounted to 29 %. If we add foreign investment in sugar refining and distilling to total foreign joint-stock capital in the food industry, foreign participation in this branch of industry rises from 4 %[2] to 17 %, whilst the proportion of foreign to domestic capital remains at 48:52. In the glass, porcelain and ceramics industry, and in the paper, wood and building industries foreign capital participation averaged around 20 % of the total nominal joint-stock capital, as shown in Table II. For a clearer survey of the percentage share of direct foreign investment in the capital of joint-stock companies in which foreign participation was identified, Table III presents the distribution of foreign capital in order of magnitude and according to branches of industry.

It is apparent from Tables I to III that at the end of 1937 foreign capital was directly invested in a substantial majority of the enterprises in the mining and metallurgy industry and in the mineral and vegetable oil industry, that it participated widely in the chemical, textiles and electrical industries, and held a comparatively smaller share of the wood, building, glass, porcelain, ceramics, food, engineering and paper industries in Czechoslovakia. There was also considerable foreign capital in Czechoslovak insurance and banking. It can be maintained without exaggeration that before 1938 there was no significant branch of industry in Czechoslovakia in which foreign capital was not directly invested.

[1] Estimates for the total joint-stock capital in the mineral and vegetable oil industry were derived from data in *Statistická ročenka* (1941) and *Compass* (1939), pp. 997–1010.

[2] See Table II – Food Industry.

Table III. *Share of direct foreign capital investment in the basic nominal capital of joint-stock companies* by branch of industry in Czechoslovakia – 31 December 1937*

Industries†	Share of foreign investment in Czechoslovakia: In all companies (%)	In companies containing foreign investment (%)
Mineral and vegetable oils	97	97
Mining and metallurgy	64	64
Musical instruments	41	100
Chemical industry	33	46
Textile industry	29	51
Electrical industry	26	52
Wood industry	23	78
Building industry	22	24
Glass, porcelain and ceramics	18	32
Food industry	17	52
Engineering industry	16	40
Paper industry	16	26
Commercial companies	9	74
Transport companies	5	22
Insurance companies	26	40
Banks	15	42

* Including one mining company, see explanation in Table I.

† The industries are ordered according to the amount of foreign participation in the total basic nominal capital.

In the preceding statistical analysis foreign direct investment has been conceived as an undifferentiated entity distributed over the field of industry, commerce and banking in Czechoslovakia. This is, however, only one aspect of its distribution. The other, complementary, aspect is its distribution according to the countries of origin. In this respect substantial changes took place in the structure of foreign investment in post-1918 Czechoslovakia, which largely reflect competitive struggles in the international capital export market.

In ascertaining the countries of origin of foreign investment in Czechoslovakia before 1938 a number of problems arise, mainly connected with the complex structure and interrelationships of international capital. The salient factors in deciding the source of a capital investment are different from case to case, and many questions have to be considered. For instance: which person, company or bank actually holds shares or stocks and of which kind; where is the international investor, combine or company based; where are profits and dividends from the Czechoslovak enterprise remitted; which countries do foreign members of the board of directors of Czechoslovak companies come from; where are the centres of control situated which influence the production, technology, finance and trade of the Czechoslovak enterprise in question; if there is a group of foreign investors in the same enterprise, what are the mutual relations of their individual shares; how do relations between foreign and domestic capital differ in the individual enterprises; and many other specific problems. By applying this questioning as thoroughly as possible and supporting my conclusions on the nationality of the investment with evidence wherever relevant material was available, I arrived at the results shown in Table IV. This table contains an analysis of the territorial distribution of total foreign investment, as well as the territorial distribution of foreign investment in the individual branches of industry and finance within the Czechoslovak economy.

Thus, before the *Anschluss* of Austria and before Munich eleven countries participated in direct capital investment in Czechoslovakia. From Table IV the striking prominence of Western European direct investment in banks and industrial enterprises emerges, with British, French, Dutch and Belgian participation amounting to 68 % of total direct foreign investment. Germany took fifth place after Holland, holding just over 7 %. Great Britain and France possessed by far the greatest share of direct foreign investment in Czechoslovakia, holding between them more than half of the total, i.e. more than all the other countries taken together. This percentage was arrived at in spite of the fact that British and French investment was probably underestimated in my calculations, while Austrian participation was probably inflated. For Austrian investments in the ČSR, which come third in Table IV, frequently included undetectable British, French, American or other participation. As no reliable source material about direct foreign investment in Austria is accessible, Austrian holdings in Czechoslovakia

Table IV. *Direct foreign capital investment in Czechoslovak enterprises* – 31 December 1937*

Investment in banks and branches of industry	Origin of investment											
	Great Britain		France		Austria		Holland		Germany		Belgium	
	In 1,000 Kč	%	In 1,000 Kč	%	In 1,000 Kč	%	In 1,000 Kč	%	In 1,000 Kč	%	In 1,000 Kč	%
Banks	54,425	24.2	100,068	44.5	—	—	—	—	—	—	38,320	17.1
Mining and metallurgy	706,912	61.0	174,001	15.0	102,340	8.8	—	—	117,694	10.1	24,348	2.1
Mineral- and vegetable-oil industry	5,638	1.4	42,950	10.5	—	—	256,719	62.1	—	—	—	—
Chemical industry	76,615	24.8	78,409	25.3	25,575	8.3	—	—	25,475	8.2	83,743	27.1
Textile industry	56,929	25.0	35,473	15.6	78,608	34.5	7,780	3.4	2,020	0.8	11,749	5.3
Engineering industry	9,596	4.4	164,319	73.8	11,600	5.2	2,000	0.9	4,900	2.1	7,637	3.4
Sugar refining	8,710	4.9	59,380	33.7	82,942	47.1	—	—	—	—	20,417	11.6
Electrical industry	14,409	10.8	6,701	5.1	3,623	2.7	11,400	8.5	44,376	33.3	16,271	12.2
Glass, porcelain, ceramics	22,322	30.2	10,500	14.2	8,000	10.8	1,299	1.8	11,993	16.1	4,142	5.6
Food industry	3,716	6.4	—	—	45,163	77.3	4,000	6.8	—	—	2,586	4.4
Paper industry	2,483	7.0	1,644	4.6	16,145	45.5	—	—	—	—	14,278	40.2
Commercial companies	249	0.7	—	—	29,732	88.5	—	—	—	—	640	1.9
Insurance companies	—	—	—	—	—	—	—	—	8,014	24.4	—	—
Wood industry	2,270	8.5	—	—	—	—	—	—	—	—	560	2.1
Transport	7,731	30.5	710	2.8	—	—	—	—	12,160	48.0	—	—
Building industry	12,170	58.2	—	—	—	—	—	—	3,360	16.0	1,934	9.3
Distilleries	64	0.5	—	—	13,175	96.2	—	—	—	—	493	3.3
Miscellaneous†	—	—	—	—	1,130	100.0	—	—	—	—	—	—
Total	984,239	30.8	674,155	21.4	418,033	13.1	283,198	8.8	229,932	7.2	227,064	7.1

Investment in banks and branches of industry	Origin of investment										Total	
	Switzerland		U.S.A.		Italy		Sweden		Hungary			
	In 1,000 Kč	%	In 1,000 Kč	%	In 1,000 Kč	%	In 1,000 Kč	%	In 1,000 Kč	%	In 1,000 Kč	%
Banks	—	—	8,004	3.6	24,000	10.6	—	—	—	—	224,817	100
Mining and metallurgy	1,000	—	5,998	0.5	6,077	0.6	10,348	0.9	12,140	1.0	1,160,858	100
Mineral- and vegetable-oil industry	39,552	9.6	69,662	16.4	—	—	—	—	—	—	414,521	100
Chemical industry	2,413	0.8	11,000	3.6	5,080	1.6	750	0.3	—	—	309,060	100
Textile industry	28,002	12.3	180	—	7,196	3.1	—	—	—	—	227,937	100
Engineering industry	6,296	2.8	3,670	1.6	1,440	0.6	11,600	5.2	48	—	223,106	100
Sugar refining	—	—	812	0.5	3,888	2.2	—	—	—	—	176,149	100
Electrical industry	22,764	17.1	7,420	5.6	—	—	6,240	4.7	—	—	133,204	100
Glass, porcelain, ceramics	6,300	8.5	2,332	3.2	2,680	3.6	—	—	4,500	6.0	74,008	100
Food industry	2,930	5.1	—	—	—	—	—	—	—	—	58,395	100
Paper industry	—	—	—	—	960	2.7	—	—	—	—	35,510	100
Commercial companies	3,000	8.9	—	—	—	—	—	—	—	—	33,621	100
Insurance companies	4,000	12.2	—	—	20,796	63.4	—	—	—	—	32,810	100
Wood industry	22,979	85.5	90	0.3	960	3.6	—	—	—	—	26,859	100
Transport	4,006	15.9	700	2.8	—	—	—	—	—	—	25,307	100
Bulding industry	2,400	11.5	750	3.5	320	1.5	—	—	—	—	20,934	100
Distilleries	—	—	—	—	—	—	—	—	—	—	13,678	100
Miscellaneous†	—	—	—	—	—	—	—	—	—	—	1,130	100
Total	145,642	4.5	110,618	3.5	73,397	2.2	28,938	0.9	16,688	0.5	3,191,904	100

* Including all enterprises irrespective of their legal status.

† Musical instruments Kč 1,000,000; leather industry Kč 130,000.

could not be broken up statistically into their component parts. The actual share of British investment, which takes first place in Table IV, amounts to just under one-third of total foreign investment in Czechoslovakia, but was almost certainly higher, because some significant Dutch holdings in the mineral and vegetable oil industry consisted of mixed Anglo-Dutch investment. In this case it was not possible to differentiate statistically between Dutch and British participation; the headquarters of the investing combines were in both Holland and Britain but dividends from Czechoslovakia were sent mainly to Holland. In my statistical estimates I therefore regarded these investments as Dutch. Judging from the situation and mutual relationships in international investments generally (see chapter 1), it is quite likely that a large part of the capital exported from Austria, Holland, Belgium, Sweden and other countries could have originated in Britain, the U.S.A. or France, but there is no reliable information which would justify qualifying these relationships.

Table IV also shows which countries invested most in the individual branches of Czechoslovak industry. Great Britain participated predominantly in the mining and metallurgy industry, and also in the chemical and textile industries and in banks. She also had a greater share than other countries in the glass industry. French direct investment was mainly in mining, metallurgy and engineering, but also in banking and the chemical, sugar refining and mineral-oil industries. Austrian capital was invested in the mining and metallurgy industry, sugar refining, textiles and the food industry, that is, those branches of industry where links had already existed between the Czech territories and Austria before the First World War. Dutch investment was mainly concentrated in the mineral- and vegetable-oil industry, while German capital participated above all in the Czechoslovak mining and metallurgy industry, and in the electrical and chemical industries. Investment from Belgium found its way especially into the chemical industry and also into banking. Swiss capital held shares in the mineral- and vegetable-oil industry and in the electrical and wood industry. The most significant American investment was in the mineral-oil industry; in other fields of Czechoslovak industry American direct capital participation was comparatively small. Italian capital participated in banks and insurance companies. Sweden invested in metallurgy and engineering and Hungary in the mining and metallurgy industry.

There can be no doubt that foreign capital played an important role in the economy of Czechoslovakia and that a large proportion of domestic enterprises in all basic industries were directly linked to various international financial and business groups.

In addition to the foreign capital investment in companies and financial institutions registered as domestic enterprises which did not appear in published statistics, several branches of foreign companies operated in Czechoslovakia directly and appeared in official statistics. Although their basic capital in the ČSR was insignificant in comparison with the total basic capital of all domestic companies, or even in comparison with the total amount of direct foreign investment in domestic enterprises, their existence cannot be overlooked in a quantitative estimate of foreign capital in the economy as a whole.

According to most recent data for foreign enterprises officially registered in the pre-Munich ČSR, there were 70 joint-stock and 43 limited companies at the end of 1937,[1] which were backed by the capital of their parent companies abroad, amounting in the case of joint-stock companies to a total of Kč 26,137.4 million and in the case of limited companies to Kč 251.7 million.[2] Thus the aggregate joint-stock capital of the foreign parent companies of those 70 branches registered in Czechoslovakia was almost three times the total joint-stock capital of all domestic companies.[3] Of course, the branches of foreign enterprises did not operate with the total basic capital of their concerns, but only with the amounts allocated for Czechoslovakia. Unfortunately, no returns were published for 1937 and the latest data relate to balances of 1935,[4] when the total basic nominal capital allocated to branches of foreign joint-stock companies in Czechoslovakia amounted to Kč 61.7 million and in limited companies to Kč 6.6 million, of which over 50 % was in industrial enterprises, 15 % in transport companies, over 20 % in commercial firms and almost 10 % in agriculture.[5]

[1] *Statistická ročenka* (1941), 175.
[2] *Statistický zpravodaj* (1938), I, 213.
[3] Ibid. and *Statistická ročenka* (1941), 175.
[4] *Statistická ročenka* (1938), 108–9.
[5] *Statistický zpravodaj* (1938), I, 213.

Table V. *Joint-stock and basic capital of domestic and foreign companies in the ČSR in 1935 (in million Kč)*

Enterprise	Joint-stock companies		Limited companies	
	Domestic	Foreign	Domestic	Foreign
Agriculture	50.2	4.3	5.5	—
Mining	992.5	1.0	36.0	—
Stone and earthenware	442.3	4.2	52.6	0.9
Glass industry	229.3	12.0	13.5	—
Metal industry	1,341.1	4.2	72.1	3.6
Chemical industry	873.4	—	30.1	1.1
Textile industry	724.0	2.5	36.2	—
Paper industry	209.8	0.5	10.2	0.4
Graphic industry	104.4	—	24.1	—
Leather industry	51.1	—	1.4	—
Rubber and asbestos industry	36.4	1.5	1.9	—
Wood industry	82.3	0.4	10.5	—
Food industry	1,349.2	—	88.9	0.2
Clothing and boot industry	579.4	—	5.4	—
Building trade	72.2	2.9	19.7	—
Electricity and gas	610.2	5.4	201.9	—
Other industries	8.8	—	3.0	—
Hotels	13.0	—	3.9	—
Commerce	423.7	13.9	177.8	0.4
Transport	229.6	8.9	9.5	—
Other enterprises	41.4	—	9.4	—
Total	8,464.3	61.7	813.6	6.6

Table V shows the distribution of foreign companies between the branches of Czechoslovak industry, in comparison with domestic companies.[1] In 1935 there were only 38 active branches of foreign companies, although 81, with an aggregate capital of Kč 22,000 million, were entered in the Commercial Register of the ČSR;[2] their territorial distribution is shown in Table VI.[3] The effective economic force of these foreign companies in Czechoslovakia lay, of course, in their parent companies, but the capital placed at their disposal for business in Czechoslovakia amounted to no more than 1 % of the total joint-stock capital of domestic companies. On the basis of these figures the Statistical Reporter of 1938 came to the unjustified conclusion that foreign capital played an insignificant role in the Czecho-

[1] Ibid. [2] *Statistická ročenka* (1937), 108–9.
[3] *Statistický zpravodaj* (1938), 309 and *Statistická ročenka* (1938), 108.

Table VI. *Territorial distribution of foreign joint-stock companies* actively operating in the ČSR in 1935*

States	Percentage of total capital in ČSR	Number of foreign companies	Capital of parent company (million Kč)	Capital in ČSR (million Kč)
England	—	1	73.1	2.8
Belgium	22.7	2	413.4	14.0
France	—	3	692.1	0.4
Holland	—	1	325.9	0.4
Italy	—	2	656.1	0.9
Yugoslavia	—	1	11.1	0.2
Hungary	—	2	138.5	1.1
Germany	27.9	10	812.2	17.2
Poland	—	1	40.9	—
Austria	23.7	13	284.7	14.6
Switzerland	—	1	0.4	0.1
U.S.A.	16.2	1	240.7	10.0
Total	—	38	3,689.1	61.7

* Number and capital of domestic companies: 1,032, 8,464.3.

slovak economy.[1] In the light of such superficial statistical enquiries into the role of foreign capital in Czechoslovakia, the importance of an appreciation of direct foreign capital investment in the economy of the pre-Munich Czechoslovak Republic becomes evident.

Here a purely statistical analysis of the state of direct foreign investment at the end of 1937 has been presented. These data can and do provide an approximate measure of the extent to which direct foreign investment participated in the various sectors of the Czechoslovak economy, the probable ratio between foreign and domestic capital as a whole and in the individual branches of industry, and the quantitative relations between the participants in foreign investment from different countries. However, statistics are only a starting-point and cannot alone do full justice to the wide range and the actual depth of the influence of foreign capital, which operated most intensively through its direct investment in the economy of Czechoslovakia before Munich.

[1] Ibid.

2 International cartels in the Czechoslovak economy 1929–38[1]

The spheres of influence of foreign capital investment in the Czechoslovak Republic before the Munich Agreement were – as we have shown – mainly divided between business and financial groups in Western Europe. It would not have been to their advantage simply to withdraw their direct longterm investment from Czechoslovakia because this relatively advanced industrial country provided a jumping-off point for further widely ramified investments in Southeastern Europe. The Anglo-French orientation of Czechoslovak foreign policy corresponded on the whole to the reality of economic conditions. Thus in the field of foreign investment German big business encountered opposition from British and French capital in its untiring efforts for economic expansion and political revision in the countries of the Little Entente and, above all, in Czechoslovakia, the most loyal ally of France.[2] However, the Little

[1] This section is partly based on my article 'Über das Eindringen des deutschen Finanzkapitals in das Wirtschaftsleben der Tschechoslowakei vor dem Münchener Diktat' which was published in *Zeitschrift für Geschichtswissenschaft* (1957), v/6, 1160–80.

[2] The attempts of German big business to expand were expressed by Carl Duisberg, the head of the I.G. Farbenindustrie A.G. in 1931: 'Aus der Enge des nationalen Wirtschaftsraumes streben kräftige Industriestaaten ebenso wie absatzsuchende Agrarstaaten nach größeren internationalen Wirtschaftsräumen, die für einen größtmöglichen Anteil der Produktion Ausgleich in sich bieten und nach außenhin als starke Handelsvertragspartner auftreten können... Auch in Europa scheint dieses Ziel des regionalen Wirtschaftsraumes allmählich festere Formen anzunehmen. Für die südosteuropäischen Staaten sowie Jugoslawien, Rumänien und Ungarn wird die Absatzfrage für ihre landwirtschaftlichen Produkte nachgerade zu einer Existenzangelegenheit. Den notwendigen Absatz finden sie zum überwiegenden Teil in Deutschland. Was liegt für diese Staaten näher, als mit Deutschland, dem kräftigsten Partner, eine Verständigung auf wirtschaftlichem Gebiet zu suchen? Deutschland auf der einen Seite hat mit Österreich erhebliches Interesse an der Entwicklung des südosteuropäischen Absatzmarktes für industrielle Produkte. Wenn im gegenwärtigen Zeitpunkt auch die Frage noch nicht so weit ist, so steht doch zweifellos fest, daß die wirtschaftliche Entwicklung dieses Raumes, die durchaus schon in den nächsten Jahrzehnten möglich ist, die Aufnahme industrieller Produkte aus Deutschland um das Mehrfache steigern kann. Handelspolitisch wird letzten Endes eine Verständigung zwischen Deutschland, Österreich und den südosteuropäischen Staaten die Form einer Zollunion finden müßen, da durch Vereinbarungen auf diesem Gebiete der übrige deutsche Export nicht gefährdet werden darf. Nur die Zollunion bleibt im Rahmen des Meistbegünstigungsprinzips, das unbedingt aufrechterhalten bleiben muß.

Durch diese regionale Wirtschaftskombination kann das europäische Problem von der Südostecke aufgerollt werden. Selbst, wenn es gelingt, im Südosten zu

Entente was, at the same time, a political expression of the expansive efforts of Czechoslovak business and banking circles. Although the post-war system of international treaties with Central and Southeast European countries originated mainly as an instrument of French foreign policy, it also represented – within certain limits, of course – the basis of an independent economic and foreign policy for pre-Munich Czechoslovakia.[1] German business and banking interests endeavoured to undermine the political ties between the states of the Little Entente and their alliance with France, as well as their economic relations with Great Britain, in order to create more favourable conditions for intensifying their economic penetration of Central and Southeastern Europe.

The world economic crisis of 1929–33 shook the foundations on which all international agreements were built; the system of Versailles began to crumble rapidly and, at the same time, the long drawn-out disintegration of the Little Entente commenced. In the 1930s the competitive struggle between the Great European Powers (Germany, Great Britain, France and Italy) also intensified in the area of Central and Southeastern Europe, and within its framework fierce competition between German and Czechoslovak business interests took place. So far Marxist historiography in Czechoslovakia has paid attention mainly to German aggressiveness and penetration in the political and diplomatic field[2] before Munich; however, the German economic offensive has not yet been sufficiently thoroughly investigated.

In its expansive efforts German capital generally penetrated the Czechoslovak economy and Southeastern European markets by means other than direct capital investment. The

einer tragbaren Regelung zu kommen, bleibt doch für eine endgültige Regelung des europäischen Problems die Frage einer wirtschaftlichen Verständigung mit Frankreich zu lösen. Erst ein abgeschloßener Wirtschaftsblock von Bordeaux bis Sofia, wird Europa das wirtschaftliche Rückgrat geben, dessen es zur Behauptung seiner Bedeutung in der Welt bedarf...'. Carl Duisberg, *Abhandlungen, Vorträge und Reden aus den Jahren 1922–1933* (Berlin, 1933), pp. 172–3.

[1] Cf. Kl. Gottwald, *Spisy* (Collected Works), p. 166.

[2] Cf. particularly J. César–B. Černý, *Politika německých buržoasních stran v Československu* (The Policy of the German Bourgeois Parties in Czechoslovakia between 1918 and 1938), Vol. I (Praha, 1961), Vol. II (Praha, 1962); K. Gajan, *Německý imperialismus a československo–německé vztahy v letech 1918–1921* (German Imperialism and Czechoslovak–German Relations 1918–1921) (Praha, 1962).

Table 1. *Survey of cartel agreements of Czechoslovak industrial and commercial companies with foreign firms (1926–September 1938)*

Year of cartels' registration	Number of cartel agreements	Total number of cartel partners	Nationality of cartel partners: ČSR	Germany	Austria	France	Poland	Great Britain	Belgium	Hungary	Italy	Holland	Switzerland	U.S.A.	Sweden	Yugoslavia	Norway	Denmark	Spain	Canada	Romania	Finland	Luxemburg	Chile	U.S.S.R.	Estonia
1926	7	76	21	13	9	7	3	6	3	3	2	1	1	—	3	2	—	1	—	—	1	—	—	—	—	—
1927	12	193	67	89	12	6	—	2	6	6	—	1	1	1	—	2	—	—	—	—	—	—	—	—	—	—
1928	7	47	22	17	7	—	—	—	—	—	1	—	—	—	—	—	—	—	—	—	—	—	—	—	—	—
1929	11	48	22	11	7	3	—	1	1	2	7	1	—	—	—	—	—	—	—	—	—	—	—	—	—	—
1930	23	222	63	61	9	33	9	5	8	5	3	1	3	11	2	—	—	1	2	2	—	—	—	—	—	—
1931	13	107	32	32	9	3	3	4	4	6	3	4	1	—	1	—	2	2	—	—	—	1	—	—	—	—
1932	11	111	46	20	9	2	15	3	—	8	2	1	1	—	—	2	1	—	—	—	—	—	—	—	—	—
1933	36	221	82	61	16	12	14	19	3	3	2	—	5	—	—	2	—	—	1	—	1	—	—	—	—	—
1934	25	142	39	19	8	15	9	16	14	6	3	8	1	1	—	1	1	—	—	—	—	—	1	1	—	—
1935	16	105	37	14	16	1	6	5	13	—	—	2	1	—	2	1	1	—	—	—	1	1	—	—	1	—
1936	21	162	119	19	5	1	7	1	—	4	7	—	2	—	2	—	—	—	—	2	—	—	—	—	—	—
1937	21	149	42	37	14	12	6	4	3	5	2	2	7	2	3	—	1	1	2	—	—	—	—	—	—	1
1938	9	72	18	20	2	—	12	2	9	1	—	4	1	—	—	—	1	—	—	—	—	—	—	—	—	—
Total number	212	1,655	610	413	123	95	84	68	64	49	32	25	24	15	13	10	7	5	5	4	3	2	1	1	1	1

Total number of registered cartels up to 30 September 1938: 1,152.
Source: Compiled from data in the Czechoslovak Cartel Register, SÚA–KR, Prague.

greatest efforts of German big business was directed towards tying important Czechoslovak industrial combines to the powerful German monopolies by way of cartel agreements.

In 1933 the Czechoslovak government passed the Cartel Act,[1] which required the registration of all valid cartel agreements. It is a characteristic feature of cartels that their terms are secretly agreed upon and the partners are bound not to divulge their contents. Although cartels are private understandings, they are in almost all cases directed against the consumer and towards an effective control of the market; often the significance and effectiveness of international cartels are equal to or greater than those of agreements between states. An effective cartel is an expression of the balance of economic power between the partners to the agreement at the time of its conclusion. The Czechoslovak Cartel Act was hailed as a step towards consumer protection, but in reality the law protected the parties to a cartel, by endorsing the secrecy of agreements.[2] However, the provision of the Act that all cartels must be registered and that legally verified copies of the terms of agreements had to be deposited, under strict conditions of secrecy, in the archives of the Czechoslovak State Statistical Office in Prague led to the establishment of almost perfect records on cartels in the 1930s, which are available for historical research in the Cartel Register of the Central State Archives in Prague.[3]

The following statistical table of cartel agreements between Czechoslovak and foreign companies during the time of the pre-Munich Republic (1926–30 September 1938) is compiled from this material (Table 1).[4]

My statistical results differ from the data in the commercial publication 'Československé kartely' (Czechoslovak Cartels) and in the Statistical Yearbooks, because in the official statistics

[1] Sb.z. a n. (Collection of Laws and Regulations), No. 14/1; APSNS, Prints XII, 1933/III, Print 2320.

[2] The deputy who introduced the law, a representative of the People's Party named Dolanský, was himself one of the leading businessmen in Czechoslovakia. Cf. APSNS, Těsnopisecké zprávy (Stenographed records) 1933/III, 291st meeting, pp. 8–9.

[3] SÚA–KR – (even so, some cartels circumvented the law's requirements).

[4] Table 1 was compiled and calculated from data in KR (the Cartel Register) in the SÚA (State Central Archives) of Prague. 1926 was chosen as the starting date because the Cartel Register gives only incomplete information about the preceding years.

only the numbers of registered cartels were counted, whereas in Table 1 a renewed cartel agreement is included if its content was different from the text of the original agreement. Renewed agreements were entered in the Cartel Register, with an indication of the number of times the cartel had been renewed; only the text of a renewed agreement reveals how the new terms differed from the previous agreement. Numbers of cartels in themselves cannot, of course, clarify the whole complex problem of cartels; at the most they can provide a starting-point for an investigation. In all cases a deeper analysis of the content of the cartel agreements is essential, but so far no serious attempt has been made to examine this side of the cartel problem. The only occasion on which some of the negative aspects of the activities of cartels in Czechoslovakia were raised was in a speech in the Czechoslovak Chamber of Deputies, later published as a political pamphlet, by Rudolf Slánský.[1] There exists, however, a very prolific economic, political and economic-historical literature, especially in English, American and German publications.

Table 1 does not confine itself to the number of international agreements, but also gives information on the nationality of the participants in these cartel agreements. International cartels comprised almost one-fifth of all valid registered agreements up to 30 September 1938,[2] and the statistical analysis shows that amongst the foreign partners of Czechoslovak firms German companies predominated. Further, a marked rise in the number of international agreements with Czechoslovak participation is apparent in 1930 and 1933. By 1930 the world economic crisis affected almost all European countries and with this decline of economic opportunities efforts to rationalize and cartelize industry increased, aiming at protecting profit margins, restricting production and artificially curbing competition. In 1933, with the seizure of power by the National Socialists in Germany, a consciously aggressive and officially directed cartel policy was conducted. The cartel system was used by Hitler's Germany as an important instrument for furthering capital

[1] Cf. R. Slánský, *Stati a projevy* (Articles and Speeches) 1 (Praha, 1951), pp. 287–328.

[2] Up to 30 September 1938, 1,152 cartel agreements had been registered, of which 212 were with foreign partners (calculated from SÚA–KR).

expansion.[1] This fact explains, to a large extent, the relatively high number of Czechoslovak cartel agreements with German participation. It is also significant that the majority of cartel agreements with German firms were concluded in those branches of Czechoslovak industry in which Western direct capital investment was strongest. One of the very likely reasons for this phenomenon is the economic reality in which German capital was unable to wield a direct controlling influence in these spheres of production. Thus international cartels were most active in the mining and metallurgical industry and in the engineering, electrical and chemical industries (Table 2). Separate sections are therefore devoted to cartels in these industries (chapters 3, 4 and 5).

While German capital played a less important role in the field of direct longterm investments in Czechoslovakia than Western European interests, it gained influence in the basic industries of Czechoslovakia by means of cartel agreements. The relatively powerful German cartel partners tried to get Czechoslovak companies to agree to conditions that would enable them to penetrate or gain bigger shares in the traditional Czechoslovak export markets, as well as obtaining, wherever possible, a stake in the domestic market of Czechoslovakia. These factors led to the deepening of contradictions in the Czechoslovak economy and contributed to the worsening of the economic and political position of Czechoslovakia as a whole.

It is, of course, also necessary to consider the other side of the picture when investigating the participation of Czechoslovak producers in international cartels between the two world wars. The relations between cartel partners varied according to their relative economic strength, whereas in the area of foreign direct investment in Czechoslovak joint-stock companies the relationship was predominantly one of direct subordination of the Czechoslovak firm to the foreign investor, especially in the case of foreign majority holdings. The participation of Czechoslovak firms or Czechoslovak national cartels in international cartels meant that Czechoslovak industrial capacity had to be taken into account by international producers. Cartel relations could,

[1] Cf. A. Norden, p. 124; also Wendell Berge, *Cartels – Challenge to a Free World* (Washington, 1946), p. 231; TNEC, Final Report and Recommendations, Exhibit No. 2789, The German Invasion of American Business.

Table 2. *Survey of cartel agreements between Czechoslovak industrial and commercial companies and foreign firms (1926–September 1938]*

Year of cartels' registration	Number of cartel agreements	Branch of industry											
		Chemical industry	Mining and metallurgy	Engineering industry	Electrical industry	Ceramics	Rubber industry	Textile industry	Glass	Paper industry	Food industry	Wood industry	Miscellaneous
1926	7	3	1	1	—	2	—	—	—	—	—	—	—
1927	12	—	7	—	—	3	—	—	2	—	—	—	—
1928	7	1	3	1	—	1	—	1	—	—	—	—	—
1929	11	5	4	—	—	2	—	—	—	—	—	—	—
1930	23	6	3	—	14	—	—	—	—	—	—	—	—
1931	13	—	3	4	2	—	1	2	1	—	—	—	—
1932	11	3	3	3	1	—	—	—	—	—	1	—	—
1933	36	23	4	5	1	2	—	—	—	—	1	—	—
1934	25	11	7	2	2	1	2	—	—	—	—	—	—
1935	16	9	—	7	—	—	—	—	—	—	—	—	—
1936	21	3	6	7	2	—	1	—	—	—	—	2	—
1937	21	5	5	5	1	—	1	1	—	1	—	—	2
1938	9	5	2	1	—	—	—	—	—	1	—	—	—
Total	212	74	48	36	23	11	5	4	3	2	2	2	2

Source: Compiled from data in the Czechoslovak Cartel Register, SÚA–KR, Prague.

for instance, act more or less in accordance with capital relations, as was the case particularly in the Czechoslovak iron and steel industry; they could, on the other hand, be acting in an inverse relationship to capital ties, i.e. in the opposite direction to foreign capital investment, as was markedly the case in the chemical industry. On the whole, it can be said that cartels are more changeable, more mobile, and register changes in relative economic forces and in political life more quickly than direct capital investments.

The problems of cartel policy in the pre-Munich Republic have been outlined in order to focus on the complexity of international capital relations and on the variety of monopoly practices. This raises a number of questions which will be investigated and analysed on the basis of archive material in the following chapters. The study of these sources leaves little doubt that the structure of the main branches of industry, and especially of foreign trade, in Czechoslovakia changed in conditions of the world economic crisis, largely because of international, and especially German, cartel policy. International cartels influenced the production and trade of the basic industries of the Czechoslovak Republic in the 1930s and thus contributed to the relative restriction of production and to a less favourable reorientation of Czechoslovak foreign trade.

3

Mining and metallurgy

1 Direct foreign investment in the mining and metallurgy industry in Czechoslovakia

In the period between the two world wars foreign capital played an important role in the mining and metallurgy industry of Czechoslovakia. The tables showing the structure of direct foreign investment in the various branches of industry (Table 1 in the previous chapter) show that direct foreign investment was highest in the mining and metallurgy industry. It existed in 37 companies out of a total of 70. Expressed as a percentage this amounted to 53 % of all mining and metallurgy companies, but the basic nominal capital of these 37 companies totalled 98 % of the total in this strongly concentrated industry. The estimated direct foreign longterm investment in this industry on 31 December 1937 was Kč 1,160,858,000, i.e. 64 % of the total nominal capital.[1] The countries in which these foreign investments originated are shown in Table 1.[2]

Foreign participation was therefore obviously very high in this industry, which was one of the main branches of modern production in the Czechoslovak economy, which provided the basis for a relatively advanced engineering and electrical industry and a number of other metal working industries. Especially prominent was the share of Anglo-French capital, which penetrated primarily because of shifts in property relations within the newly established independent Republic, and the changed balance of forces between the victorious and defeated powers after the First World War. The question to be

[1] Calculated from data in Table I, Chapter 2.

[2] Computed from material in Works Archives and the Central State Archives in Prague (SÚA).

Table 1. *Territorial distribution of direct foreign capital investment in the mining and metallurgy industry of Czechoslovakia (31 December 1937)*

Country of origin	In 1,000 Kč	In %
Great Britain	706,912	61
France	174,001	15
Germany	117,694	10.1
Austria	102,340	8.8
Belgium	24,348	2.1
Hungary	12,140	1
Sweden	10,348	0.9
Italy	6,077	0.6
U.S.A.	5,998	0.5
Switzerland	1,000	—
Total	1,160,858	100

investigated is the extent to which foreign capital, with such a high rate of participation in the mining and metallurgy industry, actually controlled this extremely important section of the Czechoslovak economy and which groups played a decisive role.

Foreign capital held a larger share in mining and metallurgy than in any other industry, accounting for 36 % of total foreign investments in all Czechoslovak industrial enterprises.[1] This branch of industry attracted foreign investment mainly because of its international importance, but also because of the significant position it held in the economy of Czechoslovakia, and because of the exceptionally strong concentration of production in large works which, as a rule, were subsidiaries of a very few centralized combines.

The significance of the mining and metallurgy industry in world and Czechoslovak production

The Czechoslovak mining and metallurgy industry was among the ten biggest producers in the world before the Second World War. In the official statistics of the Czechoslovak Republic

[1] Calculated from Table IV, Chapter 2.

Table 2. *Output and employment in mining in Czechoslovakia, 1937*

Branch of mining	Share of the total output		Workers	
	In 1,000 tons	In %	Number	% of total
Coal	16,778	45	43,392	51
Lignite (brown coal)	17,895	48	29,761	35
Coal total	34,673	93	73,153	86
Iron ore	1,836	5	6,167	7
Other ores*	560	1.5	4,240	5
Other minerals†	193	0.5	2,000	2
Total	37,262	100	85,560	100

* Other ores: manganese, gold, silver, zinc, lead, mercury, antimony, arsenic, uranium, aluminium.

† Other minerals: graphite, salt, sulphur, petroleum, natural gas.

Source: computed from *Statistická ročenka Protektorátu Čechy a Moravy*, 1941, p. 166.

Table 3. *The value of mining output in Czechoslovakia, 1936*

Branch of mining*	Value of output in 1,000 Kč	% of total value
Coal	1,212	58
Lignite (brown coal)	806	38
Coal total	2,018	96
Iron ore	61	2.9
Other ores	29	1.1
Total	2,108	100

* Without 'other minerals': see note to Table 2.

Source: Statistická ročenka, 1938, p. 62; *Compass, Čechoslovakei*, 1939, p. 679.

mining comprised coal, iron and other ores, as well as all mineral raw materials extracted in the territory of Czechoslovakia.[1] However, although the mining of iron, manganese, antimony and graphite was not insignificant, the decisive factor

[1] Cf. *Statistické ročenky Republiky Československé* (Statistical Yearbooks of the Czechoslovak Republic), Part v, Industry, Trade and Commerce.

in the mining industry was coal.[1] Almost all mines, whether manganese, iron or coal, were dominated by the large iron and steel combines of Czechoslovakia.[2] The significance of the coal industry compared with other branches of mining is set out in Tables 2 and 3. Table 2 shows that coal accounted for 93 % of all mining production in Czechoslovakia and employed 86 % of the total number of workers engaged in mining in 1937.[3] Table 3 confirms these data by showing that 96 % of the total value of mined products came from coal and lignite.

Czechoslovakia was among the biggest world producers of coal and lignite. In the mining of black coal between 1929 and 1937 she took up ninth place in world production and seventh place in Europe;[4] in lignite she occupied second place after Germany.[5] The main mining companies were situated in North Bohemia, where 93 % of lignite production was concentrated,[6] and in most cases they were subordinated to the great banks or coal trading companies in Prague. The black coal-mines, especially in the Ostrava–Karviná area where about 75 % of black coal was mined, delivered the required amounts for coking to the foundries. As a rule they belonged to the great mining and iron and steel combines.

The international significance of the iron and steel industry in Czechoslovakia was greater than that of the mining industry, as iron and steel formed the backbone of her modern production. Czechoslovak foundries produced the whole range, from pig iron and steel to a great variety of rolled materials. In world steel production between 1929 and 1937 Czechoslovakia held, on average, ninth place.[7] Table 4 shows the relative shares of the

[1] Cf. P. Eisler, *Monopoly v hornictví kapitalistického Československa*, (Monopoly in the Mining Industry of Capitalist Czechoslovakia), p. 4; also F. Píšek–L. Jeníček, *Nauka o materiálu* (Science of Materials), III/2 (Praha, 1962), Chap. 43.

[2] Cf. also P. Eisler, p. 13.

[3] The proportions were similar in 1929, when coal mining employed 88.1 % of all workers in the mining industry, and in 1935 when the proportion was 89 %. Cf. P. Eisler, p. 4.

[4] Calculated from data in *Compass, Čechoslovakei*, 1939, pp. 2028–9 and *Statistické ročenky* (Statistical Yearbooks), Part XVII.

[5] Ibid.

[6] Calculated from data in *Statistická ročenka*, 1938, p. 62.

[7] Calculated from statistics of 'Stahl-Production der Welt', *Compass, Čechoslovakei*, 1939, p. 2051. The cartel organization of the United Czechoslovak Iron Works, i.e. the Selling Agency of the United Czechoslovak Iron Works, kept a close watch on the development of world production and compiled the material which

Table 4. *Distribution of world steel production, 1929–36* (%)

Year	Europe	America	Asia	Australia	South Africa	Total	In 1,000 tons
1929	48.521	48.682	2.404	0.361	0.032	100	121,981
1930	51.902	44.631	3.092	0.333	0.042	100	96,001
1931	56.924	39.047	3.637	0.331	0.061	100	70,062
1932	65.372	28.228	5.876	0.440	0.084	100	51,173
1933	58.231	35.359	5.742	0.581	0.087	100	68,676
1934	60.334	33.242	5.676	0.627	0.121	100	82,869
1935	57.470	36.143	5.433	0.703	0.251	100	99,409
1936	53.997	40.213	4.987	0.586	0.217	100	124,526

Source: ANTM, SDS, fond 413, box 15/3 – Report on the development of the market for steel and rolled material and pig iron, including compounds of iron, in 1936, p. 3.

Table 5. *Distribution of pig iron production, including compounds of iron, 1929–36* (%)

Year	Europe	America	Asia	Australia	South Africa	Total	In 1,000 tons
1929	51.141	45.147	3.220	0.475	0.017	100	98,852
1930	54.276	41.463	3.832	0.391	0.038	100	80,090
1931	59.986	34.613	4.960	0.425	0.016	100	55,768
1932	69.628	23.057	6.791	0.486	0.038	100	39,688
1933	64.347	28.165	6.744	0.692	0.052	100	49,452
1934	65.740	26.950	6.436	0.715	0.159	100	62,954
1935	62.424	30.388	6.067	0.878	0.243	100	74,061
1936	58.345	35.677	5.046	0.713	0.219	100	91,165

Source: ANTM, SDS Report, as in Table 4, p. 26.

various continents in steel production, with Europe producing more than half the world's steel in the 1930s. In world production of pig iron the European share was somewhat larger, averaging 62 % between 1929 and 1936[1] (Table 5). Czecho-

it received as a member of the International Steel Cartel and which served as a basis for negotiations about Czechoslovak production policy. Because the data of the Selling Agency, extant in its archives, are more precise than official statistics, I have relied on them wherever this was possible; I also quote them more fully, as they have not been published before.

[1] ANTM, SDS, 413, box 15/3, Report on the development of the market for steel and rolled material and pig iron, including compounds of iron in 1936, p. 26.

slovakia was eighth in the statistics of world pig iron production.[1] In European production of steel and pig iron Czechoslovakia was seventh; however, she held first place among the Successor States between the two world wars. Tables 6 and 7 show the relative output of pig iron and steel of the most important producing countries in Europe. The large steel corporations had to take account of Czechoslovak productive capacity, because it far exceeded the demand of her home market, and thus she was a potential competitor in world trade. Foreign combines therefore attempted to gain a decisive influence in the capital of Czechoslovakia's mining and metallurgy industry and to subordinate it to the interests of the international steel cartel.

Foreign investors saw, above all, opportunities for maximizing profits in the Czechoslovak mining and metallurgy industry. The significant position of this industry in the Czechoslovak economy, as the basis for a relatively large production of armaments and also as a key industry for almost all productive activity in the country, provided favourable conditions for investment. The Czechoslovak State Statistical Office's enquiry into the condition of industrial enterprises (27 May 1930) ascertained that 11 % of all active persons were employed in mining, in briquette and coke production and in metallurgy, and that 20 % of the total horse-power of all active driving motors producing mechanical energy, and 31 % of the total horse-power of all motors providing mechanical energy for working machines, were consumed by these branches of industry.[2] The share of the mining and metallurgy industry in the total number of workers employed and in the total consumption of mechanical energy in Czechoslovakia increased relatively in the 1930s, because

[1] Calculated from *Compass, Čechoslovakei*, 1939, p. 2049.

[2] Calculated from *Statistická ročenka*, 1938, p. 67. In K. Maiwald's work, 'Index průmyslové výroby v Československu' (Index of industrial production in Czechoslovakia), special off-print from *Obzor národohospodářsky* (Economic Horizon) 6 (1934), the prime significance of mining and metallurgy is even more striking (cf. his table on 'The Relative Significance of Industries' on pp. 8–9). The share of employed persons in mining and the metal-working industries is calculated from the census of 1930 as 22.3 %, and the share of mining and the metal-working industries in the total amount of horse-power used is calculated from the census of bigger enterprises as 43.8 %. Although I believe that these data are probably reliable, I could not use them, because in column 9 of the table I referred to there is an arithmetical error, which unfortunately reduces the value of the statistics.

Table 6. *Steel production in the main European countries, 1929–37* (*in 1,000 tons*)

Country	1929	1930	1931	1932	1933	1934	1935	1936	1937
Germany	16,246	11,539	8,292	5,770	7,612	11,916	16,447	19,208	19,820
Saar	2,209	1,935	1,538	1,463	1,676	1,950			
Russia	4,903	5,798	5,416	5,900	6,900	9,563	12,211	16,083	17,830
Great Britain	10,122	7,716	5,466	5,505	7,313	9,191	10,190	12,092	13,170
France	9,800	9,447	7,822	5,640	6,531	6,174	6,277	6,703	7,900
Belgium	4,122	3,365	3,110	2,791	2,732	2,947	3,027	3,175	3,870
Luxemburg	2,702	2,270	2,035	1,956	1,845	1,932	1,837	1,981	2,510
Czechoslovakia	2,145	1,836	1,527	683	747	953	1,196	1,559	2,320
Italy	2,253	1,867	1,527	1,497	1,882	1,950	2,200	2,500	2,090
Poland	1,377	1,237	1,037	551	817	845	945	1,141	1,450
Sweden	730	637	552	537	642	878	919	1,000	1,110
Hungary	513	369	316	180	228	315	446	520	670
Austria	632	468	322	205	226	309	364	418	660
Romania	161	157	114	106	155	171	220	240	240
Spain	1,007	929	648	534	509	649	586	350	100
Yugoslavia	85	76	60	50	60	65	70	75	—
Finland	26	28	18	35	36	40	45	45	—
Norway	4	3	2	—	—	—	—	—	—
Other countries	150	150	80	50	80	150	150	150	—
Europe	59,187	40,827	39,882	33,453	39,991	49,998	57,130	67,240	—
World production	121,891	96,001	70,062	51,173	68,676	82,869	99,408	124,526	135,500

Source: as in Table 4, pp. 3 and 5; the column for 1937 is compiled from *Compass, Čechoslovakei*, 1939, p. 2051; the countries are ordered according to production figures for 1937.

Table 7. *Pig iron production (including compounds of iron) in the main European countries, 1929–37 (in 1,000 tons)*

Country	1929	1930	1931	1932	1933	1934	1935	1936	1937
Germany	13,401	9,695	6,063	3,933	5,267	8,742	12,842	15,303	15,960
Saar	2,105	1,912	1,515	1,349	1,592	1,826			
Russia	4,321	5,001	4,856	6,217	7,189	10,438	12,311	14,093	14,520
Great Britain	7,711	6,292	3,833	3,631	4,202	6,065	6,529	7,809	8,630
France	10,364	10,035	8,199	5,537	6,324	6,151	5,789	6,237	7,920
Belgium	4,041	3,365	3,198	2,749	2,710	2,953	3,060	3,207	3,840
Luxemburg	2,906	2,473	2,053	1,960	1,888	1,955	1,872	1,987	2,510
Czechoslovakia	1,645	1,437	1,165	450	499	600	811	1,140	1,680
Italy	727	588	553	495	567	573	700	775	860
Poland	704	478	347	199	306	382	394	584	720
Sweden	524	496	418	282	347	558	613	610	690
Austria	462	287	145	94	88	134	193	248	390
Hungary	368	257	160	66	93	140	186	306	360
Romania	73	69	43	9	1	59	150	165	130
Spain	753	622	479	301	339	372	356	250	110
Yugoslavia	31	35	38	9	31	33	19	46	40
Norway	153	145	119	103	113	127	131	135	—
Finland	11	10	12	14	12	20	20	20	—
Other countries	254	273	257	236	253	258	256	275	—
Europe	50,554	43,470	33,453	27,634	31,821	41,386	46,232	53,190	—
World production	98,852	80,090	55,768	39,688	49,452	62,954	74,061	91,165	104,000

Source: as for Table 6.

between 1929 and 1937 a shift from light to heavy industry took place within the economy which was caused, to a significant extent, by rising armament production.[1] While mining output was, on average, about 11 % of total industrial production between 1923 and 1937,[2] the share of metallurgy rose from 5.4 % in 1923 to 8.4 % in 1937.[3] In 1937 mining and metallurgy advanced to first place in the statistics for the value of production of the various branches of industry, a place which had been taken by the textile industry until the first half of the 1930s.

In the foreign trade of Czechoslovakia the importance of mining and metallurgy increased in the 1930s. Coal, iron and steel products contributed substantially to the active trade balance of the pre-Munich Republic.[4] The share of iron and steel products in Czechoslovak exports rose from 12 % to 15.2 % between 1934 and 1937; if we add 5.2 %, representing exports of coal and peat in 1937, then coal, iron and steel constituted more than one-fifth of total Czechoslovak exports.[5]

These economic realities undoubtedly contributed to the active interest taken by foreign investors in the mining and metallurgy industry of Czechoslovakia, which attempted after 1918 to detach itself from German and Austrian influence. The powerful foreign business groups which entered the Czechoslovak capital market were able to obtain important positions by investment in mining and metallurgical enterprises, because of this industry's exceptionally high degree of concentration and monopoly.

Monopoly in the iron and steel industry

Within the Czechoslovak iron and steel industry a well-organized monopoly structure of national dimensions developed. This was probably the tightest monopoly in steel production anywhere in the world, and was based on an effective cartel

[1] Cf. A. Dobrý, pp. 102–15; also R. Olšovský *et al.*, p. 346; also ADWI–05674.

[2] K. Maiwald mentions 11 % in 1930; L. Šauer, *Co nám říkají data o průmyslové výrobě* (What do facts about industrial production tell us) (Praha, 1940), mentions 11.6 % in 1935; P. Eisler mentions 11 % for the average between 1923 and 1937, p. 3.

[3] Calculated by P. Eisler, p. 3.

[4] Cf. ANTM, SDS, 413, box 15/3, p. 25.

[5] Calculated from *Statistická ročenka*, 1937, p. 134; 1938, p. 137; and in *Zahraniční obchod Republiky československé* in 1937 (Foreign Trade of the Czechoslovak Republic) (Praha, 1938), pp. 28–9. Czechoslovakia was one of those countries of which it was said in an 'expertise' of the TNEC, that it must export in order to survive. Cf. TNEC, Hearings, Part 20, p. 10924.

organization. The biggest iron and steel works had already joined a cartel in the period of the Austro-Hungarian Monarchy, but this was dissolved during the First World War. A new cartel agreement within the new frontiers of Czechoslovakia was negotiated only after a violent competitive struggle between the largest iron and steel combines – the Vítkovice Mining and Foundry Works in Ostrava, the Mining and Metallurgic Company in Třinec and the Prague Iron Company in Kladno. According to the records of the old Austrian cartel of 1913, 98.34 % of pig iron, 69.46 % of steel and almost 72 % of all rolled materials were produced by these three most influential combines, which competed for more favourable positions in the post-war period, and also started negotiations about production quotas.[1] The negotiations between the representatives of these three leading iron and steel producers which took place in the first half of 1921 were conducted from 'positions of strength'[2] and the result was an agreement[3] which practically cartelized the whole Cechoslovak iron and steel industry.

On 1 October 1921[4] the Selling Agency of the United Czechoslovak Iron Works[5] was founded as a joint-stock company with a nominal capital of Kč 1,000,000. Control was divided according to production quotas agreed on the basis of the comparative strength of the partners. The largest share of the quotas and the largest number of votes rested with the three main combines, which in the Selling Agency records are called 'The Big Three'.[6] Their relative positions were clarified and more or less stabilized during the process of concentration of the 1920s, when they either incorporated or liquidated smaller foundries and iron works and divided their production quotas amongst themselves.[7] In the 1930s the Big Three participated

[1] Cf. G. Günther, *Lebenserinnerungen* (Wien, 1936), pp. 220–1.

[2] Cf. ANTM – Vzpomínky J. Tilleho (Memoirs of J. Tille). [3] SÚA-KR–28/1.

[4] The year 1922 is mistakenly quoted for the foundation of the Selling Agency of the United Czechoslovak Iron Works in both P. Eisler, p. 15 and G. Günther, *Dvacetpět let Bánské a hutní společnosti* (Twenty-five Years of the Mining and Metallurgic Company) (Praha, 1931), p. 45.

[5] Cf. AÚLSMHD – Statutes of the Selling Agency of the United Czechoslovak Iron Works in Prague.

[6] Cf. ANTM, SDS, 413; also AÚLSMHD–10008.

[7] Cf. G. Günther in *Dvacetpět let Bánské a hutní společnosti*, p. 49; also P. Eisler, pp. 16–17; also *Sto let kladenských železáren* (A Hundred Years of the Kladno Iron Works), p. 340.

in 92.785 % of the joint-stock capital of the Selling Agency; the Vítkovice Mining and Foundry Works had 43.595 %, and the Mining and Metallurgic Co. and the Prague Iron Co. both had 24.595 %.[1] The state-owned iron works was also a founder member of the cartel, with a quota of 3.608 %, and was represented by a high official of the Ministry of Trade,[2] who was doubtless in an extremely weak position. The state-owned enterprise was insignificant in comparison to the economic power wielded by the Big Three. This is an example of the interweaving of private and public enterprise, which is not an infrequent phenomenon in the economic structure of this period.[3] Although outsiders did exist during the period of the Selling Agency's activities,[4] they could not seriously influence economic policy in their own branch of production.

Thus in the period between the two world wars the most comprehensive monopoly structure and the most watertight controls in steel production in the world were to be found in Czechoslovakia,[5] in the form of a national cartel organized as a joint-stock company. It dominated the production, prices and marketing of iron, steel and rolled materials on the domestic market, divided export quotas among its members and, at the

[1] Data from ANTM, SDS, 413; PA–VŽKG, Ostrava, List of the combine's subsidiaries; B. Stočes, *Dvacetpět let Bánské a hutní společnosti*, p. 60; G. Günther, *Lebenserinnerungen*, p. 221.

[2] Cf. ANTM, Protocols of Meetings of Members of the Selling Agency; also E. Hexner, *The International Steel Cartel* (Chapel Hill, 1946), p. 127.

[3] Cf. V. I. Lenin, *Collected Works*, Vol. 22, p. 251.

[4] Until 1937 the following firms remained outsiders: Rokycany, Jouza, Mědárny Čechy, Müller-Tele, Voigtmann-Janovice (ANTM–SDS, 413, box 15/3, Report on the development of the market for steel and rolled material and pig iron, including compounds of iron in 1936, p. 19). The Poldina huť also remained outside the cartel, but as the only producer of high-quality steel, the company dominated the Czechoslovak market and did not threaten other companies with competition.

[5] Cf. E. Hexner, p. 127, the former general director of the Selling Agency of the United Czechoslovak Iron Works and its representative in the International Steel Cartel, gives an informed estimate of the position of the Czechoslovak iron and steel industry in the international cartel system. This of course does not mean that the metallurgical industry in Czechoslovakia was the strongest measured on a world scale. International combines in the steel industry, such as the United Steel Corporation of the U.S.A., Vickers-Armstrong of Great Britain, Schneider–Creusot of France and Vereinigte Stahlwerke in Germany, were incomparably stronger as to capital, volume of output and numbers of workers. The priority of the Czechoslovak iron and steel industry on a world scale relates only to its degree of monopolization.

Table 8. *Share of the cartelized and non-cartelized metallurgy industry in Czechoslovak production of crude steel, 1921–36*

Year	United Czechoslovak Iron Works (Tons)	United Czechoslovak Iron Works (%)	Other steel producers (Tons)	Other steel producers (%)	Total Czechoslovak crude steel production (Tons)
1921	888,568	91.15	86,316	8.85	974,884
1922	712,230	94.03	45,239	5.97	757,469
1923	1,145,196	94.49	66,842	5.51	1,212,038
1924	1,210,773	92.28	101,346	7.72	1,312,119
1925	1,356,462	91.99	118,142	8.01	1,474,604
1926	1,251,395	92.68	98,775	7.32	1,350,170
1927	1,558,458	92.25	130,879	7.75	1,689,337
1928	1,794,224	90.65	185,132	9.35	1,979,356
1929	1,938,196	90.34	207,156	9.66	2,145,352
1930	1,664,073	90.64	171,907	9.36	1,835,980
1931	1,390,179	91.01	137,313	8.99	1,527,492
1932	617,158	90.35	65,950	9.65	683,108
1933	655,320	87.69	92,016	12.31	747,336
1934	813,955	85.43	138,865	14.57	952,820
1935	1,010,471	84.44	186,233	15.56	1,196,704
1936	1,331,732	85.39	227,855	14.61	1,559,587

Source: ANTM, SDS.

same time, supervised a whole system of domestic and international cartel agreements. All effective power, however, was vested in the Big Three. According to § 10 of the Agreement these formed a special committee in the Selling Agency of the United Czechoslovak Iron Works, which had the right to represent the Czechoslovak iron and steel industry in all domestic and foreign negotiations and to make decisions without reference to the other members, who were only entitled to be informed of the results.[1] The selling organization of the syndicated Czechoslovak iron works became the instrument of the three biggest combines for dominating the whole industry, and also affected the related economic and political areas which were dependent on it.

The share of each member of the Selling Agency in total steel production determined the quotas, and also its influence on

[1] Cf. SÚA–KR–28/1 'Agreement of the United Czechoslovak Iron Works', p. 23.

Table 9. *Share of the Big Three in Czechoslovak crude steel production, 1921–36*

Year	1,000 tons	Share of production of the United Czechoslovak Iron Works (%)	Share of total production (%)
1921	585	65	65
1922	497	71	71
1923	905	88	75
1924	982	82	70
1925	1,114	80	74
1926	1,037	80	74
1927	1,315	82	77
1928	1,564	86	78
1929	1,694	89	77
1930	1,475	85	82
1931	1,249	89	83
1932	535	89	76
1933	568	94	81
1934	746	93	83
1935	908	90	75
1936	1,173	90	78

Source: Computed from Table 8 and data in *Sto let kladenských železáren* (A Hundred Years of the Kladno Iron Works), p. 566.

industrial policy. The distribution of steel production between the cartel and outsiders from the origin of the cartel until 1936 (Table 8) clearly shows the monopoly position of the Selling Agency.

The share of the United Czechoslovak Iron Works in the total steel production of Czechoslovakia exceeded 90 % until 1932, and fell to an average of about 85 % between 1934 and 1936, i.e. in the period when an armament boom in which outsiders were able to take part was beginning (viz. column 'other Czechoslovak steel producers' in Table 8). The primacy of the cartel in quantities produced lasted throughout the period of the pre-Munich Republic, although the productive capacity of the United Iron Works fell far short of being fully utilized. The cartel restricted and regulated production to prevent a decrease in prices and a threat to profits. Only 54 % of the productive capacity of the United Czechoslovak Iron Works, which amounted to about 2,300,000 tons of steel annually, was therefore utilized on the average between 1928 and 1937.[1] This policy was systematically pursued by the Big Three, who consolidated their position within the cartel by bringing about the suspension of production in competitive plants or by buying up the works and appropriating the production quotas of their weaker competitors, until they gained a decisive voice, not only in the Czechoslovak cartel, but also in the whole Czechoslovak metallurgical industry. This process is clearly demonstrated in Table 9, which shows the course of development of the share of the Big Three in the steel production of Czechoslovakia between 1921 and 1936.

'The Big Three'

After the Selling Agency of the United Czechoslovak Iron Works was founded on the initiative of the Big Three, they proceeded deliberately to dominate all the other members and systematically acquired further production quotas. From a 65 % share in 1921, their participation in the steel production of the Agency increased 23 % by 1923, mainly by appropriation of the shares of the former Hungarian Hornad Iron Works in Krompachy (Slovakia) and of the Iron and Iron Sheet Company Union in Bratislava (Slovakia), which were divided equally between the Vítkovice Mining and Foundry Works and the Mining and Metallurgic Co. Later the Big Three gained steadily higher quotas, the additions usually being shared equally between them.[2] The consolidation of the Big Three can be clearly traced. At the beginning, in 1921, their share amounted to 65 %; in 1936 they had acquired 90 % of the steel production which formed the basis for the quota allocation, and thus dominated the Czechoslovak cartel. In addition, at least 75 % of total Czechoslovak steel production was continuously

[1] Calculated from ANTM, Reports on the development of the market for steel and rolled products 1928–36, and AÚLSMHD, Report for 1938.

[2] Cf G. Günther in *Dvacetpět let Bánské a hutní společnosti*, p. 49; Complement to the 'Agreement' confirms this distribution: cf. AÚLSMHD – 'Agreement' of 1 October 1931 changed the relative proportions of the participants from those of the original 'Agreement' of 23 May 1922, and in addition, in the 'Complement to the Agreement' of 12 May 1937, the position of the Mining and Metallurgic Co. is strengthened in relation to the other partners.

in the hands of the Big Three. It can be stated without exaggeration that the Big Three played a decisive role in the Czechoslovak metallurgy industry, and the forces which controlled the Vítkovice Mining and Foundry Works, the Mining and Metallurgic Co. and the Prague Iron Co. also dominated the whole industry. Foreign capital participation was strongest in these combines and penetrated through their subsidiaries into the most important related branches of industry.

However, competition among the members of the Big Three did not cease at any time. On the contrary, sharp struggles took place about quantities to be produced, about extraordinary export quotas (the so-called ex-contingent), about the acquisition of further plants and about the exemption of deliveries to their own subsidiaries from the quota allocations. Other complicated forms of competition in the production process and in domestic and foreign trade practices were also brought into play by these combines against each other. Influential international finance and business groups were participants in the capital of the three great combines, and were thus powerful factors in these competitive struggles, either together with the Czechoslovak groups or against them. In this connection, however, the economic strength and potential productive capacity of the individual partners of the Big Three were decisive.

The Vítkovice Mining and Foundry Works

A comparison of the annual output of steel, pig iron and rolled material of each partner of the Big Three between 1919–37 shows that the Vítkovice Mining and Foundry Works was the biggest producer and was also financially the most powerful, with the strongest capital base in the mining and metallurgy industry of Czechoslovakia. The basic capital of the Vítkovice Mining and Foundry Works consisted of 100 mining shares (Kuxe) which fell within the sphere of interest of the international banking house of Rothschild.

Relationships among the owners of shares in the Vítkovice Mining and Foundry Works had always attracted the attention of Czechoslovak financial circles. The Živnostenská Bank (Trade Bank) in particular had been interested for many years in Vítkovice mining shares. The director-general of the Živnostenská Bank, Dr Jaroslav Preiss, who was also the most prominent personality on the Czech financial scene, intended to buy shares in the Vítkovice Works as early as 1928, as part of the scheme of 'nationalization of foreign property on the territory of Czechoslovakia' in favour of Czech capital; and it seems that he had managed to concentrate sufficient financial means for this purpose.[1] However, Czech finance capital did not succeed in gaining control of the Vítkovice combine, which remained in the hands of the Rothschild group for the whole period of the existence of the independent Czechoslovak state. The world-wide capital operations of the House of Rothschild have been regarded in modern economic history as a classical example of international high finance, whereby changes in property relations occurred also within the widely ramified Rothschild family.[2] The dominating influence of the Viennese branch of the group had already begun to fall off in 1911. After the war of 1914–18 the leading role shifted – in accordance with the general trend in international relations – first to the Rothschilds in Paris and later to London, the seat of the financially strongest branch.

This development is also borne out by the transactions involving the Vítkovice Mining and Foundry Works. Table 10 shows changes in the ownership relation of the Vítkovice combine between 1918 and 1938. At the founding of the mining and metallurgical works in 1873 in Ostrava, the shares (Kuxe) were divided equally between two eminent Viennese banking families – the Gutmanns and the Rothschilds – each owning fifty shares (Table 10A). Net profits were regularly remitted in equal parts to the brothers Gutmann and to the banking house of S. M. von Rothschild in Vienna until the beginning of the 1930s and the onset of the world economic crisis.[3] It seemed that no changes had occurred in the conditions of ownership after the First World War and the establishment of the Czechoslovak Republic and this might have led to the superficial and incorrect inference that 'the capital participation in the Vítkovice Iron

[1] Cf. PA-VŽKG, Ostrava, Gen řed. (unmarked); on the interest of the Živnostenská Bank to nationalize the Vítkovice Mining and Foundry Works see also V. Král, II, p. 59.

[2] F. Morton, *Die Rothschilds, Porträt einer Familie* (München, 1962); also Richard Lewinsohn, *Die Umschichtung der europäischen Vermögen* (Berlin, 1925), p. 252.

[3] PA-VŽKG, Ostrava, VHHT 39.

Table 10. *Changes of ownership relations in the Vítkovice Mining and Foundry Works, 1918–38*

(A) *31. 12. 1931*

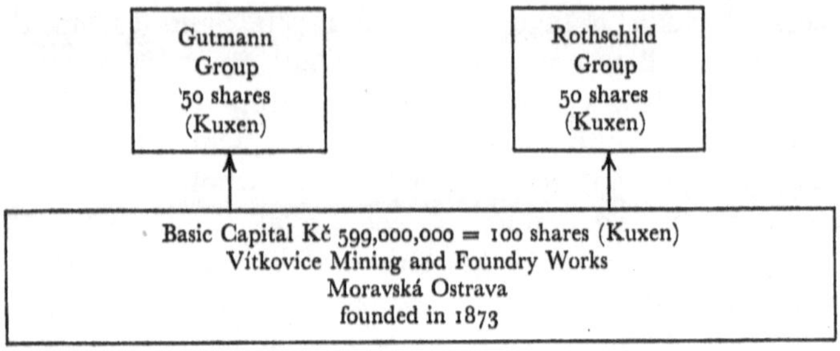

Dividends paid to banking house S. M. v. Rothschild in Vienna

(B) *Period of 'standstill agreement' (14 June 1933 – 8 May 1937)*

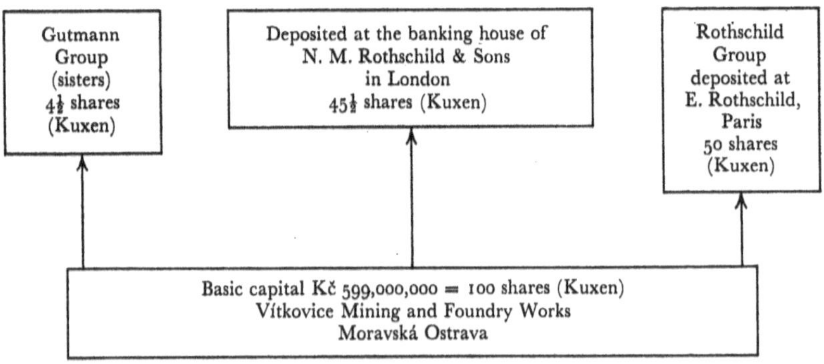

Dividends paid to banking house N. M. Rothschild & Sons in London

(C) *From 8 May 1937 ('transfer agreement') to the end of 1938*

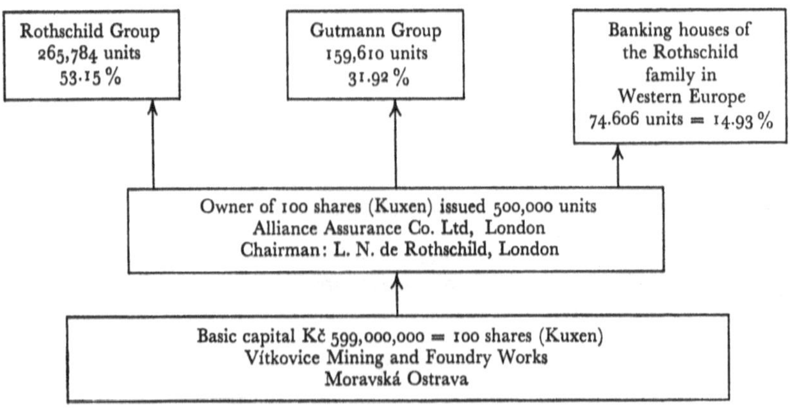

Dividends paid to the Alliance Assurance Co. in London

Works represented old Viennese capital from the period of the Austrian Monarchy, which in 1938 was still in the hands of Louis Rothschild and partly also of Wilhelm Gutmann'.[1] This so-called 'old Viennese capital' had ceased to exist with the defeat and the break-up of the Austro-Hungarian Monarchy and the concept loses its significance in the period between the two world wars, particularly during the 1930s. Vienna could no longer hold its own as one of the centres of European finance and had to submit to the financial dominance of the Entente.[2] The experienced bankers of the Rothschild group drew appropriate conclusions from post-war developments and the Viennese branch transferred its interests to economically and politically stronger centres. This stands out markedly in relation to the Vítkovice mines and iron and steel works, which represented one of the most valuable investments of the Viennese bankers in Central and Southeast Europe after their enormous losses in Russia. The accounting of this great mining and industrial combine of Vítkovice was conducted from Paris[3] and the authorized representative of the Rothschild group was the Frenchman Eugène Rothschild, who also signed international cartel agreements on behalf of the Vítkovice Mining and Foundry Works.[4] It is interesting in this connection that the English Rothschilds held a protecting hand over the indivisibility of the Vítkovice possessions during the frontier dispute between Poland and Czechoslovakia in 1920.[5]

The Gutmann group could not rely on such influential international financial backing or such powerful connections as their partners in the Vítkovice Works. Gradually the Gutmanns had to succumb to the violent competitive struggles, the chronic crisis conditions in the Austrian economy and the pressure of

[1] Cf. V. Král, Review of my 'Příspěvek k poznání zahraničních spojů finančního kapitálu v Československu' (Foreign Links of Finance Capital in Czechoslovakia), *ČSČH*, VI (1958), p. 544; V. Král repeats his assertion in 'K úloze zahraničního kapitálu v Československu před rokem 1938' (The Role of Foreign Capital in Czechoslovakia before 1938), *ČSČH*, VII (1959), p. 476.

[2] Cf. K. W. Rothschild, *Austria's Economic Development between the Two Wars* (London, 1947).

[3] Cf. PA–VŽKG, Ostrava, VHHT 39.

[4] Cf. SÚA–KR 292/1 of 1925; SÚA–KR 234/1 of 1929.

[5] Cf. J. Valenta, 'Plány německé buržoasie na neutralizaci Ostravska a Těšínska v letech 1918–1920' (Plans for the Neutralization of Ostrava and Těšín put forward by the German Bourgeoisie in 1918–1920), *Slezský sborník* (Silesian Collection) (1960), p. 310.

their creditors (the Rothschilds among them, particularly the London branch).[1] This became especially evident at the beginning of the world economic crisis in 1931, after the collapse of the largest Austrian bank, the Österreichische Credit-Anstalt für Handel und Gewerbe, on which 75 % of Austrian industry depended.[2] The leading force in the Österreichische Credit-Anstalt was the Viennese Rothschilds, and they therefore participated with the Austrian National Bank in the reconstruction and stabilization of this bank, on which the whole of the Austrian banking system depended.[3] The financial pressure on the Viennese banking house of S. M. von Rothschild as a result of these operations was extraordinary and under these circumstances its influence decreased in comparison with other international banking groups in Austria. Consequently, the Viennese branch of the Rothschild group never again attained its former significance in Central and Southeastern Europe. At the same time the indebtedness of the banking house Brüder Gutmann in Vienna rose considerably. When in addition the accounts of the Vítkovice Mining and Foundry Works for 1932 showed a large loss,[4] which was divided among the mining shareholders in the same way as profits, the Gutmann group could not meet its obligations and a settlement had to be reached between the two groups, which changed the balance of power among the mining shareholders of the Vítkovice Works. On the basis of a moratorium, the so-called Standstill Agreement of 14 June 1933, the brothers Gutmann pawned their 45½ mining shares at the banking house N. M. Rothschild and Sons in London. From that time onwards dividends were regularly paid to the London Rothschilds[5] (Table 10B). Only 4½ mining shares remained in the hands of three women members of the Gutmann family, to whom the dividends for 1½

[1] PA-VŽKG, Ostrava, Memorandum über die Witkowitzer Bergbau- und Eisenhütten-Gewerkschaft (unmarked).

[2] Cf. J. Pátek, 'Poznámky k některým problemům v československo-rakouských vztazích na počátku světové hospodářské krize' (Comments on some problems in Czechoslovak–Austrian relations at the beginning of the world economic crisis), *Sborník Vysoké školy pedagogické* (Collected Studies of the University of Education), Historie II (Praha, 1959), p. 61.

[3] Ibid., p. 60; also *Hospodářská politika* (Economic Policy) (1931), p. 409.

[4] PA-VŽKG, Ostrava, VHHT 50; the only year which showed losses between the two world wars – PA-VŽKG, Ostrava, Profits and Losses 12.

[5] PA-VŽKG, Ostrava, VHHT 39.

shares each were sent to Austria, Italy and Slovakia respectively.[1] The owners of these comparatively insignificant shares never brought any pressure to bear on the management of the works.

The uncertain ownership relations of the Vítkovice Mining and Foundry Works were no secret in financial circles in Czechoslovakia or, especially, in France and Switzerland. It was expected that the mining shares pawned in London would come up for sale eventually.[2] These speculations called forth potential competition among domestic and foreign financial groups for control of the Vítkovice Works, which was the largest mining and metallurgical combine in Czechoslovakia. The Mining and Metallurgic Company's management zealously collected information about the intentions of the owners of the Vítkovice shares. Behind this activity the interests of the Schneider group and the Živnostenská Bank were easily discernible.[3] A further French group which had apparently made an unofficial offer to purchase the Vítkovice mining shares was the bank Crédit Lyonnais.[4] Between 1932 and 1934 the owners of the Vítkovice Works discussed transforming the mining company into a joint-stock company. At the meetings of the mining share owners on 10 December 1932 and 21 April 1934 the nominal amount of the basic joint-stock capital was agreed upon and the proposal for the establishment of a joint-stock company was passed.[5] However, the joint-stock company was never formally legalized. The material in the archives suggests that the Rothschild group reconsidered this decision, mainly because the profitability of the Vítkovice Mining and Foundry Works began to rise again after 1932, but also for reasons of competition. Evidently, the penetration of Czecho-

[1] PA–VŽKG, Ostrava, VHHT 43.

[2] Cf. *Hospodářské hovory* (Economic Conversations), 14 February 1938; also PA–VŽKG, Ostrava, Gen. řed. (unmarked).

[3] Cf. AÚLSMHD–BHS, Executive Committee, 1932–36.

[4] Cf. *Hospodářské hovory* (Economic Conversations); this information I was unable to verify. However, with the Živnostenská Bank French capital could have penetrated the Mining and Metallurgic Co., the greatest competitor of the Vítkovice Works in Czechoslovakia.

[5] PA–VŽKG, Ostrava, VHHT 50; V. Král mentions negotiations between Baron Louis Rothschild and the Živnostenská Bank about its participation in the Vítkovice combine in his book *Otázky hospodářského a sociálního vývoje v českých zemích 1938–1945*, II, p. 59. There was no evidence of this in the archives of the Vítkovice Iron Works.

slovak competitors into the management was feared, for two reasons. Firstly, according to the law relating to joint-stock companies the majority of the members of boards of directors had to be citizens of the Czechoslovak Republic and would necessarily therefore represent the interests of one or other of the Czech groups, as well as, probably, the interests of foreign capital. Also, the penetration of a group around the Živnostenská Bank into the Vítkovice Mining and Foundry Works would have been difficult to prevent. One indication of the possibility of such a development was the great indebtedness of the Gutmann brothers to the Živnostenská Bank. As a result of this, the firm of the brothers Gutmann in Prague, a large coal trading enterprise, passed into the sphere of influence of the Živnostenská Bank at just this time (1933).[1]

The Rothschild group obviously decided not to relinquish control of the Vítkovice Mining and Foundry Works. By a formal agreement on the transfer of all mining shares to the Alliance Assurance Co. Ltd in London, the 'Transfer Agreement' of the international House of Rothschild ensured that its influence in the management of the combine would continue to be decisive (Table 10C). The transfer of all 100 mining shares to the Alliance Assurance Co. Ltd in London was according to the Mining Law of Czechoslovakia entered in the Mining Book of Ostrava in the middle of 1937.[2] The Alliance Assurance Co. issued the former mining share owners with certificates to a total of 500,000 units (each mining share amounted to 5,000 units), which entitled them to receive dividends – not, however, from the Vítkovice Mining and Foundry Works, but from the English insurance company as their trustee.

The distribution of the units among the members of the Rothschild and Gutmann groups is shown in Table 10C and their territorial distribution on 31 December 1937 in Table 11. It is clear that a change in ownership relations had taken place and that the share of the Rothschild group increased by almost

[1] Cf. V. Král, II, p. 290.

[2] Cf. PA–VŽKG, Ostrava, Transfer Agreement (unmarked); P. Eisler writes of 'a transfer of share holdings to the London branch of this international banking dynasty', p. 22; cf. further copy of the registration in the Mines Book in PA–VŽKG, Ostrava, VHHT 40; R. Wagner mentions the Alliance Assurance Co. Ltd. as already the owner of the shares in 1932, but this does not accord with the documentary evidence in the archives; cf. R. Wagner, p. 81.

20 %. According to the 'Transfer Agreement' the holders of certificates had no powers whatsoever in the management of the Vítkovice Mining and Foundry Works. Only the Alliance Assurance Co. Ltd, as the owner of the mining shares, could vote at the assembly of owners and receive dividends.[1] The agreement, however, transferred both these decisive functions to the representative of the London banking house L. N. de Rothschild.[2]

Most of the legal operations of combines and banks disguise rather than clarify the mechanism of finance and capital movement.[3] That this danger was present in this complicated legal transaction is clear without further analysis.[4] It is particularly important to ascertain the character of the Alliance Assurance Co. Ltd and the connection of the Vítkovice combine with British finance.

The Alliance Assurance Co. was not formed – as has been maintained – as a sham company for the take-over of the Vítkovice mining shares, but was founded in 1886 by the English bankers of the Rothschild family.[5] In the 1930s the chairmanship of the board of directors was still held by the head of the London banking house, Lionel N. de Rothschild. With a nominal joint-stock capital of £5,450,000, it was one of the biggest insurance and investment firms in Britain.[6] Among its directors were representatives of the foremost British banks and insurance companies, and of the most powerful combines in the oil, rubber, steel, shipping and coal industries, as well as of land- and sea-transport companies, all with a wide network of interests in the British Empire and in other countries.[7]

[1] Cf. PA–VŽKG, Ostrava, Transfer Agreement, Deed of Trustee; also IMT, Nr. IV, Fall XI, pp. 17560/61.

[2] Cf. PA–VŽKG, Ostrava, Transfer Agreement; a Memorandum.

[3] Cf. V. I. Lenin, *Collected Works*, Vol. 22, p. 227.

[4] Cf. V. Král, 'K úloze zahraničního finančního kapitálu v Československu před rokem 1938' (The Role of Foreign Finance Capital in Czechoslovakia before 1938), pp. 476–7.

[5] Cf. Ibid., p. 476.

[6] Cf. *The Stock Exchange Official Intelligence* (London, 1930); *The Stock Exchange Year Book* (London, 1932–7), *The Bank and Insurance Shares Year Book* (London, 1937, 1938–9).

[7] Cf. *Directory of Directors* (London, 1937–40). Of the board of directors of the Alliance Assurance Co. Ltd, 21 members held 144 seats on boards of a number of powerful combines in industry and banking. A significant place was also held by Sir William John Firth, a representative of the British steel and shipping industry in the Vickers combine.

Table 11. *Combine of the Vítkovice*

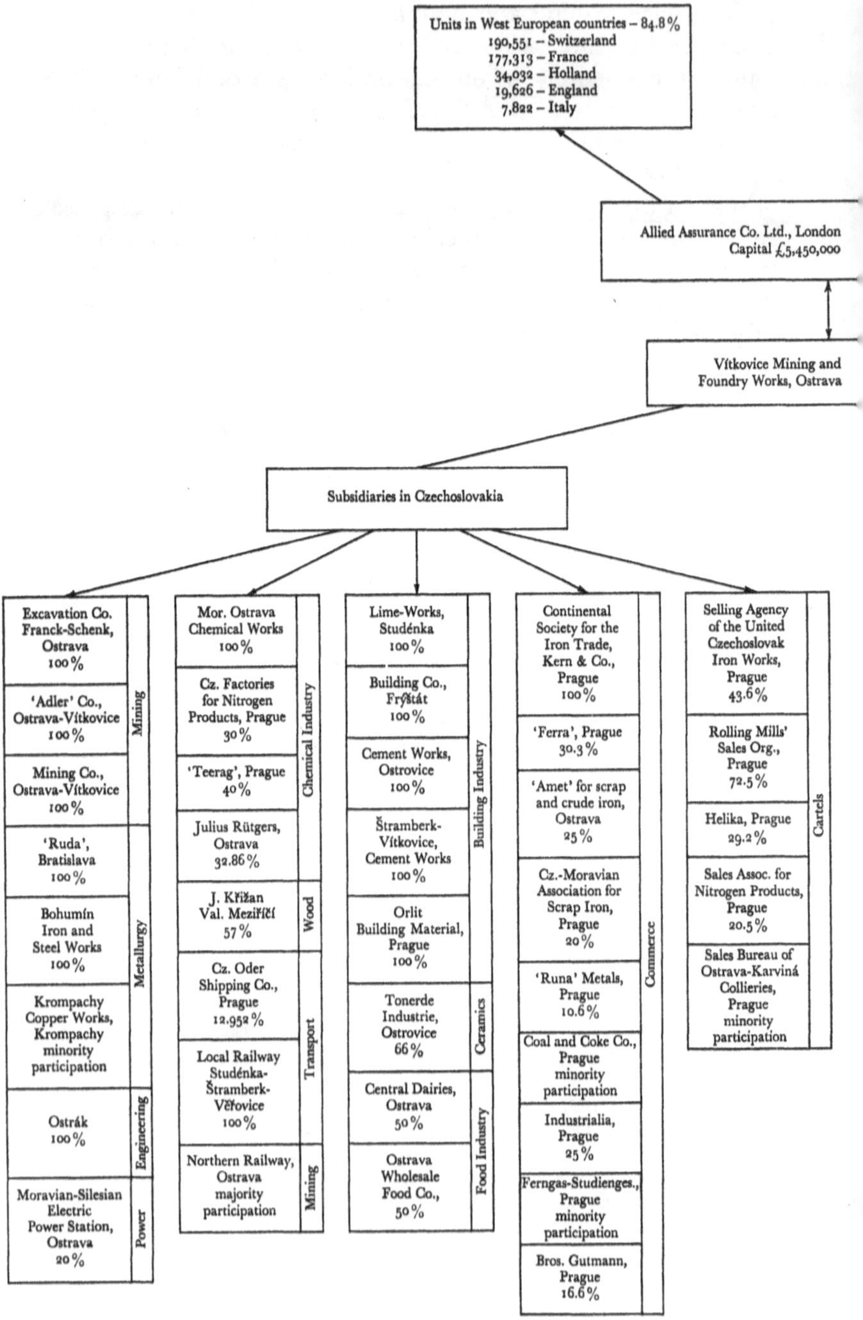

Mining and Foundry Works, 31 December 1937

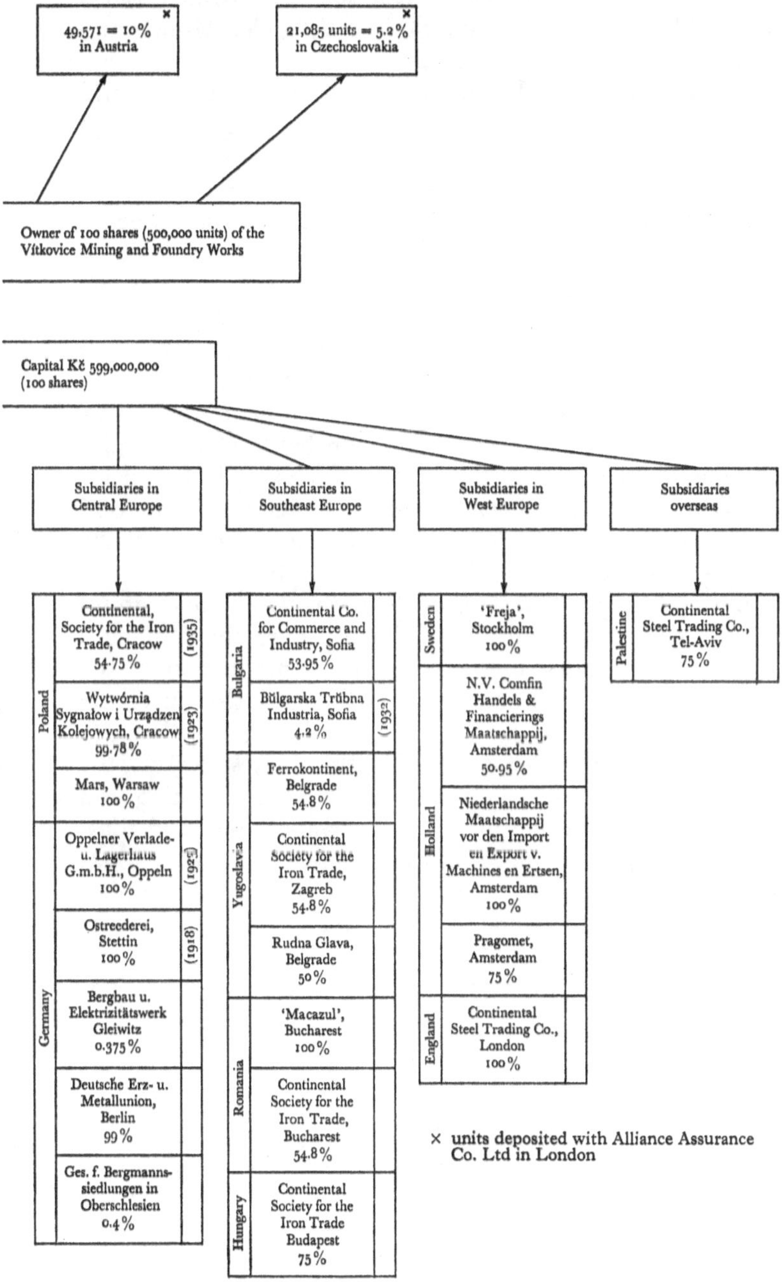

This capital and financial strength, together with the banking and industrial connections of the Rothschilds, provided a firm basis for the competitive position of the Vítkovice Mining and Foundry Works in Central Europe.

The link between the Vítkovice Mining and Foundry Works and British capital also had roots in its long-standing cooperation with the most powerful British steel and shipbuilding combine, Vickers Ltd., for whom the Vítkovice steel works produced rolled material and especially heavy sheets.[1] In the Czechoslovak United Iron Works cartel the exceptional relationship between Vítkovice and Britain was recognized, and in the agreements of the 1930s the export of shipbuilding material and of a fixed quantity of heavy sheets by the Vítkovice Works to Britain was allowed for outside the quota system.[2] The connection which secured Vítkovice standing orders from Vickers was not accidental, because the banking house of Rothschild in London participated in the capital of Vickers Ltd. and for many years both firms had a common director. The mutual linking of interests of the Rothschild bank in London and the Vickers works originated at the beginning of the century.[3] Thus it appears that the British branch of the Rothschild group gradually gained a controlling influence over the Vítkovice combine and guaranteed a market for its production in the British steel industry. These facts justify the inclusion of the foreign capital invested in the Vítkovice Mining and Foundry Works before 1938 in the sphere of British interests.[4]

Table 11 shows the structure of the Vítkovice Mining and Foundry Works combine up to 31 December 1937 and illustrates the key position of its central management, which was able through its numerous subsidiaries to intervene in a number of important industries in Czechoslovakia and which penetrated into most of the Central and Southeast European countries as well as into Western Europe. The direct participation of foreign capital in the Vítkovice combine, represented by

[1] Cf. ANTM–SDS 413, box 1.

[2] Cf. AÚLSMHD–10008, enclosure 31.

[3] Cf. J. D. Scott, *Vickers* (London, 1962), p. 62.

[4] The discussion between V. Král and myself in the Czechoslovak Journal of History (*ČSČH*, 1958–9), and my researches in the works archives of the Vítkovice Mining and Foundry Works in Ostrava and in London contributed towards a clarification of this question.

the Alliance Assurance Co. Ltd, brought with it indirect participation in a further 37 industrial, commercial and cartel companies in Czechoslovakia and 22 other enterprises outside Czechoslovakia. By means of its direct investment in the Czechoslovak combine foreign capital penetrated, above all, into heavy industry in Central and Southeastern Europe, and these so-called Czechoslovak investments abroad belonged, in the last analysis, to the group centred around the British banking house of the Rothschilds.

The Vítkovice Mining and Foundry Works constituted the largest industrial combine in pre-Munich Czechoslovakia, and was continuously strengthening its position, either by acquiring new subsidiaries or by increasing its participation in the capital of its existing subsidiary companies. On the eve of the Second World War the Vítkovice Works increased its direct investment in subsidiary enterprises, from about Kč 166 million in 32 companies in 1935 to about Kč 200 million in 37 companies in 1937, i.e. by more than 20 %.[1] At the same time opportunities for profit increased, not only because of the automatic increase in dividends and commissions, but also by the rationalization of production and the elimination of middlemen or other connecting links in the production and selling process. Evidence of this is given by the balance sheets, which show a net profit for the whole combine, including the Czechoslovak subsidiaries, of Kč 42,377,100 in 1935, which rose to Kč 100,251,100 in 1937.[2] Even at the height of the boom of 1929 the Vítkovice combine did not achieve such a profit. Until 1935, apart from the losses in 1932, the dividends that were sent to Vienna in the 1920s and then to London in the 1930s amounted to Kč 40–60 millions annually. In the period 1935–8 the dividends paid out of Czechoslovakia rose together with the rising net profits and, according to the official accounts of the Vítkovice Works,[3] reached Kč 80 millions in 1937. The sharp rise in profits reflects on the one hand the expansion of capacity and the strengthening of the position of the Vítkovice Mining and Foundry Works, and on the other hand its important share in the armament boom in Czechoslovak heavy industry in the

[1] Calculated from PA–VŽKG, Ostrava, VHHT 40 and Profits and Losses 12.

[2] PA–VŽKG, Ostrava, Profits and Losses 12.

[3] PA–VŽKG, Ostrava, VHHT–Vedení (Management) 41.

second half of the 1930s. It also shows that foreign investors regularly skimmed off almost the whole net earnings of the Vítkovice combine, a fairly significant part of the Czechoslovak national income.[1]

The structure of the Vítkovice combine was that of a vertical monopoly, controlling the whole production process from coal and iron-ore mines, coke and cement works, sawmills, electrical power stations and chemical works to iron and steel and engineering works; and extending to transport companies and selling agencies for coal, coke, chemical products and steel goods. This structure was also reflected in the subsidiary enterprises outside Czechoslovakia, which included iron-ore mines, especially in Sweden and Yugoslavia; iron and steel works in Poland, Germany, Bulgaria, Yugoslavia and Romania, and shipping companies in Germany. The latter handled most of the raw material supplies and the export of the products of Czechoslovak iron and steel works, which were transported on the big German rivers. In addition, the Vítkovice Mining and Foundry Works combine built up a network of sales agencies, which were controlled by a subsidiary, the Continental Society for the Iron Trade Kern & Co. in Prague.[2] The subsidiaries in Holland, England and Palestine consisted entirely of commercial companies, and the Amsterdam trading and financial house N.V. Comfin Handels en Financierings Maatschappij also belonged to the Rothschild sphere of interest in Western Europe.[3]

Sixty per cent of all the iron-ore consumed by furnaces in Czechoslovakia was imported.[4] The Vítkovice Iron Works had its own iron-ore mines in Slovakia, although a substantial part of the ore it used came from mines in Sweden, through its company 'Freja' Bergwerks Aktiebolaget in Stockholm.[5] In this field the Vítkovice Mining and Foundry Works had a considerable advantage over other iron and steel producers, because deliveries of high quality iron-ore from its own subsidiary were obtained at a lower cost than was possible for its

[1] This conclusion results from the data of PA-VŽKG, Ostrava, VHHT 40, Balance Reports (Bilanční zprávy).

[2] On joint participations of the Mining and Metallurgic Co. and the Vítkovice Mining and Foundry Works, see below, pp. 112–113.

[3] Cf. PA-VŽKG, Ostrava, VHHT (unmarked).

[4] Cf. *Statistická ročenka*, 1938, p. 67.

[5] Viz. Table 11.

biggest competitor. This was the Mining and Metallurgic Co., which also used Swedish ore but depended to a large extent on deliveries from Yugoslavia, the Soviet Union and through its French shareholders on iron-ore from North Africa.[1] From this point of view the production costs of the Vítkovice Works were relatively lower and profits thus relatively higher.

Further positive advantages were gained by the Vítkovice Iron Works through its subsidiary transport companies. In the efforts to reduce transport costs a special role was played by the Czechoslovak Oder Shipping Co., which also belonged to the Vítkovice combine. This company provided shipping on the Oder from Stettin (Szczecin) and was founded in 1924 by the Czechoslovak state, which held 72 % of the joint-stock capital. The services of the Czechoslovak Oder Shipping Co. were almost exclusively used by the iron and steel works of Ostrava and the state therefore transferred the management of the company to its private shareholders, i.e. the Mining and Metallurgic Co., whose participation amounted to 15.05 % and the Vítkovice Mining and Foundry Works, with a share of 12.95 %.[2]

The general directors of both combines were members of the board of this essentially state-owned enterprise,[3] but the practical running of the company was in the hands of the Vítkovice combine, because the Czechoslovak Oder Shipping Co. was managed by the transport department of the Vítkovice Mining and Foundry Works.[4] The company's operations were thus managed in conjunction with those of the other transport subsidiaries of Vítkovice providing shipping on the Oder, the Oppelner Verlade und Lagerhaus Gesellschaft in Oppeln and the Ostreederei Gesellschaft m.b.H. in Stettin. However, the state-owned shipping company, in which the private combines had minority shares, showed rather large losses in its balance sheets every year – half a million Czechoslovak Crowns on the average[5] – which were regularly met by the biggest shareholder, i.e. the Czechoslovak state.

In addition the Ministry of Public Works paid subsidies to

[1] Cf. ANTM – Vzpomínky J. Tilleho (Memoirs of J. Tille).
[2] Cf. *Compass*, Čechoslovakei (1929–39); viz. Tables 11 and 12.
[3] Cf. *Compass*, Čechoslovakei.
[4] Cf. ANTM – Vzpomínky J. Tilleho.
[5] Calculated from the balance reports in *Compass*, Čechoslovakei.

the company, partly to cover its losses and partly for the servicing of its freighters.[1] The Ministry for Industry and Trade justified this financial policy by declaring it to be its duty to make the biggest possible contribution to the overall prosperity of Czechoslovak industry.[2] In comparison with the chronic passivity of the state-owned transport company under the management of private combines, the subsidiary transport companies in Oppeln and Stettin, whose capital was wholly owned by the Vítkovice Mining and Foundry Works, were continuously profitable. It seems that the managements of Vítkovice and of the Třinec Mining and Metallurgic Co. lowered transport costs and thus production costs by depending heavily on the tax-payers.

In monopolistic organizations the tendency for production costs to fall can also be reflected in technical improvements and in the introduction of the latest production methods, which is as a rule accompanied by a reduction in the labour force. This course, which in time usually leads to an increase in profits as well, requires longterm and sometimes very substantial investment. Whenever it was possible to postpone technical improvements, the Vítkovice Mining and Foundry Works did so. It followed an exceptionally cautious investment policy[3] and relied more on its network of selling agencies abroad to raise and transfer profits. One important channel for transferring profits from the Vítkovice combine in Czechoslovakia to the shareholders abroad was the Continental Society for the Iron Trade Kern & Co. This company obtained products of the Vítkovice Iron Works on preferential terms and sold them abroad at prices protected by the International Steel Cartel. The profits from these sales were, as a rule, not accounted for in the central accounting office of Vítkovice in Czechoslovakia, but directly with the banking houses of the Rothschild group. The Třinec Mining and Metallurgic Co. also took part in these transactions, as a minority shareholder in the Continental Society for the Iron Trade Kern & Co. The operations within a ramified combine with subsidiaries at home and abroad are so compli-

[1] Cf. *Compass*, Čechoslovakei (1939), p. 1534.
[2] Cf. ANTM – Vzpomínky J. Tilleho.
[3] Cf. Ibid., and investments in construction in Balance Reports, PA–VŽKG, Ostrava.

cated that it is difficult to estimate the real size of the drain of Czechoslovak national income to foreign investors, over and above dividends and commissions actually accounted for in the balance sheets of the corporations.

The Vítkovice Mining and Foundry Works combine occupied an important place in European economic relations, which was contested by Czechoslovak and foreign competitors in big business and finance, especially in the 1930s. Above all, the interests of West European and German groups clashed in this area. After Hitler came to power, the well-known conscious longterm objective of German heavy industry, to penetrate into Czechoslovak industrial and banking combines in order to attain a basis for further advances into Southeast Europe, was openly and aggressively pursued by German political and economic representatives. It is therefore highly probable that the changes and the new structure of ownership relations in the Vítkovice combine, which have been traced up to the end of 1937, were a result of a competitive struggle. In the course of this the Rothschild group shifted the centre of its interests to London so as to strengthen its position in Czechoslovakia, because from there its capital investments branched out into Central and Southeast Europe.

The transactions affecting the Vítkovice Mining and Foundry Works do not in any way suggest a voluntary withdrawal from the Central and Southeastern European area 'in favour of German capital'.[1] The Rothschild group, together with the Gutmann family, only agreed to negotiate the sale of the Vítkovice Iron Works in 1938, and in particular after Munich,[2] after threats of physical violence against Baron Louis Rothschild – a member of the Viennese branch of the family who had been arrested by the Gestapo after the *Anschluss* of Austria. The documents of the Nuremberg economic trials tell us something about the course of the negotiations and their failure.[3] The impatience of German heavy industry, especially the Goering combine, and the value the Fascist leaders attached to the Vítkovice Iron Works, are evident from Hitler's order to Keitel, issued on the afternoon of 14 March 1939. General Keitel was ordered to occupy Vítkovice before the general military invasion

[1] Cf. V. Král, II, p. 59.
[2] Cf. IMT - Nr. IV, Fall XI, 17563.
[3] Cf. V. Král, II, pp. 58–72.

of the Czech Lands on 15 March 1939, in order to prevent Poland from taking over the rolling mills before the arrival of the German army.[1] The attempt of the German Fascists to take over the Vítkovice Mining and Foundry Works by force provides evidence that the groups which owned the Vítkovice combine did not retreat slowly from the field under pressure from German capital long before Munich. The preceding analysis has rather suggested the existence of forces which acted in the opposite direction at this time.

It is quite understandable that the British government took an active interest in the negotiations between Baron Eugène Rothschild and the representative of the Dresdner Bank, Karl Rasche, which took place in 1939. After long negotiations and delays a deed of sale was agreed upon by Rasche and the representative of Eugène Rothschild. It was, however, only signed conditionally, for the Rothschild group in Paris had to refer back to their 'London advisers' to obtain the approval of the British government to the sale of the Vítkovice Mining and Foundry Works.[2] In the meantime the Second World War broke out and Germany was informed through British government channels that the deed of sale concerning the Vítkovice Mining and Foundry Works had lost its validity.[3]

The Mining and Metallurgic Company

Very soon after the First World War the Mining and Metallurgic Co., with its rich coal-mines in the Ostrava–Karviná region and its main foundry in Třinec, became the second most influential member of the Big Three. Its combine expanded considerably during the period of the pre-Munich Republic and a significant proportion of its joint-stock capital was in the hands of foreign, predominantly French, shareholders from 1920 to 1940 (Table 12).

The history of foreign capital participation in the Mining and Metallurgic Co. provides an almost classic example of the shifts

[1] Cf. Keitel's testimony IMT–1400–1700, 5 April 1946.

[2] Cf. DZAP–B202–NID 15625, also 15551.

[3] Because there is no access to the relevant material, the circumstances under which Eugène Rothschild negotiated with the British government or British authorities on the sale of the Vítkovice Works in the spring or summer of 1939 cannot be satisfactorily clarified.

in property relations between the bankers and industrialists of the victorious and defeated countries resulting from the new division of the world's spheres of interest after the First World War. From its foundation as a joint-stock company until 1920 the Archduke Friedrich von Habsburg and the Österreichische Boden-Credit-Anstalt in Vienna held a controlling interest[1] in the Österreichische Berg- und Hüttenwerks-Gesellschaft A.G., and a minority holding belonged to Reichs-German holders.[2] Since 1909 financial and technological matters had been in the hands of Georg Günther, who was also a director of the Österreichische Boden-Credit-Anstalt.[3] Günther's undoubted organizational talent and his sound technical knowledge, as well as his determined drive to reduce production costs and to increase profits, laid the foundation for the company's competitive strength, especially during the First World War when the Austro-Hungarian Iron and Steel Cartel was suspended. The Mining and Metallurgic Co. had already competed effectively with the leading combines of the Austrian Monarchy, the Prague Iron Co. and the Alpine Montangesellschaft.

After the defeat of the Central Powers and the establishment of the Successor States, the continued existence of the combine as a unit depended on the solution of controversial international issues, especially those connected with the frontier dispute between Poland and Czechoslovakia. The main foundries of the Mining and Metallurgic Company were situated in Třinec, i.e. on the disputed so-called plebiscite territory in Těšín; another part of the works was in Węgierska Górka in Poland; the coal-mines were located in the Ostrava–Karviná region and the sheet-rolling mills in Karlova Huť in Czechoslovakia. The general and commercial management, on the other hand, remained in Vienna, entirely separated from the production base. Thus the eventual fate of the combine of the Mining and Metallurgic Co. was to be determined by geographical, economic and political considerations, which found expression in a complicated competitive tug-of-war between influential business groups of

[1] Cf. Stočes, pp. 23, 24, 66.

[2] DZAP – RWiM 13756, fol. 102–3.

[3] G. Günther, *Lebenserinnerungen*, p. 224. Günther belonged to the leading group of Austrian bankers and industrialists, although he was of Prussian origin. His most influential post was as a leading executive of the Österreichische Boden-Credit-Anstalt, in which he remained until its collapse in 1929–30.

Table 12. *Combine of the Mining*

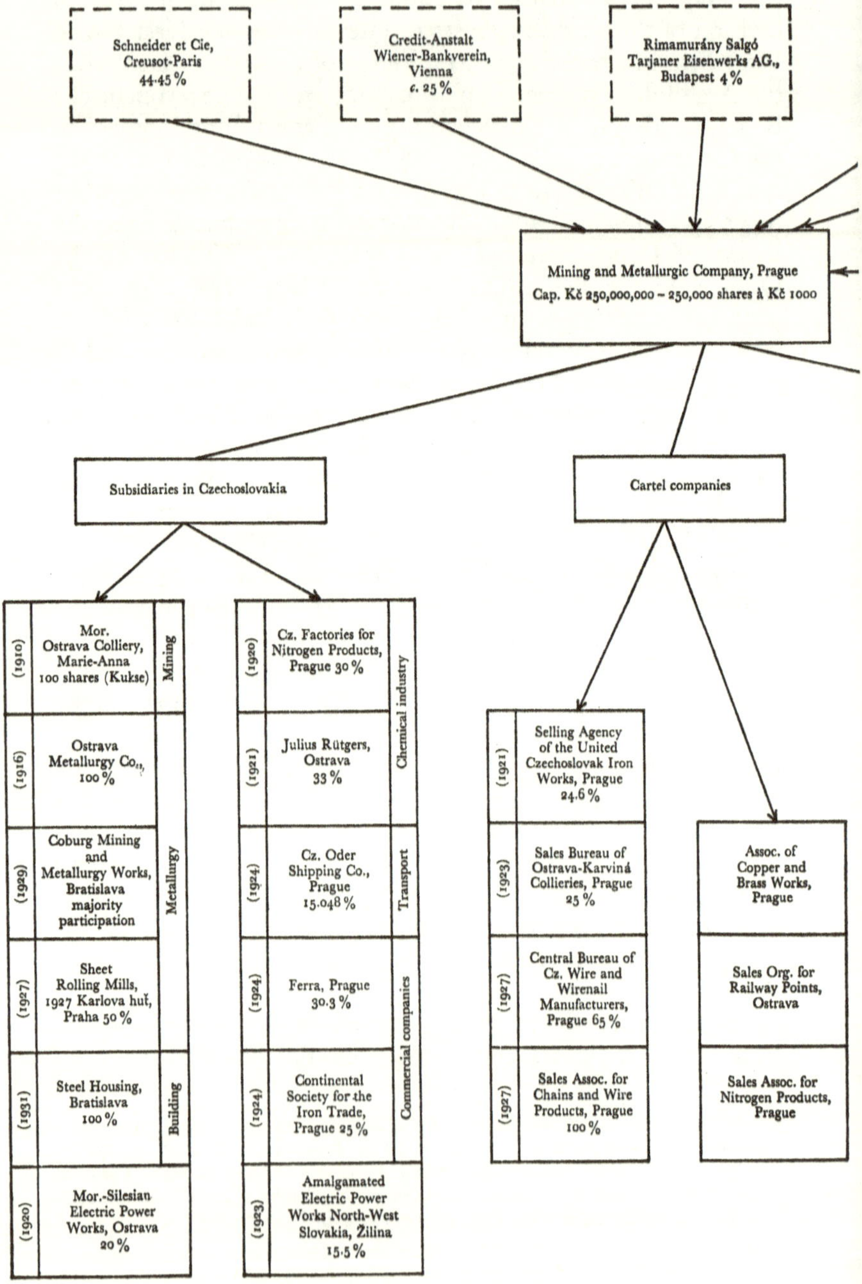

and Metallurgic Company, 31 December 1937

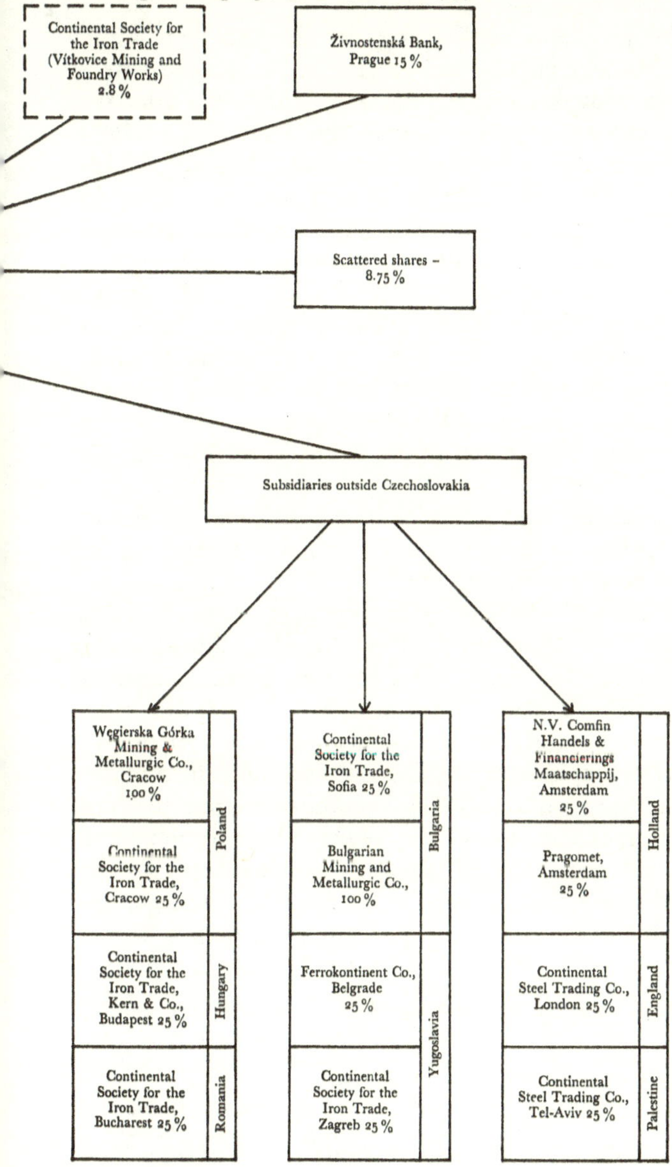

the Entente Powers for the positions of the defeated Germans, Austrians and Hungarians.

One of the problems confronting the shareholders of the Mining and Metallurgic Co. and of similar large-scale enterprises in Czechoslovakia was the demand of the revolutionary working-class movement, especially in the Ostrava–Karviná–Těšín area, for the socialization of large-scale industry.[1] This claim was reinforced by widespread and militant strikes in Ostrava and Těšín during 1920, which developed into political protest strikes against the transit of arms through Czechoslovak territory to Poland for use in the Polish–Soviet War.[2] Unrest in Polish, and particularly in Czechoslovak, industrial areas, as well as the unexpected advance of the Red Army towards Warsaw, induced the Great Powers and the Successor States to reach a speedy solution of the Těšín problem, thus, at the same time, settling the destiny of the Mining and Metallurgic Company.

In addition to the class struggles in the area, financial and business groups among the Entente Powers were competing for control of this economically extremely important region, as part of the new division of international spheres of interest. The Paris Peace Conference had set up an Inter-Allied Commission, in whose deliberations the Anglo-American standpoint, as distinct from the French, is clearly discernible. On the one side, American circles around Herbert Hoover – evidently supported by the American representative, Dubois, and the British representative, Coulson, on the Těšín Commission – put forward plans for the neutralization of this region. They proposed to make it an internationalized territory administered by the United States and Great Britain, which would be a large, undivided raw-material and industrial region, comprising Upper Silesia, Ostrava and Těšín and which would control the main

[1] Cf. J. Valenta, 'K počátkům internacionalistického směru v dělnickém hnutí na Ostravsku a Těšínsku v letech 1918–1920' (The Beginnings of Internationalism in the Working Class Movement of Ostrava and Těšín in 1918–1920), *Slezský sborník* (Silesian Collection) (Opava, 1961), p. 190.

[2] Cf. M. Otáhal, *Dělnické hnutí na Ostravsku v letech 1917–1921* (The Working Class Movement in Ostrava 1917–1921) (Ostrava, 1955), p. 76; also *O československé zahraniční politice 1918–1939* (Czechoslovak Foreign Policy 1918–1939) (Praha, 1956), p. 68 passim; also V. Olivová, *Československo-sovětské vztahy 1918–1922* (Czechoslovak–Soviet Relations 1918–1922) (Praha, 1957), p. 212.

routes to Southeastern Europe.[1] Such a solution would have satisfied the interested German and Austrian bankers and industrialists, because it would have enabled them to hold on to many of their possessions and to retain some of their powerful positions in this rich area, from which they could further have influenced the economic life of the Successor States, especially Czechoslovakia.[2] They hoped to benefit from the differences amongst the Great Powers, because in Washington, and to some extent in London,[3] there were plans to counter French efforts to build a system of alliances in Central and Southeastern Europe aimed at French hegemony in Europe. On the other side, the French representatives in Paris and in the Těšín Inter-Allied Commission defended their proposal to assign the disputed territory to Czechoslovakia,[4] which fitted in with the aims of French power politics in Europe. The official French standpoint on the Těšín question coincided with the attempts of French capital to gain control of the Mining and Metallurgic Co. In these complicated relations French finance found itself in a favourable situation compared with other Entente groups, as the French Military Mission held a powerful position in the new Czechoslovak state.

At the same time a violent competitive struggle developed between the Czech bourgeoisie, who had taken over the Czechoslovak government, and the politically weakened German and Austrian bourgeoisie, who still held key positions in industry and banking in the newly established state. For this reason Czech financial circles were not indifferent to German and Austrian participation in the joint-stock capital of the Mining and Metallurgic Company. In accordance with the

[1] J. Valenta, 'Plány německé buržoasie na neutralizaci Ostravska a Těšínska v letech 1918–1920' (Plans for the Neutralization of Ostrava and Těšín put forward by the German Bourgeoisie 1918–1920), *Slezský sborník*, particularly p. 303.

[2] Cf. Ibid., p. 295.

[3] The position of the British government was not wholly explicit. During the talks between the Foreign Ministers of Czechoslovakia and Great Britain, Dr Beneš and Lord Curzon, the latter supported a frontier along the river Olše, which meant that the main coal-mines would remain on the territory of Czechoslovakia. Cf. *O československé zahraniční politice*, p. 69.

[4] Cf. J. Valenta, p. 304, footnote 105 on p. 307. Valenta's surmise that the Schneider combine's bank, L'Union Européenne Industrielle et Financière, sympathized with plans for neutralization does not seem very likely, because its explicit function was to look after the investments of the Schneider combine in Central and Southeast Europe; cf. J. Valenta, p. 229 and footnote 60.

nationalization programme the Czechoslovak Chamber of Deputies passed the Nostrification Act at the end of 1919, which required every joint-stock company to transfer its headquarters to the territory of the new state in which its plants were situated.[1] At the same time, other legislation also furthered the process of nationalization, e.g. the transfer of foreign-owned property wherever possible into Czech ownership. The Currency Separation Act of March 1919, in particular, made it impossible for Viennese banks to finance direct from Vienna their own Czechoslovak subsidiaries in industry, commerce and banking. Thus opportunities arose for the big Czech banks, particularly the leading institution, the Živnostenská Bank, to gain financial influence in these enterprises.[2] Another law concerning domestic joint-stock companies decreed that at least half the members of boards of directors had to be Czechoslovak citizens and that the general director must be a Czechoslovak citizen permanently domiciled in Czechoslovakia. This legislation undermined the power of the Viennese banks in the Czechoslovak economy and particularly weakened the position of the Österreichische Boden-Credit-Anstalt, which had most of its shares in industrial companies on Czechoslovak territory.[3] The Mining and Metallurgic Co. was among the most valuable industrial possessions of this bank and under the new conditions management and financial transactions with the Viennese central offices were greatly impeded.

The unfavourable situation, together with strong tendencies towards socialization and uncertainties about the territorial division of the combine, adversely affected quotations of the Mining and Metallurgic Co.'s shares on the stock-exchange.[4] Under these pressures the Austrian and German shareholders of the company agreed to enter into negotiations about selling their shares. However, even the strongest Czech financial

[1] Act passed 11 December 1919, No. 12, Sb.z. a n. (Collection of Laws and Regulations, 1920). On the significance of nostrification generally viz. R. Olšovský *et al.*, p. 34.

[2] Cf. A. Pimper, *České obchodní banky za války a po válce* (Czech Commercial Banks during the War and after the War) (Praha, 1929), p. 138.

[3] Cf. *Compass, Österreich* 1919; also G. Günther, *Lebenserinnerungen*, p. 244.

[4] Cf. A. Dobrý on nostrification and the fall in the value of shares on the stock-exchange, p. 20. However, Dobrý underestimates the role of foreign investment by the Western Powers in the process of so-called nationalization, cf. especially pp. 21–3.

groups did not have enough capital to obtain a majority holding – a situation which, incidentally, also occurred in other so-called 'nationalization' processes initiated by Czech banking and business circles. Finally the Czech Živnostenská Bank became the junior partner of the biggest French iron and steel combine, Schneider et Cie., which was greatly aided by the legislative measures of the Czechoslovak government in gaining a significant share in the joint-stock capital of Czechoslovakia's heavy industry.

At the end of spring 1920 the management of Schneider et Cie–Creusot concluded that the time was ripe to purchase a controlling share in the Mining and Metallurgic Co. For this purpose representatives were sent to Vienna. Negotiations about the transfer of shares took place between the general director of the Paris central offices, Fournier, for the Schneider group and the general director of the Mining and Metallurgic Co., Günther, for the Österreichische Boden-Credit-Anstalt.[1] The two sides reached an agreement in a comparatively short time, mainly because Günther was a realistic judge of the political and economic situation and believed that the economic and military strength of France offered the best guarantees, firstly against socialization and secondly against a territorial division of the works and plant which would separate the foundries from their coal supplies. Günther drew special attention to these dangers during the negotiations with the Schneider representatives.[2] His views coincided with those of his great rival, as well as business associate in the Ostrava–Karviná region, the general director of the Vítkovice Mining and Foundry Works, Dr Adolf Sonnenschein, who became convinced that under the new circumstances the profitability of the iron and steel industry would be best secured within the Czechoslovak state but with decisive participation of Western capital investment.[3] Very soon after the Vienna meeting the majority of the Mining and

[1] Cf. G. Günther, p. 219.

[2] About his decision to obtain the desired package of shares for Schneider Günther writes: 'Wenn ich ihn (den Entschluß – A.T.) dennoch fasste, so tat ich es in der Annahme, daß die erwähnten und die noch zu befürchtenden Schwierigkeiten durch französischen Einfluß noch am ehesten überwunden werden konnten.' G. Günther, *Lebenserinnerungen*, p. 218; cf. also B. Stočes, p. 52.

[3] Cf. G. Günther, p. 219; also Stočes, p. 53; J. Valenta, p. 294, footnote 29 and p. 303, footnote 89.

Metallurgic Co.'s shares were transferred to Schneider et Cie–Creusot in Paris; the shares in question came partly from the holdings of the Österreichische Boden-Credit-Anstalt in Vienna and partly from Switzerland, where the largest shareholder, the Archduke Friedrich of Habsburg, had managed to deposit his shares shortly before the collapse of the Austro-Hungarian Monarchy.[1] The connection with the Viennese bank was not wholly severed, for approximately 25 % of the company's joint-stock capital remained in its hands. At the same time as French participation began, the Živnostenská Bank also penetrated into the company, gradually gaining about 15 %. The decisive influence, however, went to the Schneider group, whose participation amounted to about 50 % throughout the period of existence of the pre-Munich Czechoslovak Republic (Table 12).

On 3 July 1920 two general directors of the Schneider iron and steel works in France, Jules Aubrun and André Vicaire, joined the board of directors of the Mining and Metallurgic Co.; with them were two representatives of the Schneider group's Polish subsidiary combine Huty Bankowé, Joseph Chanove and Robert Huet.[2] It was not accidental that an officer of the French army, Colonel Ernest Weyl, became a member of the board of directors at the same time. He too represented the Schneider interests and had already made it quite clear on a previous occasion, when, as a member of the board of directors of the Škoda-Works, he addressed the first board meeting, that French capital was pursuing not emotional aims but a level-headed profit policy.[3] Colonel Weyl held an important post for the Schneider interests in Czechoslovakia as the 'administrateur délégué' of their holding company, L'Union Européenne Industrielle et Financière, and also as head of a small delegation from Schneider et Cie which was permanently domiciled in Czechoslovakia.[4]

At that time preparations for a plebiscite in the Těšín area were suddenly cancelled and, instead, negotiations about the disputed boundaries between Poland and Czechoslovakia took place on 10 July 1920 in Spa, between representatives of Czechoslovakia, France and Great Britain. As a result, Poland

[1] Cf. ANTM – Vzpomínky J. Tilleho; also G. Günther, p. 219.
[2] Cf. B. Stočes, p. 20.
[3] PA–ZVIL, GŘ 2, 21 May 1920. [4] Ibid.

and Czechoslovakia agreed to accept the arbitration of the Great Powers. During the final stage of the Těšín dispute Anglo-French opinion inclined towards the Czechoslovak side.[1] The most influential business and government circles of Western Europe obviously considered Czechoslovakia capable of giving better guarantees than post-war Poland of the success of their economic and political policy in Central and Southeastern Europe. As a consequence the Ambassadors' Conference of 28 July 1920, Těšín was divided in such a way that the Karviná coal-fields and the whole Košice–Bohumín railway, together with the Těšín railway station, came under the jurisdiction of the Czechoslovak state, while the eastern part of the town of Těšín and the country area east of the river Olše went to Poland.[2] The iron works of Třinec, which were situated east of the Olše, were included in the Czechoslovak territory, and thus Czechoslovakia gained a narrow strip of territory on the right bank of the river Olše and the boundary with Poland was shifted slightly to the east. The coal-mines and iron and steel works of the Mining and Metallurgic Company remained united in Czechoslovak territory. For the shareholders of the company the Allied decision was of far-reaching significance, for the collieries of Karviná delivered high-grade coal, which was admirably suited for coking, to the blast-furnaces in Třinec.[3] Only the iron foundry of the Mining and Metallurgic Co. in Węgierska Górka remained on Polish territory; that plant also became part of the reorganized combine under French control. Through their capital participation in the Mining and Metallurgic Co. the Schneider group gained another key position in Czechoslovakia, especially after the Těšín decision; the previous year they had obtained a controlling holding in the joint-stock capital of the Škoda-Works.[4] French capital investment in these areas strengthened the Czechoslovak government and business circles and at the same time hindered the socialization of heavy industry.

[1] Cf. J. Valenta, p. 310, footnote 129.

[2] Cf. *O. československé zahraniční politice*, p. 72.

[3] Cf. B. Stočes, pp. 52–3; also ANTM – Vzpomínky J. Tilleho; also G. Günther, p. 219.

[4] Cf. V. Jíša–A. Vaněk, *Škodovy závody 1918–1938* (Škoda-Works 1918–1938) (Praha, 1962), p. 118; the analysis of French direct investment in the Škoda-Works is dealt with in Chapter 4.

The identity of interests between French foreign policy and the foreign investment of French business was remarkable, but it undeniably existed. In this case, Schneider et Cie, which, as the most powerful company in the French iron and steel industry, headed the Comité des Forges, pursued a policy of penetration of French interests into Czechoslovak heavy industry and through these connections, further eastwards,[1] in the process taking over capital which had formerly been German and Austrian. Czech businessmen and bankers, particularly the Živnostenská Bank, participated actively in this investment policy, using the aspirations for national liberation of the peoples of Southeast Europe and the conditions of the peace treaties to their own advantage. In the case of the Mining and Metallurgic Co. the Czechoslovak government applied paragraph 297 of the Versailles Peace Treaty, which gave it the right to liquidate the capital participation of German citizens in railways, mines, foundries and spas. In spite of the fact that the Czechoslovak government withdrew a substantial number of its claims during the Czechoslovak–German negotiations over the liquidation of German property in these areas of the economy, which extended over several years, it insisted (in the final 'Maximum Liquidation Programme' of 1 November 1924) on the transfer of bonds of the Košice–Bohumín railway and shares in the Mining and Metallurgic Co. to Czech ownership.[2] In this way, the participation of the Živnostenská Bank in the joint-stock capital of the Mining and Metallurgic Co. was somewhat increased.

In these transactions the Živnostenská Bank cannot be considered an equal partner with the powerful monopolist companies which made up the Schneider combine. The head of Schneider et Cie, Eugène Schneider, exerted considerable influence on French policy as a leading representative of the powerful Comité des Forges, an association of 250 French iron and steel plants.[3] Eugène Schneider was also connected with other internationally influential combines in the period

[1] Cf. *Milliarden Truste in Frankreich*, p. 92.

[2] DZAP–RWiM 13756; negotiations lasted from 1920 to 1925.

[3] Cf. M. Thorez, *France To-day* (London, 1936), p. 40; Eugène Schneider was president of the Comité des Forges until 1923 and after that was one of its 30 permanent directors. Cf. also A. Plummer, *International Combines in Modern Industry* (London, 1949), p. 234.

between the two world wars; he was on the board of directors of one of the four leading French banks, the Crédit Lyonnais in Paris, and was also head of the Schneider family's banking-house, L'Union Européenne Industrielle et Financière, which was based in Paris, where all the Central and Southeastern European investments and financial interests of Schneider et Cie were also concentrated. Table 13 shows the main capital interests of Eugène Schneider; each presidency and vice-presidency signifies a controlling influence at the centre of this enormous combine.

As early as 1919 Eugène Schneider became the first vice-president of the board of directors of the Škoda-Works in Plzeň; after the transfer of the Mining and Metallurgic Company's headquarters from Vienna to Brno, as a result of the Nostrification Act, he became the company's president in 1921.[1] He retained these posts until the break-up of the pre-Munich Republic. Clearly, the Czechoslovak combines were considered to be of key importance in the Schneider spheres of interest, because Eugène Schneider refused to accept similar offices in 19 other subsidiary enterprises in Central and South-eastern Europe.[2] From the minutes of the meetings of the board of directors and the executive and management committees, it appears that Schneider himself and his representatives made it quite clear which was the most powerful interest in enterprises subordinated to the Schneider combine.[3]

When the board of directors of the Mining and Metallurgic Co. was reorganized in 1921, Czech bankers and industrialists became members, in accordance with the legal requirements of the Czechoslovak state. They joined the board at the same time as representatives of the French shareholders and the director-general of the Živnostenská Bank, Dr Jaroslav Preiss, became the most important representative of Czech interests. However, the continuity with the former owners was retained and, although the Österreichische Boden-Credit-Anstalt became a minority shareholder, its governor, Dr Rudolf Sieghart, formerly

[1] Cf. PA-ZVIL, Plzeň, GŘ 2; also B. Stočes, p. 53.

[2] In the minutes of the inaugural meeting of the board of directors of the Škoda-Works this attitude of Schneider is interpreted as a sign of particular affection for Czechoslovakia; cf. PA-ZVIL, GŘ 2, 25 September 1919.

[3] Cf. PA-ZVIL, Plzeň, GŘ 2-3; AÚLSMDH/Board of Directors, Executive Committee, BHS.

Table 13. *Eugène Schneider's most important directorships, 1921–37*

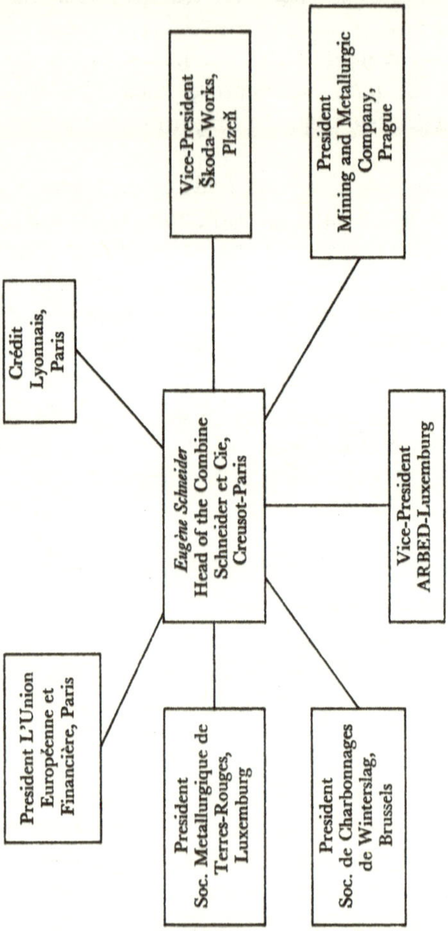

president of the Mining and Metallurgic Co., remained on the board as vice-president until 1929. The director-general of the Österreichische Boden-Credit-Anstalt also had a seat on the board until the end of 1929. After the failure of the Austrian bank at the beginning of the world economic crisis and its merger with the Österreichische Credit-Anstalt für Handel und Gewerbe, Viennese participation was represented on the board by Ludwig Neurath, the director of the Österreichische Credit-Anstalt.[1] The whole character of the so-called Austrian capital participation in the company is problematical, because the capital structure of both Viennese banks was permeated by Anglo-American capital after the First World War. The Österreichische Credit-Anstalt für Handel und Gewerbe, in particular, was in the sphere of interest of the international House of Rothschild. The entire Austrian banking system was reconstructed during the world economic crisis and the Österreichische Credit-Anstalt-Wiener-Bankverein, which became the leading financial institution, was even more firmly tied to international finance, mainly to the Anglo-International Bank in London, the International Acceptance Bank in New York and the Rothschild bank.[2] From this point of view a large proportion of the capital participation of the Viennese banks in the Mining and Metallurgical Co. can be regarded as Anglo-American.[3] After the economic crisis no more representatives of the Österreichische-Credit-Anstalt-Wiener-Bankverein were delegated to the board of directors of the Mining and Metallurgic Co. The only remaining Austrian board member was the former director-general of the company, Georg Günther. However, his active participation in management ended for practical purposes in 1927.[4]

The importance of Czech capital in the Mining and Metallurgic Co. increased with the declining influence of Austrian finance capital. More Czech directors were appointed to the board; however, their number only rarely exceeded the legal minimum, i.e. half the members. The other half of the seats was

[1] Cf. Stočes, pp. 19ff.; also *Compass, Čechoslovakei*, 1921–9.

[2] Cf. Rothschild, *Austria's Economic Development*; *Compass, Österreich* (Wien, 1938), pp. 281 ff.

[3] P. Eisler also draws attention to this aspect of the foreign investment in the Mining and Metallurgic Co. in his *Monopoly v hutnictví* etc., p. 23.

[4] Cf. G. Günther, p. 221.

firmly in the hands of Schneider's representatives. When Dr Sieghart of the Österreichische Boden-Credit-Anstalt resigned his seat in 1929, Dr Jaroslav Preiss became vice-president, a post which he held until the Nazi occupation of Czechoslovakia. The composition of the Czech membership of the board of directors of the Mining and Metallurgic Co. between the two wars is significant, for it reflects the relations between the Czech and the French shareholders. In addition to representatives from the Živnostenská Bank (the directors J. Preiss and A. Tille, and the managers of their Moravian branch, H. Bulín and K. Fajfrlík) and representatives of large subsidiaries of the Živnostenská Bank (J. Jahn and František Ringhoffer), who were listed in the commercial directories, influential statesmen of the period also at times held seats on the board, when they were not in office. Their names were not listed in directories of directors of banks and industrial companies. Most influential among them was Dr Karel Engliš, minister of finance and later governor of the Czechoslovak National Bank, and Dr Vilém Pospíšil, also governor of the Czechoslovak National Bank and economic adviser to the Ministry of Foreign Affairs, as well as chairman of the Czechoslovak Committee for Central European Cooperation.[1] On the whole, their functions and their contacts were useful to the Mining and Metallurgic Co. Thus in Czechoslovakia, as in the heavy industry of other industrially advanced Western countries, the interrelationship between banking, business, government and foreign investment was very close.[2]

The post of director-general of the Mining and Metallurgic Co. remained unfilled for an unusually long time, even though the structure of the shareholdings had already been settled by 1920. In the negotiations between M. Fournier of Schneider et Cie and Ing. Günther in Paris it was agreed contractually that the general directorship was to go to Günther.[3] Until 1923 Günther actually discharged the duties of the director-general.

[1] Cf. B. Stočes, p. 21; AÚLSMDH – Board of Directors (unmarked). Preiss became vice-president of the board of directors in 1929, and not in 1920 as stated in *Přehled československých dějin* (Survey of Czechoslovak History), III, p. 51.

[2] Cf. A. Teichová, 'O výdělečné činnosti členů poslanecké sněmovny ve volebním období 1929–1935' (Deputies in the Czechoslovak Parliament and their Business Interests 1929–1935), *ČSČH*, 1/1955, pp. 116, 119.

[3] Cf. G. Günther, p. 219.

This was definitely an infringement of the laws of the Czechoslovak Republic, for domestic joint-stock companies were required to appoint as director a Czechoslovak citizen domiciled within the state territory. The French shareholders were not in any hurry to comply with this law; on the contrary, they wanted to appoint a Frenchman from the Schneider group.[1] Later, however, they abandoned this aim so as to meet the nationalization demands of the Czechoslovak government, and a Czech with an engineering background, Otakar Kruliš-Randa, who had been in charge of the company's dealings with the Prague central government, was officially appointed to the post of director-general, which he held until the Second World War. Until 1927 Kruliš-Randa was strongly influenced by Günther in questions of management, but his general policy was, above all, dictated by the main shareholder, the firm of Schneider. Kruliš-Randa was himself, at the same time, a member of the board of directors of the Živnostenská Bank, as well as being on the boards of several of the bank's subsidiaries. This is symbolic of the close connections of the Živnostenská Bank's combine with strong foreign groups and their subsidiary companies in Czechoslovakia. However, the decisive role in the finance, commerce and technology of the Mining and Metallurgic Co. was undeniably played by Schneider et Cie, through the director-general of L'Union Européenne Industrielle et Financière, Ing. Aimée Lepercq, who also held the controlling seat on the board of directors of the company.[2]

As an executive of the Schneider group, Lepercq played a significant part in the management of numerous important subsidiary companies, particularly in Central and Southeast Europe (Table 14). In close cooperation with Günther and Kruliš-Randa he paid particular attention to the growth of the Mining and Metallurgic Co. as a basis for further French investments. The exceptional technical and organizational abilities of Lepercq were recognized in Czech industrial circles. It was known that he held strong anti-German sentiments, especially against the German *Drang nach Osten*, and he therefore uncompromisingly implemented the policy of French capital penetration to the East through the bank L'Union Européenne

[1] Cf. ANTM – Vzpomínky J. Tilleho.

[2] Cf. Ibid.; also *Compass, Čechoslovakei* (1922–1940).

Table 14. *Directorships of Aimée Lepercq, representative of Schneider et Cie*, 1922–38

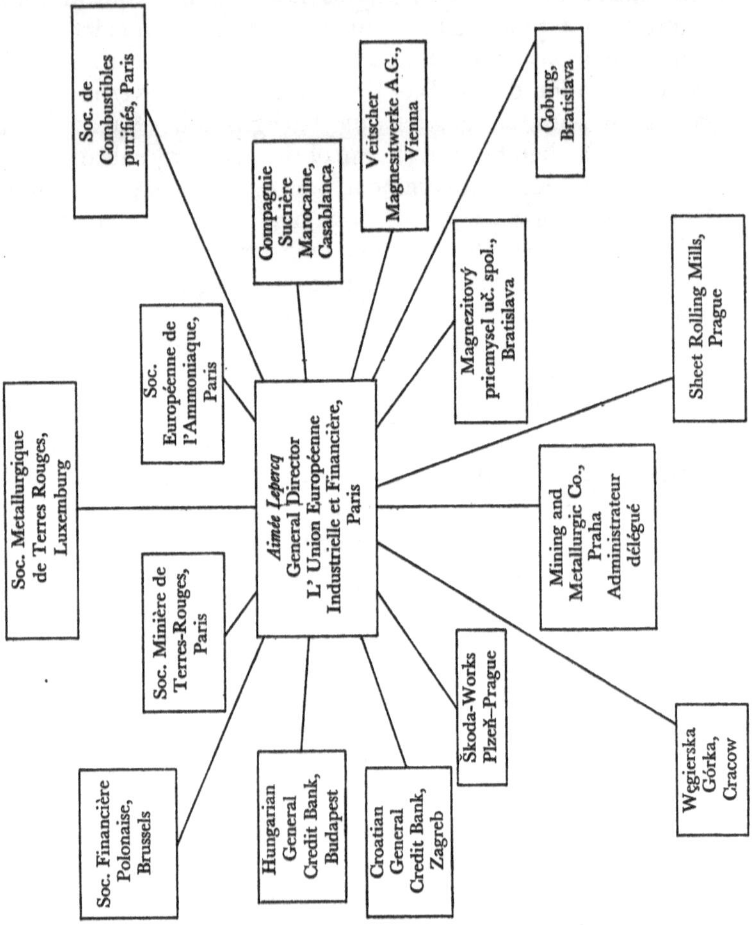

Industrielle et Financière.[1] Lepercq's activity in the Mining and Metallurgic Co. was fully consistent with these aims. He followed the financial performance of the company very carefully, insisting on detailed monthly situation reports and balances, which had to be completed by the managing directors of the financial, accountancy and commercial departments according to precise instructions from the central offices of Schneider et Cie. These had to be in Paris at the L'Union Européenne by a certain stipulated time. On examination of the balance sheets further instructions for production, financial and commercial policy were issued to the director-general in Czechoslovakia. In this way the Schneider group watched and directed the all-round policy of all their subsidiary firms and harmonized their financial policy from the Paris centre. Thus the Mining and Metallurgic Co. received its basic instructions from Paris through Lepercq and not, as has often been suggested, from Prague through the Živnostenská Bank and Kruliš-Randa. These latter accepted and followed the main lines of policy from Paris because, in practice, their financial interests coincided with those of their French partners.

At the same time, Lepercq also kept the technical management under his control. After the departure of the leading German technical staff he called in mainly French engineers from the iron and steel works of Schneider et Cie at Terres Rouges.[2] Under Lepercq's guidance the mines, foundries and iron and steel works (especially the steel works in Třinec) were extensively modernized in an effort to reach a scale of production as large as that of the Vítkovice Works.[3] It was one of the longterm aims of Schneider policy to transfer the basis of the steel industry in Czechoslovakia to Třinec. Besides the

[1] Cf. ANTM – Vzpomínky J. Tilleho. In the executive body of the L'Union Européenne Industrielle et Financière the interests of French high finance were closely interlocked (Schneider and de Neuflize, Rothschild and de Wendel). At the same time these financial families held 'Regents' seats in the Bank of France, which the French financial oligarchy had controlled since the beginning of the nineteenth century.

[2] Until 1934 the technical director was Georges Thédrel, who had formerly served successfully in the Schneider iron and steel plants of Terres Rouges. However in Czechoslovakia he adopted a colonialist attitude, according to Tille (cf. ANTM – Vzpomínky J. Tilleho). He was later replaced by Ing. Louis Rocaut, also a leading technical director of the French Schneider works.

[3] This conformed with Günther's endeavours and he and Lepercq understood each other well. Cf. ANTM – Vzpomínky J. Tilleho.

technical improvements in the main work, Lepercq, with profitability always uppermost in his mind, pursued the aim of enlarging the combine, particularly in Slovakia. The Mining and Metallurgic Co. bought up competitors, either with a view to complementing its own production programme or to close down their production and to acquire their quotas. In this way it strengthened its own position in the Czechoslovak steel cartel against the other members of the Big Three. At the same time, however, the Mining and Metallurgic Co. often cooperated with the Vítkovice Mining and Foundry Works in achieving its programme of expansion and this, in effect, increased the influence of foreign capital in the Czechoslovak economy.

Although the Ostrava and the Třinec combines competed with each other, there also existed a great deal of cooperation between them. Taken realistically, this cooperation was, in fact, a result of the permanent competition which led to the division of some significant investments between them in the period between the two world wars (viz. Table 11 – Vítkovice Mining and Foundry Works, and Table 12 – Mining and Metallurgic Co.). In the process of pushing former enemy capital out of Czechoslovakia, the Mining and Metallurgic Co. took over the Hornád Iron Works Ltd. from the Hungarian Rimamurány Iron Works Ltd. (RIMA)[1] and the Bratislava steel plate factory, Union, from German and Hungarian owners,[2] stopped their production in Slovakia and shared their quotas with the Vítkovice Iron Works. By an exchange of shares, the Budapest iron works RIMA received 4 % of the joint-stock capital of the Mining and Metallurgic Co. The Coburg iron foundries in Slovakia also ceased production of pig iron in favour of the Mining and Metallurgic Co., in accordance with the terms of the cartel agreements of 1922 and 1931.[3] As a result of this

[1] PA–TŽ–BH Třinec, Statutes of the Mining and Metallurgic Co., Brno 1927, p. 6; also B. Stočes, p. 44.

[2] PA–TŽ–BH Třinec, Statutes of the Mining and Metallurgic Co.; DZAP–RWiM 13756.

[3] SÚA–KR 28/1; also AÚLSMHD – Agreement 11. For effects on the Slovak economy see J. Kramer, *K dejinám priemyslu na Slovensku za prvej ČSR* (History of Industry in Slovakia during the First ČSR) (Bratislava, 1955), particularly pp. 75, 79, 97; also M. Strhan, 'Odbúravanie banského a železiarského priemyslu na Slovensku v rokoch 1921–1923' (The Dismantlement of the Mining and Iron Industry in Slovakia 1921–1923), *Historický časopis* (Historical Journal) (1954).

policy of the big combines in the iron and steel industry the majority of blast furnaces in Slovakia were gradually put out of production. This had disastrous consequences for the development of Slovakia and also, eventually, for the ability of the Czechoslovak state to build up its defence system.

The Mining and Metallurgic Co. and the Vítkovice Mining and Foundry Works participated together with the Czechoslovak state in the joint-stock capital of the Moravian–Silesian Electricity Power Plant and the Czechoslovak Oder Shipping Company. This connection enabled the iron and steel works to reduce its costs for the consumption of electric energy and river transport.[1]

For the profitable utilization of the by-products of their coking plants the Mining and Metallurgic Co. and the Vítkovice Mining and Foundry Works bought an important tar distilling works in Moravská Ostrava in 1921, which had previously belonged to the German chemical combine Julius Rütgers.[2] In this area of production as well, German capital had to retreat in favour of West European and Czech capital. At almost the same time the two combines started to produce synthetic ammonia jointly in the chemical works, Czechoslovak Factories for Nitrogen Products. This enterprise developed in competition with the Association for Chemical and Metallurgical Production in Ústí nad Labem, in the joint-stock capital of which the Belgian group Solvay et Cie participated. In 1927 a cartel company was founded, the Sales Association for Nitrogen Products Ltd, which acquired sole rights for the sale of its members' products.[3] The resulting quota system was a measure of the respective strength of the manufacturers of nitrogen substances, who also reached an agreement which conceded a 14.5 % participation in the joint-stock capital of the Czechoslovak Factories for Nitrogen Products in Moravská Ostrava to the Association for Chemical and Metallurgical Production in Ústí. The Vítkovice Mining and Foundry Works and the Mining and Metallurgic Co. continued to hold a majority share, i.e. 30 % each.[4] Whilst foreign investments in

[1] On the mechanism of accountancy see the section on the Vítkovice Mining and Foundry Works, pp. 89–90.

[2] PA–TŽ–BH Třinec, Konzern 'Berghütte'.

[3] SÚA–KR 247/1.

[4] Viz. Tables 11 and 12, also Table 2 in Chapter 5 (1) See p. 121 – Association for Chemical and Metallurgical Production.

the plants manufacturing nitrogen substances remained unchanged, this whole branch of industry was gradually subordinated to the International Nitrogen Cartel.[1]

The two iron and steel combines, the Vítkovice and the Třinec works, competed with each other; they also, however, cooperated against other competitors. This was especially apparent in the cartel associations which they jointly founded and in which they invested together with the Prague Iron Co. The most important cartel was, of course, the Selling Agency of the United Czechoslovak Iron Works. The Big Three also participated in the trading company 'Ferra', each holding a third of the joint-stock capital of Kč 20 million. In 1923 the Mining and Metallurgic Co. together with the Vítkovice Works founded the Sales Bureau of the United Ostrava–Karviná Collieries, which controlled practically the whole output and marketing of black coal in Czechoslovakia (viz. Table 12). Thus in this area of production, too, there was a significant degree of dependence on foreign capital investment.

The relative positions of the mining and metallurgical combines often changed as a result of the continuous competitive struggle between them. An example is provided by their changing relations in the export trade. In 1924 the Vítkovice Mining and Foundry Works were obliged to grant a 25 % share in their trading firm, the Continental Society for the Iron Trade Kern & Co., to the Mining and Metallurgic Co.[2] In return the Mining and Metallurgic Co. abandoned its connections with the Hamburg export firm of Coutin Caro & Co., and Kern & Co. was entrusted with the entire export sales of both combines.[3] In addition, in 1925 the Mining and Metallurgic Co. gave part of its own shares, amounting to 2.8 % of its own joint-stock, to the Continental Society for the Iron Trade Kern & Co., in exchange for the transfer of the above-mentioned 25 % of their shares.[4] In this way interlocking took place between the Schneider and the Rothschild groups. Günther valued the participation in the Continental Co. extremely highly, as it contributed to the increasing power of the Mining

[1] SÚA–KR 385, 246, 689. [2] Cf. B. Stočes, p. 67; viz. Tables 14 and 15.
[3] Cf. ANTM – Vzpomínky J. Tilleho.
[4] Cf. PA–TŽ–BH, Statutes of the Mining and Metallurgic Co., p. 6; ASÚS–cizí účasti, Expertise No. 16; PA – VŽKG–Koncernové podniky (Subsidiary companies of the combine); also B. Stočes, p. 67.

and Metallurgic Co.[1] In the 1930s especially the Continental Co. gained markets through its extensive international connections, to the detriment of the Prague Iron Co., whose exports were administered by the Mannesmann sales agencies.[2]

In its drive for concentration and rationalization the Mining and Metallurgic Co. drew the Iron Works Rotava-Nýdek into its combine (on 1 January 1928), in order to rationalize their sheet rolling mills.[3] In this transaction Franco-Czech capital in the Mining and Metallurgic Co. was involved on the one side, and the Austrian capital of the House of C. T. Petzold & Co. in Vienna, as the main shareholder of the Rotava-Nýdek Iron Works, was involved on the other, besides three Prague commercial banks (the Czech Escompte Bank, the Czech Bank Union and the Anglo-Czechoslovak Bank). The merger followed a sharp competitive struggle, in which the Mining and Metallurgic Co. endeavoured to gain a quota of white sheet production at the expense of the Iron Works Rotava-Nýdek. However, in the Czechoslovak steel cartel the firm of Rotava-Nýdek had exclusive rights to produce 100 % of the Czechoslovak white sheet quota,[4] and this fact strengthened its bargaining position vis-à-vis the Mining and Metallurgic Co. It is significant that the final negotiations and the signing of the agreement between them took place in Paris at the central offices of Schneider et Cie.[5] The Paris Agreement clearly shows the comparative strength of both partners. The Mining and Metallurgic Co. took possession of the Rotava-Nýdek's quota, although the Austrian shareholder did not leave empty-handed. As a result of the agreement, production in the iron works of Rotava-Nýdek in the Karlovy Vary (Karlsbad) area was discontinued and gradually transferred to Karlova Huť, where a large steel plate rolling mill was erected in which both companies had equal shares (50:50).[6] The joint-stock company

[1] Cf. B. Stočes, p. 50.

[2] Cf. e.g. the allocation of the Czechoslovak quota in Austria exclusively to the Continental Society for the Iron Trade Kern & Co. by the Austrian Syndicate of Wholesalers. The Prague Iron Co. protested against this procedure at the meetings of the Big Three, but to no avail. ANTM–SDS–413, box 1, 17 August 1933.

[3] AÚLSMHD – Agreement 12.

[4] Ibid.

[5] AÚLSMHD–BH–Pariser Übereinkommen.

[6] Cf. PA–TŽ–BH Konzern 'Berghütte'; also ANTM – Vzpomínky J. Tilleho; P. Eisler, p. 49.

Rotava-Nýdek became a mere holding company, with 50 % of the shares of the Válcovna plechů a.s. (Sheet Rolling Mill), but without its own production facilities.[1] The new rolling mill in Lískovec was constructed between 1929 and 1931 and was one of the three most technically advanced in Europe, with an annual capacity of *c.* 150,000 tons at considerably reduced costs.[2] Both partners sought to maximize profits; in the Paris Agreement the Třinec iron works was granted the exclusive right to deliver crude steel and semi-finished goods to Karlova Huť, and Petzold & Co. obtained the exclusive right to the sale of thin plate manufactured in the new rolling mill.[3] From the point of view of the role of foreign capital in Czechoslovakia, this big transaction shows that foreign financial groups competed with each other inside the Czechoslovak economy, and made decisions about capital transfers and the quantity of production, while Czechoslovak banks played what was often an auxiliary or mediating role.

As the productive capacity of the rolling mill in Karlova Huť grew, the discrepancy between the rising output of the Mining and Metallurgic Company and the restrictive tendencies of the steel cartel became greater. The management of the Mining and Metallurgic Co. therefore exerted considerable efforts to push other plants out of production or force them into the cartel, in which, as a member of the Big Three, it had a controlling influence. In the manufacture of thin and galvanized sheets the Mining and Metallurgic Co. attained complete cartelization only at the beginning of 1935, when the last outsider, the Plants for the Manufacture of Galvanized Metals in Chomutov – Bablík Brothers, which was in Austrian ownership,[4] was manœuvred into the cartel and had to produce according to an allocated quota.

Between 1929 and 1937 the Mining and Metallurgic Co. gained unqualified control over the Coburg Mining and

[1] Cf. DWI–01259. [2] Cf. Ibid.; also Stočes, p. 41.

[3] Information and reminiscences of P. Polánský, formerly chief clerk of the Válcovna plechů (Sheet Rolling Mill) have helped me to understand the intricate relationships and agreements surrounding this transaction and I am very grateful to him. A patriot who wanted to rescue some of the machinery for the Czech Lands after the Munich Agreement, Mr Polánský was arrested by the Gestapo during the German occupation of Czechoslovakia and spent the rest of the war in the concentration camp of Buchenwald.

[4] ANTM–SDS–413, box 1.

Metallurgic Works in Bratislava, by taking over their shares from the German Mannesmann group (viz. Table 12). In this way the dominance of the Mining and Metallurgic Co. over the Coburg works reached its culmination, for it had already acquired Coburg's production quota in the 1920s; in the 1930s the management of Coburg transferred all its rights in the cartel irrevocably to the Mining and Metallurgic Co., whose approval of decisions within the cartel 'brought with it the automatic approval of Coburg'.[1] The cartel agreement quoted in this context reflects the takeover of the Coburg plants by the Mining and Metallurgic Co. In analysing these concrete relationships the process of concentration and monopoly formation can be traced, as well as the longterm competition between French and Czech finance capital, on the one hand, and Austro-German capital investment in Czechoslovak heavy industry, on the other.

The management of the Mining and Metallurgic Co. also continued to enlarge its sphere of influence in the field of further processing of steel, because the capacity of its blast furnaces in Třinec steadily increased and a market for crude and semi-finished steel had therefore to be secured.[2] As deliveries of crude and semi-finished steel to the combine's own subsidiary plants were not included in the quotas allocated by the cartel[3] and did not enter into the cartel's accounts, the steel works in Třinec could increase deliveries of their products within their own combine and also increase profits, without any danger of being fined for 'illicit' production under the cartel's rules. For this reason the management of the Mining and Metallurgic Co. tried to subordinate its competitors in iron and steel manufacture and related fields to its own combine. In 1923 it bought a wire mill in Bohumín and a chain producing plant in Malá Moravka. The Bohumín wire mill was modernized and became one of the largest in Europe,[4] reducing production costs considerably and gaining an unassailable competitive position among wire rod manufacturers in Czechoslovakia. Soon it dominated the whole branch of the industry and became the exclusive supplier to all manufacturers of wire products of the semi-finished material

[1] AÚLSMHD – First complement to the Agreement, 1937.

[2] ANTM – Vzpomínky J. Tilleho; cf. also P. Eisler, about the growth of the capacity of blast-furnaces in general, pp. 51, 56.

[3] Cf. AÚLSMHD – Agreement 12.

[4] Cf. Stočes, p. 41; also ANTM – Vzpomínky J. Tilleho.

they required. A cartel organization, the Central Bureau of Czechoslovak Wire and Wire Nail Manufacturers, founded in 1927, in which the Mining and Metallurgic Co. owned 65 % of the joint-stock capital, served as the instrument of domination. The general director of the Mining and Metallurgic Co., O. Kruliš-Randa, became its chairman and the second biggest firm in the field of wire production in Czechoslovakia, the Steel Industry in Most, participated in it. Almost all wire manufacturers in Northwestern Bohemia belonged to the combine of the Steel Industry in Most, which in turn was controlled by Swedish capital (62.3 % of the joint-stock).[1] As the Mining and Metallurgic Co. was unable to include these enterprises in its own combine, it proceeded to build up a watertight cartel in cooperation with the Swedish–Czechoslovak combine. Up to that time all Northwest Bohemian manufacturers had been supplied with wire rods from the Prague Iron Co. in Kladno for their needs additional to the supplies they received from their own combine's steel plants in Most. Because this market went to the Třinec works after the formation of the cartel, the marketing problems of the Kladno iron and steel works were increased. The Prague Iron Co. waged a long and unsuccessful battle at meetings of the Big Three against the quota system in wire production and against the cartel's approval of the Mining and Metallurgic Co. supplying wire rods to its own former customers without accounting for it to the cartel. The Prague Iron Co., on the other hand, had to account for all its deliveries of wire rod to the Selling Agency of the United Czechoslovak Iron Works.[2]

The minutes and protocols of meetings of the board of directors of the Central Bureau of Czechoslovak Wire and Wire Nail Manufacturers over the period 1927–36 reveal a history of buying up and scrapping machinery and of stopping outsiders' production,[3] in order to be able to raise prices after completing

[1] Bechert & Co., Žatec; Richard Hirsch in Plzeň; Leopold Telatko, Žatec; Simon Semler, Plzeň; Eisner & Levit, Lobzy. Cf. AÚLSMHD–Agreement. The central offices of the Swedish combine, Aktiebolaget O. Mustad Sön, were in Gothenburg (ASÚS – cizí účasti).

[2] ANTM–SDS–413, Minutes of the meetings of the Big Three. The protests of the Prague Iron Co. are repeatedly recorded, cf. particularly minutes of 23 June 1933.

[3] Cf. AÚLSMHD – Board of directors of the Central Bureau of the Czechoslovak Wire and Wire Nail Manufacturers in Prague, 1 January 1927–30 June 1936,

the cartel. At the same time, they show transfers of quotas and shares belonging to those firms which succumbed in the war with the cartel to the Mining and Metallurgic Co. and, less frequently, to the Steel Industry in Most.[1] The same aims were pursued by the Sales Association for Chains and Wire Products which the Mining and Metallurgic Co. developed as an absolute monopoly in the Czechoslovak economy. All these efforts, which culminated in the 1930s, were extremely beneficial to the French, Swedish and Czech owners of the steel combines and were, at the same time, an expression of objective trends towards monopoly in the Czechoslovak economy.

The Mining and Metallurgic Co. combine grew most quickly between 1921 and 1931, when most of the constructive investments were also made; however, efforts at expansion also continued into the 1930s. At the end of the 1930s the rearmament boom brought large profits to the shareholders; in 1937–8 these reached the same peak as at the high-point of the 1929–30 boom, i.e. about Kč 40 million net profits.[2] About 75 % of the dividends and more than half the board of directors' receipts found their way out of Czechoslovakia, in addition to those profits that were obtained by transactions within the powerful international combine of the Schneiders.

Our rather detailed analysis of the growth of the Mining and Metallurgic Co.'s combine provides a concrete demonstration of the extent of French influence (represented in the field of heavy industry by the Schneider group) on the economic life of Czechoslovakia, and also shows how this French group competed as well as cooperated with other foreign financial groups operating in the economy. Further, it becomes clear, as in the case of the Vítkovice combine, that French capital did not withdraw voluntarily from the mining and iron and steel industries of Czechoslovakia long before Munich in order to make room for German capital but, on the contrary, held on to

also ibid. Executive Committee, Special Committee 1935–6. (The following firms were either pushed out of production or subordinated to the cartel: Fa. Kratochvil; Albrecht Dubský, Drnovice; Prague Wire Factory Pánek, Praha-Vysočany; Budějovice Screw Factory; Fanny Valečka, Opava; Karel Fischer, Nepomuk; Alfred Reiss & Sons, Nové Mesto n.V. and many smaller firms.)

[1] Ibid.

[2] Cf. balance sheets of the Mining and Metallurgic Co. – AŮLSMHD; also *Compass*, Čechoslovakei, relevant annual statistics.

its investments and continued to pursue an expansive policy in heavy industry up to the eve of the Second World War. The world economic crisis of 1929–33 naturally slowed down investments and expansion, and as a result of the crisis competition amongst the powerful combines in heavy industry increased, particularly in Central and Southeast Europe, where French capital defended its position under changing political conditions. However, only violent intervention, arising out of German Fascist aggression in the period from the Munich Pact to the Fall of France, led in 1940 to the transfer of the French participation in the joint-stock capital of the Mining and Metallurgic Co. into the hands of a group of German banks headed by the Deutsche Bank. The Živnostenská Bank joined the group of German banks which bought the Schneider shares.[1] German finance and industry succeeded in dominating the Upper Silesian and Ostrava–Těšín industrial region only after Germany went to war with Poland, France and Great Britain.

In the period of the pre-Munich Republic, leading Czech bankers and industrialists participated actively in the policies of the Schneider group, which was also the decisive force in the Mining and Metallurgic Co.'s combine. A more detailed analysis of the expansion of this combine in Czechoslovakia's mining and iron and steel industries shows clearly that the so-called nationalization process in this branch of industry consisted largely of transferring German, Austrian and Hungarian property into the hands, mainly, of the French, and to a far less extent into Czech ownership. In this process of changing ownership relations the Czechoslovak government passed laws which encouraged the influx of French investments into key areas in the heavy industry of Czechoslovakia.[2] Anglo–French capital in Ostrava and Těšín doubtless supported the Czechoslovak government in its efforts to strengthen domestic enterprise against the formerly predominant German and Austrian influence. It also helped to prevent the socialization of mines and foundries in Czechoslovakia.

1 Cf. V. Král, II, p. 200.

2 From the concept of 'the monopoly of state power' in the hands of the Czech bourgeoisie V. Král derives the decisive role of domestic capital as against foreign capital. In the Mining and Metallurgic Co. the decisive influence remained in the hands of the Schneider group, although state power reposed undoubtedly with the Czech bourgeoisie. Cf. V. Král, *ČSČH*, 3, 1959, p. 474.

The Prague Iron Company

The situation of the third member of the Big Three, the Prague Iron Co., with its production base in Kladno, is to some extent deducible from the analysis of the two leading combines in this constellation. In a period of particularly fierce competition with the two stronger partners in the aftermath of the First World War, the Prague Iron Co. lost its leading place in the iron and steel cartel of Austria-Hungary and fell back to third place in the Czechoslovak steel cartel. As with the Ostrava and Třinec combines, foreign capital was also invested in the Kladno works. The Mannesmann–Röhrenwerke of Düsseldorf gradually acquired shares, obtaining 25.7 % of the joint-stock capital by the end of 1937.[1] Although this was not a majority participation, and although other financial groups also held shares, the Mannesmann group influenced production and the commercial policy of the company in a decisive manner.

Before 1918 the Prague Iron Co. was the leading steel producer in the Austro-Hungarian Monarchy and, at that time, owned a majority of shares in the Österreichische Alpine Montangesellschaft. However, it was itself a subsidiary company of the Niederösterreichische Escompte Gesellschaft in Vienna, which, in this way, gained financial control over both iron and steel works. The investment policy of the Viennese bank encouraged the modernization and expansion of the Austrian iron and steel works, while in the Bohemian works in Kladno tendencies towards stagnation had already appeared before the First World War.[2] The longterm effect of the technical backwardness of the Prague Iron Co. in comparison with the Vítkovice Mining and Foundry Works and the Mining and Metallurgic Co. became fully apparent only between the two world wars, because in that period no basic technical improvements were undertaken.[3]

The fall of the Austro-Hungarian Monarchy in 1918 and the emergence of the independent Czechoslovak state shook the capital position of the Prague Iron Co. considerably. In the

[1] ASÚS – cizí účasti, Expertises 19, 20, 21.

[2] *Sto let kladenských železáren* (A Hundred Years of the Kladno Iron Works), pp. 157 and 341.

[3] Ibid., p. 363.

spring of 1919 its main shareholder, the Niederösterreichische Escompte Gesellschaft, bought out the shares of the Österreichische Alpine Montangesellschaft (henceforth referred to as 'Alpine'), which had been in the possession of the Prague Iron Co.,[1] in order to prevent Czech capital from gaining a decisive foothold in Austrian heavy industry. Later, the majority of the Alpine's joint-stock capital, i.e. 57 %, was transferred to the ownership of the powerful German Vereinigte Stahlwerke, which were founded in 1926.[2] As a result of these property transfers the relationships were reversed, so that German and Austrian capital influenced the Prague Iron Co. through the Alpine on the one hand, and the Niederösterreichische Escompte Gesellschaft on the other. Although this did not amount to a decisive influence, the capital connection with the Viennese bank survived until 1936 and was also maintained through the Czech Escompte Bank and Credit Institute in Prague, which before nostrification had been a branch of the Niederösterreichische Escompte Gesellschaft in Vienna and which in the 1920s held more seats on the board of directors of the Prague Iron Co. than any other participant in its joint-stock capital.[3]

In addition, the Niederösterreichische Escompte Gesellschaft appointed two representatives to the Prague Iron Co.'s board of directors, who personified the affinity of interests of their bank and the combine. Johann Fürstenberg, who held a seat on the board until the end of 1937, deserves special mention.[4] He was also a partner in the well-known Berliner Handelsgesellschaft and a member of the boards of directors of the Alpine and the Niederösterreichische Escompte Gesellschaft. There was also

[1] Ibid., p. 341.

[2] Cf. *Compass, Österreich* (1938); also P. Eisler, p. 24; *Sto let kladenských železáren*, p. 345.

[3] Chairman of the Prague Iron Co. – Dr Adolf Stránský; vice-chairman – Dr Otto Feilchenfeld; members of the board of directors: Dr Václav Bouček, Otto Klesper, Wilhelm Kux, Dr Arthur Löb, Cf. *Compass, Čechoslovakei* (1929–37).

[4] Cf. ADWI–05981; *Compass, Čechoslovakei* (1929, 1938); *Compass, Personenverzeichnis* (1934). After the attack on Ernst von Rath, an attaché of the German Embassy in Paris, in November 1938, Goering and Goebbels organized pogroms of Jews in Germany and Jewish possessions were confiscated and transferred to German businesses and banks. 'Herr Herbert Goering, a member of the Air Minister's family, entered the Berlin Handelsgesellschaft and replaced the Jewish partner of the bank Johann Fürstenberg.' A. Norden, *Zákulisí německého imperialismu* (The Background of German Imperialism) (Brno, 1950), p. 139.

the director of the Austrian bank, Wilhelm Kux, in whose person the Austro-Hungarian–Czechoslovak interests of the Niederösterreichische Escompte Gesellschaft were combined; of these the Prague Iron Co. and the Poldina huť in Czechoslovakia were important parts.[1] During the world economic crisis and the failure of the Viennese banks, Anglo-American capital took over a substantial part of the shares of the Niederösterreichische Escompte Gesellschaft;[2] thus the original Austrian participation in the Prague Iron Co. became to a large extent an indirect Anglo-American investment.

The participation of the Czech Escompte Bank and Credit Institute in the joint-stock capital of the Prague Iron Co. also partly constituted an indirect Anglo-American–Belgian investment, for financial groups in these countries had invested in the Czech bank's joint-stock capital. Of these foreign investors the Belgian bank, Banque de Bruxelles, and the British bank, Kleinwort Sons & Co., remained shareholders until the end of the Czechoslovak Republic's existence, and thus they indirectly participated in the bank's subsidiary companies.[3] Through participation in the Czech Escompte Bank the Živnostenská Bank also gained an indirect investment in the Prague Iron Co., because in the process of nostrification in 1919 it obtained a decisive share in the joint-stock capital of the Czech Escompte Bank and Credit Institute from the Niederösterreichische Escompte Gesellschaft.[4] In the ensuing period, however, the Živnostenská Bank's direct investment in the Czech Escompte Bank decreased, falling to 11 % by 1937.[5] Its indirect invest-

[1] Wilhelm Kux belonged to the following boards of directors: Niederösterreichische Escompte Gesellschaft, Wien; Czech Escompte Bank and Credit Institute, Prague; Steiermärkische Escompte Bank, Graz; Wiener Giro- und Cassen-Verein, Wien; Österreichische Immobiliar A.G., Wien; Poldina huť, Prague; Prague Iron Co., Prague; Vereinigte Brauereien Schwechat, St Marx, Simmering, Hütteldorf; A.G. Ignaz Kuffner und Jacob Kuffner, Ottakring-Döbling; Hauser und Sobotka A.G., Wien; Brüder Reininghaus A.G. für Brauerei- und Spiritusindustrie, Steinfeld bei Graz; Hofherr-Schrantz-Clayton-Shuttleworth A.G., Wien; Kurz A.G., Fabrik für maschinelle und gesundheitstechnische Anlagen, Wien; Ungarische Stahlwarenfabrik A.G., Budapest; A.s. Červenokostelecké a erlašské přádelny a tkalcovny, Prague; Donau Allgemeine Versicherungs A.G., Wien. Cf. *Compass, Personenverzeichnis* (1934).

[2] Cf. *Compass, Österreich* (1934–8).

[3] Viz. Table 7, Chapter 6 (1) – The Czech Escompte Bank and Credit Institute – Foreign Investments.

[4] Cf. A. Pimper, p. 491; also *Sto let kladenských železáren*, p. 344.

[5] DZAP–B 186–NID 13405 – Dokumentenbücher.

ments in the subsidiary companies of the Czech Escompte Bank, of course, diminished in the same proportion.

Apart from its indirect participation, the Živnostenská Bank also invested directly, and thus more effectively, in the Prague Iron Co. When the Prague Iron Co. transferred its seat from Vienna to Prague under the Nostrification Act of 1919 the Živnostenská Bank began to finance a great deal of the mining and iron and steel production in the Kladno collieries and plants and soon became the main creditor of the company.[1] During the Czech government's endeavours to nationalize mines and foundries in German possession efforts were made to liquidate German participation in the Prague Iron Co. and transfer it to Czech ownership. The German Ministry of Foreign Affairs, however, objected, maintaining that 'the Prague Iron Co. cannot be classified as a mining and metallurgic enterprise because out of a joint-stock capital of 72 million Kč only 3,336,000 Kč consisted of collieries'.[2] Although it could hardly be denied that the Prague Iron Co. was, in fact, a mining and metallurgic combine, it was excluded from the liquidation programme. In this case the Živnostenská Bank was unable to use nationalization methods to increase its capital investments. However, it used its influence on the board of directors of the Prague Iron Co.; the deputy director of the Živnostenská Bank, Jindřich Bělohříbek, became vice-chairman, and the director-general, Dr J. Preiss, and another member of the Živnostenská Bank's board, J. Pospíšil, became members. In 1929 three seats were occupied by the Živnostenská Bank respresentatives, as against six for the Czech Escompte Bank and Credit Institute. The Živnostenská Bank gradually raised the number of its representatives until in 1937 it held eight seats out of seventeen, and membership from the Czech Escompte Bank had fallen to five. After 1931 the chairman of the board of the Prague Iron Co. was always a representative of the Živnostenská Bank.[3]

Up to the mid-1930s the Živnostenská Bank's direct capital investment was comparatively small, but its credits to the Prague Iron Co. grew from year to year. As a result of relatively

[1] Cf. *Sto let kladenských železáren*, p. 344.

[2] DZAP–RWiM 13756 – Verbalnote des Auswärtigen Amtes vom 9. Januar 1923.

[3] AÚLSMHD–PŽ – Board of directors: first J. Bělohříbek and then Jan Dvořáček (Preiss' son-in-law).

high production costs, the indebtedness of the company steadily increased with all banks which participated in its joint-stock capital, particularly the Živnostenská Bank and the Czech Escompte Bank.[1] These two banks, in close cooperation with the Niederösterreichische Escompte Gesellschaft and the Berliner Handelsgesellschaft, formed the controlling group in the Prague Iron Co. by virtue of their position as creditors and also because no single majority shareholder existed.[2] This situation was, on the whole, acceptable to the banks, because they received high interest rates on their loans, although dividends were low or (as between 1931 and 1936) were not distributed at all.[3] According to the profit and loss accounts for the years in which the company did show a profit, the interest paid to the banks was higher than the net profit and greatly exceeded the dividends that were distributed. During 1932–5 the Prague Iron Co. suffered losses, which it covered with new loans from banks, paying them interest of many million Czechoslovak Crowns.[4] Both Czech banks thus provided loans, managed the finances of the company and protected their financial interests on the board of directors. However, the production programme and commercial policy of the Prague Iron Co. were strongly influenced by the conditions which the main German shareholder, the Mannesmann–Röhrenwerke, had laid down. As a result of the Mannesmann conditions, the Czechoslovak banks, in effect, provided financial support (obtaining, of course, a satisfactory rate of profit and/or interest) for the Mannesmann combine, which derived substantial benefits from their connection with the Prague Iron Co.

The Mannesmann–Röhrenwerke A.G. in Düsseldorf had acquired shares in the Prague Iron Co. as early as 1921, when their subsidiary plant, the Mannesmann–Röhrenwerke in

Ibid. – Creditors, 1938 (the item 'creditors' of the Prague Iron Co. increased from Kč 132 million in 1921 to Kč 336 million in 1937, whilst the item 'debtors' varied in the same period between Kč 60 and Kč 150 million). Cf. *Compass, Čechoslovakei* (1939), p. 741. Even in the boom of 1929 the bank debt of the company amounted to Kč 78 million; in 1936 it was Kč 48 million, in 1937 Kč 62 million and in 1938 Kč 81 million; the joint-stock capital was nominally Kč 72 million; compiled from ADWI–05981 and AÚLSMHD – Creditors.

[2] ADWI–05981.

[3] Cf. balance sheets of the Prague Iron Co. 1920–1921–1937, *Compass, Čechoslovakei* (1939), p. 741.

[4] AÚLSMHD – Profit and Loss Accounts (about Kč 10 million in annual interest, most of which went to the Živnostenská Bank).

Chomutov, acquired 35,000 shares out of a new issue of 72,000.[1] With this investment, which amounted between 1921–6 to 24.3 % of the Prague Iron Co.'s joint-stock capital, the Mannesmann combine secured a source of raw materials for its tube manufacture in Chomutov. In July 1921 the Prague Iron Co. and the Chomutov Mannesmann–Röhrenwerke signed a long-term contract, which put the Prague Iron Co. under an obligation to deliver a quarter of its total output of ingot and semi-finished material regularly to the Chomutov works. This provided a guaranteed market for a significant part of the Prague Iron Co.'s produce, but the technical and delivery conditions were so unfavourable and the agreed level of prices so low that they did not fully cover costs, and the Prague Iron Co. suffered continuous losses from this unequal association.[2] The contractual obligations of the Prague Iron Co. to the Mannesmann–Röhrenwerke in Chomutov were fully recognized in the cartel agreement of the Selling Agency of the United Czechoslovak Iron Works. As with other inter-combine relationships, deliveries to the Mannesmann works in Chomutov from the Kladno steel plants were also exempt from the joint-selling activity of the cartel and were not accounted for in the quotas of the Prague Iron Co.[3] In practice, the Prague Iron Co. was a subsidiary of the Mannesmann combine, and it was possible to transfer profits from one subsidiary company to another by means of deliveries over and above the quota system at extremely favourable conditions and prices. The Mannesmann–Röhrenwerke in Chomutov showed steady and substantial net profits during the inter-war period, in contrast with the Prague Iron Co., whose net profits were relatively low and which incurred losses amounting to about Kč 30 million annually in the 1930s up to the rearmament boom in 1936.[4]

[1] ASÚS – cizí účasti, Expertises 19–21.

[2] ANTM – Vzpomínky J. Tilleho; *Sto let kladenských železáren*, p. 347; *Compass, Čechoslovakei*, mentions the Delivery Agreement in all its annual publications, beginning with 1921, in connection with the Prague Iron Co. and the Mannesmann-Röhrenwerke in Chomutov. V. Král is under the impression that the unfavourable delivery agreement, which imposed continuing losses on the Prague Iron Co., was an outcome of the German occupation of the Czech Lands and derives from this mistaken view 'a picture of a tenacious duel' between the Živnostenská Bank and the Mannesmann combine. Cf. V. Král, II, p. 296.

[3] AÚLSMHD – Agreement 6c, and 12, III, 1931.

[4] AÚLSMHD – Profit and Loss Account; *Compass, Čechoslovakei* (1929–39).

The export quotas of the Prague Iron Co. were allocated by the Selling Agency to the Mannesmann Trading Co., which provided another way of transferring profits from the sales of the Prague Iron Co.'s products abroad to the Mannesmann combine.[1] The participation of the Mannesmann–Röhrenwerke in the Prague Iron Co. consisted of investment in the joint-stock capital and contractual and commercial ties. This resulted in subordinating the production as well as commercial and financial policy of the Prague Iron Co. to the interests of the Mannesmann combine in Germany.

Mannesmann interests penetrated into Czechoslovakia through their own subsidiary enterprise in Chomutov and these, in turn, pushed their way further into Southeast Europe by additional capital investment (Table 15). An additional part of this expansion was investment in the Prague Iron Co. In fact, the Mannesmann participation in Czechoslovak heavy industry represented the most important stake of German capital in the Czechoslovak economy between the two world wars. The Mannesmann–Röhrenwerke A.G., Düsseldorf, constituted a significant economic force in Germany; it was one of the leading industrial combines which had been in the forefront of German economic expansion since the end of the nineteenth century.[2] It is therefore not particularly surprising that we find the Mannesmann group supporting the programme of the NSDAP, and, like others in big business, contributing to the funds of the Nazi Party even before it came to power.[3] In 1934 the Mannesmann–Röhrenwerke were included in the giant combine of the Deutsche Bank[4] and the director-general of the Düsseldorf works, Heinrich Bierwes, became a member of the board of directors of the Deutsche Bank.[5] Since the 1920s Heinrich Bierwes had also represented the Mannesmann interests on the board of directors of the Prague Iron Co., as well as the Chomutov works and the Královdvorská cementárna (cement plant). Alongside him a representative from the Deutsche Bank and the Mannesmann works in Düsseldorf, Max Steinhal, held seats on the boards of

[1] ANTM–413 – Meetings of the Big Three.

[2] The Mannesmann company was founded in 1889 and derived its monopoly from the invention of seamless tubes by Reinhard Mannesmann.

[3] Cf. A. Norden, p. 96.

[4] Cf. G. Baumann, *Eine Handvoll Konzernherren* (Berlin, 1953), p. 191.

[5] Cf. H. Radandt, *Kriegsverbrecher-Konzern Mansfeld* (Berlin, 1957), p. 166.

Table 15. *Position of the Prague Iron Company in the Mannesmann combine, 31 December 1937*

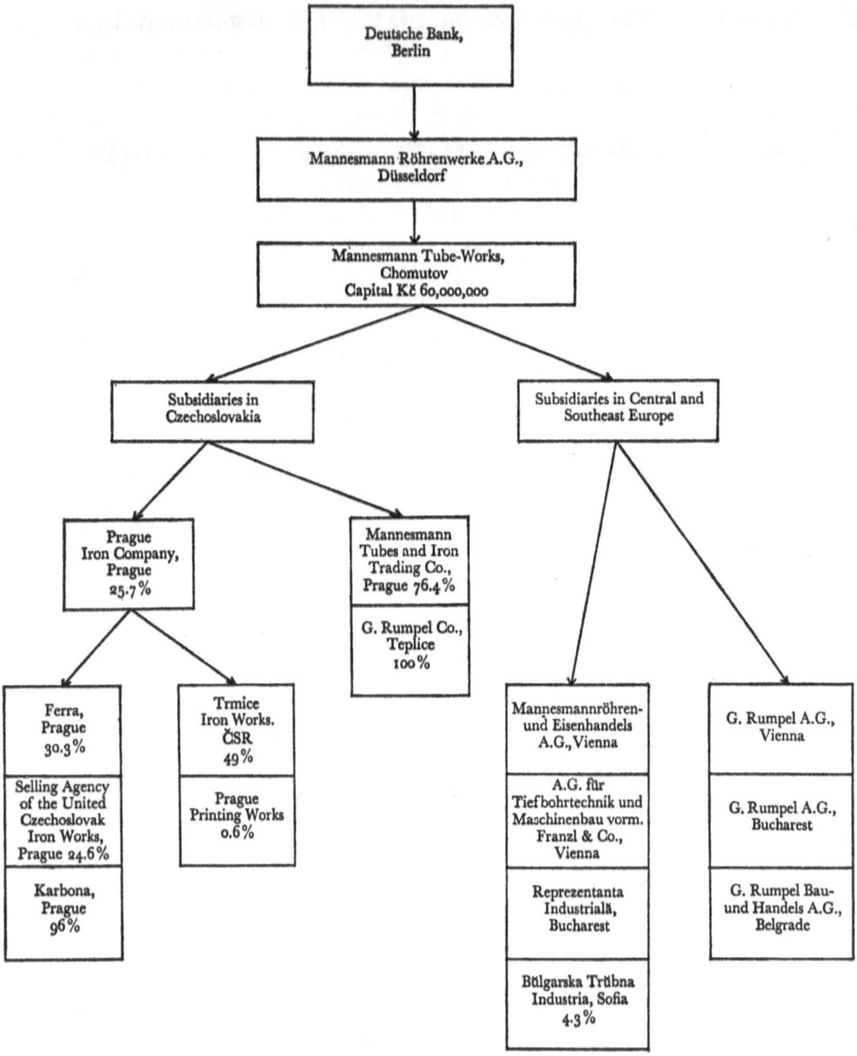

directors of these Czechoslovak firms.[1] In 1934 the Deutsche Bank entrusted Wilhelm Zangen with the leadership of the extensive Mannesmann combine;[2] he soon replaced Bierwes as the head of the boards of directors of the Czechoslovak Mannesmann subsidiaries and as a member of the board of the Prague Iron Co.[3] Wilhelm Zangen played an active part in the economic preparations of Fascist Germany for the Second World War and in October 1938 became the head of the Reichsgruppe Industrie.[4]

The Mannesmann participation in Czechoslovak enterprises had the backing of the powerful capital located at the centre of the combine in Düsseldorf and in the Deutsche Bank. Although the German group was represented in the Prague Iron Co. by only three members, there can be no doubt that their word carried greater weight than their numerical representation would warrant. Thus it clearly appears that the Mannesmann combine derived its directive influence in the Prague Iron Co. from its great capital strength, which significantly overshadowed that of the other shareholders. In addition, the Mannesmann group were making continuous and consciously directed efforts to push out other shareholders of the Prague Iron Co., especially those connected with the Niederösterreichische Escompte Gesellschaft and the Berliner Handelsgesellschaft. Here German capital also penetrated into the sphere of interest of Austrian finance.

Foreign capital participation in the Ostrava and Těšín iron and steel combines was, of course, much more significant than in the Kladno works. While the capital of the West European investors sought profitable investments from the position of creditor states, the expansion of German capital investment took place from the position of a debtor state. Frequently, German investments in Central and Southeast Europe really consisted of mixed American–German or indirect American participation.[5] German investors therefore tried to hold on to and to expand

[1] Cf. *Compass, Čechoslovakei* (1929–39); *Compass, Personenverzeichnis*; *Sto let kladenských železáren*, p. 347.
[2] Cf. G. Baumann, p. 191.
[3] Cf. *Compass* (1938–9); also AÚLSMHD-PŽ – Board of directors.
[4] Cf. G. Baumann, p. 189.
[5] Cf. K. Obermann, *Die Beziehungen des amerikanischen Imperialismus zum deutschen Imperialismus in der Zeit der Weimarer Republik (1918–1925)* (Berlin, 1952).

their relatively small foreign investments by all available means. In the case of foreign investment in the mining and metallurgic industry of Czechoslovakia before the Second World War, the greater strength of French and British capital gave the Ostrava and Těšín plants more support and freedom of movement, as long as they fulfilled the main function of a capitalist enterprise and secured satisfactory profits. This was not so with the Mannesmann investment; for the German shareholder could not with equal confidence control the Prague Iron Co. by mere capital participation, and had to secure its influence contractually by means of tough conditions. The role of German investors therefore appears in a more aggressive light[1] than that of the British or the French, although their aims in the Czechoslovak mining and metallurgic industry were virtually identical.

The whole capital structure was reflected in the relative positions of the members of the Big Three in the cartel of the United Czechoslovak Iron Works. The tough competition between them can, in a sense, be regarded as a reflection of the wider competitive struggle between Anglo-French and German capital in Czechoslovakia before Munich. Because German shareholders remained in the Prague Iron Co. after the First World War, the company's situation in the cartel was weakened from the outset. When cartel conditions were negotiated between the Big Three, the representatives of the Vítkovice Works and of the Mining and Metallurgic Co. (Sonnenschein and Günther) dominated the field entirely; not only did the Prague Iron Co. come away with reduced quotas, but some of the provisions of the 'Agreement' affected it adversely.

This was particularly true of the provision for dividing orders according 'to the criterion of the lowest transport costs between the sending-off station and the receiving station'.[2] This condition, apparently perfectly logical, nevertheless concealed the commercial interests of both Ostrava–Těšín combines. Before

[1] For instance J. Tille is under this impression in his memoirs, where he writes about the contractual relations between Mannesmann and the Prague Iron Co. Cf. ANTM – Vzpomínky J. Tilleho. The authors of *Sto let kladenských železáren* express a similar opinion (p. 347). This is certainly the case, but the foreign shareholders in the other steel works also wished to maximize profits. Their stronger capital position permitted them to achieve this by more acceptable methods.

[2] AÚLSMHD – Agreement, 15, 2b.

the formation of the cartel it had been the general practice in the iron and steel trade to execute orders from the Eastern foundries with the endorsement 'Transport Basis Kladno' and steel plates with 'Transport Basis Dvůr Králové', which meant that the difference in transport costs between Ostrava or Třinec and Kladno and the place of delivery had to be met by the Vítkovice Mining and Foundry Works or the Mining and Metallurgic Co.[1] This arose because most metal-working factories and the biggest trading firms were situated in Bohemia, nearer to Kladno than to Ostrava or Třinec. When in 1921 the Selling Agency of the United Czechoslovak Iron Works began, according to the 'Agreement', to distribute orders to those works which from the point of view of transport were situated nearest to the place of delivery, the Prague Iron Co. quite soon naturally had a considerable advantage in orders, which in fact exceeded its quota. Those orders which the Prague Iron Co. was unable to execute were then re-allocated by the Selling Agency to Ostrava or to Třinec. The difference in transport costs, however, appeared in a reduction in the prices paid by the cartel to the Prague Iron Co. which did not apply to the other members. Besides this, another condition of the 'Agreement' provided that those firms 'which had a start' in orders must pay compensation to the cartel members who lagged behind, i.e. 10 % of the average basic price obtained for each 100 kg of the advance orders.[2] Thus the Prague Iron Co. had to compensate the works in Ostrava and Těšín for their unfavourable geographical situation on the domestic market. Of course, their location near the Oder was very convenient for foreign trade. The Prague Iron Co. could not carry this growing financial burden for long, as the quotas of the Vítkovice Mining and Foundry Works and the Mining and Metallurgic Co. were larger than its own and each delivery in excess of the quota had to be accounted for to the Selling Agency. It was forced to request new negotiations, which resulted in the 'Brno Agreement' between the members of the Big Three. The Vítkovice Mining and Foundry Works and the Mining and Metallurgic Co. accepted a division into three equal parts of deliveries which fell under the terms of the 'Agreement'.[3] However, they did not

[1] Cf. ANTM–Vzpomínky J. Tilleho; also *Sto let kladenských železáren*, p. 340.
[2] AÚLSMHD – Agreement, 26, 1 a, b. [3] Cf. ANTM–Vzpomínky J. Tilleho.

agree on any changes in the allocation of quotas. Transport costs from Ostrava and Třinec were still lower than they had been before the original 'Agreement' was concluded, while the unfavourable situation of the Prague Iron Co. was only slightly alleviated.

Production costs played an extraordinarily important part in the cartel, as they became one of the main vehicles for maximizing profits. The cartel partners had, according to the terms of the 'Agreement', relinquished direct independent sales and had transferred this activity to the Selling Agency, which paid them a uniform average price for each of their products, irrespective of the production costs they incurred. The lower the costs, the greater the profits. On the one side, average prices gave less profitable enterprises the possibility of a certain profit margin; on the other side, however, they encouraged technical improvements, rationalization of the production process and every effort to decrease costs in order to attain the highest possible rate of profit.[1] The Vítkovice Mining and Foundry Works and the Mining and Metallurgic Co. achieved the lowest production and transport costs and therefore benefited most from membership of the cartel. The Prague Iron Co. succumbed in competition with them, particularly in the area of production costs. It drew on comparatively low-grade iron-ore from Nučice, which contained a large amount of acidic waste rock and used up greater quantities of coke and lime. In addition, the yield of its own iron-ore mines gradually deteriorated and neither in the collieries nor in the iron and steel works was the necessary large-scale investment made. Thus production costs could not be radically reduced.[2] The financial policy of the main shareholders and the condition of the contract with the Mannesmann–Röhrenwerke made the necessary investments impossible.

As well as the unfavourable contract with Mannesmann, the Prague Iron Co. had been drawn into a relatively unfavourable agreement with the Králodvorská cementárna (Králodvorská cement plant), which owned 25 % of the Prague Iron Co.'s joint-stock capital from 1929 to 1936.[3] The Králodvorská

[1] Cf. AÚLSMHD – Agreement about accounting quantities; also P. Eisler, *Monopoly v hutnictví kapitalistického Československa* (Monopoly in the Metallurgical Industry of Capitalist Czechoslovakia), p. 50.

[2] AÚLSMHD–PŽ – Prague Iron Co., 1938.

[3] Cf. *Sto let kladenských železáren*, p. 347; *Compass, Čechoslovakei* (1938–9).

cementárna, with its nominal joint-stock of Kč 48 million, was the strongest enterprise in this branch of industry in the pre-Munich Republic and succeeded in monopolizing the production of cement.[1] The same groups were represented on its board of directors as on that of the Prague Iron Co. Heinrich Bierwes of Mannesmann was a permanent member of the board; however, the proportions of shares held by the Živnostenská Bank and the Czech Escompte Bank respectively were reversed, i.e. the Czech Escompte Bank owned a majority and nominated the president of the company.[2] An agreement between the Králodvorská cementárna and the Prague Iron Co. had been in existence since 1900 about deliveries of blast-furnace slag from Kladno and Králův Dvůr at very low prices and with unfavourable transport conditions.[3] When the Prague Iron Co. wanted to rid itself of these irksome conditions and planned to build its own cement plant, the Králodvorská cementárna, with the help of the participating banks, acquired 25 % of its shares in order to forestall the project.[4] The Prague Iron Co. was put under pressure in 1936 to renew the delivery agreement until 1990; in addition, both companies promised not to interfere with each other's production and delivery programmes.[5] The unfavourable contract was thus prolonged and, although the Králodvorská cementárna later sold its shares in the Prague Iron Co. to the Živnostenská Bank, conditions remained unchanged.

In comparison with the iron and steel works in Ostrava and Třinec, which had their own lime stone quarries, coal-mines and cokeries, the situation of the Prague Iron Co. was less favourable. Furthermore, the Kladno iron and steel works depended on coke imported either from Germany or from Ostrava, where all sales of coke were monopolized by the Vítkovice Mining and Foundry Works and the Mining and Metallurgic Co., through their Sales Bureau of the United Ostrava–Karviná Collieries.

The Prague Iron Co. was thus forced to buy coke from its

[1] Cf. also V. Král, II, p. 320.

[2] Cf. Ibid., p. 322; also *Sto let kladenských železáren*, p. 347; *Compass, Čechoslovakei* (1938–9).

[3] Cf. *Sto let kladenských železáren*, ibid.

[4] Ibid.; also V. Král, II, p. 321.

[5] Cf. ibid.; *Compass, Čechoslovakei* (1938), p. 587.

competitors at monopoly prices.[1] In all these areas it was not able to stand up to competition. These factors help to bring out the relatively weaker position of German and Austrian capital in the mining and metallurgy industry of Czechoslovakia before Munich.

Not even a re-shuffle in the ownership relations of the Prague Iron Co., undertaken in 1936–7, could alter the company's situation or significantly strengthen the Kladno works. During the armament boom the Mannesmann–Röhrenwerke in Chomutov and the Živnostenská Bank formed a shareholders' syndicate, in which they had almost a majority holding (Mannesmann 25.6 % and the Živnostenská Bank 20.21 %).[2] If controlling influences on production and trade are added to the capital investment, the priority of the Mannesmann interests cannot be doubted. At the same time, the Mannesmann group consolidated its position in all its Czechoslovak subsidiary companies from which the Austrian bank, the Niederösterreichische Escompte Gesellschaft, and the German bank, the Berliner Handelsgesellschaft, had been ousted.[3] At that time Wilhelm Zangen already represented the Deutsche Bank and the Mannesmann combine in Czechoslovakia, and was determined to expand German economic influence in Central and Southeast Europe. The board of directors of the Prague Iron Co. approved a five-year investment programme in 1936, by which time the company had recovered and again showed a positive profit. The investments were aimed at securing the company a better basis for the negotiations about the renewal of the steel cartel which were to begin in 1940.[4]

[1] Cf. *Sto let kladenských železáren*, p. 342.

[2] Cf. ASÚS–cizí účasti, Expertises 19–21; also ADWI–05981.

[3] Cf. ADWI–05981.

[4] Cf. ADWI–05981; also AÚLSMHD–PŽ – Board of directors meetings 1936, 1937. V. Král considers the plan for technical improvements in the works as a thorough preparation for the time when the Prague Iron Co. would exclusively serve the war needs of Hitler's Germany. (Cf. V. Král, II, p. 297.) No doubt the Mannesmann combine also endeavoured to realize these objectives. However, the investment programme was not particularly large and was estimated at a cost of Kč 100–125 million, i.e. about Kč 20–25 million annually. These were not meant to be investments for expansion, but were rather intended to catch up with neglected investments, so that by the time of the expiration of the cartel agreement, at the end of 1940, the Prague Iron Co. would have reached a more consolidated position and a better starting situation for negotiations about new cartel conditions.

However, in 1938 profits fell sharply and indebtedness rose once more, so that the investment programme could not be properly started and the situation of the company remained practically unchanged until the violent intervention of German interests in 1939.

By its participation at the centres of the combines of the Big Three, foreign capital investment spread into almost all enterprises in the mining and metallurgic industry and into a large number of companies in related industries in Czechoslovakia. At the same time the central managements of the combines in Czechoslovak territory helped foreign investors to expand further into Central and Southeast European countries (viz. Tables 11–15). An increasing number of enterprises in the metallurgy and metal-working industries in Czechoslovakia were being drawn into the sphere of interest of the Big Three and into the steel cartel, the Selling Agency of the United Czechoslovak Iron Works, which was dominated by one or the other of the Big Three and usually by all the three combines together.

Foreign investment also found access to relatively smaller mining and metallurgic companies in Czechoslovakia. Their significance consisted mainly in their specialized production, their favourable export situation, or their mining of rare metals or minerals. As mentioned earlier in another connection, Swedish capital, in the form of the firm Mustad et Sön of Gotheburg, held a majority of the shares of the mining and metallurgic combine, the Steel Industry in Most, and by this participation it gained indirect control over the Steel Industry's subsidiary companies. The Mining and Metallurgic Co., as was shown above, gained a significant influence over the sales of the combine of the Steel Industry through their Central Bureau of Czechoslovak Wire and Wire Nail Manufacturers and their Sales Association for Chains and Wire Products. Here French, Swedish and Czech capital cooperated in monopolizing and rationalizing this branch of production. The Big Three also forced the Chomutov manufacturers of galvanized plates, the Brothers Bablik of Austria, into the steel cartel and, as the stronger partners, imposed production and trading conditions on them.

Foreign investors were also interested in the shares of the mining and metallurgic combine of the Poldina huť, which was not among the largest in Czechoslovakia, although its nominal joint-stock capital was fairly high, amounting to Kč 125 million.[1] The Poldina huť attracted foreign investment because of its specialized production of high-quality steel and its widespread network of sales agencies abroad, which handled 60–75 % of the products of its Kladno and Chomutov works; thus only a very small part of its output served the domestic market.[2] The controlling shareholder in the Poldina huť was the Czech Escompte Bank and Credit Institute in Prague (with about 25 %),[3] whose director was also the chairman of the board of directors of the Poldina huť; the Niederösterreichische Escompte Gesellschaft also had shares and its representative, Wilhelm Kux, was vice-chairman of the Poldina huť for 22 years until the withdrawal of the Austrian bank's participation in 1937.[4] Financial groups from Belgium, Great Britain and the United States have to be regarded as indirect investors in the Poldina huť, because of their direct participation in the joint-stock capital of the Prague and Viennese banks which held the majority of the Poldina huť's shares. The Živnostenská Bank also owned a rather insignificant share in the combine (about 4 %);[5] it could use its influence indirectly,[6] but this influence could not be decisive. This appears clearly in the failure of a long-planned project of the Živnostenská Bank and the Prague Iron Co. to build a united raw material and electric power plant for the Kladno works of both combines.[7] Such a project would, on the one hand, have removed the unfavourable conditions of the Prague Iron Co. and, on the other hand, would have reduced production costs considerably in the Kladno works of both combines; but there would have been an acute danger of penetration by German capital (of Mannesmann and the Deutsche Bank) into the Poldina huť. It is evident that the interests of the financial groups which participated in the Poldina huť and those which participated in the Prague Iron

[1] Cf. *Sto let kladenských železuren*, p. 369.
[2] Cf. ADWI–05674. Poldina huť had 78 sales agencies abroad in 38 countries in all continents, cf. *Sto let kladenských železáren*, p. 363.
[3] ASÚS–cizí účasti, Expertise No. 12.
[4] Cf. ADWI–05674; also *Compass, Čechoslovakei*, relevant years.
[5] Cf. ASÚS–cizí účasti, Expertise No. 12.
[6] Cf. IMT–Nr. IV, Fall XI–8322; also V. Král, II, p. 46.
[7] Cf. ADWI–05674; also V. Král, II, p. 295.

Co. were antagonistic. Western and Austrian capital tried to prevent an expansion of German capital into this sphere of interest.

The Poldina huť was among those economic entities in Czechoslovakia which aroused an extraordinarily lively interest in German big business. The intelligence department of the Deutsche Bank watched the development of the combine carefully in the 1920s and even more intensely in the 1930s, and the reports expressed appreciation of the quality and reputation of its products and its large exports.[1] The bank and the German Ministry of Finance were aware of the industrial potential and the well-established exports of the Poldina huť, 'whose products necessarily must have a great significance for the German economy and especially for the army'.[2] However, German capital was able to absorb the Poldina huť only after the annexation of the border regions of Czechoslovakia and the occupation of the Czech Lands.[3] Until then West European and Czech financial groups predominated in the combine.

Another comparatively significant foreign investment in the Czechoslovak metallurgical industry was that of the Viennese Banking House Reitzes, which owned 65.25 % of the joint-stock of the Válcovny kovů a.s. (Metal Rolling Mills) in Moravská Ostrava–Přívoz.[4] Also, an American firm from Connecticut owned 97.1 % of the shares of the Branecké železárny a.s. (Branka Iron Works) in Branka near Opava.[5] In both companies foreign shareholders were represented on the board of directors and production and commercial policies were directed by the foreign investors.

One of the strongholds of foreign investment – above all from France and the United States – was in the magnesite industry of Austria and Czechoslovakia. Magnesite is the source of magnesia and also forms the raw material for fireproof products, especially for the basic walling of blast-furnaces. In 1937 Austria was the second largest producer of magnesite in the world and Czechoslovakia the sixth. The richest deposits occurred in Veitsch (Austria) and in Slovakia.[6] The leading

[1] Cf. ADWI–05674.
[2] Cf. DZAP–B 187–NID 10639.
[3] Cf. IMT–NID 13399; 10639; also ASÚS – cizí účasti, Expertise No. 12; also V. Král, II, p. 47.
[4] Cf. ASÚS – cizí účasti, Austrian capital participation in 1938.
[5] Cf. Ibid.; also *Compass, Čechoslovakei* (1938).
[6] Cf. W. R. Jones, p. 73.

French mining and metalluric combines, Schneider et Cie and de Wendel, participated in the Veitscher Magnesitwerke A.G. in Vienna and in the Magnezitový priemysel úč. spol. in Bratislava.[1] Their representatives held seats on the board of directors of the Slovak company, where Schneider had nominated Aimé Lepercq and the interests of de Wendel were entrusted to a member of the family, who was also a member of the French senate – Guy de Wendel. In addition, French investments acted indirectly on the Slovak Magnezitový priemysel through its other shareholders, the Austrian Veitscher Magnesitwerke and the Hungarian Allgemeine Credit Bank, which themselves were subsidiaries of Schneider's L'Union Européenne Industrielle et Financière. The capital ties between the Austrian and Slovak magnesite industry and the French combines were fully recognized in the international cartel organization 'Vereinigung der Magnesitwerke' and in the cartel agreement deliveries of magnesite products for the needs of the Mining and Metallurgic Co. and for all other Schneider subsidiaries were not included in the quotas.[2] The activities of foreign capital and of the international cartel resulted in strict control of the output of magnesite and magnesite products in Czechoslovakia, which also applied to the West-Bohemian Kaolin and Fire-Brick Manufacture and Slovak Magnesite Works (Západočeské závody kaolinové-šamotové a slovenské magnesitové),[3] in spite of the fact that the latter belonged to the combine of the Živnostenská Bank.

Our analysis in this chapter has shown that one of the technically most advanced and economically most important industries of the Czechoslovak economy, the mining and metallurgical industry, was definitely controlled by foreign capital, with Anglo-French investors holding the first place followed by German investors. At the same time, it is interesting to see that the most powerful representative of domestic

[1] Cf. ASÚS–cizí účasti; also *Compass, Čechoslovakei* (1929–38). I was unable to find evidence of an American investment which V. Král mentions (op. cit., II, p. 317). According to the international cartel agreement, American capital participated in the Österreichisch-Amerikanische Magnesit A.G. Radenthe in Kärnten, Austria (cf. SÚA–KR–175). As far as Slovak enterprises are concerned the decisive influence among foreign investments was French.

[2] Cf. SÚA–KR 175 (16 October 1929–31 December 1939).

[3] Ibid.

Czech finance, the Živnostenská Bank, actively participated, as the weaker partner, in the Mining and Metallurgic Co. in the French sphere of influence, and in the Prague Iron Co. in the German sphere of influence. It can be maintained that the position of the Živnostenská Bank reflects two lines of policy pursued by Czechoslovak bankers and industrialists in relation to the struggle for predominance which was waged by British, French and German big business in Central and Southeastern Europe.

2 The participation of the Czechoslovak iron and steel industry in international cartels, 1926–38

In order for the producers of a certain country to be able to participate in an international cartel, it is generally necessary for them to have a national cartel capable of ensuring the operation of the international cartel as agreed, without interference from regional competition.[1] The high degree of monopolization and the comprehensive cartelization of the Czechoslovak iron and steel industry provided a basis for effective control of the domestic market by the Selling Agency of the United Czechoslovak Iron Works (hereafter referred to as 'the Selling Agency'). Thus, very soon after the First World War, favourable conditions arose for the Czechoslovak steel industry to negotiate with its foreign competitors and also with the European Steel Cartel about problems of production, prices and marketing. Essentially, it was representatives of the Big Three who negotiated, concluded, changed or dissolved international cartel agreements, as this privilege was reserved for them by the above-mentioned Agreement within the framework of the Selling Agency.[2]

The interests of the Czechoslovak steel producers fitted in with the efforts of the most powerful iron and steel combines of post-war Europe to regulate competition on world markets – especially with a view to the potential strength of German

[1] Cf. Corwin D. Edwards, *Economic and Political Aspects of International Cartels*, Senate Committee Print – Monograph No. 1, 78th Congress 2nd Session – Committee on Military Affairs, Subcommittee on War Mobilization (Washington, 1944), p. 1.

[2] Cf. SÚA–KR 28/1, Agreement of the United Czechoslovak Iron Works, p. 23.

heavy industry – and to adapt the steel industry on the continent to the economic and political situation brought about by the Peace Treaties of 1919–20. Besides, the iron and steel trade had a significant influence on the economic life of most countries, especially those which had to export in order to survive economically between the two world wars. In Central Europe this applied above all to Czechoslovakia, whose steel exports amounted to about one-third of total production between 1924 and 1936.[1]

The Czechoslovak steel cartel tried to protect its own home market against foreign competition and at the same time to secure the largest possible share of the world market, particularly its traditional markets in the territory of the former Austro-Hungarian Monarchy. To some extent the Czechoslovak iron and steel industry was in a relatively better position than its main competitors in the neighbouring defeated countries, because through its economic ties and the political orientation of the new Czechoslovak state, it could count on the support of some of the most powerful steel combines in the countries of the Entente, which incidentally belonged to the founders of the European Steel Cartel. This was also one of the reasons why Czechoslovak producers joined the European Steel Cartel very soon after its formation.

The origin of the Entente Internationale de l'Acier (EIA) and the membership of the Czechoslovak iron and steel industry

International steel cartels already existed before the First World War, between the European countries as well as in the United States of America, but each cartel organization concentrated mainly on one particular product. One of the oldest of this kind was the International Railmakers Association – IRMA – founded in 1883 and renewed in a tighter and amazingly durable organizational form in 1904.[2] However, at the beginning of the 1920s the most important European producers and exporters of steel discussed much more ambitious plans for international cartelization. They joined in an attempt

1 Calculated from data in ANTM–413/15, No. 3 – Reports on the development of the market for steel and rolled products 1928–36 give the amount of exports as 32 % of total production.

2 Cf. Robert Liefmann, *Cartels, Concerns and Trusts* (London, 1932).

to establish a super-cartel, which would control the export of steel products all over the world. Negotiations were complicated and often had to be discontinued, because the rival interests of the negotiators were so strong as to appear irreconcilable. The difference between the favourable political situation of the steel industries in victorious countries and the situation of the German steel industry was particularly marked. Moreover, some representatives could not speak for the whole of their national steel industries, because cartelization in their countries had not progressed sufficiently. This was especially true of Belgium. At the end of September 1926, however, an agreement was signed by the representatives of five national groups – France, Belgium, Luxemburg, Germany and the Saar, the so-called Founder Groups – setting up the first international steel cartel, the Entente Internationale de l'Acier (EIA), also known as the Rohstahlgemeinschaft or European Steel Cartel, as from 1 October 1926.

Clearly the most powerful European steel producers did not arrive accidentally at a time for the formation of the cartel. After the occupation of the Ruhr a provisional settlement was reached between the steel combines of France and Germany, which played a decisive role in the background of the Franco-German dispute. In 1925 a partial international stabilization followed the signing of the Locarno Treaty, and in September 1926 – at the same time as the representatives of the five largest steel combines set up the EIA – Germany joined the League of Nations. Parallel to these international events, which led to a certain stabilization of the post-war world, the German steel industry formed a tight cartel, the renewed Stahlwerks-Verband,[1] which was dominated by the Vereinigte Stahlwerke, which was formed at almost the same time and was the strongest German trust in the industry.[2] The head of the Vereinigte Stahlwerke was Dr Fritz Thyssen, who was also the

[1] The Stahlwerks-Verband was founded in 1904 but disintegrated after the cartel agreement expired in 1917 and survived only as a registered commercial company. In summer 1925 the agreement was renewed and covered practically the whole German steel industry. It had the approval and direct support of the German government.

[2] The Vereinigte Stahlwerke arose out of the merger of four large groups of steel producers (Rhein-Elbe-Union, Phoenix, Thyssen and Rheinstahl) on 1 April 1926 and became the most powerful steel combine in Europe.

dominant personality among the German group in the negotiations about the EIA. Supported by his government,[1] he took an active part in the preliminary negotiations and decisively influenced formulation of some of the cartel statutes. His most active opponent during this time was Dr Emil Mayrisch from Luxemburg. As president of the Luxemburg combine ARBED (Arciéries Réunies de Burbach-Eich-Dudelange) he could come forward with at least an appearance of neutrality between France and Germany. However, in reality he was influenced by the French Comité des Forges, especially by Eugène Schneider, who was also vice-president of ARBED. Thus Mayrisch effectively represented the Franco-Belgian–Luxemburg group. The steel combines of these three groups were closely interlocked by mutual capital investments, chiefly as a result of the large shifts of capital in favour of the French Schneider group after the First World War.[2] Dr Mayrisch became president of the EIA and retained this post until his death in 1928, representing in fact the interests of the steel industry of the victorious nations. According to the statutes of the EIA the presidency should have been taken in turn by each of the Founder Groups.[3] However, after the death of Dr Mayrisch his successor in ARBED, Dr Aloys Meyer, also took over the presidency of the EIA, which he held until the outbreak of war in 1939, when the cartel disintegrated. This course of events reflects the changing balance of power in Europe in this extremely important economic field.

The member countries of the EIA produced only about 30 % of the world's steel; after the formation of the cartel, however, they controlled 65 % of the world's steel exports.[4] This factor played a decisive role when the cartel was founded, for its ultimate aim was to control the whole of the international trade in steel. The highest degree of control was achieved by the International Steel Cartel after the world's largest producers, the U.S.A. and Great Britain, joined in the middle of the 1930s.

[1] Cf. Stresemann's enthusiastic coverage of the founding of the EIA in *Frankfurter Zeitung*, 2 October 1926, No. 735, p. 1.

[2] In the French Parliamentary Investigation these transfers of ownership were characterized as the greatest war loot in the history of France. Cf. Chambres des députés, Documents Parlamentaires, Annex No. 5367, 19 January 1928, p. 186, cited by E. Hexner, *The International Steel Cartel* (Chapel Hill, 1943), p. 54.

[3] International Steel Agreement, 30 September 1926, Article 2. Cf. E. Hexner, Appendix III.

[4] E. Hexner, *International Cartels* (London, 1946), pp. 270f.

At this point the cartel reached its peak, but it collapsed almost immediately, in September 1939.

The cartel was administered through the so-called National Groups – Comptoir Sidérurgique de France, Comptoir de Vente de la Sidérurgie Belge 'Cosibel', Stahlwerks-Verband A.G. – which were responsible for ensuring adherence to the statutes of the cartel in their respective countries. In due course the central office of the cartel in Luxemburg built up a net of export and sales organizations, which, in effect, formed a further system of international cartels for certain specific products (semi-finished goods, structural shapes, merchant bars, plates of various kinds, universal steel, etc.). In contrast with other international cartels, especially in the chemical and electro-technical industry, the conditions agreed upon by the members of the EIA were not concerned with patents or secret technological processes; neither was there any explicit intervention in production methods or a ban on production. However, the cartel influenced the quantity of production indirectly, by its quota system for individual National Groups. In addition, the agreement included a regulated price policy, which was to lead to the stabilization of prices at the highest possible level and to the mitigation of price fluctuations in times of crisis. The members of the cartel were assured of the protection of their home markets and were to unite in opposition to outsiders and, if necessary, to liquidate external competition completely.[1] A complicated system of controls, sanctions, fines and other economic mechanisms was set up to resolve competitive conflicts by negotiations wherever possible, with the aim of maximizing profits under given economic and political conditions.

From 1 January 1927 Czechoslovak producers, represented by their national cartel, the Selling Agency of the United Czechoslovak Iron Works, became associate members of the EIA. They could not participate on an equal footing with the Founder Groups, who alone were entitled to determine the economic policy of the cartel; and unlike the Founder Groups they could not claim compensation for losses incurred in a price-cutting campaign against outsiders. Together with the Czechoslovak Group, the Austrian and Hungarian steel producers also joined the cartel; these three national groups were regarded by

[1] Cf. Basic Cartel Agreement, AÚLSMHD–10008.

Table 1. *Quotas in the International Steel Agreement of 30 September 1926*

Country	Percentage
Germany	40.45
France	31.89
Belgium	12.57
Luxemburg	8.55
Saar	6.54

the leading organs of the EIA as one unit, the so-called Central European Group (Zentraleuropäische Gruppe – ZEG).[1] According to the agreement signed on 4 February 1927, a joint quota was allocated to the Central European Group amounting to 7.272 % of the total production of the founder members of the EIA, to be divided among themselves by the members of the ZEG.[2] Czechoslovakia dominated the ZEG. Her quota came to more than two-thirds of the total allocated to the ZEG and, as a rule, Czechoslovak steel producers represented the ZEG in international negotiations.

In the first years of the EIA's existence quotas were calculated on the basis of the quantity of crude steel contained in steel products. In this way the quotas indirectly influenced the quantity of steel produced in the member countries. The cartel determined the quantity of crude steel which each national group was allowed to produce in the following quarter by basing its calculations on production figures for the first quarter of 1926. The quota shares were divided according to an estimated annual production of 25,278,000 tons of crude steel (Table 1).[3]

At the same time a pool was established in Luxemburg, into which each National Group put $1 for each ton of crude steel actually produced. National groups who exceeded their quotas had to pay a fine of $4 for each ton produced in excess, but in cases of under-production the groups who did not fulfil their

[1] This was also the practice in the international railmakers' cartel IRMA. Cf. SÚA–KR 207 and 209.

[2] Cf. AÚLSMHD–10008.

[3] Cf. Share Quotas in the International Steel Agreement of 30 September 1926, published by E. Hexner, The International Steel Agreement, Appendix IIIA.

Table 2. *Actual balance sheet of the EIA, October 1926–March 1927*

Country	Levies at \$1 per ton	Over-production fines (\$4 per ton)	Compensation for under-production (\$2 per ton)	Resulting amount for distribution after administrative expenses
				(\$)
Germany	7,694,000	6,044,000	...	13,738,000
France	4,202,000	...	470,000	3,732,000
Belgium	1,883,000	885,000	...	2,768,000
Luxemburg	1,181,000	...	8,000	1,173,000
Saar	932,000	428,000	...	1,360,000
Total	...	...	...	22,771,000

quotas obtained compensation payments of \$2, for each ton they did not produce. From 1927 onwards the accounts of the pool were balanced quarterly and, after deduction of the costs of running the cartel, the National Groups divided the surplus among themselves. The first balance sheet of the EIA confirms and illustrates this system (Table 2).[1] Although the quota system was on the whole relatively elastic, as the calculations took into account expert estimates of future demand on world markets, the international cartel had a basically restrictive effect: the expansion of productive capacity was penalized while its contraction was rewarded.

At the time when the cartel's operations began, competition was partly transferred into the sphere of the division of quotas between the members. Great Britain and the United States remained outside the cartel and Polish steel producers did not submit to pressures and join until 1935. From the beginning, differences within the cartel were very great and each point of agreement represented a truce in economic warfare which was dictated by the balance of power among the competitors. German producers had already put forward a demand for larger quotas when negotiating the foundation agreement, because they considered that the level of production which they

[1] Ibid., p. 76.

Table 3. *Quotas in the International Steel Agreement of November 1926*

Country	Percentage
Germany	43.18
France	31.18
Belgium	11.56
Luxemburg	8.30
Saar	5.78

For comparison: Central European Group from 1 January 1927, 7.272 %.

were permitted in the first quarter of 1926 put them at a disadvantage in comparison with France and Belgium. They succeeded in gaining a somewhat larger quota by November 1926. The maximum annual amount of crude steel production was raised by 4 million tons and the proportions were adjusted in favour of Germany (Table 3).[1] The German quota was increased by 2.73 %, but German production exceeded its quota by more than half a million tons almost immediately and the Stahlwerks-Verband had to pay a fine of more than six million dollars into the pool, as is shown in the balance sheet of the EIA for the first half-year. The very existence of the cartel – especially in Europe – depended essentially on the degree of cooperation of German producers and on their willingness to abide by the rules of the game.

The Czechoslovak cartel also had to fight for its production quota and, in particular, tried to secure and protect its markets, on the one hand, against the powerful cartels of the Founder Groups, and on the other against its partners in the ZEG, which was not by any means a harmonious unit. In addition to the agreement by which the Czechoslovak Group joined the EIA, the Selling Agency concluded a number of international cartel agreements with foreign steel cartels or steel combines which were dominant in their own domestic industries. The structure of these international cartel agreements was, of course, influenced by complicated trade and production relations. The entire steel exports of Czechoslovakia were tied up in cartel agreements, and only an analysis of these can provide an under-

[1] Ibid., Appendix III A.

standing of the decisions which were made about the amount and direction of foreign trade in Czechoslovak iron and steel products.

The position of the Czechoslovak steel industry in the Central European Group (ZEG) in the 1920s

The largest and most vital markets of the Czechoslovak steel industry were in the so-called 'original' territory, which comprised Austria, Hungary, Yugoslavia, Romania, Bulgaria, Italy, Turkey and Albania. In these markets the world's big steel combines and cartels competed fiercely, but the cartelized Czechoslovak industry persisted in trying to protect at least part of its traditional access to them. Apart from direct participation by Czechoslovak iron and steel combines in the steel industry of most of these countries, through their own subsidiary works or capital investment in indigenous enterprises, the Selling Agency of the United Czechoslovak Iron Works attempted to maximize its share in the imports of Central and Southeast Europe. Shortly before the ZEG entered the international steel cartel, the Selling Agency concluded a cartel agreement, on 1 January 1924, with the Austrian producers, represented by the Alpine, concerning not only crude iron and steel production but also rolled material (semi-finished steel, merchant bars, beams, rails, cross ties, thick plates). One part of the agreement provided for the protection of the Czechoslovak domestic market; Austrian exports to Czechoslovakia were prohibited, because the Selling Agency had the exclusive right to supply the home market with all except a few kinds of special steel which the Czechoslovak works did not produce. However, on Austrian territory the Alpine and the Selling Agency divided the market for cast-iron and haematite pig iron in a ratio of 2:1 in favour of the Czechoslovak producers, and on the average 18–25 % of the Austrian market for rolled products was allocated to the Czechoslovak works.[1] The second part of the agreement divided steel exports to the 'original' territory between the Selling Agency and the Alpine, generally on a proportional basis of 70:30 in favour of the Czechoslovak works.[2]

[1] ANTM–SDS 413/4, Uebereinkommen (Oesterreich-Tschechoslowakei).

[2] AÚLSMHD–10008 – Territorialschutz-Uebereinkommen, Oesterreich-Čechoslovakei, Export Uebereinkommen, 29 January 1926.

In Hungary, Czechoslovak deliveries accounted for about 83 % of consumption of cast-iron in the 1920s, while the Czechoslovak market remained almost entirely protected against Hungarian imports.[1]

In accordance with their role as the main economic force in the Central European Group, the leading personalities of the Czechoslovak iron and steel industry endeavoured to strengthen their positions in the foreign trade of Romania and Yugoslavia during 1925 by negotiations, economic pressures and market operations. It does not seem to be entirely accidental that the intensified drive of the Czechoslovak steel industry into this area came at a time when the Czechoslovak–French alliance was confirmed in an official diplomatic and military treaty and when the efforts of the Czechoslovak Republic to play a leading role in the Little Entente assumed concrete form. On the other hand, the Czechoslovak steel cartel's attempt to conclude bilateral international cartel agreements can be explained by the desire of the Czechoslovak producers to organize their markets so that they could negotiate from a stronger position about the conditions for their entry into the international steel cartel.

As a rule the representatives of the Big Three (the president of the Mining and Metallurgic Company, Ing. Günther, the director-general of the Vítkovice Mining and Foundry Works, Dr Sonnenschein, and the director-general of the Prague Iron Company, Dr Hořovský) conducted all decisive international negotiations, together with the director of the Selling Agency, Dr Brenner. In the case of Romania they negotiated about conditions for the import and export of steel products with the representative of Romania's most influential iron and steel works 'Reşita', director Hajts, who relinquished any claims to exports from Romania and agreed to guarantee to Czechoslovak exporters a third of the Romanian market for iron and steel and rolled materials.[2]

Negotiations with Yugoslavia, however, did not proceed quite so smoothly. Yugoslav industrialists argued against the pressures put on them by the ZEG, pointing out that their government did not permit cartels and also preferred to give orders for rolled products to domestic works. The Yugoslav negotiator, director-general von Noot, indicated nevertheless

[1] AÚLSMHD–10008, supplement 9. [2] AÚLSMHD–10015.

that his government would not prevent the conclusion of a cartel agreement if its conditions were acceptable to the Yugoslav iron and steel works, who were demanding a higher quota in their own home market than the ZEG was prepared to concede; in return the ZEG would be able to share government orders and the Yugoslav government might even approve a rise in prices. The cartel conditions formulated by Dr Sonnenschein of Vítkovice were the following: (1) the Yugoslav market was to be divided between the Yugoslav works and the ZEG in the ratio 2:1; (2) the Yugoslav government was to place its orders with a selling agency to be established by the ZEG in Yugoslavia, which would get preferential prices at least 10 % higher; (3) if the Yugoslav government failed to adhere to these conditions the agreement would become invalid; (4) the Yugoslav works were to relinquish their rights to expand their production programme of rolled steel goods and were not to change their situation in any way that might be detrimental to the ZEG; (5) the Yugoslav works were to give up exports to Czechoslovakia, Austria, Hungary, Romania, Bulgaria, Albania, Greece, European Turkey, Italy and Poland; (6) the ZEG was to have priority in deliveries to Yugoslavia, of foreign crude steel and semi-finished steel as well as those steel products which the Yugoslav works did not produce.[1]

These severe conditions are proof of the strong position of the ZEG, especially of the Czechoslovak iron and steel combines. On the other hand the arguments used by the Yugoslav industrialists show that they were able to enlist the aid of their government in their efforts to gain somewhat better conditions in the cartel and that, although they were private businessmen, they could safely promise government orders, higher prices and the evasion of the anti-cartel legislation. The interrelation of the domestic steel industry and the government is quite evident from the discussion between Dr Sonnenschein and the Yugoslav Minister for Forestry and Mining which took place on 15 May 1925.[2] As a result of these negotiations the basic principles were laid down for an international cartel 'concerning the marketing of rolled products in the Kingdom of Yugoslavia' which was signed by the Yugoslav works (in Zenica, Jesenica and Storé) and the ZEG (i.e. by the Selling Agency for Czechoslovakia,

[1] AÚLSMHD-10014. [2] AÚLSMHD-10015.

the Alpine for Austria and the RIMA for Hungary) on 31 May 1925.[1] The Czechoslovak negotiators succeeded in their demand for a 33½ % share in the Yugoslav market for the ZEG, even though their Yugoslav partners continually raised the question of a 70 % quota for themselves on their own home market.[2] A selling agency was established in Yugoslavia, which was to get government orders and preferential prices on condition that the Yugoslav works participated in it. The Yugoslav works agreed to restrict their production of rolled goods and to abstain from exports to Czechoslovakia, Austria and Hungary. If they wanted to export to other countries, they would have to come to an agreement with the ZEG first.[3] The cartel conditions did not satisfy the Yugoslav industrialists and in the same year they tried, unsuccessfully, to renew negotiations on extraordinary quotas for government orders, the expansion of production in their rolling mills and restricting the imports of the ZEG into Yugoslavia.[4]

The Central and Southeastern European markets for steel and rolled materials, which were tied to the Czechoslovak, Austrian and Hungarian steel industry by cartels, became a protected area for the Central European Group within the EIA but not to the extent which the Czechoslovak producers had envisaged. As well as the domestic markets of the ZEG members, the European Steel Cartel also respected Albania, Yugoslavia, Trieste, Fiume and New Italy as protected areas. Here other members of the EIA were to refrain from competition with Czechoslovak, Austrian and Hungarian steel producers.[5] In return for this protection, the Central European Group, on joining the EIA at the beginning of 1927, had to undertake not to export to the markets of the Founder Groups. This meant not only their domestic markets, but in case of Belgium and France their colonial territories as well, as in the case of Germany Danzig and all free ports.[6]

Czechoslovak–German relations in the steel cartel

Although at the beginning of 1927 the signatories of the international convention of the EIA had pledged absolute mutual

[1] SÚA–KR 39.
[2] AÚLSMHD–10017, 10017a.
[3] SÚA–KR 39.
[4] Cf. AÚLSMHD–10017a, 10017.
[5] SÚA–KR 59.
[6] Cf. SÚA–KR 673.

territorial protection, competition obviously did not cease in the markets of Central and Southeastern Europe, especially between Czechoslovak and German iron and steel works. After negotiations between the Selling Agency of the United Czechoslovak Iron Works and the Roheisenverband in Essen, a separate understanding about the mutual protection of their respective home markets was reached on 11 May 1927. Deliveries of haematite pig iron with poor phosphor content were, however, to be allowed from Germany into Czechoslovakia when the Czechoslovak works were not producing this commodity or when Czechoslovak purchasers refused to buy haematite iron from domestic producers; in each case the German suppliers had to obtain the agreement of the Selling Agency.[1] A similar understanding on mutual territorial protection concerning rolled steel products was signed on 23 May 1927, after negotiations in Berlin and Düsseldorf, between the Selling Agency, the Alpine and RIMA (i.e. ZEG) on the one hand and the Stahlwerks-Verband on the other.[2] While the Stahlwerks-Verband accepted the clause for the mutual protection of domestic markets, it claimed the right to deliver rolled bands to Trieste and conveyed an emphatic demand from the German cartel, the Roheisenverband, to be allowed to export its special steel products into the protected areas of the ZEG.[3] There were long drawn-out negotiations and exchanges of letters on this issue, and these were accompanied by competitive manœuvres, whereby the German producers tried to penetrate into these contractually forbidden markets.

German and Czechoslovak steel works competed in all products which were subject to the international cartel agreement on mutual market protection; their interests clashed not only in Romania, Yugoslavia and Bulgaria, but also in the home markets of the ZEG, in Hungary and Austria, where German producers obtained orders by offering lower prices and more favourable conditions for deliveries and payment than were permitted by the cartel. At this time the drive of the German steel industry into Central Europe increased in vigour, particularly because the degree of concentration in the industry increased (for instance, a majority participation in the joint-

[1] AÚLSMHD–10008, supplement 8; SÚA–KR 55.
[2] SÚA–KR 54. [3] Ibid.

stock capital of the Österreichische Alpine Montangesellschaft was acquired by the Vereinigte Stahlwerke),[1] but also as the result of a large inflow of American investments and credits into German heavy industry.

By their open competition in areas which the International Steel Cartel had allocated to the ZEG the German steel producers were not, of course, aiming at absolute control of these markets – the economic conditions were not yet ripe for this – but they felt that, with sufficient pressure, the Czechoslovak steel cartel could be forced to part with a certain share of its markets in favour of German products. Proof of this was provided on 18 April 1929, by the negotiations in the Viennese central offices of the Alpine between the Selling Agency and the Roheisenverband, which led to a new cartel agreement. The German cartel accepted a 17 % share in imports of steel to Hungary, leaving the Czechoslovak Group with 83 %; but at the same time the Austrian market was divided into three equal parts among the Selling Agency, the Alpine and the Roheisenverband, with an accompanying rise in prices for all kinds of steel. In these transactions the German participation in the Alpine, the largest Austrian combine, becomes clearly apparent. In return the German party to the cartel undertook to abstain from further exports to Bulgaria, Yugoslavia and Romania, except for special kinds of steel. All present expressed a desire to reach an understanding with the French–Belgian–Luxemburg Groups as well, but agreed to keep secret their undertaking, which was to remain in force until the end of 1940.[2] A few days after signing this agreement the Roheisenverband announced to the Selling Agency that the German works had withdrawn from the area concerned and that Czechoslovak producers would not meet with their competition any more.[3]

The German–Czechoslovak cartel agreement on the production of pig iron and steel reflected the relative economic and political strength of the partners in the period lasting approximately until the Munich Agreement. It remained intact during the temporary disintegration of the EIA. During the world economic crisis, when political relations between Czechoslovakia and Hungary deteriorated, the Roheisenverband

[1] Viz. p. 120. [2] AÚLSMHD–10008, supplement 9.
[3] Ibid. – letter of 24 April 1929.

obtained the consent of the Selling Agency (during negotiations in Vienna on 16 August 1932) to the opening of the Hungarian market to German products as long as the Czechoslovak–Hungarian rift lasted, while leaving the previously agreed conditions unchanged.[1] Partners in the cartel similarly did not hesitate to appropriate each other's quotas. In 1935 the Selling Agency and the Roheisenverband divided the share of the Alpine, amounting to a third of the Austrian demand for cast-iron and haematite pig iron and steel, equally between them. The Alpine was compensated with 5–6 Austrian Schillings for each ton it did not produce and undertook to persuade the Austrian authorities to stop imports of Russian cast-iron and haematite pig iron and steel; the Czechoslovak and German works would not have been able to compete with Russian products on the Austrian market.[2]

Very soon another competitor appeared on the Austrian market for pig iron, in the shape of the Dutch combine, Koninklijke Nederlandsche Hoogovense Staalfabrieken, N.V., Ijmuiden (which we shall refer to as 'Ijmuiden'), which had been delivering increasing quantities of pig iron to Austrian customers since 1933. All three Groups – the Czechoslovak, Austrian and German – united to defend their cartel privileges in Austria. Consequently a price war developed with the Dutch combine, which ended with the entry of the Dutch steel works into the cartel. In the agreement between the Selling Agency, the Alpine and the Roheisenverband on the one hand, and the Ijmuiden works on the other, the Austrian market for cast-iron and haematite iron was divided in the ratio 75:25 from 1 November 1936; at the same time it was agreed to raise the price of pig iron at once by 20 Austrian Schillings a ton.[3] At the same time the Selling Agency concluded a separate agreement with the iron and steel works in Ijmuiden concerning the mutual protection of their home markets, by which the Big Three also undertook to obtain all their supplies of haematite pig iron with low phosphor content from the Dutch firm, giving it orders in

[1] Ibid. – Niederschrift vom 6. August 1932.

[2] Ibid. – Abkommen wegen Ankauf des Alpine-Roheisenanteiles in Österreich – 3., 4. und 5. Juni 1935.

[3] Ibid. – Abkommen in Angelegenheit der Belieferung des Österreichischen Marktes mit Giesserei- und Hämatitroheisen – 16. Oktober 1936 bis 31. Dezember 1937.

preference to other competitors, provided that quality and prices were equal.[1] It is interesting to note that by this undertaking the Czechoslovak works gave preference to the Dutch supplier over the Roheisenverband, which had been permitted certain limited and very closely defined deliveries into Czechoslovakia in the 1920s.[2] Relations between partners in cartels vary according to changing economic circumstances, and depending on where the greater economic advantage lies.

On the whole, as is shown by the above analysis, German and Czechoslovak steel producers tried to settle their differences on Central European markets by concluding separate cartel agreements, which altered relationships in the EIA to some extent, because they included partial concessions by the Czechoslovak Group, faced with the economic reality of German competition.

The disintegration of the EIA

Although Czechoslovak–German cartel relations became more or less stabilized, the German Group became increasingly dissatisfied with the quota system and the division of markets in the European Steel Cartel and on 1 May 1929 they gave notice of their withdrawal from the EIA. Other members had also violated the agreement and the management of the cartel in Luxemburg was not strong enough to enforce the hoped-for cooperation between the national steel monopolies on the world markets, especially at a time of economic boom, in which exporters tried to secure the biggest possible share of the market for themselves as a safeguard against the eventual worsening of market conditions. When the German Group seceded from the EIA on 30 October 1929, the organization became practically ineffective, although it was not liquidated; the remaining National Groups extended the validity of the cartel on a monthly basis and the Czechoslovak producers promised to cooperate with the cartel in spite of the fact that no longterm agreement existed. During the years of the deepening world economic crisis various unsuccessful attempts were made to

[1] SÚA–KR 1001.

[2] SÚA–KR 55; also AÚLSMHD–10008, supplement 8, letter from the Selling Agency of 11 May 1927.

revive the cartel, which was again to allot production quotas to the National Groups, but this time separately for the home market and for exports; fines for exceeding stipulated quotas were also to be reduced. The administrative centre of the EIA in Luxemburg continued its coordinating work, establishing common export agencies – i.e. sales syndicates – of the Founder Groups for certain specified steel products (semi-finished steel, structural shapes, merchant bars, plates); the Central European Group agreed to cooperate in cartelizing exports of these products.

However, export markets diminished continuously in the prevailing crisis conditions and the members of the cartel competed against each other by undercutting prices, and by encroaching on their mutually protected territories in disregard of their contract obligations. The original international cartel, the EIA, collapsed in the middle of 1931. Persistent competition ruined weaker enterprises and was especially fierce in export markets. Each national group attempted to consolidate its position on the world market, hoping for higher quotas when the cartel was restarted, as they expected it would be very soon.

The world economic crisis of 1929–33 shook the foundations of all international agreements; the system of the Versailles Treaties began to crumble and at the same time the Little Entente began its slow process of disintegration. Cartel relations in general, and those of the steel industry in particular, reflected changes in international politics very accurately, and often foreshadowed such changes, especially in Central and Southeastern Europe, where competition between the European powers (Germany, Great Britain, France and Italy) was enormously intensified. Under the impact of the crisis, existing international steel cartels either collapsed completely or temporarily discontinued their activities. As a rule, cartel partners who had weathered the competitive storms on the world markets altered the conditions of their agreements in a manner that reflected amazingly closely the changed balance of economic forces. The economic crisis also brought about the growth of entirely new international cartels. The disintegration of the ZEG was part of this many-sided process.

Only two international cartels in the steel industry survived the world economic crisis basically unshaken, and managed to accommodate changes in the economic relationships of their members by altering their original agreements. In particular, the oldest and most tightly organized rail cartel, IRMA, strongly influenced by British steelmakers, controlled quotas and prices strictly and enforced a system of severe fines and compensation payments on its members through its London Committee. It had complete control over exports of heavy rails on world markets; all orders were sent to the London offices, where it was decided who was to execute them, and only then were the orders allotted to the national groups with precise instructions on prices and conditions of delivery. All member countries had their permanent representatives on the London Committee, but their voting power varied according to the size of their respective quotas. In this way the strongest producers with the largest quotas also had a decisive voice in decision-making (i.e. Great Britain, Germany, France, Belgium, Luxemburg and, after 1929, the United States). In addition to the national groups, two large Belgian combines, the works in Ougrée-Marihaye, with rolling mills in France, Belgium and Luxemburg, and the firm of Beame and Nimy, enjoyed special quotas.

The ZEG became a member of IRMA on 1 January 1927, and was represented on the London Committee by the Selling Agency of the United Czechoslovak Iron Works.[1] As in the EIA, in IRMA the Central European Group received a common quota of 3 % of total world exports of heavy rails. In addition, IRMA strictly pursued the principle of mutual market protection among its members.[2] The Yugoslav and Bulgarian markets were added to the ZEG's domestic markets as protected areas. In the first half of the 1930s the Hungarian works broke with the ZEG, as a result of Czechoslovak–Hungarian competitive conflicts and tried to get an independent and more favourable quota in the international cartel. In the IRMA agreement of 1 August 1935, only Czechoslovakia and Austria were still represented by the Czechoslovak Selling Agency. The Czechoslovak–Austrian quota fell to 2.68 %, because all cartel members had to transfer 10 % of their original quota to the Polish Group, which joined IRMA in 1935 and because they also had to contribute 0.02 % of their quotas to increase the

[1] SÚA-KR 207, 209.

[2] AÚLSMHD-10008, supplement 24.

Table 4. *Percentage shares in export quotas of heavy rails in IRMA, February 1937*

Country or company	Percentage
Great Britain	28
Germany	15.603
France	14.421
U.S.A.	12.471
Poland	9.412
Belgium	6.940
Ougrée	4.303
Luxemburg	3.282
Czechoslovakia	1.788
Hungary	1.740
Beame & Nimy	1.306
Austria	0.734

British share – Great Britain was traditionally the strongest member of the rail cartel. At the same time the management of IRMA asked the ZEG to waive part of its quota for an agreed compensatory payment. The Selling Agency and the Austrian Alpine divided the allotted quota between them in a ratio of 70.883 % : 29.117 % (i.e. the Czechoslovak producers could count on 1.9 % and the Austrian producers on 0.78 % of the world's exports of heavy rails in 1935); they divided the Yugoslav and Bulgarian markets among themselves in the same proportions.[1] As a settlement could not be reached with Hungary, an additional understanding was signed in 1936, further reducing the Czechoslovak–Austrian quota to 2.522 %, although the internally agreed proportions were changed slightly in favour of the Czechoslovak Group as against the Austrian producers (70.896 % : 29.104 %); overall, however, the Czechoslovak producers received a quota of 1.79 % of the world's heavy rail exports. The mutual quota relationships of the ZEG within IRMA were henceforth specified independently for each country[2] (Table 4). Even though the Czechoslovak share remained the largest among the Central European

[1] Ibid., supplement 25. The proposal that the Selling Agency should refrain from selling a certain part of its quota and receive compensation for so doing was negotiated in Brussels on 24 July 1935. (Cf. ANTM–413, box 1/1.)

[2] AÚLSMHD–10008.

members of the cartel, there can be no doubt that Czechoslovak producers could no longer control the size of quotas of the other members of the ZEG and that they lost some ground within the international rail cartel in the Central European market in the 1930s.

While the international rail cartel allotted orders to its members and controlled the export trade, the other international cartel in the steel industry which came through the world economic crisis practically unharmed was strictly a selling syndicate. The International Cartel for the Protection and Sale of Wire Products was set up by an agreement among German, Belgian, Dutch and Czechoslovak producers not to compete on their respective home markets; later the understanding was widened to include price fixing of wire products and on 30 November 1931 a cartel agreement was signed, setting up a selling agency, the Compagnie Internationale pour l'Exportation des Produits Tréfilés, Société Cooperative (henceforth referred to as IWECO = International Wire Export Company). Its headquarters were in Brussels but it was dominated in practice by the German cartel, Drahtverband G.m.b.H., based in Düsseldorf. Czechoslovak producers had a comparatively influential position in the IWECO, and Ing. Kruliš-Randa of the Czechoslovak Mining and Metallurgic Co. became its vice-chairman. In 1932 the member groups agreed to a set of rules based on production in 1931. No production increases above the 1931 level were permitted; it was also forbidden to build new works or to acquire majority shares in enterprises of the member countries without the approval of the cartel.[1] The activity of the international cartel coincides markedly in time and in content with the monopolizing and restrictive efforts of its Czechoslovak member, the national cartel organization Central Bureau of Czechoslovak Wire and Wire Nail Manufacturers, which was controlled by the Mining and Metallurgic Co. and whose chairman was also Ing. Kruliš-Randa. All members of the IWECO relinquished their rights to independent export sales, all marketing was to be carried out on behalf of members by the Brussels offices, where earnings were pooled and profits divided according to quotas. Table 5 shows the relations between member groups in 1932 and 1937.[2]

[1] SÚA-KR 33. [2] Ibid.

Table 5. *Percentage shares in the export of wire products within IWECO*

Group	1932* (%)	1937† (%)
German	53.37	50.0
Belgian	35.17	32.9
Czechoslovak	6.03	5.9
Dutch	0.61	5.8
Polish	—	2.7
Austrian	—	1.2
Hungarian	0.86	0.8
Danish	0.61	0.7

* Total quantity 718,926 tons. † Total quantity 776,920 tons.

Even though, historically, IWECO was one of the best organized of the syndicates which controlled quantities to be produced and tried to enforce its monopoly on world markets, it did meet with occasional competition. The production of wire and wire products did not require very large investments or particularly complicated and expensive machinery in comparison with other steel products; outsiders therefore periodically managed to get into export markets by undercutting the artificially high prices of these cartelized products. As a result, IWECO began to cooperate with the cartel of wire rod producers, the Internationaler Walzdrahtverband (IWV) which contained the largest European producers, and of which the Czechoslovak Selling Agency was thus also a member. As a rule, the large wire rod producers also controlled wire products – in Czechoslovakia the works of the Mining and Metallurgic Co., the Prague Iron Co. and the Steel Industry in Most – and in accordance with the cartel policy of IWECO the IWV also restricted its customers for wire rods to members of IWECO, in order to prevent the production of wire goods in works not belonging to IWECO. In this way both international cartels, IWECO and IWV, effectively controlled the world market for their products.

The Czechoslovak Group joined the IWV on 1 January 1930, and with the Austrian and Hungarian works formed the Central European Group within this international cartel (ZEG). As the largest producer the Czechoslovak Group retained about 60 % of the total ZEG quota, until the Munich events in 1938 (Czechoslovak Group – Selling Agency 59.067 %; Austrian Group–Alpine 28 %; and Hungarian Group–RIMA 12.933 %). When the Czechoslovak works settled the internal division of their quota in the IWV between themselves the interests of the two biggest competitors, the Mining and Metallurgic Co. and the Prague Iron Co., clashed sharply. The representatives of the two combines reached an agreement fairly easily to allocate an annual production quota of 1,500 tons to the third biggest works, the Steel Industry in Most, and also recognized their quotas of free deliveries of wire rods to foreign shareholders. However, during negotiations in 1931[1] Ing. Kruliš-Randa and Ing. Lepercq of the Mining and Metallurgic Co. insisted on an equal share of the remaining quota for their works and for the Prague Iron Co., instead of the 40:60 proportion agreed on in 1928.[2] They refused to enter into any discussions about this with the director-general of the Prague Iron Co., Dr Hořovský, who demanded recognition of the original cartel conditions but who had to give in to the stronger competitor. The Czechoslovak share of the export quotas of the IWV was as follows: ZEG total – 13.02 %, of which the Selling Agency got 7.6905 %, the Alpine 3.6456 % and RIMA 1.6839 %.[3] The Central European Group in the IWV did not fall apart in the 1930s and, represented by Ing. Kruliš-Randa, remained undivided in this international cartel until August 1938. In particular it kept a close watch on the German Group, in order to prevent it from encroaching on its protected markets, which included the territory of Southeast Europe. German suppliers were fined Kč 3.50 for every 1,000 kg of wire rods delivered to areas protected by the treaty.[4]

In 1935 the Polish Group joined the IWV and the relationship between the ZEG and the Polish Group on the Bulgarian market was adjusted so that the Polish works got 22 % of the 40 % previously allotted to the ZEG. The Czechoslovak Group were displeased with this arrangement and tried to get the unfavourable ratio changed, or, alternatively, to obtain permission

[1] AÚLSMHD–10008, supplement 22 of 14 October 1931.
[2] Ibid., supplement 23 of 15 October 1928.
[3] SÚA–KR 40 and AÚLSMHD–10008, supplement 18.
[4] Ibid., supplement 18.

from the IWV to export 70,000 tons of wire rods to the Soviet Union without incurring a fine. These efforts were, however, unsuccessful. In 1936, during negotiations about the proposed renewal of the general cartel agreement until 1941, further serious internal differences appeared within the IWV. Up to that time the German Group had been granted 20 % of the total IWV quota, but it now demanded an increase to 40 %. Among the Founder Groups of the revived International Steel Cartel (ISC), to which the IWV was subordinated, it was generally considered that the quota of the German Group, i.e. the Deutsche Drahtwalzwerke A.G., Düsseldorf, might be raised to 35 %.[1] However, no new longterm agreement was concluded by the IWV and from 1937 onwards the previous cartel was renewed repeatedly, but only for short periods. A formal cartel agreement was finally signed in May 1939 in Belgium, which collapsed with the outbreak of war.[2]

The ZEG retained its membership of the IWV. This was of particular value to Czechoslovak producers in their relations with German works. Even after the *Anschluss* of Austria by Germany, German producers did not attempt to increase their share of Czechoslovak wire production, although they acquired the Austrian quota. In confidential negotiations between the ZEG and the Deutsche Drahtwalzwerke A.G. in Munich on 10 August 1938, the Alpine Montangesellschaft withdrew from the ZEG and the Austrian quota in the ZEG was transferred to the German Group, whose quota consequently rose by 3.6456 %. The Czechoslovak–Hungarian share remained unchanged, although the Hungarian representative from RIMA, Director Mátyás, declared that he could not express any views about the future of the ZEG.[3] This was one of the few cases where quotas were not changed immediately. The annexation of Austria by Germany certainly brought about a shift in economic and political forces in the Central European market, which adversely affected the Czechoslovak position in all fields of production. The International Wire Rod Association (IWV) belonged to that category of export cartels which had arisen as subordinate selling agencies for specific steel products after the renewal of the international steel cartel in 1933.

[1] Ibid., Niederschrift Besprechung der ZEG 21 November 1936 in Wien.

[2] Cf. E. Hexner, p. 151.

[3] SÚA–KR 40.

The renewal of the international steel cartel

The impulse to revive plans for a world-wide steel cartel came in 1932, when the greatest slump in steel prices yet experienced occurred, while world prices for cartelized products, such as rails, rolled wire and tubes, remained relatively stable (see Table 19, p. 185). At the same time the founders of the first EIA closed their ranks against the protective policy of Great Britain, which imposed a 10 % import duty on steel products in the same year. At the end of 1932 representatives of the four big national founder cartels – Comptoir de Vente de la Sidérurgie Belge, 'Cosibel', Le Groupement des Industries Sidérurgiques Luxembourgeoises, Comptoir Sidérurgique de France and Stahlwerks-Verband for Germany and the Saar – began negotiations about a new system of controlling the world steel market. A new general agreement was signed in Luxemburg on 25 February 1933, dealing only with the export market; unlike the former cartel it did not try to regulate the domestic markets of its members, who were to observe absolute mutual market protection.

The export of certain categories of steel products was managed on a quota system by selling agencies, whose activities were directed and coordinated by the European Steel Cartel (ESC), and after 1935, i.e. after the entry of Great Britain and the U.S.A., by the International Steel Cartel (ISC). Six main syndicates dealt with the export of semi-finished goods, structural shapes, merchant bars, steel rods, thick plates, medium plates and universal steel. A special cartel for each product regulated price and market conditions, in accordance with the general directions of the ISC convention. The members' quotas in the export trade were based on the crude steel content of steel products and on the actual exports in the first half of 1932, along with an average of exports between 1 January 1928 and 31 October 1929.[1] Thus an average was obtained between crisis and boom conditions. At the same time quotas were fixed so as to make allowance for exports being substantially smaller or larger than the agreed mean. Judging from the minutes of the negotiations in 1933, a balance of relative forces was reached which reflected the outcome of the preceding period

[1] ANTM-SDS-413, box 3/15.

Table 5.a *The participation of the Czechoslovak steel industry in the International Steel Cartel, 1938*

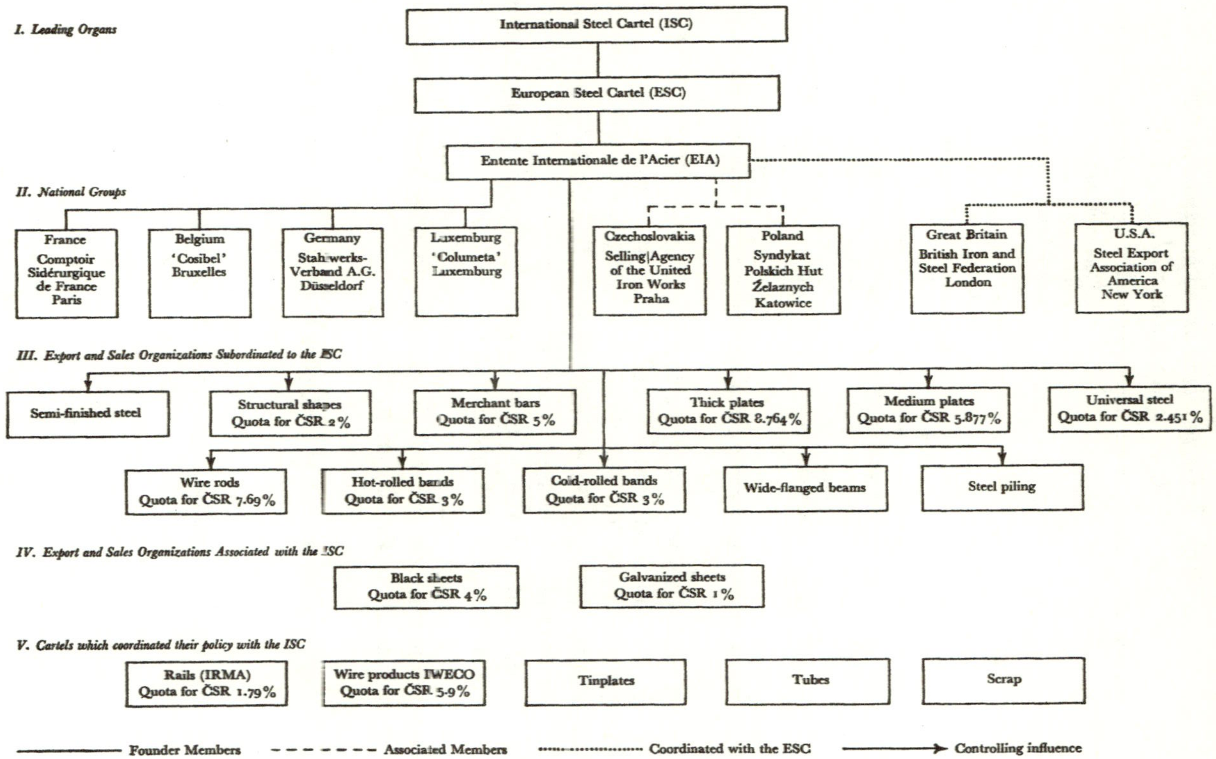

Table 6. *Quota scheme agreed by members of the ESC on 25 April and 5 May 1933*

Country	Total annual crude steel value of exported commodities: 6.8 million metric tons or less (%)	Total annual crude steel value of exported commodities: 11.5 million metric tons or more (%)
Germany–Saar	29.2	33.7
Belgium	29.0	26.0
France	20.6	23.5
Luxemburg	21.2	16.8
	100.0	100.0

of fierce competition in the new quota system (Table 6).[1] It was tacitly assumed that as well as the six export sales cartels, IRMA, IWECO, the International Tube Cartel and IWV would also cooperate with the ISC. Gradually a number of additional syndicates came into existence within the ISC, concerned with the export of specific steel products, for example rolled bands, black plates and galvanized plates. The diagram on page 161 illustrates the structure of the ISC when its influences was greatest, in the second period of its existence, i.e. at the beginning of 1938.

The position of the Czechoslovak steel industry in the international cartels of the 1930s

By June 1933 the Czechoslovak Group which controlled the ZEG was already a member of the revived European Steel Cartel and generally agreed to cooperate in exports of all rolled materials. This cooperation involved a pledge of mutual market protection by the Founder Groups on the one side and the ZEG on the other, and adherence to cartel conditions.[2] Because the problem of export quotas on the Central European steel market could not be satisfactorily solved, the previous agreement was

[1] Cited by E. Hexner, p. 84, footnote 40.

[2] SÚA–KR 673/1.

Table 7. *Export quotas of the Central European Group in Southeast Europe from 1 January 1930 to 30 June 1934*

Markets	Percentage share of RIMA	Percentage share of Czechoslovak and Austrian Group
Albania, Bulgaria, Yugoslavia, Romania	29	71
Italy only, material for ship-building	7	93

twice prolonged for a provisional period of a month.[1] In the end no new agreement between the ESC and the ZEG was concluded, and the Czechoslovak Group alone formally joined the international sales agencies of the ESC for thick plates, medium plates and universal steel on 1 July 1934 for a period of five years.[2] This situation reflects the weakened position of the Czechoslovak Group in the ZEG: the Czechoslovak cartel was no longer in a position to represent the Austrian and Hungarian works in the international cartel organization and could not always influence the allocation of quotas to its partners in the ZEG as it had in the 1920s. The Czechoslovak Selling Agency had tried to retain its position and to make it a condition of its entry into the ESC that the Austrian, Hungarian and Polish industries must also join, but without success.[3]

As a result of the economic crisis, of the efforts of the revisionist powers in Europe and a general deterioration in international relations, the common quota system of the ZEG also disintegrated. The mutual relationship between the Czechoslovak, Austrian and Hungarian steel industries changed, firstly because the Austrians and Hungarians were opposed to Czechoslovak predominance, secondly because they tried to defend their home markets against the inflow of Czechoslovak products, and thirdly because they demanded a greater share in steel exports to Southeast Europe. There the Czechoslovak cartel also met with increased competition from Germany and Western countries.[4]

[1] SÚA–KR 673/2, 673/3.
[2] SÚA–KR 673/4.
[3] ANTM–413, box 1/1.
[4] Cf. ANTM–413, box 2/A2.

Czechoslovak–Austrian cartel relations

The Austrian works represented by the Alpine pressed for changes in Czechoslovak–Austrian cartel relations from the middle of the 1920s onwards. By 1926 – immediately after the decisive participation of the Vereinigte Stahlwerke in the capital of the Alpine – the Austrian side had obtained certain concessions from the Czechoslovak Group in relation to the agreement of 1924. The agreed share of Czechoslovak producers in the Austrian market for cast-iron was reduced from 66⅔ % to 50 %, and for rolled material from 18 % to 9 %.[1] In the crisis years these conditions were changed again (on 7 April 1932), by allowing the Alpine to deliver the same amount of crude steel to Czechoslovakia as Czechoslovak producers delivered of cast-iron to Austria. The Czechoslovak Selling Agency reserved its exclusive rights to sell Austrian crude steel to its own home market, but it had to give way on the condition of the original cartel agreement of 1924, i.e. that the Czechoslovak market was to be absolutely protected against all Austrian steel products which were also produced by Czechoslovak works.

At the same time the Czechoslovak Group had to surrender the 9 % share – which up to that time had been guaranteed – of the Austrian market for all kinds of rolled material. This was in return for a general statement by the Alpine that it would try to let the Czechoslovak Group supply the Austrian requirements of thick plates, semi-finished steel and other rolled material, should these not be included in the production programme of the Austrian works.[2] This agreement was cancelled on 2 November 1933 and was not formally extended 'because of certain obstacles during negotiations',[3] according to the minutes of the partners' meeting. The Czechoslovak Selling Agency met with obstacles on the Austrian market when its formerly guaranteed position was more forcefully challenged by competition from the Austrian Syndicate of Wholesalers, which preferred to buy its rolled steel material from the Viennese Kontinentale Eisenhandelsgesellschaft Kern & Co.[4] This state of affairs is reflected

[1] ANTM–SDS–413, box 4.
[2] SÚA–KR 38/1 – Territorialschutzabkommen.
[3] Ibid., letters of the Selling Agency of 22 October 1934 and 21 June 1935.
[4] ANTM–SDS–413, box 1/7.

Table 8. *Exports of steel products from Czechoslovakia to Austria, 1926–37** (*in metre centners*)

Year	Spiegel iron	Thick plates: 1 mm or stronger	Thick plates: 2 mm–1 mm	Thick plates: 1 mm–0.6 mm	Thick plates: 0.6 mm–0.4 mm
1926†	4,930	134,255	10,172	9,328	27,726
1927	9,550	141,071	7,751	4,236	15,797
1928	9,113	215,172	18,291	15,961	17,772
1929	8,460	241,216	16,289	11,175	8,892
1930	4,913	130,254	10,319	7,816	12,083
1931	3,165	76,478	3,979	1,575	11,483
1932†	1,513	50,409	939	976	5,289
1933	2,320	26,348	536	683	4,551
1934†	4,550	3,058	342	1,547	6,939
1935	8,750	6,703	1,059	2,152	6,671
1936	4,900	6,950	769	1,311	7,005
1937†	4,970	8,149	369	1,371	5,280

Year	Galvanized, tin and lead plates: 1 mm or stronger	Galvanized, tin and lead plates: 1 mm–0.6 mm	Galvanized, tin and lead plates: 0.6 mm–0.4 mm	Galvanized, tin and lead plates: Under 0.4 mm	Pig iron: Exports	Pig iron: Imports
1926†	974	3,811	10,048	5,604	74,475	—
1927	879	4,710	10,693	2,382	88,326	—
1928	1,001	3,240	9,669	359	94,615	6,396
1929	2,385	10,862	24,641	609	116,488	8,124
1930	709	2,726	7,081	6,465	73,964	1,504
1931	330	1,164	1,264	3,322	44,758	407
1932†	513	424	665	144	17,451	359
1933	115	127	43	—	12,852	5
1934†	249	—	—	—	30,000	164
1935	397	—	—	—	42,249	4,374
1936	330	1,352	2,320	—	56,378	7,370
1937†	268	10	—	—	76,038	34,583

* *Zahraniční obchod Republiky československé* (Foreign Trade of the Czechoslovak Republic).

† Dates of cartel agreements.

Imports from Austria to Czechoslovakia were insignificant except for pig iron.

in the statistics of Czechoslovak foreign trade with Austria (Table 8). In the ensuing period of general price cutting Czechoslovak and Austrian works competed, particularly on the Austrian market for steel plates of all kinds, until in 1934 the

Czechoslovak quota in this market was reduced from 20 % to 15 %, and in galvanized plates from 17 % to 12½ %.[1]

The relative shares of the Czechoslovak and Austrian steel industries were revised again in a new system of Czechoslovak–Austrian cartels negotiated between April and June 1937. Its characteristic features were further concessions by the Czechoslovak partners. The Czechoslovak Selling Agency undertook to abstain from offering and delivering crude steel, spiegel iron and rolled steel material to Austria, to surrender the sales activities for cartelized products from Czechoslovak works on the Austrian market to the Viennese wholesale firms, the Kontinentale Eisenhandelsgesellschaft Kern & Co. (belonging to the Rothschild group) and the Mannesmannröhren- und Eisenhandels A.G. (belonging to the Mannesmann combine), who were to fix their relative sales quotas in agreement with the Alpine. In return for these concessions the Czechoslovak Group was allowed free sale of processed steel plates in Austria, as long as they were at least 50 % dearer than Austrian wholesale prices.[2] This agreement did not include thin, galvanized and black plates of Czechoslovak origin on the Austrian market, which were regulated by a separate understanding of 16 June 1937. According to this the Czechoslovak works could deliver 10 % of the total requirements of thin and black plates[3] and 8 % of galvanized plates[4] to the Austrian market. This meant a further reduction of the Czechoslovak import quota as against 1934 (Table 8). On the other hand, the Czechoslovak market remained for all intents and purposes closed to Austrian producers (except for very small amounts of plates: 1,534 centner annually for the firm of Schoeller–Bleckmann, 200 centner for the firm of Bablik, and 270 centner for the firm of Boschan). In the agreement it was provided that the Selling Agency alone was to control its sales of cartelized goods in Austria and the Austrian Group was to keep accounts of imported quantities and to impose fines of 1.50 Austrian Schillings for every metric centner delivered in excess of the quota.[5]

[1] SÚA–KR 55, KR 35.
[2] SÚA–KR 38/7.
[3] AÚLSMHD–10008, supplement 32; also SÚA–KR 35/8.
[4] SÚA–KR 53; also AÚLSMHD–10008, supplement 34.
[5] SÚA–KR 35/8; the accounts were kept in the Evidenzbüro in Austria and the Czechoslovak Group paid 0.10 Austrian Schillings for every 100 kg of goods delivered to Austria from Czechoslovakia.

At the same time as cartel arrangements between the Selling Agency and the Alpine underwent adjustments by which the Czechoslovak position on the Austrian market was relatively weakened, the Austrian steel industry also attacked the relative quotas of Czechoslovak and Austrian exports in their common markets in Southeastern Europe. This resulted in changes in the Export Agreement, in June 1932, which gave the Alpine a larger share in the market for semi-finished steel and rolled goods in the so-called contracting countries (Albania, Bulgaria, Romania, Italy and Yugoslavia). The Alpine's former 30 % participation was increased to 31½ % and the Czechoslovak share was reduced from 70 % to 68½ %. Although the Alpine was to get 31½ % of these exports it could ask for 40 % of the orders from Yugoslavia and Italy if it gave up its 31½ % share of the Bulgarian and Romanian markets in favour of the Czechoslovak Group.[1] In spite of this adjustment competition continued on the Southeastern European markets and led to a new understanding in June 1937, which again raised the proportionate share of the Austrian Alpine in the markets of all 'contracting' countries at the expense of the Czechoslovak Group, i.e. to 33⅓:66⅔; alternatively, the Alpine could always decide three months in advance whether it preferred 40 % of the Albanian, Italian and Yugoslav markets to a third of the Bulgarian and Romanian. The Czechoslovak Group, i.e. the Selling Agency, retained the right to allocate and keep account of quotas. Deliveries exceeding quotas by less than 10 % were fined ten gold Schillings and over 10 % twenty gold Schillings for every 1,000 kg of crude steel. But sales did not remain exclusively in the hands of the Selling Agency, as before. The Alpine was to take care of export sales to Albania, Italy and Yugoslavia and the Selling Agency was to deal with exports to Bulgaria and Romania.[2]

The analysis of Czechoslovak–Austrian cartel relations on their respective home markets, especially the Austrian, and also on their common export markets, indicates that in the 1930s, under pressure of competition, the Czechoslovak steel industry had to make concessions to its Austrian cartel partner, which became increasingly interlocked with German steel combines.

[1] ANTM–413–box 2/A2.

[2] AÚLSMHD–10008, supplement 12; also 10009, supplement 15.

Czechoslovak–Hungarian cartel relations

Differences between the Czechoslovak and Hungarian steel industries developed much more markedly than was the case in Czechoslovak–Austrian cartel relations; in the first half of the 1930s they reached such a pitch as to bring about the break-up of the ZEG. Before the entry of the ZEG into the first international steel cartel, the EIA, a separate cartel agreement, known as RIMA-Übereinkommen, had regulated economic policy between the Czechoslovak, Austrian and Hungarian steel industries, especially with regard to the division of the Balkan markets for exports of rolled steel goods.[1] In the RIMA-Übereinkommen the Czechoslovak cartel was dominant. The Selling Agency stood at the centre of the Central European cartel system, supervised adherence to agreed conditions, usually carried through the export sales of all ZEG partners, and functioned as a controlling organization, keeping accounts of quantities exported, imposing fines and allocating compensatory payments.

The Hungarian steel industry resented the tutelage of Prague in the ZEG, particularly in allotting production and export quotas and in dividing up the Southeastern European markets, and tried to counter the penetration of Czechoslovak steel products into its own home market. Soon a cartel was formed on the Hungarian market, in which the privately owned combine Rimamurány Iron Works (RIMA) had a controlling influence and spoke on behalf of the other partner, the Hungarian State Iron Works 'Diosgyör', which did not officially join any international cartel. All the latent Czechoslovak–Hungarian differences came to the fore when the original agreement expired at the end of 1929.

After lengthy and difficult negotiations the representatives of the Selling Agency, the Alpine and the RIMA signed a renewed agreement (RIMA-Übereinkommen) in Trenčianské Teplice on 30 May 1930, in which the Hungarian negotiators managed to obtain certain concessions from their stronger partners.[2] The agreement applied to the usual kinds of semi-finished and rolled steel products and ensured the mutual protection of the state territory of each party. Thus exports of

[1] SÚA–KR 37.

[2] AÚLSMHD–10008, supplement 13.

Table 9. *Export of steel products from Czechoslovakia to Hungary, 1926–37* (in metre centners)*

Year	Pig iron	Spiegel iron	Thick plates: 2 mm or stronger	Thick plates: 2 mm–1 mm	Thick plates: 1 mm–0.6 mm	Thick plates: 0.6 mm–0.4 mm
1926†	144,251	8,997	335	493	23	1,936
1927	220,666	7,777	1,391	173	828	3,551
1928	228,671	7,250	2,126	263	—	8,013
1929	245,336	5,151	292	342	83	7,833
1930†	100,659	2,355	259	176	12	—
1931	7,026	200	110	18	15	—
1932	11,148	—	6	—	—	—
1933	750	—	21	—	—	—
1934	300	—	12	—	—	—
1935	—	—	1	—	1	—
1936	—	—	3	—	158	—
1937	—	1,000	160	—	92	—

Year	Galvanized, tin and lead plates: 1 mm or stronger	1 mm–0.6 mm	0.6 mm–0.4 mm	Under 0.4 mm
1926†	51	57	54	762
1927	484	52	69	1,127
1928	116	82	163	767
1929	304	42	38	905
1930†	139	22	85	327
1931	—	—	—	—
1932	—	—	—	—
1933	—	—	—	—
1934	—	—	—	—
1935	—	—	—	—
1936	—	—	—	—
1937	—	—	—	—

* *Zahraniční obchod Republiky československé.*
† Dates of cartel agreements.
Imports from Hungary to Czechoslovakia were insignificant.

these products from Czechoslovakia to Hungary practically ceased after 1931 (Table 9). RIMA succeeded in getting a separate quota on the formerly common markets, the so-called contracting territory, of the Central European Group, in return for compensation payments to the Czechoslovak and Austrian Groups. The agreement permitted Hungarian exports of rolled goods up to a maximum content of 232,000 centner of crude steel to Albania, Bulgaria, Yugoslavia and Romania. Table 7 shows the division between RIMA and the Czechoslovak–Austrian Group.[1] For the transfer of the export quota RIMA was obliged to pay Kč 8,621 per hundred centners up to 116,000 centners of crude steel content and Kč 13,793 for each hundred centners exported to the Austrian–Czechoslovak Group above this. The relevant accounts were kept by the Selling Agency, which collected quarterly compensatory payments from the Hungarian Group. Cartel conditions were enforced by an executive committee on which the Czechoslovak Group had a majority of three members as against one each from the Alpine and the RIMA; the Selling Agency administered the cartel, controlled prices, allocated orders, saw to it that the members adhered to decisions, in particular that no new products were included in production programmes and no new works built and that the partners neither bought nor sold enterprises without the consent of the executive committee.[2]

This state of affairs prevailed until 1934, except for some minor adjustments: e.g. RIMA surrendered its Bulgarian orders to the Selling Agency[3] and relations with Yugoslavia also changed. No further understanding was signed and from 1935 only a verbal promise of mutual market protection was given, in the form of a Gentleman's Agreement.[4] In the same year the Hungarian Group severed its connection with the ZEG and began to act independently of it. The results of cartel agreements can be traced with remarkable precision in the development of Czechoslovak trade in steel products with the countries of the ZEG. They played a decisive role in determining prices and quantities produced, as well as quantities exported and the direction of Czechoslovak foreign trade, in this branch of industry. Tables 8 and 9 show how exports of steel products from Czechoslovakia to Austria and Hungary fell. Every important change affecting trade in steel and steel products

[1] Ibid. [2] Ibid.

[3] Ibid., Aktennotiz 14 June 1930 (Wien, Alpine).

[4] Ibid., Aktennotiz 29 May 1935 (Wien, Kontinentale).

between Czechoslovakia, Austria and Hungary can be directly associated with the conditions of cartel agreements concluded between the steel industries of these countries.

The position of the Czechoslovak steel cartel in the markets of Southeast Europe

Tendencies similar to those in the ZEG also appeared in the relations of the Czechoslovak steel industry in the so-called 'original territory', where intensified competition among the members of the Central European Group led to its slow disintegration and to a weakening of the influence of the Czechoslovak Group. This eventually resulted in a shift of forces within the Central European cartel structure. As a consequence of the new cartel conditions Czechoslovak foreign trade with Southeastern Europe declined considerably.

After many unsuccessful attempts, the Yugoslav works managed in 1932 – in a complicated general crisis situation – to obtain a promise from the ZEG that it would not force the sale of its products on the Yugoslav market. Later they gained more favourable conditions, in the renewed cartel agreements of 22 July 1932 and 11 September 1934. While in the agreement of 1927 the whole territory of Yugoslavia was considered as a joint market of the ZEG and the Yugoslav works, divided in the proportions $\frac{1}{3}:\frac{2}{3}$, the new agreement of 1932 covered only part of Yugoslavia. The ZEG waived its right to deliveries of all products in the rest of the country, except for wire rods and those products which the Yugoslav works did not themselves produce. Thus the $33\frac{1}{3}$ % share of the ZEG in the Yugoslav steel market remained valid only for part of Yugoslav territory, including all seaports.[1]

The cartel agreement guaranteed the members of the ZEG priorities in Yugoslav orders for steel products which Yugoslav works required but did not produce themselves.[2] In these agreements the combined works of the ZEG constituted one cartel partner and four Yugoslav works the other (Eisenindustrie-A.G., Zenica; Krainische Industrie Gesellschaft, Jesenice; Berg- und Hüttenwerke, Stora, and (after 1934) Jurja Grofa Thurnskega jeklarnana Ravnah d.d., Gustanj-Ravne). Those

ANTM–SDS–413, box 2/A2. [2] Cf. AÚLSMHD–10008, supplement 16.

partners who exceeded their quotas had to pay fines to those who did not fulfil their share. The Yugoslavs, whose productive capacity increased, ran into considerable debts and repeatedly demanded a reduction in compensatory payments. This was granted only in the most acute crisis years. However, in the agreement of 1934 the representatives of the Czechoslovak, Austrian and Hungarian groups enforced a substantial increase in fines,[1] which forced the Yugoslav industry into still greater indebtedness to the stronger Czechoslovak, Austrian and Hungarian iron and steel works. As late as February 1938 the Yugoslav works applied to the Czechoslovak Group for a reduction of their debt.[2] On the one hand the Central European Group had to make concessions on the Yugoslav market, but on the other hand it retained a substantial influence over the Yugoslav iron and steel industry.

The cartel relations in the Central and Southeast European steel industry (except for Poland between the wars), in which the Czechoslovak Group maintained its leading position, were not only tolerated but supported by the leading circles of the ESC and later also the ISC. However, the foregoing analysis of the cartel agreements shows that the Czechoslovak steel cartel had to retreat under the pressure of changing economic and political conditions, had to resort to compromises and had to agree to the entry of German and West European competitors into markets which the international cartel had allotted to its sphere of influence. The export statistics of this period reflect this cartel policy: Czechoslovak steel exports to the 'original' territories fell, while exports to the Soviet Union increased significantly (Table 10).[3]

[1] Cf. AÚLSMHD–10008.

Agreements	31 May 1927	22 July 1932	11 September 1934
Fines (in dinars) for exceeding quotas (per 100 kg)			
To 3%	3.0	6.0	6.0
From 3 to 5%	7.50	Temporarily reduced to Din. 1.0	15.0
Over 5%	15.0		30.0

[2] AÚLSMHD–10008, supplement 16, Minutes of the meeting of the Joint Executive Committee of 22 February 1938. [3] ANTM–SDS–413–3/15.

Table 10. *Total direct exports of steel and rolled products from Czechoslovakia (all deliveries)*

	Exports to Austria, Hungary, Yugoslavia, Romania, Bulgaria, Italy, Turkey, Albania, i.e. 'original territory'		Exports to 'other markets'		Total		Exports to Russia (amount and percentage of total)	
Year	Tons	%	Tons	%	Tons	%	Tons	%
1924	99,377	52	90,094	48	189,471	100	789	—
1925	172,648	62	104,241	38	276,889	100	763	—
1926	135,187	54	114,733	46	249,920	100	4,406	2
1927	153,541	41	224,016	59	377,557	100	29,913	8
1928	167,695	42	227,240	58	394,035	100	80,263	20
1929	177,417	45	214,673	55	392,090	100	89,048	23
1930	123,895	30	293,680	70	417,575	100	165,898	40
1931	70,381	17	338,737	83	409,118	100	262,730	64
1932	27,352	57	20,604	43	47,956	100	4,841	10
1933	14,165	24	45,327	76	59,492	100	24,446	41
1934	27,747	30	65,983	70	93,730	100	9,793	10
1935	34,421	26	96,641	74	131,062	100	30,232	23
1936	44,379	25	129,866	75	174,245	100	19,163	11

Although the Czechoslovak Group was relatively weakened in the 1930s, the most powerful cartel organizations still considered it to be the biggest and most influential steel producing national cartel in Central and Southeast Europe.[1] The Czechoslovak industry held this position up to Munich, despite the growing intensity of German and West European competition and the increasing industrialization of the Southeast European countries, which sought to protect their own home markets.

Czechoslovak–Polish cartel relations in the steel industry

With the conclusion of the cartel agreement of 1 July 1931[2] between the ZEG and the Polish steel works associated in the Syndikat Polskich Hut Żelaznych, foreign trade in steel and

[1] Cf. ANTM–SDS–413, box 4, e.g. negotiations about the entry of the Czechoslovak Group into the International Cartel for Band and Tube Iron in Prague, 9 January 1936.

[2] SÚA–KR 205.

Table 11. *Trade in steel products between Czechoslovakia and Poland (1926–37)* (in metre centners)*

	Pig iron		Thick and black plates: 2 mm or stronger		Thick and black plates: 2 mm–1 mm		Thick and black plates: 0.6 mm–0.4 mm	
Year	Export	Import	Export	Import	Export	Import	Export	Import
1926	19,505	17,126	20,056	—	16	433	755	68
1927	10,694	6,421	20,079	—	8	175	132	109
1928	2,128	282	13,334	—	—	61	—	—
1929	250	2,675	4,048	—	—	65	167	10
1930	—	400	6,564	—	—	—	—	—
1931†	—	503	981	—	—	—	14	—
1932	—	—	—	—	—	—	—	—
1933	150	—	65	—	—	—	—	—
1934	—	—	—	—	—	—	—	—
1935	—	—	46	—	—	—	—	—
1936†	—	—	10	—	—	—	—	—
1937	—	—	—	—	—	—	—	—

	Galvanized, tin and lead plates: 1 mm or stronger		Galvanized, tin and lead plates: 1 mm–0.6 mm		Galvanized, tin and lead plates: 0.6 mm–0.4 mm		Galvanized, tin and lead plates: Under 0.4 mm	
Year	Export	Import	Export	Import	Export	Import	Export	Import
1926	19	—	309	382	438	228	2,030	—
1927	55	9	270	151	410	652	1,591	—
1928	58	—	257	110	128	1,552	45	50
1929	95	—	62	—	39	—	38	—
1930	57	—	134	—	190	—	2,406	—
1931†	94	—	98	—	87	—	516	—
1932	28	—	21	—	10	—	—	—
1933	—	—	—	—	—	—	—	—
1934	22	—	—	—	—	—	—	—
1935	27	—	—	—	—	—	—	—
1936†	26	—	26	—	—	35	—	—
1937	30	—	—	—	—	—	—	—

* *Zahraniční obchod Republiky československé.*

† Dates of cartel agreements.

steel products practically ceased between Poland and Czechoslovakia. Czechoslovak foreign trade statistics provide evidence of the impact of the cartel (viz. Table 11). The agreement covered crude steel and all rolled material, and allowed for mutual protection of the partners' respective domestic markets. The ZEG agreed to pay the Polish Group £6,000 annually in return for refraining from deliveries of thin and galvanized plates to Czechoslovakia, of which the Czechoslovak Group bore 61.645 %, i.e. £3,699 5*s*., annually.[1] Table 11 demonstrates strikingly the immediate effect of the cartel agreements on Polish steel plate imports to Czechoslovakia. Except for similar payments to the German Bismarckhütte, these were the only regular obligation of this kind undertaken by the Czechoslovak steel cartel. In spite of the efforts of representatives of the Selling Agency to urge the Polish works not to insist on compensatory payments, when the agreement expired at the end of 1936 it was extended practically unchanged. The Czechoslovak Group had already negotiated the renewed agreement independently, while the Austrian and Hungarian Groups also concluded separate agreements with the Polish works. In the new understanding the Czechoslovak Group succeeded in getting a 25 % reduction in compensation payments (i.e. £2,774 8*s*. 7*d*.), but the Polish import tax was also raised by 12 %.

An interesting new element appeared, however, in the cartel agreements with the Polish iron and steel industry. As part of the protected territories of the Polish home market, the town and port of Danzig was specifically mentioned. In agreements before 20 March 1936 it had been invariably included in the protected territory of the German home market. All international cartel agreements were changed in this way during 1936.[2] This was undoubtedly connected with Poland's conditions of entry into the organization of the International Steel Cartel. This state of cartel relations was to last until the events of Munich, after which it was only partly valid, especially on the question of Danzig, until the outbreak of the Second World War.

[1] ANTM–SDS–413, box 2/A2.

[2] SÚA–KR 43, 54, 205/4, 692, 693; also AÚLSMHD–10008.

Implications of the entry of the Czechoslovak steel industry into the associations of the international steel cartel in the 1930s

Czechoslovak steel production occupied a special place in the ISC, mainly because of its close capital integration with the big West European steel combines. The Czechoslovak works were not actually considered as unfriendly competitors, even when no formal agreement existed between them and the ISC and the Czechoslovak steel industry was, to some extent, competing with members of the international cartel. On the contrary, throughout the international cartel's existence the Czechoslovak Selling Agency administered a number of Central European and Southeast European cartel agreements as the ISC's representative and also discharged part of the export business of some of the subsidiary syndicates for Central European and Southeast European markets. The renewed general cartel agreement between the ISC and the Selling Agency was formally negotiated and signed during 1936; it came into force on 1 January 1937 and lasted until the beginning of the Second World War. The particular situation of the Czechoslovak producers arose on the one hand quite naturally out of the investment interests of the West European Groups in Czechoslovak iron and steel works, and on the other from the common interests of the Anglo-French–Belgian and Czechoslovak combines in their competition with the German steel producers in the ISC. It also arose out of a desire to give Czechoslovak producers room for manœuvre in the markets dominated by the cartel, in order to prevent more extensive exports of Czechoslovak steel products to the Soviet Union.

These factors were reflected in the quotas allocated to the Czechoslovak Group, from which the works of the Big Three benefited most. A classic example of the division of export quotas among the Founder Groups of the ISC and the Czechoslovak Group is provided by the calculations of quotas on the entry of the Selling Agency into three of the subsidiary cartel associations of the ISC, i.e. for thick plates, medium plates and universal steel, in 1934, when the Czechoslovak Group gained 8.764 %, 5.877 % and 2.451 % respectively of the total exports of these cartelized products. On the basis of these quotas the Selling Agency calculated the shares in exports of each product

Table 12. *Exports of the ISC and Czechoslovak Group**
(*deliveries abroad in tons*)

1936 month	Semi-finished steel			Merchant bars		
	ISC†	ČSR	Total	ISC†	ČSR	Total
June	67,766	97	67,863	99,738	4,652	104,390
July	100,600	327	100,927	141,390	5,202	146,592
Total	168,366	424	168,790	241,128	9,854	250,982
	99.75 %	0.25 %	100 %	96.07 %	3.93 %	100 %
Quotas of the Czechoslovak Group as % of total ISC exports.						
		2 %			5 %	

1936 month	Structural shapes			Rolled bands		
	ISC†	ČSR	Total	ISC†	ČSR	Total
June	28,864	500	29,364	10,102	—	10,102
July	42,284	382	42,666	22,430	796	23,226
Total	71,148	882	72,030	32,532	796	33,328
	98.78 %	1.22 %	100 %	97.61 %	2.39 %	100 %
Quotas of the Czechoslovak Group as % of total ISC exports.						
		2 %			3 %	

* According to data of the Selling Agency of 9 September 1936 and allocated quotas.

† Founder Groups.

of the members of the Big Three: the largest share was allocated to the Vítkovice Mining and Foundry Works (98.14 %, 73.081 % and 54.549 % respectively), the next to the Mining and Metallurgic Co. (1.289 %, 15.331 % and 24.317 % respectively), and the smallest to the Prague Iron Co. (0.571 %, 11.588 % and 11.134 % respectively).[1]

During 1935 and 1936 negotiations continued in the committees of the ISC on Czechoslovak participation in the international cartels which regulated the exports of specific steel products. While the Czechoslovak producers on the whole observed the rules of the international cartel, they were in no particular hurry to join further syndicates and tried to gain

[1] ANTM-SDS 413-3/15.

Table 13. *Calculations of export quotas for merchant bars according to a communication from ISC of 22 January 1937*

Country	Total exports 161,403 tons or less (%)	Total exports 357,327 tons or more (%)
Germany	26.350	28.162
Belgium	36.663	32.307
France	11.160	11.928
Luxemburg	25.827	27.603
Founder Groups' total	100	100
Founder Groups	95	—
ČSR	5	—
Founder Groups and ČSR	100	—

more favourable trading positions by undercutting cartel prices on the world market. However, they were forced into these cartels by competition from imports of steel products, above all thin and black plates, which led to the granting of a 3 % bonus to domestic customers.[1] However, the situation deteriorated for the Czechoslovak works due to further international price cutting and the Czechoslovak Group found it necessary formally to join the other international associations in the ISC from 1 January 1937.

In spite of the fact that the Czechoslovak Group did not have a very significant share in world exports of semi-finished steel, merchant bars, structural shapes and steel strips, the ISC granted relatively high quotas to the Czechoslovak producers.[2] The actual division of exports between the Founder Groups and the Czechoslovak Group for June and July 1936 compared with the allotted quotas, is shown in Table 12.[3] At the same time it was decided that the Czechoslovak Group was not to get any compensatory payments if it did not fulfil its export quotas; only the Founder Groups could claim such compensation.

After a relatively competitive period on the markets for thin, black and galvanized plates, the Czechoslovak Group acquired

[1] Cf. ANTM-413, box 1/3. [2] Cf. ANTM-413, box 2/A2.
[3] Compiled from data of ANTM-413, box 4 and box 2/A2.

Table 14. *Quota shares in the ISC in percentages of total exports (1937–8)*

Products	ISC*	Poland	ISC*	Great Britain
Pig iron	95.803	4.197	—	—
Semi-finished steel	—	—	95.96	4.04
Structural shapes	97.776	2.224	90.91	9.09
Merchant bars	95.767†	4.233	91.326†	8.674
Thick plates	98.254	1.746	69.710	30.290
Medium plates	96.625	3.375	86.759	13.241
Universal steel	92.844	7.156	61.175	38.825
Rolled bands	—	—	93.350	6.650
Wire rods	—	—	98.92	1.08
Black plates	—	—	—	—
Galvanized plates	—	—	—	—

	ISC*	ČSR	ISC§	U.S.A.
Pig iron	—	—	—	—
Semi-finished steel	98	2‡	93.981	6.019
Structural shapes	98	2‡	95.606	4.394
Merchant bars	95	5‡	98.513	1.487
Thick plates	91.236	8.764	85.993	14.007
Medium plates	94.123	5.877	85.993	14.007
Universal steel	97.549	2.451	85.993	14.007
Rolled bands	97	3‡	—	—
Wire rods	92.31	7.69	85.308	14.692
Black plates	98‖	2	—	—
Galvanized plates	99.5‖	0.5	—	—

* Founder Groups. † Without Belgian works.
‡ Proposed quota. § Founder Groups and Great Britain.
‖ Founder Groups, Great Britain and Poland.

fairly advantageous quotas on joining the respective international cartels. In the case of black plates the Czechoslovak steel works got 2 % of the total world exports, not only of the four Founder Groups but also of the British and Polish Groups, and were to have no fines imposed until they exported more than an additional 2 % of total world exports. Similarly, 0.5 % of total world exports of galvanized plates was allocated to the Czechoslovak Group, with an additional allowance of 0.5 % free of fines.[1] Thus the Czechoslovak works could double their

[1] Cf. ANTM-413, box 2/A2.

Table 15. *Distribution of export quotas among members of the Big Three (10 June 1936)*

Products	BHS (%)	PŽ (%)	VHHT (%)	Czechoslovak quotas as % of ISC
Semi-finished steel	30	40	30	100 = 2
Structural shapes	33·3	33·3	33·3	100 = 2
Merchant bars	30	20	50	100 = 5
Rolled bands	32.5	5	62.5	100 = 3

BHS = Báňská a hutní společnost (Mining and Metallurgic Co.).
PŽ = Pražská železářská společnost (Prague Iron Co.).
VHHT = Vítkovické horní a hutní těžířstvo (Vítkovice Mining and Foundry Works).

export quotas of these goods without having to pay fines into the cartel pool.

The position of Czechoslovak production in the International Steel Cartel can be seen more clearly by comparing the relative quotas of the Founder Groups and the Czechoslovak Group in exports of merchant bars, which were generally used as a basis for calculating the mutual relations between member countries (viz. Table 13).[1] Comparative Czechoslovak quotas appear even more distinctly in the following table (Table 14),[2] because it shows export quotas of specific products for countries which joined the cartel after 1934, i.e. Poland, Great Britain, Czechoslovakia and the U.S.A., in relation to the Founder Groups of the ISC, at the height of its effectiveness in 1937 and 1938. A comparison of these quotas shows that Czechoslovak exports of steel products were not negligible, and ranged from 2 to 9 % of cartelized world exports on the eve of Munich.

The Big Three almost invariably divided all export quotas allocated by the ISC to the Czechoslovak Group among themselves in agreed proportions (viz. Table 15),[3] although other producers were also members of the various groups within the Czechoslovak cartel. However, the initial Agreement, as was

[1] Compiled from data of AÚLSMHD–10007.
[2] Compiled from data of AÚLSMHD–10007 and ANTM–413.
[3] According to the minutes of the meeting of the Big Three, 10 June 1936, ANTM–413, box 1/1.

mentioned above, had transferred exclusive authority to the Big Three to negotiate and conclude international agreements.[1] Cartel relations can in no way be appraised on moral grounds. The only valid criterion for the allocation of quotas in international as well as national cartels is the relative economic strength of the partners, and this also applies to cartels in the steel industry.

Market relations in the cartel

By joining the international cartel organizations of the ISC the Czechoslovak Group in fact curtailed the export activity of Czechoslovak iron and steel works. The least affected were the main combines of the Big Three, which as a rule appropriated the entire export quota of the Czechoslovak Group. All the same, the quota system absolutely restricted export prospects for steel products from Czechoslovakia. It also limited the range of export activities of Czechoslovak producers, through the clause on mutual market protection in the agreement, which covered all domestic markets and also all colonies and other protected territories of ISC members. Thus a vast area remained closed to the Czechoslovak steel industry, including the desirable markets of Czechoslovakia's Western Allies. The fact that the Czechoslovak steel cartel was able to dominate its home market without serious outside competition only partly compensated for this.

As a member of the ISC the Czechoslovak Group was permitted to participate in a strictly controlled manner in imports to countries whose markets for steel products were monopolized by the International Steel Cartel. These countries had become part of the ISC's sphere of influence because of their dependence on steel imports and they formed the so-called 'organized' markets of the ISC, where member groups had to adhere to agreed import quotas. The position of the Czechoslovak Group in the 'organized' markets of the ISC is shown in Tables 16, 17 and 18, which record the relative quotas in merchant bars, structural shapes and thick plates at the end of 1937.[2] Czechoslovak producers could thus count on a guaranteed but limited

[1] Cf. AÚLSMHD–10008, state of international agreement 1 March 1938.

[2] The tables are compiled from material in AÚLSMHD and from data published by E. Hexner, pp. 168 f.

Table 16. *Distribution of import quotas in 'organized' markets for merchant bars among members of the ISC, December 1937*

'Organized' markets: importing country	Quota (%)						
	Germany	Belgium	France	Luxemburg	Poland	Czechoslovakia	Total
Great Britain	14.095	50.280	13,424	22,201	—	—	100
Switzerland	28.205	—	52.301	13.494	—	6.000	100
China	30.000	29.400	6.240	34.360	—	—	100
Norway	15.523	19.127	14.493	34.285	11.199	5.328	100
Sweden	22.802	21.556	13.615	35.881	3.243	2.903	100
Denmark	35.428	22.509	11.120	28.943	—	2.000	100
Syria	—	22.312	24.575	46.145	6.968	—	100
Palestine	26.471	19.182	9.854	22.988	12.784	8.721	100
Egypt	6.384	19.520	13.696	45.388	7.622	7.390	100

Table 17. *Distribution of import quotas in 'organized' markets for structural shapes among members of the ISC, December 1937*

'Organized' markets: importing country	Quotas (%)						
	Germany	Belgium	France	Luxemburg	Poland	Czechoslovakia	Total
Great Britain	8.037	21.678	50.448	19.837	—	—	100
Holland	49.907	18.567	20.203	4.159	5.269	1.895	100
Switzerland	48.562	—	46.786	4.152	—	0.500	100
Norway	24.417	10.572	44.267	7.692	11.277	1.775	100
Sweden	28.788	11.930	45.758	11.645	0.387	1.494	100
Denmark	31.683	11.916	42.896	11.605	—	2.000	100
Syria	—	12.406	74.129	8.095	5.370	—	100
Palestine	27.110	9.236	42.458	7.885	3.679	9.632	100
Egypt	10.288	11.179	62.783	7.689	5.218	2.843	100

quantity of exports to markets controlled by the ISC. In such cases competition took place within the cartel on each fraction of a percentage in the division of export quotas; the share of the Czechoslovak steel industry in all these quotas had to be fought for, especially against German opposition.

The ISC only recognized the priority of the Czechoslovak Group in the markets of Southeastern Europe, and the exact limits in this area were defined by the cartel. In Yugoslavia the

Table 18. *Distribution of import quotas in 'organized' markets for thick plates among members of the ISC, December 1937*

'Organized' markets: importing country	Quotas (%)							
	Germany	Belgium	France	Luxem-burg	Poland	Czecho-slovakia	Austria	Total
Great Britain	36.433	45.181	16.281	2.105	—	—	—	100
Holland	47.433	46.046	4.029	0.462	2.030	—	—	100
Switzerland	28.972	—	56.358	2.840	—	8.830*	3.00	100
Norway	40.330	43.753	10.437	2.320	3.160	—	—	100
Sweden	49.327	45.032	3.967	1.344	0.330	—	—	100
Denmark	49.030	45.181	4.194	1.595	—	—	—	100
Syria	—	41.911	42.910	13.149	2.030	—	—	100
Palestine	41.000	42.779	5.630	10.591	—	—	—	100
Egypt	5.687	44.264	35.795	12.224	2.030	—	—	100

* No agreement could be reached about the Czechoslovak quota in other 'organized' markets.

Czechoslovak Group was the recognized representative of the ZEG, and the entry of Czechoslovak producers to the markets of Albania, Bulgaria and Northern Italy was guaranteed by the cartel. Despite these safeguards the Czechoslovak steel industry did encounter competition in these areas and, in particular, met with the untiring efforts of Germany to increase her exports to Southeastern European countries. The United Czechoslovak Iron Works tried to control this situation by concluding a number of additional bilateral cartel agreements, which together with the understandings with the ISC formed a whole system of interrelated cartels. These regulated the quantity and the geographical direction of steel exports from Czechoslovakia. In these cartel agreements the efforts of the Czechoslovak steel industry in conjunction with its Western partners to limit the German steel producers' access to the markets of Southeast Europe can be clearly seen. The repeated demands of the German partners in the ISC for increased quotas, especially in 1936 and 1937, coincide with the economic and political drive of National Socialist Germany for an increase in her share of the foreign trade of Central and Southeast Europe.[1]

[1] Cf. A. Teichová, 'Great Britain in European Affairs', *Historica* III (Praha, 1961).

Price relations in the cartel

Although the principle of mutual market protection in the ISC restricted the area and the volume of Czechoslovakia's steel exports, the Czechoslovak cartel derived advantages from its membership on its own home market. The Czechoslovak works were, on the whole, effectively protected against foreign competition and their sales on the home market increased in proportion to the decreasing import figures. At the same time they could fix and regulate prices of crude steel and rolled steel products in Czechoslovakia more easily between 1926 and 1938. This is proved by the relative stability of prices. In 1930 steel prices fell on the average by 7 %, but in the following years they remained stable, despite severe crisis conditions and enormous reductions in world prices.[1] By maintaining a high price level on the domestic market the cartel of the United Czechoslovak Iron Works ensured for its members a higher rate of profits, which at least partly outweighed relatively smaller profits from exports, where quantities and prices had to be adjusted to conditions on the world market and to the price scales fixed by the ISC.

Although world prices in the ISC were lower than those which each national cartel obtained on its domestic market, the cartelized Czechoslovak producers still gained by joining the ISC, for the world prices fixed by the ISC were higher than they would otherwise have been. Table 19 shows world price movements of steel products when the cartel was functioning and when it was disintegrating.[2] The relationship between price movements and the activities of the cartel is quite evident. Prices of standard rails and wire rods also remained remarkably stable in the crisis years when the organization of IRMA and IWV remained intact and thus prevented drastic decreases in prices. However, prices of other steel products fell severely between 1930 and 1933 when the EIA disintegrated, and in 1932 reductions in steel prices amounted to more than 50 %. Table 19 also shows clearly that the conclusion of each new cartel agreement was followed by an increase in prices. Until

[1] Cf. ANTM-413/3.

[2] Table 19 is compiled from data of the *Statistisches Jahrbuch für das Deutsche Reich*, Internationale Übersichten (Berlin, 1938), E. Hexner, pp. 190 f. and AÚLSMHD-10007, 10008 and 10009.

Table 19. *World price movements of some steel products from June 1926 to December 1937 with special reference to the effectiveness of international cartels (prices in gold £ f.o.b. Antwerp)*

Dates	Merchant bars	Structural shapes	Thick plates	Black plates	Standard* rails	Wire† rods	Validity of cartel agreements
	£ s d	£ s d	£ s d	£ s d	£ s d	£ s d	* IRMA and † IWV
June 1926	4 14 6	4 12 0	5 0 0	9 5 0	6 0 0	5 8 0	EIA founded 1 October 1926
December 1926	5 12 0	5 11 6	6 7 6	11 10 0	6 0 0	6 2 6	
June 1927	4 14 9	4 13 9	6 1 0	9 18 0	6 5 0	5 10 0	Czechoslovak Group enters ZEG
December 1927	4 16 0	4 8 0	5 19 0	9 14 0	6 7 6	5 10 0	
June 1928	5 15 0	4 18 0	6 7 9	10 14 0	6 7 6	5 16 9	
December 1928	6 2 6	5 1 0	6 6 6	10 3 9	6 10 0	6 2 6	
June 1929	5 18 9	5 4 9	6 7 6	10 2 6	6 10 0	6 7 6	
December 1929	5 5 0	4 17 9	6 4 0	10 15 0	6 10 0	6 7 6	
June 1930	5 4 6	5 1 6	6 10 6	9 15 6	6 10 0	6 5 0	Germany leaves EIA
December 1930	4 6 0	3 15 0	4 17 0	8 6 9	6 10 0	6 0 0	
June 1931	3 7 0	3 5 6	4 0 0	8 0 0	6 10 0	5 0 0	Disintegration of EIA
December 1931	2 14 0	2 13 0	3 7 0	6 17 6	5 17 6	5 0 0	
June 1932	2 2 0	2 0 0	2 13 0	5 6 0	5 10 0	4 10 0	
December 1932	2 13 0	2 2 6	3 1 0	5 17 6	5 10 0	4 10 0	
June 1933	3 0 0	2 15 0	3 18 6	5 17 6	5 10 0	4 10 0	ISC renewed 1 June 1933
December 1933	3 2 6	2 17 6	4 1 0	5 15 0	5 10 0	4 10 0	
June 1934	3 3 6	3 1 6	4 2 6	5 10 0	5 10 0	4 10 0	Promise of ČSR to cooperate with ISC
December 1934	3 3 6	3 1 6	4 2 6	5 16 0	5 10 0	4 10 0	ČSR joins 3 subsidiary cartels
June 1935	3 3 9	3 1 6	4 2 6	5 16 0	5 10 0	4 10 0	Poland, Great Britain and U.S.A. join ISC
December 1935	3 3 9	3 1 6	4 5 0	5 16 0	5 10 0	4 10 0	
June 1936	3 3 9	3 1 6	4 5 0	5 16 0	5 10 0	4 10 0	
December 1936	4 2 6	3 10 0	4 7 6	6 15 0	6 0 0	4 10 0	ČSR joins other subsidiary cartels and enters into
June 1937	6 0 0	4 17 6	6 2 6	8 10 0	5 15 0	7 0 0	formal agreement with ISC
December 1937	6 0 0	5 7 6	7 2 6	8 15 0	5 15 0	6 0 0	

* Cartel IRMA was valid for the whole period (ČSR was a member).
† Cartel IWV was valid for the whole period (ČSR was a member).

1936 rising prices were, above all, the result of the activity of the international cartel; they did not arise from a substantial increase in the demand for steel products. However, from the middle of 1936 incipient boom conditions, together with cartel practices, influenced the rising prices of steel products.

The participation of the highly concentrated and tightly cartelized steel industry of Czechoslovakia in international cartels, particularly in the central cartel of the EIA and later of the ISC, ensured a relatively higher level of prices, especially on the home market, and a higher rate of profits for the Czechoslovak combines. At the same time, they could rely on a relatively protected home market against foreign competition.

Our analysis of cartel agreements between Czechoslovak and foreign producers shows that the quantity and the direction of Czechoslovak steel exports were decisively determined and regulated by international cartel agreements and were not by any means the outcome of a free play of economic forces in foreign trade; neither were they a reflection of a foreign trade policy guided by the needs of the independent Czechoslovak state.

The extremely complicated and largely effective system of international cartels in the steel industry so often reflects the pattern of international politics that these phenomena cannot be regarded as wholly accidental. At the beginning of section 2 of this chapter I discussed the efforts of the great West European steel combines to bring about a balance of forces in the international cartel which would correspond to the new situation in Europe at the end of the First World War, a situation which, on the whole, suited the Czechoslovak industry. The political stabilization of the capitalist countries of Europe and the fairly extensive recognition of Germany as an equal partner in the Western world during 1925 and 1926 undoubtedly contributed to the foundation of the first international steel cartel. Without doubt, the strengthening of Germany and the ensuing economic crisis also led to the subsequent disintegration of the cartel. However, the same crisis engendered new cartels, which in an apparent economic impasse preserved the profits of the strongest combines. The World Economic Conference in 1933 in London did not achieve any significant economic or political successes, but it did stimulate greater international cartelization. In this context the revival of the international steel cartel, the ISC, can be better appraised. We can also see why the German steel industry, which had been badly shaken by the crisis, joined the ISC again and accepted only slightly altered conditions, although in 1929 they had been unacceptable to the German producers. Very soon attacks on the ISC appeared in the German economic press, complaining of disappointed hopes in this field of production.[1]

Some economic circles in Europe expected a strengthening of Pan-European trends in heavy industry, under French and German leadership, to result from the revived international cartel, and expected this to counterbalance the pressures of Anglo-American heavy industry.[2] However, shortly after this the Anglo-German Naval Treaty was signed and the British Iron and Steel Federation, and later the steel cartel of the U.S.A., joined the recently established International Steel Cartel. Quite clearly the new division of markets and export quotas did not satisfy the German steel producers, who again fought for larger export opportunities, opposing the mutual protection of all members' home markets. For example, in the case of Danzig, which was taken out of the German market and allocated to the Polish domestic market, German export opportunities were reduced.

In this constellation of forces the Czechoslovak industry enjoyed guarantees within the ISC on the protection of its own home market and certain fixed export quotas which, despite some changes, showed some continuity with the conditions of the 1920s. From this point of view the international cartel structure reflects the dependence of the Hungarian and Austrian steel industry on that of Czechoslovakia, especially in the sphere of exports to Southeast European markets. Due to the *Anschluss* of Austria in March 1938 the balance of forces in the cartel structure of Central and Southeast Europe was suddenly upset. A number of basic cartel agreements between the Czechoslovak steel industry and Austrian works were incorporated into the German cartel system which had taken over the Austrian steel

[1] E.g. *Wirtschaftskurve*, July 1933.

[2] Cf. R. D. Charques and A. H. Ewen, *Profits and Politics in the Post-War World* (London, 1934), p. 278.

works. This created an extremely serious situation for the Czechoslovak steel industry, which, however, managed to preserve its shaken position until the signing of the Munich Agreement in September 1938. With the implementation of the Munich Dictate and the separation of the frontier areas in the Northwest and Southwest from the state territory of Czechoslovakia, the whole cartel structure, which had expressed the relations of economic forces in the steel industry from the mid-twenties to September 1938, collapsed.

4

Mechanical and electrical engineering

1 Longterm direct investments of foreign industrial combines and banks in the engineering and electrical industry in Czechoslovakia

The effect of foreign investment in the iron and steel industry on the engineering industry

Direct foreign investment decisively influenced the iron and steel industry of pre-Munich Czechoslovakia (viz. Chapter 3) and, because of the industry's key position in the national economy, it also had a significant effect on those branches of industry which were dependent on supplies of raw materials and semi-finished products from iron and steel works. The connection between the iron and steel and engineering industries[1] was of course especially close.

The structure of demand for iron and steel products from the individual branches of industry on the Czechoslovak domestic market before 1938 cannot, unfortunately, be precisely ascertained, because of the lack of reliable statistics. However, according to my calculations based on the archives of the Czechoslovak iron and steel cartel, the United Czechoslovak Iron Works, covering the 1930s and 1940s,[2] the engineering industry absorbed about 50 % of the total output of rolled iron and steel products; about 18 % was used by building, transport, independent craftsmen and services, and exports amounted to 32 %, on the average between 1924 and 1936.[3] This demand structure was reflected in the production programme (including

[1] I. Kruliš-Randa, 'Situace železářského průmyslu' (The situation of the iron industry), *Hospodářský rozhled* (Economic View), 24 May 1928.
[2] ANTM–SDRUŽEL, Group S.
[3] Calculated according to data in ANTM–413/15, No. 3.

armaments) of the two largest engineering combines in Czechoslovakia – the Škoda-Works (A.s. dříve Škodovy závody)[1] and the Czech-Moravian-Kolben-Daněk Co. (Českomoravská Kolben-Daněk a.s.)[2] in the period 1929–38.

Mutual interests as well as conflicting relations led to mergers and other forms of combination between suppliers and purchasers within Czechoslovakia. Iron and steel works tried through their tight cartel to sell their products at the highest possible prices, and engineering plants attempted to reduce the cost of their raw materials and semi-finished products. A similar process can be observed in other industrially advanced economies.[3] As a rule, the iron and steel works emerged as the leading force, acquiring direct investments in or controlling through cartels foundries, wire mills, chain factories, locomotive-building and bridge-building plants, screw factories and engineering works.[4] Conversely, the Škoda-Works, the most important engineering combine in Czechoslovakia, owned iron and steel works in Hrádek which in turn supplied the engineering plants in Plzeň with part of their raw material requirements as well as semi-finished products.

The most significant and, in a way, indirect links between a combine supplying steel and a combine purchasing it existed in Czechoslovakia in the period 1920–38, when a connection was established between the Mining and Metallurgic Co. and the Škoda-Works through their common French shareholder, Schneider–Creusot, who played a controlling role in both concerns.[5] The iron works in Hrádek and the steel works of the Mining and Metallurgic Co. in Těšín produced a substantial proportion of the raw materials needed by the Škoda-Works. For this reason the Škoda-Works undertook – apparently

[1] Cf. PA–ZVIL, GŘ 287 – circular gen. řed. No. 2.

[2] Cf. J. Petráň and V. Fuchs, *90 let práce a bojů* (90 years of work and struggle) (Praha, 1961).

[3] TNEC, Final Report of the Executive Secretary, p. 25.

[4] Viz. Tables Nos. 11, 12 and 15 in Chapter 3/1.

[5] It is surprising that neither previous publications nor the authors of the latest monograph on the history of the Škoda-Works during the inter-war period pay any attention to the connection between the Mining and Metallurgic Co. and the Škoda-Works through their common shareholder, Schneider et Cie., although they mention some of the French directors who held seats on the boards of both companies. See V. Jíša and A. Vaněk, *Škodovy závody* (The Škoda-Works) (Praha, 1962), p. 136.

without much protest – in the Cartel Agreement of the United Czechoslovak Iron Works 'not to expand the production programme of their rolling mills in Hrádek, and to abstain from deliveries of semi-finished steel of all kinds to other outside firms',[1] which meant, in effect, that the steel plants in Hrádek were to produce exclusively for the requirements of the Škoda-Works and their subsidiaries. Preference in other orders for steel products from the Škoda-Works, especially thin sheets, was given to the Mining and Metallurgic Co. Cartelized selling organizations respected this arrangement between the two Schneider-controlled concerns when allocating orders from engineering works to iron and steel works.[2] In this way the Schneider organization created favourable conditions within the Czechoslovak iron and steel and engineering industries for price and profit transfers inside their combines, in order not only to maximize profits but also to gain effective control, and to attain as high a degree of efficiency of production as given conditions permitted.

The large concerns in the iron and steel industry did not only influence the engineering industry through their direct and indirect investments in engineering firms. However violently they competed with each other the partners in the national steel cartel took a common stand against the engineering industry, mainly by agreeing on prices and conditions of delivery and by controlling the quality of their commodities.[3] The almost im-

[1] AŮLSMHD–Agreement, 1931, §19.

[2] PA–VILZ – Agenda gen. řed. Rochette. The French head office insisted that all Škoda orders should be executed by the Mining and Metallurgic Co. and protested vigorously when the Selling Agency or Petzold sent these orders to the Prague Iron Company. Cf. for instance ibid., Aktová noticka pro pana gen. řed. Rochette (business note for director-general Rochette), 31 March 1934.

[3] In a closely argued draft of 5 March 1938 prepared by the Škoda-Works, the ČKD and the Brno Armaments Works for the Ministry of Finance, the following complaint was made: 'The deliveries of raw material and semi-finished goods which our plants convert into further products of the engineering, metallurgic and electrical industries are controlled by a number of highly effective cartels. Therefore, the domestic market of these raw materials and semi-finished goods and to a large extent also their imports are organized in such a way as to exclude free competition.

The prices of these raw materials are therefore substantially higher than they would have been if free competition had existed. Prices especially of the following raw materials and semi-finished goods are affected by these cartel agreements: crude and rolled steel, copper, cables, insulators, porcelain products, wood, coal and coke, electric current, oil and others...' PA–ZVIL–GŘ 287.

penetrable domestic cartel, represented by the Selling Agency of the United Czechoslovak Iron Works, maintained its supremacy in the home market.[1] Purchasers in the engineering, building and other industries therefore had to pay relatively high prices in comparison with other European countries and particularly in comparison with the export prices obtained by the Czechoslovak steel industry.[2]

The Czechoslovak engineering industry fought a losing battle with the steel concerns. In the negotiations between the Selling Agency of the United Czechoslovak Iron Works and the employers' organization of the engineering industry, the Association of Metalworks, the engineering industry representatives, who had hoped to be able to reduce their costs, were unable to obtain any price reductions for steel products.[3] An idea of the Czechoslovak steel cartel's strength on the domestic market may be obtained from the remarkable stability of steel prices between 1930 and 1936, i.e. in a period of severe crisis conditions and rapidly falling world prices, when domestic prices of steel and rolled products remained unchanged, apart from a comparatively small price reduction on 26 November 1930.[4] The steel concerns were thus able to absorb part of the profits which would otherwise have accrued to the engineering industry or could alternatively have benefited the consumer of finished engineering products.

The influence of the metallurgical industry on engineering made itself felt in at least two ways: in the first place, indirectly,

[1] The international cartel system, on the other hand, caused a decline in the exports of the Czechoslovak steel industry. See Chapter 3 (2).

[2] ANTM–fond 413/3.

[3] Differences between the Selling Agency and the Association of Metalworks continued and the steelworks allowed the engineering firms an 'export bonus' only if they could prove that the ordered material would be used for export (in the terminology of the Selling Agency this was to be 'indirect export' which amounted to about 10% of total steel production between 1924 and 1936). However, even after deducting the 'export bonus', domestic prices were appreciably higher than world prices. Cf. ANTM – Memoirs of J. Tille; also calculations of the average share of indirect export from steelworks in Czechoslovakia. ANTM–fond 413/3.

[4] According to statistics on the Brussels Stock Exchange prices of merchant bars fell by 47.14% between 1930 and 1933; from 1930 to 1935 the average fall in prices was 20% of the level at January 1930. In Czechoslovakia prices of steel and rolled products were reduced by 7% on 26 November 1930 and remained stable after that. Cf. ANTM–fond 413/3, Reports on the development of the market for steel and rolled products 1928–36.

through its dominating position as a basic supplier for the metal-working industry and its cohesive monopoly structure; in the second place, more directly, by controlling engineering firms which were subsidiaries of the leading iron and steel combines dominated by foreign majority shareholders. In this way, although it cannot be quantified, the role of foreign investment in the Czechoslovak engineering and electrical industry, which included a large armament sector, was increased.

The mechanical engineering industry

However, the most immediate influence was that of direct foreign participation in the Czechoslovak engineering industry, which according to my calculations amounted to Kč 223,106,000 at 31 December 1937, i.e. 16 % of the total nominal capital in this branch of industry. Direct foreign capital participation in 36 companies with a total capital of Kč 565,625,000 amounted to 40 %. Foreign direct investment existed in only 9.4 % of the total number of joint-stock companies and limited companies, although these firms controlled over 35 % of the basic capital in the industry as a whole.[1] These figures provide proof of a significant degree of concentration in the Czechoslovak engineering industry and, at the same time, of the existence of a considerable number of lesser factories and workshops. They also show that foreign capital participated in the financially strongest and most concentrated enterprises. The territorial distribution of foreign investment is shown in Table 1.[2]

It emerges from Table 1 that French capital predominated over investment from other countries, which mainly consisted of shares held through iron and steel concerns or banks. Although total foreign investment in the metal-working industry was by no means as large as in the mining and metallurgical industry, its importance lay in the controlling interest held by the French Schneider combine in the leading Czechoslovak engineering and armament concern, the Škoda-Works. Schneider's interest in the Škoda-Works is shown graphically in Table 3, which gives the situation from 29 January 1937 to 30 September 1938. The

[1] Calculated from data in *Statistická ročenka* (1941); *Compass, Čechoslovakei* (1939), 774 and Tables III and IV in Chapter 2 (I).

[2] Cf. Table IV, Chapter 2 (I).

Table 1. *Territorial distribution of direct longterm foreign investment in the engineering industry of Czechoslovakia, 31 December 1937*

Country of origin of investment	Nominal value in 1,000 Kč	Percentage of total foreign investment
France	164,319	73.8
Austria	11,600	5.2
Sweden	11,600	5.2
Great Britain	9,596	4.4
Belgium	7,637	3.4
Switzerland	6,296	2.8
Germany	4,900	2.1
U.S.A.	3,670	1.6
Holland	2,000	0.9
Italy	1,440	0.6
Hungary	48	—
Total	223,106	100.0

Calculated from data in V. Jíša–A. Vaněk, p. 500; V. Petráň–V. Fuchs, pp. 131, 164, 181; V. Král, II, p. 308; PA–ZVIL, GŘ 267; *Compass, Čechoslovakei* (1939).

Škoda-Works was the most important Czechoslovak engineering firm, occupying the same place in Central Europe as Vickers in Great Britain, Schneider in France and Krupp in Germany. It is, therefore, not surprising that it became attractive to foreign investors when spheres of interest changed after the First World War.

The second largest engineering and armaments plant in Czechoslovakia between 1929 and 1938 was the Czech-Moravian-Kolben-Daněk Co. (ČKD). However, in terms of capital, volume of output, number of workers and, especially, international standing, it was considerably weaker. Table 2 shows some aspects of ČKD's size compared with that of the Škoda-Works; it appears that the ČKD had roughly one-third of the Škoda-Works' capacity.[1]

The director-general of ČKD, V. Koula, emphasized in his article celebrating the first decade of the Czechoslovak Republic's existence 'that the company has its roots in the soil of the Czechoslovak Republic and contrary to many domestic joint-stock companies has only domestic share capital'. The second director, F. Hoffmann, pointed out in his article 'Ways and

Table 2. *Comparative state of the Škoda-Works (ŠZ) and the Českomoravská-Kolben-Daněk (ČKD) on 31 December 1937 (in millions Kč)**

Item	ŠZ	ČKD	ČKD as % of ŠZ
Joint-stock capital	220	37·5	17
Profits	61	14	23
Balance of accounts	2,678	766	28
State of orders	2,051†	819	41
Number of workers and office employees	32,000	12,000	37·5

* Figures have been rounded.
† On 31 December 1936.

Aims of our Commercial Policy', that 'no foreign money financed the production of the ČKD', and that 'never were any pure profits transferred across the border which cannot be said of any of the other large domestic concerns in our industry'.[1] Both concerns waged a continuous competitive war which, in a way, was a form of competition between domestic and foreign capital. The weaker contestant eventually had to compromise and the balance of power was formalized in a cartel agreement between the Škoda-Works and the ČKD on 1 January 1935.[2]

The process of ousting German, Austrian and Hungarian capital also began in the engineering industry after the establishment of the independent Czechoslovak state. In this area the so-called nationalization policy also, in effect, paved the way for Western European capital investment. The earliest and most important foothold was obtained, not by Czech capital, but by the French, immediately after the conclusion of the Peace of Versailles, when 73 % of the joint-stock capital of the Škoda-Works in Plzeň was transferred to Schneider et Cie. in Paris.[3]

While peace was still being negotiated at Versailles, Dr Beneš, the Czechoslovak Minister for Foreign Affairs, was attempting to attract West European investment, especially in those enterprises which had been dominated by German or Austrian

[1] 'Der Aufstieg einer Grossindustrie-Čs. mor. Kolben-Daněk A.G.', *Prager Presse*, Sonderbeilage, 29 January 1928.
[2] Cf. PA–ZVIL – Agenda Rochette – Products under the Agreement.
[3] V. Jíša–A. Vaněk, p. 120.

shareholders. During his stay in Paris he was actively engaged in discussions with the French Ministries of Foreign Affairs and Finance and with representatives of Schneider, which led to Schneider's investment in the Škoda-Works. At the same time the Živnostenská Bank, with the approval of the Czechoslovak government, acted as mediator in Vienna between Eugène Schneider and Dr Karel Škoda, from whom it obtained the Škoda-Works' shares, which it then transferred into French hands.[1] A month after the signing of the Versailles Peace Treaty, Dr Beneš informed the Škoda-Works and the Živnostenská Bank that he had reached full agreement with Schneider's representative, Ing. Victor Champigneul, and that a general meeting should be called of the company.[2]

After the German–Austrian members of the board of directors had resigned[3] and the company's central office had been moved from Vienna to Prague,[4] the transfer of the Škoda shares to the Schneider combine was completed, at the general meeting on 25 September 1919. On the same day the constituent meeting of the new board of directors took place and the minutes confirm that so far 225,000 shares had been handed over to Schneider et Cie. in Paris.[5] Altogether, with the shares obtained from the former owners, the Schneider concern held 325,000 shares out of a total of 450,000,[6] thus gaining an absolute majority and a controlling interest.

This transaction became a model for further changes in property relations in the Czechoslovak economy, which reflected the new distribution of spheres of influence in Europe. The incorporation of the largest armaments works in Central Europe into the Schneider combine corresponded with the intentions of French power politics and, at the same time, constituted a decisive step towards implementing the political

[1] For further details of the transfer see V. Jíša–A. Vaněk, Part II, Chapter I.

[2] Cf. telegram dated 19 August 1919 from Dr Beneš in Paris to the Ministry of Foreign Affairs in Prague. Quoted by V. Král, *O Masarykově a Benešově kontrarevoluční protisovětské politice* (Masaryk's and Beneš' counter-revolutionary and anti-soviet policy) (Prague, 1953), p. 129.

[3] Cf. PA-ZVIL, GŘ 2, 25 September 1919.

[4] Cf. 'Die Škodawerke nach dem Kriege; Zehn Jahre Friedensarbeit der Škodawerke', *Prager Presse*, Sonderbeilage (1928).

[5] Cf. PA-ZVIL, GŘ 2 – Protocol of the constituent meeting of the board of directors, 25 September 1919.

[6] Cf. V. Jíša–A. Vaněk, p. 120.

conception of the most influential Czechoslovak governing circles around T. G. Masaryk and Eduard Beneš.[1] Seen from this angle, the close connection between leading Czech bankers, businessmen and statesmen and the French shareholders of the Škoda-Works can be better understood, as can Beneš' satisfaction with the accomplished transfer. He expressed this in a letter of 22 October 1919 to the general management of the Škoda-Works: 'Now the Škoda-Works, by their fusion and by increasing their Czech and French capital, have completely freed themselves of any influence which the company could call foreign.'[2] Its wider implications were, however, that the great trust of Schneider–Creusot, aided by the Czechoslovak government, gained a foothold in Central Europe for further expansion into Eastern and Southeastern Europe.

There can be little doubt that power politics was one of the main forces behind longterm French direct investment in the Czechoslovak mining, metallurgic, engineering and armaments industries. Thus one of the main objective reasons for Schneider's participation in the Škoda-Works, and somewhat later in the Mining and Metallurgic Co., can be seen in the attempts of this influential representative of French high finance and heavy industry to facilitate economic expansion and to take over economic positions from his former rivals, now defeated. The transaction involving the Škoda-Works was accordingly evaluated by the German Ministry of Interior's department for Czechoslovak affairs, not as a move in the direction of Czech nationalization, but as the first serious attack on German economic interests in this area.[3]

Schneider's efforts to exclude the Škoda-Works from competition in Central Europe must also be judged in the light of this ambitious policy.[4] The Schneider combine aimed at a strict

[1] During the peace negotiations in Paris in 1919 Harold Nicolson had a conversation with Eduard Beneš, of whose foreign policy aims he wrote: 'Bohemia wants to reconstruct Mittel Europa on a new basis which is neither German nor Russian. She therefore bases her claims "not so much on national as on international justifications". For her, although national unity comes first, and national prosperity second, the ultimate aim is the stability of Central Europe...' Harold Nicolson, *Peacemaking* (London, 1944), p. 239. In his policy speeches between 1919 and 1931 Beneš continually returned to this conception of Czechoslovakia's role in Europe.

[2] Quoted by V. Jíša–A. Vaněk, p. 123.

[3] DZAP–RMdI–5819.

[4] V. Jíša–A. Vaněk, pp. 118, 235–6.

delimitation of production and armaments programmes, as well as a division of markets between Schneider–Creusot and the Škoda-Works in Plzeň, in which the latter generally had to submit to the demands of the former. Nevertheless, the common economic and political interests of the Czech and French governments also favoured the strong participation of French capital in the Škoda-Works because from the point of view of internal Czechoslovak policy, Czechoslovak industrial and banking circles saw in it an effective guarantee against incipient popular demands for the socialization of armaments works and heavy industry as a whole.[1] The general significance of the Škoda-Works extended beyond the regional and national framework and its fate often reflected the economic and political development of the country in relation to international events.[2]

French influence in the Škoda-Works was decisive from the time of Schneider's original investment in September 1919 until the sale of the Schneider shares in December 1938, following the signing of the Munich Agreement. Naturally, there were disagreements within the management of the Škoda-Works between domestic Czech interests and those of the foreign shareholder and attempts were made by the Czechs to obtain greater freedom from French control. However, these attempts did not, on the whole, change the balance of power between the participating groups. The minutes and protocols of the board meetings, of the smaller but often more important body, the Executive Committee, and particularly an examination of organization at the highest levels in the Škoda-Works[3] make it quite obvious that the main policy decisions on production, commerce, trade and finance were taken in the central offices of the French concern in Paris.[4]

The decisive influence of the French shareholder was not only based on its majority holding but also secured by a network of financial, contractual and personal relations. However, the direct investment of the Schneider combine provided the basis for exercising a controlling influence. From this point of view the history of the French investment is of more than academic interest.

While the absolute number of Škoda shares in Schneider's

[1] Ibid. Both authors produce convincing evidence in Part 1, Chapter 5.
[2] Ibid. p. 234.
[3] PA–ZVIL, especially GŘ 267 and Agenda Rochette.
[4] PA–ZVIL, GŘ 2, 3, passim.

holding company, L'Union Européenne Industrielle et Financière, remained unchanged over the whole period, its proportion fell with every new issue of shares. As a rule the joint-stock capital was increased when mergers took place and the shares of the merged company were converted into a new issue of Škoda shares, as was, for instance, the case with the United Machine Factories (Spojené strojírny).[1] In the cases of other mergers, such as the iron works in Hrádek-Rokycany, the car factory Laurin and Klement and other engineering plants, the necessary number of shares was usually withdrawn from the free market. Sometimes the Union Européenne also put some of its shares temporarily at the disposal of the Škoda-Works,[2] and they were then given to the former owners of the incorporated enterprises in lieu of payment, mostly along with seats on the board of directors of the Škoda-Works.[3] In 1924 the Škoda-Works became partners with the Czechoslovak state in a joint-stock company, the Czechoslovak Armament Works in Brno (Československá zbrojovka v Brně), acquiring a 20.5 % participation. Thus the Schneider concern also gained an indirect interest in this Czechoslovak state enterprise.[4]

[1] Cf. V. Jíša–A. Vaněk, p. 132; also PA–ZVIL, GŘ 2, Protocol of the meeting of the board of directors, 1 October 1921. [2] Cf. V. Jíša–A. Vaněk, p. 209.

[3] Such an action was taken during the merger with Laurin & Klement in 1925 when Václav Klement and Dr Emil Miřička were co-opted onto the board of directors. PA–ZVIL, GŘ 2, Protocol of extraordinary meeting of the board of directors, 20 July 1925.

[4] With the participation in the Czechoslovak Armament Works in Brno in 1924 two directors of the Škoda-Works joined the board of the Brno company and one director from Brno became a member of the Executive Committee of the Škoda-Works. PA–ZVIL, GŘ 2, Protocol of extraordinary meeting of the board of directors, 3 November 1924. With every increase in the capital of the Armament Works in Brno the share of the Škoda-Works rose proportionately and their influence in the management was retained, as the following table shows.

*Changes in the joint-stock capital of the Czechoslovak Armaments Works in Brno**

Year	Total capital (million Kč)	Total number of shares	Owners of shares		
			State	Škoda	Others
1924	30	75,000	56,639	15,098	3,263
1934	70	175,000	135,533	36,071	3,396
1937	120	300,000	235,528	61,071	3,401

* DZAP–IMT–B 187–NID 7088.

Table 3. *Škoda-Works combine,*

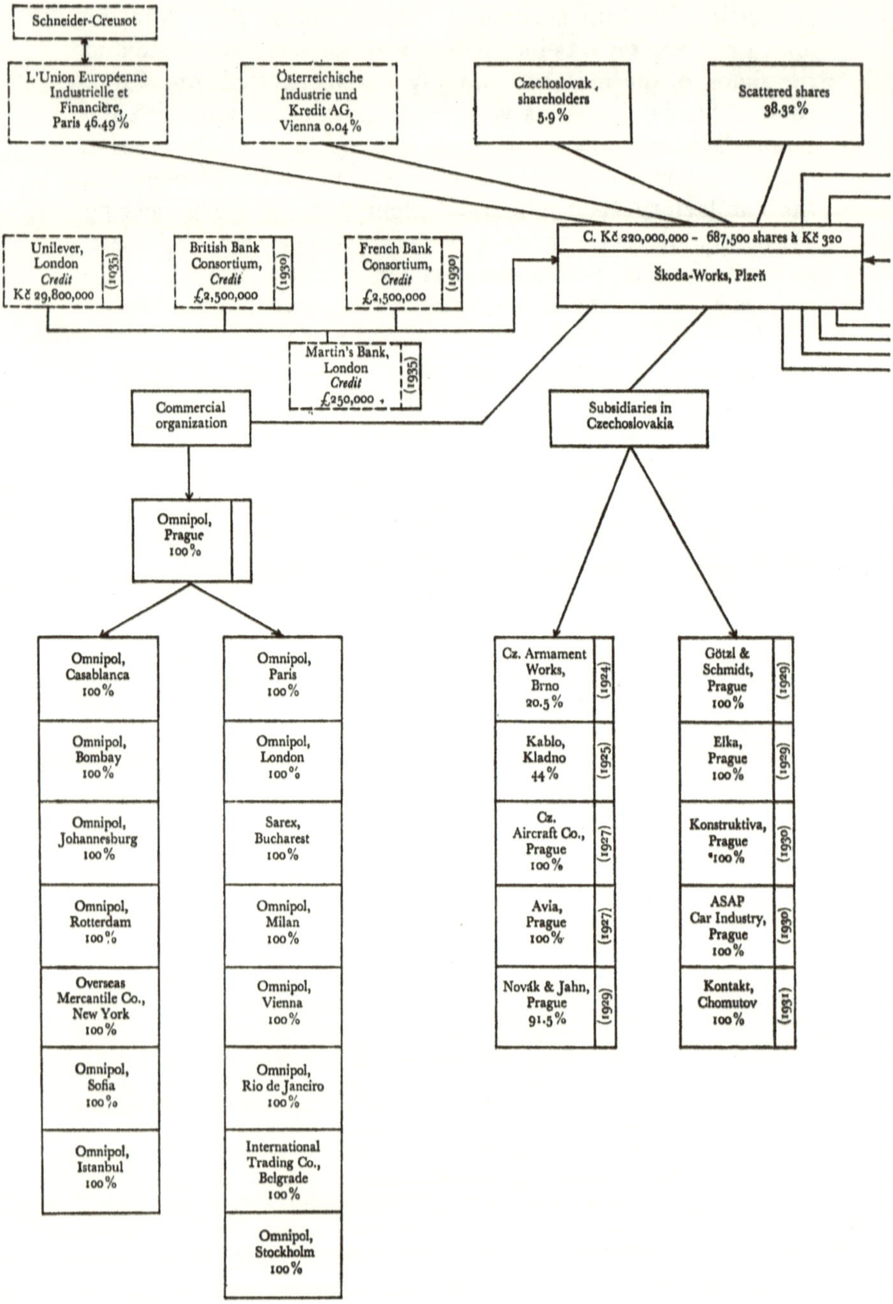

29 January 1937–30 September 1938

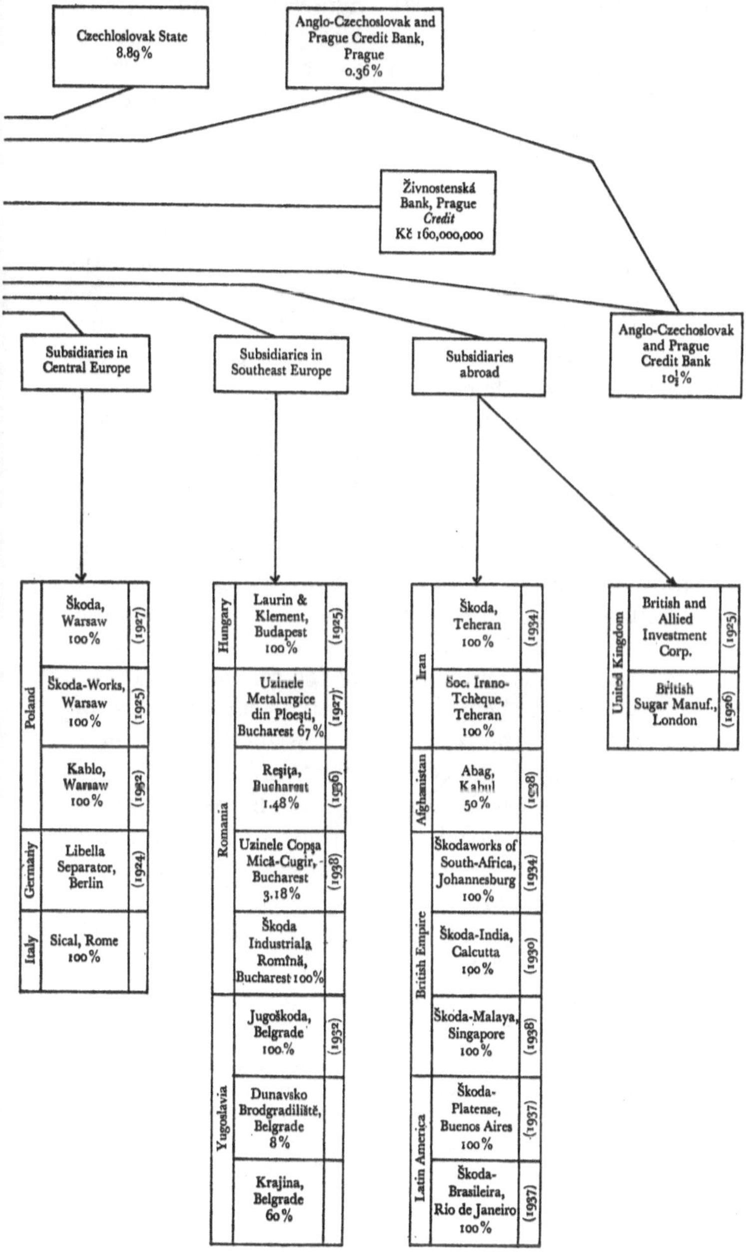

The growth of the Škoda concern was carefully watched by the French shareholder.[1] Its expansion developed generally along the lines of a horizontal monopoly,[2] which gradually dominated the whole Czechoslovak engineering industry, encroached upon the electrical industry and played a significant part in the foreign trade of the country through its commercial organization 'Omnipol' (Table 3). It further consolidated its leading position in 1935, by concluding the previously mentioned far-reaching cartel agreement with its most persistent competitor on the home market, the Czech-Moravian-Kolben-Daněk Company, which all other important domestic firms were also obliged to enter. The chairman of the board of directors of the Škoda-Works, Dr Karel Loevenstein, subsequently announced with great satisfaction in his report to the board at the end of 1935 that the engineering cartel in Czechoslovakia was almost complete.[3]

The Škoda-Works grew steadily from 1921 to 1938, with only one short break in the worst crisis year of 1933; it expanded both within and beyond the frontiers of Czechoslovakia, particularly into Central and Southeast Europe. Infiltration into this area took place against a favourable background of political, military and economic treaties in the framework of the Little Entente. Table 3 shows the chronology and the direction of growth as well as the predominantly horizontal expansion of the Škoda combine. These factors and the transactions associated with them did not impair the influence of Schneider–Creusot; on the contrary, it was increased in proportion to the increase in the economic strength of the Škoda-Works. The rising number of subsidiaries of the Škoda-Works at home and abroad involved an extension of the Schneider interests into these countries as well, because the Škoda-Works were really part of the European Schneider combine.

With the last issue of Škoda shares before Munich (at the extraordinary general meeting of shareholders on 29 January 1937), when the company's joint-stock capital was increased from Kč 200 million to Kč 220 million by an issue of 62,500

[1] Regular reports on the investment activity and financial performance of the subsidiary companies were sent from Prague to Paris for the L'Union Européenne Industrielle et Financière. PA–ZVIL, GŘ 267, Reports Union.

[2] Cf. also V. Jíša–A. Vaněk, p. 214.

[3] PA–ZVIL, GŘ 3, Ředitelská zpráva (Director's Report), 9 December 1935.

shares for the Czechoslovak state, French participation fell from an absolute majority holding to 46.49 % (Table 3).[1] However, this did not seriously weaken Schneider's decisive influence, because neither the holding of the Czechoslovak state (8.89 %) nor that of the Anglo–Czechoslovak and Prague Credit Bank (0.36 %) was comparable in size with the French investment; the remaining shares were scattered among a large number of shareholders.[2] This situation is convincingly demonstrated by the list of persons present at the meeting on 29 January 1937. The sixteen shareholders who attended held between them 360,542 shares, i.e. 58 % of the total joint-stock capital. Of these, representatives of Schneider et Cie owned 319,632, which, according to the statutes of the Škoda-Works, gave them 88 % of the vote.[3] However, opposition never occurred during voting because the agenda of every general meeting was invariably settled beforehand in the meetings of the Executive Committee and the board of directors, where the predominance of the Schneider representatives was fully recognized.[4]

A superficial judgement of holdings in the Škoda-Works after January 1937 might suggest that after the Czechoslovak state became a substantial shareholder the Czech element in the Škoda-Works would be able to use state powers to give themselves a decisive influence in management. However, closer investigation reveals that, given the prevailing financial and

[1] PA–ZVIL, GŘ 267, Protocol of General Meeting, 29 January 1937.

[2] It is, therefore, erroneous to suppose that a formal majority of Škoda shares passed into the hands of Czech agrarian finance capital in 1937, as is maintained by V. Král (II, p. 72). In his contribution to the discussion with me, on the other hand, he asserts that the formal majority was in the hands of foreign shareholders (cf. 'K úloze zahraničního kapitálu v Československu před rokem 1938' [The Role of Foreign Capital in Czechoslovakia before 1938], *ČSČH*, 7 (1959), 474). In any case, in his critical review of my article Král refers to the well-known economic fact that a minority participation can be decisive in cases where other shares are widely scattered. Cf. *ČSČH*, 6 (1958), 544.

[3] Calculated from data on the list of shareholders present at the General Meeting of 29 January 1937. PA–ZVIL, GŘ 267.

[4] This principle was preserved in the Syndicate Agreement between the L'Union Européenne Industrielle et Financière, the Czechoslovak state and the Anglo-Czechoslovak and Prague Credit Bank in 1936. Article VIII of this agreement laid down that the Syndicate Committee, on which the French had a two-thirds representation, had to agree on the agenda of general meetings before convening them, as well as on the text of the resolution and on the way the members of the Syndicate were to vote. Cf. PA–ZVIL, GŘ 267, Syndicate Agreement.

capital structure, Czech capital was not strong enough to press its claims to decision-making, in spite of the potential powers of the Czechoslovak government. If it had been able to, this would have meant an appreciable weakening of one of the main links in Schneider's European combine. In this connection it is important to realize that Schneider's total capital holdings were larger than those of Czechoslovakia's whole heavy industry and were closely connected with the Banque de France and the French government.

The Czechoslovak state was undoubtedly involved with the Škoda-Works from the start of the French participation, which – as mentioned before – was itself made possible largely by the active mediation of Czechoslovak politicians. The Czechoslovak state was, in addition, one of the main purchasers of the Škoda-Works' products through its ministries; most important, of course, were government orders for armaments, which influenced Škoda's production programme decisively. This is borne out by orders and invoices for the army, which amounted to almost 70 % of the total value of orders received and about 60 % of the total value of invoices of the Škoda-Works on the average in the years 1933–6.[1] The relationship between the Škoda management and the state was very complex: it did not arise out of direct capital investment by the Czechoslovak state in the Škoda-Works, but rather depended on various connections with the state apparatus and, to some extent, on the firm's practice of secretly co-opting onto the board of directors the heads of ministries which allotted government orders or controlled financial transactions. Politicians and ministers generally joined the board after concluding their terms of office; however, the Škoda-Works informed them confidentially of their co-option while they were still in office.[2]

[1] Calculated from data prepared by the general management of the Škoda-Works for L'Union Européenne in Paris. PA–ZVIL, GŘ 267.

[2] '(2) Co-opted onto the board of directors Dr Ing. František Kovářík who resigned his former post to become Minister of Public Works.

(3) Further co-opted onto the board of directors Mr Fr. Staněk. With this decision a formal resolution is being realized which had been prepared long ago. It is resolved not to publish this decision as yet, but to inform the Minister about the co-option, as he will take up his function after his term of office finishes.' PA–ZVIL, GŘ 2, Protocol of the meeting of the board of directors, 1 October 1921.

The Minister of Finance, later Governor of the National Bank of Czecho-

Between 1921 and 1938 a number of ministers held seats on the board of directors: the Minister of Public Works (Dr Fr. Kovářík), the Minister of Agriculture and Post (Fr. Staněk), the Minister of the Interior (Dr J. Slavík), the Minister of Health (Dr V. Šrobár), the Minister of National Defence (Dr K. Viškovský) and the Minister of Trade (Ing. L. Novák). Until 1925 the Czechoslovak Ministry of National Defence was run by the French Military Mission, which provided a direct connection with the Schneider interests. A special place on the board was reserved for Dr Karel Engliš, who, at the invitation of the board, always renewed his membership when his term as Minister of Finance or as Governor of the National Bank of Czechoslovakia came to an end. If one assumes that the incomes of members of the board of directors were in the region of Kč 100,000 to Kč 200,000 annually, then it is not inconceivable that the controlling influences in the Škoda-Works used this entirely legal practice in order to involve public figures in reciprocal services. This emerges from protocols of board meetings, in which these members of the board of directors were briefed to intervene in the appropriate places on behalf of the Škoda-Works in cases of government orders and loans, or when higher prices for arms deliveries were solicited. One of the first demands of the French members of the board concerned the need for higher prices for artillery supplied to the Czechoslovak Ministry of National Defence. In order to effect this Dr Engliš was asked to approach the Minister of Finance, Dr Kovářik was to see the Minister of Trade, and also Luděk Pik, the Mayor of Plzeň and Member of the National Assembly, was to intervene with the Minister of Social Welfare.[1] Luděk Pik, a leading member of the Czech Social-Democratic Party, held a seat on the board of directors of the Škoda-Works continuously from 1919 to 1932 and actively participated in the firm's rationaliza-

slovakia, Dr Karel Engliš, became a member of the board of directors of the Škoda-Works whenever he was out of government office. A resolution was adopted by the board of directors, in the presence of Eugène Schneider, that Engliš would not be on the board during his term at the Ministry of Finance, but he was asked to rejoin afterwards. PA–ZVIL, GŘ 2, Protocol of the meeting of the board of directors, 1 February 1926, also 1929. Further data on membership of the board by ministers of the Czechoslovak government are taken from the records in PA–ZVIL, GŘ 2, 3.

[1] PA–ZVIL, GŘ 2, Protocol of the meeting of the board of directors, 27 February 1922 and others.

tion drive. He was mainly concerned with smoothing negotiations on dismissals and wage reductions; at the same time, as Mayor of Plzeň, he looked after the relations between the Škoda-Works and local government.[1] By means of these personal contacts the Škoda-Works and their French partners were connected with the Czechoslovak state long before the state acquired any shares.

Another point of contact was in the field of foreign trade. The Czechoslovak government obtained significant orders for the Škoda-Works through its diplomatic service[2] and guaranteed their credits, especially in Romania.[3] In this way the state took the risks upon itself and the Škoda-Works enjoyed much safer guarantees.

The Czechoslovak state also stepped into the breach in 1932 when the French and British banks, which had so far provided the Škoda-Works with credit, refused to renew their loans.[4] The state granted the Škoda-Works an obligatory credit to the amount of Kč 250 million and secured the right to convert this loan into a new issue of shares within four years.[5] On the basis of this agreement the Czechoslovak state then took over all the Škoda shares which were issued in January 1937, i.e. 62,500 shares, of which 2,500 were transferred to the Anglo-Czechoslovak and Prague Credit Bank; the rest was also deposited there.[6] With this transaction the Czechoslovak Republic became part-owner of the largest armament concern in the country. The absolute majority had been held by the French investor for the previous seventeen years; however, the state's

[1] On L. Pik's membership of the board of directors, see A. Teichová, 'O výdělečné činnosti členů poslanecké sněmovny ve volebním období 1929–1935' (Deputies of the Czechoslovak Parliament and their Business Interests 1929–35), *ČSČH* (1955); on L. Pik's activities in the labour movement of the Plzeň region during his membership on the board, see V. Jíša–A. Vaněk, passim.

[2] AMZV–IV. sekce (unnumbered).

[3] V. Jíša–A. Vaněk, p. 222; the Škoda-Works took part in the negotiation of the agreement between the governments of Czechoslovakia and Romania on the methods of payment for Romanian orders with the Škoda-Works. It was agreed that Omnipol would take over Romanian exports to the amount of the credit. Thus the Škoda-Works profited twice; firstly from arms delivered to Romania, and secondly from handling Romanian exports. Cf. PA–ZVIL, GŘ 267, Confidential report to the French Secretariat, 7 November 1935.

[4] Cf. PA–ZVIL, GŘ 3, Protocols of extraordinary meetings of the board of directors, 19 December 1931 and 5 August 1932.

[5] Ibid., 5 August 1932.

[6] PA–ZVIL, GŘ 267, Protocol of General Meeting, 29 January 1937.

share was not as large as had been foreseen in the loan agreement of 1932.[1] At the end of 1936 it transpired that the state loan was being repaid faster than expected, through government deliveries at artificially increased prices and through various allowances, so that the Škoda-Works was able to repay the remaining credit by a fairly small issue of shares, with a nominal value of Kč 20 million, against the originally planned sum of Kč 41,600,000.[2] Thus the capital participation of the Czechoslovak state had fallen to half the size intended and the new arrangement left the decisive role of the French shareholder essentially intact. In its relationship to the Škoda-Works, the Czechoslovak state appears, firstly, as a protector of their interests, a purchaser of their products, a channel for orders from other countries and a guarantor of their more doubtful foreign credits, as well as rescuing them from financial difficulties; only in the second place and in the last phase, does it become a relatively small participant in their share capital.

The newly formed relationship was laid down in the Syndicate Agreement between the Government of the Czechoslovak Republic and its banker, the Anglo-Czechoslovak and Prague Credit Bank, on the one side, and Schneider's bank, L'Union Européenne Industrielle et Financière in Paris, on the other, which was concluded in December 1936. In spite of the fact that state power was in the hands of the Czechoslovak group, the Syndicate Agreement of the Škoda-Works of 1936 did not so alter the position of the domestic interests in the company as to transfer a controlling influence to them.[3] French dominance

[1] 'A special provision of the agreement foresees the state's optional right to shares from our Works' new issue as follows: 60,000 shares per Kč 500, 60,000 shares per Kč 600, 130,000 shares per Kč 1,000.' PA–ZVIL, GŘ 3, 19 December 1931.

[2] Ibid., also Protocol of the extraordinary meeting of the board of directors, 16 December 1936. The nominal value is calculated from the data in the director's report of 5 August 1932. In the confidential report for the French Secretariat of 7 November 1935 the rapid repayment of the state loan and its reduction from Kč 250 million to Kč 66 million is strongly emphasized. PA–ZVIL, GŘ 267. Cf. also R. Slánský, I, p. 300. On the connection between the financial rescue of the Škoda-Works and the French government loan to the Czechoslovak state in 1932, see p. 375.

[3] In his article criticizing my contribution 'The Role of Foreign Capital in the Czechoslovak Economy before Munich', *ČSČH*, 7 (1959), 114, V. Král maintains that 'in the Syndicate Agreement of the Škoda-Works of 1936 we directly come across the formulation that according to the Czechoslovak government's wish

was explicitly recognized in the agreement, which also reiterated the continuity of the principles of management of the Škoda-Works laid down in 1920.[1] Rather than establishing the preponderance of the Czechoslovak state, the agreement defined and limited its powers and rights, and those of the Czech shareholders, in relation to the stronger French participants. Above all, the Czechoslovak side secured an option on buying French shares;[2] in addition, the Czechoslovak side was to partake in decisions affecting the interests of the Czechoslovak state through three representatives of the Anglo-Czechoslovak and Prague Credit Bank, and the Union Européenne was contractually obliged to bring its influence to bear in securing three places on the Škoda-Works' board of directors for them.[3] Until the end of 1936 the Schneider combine almost completely dominated the Škoda-Works, and some of the articles in the Syndicate Agreement did indicate a limited but definite strengthening of domestic influence. However, this in no way meant a complete reversal of the balance of power. To some extent this development reflected the competitive struggle between foreign and domestic capital, as well as the relative weakening of all French positions during the 1930s.

At a meeting of the board of directors of the Škoda-Works in January 1937 two representatives of the Anglo-Czechoslovak and Prague Credit Bank were co-opted, i.e. the bank's president Dr Antonín Schauer and Dr Václav Vaněk,[4] although the signatories of the Syndicate had agreed to three representatives.

the position of the domestic shareholders was rearranged in such a way as to give them decisive influence, even though the formal majority of capital participation was in the hands of foreign shareholders'. V. Král, 'The Role of Foreign Capital', *ČSČH*, 7 (1959), 474.

[1] A two-thirds majority on the Syndicate Committee was guaranteed to representatives of the L'Union Européenne; on all questions that could not be deferred or delayed the view of the L'Union was to prevail (§VII); in economic and financial matters the representatives of the private shareholders were to decide in the accustomed manner (§IV); serious differences were not to be resolved by the Czechoslovak state, but in the last instance by the Permanent Court of the International Justice at the Hague (§VIII). Cf. Text of Agreement.

[2] Ibid., §III.

[3] Ibid., §IV.

[4] PA–ZVIL, GŘ 3, Protocol of meeting of the board of directors, 29 January 1937. In mid-1937 Dr Václav Vaněk was appointed deputy managing director of the National Bank and resigned from the board of the Škoda-Works, where he was replaced by Bohuslav Kučera from the Anglo-Czechoslovak and Prague Credit Bank. Ibid. Protocol of 1 June 1937.

The Czechoslovak government could thus make its influence felt through the Anglo-Czechoslovak and Prague Credit Bank. Conversely, however, the Škoda-Works had held a stake in the bank since 1927,[1] when they acquired a share in its capital during nationalization; this amounted in 1937 to 10.5 %.[2] Since 1927 the chairman of the board of directors of the Škoda-Works, Josef Šimonek, and the director-general, Dr Karel Loevenstein, had been members of the bank's board of directors.[3]

The Czechoslovak state banker was fairly strongly influenced by the Czech Agrarian Party, as were some of the directors of the Škoda-Works, but other, especially foreign, groups participated in the capital of the Anglo-Czechoslovak and Prague Credit Bank as well. The complexity of the relationships can be illustrated by the position of Dr Loevenstein himself, whose political position was close to that of the Agrarian Party. At the same time, however, he was a supporter of French interests in the management of the Škoda-Works and later became chairman of the board of directors, at the suggestion of Eugène Schneider.[4]

The usefulness of each member of the board of directors of the Škoda-Works was carefully considered in the Schneider headquarters in Paris, as can be seen from the correspondence of the French representatives in Czechoslovakia.[5] With the exception of the representatives of the Anglo-Czechoslovak and Prague Credit Bank, who according to the Syndicate Agreement were appointed by the Czech side, the composition of the board reflected the economic and political interests of the Schneider combine. Apart from the representatives of the most important subsidiaries, the Czech members of the board were selected from among Ministers and Deputies in Parliament of the National Democratic or Agrarian Party, and there was one representative of the Social-Democratic Party.[6] The ratio of

[1] V. Jíša–A. Vaněk, p. 230. [2] PA–ZVIL, GŘ 143; see also Table 3.

[3] PA–ZVIL, GŘ 3; *Compass, Čechoslovakei* (1929–38); V. Jíša–A. Vaněk, p. 275.

[4] PA–ZVIL, GŘ 3, 23 June 1934.

[5] PA–ZVIL – Agenda Rochette, Correspondence with L'Union – unnumbered.

[6] Ministers were mentioned in discussion of the Škoda-Works' relationship with the state apparatus. There were the following Deputies of Parliament: National Democrat J. Maštalka (from 1922), Agrarian and industrialist V. Stoupal (1925–34), National Democrat and industrialist Ing. L. Novák (1930–8), and Social Democrat Luděk Pik (1919–32). PA–ZVIL, GŘ 2, 3.

Table 4. *Czechoslovak–French division of the board of directors of the Škoda-Works between 1919 and 1937*

Year	Number of Czechoslovak directors	Number of French directors
1919	6	3
1930	13	7
1934	9	8
1936	9	9
1937	10	9

Czech to French members of the board moved between 1919 and 1937 in favour of the French, from 2:1 to 1:1, as is seen in Table 4.[1]

A somewhat different role was played by Dr Jaroslav Preiss, the director-general of the Živnostenská Bank, who was the second vice-president of the Škoda-Works from 1919 to 1930. He directed his efforts towards obtaining a larger share in the capital and management of the Škoda-Works for the Živnostenská Bank. At the same time he attempted to create a tighter national engineering monopoly by advocating the fusion of the Škoda-Works with the ČKD concern,[2] in which French influence would be weaker. However, Dr Preiss was unsuccessful, especially after the Škoda-Works shifted the centre of gravity of their domestic banking connections towards the Anglo-Czechoslovak bank.[3]

The Škoda-Works maintained their credit connections with leading British and French banks. This weakened the influence not only of the Živnostenská Bank, but also of domestic capital in general.[4] Preiss drew the obvious conclusion from the failure

[1] Compiled from material in PA–ZVIL, GŘ 2, 3.

[2] J. Petráň–V. Fuchs, p. 104.

[3] V. Jíša–A. Vaněk, p. 275.

[4] Ibid., pp. 230, 275. A thorough analysis of the relevant capital participation and credits shows that V. Král greatly simplified the question by maintaining 'that before 1938 the Živnostenská Bank and the Anglobanka divided their influence in the Škoda-Works between themselves'. V. Král, II, p. 342. He also exaggerated the actual influence of the Živnostenská Bank through its credits to the Škoda-Works. Ibid., p. 307. The French participation cannot be ignored, neither can the enormous loans supplied by British and French banks to the Škoda-Works which were many times larger than the credits of the Živnostenská Bank.

of his plan and resigned from the board of directors of the Škoda-Works in 1930.[1] In the same year he was elected president of the board of the ČKD, in the capital of which the Živnostenská Bank had a controlling interest, and the struggle between the two engineering combines continued unabated.[2] Relations between the Škoda-Works, the ČKD and the Živnostenská Bank improved only towards the end of the 1930s, as a result of their Cartel Agreement in 1935 and the armaments boom.

In contrast to their Czech counterparts the French members of the board of the Škoda-Works represented the interests of Schneider–Creusot in Czechoslovakia unanimously and purposefully. The basic policy of Schneider's management was stated by the director-general of the Schneider holding company L'Union Européenne, Colonel Ernest Weyl, at a meeting of the board on 21 May 1920, at which the head of the Paris concern, Eugène Schneider, and the director-general of the Schneider Iron Works, Jules Aubrun, were present. The colonel outlined the main tasks[3] and thus initiated the policy which safeguarded the decisive role of the French combine in the production, trade and finance of the Škoda-Works over the next two decades.

The running of the works, calculations, book-keeping, methods of compiling and presenting reports, were all done according to instructions from the French management. In the Czechoslovak works French experts were engaged in managerial posts at various levels, but the main reins of power were held by the director-general, Christophe Rochette, who from 1923 had regular and continuous contacts on all managerial questions with the director-general of L'Union Européenne, Aimée Lepercq, in Paris. Detailed monthly and annual reports, compiled according to instructions common to all Schneider subsidiaries, always had to be sent to L'Union Européenne in Paris by the 15th of the following month. They reported on the overall progress of the works, and special regular reports gave an analysis of how the agreements of 1922 on the delimitation of armament production, especially artillery, were carried out

[1] PA–ZVIL, GŘ 3, 28 May 1930. [2] J. Petráň–V. Fuchs, p. 147.
[3] PA–ZVIL, GŘ 3, 21 May 1920; also V. Jíša–A. Vaněk, p. 124. This occurred at the same time as Schneider gained participation in the Mining and Metallurgic Co. See Chapter 3 (1), pp. 99–103.

and whether the agreed division of markets between the Schneider Works in France and the Škoda-Works in Plzeň was being adhered to.[1] The approval of the Paris central management was required for the execution of large orders. The French representatives also performed an important intelligence role, by sending reports to Paris on the economic and political situation in Czechoslovakia and drawing conclusions for the attitude to be taken by the Škoda-Works. Everything was then carefully sifted and commented upon in Paris. On the basis of information of this sort from all its subsidiaries, Schneider in Paris sent instructions, enquiries and orders to their representatives in Czechoslovakia.[2]

A network of Schneider representatives drew the Škoda-Works into the European Schneider combine: their names appear among the directors of the Škoda-Works and their tasks originated from their positions in the firm of Schneider et Cie. The head of the company, Eugène Schneider, the general director of the Schneider Iron Works in France, Victor Champigneul, and directors Jules Aubrun, de Saint-Sauveur and André Vicaire, formed the connection with the central works in France; the most important capital and commercial link was through the director-general of Schneider's holding company L'Union Européenne, Colonel Ernest Weyl and Aimée Lepercq; relations with the Mining and Metallurgic Co. in Těšín were conducted through the director-general of the Škoda-Works, Ch. Rochette, and the leading board member of the Mining and Metallurgic Co., A. Lepercq, together with two others, J. Chanzy and P. Crossé-Brissac. All these men were representatives of the executive organs of the Schneider concern

[1] PA–ZVIL, Agenda Rochette, including urgent requests for more detailed information [Rapport sommaire sur la marche des Usines Skoda; Rapport sur l'exécution des prescriptions de la lettre No. 4743 du 22, Octobre 1922, etc.] The Paris central office kept a close watch on compliance with the Entente d'Artillerie du 27 Mai 1922 and on the agreement not to supply arms to the Soviet Union.

[2] These conclusions are derived from voluminous material in the Agenda Rochette and also from the correspondence and reports for the L'Union Européenne in the works archives of the Škoda-Works in Plzeň. I believe that V. Jíša and A. Vaněk's view that Christophe Rochette took sides with Czechoslovakia against Schneider emanates from a myth which, perhaps intentionally, circulated in Plzeň. Rochette's agenda leaves no doubt that from the 1920s to 1938 his services were subordinated to the Paris central management. Cf. V. Jíša–A. Vaněk, p. 136.

and directors of its subsidiaries, first in Czechoslovakia and then in other parts of Southeast Europe.

The Škoda-Works could pursue an independent policy only as long as it did not clash with the interests of the main shareholder. In the interests of Schneider, areas of production and markets were delimited by the Artillery Agreement concluded in 1922 and renewed in 1937,[1] by the Sugar-Refinery Agreement, which was followed by agreements on markets for the equipment of breweries and distilleries, and by the General Convention Schneider–Škoda in 1922.[2] In these agreements the French side generally protected its markets in France and the French Colonial Empire and allocated markets in precisely defined spheres to the Škoda-Works. These were mainly in Eastern Europe, from Finland to Yugoslavia, in some Latin-American countries (Colombia, Uruguay), in Turkey and in Iran. In addition, the Škoda-Works were partners in numerous cartel agreements, which further restricted their export activities and by which they were invariably barred from French colonial markets.[3] Exports to the Soviet Union which could be classified as arms were strictly prohibited.[4] One of the biggest and probably most important interventions of the French investor in the structure of the Škoda-Works took place when the heavy artillery shop was dismantled, together with the large tube rolling mill whose unique machinery was transferred to the Schneider Works in France.[5] In considering the policy of the Schneider concern in the Škoda-Works one cannot avoid the impression – although no absolute and direct evidence can be cited – that the diversification of products which prevented thorough technical reconstruction and rationalization[6] was deliberately preserved and encouraged by the French directors.

Among the bans imposed by the French concern on the

[1] Ibid., p. 239.

[2] PA–ZVIL, Plzeň, Kartely.

[3] For details see Chapter 4 (2).

[4] L'Union Européenne repeatedly asked Rochette to report whether the prohibition was strictly observed. PA–ZVIL, GŘ 267 – Agenda Rochette.

[5] V. Jíša–A. Vaněk, p. 125. A Sudeten German confidant of the German Ministry of Interior in ČSR confirmed with satisfaction eye-witness reports of the transport of the largest machines from Plzeň to France. DZAP–RMdI, 5819, Report of 12 May 1924.

[6] Due to the great variety of products, standardized machines and automated conveyor belts could only rarely be installed in the Škoda-Works. Cf. V. Jíša–A. Vaněk, p. 187.

Škoda-Works was an embargo on imports of certain raw materials and semi-finished goods from Germany, because the Paris head-office reserved deliveries of these for itself.[1] During the whole period of French participation Schneider's central management was particularly sensitive about German competition and here its interests coincided with those of the Czech industrialists. Every director's report on the Škoda-Works comments carefully on the growth of German competition, especially from 1926 onwards, when 'again our most dangerous competitor on the world market raises his head'.[2] In 1935 the director's report warns that 'especially in recent times German industry, supported extraordinarily effectively by its government, is getting ready for a fierce struggle for which we must mobilize all our strength'.[3] The lists of the largest competitors of the Škoda-Works which were compiled by the commercial management between 1934 and 1938 were headed by German firms, and Friedrich Krupp of Essen was always at the top.[4] It became increasingly clear that Czechoslovakia and Southeast Europe were becoming an area of intense competition between France and Germany, and in this struggle influential Czech industrialists relied on their more powerful French partners.

French capital participation meant limits to the outlets for Škoda commodities on the one hand, but on the other hand it also brought important orders to the Škoda-Works, especially at the beginning of the 1920s, when the Czechoslovak works shared in deliveries to the war-damaged areas of Northern France.[5] In 1923 they benefited from the French occupation of the Ruhr and not only gained orders that would otherwise have been fulfilled by German works,[6] but were also able to make deliveries directly to Germany.[7] In the 1930s Schneider's Paris bank provided loans to Eastern European and South American

[1] On controversial issues the director-general of L'Union Européenne, Lepercq, asked Rochette for detailed information. As late as 1936 Rochette wrote that the Škoda-Works were trying to exclude German deliveries wherever possible. PA–ZVIL, Plzeň, Agenda Rochette.

[2] PA–ZVIL, Plzeň, GŘ 3 – 14 April 1926; similarly in all annual reports.

[3] Ibid., 9 December 1935.

[4] Cf. PA–ZVIL, Plzeň, GŘ 287.

[5] V. Jíša–A. Vaněk, p. 219.

[6] PA–ZVIL, Plzeň, GŘ 2, Report on the Situation in the Works, 13 December 1923.

[7] Cf. 'Zehn Jahre Friedensarbeit der Škodawerke, Geschäftsentwicklung und Absatzgebiete 1918–28', *Prager Presse*, Sonderbeilage (1928).

countries to enable them to pay for their arms orders from the Škoda-Works. Schneider and Škoda divided the execution of these orders between them according to the 1922 Convention.[1]

As a rule, however, the French shareholder did not provide the main credit requirements for the Škoda-Works, which needed extensive financial means to cover arms deliveries on longterm credits, mainly to the countries of the 'cordon sanitaire'.[2] With the agreement of the French directors, the management of the Škoda-Works in 1922 began to negotiate a loan in London on terms similar to those obtained for the Czechoslovak government loan of the same year; this loan was specifically to finance Romanian orders for armaments.[3] The Bank of England and the National Provincial Bank issued the Škoda loan for £1,000,000 in 1923 at 92 % with a rate of interest of 8 %.[4] After its conversion in 1926 the loan rose to £2,500,000 and was also used to cover the Yugoslav orders at the Škoda-Works.[5] In 1930 the Škoda-Works received further Romanian orders to the value of a milliard Czechoslovak Crowns and had to try to negotiate an increase of the British loan to £5,000,000. However, the British creditors were prepared only to accept a conversion of the loan at its existing level of £2,500,000. A French financial group was therefore formed, consisting of the foremost Paris banks, which remitted the remaining part of the loan, i.e. another £2,500,000.[6] The Škoda-Works were thus burdened with large foreign loans and each conversion was almost fully swallowed up by paying off old debts, commission, amortization and interest payments. In 1935 Škoda's indebtedness in Britain increased by two further loans of £250,000 each, one provided by Unilever and the other by Martin's Bank Ltd in London.[7]

In contrast with French direct investment, the British investment in the form of longterm loans influenced neither the production programme nor the commercial management of the Škoda-Works. Yet it could not but influence the financing of the

1 PA-ZVIL, Agenda Rochette.
2 V. Jíša–A. Vaněk, p. 222; also PA-ZVIL, GŘ 267, Confidential Report to the French Secretariat.
3 PA-ZVIL, GŘ 2, Protocol of the meeting of the board of directors, 17 July 1922.
4 Ibid., Extraordinary meeting of the board of directors, 16 October 1923.
5 PA-ZVIL, GŘ 143.
6 PA-ZVIL, GŘ 3, Protocol of extraordinary meeting of the board of directors.
7 Ibid., 4 July 1935; also GŘ 267, Engagements Škoda.

works. The British creditor's collateral was all the plants' immovable assets,[1] and this acted as an effective incentive towards regular amortization and interest payments. Thus after 1923 a considerable part of the Škoda-Works' income flowed into British banks and after 1930 French banks also shared in this income. The inflow of longterm loans from Western Europe, which increased in 1930 and 1935, does not support the view widely held among Czechoslovak economic historians, that a substantial flight of foreign capital from Czechoslovakia took place long before Munich.

Foreign longterm investment remained, and direct capital investment as well as loans brought profitable returns. From a confidential report of 1934 on the Škoda-Works for the French Secretariat of the Schneider concern, an indication can be gained of the proportional amounts of dividends and royalties on the one side, and interest payments to foreign creditors on the other. While dividends and royalties amounted to Kč 30 million, interest on foreign loans in 1934 reached Kč 67.4 million.[2] From this relationship no far-reaching conclusions can be drawn about the size of profits and controlling influences, because dividends are not a true measure of profits, but it gives an idea of the size of the commitments arising from foreign loans. Within the Schneider concern there were many possibilities for transferring the Škoda-Works' profits into various channels, without necessarily showing them in the ordinary profit and loss accounts.

Our analysis of the role of the Škoda-Works in the Czechoslovak engineering industry and their capital relationships before 1938 shows that French capital exerted a decisive influence on the Škoda-Works between 1919 and 1938. Three months after the Munich Agreement – in December 1938 – Schneider's holding company, L'Union Européenne, decided to sell its participation on fairly favourable terms to a consortium of Czech banks, along with the Armaments Works in Brno.[3] However, this was only a transitory solution, because the

[1] PA–ZVIL, GŘ 3. The whole complex of British loans was finally settled after the Second World War. Cf. Treaty Series No. 32 (1959), Cmd. 1009 (London, 1960).

[2] PA–ZVIL, GŘ 267, French report 1934.

[3] PA–ZVIL, GŘ 13; ASÚS–cizí účasti–Dobrozdání No. 11. For the further development of the participation and its transfer into German hands see V. Král, II, p. 73.

Czech financial position was not strong enough to resist German pressure for long without outside assistance. As a result of the political upheavals after Munich and in early 1939, changes in the balance of power created conditions in Central and Southeastern Europe which favoured the integration of the Škoda-Works into the sphere of influence of the German Reich. Before Munich the Škoda-Works and their subsidiaries represented one of the focal points of French penetration into Southeast Europe. In addition, it is clear that the Škoda-Works' credit ties with Anglo-French banks were much stronger than with domestic bankers. Although Czech capital participated profitably in all transactions, it did so in the role of a subordinate partner.

As foreign capital predominated in the largest engineering concern in Czechoslovakia, it also influenced the whole engineering industry in the country. Foreign capital also participated in other engineering firms, either directly or through banks, as can be seen from the diagrams showing investments of Czechoslovak joint-stock banks in industry (viz. Tables 4 to 8, Chapter 6 (1), but no other foreign investment in the Czechoslovak engineering industry could seriously challenge the all-pervading influence of French capital in this area of production.

The electrical industry

The influence of foreign investment in the Škoda-Works not only made itself felt in the mechanical engineering industry but also affected the electrical industry. The Škoda-Works developed their production in this field after 1918 and acquired a number of subsidiary electrical engineering plants. This fact somewhat distorts the statistics of foreign investment in the electrical industry given in Table 5, as they do not include the Škoda-Works. It was not possible to estimate the capital value of the electrical production of the Škoda-Works or to give an acceptable quantitative estimate of the role it played in total investment. However, the Škoda-Works provided significant competition for domestic and foreign producers in this branch of industry. As foreign groups, especially German and Swiss concerns, competed strongly with each other in Czechoslovakia,

Table 5. *Territorial distribution of direct longterm foreign investments in the electrical industry of Czechoslovakia, 31 December 1937*

Country of origin of investment	Nominal value in 1,000 Kč	Percentage of total foreign investment
Germany	44,376	33.3
Switzerland	22,764	17.1
Belgium	16,271	12.2
Great Britain	14,409	10.8
Holland	11,400	8.5
U.S.A.	7,420	5.6
France	6,701	5.1
Sweden	6,240	4.7
Austria	3,623	2.7
Total	133,204	100.0

they could not reconcile themselves to the competitive power of the Škoda-Works in the electrical industry.[1] Here, as in other industries, French and German interests clashed on Czechoslovak territory. On the domestic market competition was particularly fierce between the electrical products of the Škoda-Works and the ČKD. A closer investigation of the competition between these concerns shows that it emanated basically from the competitive efforts of two American multinational combines, which wanted to divide the European spheres of influence between themselves. One connection can be traced from a grouping round the General Electric Co. in the U.S.A., through the Als Thom Company in France and the Allgemeine Elektrizitätsgesellschaft in Germany to the firms of Křižík-Chaudoir in Prague and the Škoda-Works in Plzeň. The other grouping leads from the Westinghouse Electric Company in the U.S.A. through Siemens and Halske in Germany to the companies controlled by Siemens in Czechoslovakia (Elektrotechna a.s. pro slaboproudou techniku [Elektrotechna Company for Low-tension Techniques], Praha; Siemens a.s. pro výrobu elektrických zařízení [Siemens Company for the Production of Electrical Equipment], Praha; Siemens, technický průmysl a.s. [Siemens, Technical Industry Company], Praha) and to the ČKD in

[1] PA-ZVIL, GŘ 3, Director's Reports 5 June 1928 and 21 January 1929.

Prague.[1] The Cartel Agreement of 1935 brought about a temporary truce, but the groupings remained unchanged.

The connection between ČKD and Westinghouse Electric began in 1922 with licensing agreements for electrical products,[2] by which ČKD subordinated its production to the American concern's specifications. It is a well-known fact that the owner of patents consolidates and extends his influence through licensing conditions which affect not only technology but also output, export markets and other economic spheres.[3] Seen in this light, the claim of ČKD's general management to exclusively Czech national control appears highly dubious. Equally doubtful is the repeated assertion of leading figures of the ČKD that their profits never left the country, when their license payments constituted a regular flow to the U.S.A.

The competitive struggle between the Škoda-Works and the ČKD in the electrical industry also reveals the complicated international relations of big business. Behind most of the German capital participation in Czechoslovak electrical firms there was American investment, forming part of a network of investments, cartels and patents through which large American firms divided the world market among themselves. Czechoslovak business can be found on both sides of the competitive struggle. However, no clearcut line can be drawn between the contending Czechoslovak groups and they cannot be divided conveniently between the agrarian bourgeoisie and the financial oligarchy grouped around the Živnostenská Bank. For instance, Křižík-Chaudoir and the Škoda-Works had close capital ties with the Anglo-Czechoslovak and Prague Credit Bank, which in Czechoslovak historiography is generally considered to be an instrument of agrarian capital.[4] Siemens with its investments in Czechoslovakia was in the other camp, but the Siemens interests belonged to the sphere of the Agrarian Bank. On their side, then, we find ČKD representing an essential part of the concern of the Živnostenská Bank. An objective analysis shows much more complicated and variable relations, which cannot

[1] Cf. correspondence between L'Union Européenne Industrielle et Financière and the Škoda-Works. Memoranda for director-general Rochette. PA–ZVIL, Agenda Rochette from 1931 onwards.

[2] J. Petráň–V. Fuchs, p. 105.

[3] Cf. TNEC, Final Report of the Executive Secretary, p. 20.

[4] R. Olšovský *et al.*, *Přehled hospodářského vývoje*, p. 244; also V. Král, II, p. 342.

be fitted into a preconceived framework, in which one part of the Czechoslovak bourgeoisie is the ally of the Western bourgeoisie and the other of the German bourgeoisie.

With the limitations discussed above, I offer my estimate of foreign direct investment in the electrical industry of Czechoslovakia up to 31 December 1937. More than half of all registered companies contained foreign investments, which amounted to 26 % of the total joint-stock capital in the industry. In the 26 companies with foreign investment 52 % of total capital was found to be in foreign hands. The countries of origin of foreign investment in the Czechoslovak electrical industry are shown in Table 5.[1]

The largest share was invested by German companies closely associated with American concerns. A significant role was played by the participation of Siemens in Telegrafia, továrna na telegrafy a telefony (Telegrafia, Telegraph- and Telephone Factory) which belonged in the Agrarian Bank combine. But 51 % of Telegrafia's joint-stock capital was held by the International Standard Electric Corporation in New York, with a direct participation of 32.8 % and another 18. 2 % through its Berlin subsidiary, the Standard Elektrizitäts-Gesellschaft A.G.[2] The Berlin companies, Siemens & Halske and Osram, were the biggest German shareholders in the Czechoslovak electrical industry.

A relatively large proportion of the Swiss capital was held by the Schweizerische Gesellschaft für elektrische Industrie, with a 33 % participation in the Severočeské elektrárny (North-Bohemian Electric Power Works) in Podmokly, and by the well-known concern Brown Boveri et Cie., which controlled its own works in Czechoslovakia. The Belgian investment came from the Société Electricité de Transporte de l'Europe Centrale S.A. in Brussels, which in turn was associated with the Česká eskomptní banka (Czech Escompte Bank). The Dutch participation in companies belonging to Philips was associated with the Živnostenská Bank. The boards of directors of the companies in which foreign capital was invested reflected this fact by their

[1] Excerpt from Table IV, Chapter 2/1.

[2] ASÚS – cizí účasti, Dobrozdání No. 24. The participation of the Czechoslovak state cited in *Compass, Čechoslovakei* (1938), 1089, was considerably smaller and was really in the hands of the Agrarian Bank.

international composition, although in each case Czech members occupied 50 % of the places, as was required by company law. There can, however, be no doubt about the decisive role of the influential mother companies in Brussels and the Dutch centre of the great Philips concern in Eindhoven.

All the important electrical companies in Czechoslovakia thus contained foreign investment. In this branch of industry, also, the Central European area became an area of competition for large industrial concerns with world-wide interests. At the same time, this situation was reflected in far-reaching international cartel agreements, which drew the whole Czechoslovak electrical industry into their hierarchical structure.

2 International cartels in the mechanical engineering and electrical industry in the Czechoslovak Republic

Most of the output of the mechanical and electrical engineering industry was concentrated in a very limited number of large concerns, of which the Škoda-Works were the most important. Although there were strong tendencies towards monopoly by concentration and mergers, the process of cartelization was somewhat slower than in the iron, steel and chemical industries. This resulted from the great variety of products and diversity of technological methods in production in the large works, together with the existence of a significant number of medium and small-scale firms which, as a rule, specialized in certain products in order to be able to compete with the powerful concerns in the industry. For this reason no single unified cartel organization acted as a spokesman for the whole Czechoslovak engineering industry in international cartels, as was the case in the iron and steel industry (viz. Chapter 3). Specified groups of works or an influential company participated as the Czechoslovak representative in international cartel agreements, depending on which firm effectively controlled a certain product or products on the domestic market.

The engineering industry in Czechoslovakia was perceptibly affected by the steel cartel's complete domination of the home market in iron, steel and semi-finished products, and could purchase these only on terms and at prices determined by the United Czechoslovak Iron Works.

Engineering works could only get certain stipulated discounts when purchasing material for the manufacture of export goods which the member of the steel cartel classified as its own 'indirect export'. Those engineering works which were subsidiaries of the large concerns in the mining and metallurgical industry were in a relatively more favourable situation, because cartel conditions allowed them to obtain supplies from their mother companies outside the quota system. Thus the whole raw material basis for the engineering industry was strongly cartelized before it passed into the metal-working stage (particularly crude iron and steel, rolled products, copper, cables, coal, coke and electricity).[1]

Throughout the life of the pre-Munich Czechoslovak Republic the Škoda-Works, as the leading engineering concern, made attempts to cartelize the domestic engineering industry. However it was not until 1935, after a far-reaching settlement between the Českomoravská-Kolben-Daněk a.s. and the Škoda-Works had been reached, that an engineering cartel arose which comprised the most important producers of armaments, mechanical and electrical engineering products and which practically controlled the domestic market.

This certainly does not mean that cartelization in the Czechoslovak engineering industry was insignificant before 1935. On the contrary, during the world economic crisis national cartels arose which controlled key areas of the engineering industry or important mechanical or electrical engineering products. In most cases a vital semi-finished engineering product or an essential part of a larger construction – produced by one of the large works – was cartelized and the company therefore came to dominate the cartel organization. Table 1 gives a survey of cartel organizations in the metal-working industry of Czechoslovakia which were members of international cartels before 1938. In it are listed only the international agreements affecting those groups of Czechoslovak firms which were organized in domestic cartel associations. Nevertheless, it clearly emerges that international cartels affected products which were crucially

[1] Cf. PA–ZVIL–GŘ 287. The introductory part of this chapter deals with the relationships between the metallurgical and the engineering industry.

Table 1. *Participation of the Czechoslovak engineering industry in international cartels before 1938**

Czechoslovak cartel			
Domestic cartel	Czechoslovak cartel members	International cartel partners	Character of car
Accounting office for *tyres, axles and gear wheelsets*, Prague	Škoda-Works, Prague; Vítkovice Mining and Foundry Works, Ostrava	Schoeller-Bleckmann Stahlwerke A.-G., Vienna; Deutscher Lokomotiv-Radsatz-Verband	Allocation of forei trade, price cartel
Evidence Bureau for *forged pieces*, Prague	Škoda-Works; Vítkovice Mining and Foundry Works	Schoeller-Bleckmann Stahlwerke A.-G., Vienna; Schmiedestück-Vereinigung für den europäischen Kontinent, Essen	Allocation of expo
Association of Czechoslovak producers of *malleable tube fittings* and *grey cast iron straight-way and discharge cocks*, Prague	Žandov Ironworks; Janovice Ironworks; Voigtmann & Sons; Moravian Iron and Steelworks, Olomouc-Řepčín	Fittingsverband, Düsseldorf	Price cartel; divisi Czechoslovak ma
Evidence Bureau of screw mills for polished products, Prague	5 Czechoslovak works subordinated to Škoda-Works	1 Yugoslav, 5 Polish, 4 Hungarian and 4 Austrian works	Price and allocatio cartel concerning *polished screws*
Helika, Sales Bureau for screws, Prague	9 Czechoslovak works subordinated to PŽS and VHHT	1 Yugoslav, 5 Hungarian, 11 Polish and 5 Austrian works – Screw Rivet Cartel	Mutual market pr tection and expor quota allocation concerning *screws*
VRUT, selling agency for *wood screws*, Prague	Syndicalization of Czechoslovak firms by government decree 1935	Wood Screw Syndicate (Austrian, British, Polish, Hungarian and German works)	Allocation and pri cartel
Central Bureau of Czechoslovak *wire and wire nail* manufacturers, Prague	17 works subordinated to BHS	Verband österreichischer Draht- und Drahtstiftenwerke (13 factories)	Protection of dom market
Czechoslovak group of crude zinc producers	Brothers Dudek, Řetenice; Weinmannwerke, Teplice-Šanov	Internationales Zinksyndikat	Allocation of *crude* output quota
Czechoslovak group of zinc plate producers	Metal Rolling Mills, Přívoz; Bros. Dudek; Franke & Scholz, Rymařov; Czechoslovak Metal Works, Varnsdorf	Entente internationale des lamineurs de zinc, Liége	Allocation of expo quotas on world market of *zinc sh*
Czechoslovak–Hungarian group of rolled zinc products	Metal Rolling Mills, Přívoz; (Horgany-hengermü R.T., Vác)	Zinkwalzwerksverband, Berlin	Division of export markets and quot allocations of *roll zinc products*
Association of Copper and Brass Works in Czechoslovakia, Prague	8 Czechoslovak works including BHS; Křzík-Chaudoir; Czechoslovak Armament Works, Brno	Zentralverband der deutschen Metallwalzwerks- und Hüttenindustrie E.W., Berlin	Price cartel concer *copper and brass s finished materials*
Evidence Bureau for Cables, Prague	Kablo, Prague; Fr. Křížík, Prague; Cable Factory, Bratislava	International Cable Development Corporation, Vaduz	Allocation of expo quotas for *high- a low-voltage cables*
Czechoslovak group of bulb manufacturers	Elektra, Prague; Osram, Prague	Phoebus, S.A., Genève	Syndicate (*bulbs*)
Czechoslovak automobile works	ŠZ, ČKD, Ringhoffer-Tatra	Chambre Syndicale des Constructions d'Automobiles, Paris	Customs and alloc of output agreem concerning *autom*

* Compiled from material in SÚA–KR, PA–ŠZ, Praha-Legal Department and PA–VIL, Plzeň-Kartely
Abbreviations: PŽS = Prague Iron Company, Prague; VHHT = Vítkovice Mining and Foundry W Ostrava; BHS = Mining and Metallurgic Company; ČKD = Czech-Moravian Kolben-Daněk, Pr IWECO = International Wire Export Company.
Products which were the subject of international cartels are indicated by italics.

important to engineering production and could thus indirectly influence supply conditions and prices of a large range of products in the industry.

The Czechoslovak mechanical engineering industry as a partner in international cartels of railway products

Agreements between iron and steel and engineering works about prices and markets of railway products are among the oldest existing international cartels. The International Rail-makers' Association founded in 1884 has been mentioned in another context (p. 154). Also in the 1880s a cartel was established in Cisleithania which was to control the production, prices and markets of tyres for locomotives, tenders and wagons.[1] The area of cartelization of railway products in Austria–Hungary was expanded in 1902, when Austrian iron and engineering works drew the Hungarian works into a wider agreement about the division of output quotas and markets for tyres, wheels, gear wheelsets, and axles for locomotives, railway wagons and tenders.[2] About half the total quotas fixed by the cartel were as a rule allocated to the large works situated in the Czech Lands.[3] When the Škoda-Works in Plzeň joined the Austro-Hungarian cartel Tyres- und Achsenverband and Vereinigte Räderwerke on 21 April 1910, this relationship was

[1] Cf. J. Purš, 'Použití parních strojů v průmyslu v českých zemích v období do nástupu imperialismu' (The employment of steam engines in industry in the Czech Lands in the period before the rise of imperialism), *ČSČH*, III, 3 (1955), Table XXXVI, 443.

[2] Cf. Cartel Agreements in PA–ŠZ, Praha – právní oddělení (legal department), unnumbered material.

[3] In the cartel agreement on railway tyres valid from 1 January 1902 to 30 June 1912 the quotas were divided in the following proportions: Österreichische Alpine Montangesellschaft, 28.1 %; Ternitzer Stahl- und Eisenwerke von Schoeller & Co., Wien, 29.2 %; Witkowitzer Bergbau- und Eisenhüttengesellschaft, Ostrau, 30.1 %; Erzherzögliche Eisenwerke in Teschen, 12.6 %. The works of the Poldihütte discontinued their production of tyres for an annual compensation payment of Kč 25,000.

In the cartel agreement concerning railway axles valid from 1 January 1902 to 30 June 1912 the quotas were divided in the following proportions: Österreichische Alpine Montangesellschaft, 24.0 %; Ternitzer Stahl- und Eisenwerke von Schoeller & Co., Wien, 24.6 %; Erzherzögliche Eisenwerke in Teschen, 3.4 %; Witkowitzer Bergbau- und Eisenhüttengesellschaft, Ostrau, 28.0 %; Poldihütte, Kladno, 20.0 %. PA–ŠZ, Praha – právní oddělení, unnumbered material.

further strengthened by the addition of the works situated in Czech territory. On the basis of the competitive struggle which preceded this cartel agreement the Škoda-Works gained 23.5 % of the total Austro-Hungarian quota.[1] At the end of the same year Austro-Hungarian works producing wheelsets concluded an agreement with the German cartel, the Auslands-Radsatz Gemeinschaft in Düsseldorf, about deliveries for indirect exports[2] thus entering the international cartel – as in other fields of production – within the German sphere of influence.

During 1918 almost all the cartels of the Central Powers disintegrated, including those for railway products. After the substantial territorial changes resulting from the First World War and with the rise of new customs barriers, the engineering works which were formerly tied to Austro-Hungarian cartel agreements competed openly with each other for a greater share of the Central and Southeast European markets. Producers of railway materials in particular strove to obtain orders from the more backward regions of the former Habsburg Monarchy, where it was expected that the railway network would be extended. At the same time, however, they tried to prevent each other from entering the markets of their own newly established states, regarding these as their own independent customs territories. The technically more advanced and economically stronger iron and engineering works on Czech territory had already taken up a leading position in the pre-war Austro-Hungarian cartels, but they had then belonged almost entirely to the Austro-German capital sphere, from which they extricated themselves after 1918. Their new political and economic involvement with the victorious powers of the Entente strengthened their hand in relation to the Austrian works and

[1] Vertrag des Tyres- und Achsenverbandes (Achsenwerke: Österreichische Alpine Montangesellschaft; Österreichische Bergwerks- und Hüttengesellschaft in Teschen; Ternitzer Stahl- und Eisenwerke von Schoeller & Co., Wien und Witkowitzer Bergbau- und Eisenhüttengesellschaft in Ostrau; zusammen 76.5 %; Škodawerke in Pilsen 23.5 %) gültig vom 21 April 1910 bis 31 Dezember 1917. At the same time the Škoda-Works joined the cartel Vereinigte Räderwerke (Österreichische Alpine Montangesellschaft; Ternitzer Stahl- und Eisenwerke von Schoeller & Co., Wien; Witkowitzer Bergbau- und Eisenhüttengesellschaft; Ungarische Werke der österreich-ungarischen Staatseisenbahngesellschaft). PA–ŠZ, Praha – právní oddělení, unnumbered material.

[2] Übereinkommen der österreich-ungarischen Räderpaar-Werke mit der Auslands-Radsatz Gemeinschaft in Düsseldorf ddo. 7. Dezember 1910 getroffen. PA–ŠZ, Praha – právní oddělení, unnumbered material.

during the increased competition of 1918–20 they obtained a much more favourable position from which to negotiate about new cartel agreements on railway products. As in other industries, the big engineering works preferred contractual understandings to cut-throat competition. Consequently, in these agreements the changing balance of forces found a fairly reliable expression, whether they concerned the position of individual firms in a national cartel or of whole national industries in international cartels.

The first post-war cartel between Austrian and Czechoslovak producers of wagon and locomotive parts was established at the end of 1920. It contained a system of selling quotas on the respective home markets of the participants and on the markets of the Successor States. In this way the cartel regulated mutual relations in the territory of the former Habsburg Monarchy. In order to provide a basis for comparing the changing relationships in subsequent cartel agreements Table 2 gives the proportionate quotas in the cartel of 8 December 1920.[1]

From Table 2 it is apparent that the two largest Czechoslovak combines, the Vítkovice Mining and Foundry Works and the Škoda-Works, dominated the home market almost completely, secured for themselves 10–30 % of the Austrian market and obtained a majority share of the markets of the Successor States, i.e. 60–70 %. The Vítkovice concern gained the largest quota and its proportionate share in the markets of the former Austro-Hungarian area rose, compared with its quotas in the pre-war cartel.[2] On the other hand the Škoda-Works' percentage share of the domestic Czechoslovak market rose considerably (from 23.5 % to 45 % of the market for gear wheelsets and tyres, and from 23.5 % to 32.808 % of axles), but remained the same on the markets of the Successor States – i.e. 23.5 % – as in the pre-war cartels. In subsequent years the Škoda-Works succeeded in bringing about a revision of the quota system in its favour. However, at the beginning of the 1920s the proportionate shares in the Central and Southeast European markets of Austrian and Czechoslovak producers corresponded roughly

Compiled from 'Ujednání ohledně kol a soukolí' (Agreement concerning wheels and axles) of 8 December 1920. PA–ŠZ, Praha, obchodní oddělení (commercial department), unnumbered material.

[2] Cf. percentages given in footnotes on pages 224–5 with those in Table 2.

Table 2. *Cartel agreement between the Czechoslovak and Austrian manufacturers of wheels, wheelsets, axles and tyres for locomotives, tenders and wagons, concluded 8 December 1920 (valid from 1 January 1920 to 31 December 1922)*

(*a*) Division of output quotas of wheels and wheelsets in percentages

Works	On Czechoslovak market	On Austrian market	On markets of successor states
ČSR:			
VHHT	55	5·5	Not ascertained
ŠZ	45	4·5	
Austria:			
Ternitz	—	90	

(*b*) Division of output quotas of tyres in percentages

Works	On Czechoslovak market	On Austrian market	On markets of successor states
ČSR:			
VHHT	55	16.5	40.426
ŠZ	45	13·5	23·5
Austria:			
Ternitz	—	70	36.074

(*c*) Division of output quotas of axles in percentages

Works	On Czechoslovak market	On Austrian market	On markets of successor states
ČSR:			
VHHT	47·192	14.158	33·803
ŠZ	32.808	9.842	23·5
Poldi	20	6	15·3
Austria:			
Ternitz	—	70	27·397

Abbreviations: VHHT = Vítkovice Mining and Foundry Works, Ostrava; ŠZ = Škoda-Works, Plzeň; Poldi = Poldina huť, Kladno; Ternitz = Ternitzer Stahl- und Eisenwerke von Schoeller & Co., Vienna.

to their relative economic strength. Together they formed a group opposing German competition and were able to negotiate an agreement with the German producers of railway materials.

At that time the German iron and steel and engineering industries had not yet been fully cartelized. Alongside strongly competitive and centralized groups of companies there existed very strong individual outsiders. This is reflected in the cartels of 1921, concluded after fairly complicated negotiations between Czechoslovak and Austrian works on the one hand, and German works on the other. The Czechoslovak, Austrian and German representatives of the largest engineering works undertook to regulate the European market for railway components and signed three cartel agreements in which the Czechoslovak–Austrian works acted as one united Group against two groups of German works. The strongest group was organized in the cartel company Deutsche Stahlgemeinschaft G.m.b.H., Essen-Ruhr. The Czechoslovak–Austrian group, consisting of the works listed in Table 2, concluded the so-called Territorial-Abkommen and the Kontinental-Abkommen agreements with this group on the allocation of orders over and above the production of components for use in their own works for the construction of locomotives, tenders and wagons.[1]

The Territorial-Abkommen defined the regions in which each contracting party had exclusive rights of access to the market without competitive intervention from the other party. Thus the Czechoslovak–Austrian Group was allotted the markets of Czechoslovakia, Austria, Hungary and Yugoslavia and 60 % of the Polish market. Against this the German works in the Deutsche Stahlgemeinschaft were given exclusive rights on the markets of Germany, Luxemburg and Danzig and were entitled to 40 % of the Polish market. It was also agreed that whenever a cartel partner could not cover his own demand he would let the other partners have his orders. This condition gave rise to a dispute between the German and Czechoslovak representatives at a meeting in Berlin in 1923, when Director Spitzer of the Vítkovice Iron Works reproached the Stahlgemeinschaft with having, in contravention of their contract, given preference to German outsiders in allocating orders which the Stahlgemeinschaft could not fulfil because of the French occupation of the Ruhr. An agreement to extend their previous contract was reached only after the Stahlgemeinschaft undertook to transfer the orders to the Czechoslovak–Austrian cartel-partners.[2]

[1] Cf. Protocols, correspondence and text of agreements in PA–ŠZ, Praha – obchodní oddělení, unnumbered material.

[2] Cf. Aktennotiz über Aussprache in Berlin, 20 April 1923, Ibid.

The Kontinental-Abkommen required all incoming orders outside the scope of the Territorial-Abkommen to be directed to the central office of the cartel (the Geschäftsstelle) in Essen, where allocation to individual partners as well as conditions of delivery and prices were to be decided. The Geschäftsstelle was also entrusted with keeping the accounts of the cartel and producing a quarterly balance sheet for the sales of tyres, axles, carrying axles and gear wheelsets in all areas of Europe except those coming under the Territorial-Abkommen. Within the Kontinental-Abkommen the Czechoslovak–Austrian Group was to refrain entirely from selling to Holland and had to undertake generally not to sell its products in the Scandinavian countries, Switzerland and Finland, unless it was executing an isolated order. On the other hand, all members of the cartel were to have equal access to the market of Romania. On all European markets the minimum prices of the German partners were to be observed by the Czechoslovak–Austrian works. Originally, the Stahlgemeinschaft wanted to fix these prices single-handed, but the Czechoslovak negotiators insisted that prices should be determined only after consultation with the Czechoslovak–Austrian Group.[1]

In essence, the endeavours of the Czechoslovak producers and their Austrian business partners[2] were directed towards ensuring their traditional access to the markets of the former Habsburg Monarchy, by entering into cartel agreements with the Deutsche Stahlgemeinschaft. The conditions of the Territorial-Abkommen show that their plans met with only partial success in the Southeast European area and their access to other European markets was considerably curtailed by the cartel conditions enforced by their German competitors. In addition to this another large German combine demanded a share of the markets which, according to the Territorial-Abkommen with the Stahlgemeinschaft, were to be the exclusive outlet for

[1] Cf. Kontinental-Abkommen für Radsätze und Radsatzteile (Radreifen, Achsen und Radkörper) zwischen der Deutschen Stahlgemeinschaft G.m.b.H., Essen-Ruhr und den tschechoslowakisch-österreischischen Werken, 15 February 1921, PA–ŠZ, Praha - obchodní oddělení, unnumbered material.

[2] The decisive voice was that of the Czechoslovak engineering industry. The formal conditions of the Czechoslovak–Austrian agreement concerning wheels, tyres and gear wheelsets of 8 December 1920 also show a clear majority of votes on the Czechoslovak side over the Austrian firms. Ibid.

Czechoslovak–Austrian products. This claim was put forward by the concern of Otto Wolff of Cologne which until 1918 had been a business partner of the Austro-Hungarian works and which after 1918 did not belong to the German Stahlgemeinschaft. In a separate agreement, concluded on the same day as the one with the Stahlgemeinschaft, the Czechoslovak–Austrian Group regulated its relationship with the firm of Otto Wolff on the markets of Czechoslovakia, Austria, Hungary, Yugoslavia and Poland.[1] Accordingly, the Czechoslovak home market remained intact in the hands of the Czechoslovak works, and the Otto Wolff Group was to refrain from offering or supplying their products to the ČSR. On the Austrian market, however, it was to obtain a 5 % share of the total demand. The same proportion was by tacit understanding to be allotted to Otto Wolff in Hungary and Yugoslavia, although the written agreement entitled the German supplier to deliver up to 40 % of the Hungarian and Yugoslav consumption.[2] At the same time the Otto Wolff Group claimed a proportion of the Polish market, where the Czechoslovak–Austrian Group had obtained 60 % in their agreement with the Stahlgemeinschaft. In the negotiations with the representatives of Otto Wolff it was agreed to let them have 10 % of the quota, thus leaving the Czechoslovak–Austrian Group with 50 % of Poland's consumption. The cartel set up its office in the Kreditanstalt für Handel and Gewerbe in Vienna, where orders were concentrated and allocated, minimum prices fixed and income accounted for and distributed among members.[3]

The Czechoslovak works were obviously strong enough to protect their own domestic market. However, they could not prevent the infiltration of German competition into the markets of Central and Southeastern Europe and they were not able to capture a significant part of exports to the rest of Europe.

The cartel structure of 1920–1 concerning the production of railway components reflected the current balance of power between the Czechoslovak, Austrian and German producers on

[1] Cf. Protokoll vom 15 February 1921 zwischen dem Konzern der Firma Otto Wolff in Köln (Gruppe A) und den Werken der Poldihütte, Škoda-Werken, Ternitzer Stahl- und Eisenwerken von Schoeller et Co., Wien und der Witkowitzer Bergbau- und Eisenhüttengesellschaft (Gruppe B), Ibid.

[2] Ibid. [3] Ibid.

European markets. Within a very few years the changing economic and political scene, and especially the greatly accelerated process of concentration, upset the balance attained in the immediate post-war years.

In Czechoslovakia only two large combines remained in the field of railway part production, the Vítkovice Mining and Foundry Works and the Škoda-Works; they had excluded the Poldina huť which ceased this line of production completely. Together they established a cartel company Súčtovací kancelář pro obruče, nápravy a soukolí (Accounting Office for Tyres, Axles and Gear Wheelsets), with its centre at the Prague headquarters of the Vítkovice Mining and Foundry Works, where all commercial and financial records were kept. In Austria the largest concern, Schoeller, tried to create a monopoly on its home market and to reduce the Czechoslovak quota in supplies to Austria. In Germany iron and steel, and also the engineering industry became fully cartelized and all works producing railway wheels and their components were united in the cartel organization, the Deutscher Lokomotiv-Radsatz-Verband. The firm of Otto Wolff disappeared from all international cartels. By the mid-twenties the cartel conditions agreed at the beginning of the twenties already failed to correspond with the new economic relationships which had developed within the cartels as a result of mutual but not always obvious competition. These changes demanded a revision of the cartel structure, if the competitive producers were to avoid the disintegration of their cartels and a price war and its accompanying loss of profits.

In 1926 cartel agreements on railway products between the Czechoslovak combines, the Vítkovice Mining and Foundry Works and the Škoda-Works, on the one side, and the Austrian concern Schoeller-Bleckmann Stahlwerke on the other, were revised and renewed. As a result, the centre of gravity of this branch of production shifted from Vienna to Prague, where the Accounting Office for Tyres, Axles and Gear Wheelsets became the centre for conducting the business not only of the domestic cartels, as previously, but also of the international cartel agreements. All members of the cartel were obliged to announce all orders received for cartel products to the Accounting Office in Prague, where on the basis of the quota system it was decided who was to execute each order. At the same time, the Accounting Office fixed the price which was to be quoted by the chosen producer to his customer, while all other producers were to quote prices not less than 3 % higher (so-called protective prices) to ensure the successful conclusion of the business according to the cartel's intention. Should a cartel member be caught concealing orders or quoting prices other than those agreed a fine of 20 % of the invoiced quantity was to be imposed for every 100 kg thus sold. A progressive scale of prices was also agreed on, to be paid by works exceeding output quotas to compensate those cartel members lagging behind. This system undoubtedly tended to keep prices as high as possible and put difficulties in the way of increasing output. Compensation was also paid to members of the cartel who tried to annihilate outsiders by price-cutting and thus were unable to achieve the agreed cartel rate of profit. Wherever disagreements could not be resolved in the framework of the cartel they were to be taken to arbitration.[1]

The growth in the strength of the Czechoslovak concerns compared with the Austrian Schoeller-Bleckmann Stahlwerke appears particularly clearly in the changed proportions of export quotas as a result of new cartel conditions in the agreement of 10 April 1926 concerning components for locomotives, railway wagons and tenders. But the Vítkovice and Škoda-Works also tightened their monopoly on the home market and, at the same time, supplied the Austrian market, i.e. Austrian locomotive- and wagon-works which were engaged on export orders, with 'indirect exports'. The indigenous Schoeller Iron Works were to be the exclusive suppliers for Austrian domestic consumption. However, in the markets of Central and South-eastern Europe the proportionate share of the Schoeller Works decreased steadily with every renewal of the cartel between 1926 and 1938 in comparison with the export quotas of the Czechoslovak works, as is evident from Table 3.

The Czechoslovak–Austrian cartel developed against the background of its relations with the strengthened and unified German cartel, Deutscher Lokomotiv-Radsatz-Verband, which it faced as a united group in the international cartel until the

[1] SÚA–KR 214 and 215; also PA–ŠZ – obchodní and právní oddělení, unnumbered material.

Table 3. *Changes in export quotas within the Czechoslovak–Austrian cartel concerning wheelsets, tyres and axles for locomotives, wagons and tenders**

Date of conclusion of cartel agreement	Export area	Export quotas, including indirect exports				
		VHHT (%)	ŠZ (%)	ČSR (total) (%)	Schoeller, i.e. Austrian total (%)	Total (%)
10 April 1926	Hungary, Yugoslavia, Romania, Bulgaria, Poland 50 %, indirect exports to Austria	38	32	70	30	100
2 June 1928	Total exports to Europe, excluding domestic markets	40	50	90	10	100
31 December 1931	Total exports to Europe, excluding domestic markets	46	44†	90	10	100
16 October 1933	Total exports to Europe, excluding domestic markets	46	49	95	5	100
24 May 1938	—	—	—	—	Transfer of Austrian quota to Germany	—

* Compiled and calculated from data in SÚA–KR 214, 215, 170, 181 and PA–ŠZ, Praha – Commercial and Legal Department (not numbered).

† Excluding the Škoda-Works' own output for indirect export.

Abbreviations: VHHT = Vítkovice Mining and Foundry Works, Ostrava; ŠZ = Škoda-Works, Plzeň; Schoeller = Schoeller-Bleckmann Stahlwerke A.G., Vienna.

Table 4. *Czechoslovak foreign trade in railway wheels and wheelsets (diameter 36 cm and over), 1926–37*

Year	1926		1927		1928		1929		1930		1931	
	q	000 Kč	q	000 Kč	q	000 Kč	q	000 Kč	q	000 Kč	q	000 Kč
						EXPORTS						
Total	52,633	14,074	58,031	15,452	53,402	13,553	42,435	16,013	10,016	4,413	7,579	2,525
British India	36,823	8,777	7,231	2,204	1,730	731	6,647	2,096	687	276	3,254	1,302
Union of S. Africa	—	—	—	—	—	—	—	—	—	—	—	—
Great Britain	27	20	200	101	46	28	16	38	—	—	—	—
Yugoslavia	1,902	828	2,929	1,032	2,397	963	26,437	9,930	3,632	1,687	157	49
British S. Africa	—	—	2,064	1,053	1,777	854	204	93	2,103	1,118	2,644	691
China	5,910	1,979	4,853	1,233	—	—	—	—	210	139	—	—
Netherlands	—	—	718	381	—	—	—	—	—	—	—	—
Bulgaria	—	—	—	—	—	—	1	—	—	—	292	53
Sweden	152	41	445	166	205	127	189	76	70	31	51	13
Egypt	2,697	525	5,443	1,748	—	—	—	—	—	—	456	181
Romania	1,767	671	2,128	672	8,872	2,157	1,372	382	1,270	372	277	74
Austria	1,009	280	425	136	144	50	44	22	46	12	3	1
Lithuania	648	234	712	292	—	—	—	—	—	—	107	50
Denmark	403	172	254	135	538	230	58	37	526	215	107	24
Switzerland	316	145	29	20	1,073	629	2,094	1,385	82	41	—	—
Estonia	294	129	48	11	—	—	156	82	—	—	24	6
Latvia	289	64	—	—	—	—	—	—	—	—	—	—
Poland	167	44	24	18	100	58	68	35	—	—	—	—
Italy	136	95	50	17	18	9	136	55	—	—	—	—
Hungary	45	49	1	1	365	140	2,724	824	695	255	—	—
Germany	36	16	475	73	118	64	61	37	77	39	14	6
Fiume	12	5	—	—	—	—	—	—	—	—	—	—
U.S.S.R.	—	—	29,316	5,944	35,852	7,419	—	—	145	29	—	—
Abyssinia	—	—	460	143	—	—	—	—	—	—	—	—
Belgium	—	—	165	41	—	—	—	—	—	—	—	—
Norway	—	—	33	16	59	35	—	—	—	—	—	—
Chile	—	—	28	15	—	—	—	—	—	—	—	—
Spanish Morocco	—	—	—	—	98	59	—	—	—	—	—	—
Finland	—	—	—	—	—	—	2,111	883	—	—	—	—
Portugal	—	—	—	—	—	—	112	36	—	—	—	—
British E. Africa	—	—	—	—	—	—	—	—	403	166	—	—
Colombia	—	—	—	—	—	—	—	—	40	21	—	—
Greece	—	—	—	—	—	—	—	—	30	12	—	—
Argentine	—	—	—	—	—	—	—	—	—	—	193	75
Other states	—	—	—	—	—	—	—	—	—	—	—	—
Other S. American republics	—	—	—	—	—	—	—	—	—	—	—	—
Price	—	267	—	266	—	254	—	377	—	441	—	333
				IMPORTS (tariff rate: 1q 232 Kč general, 174.40 on contract)								
Total	866	268	693	286	206	64	338	116	130	71	31	22
Hungary	—	—	28	26	72	18	—	—	—	—	—	—
France	616	147	16	4	—	—	30	8	—	—	—	—
Germany	226	110	565	238	78	29	168	46	102	61	13	17
Austria	28	11	84	18	56	17	57	27	12	5	18	5
Poland	—	—	—	—	—	—	83	35	16	5	—	—
Belgium	—	—	—	—	—	—	—	—	—	—	—	—
Price	—	309	—	413	—	311	—	343	—	546	—	710

Table 4 (*cont.*)

Year	1932		1933		1934		1935		1936		1937	
	q	000 Kč	q	000 Kč	q	000 Kč	q	000 Kč	q	000 Kč	q	000 Kč
						EXPORTS						
Total	2,764	672	1,165	490	4,739	1,409	157,626	26,620	38,826	6,450	2,615	1,075
British India	—	—	—	—	3,733	1,125	3,892	1,023	3,211	840	1,488	493
Union of S. Africa	—	—	—	—	—	—	—	—	—	—	264	210
Great Britain	—	—	—	—	—	—	—	—	—	—	182	41
Yugoslavia	2,270	548	867	269	341	74	806	267	402	102	172	86
British S. Africa	—	—	—	—	—	—	—	—	—	—	156	148
China	—	—	243	183	367	110	—	—	48	29	146	25
Netherlands	—	—	—	—	—	—	—	—	199	42	111	28
Bulgaria	15	5	—	—	—	—	—	—	—	—	63	32
Sweden	—	—	32	16	55	16	20	5	—	—	33	12
Egypt	—	—	—	—	—	—	—	—	—	—	—	—
Romania	462	111	19	19	56	44	—	—	—	—	—	—
Austria	—	—	—	—	—	—	—	—	—	—	—	—
Lithuania	—	—	—	—	—	—	—	—	—	—	—	—
Denmark	—	—	—	—	8	3	—	—	—	—	—	—
Switzerland	—	—	—	—	—	—	—	—	—	—	—	—
Estonia	—	—	—	—	—	—	—	—	—	—	—	—
Latvia	—	—	—	—	—	—	—	—	—	—	—	—
Poland	—	—	—	—	—	—	—	—	—	—	—	—
Italy	—	—	—	—	14	6	—	—	—	—	—	—
Hungary	—	—	—	—	—	—	—	—	—	—	—	—
Germany	—	—	4	3	—	—	—	—	—	—	—	—
Fiume	—	—	—	—	—	—	—	—	—	—	—	—
U.S.S.R.	—	—	—	—	—	—	152,897	25,322	34,966	5,437	—	—
Abyssinia	—	—	—	—	—	—	—	—	—	—	—	—
Belgium	—	—	—	—	—	—	—	—	—	—	—	—
Norway	—	—	—	—	—	—	—	—	—	—	—	—
Chile	—	—	—	—	—	—	—	—	—	—	—	—
Spanish Morocco	—	—	—	—	—	—	—	—	—	—	—	—
Finland	—	—	—	—	—	—	—	—	—	—	—	—
Portugal	—	—	—	—	—	—	—	—	—	—	—	—
British East Africa	—	—	—	—	—	—	—	—	—	—	—	—
Colombia	—	—	—	—	—	—	—	—	—	—	—	—
Greece	—	—	—	—	—	—	—	—	—	—	—	—
Argentine	—	—	—	—	41	16	—	—	—	—	—	—
Other states	17	8	—	—	—	—	11	3	—	—	—	—
Other S. American republics	—	—	124	15	—	—	—	—	—	—	—	—
Price	—	243	—	421	—	297	—	169	—	166	—	411
				IMPORTS (tariff rate: 1q 232 Kč general, 174.40 on contract)								
Total	—	—	—	—	—	—	—	—	32	12	38	12
Hungary	—	—	—	—	37	10	—	—	—	—	38	12
France	—	—	—	—	—	—	—	—	—	—	—	—
Germany	4	2	3	3	—	—	—	—	—	—	—	—
Austria	—	—	—	—	—	—	—	—	3	1	—	—
Poland	—	—	—	—	—	—	—	—	—	—	—	—
Belgium	—	—	—	—	—	—	—	—	29	11	—	—
Price	—	—	—	—	—	270	—	—	—	375	—	316

Table 5. *Czechoslovak foreign trade in iron parts of wheels, tyres, wheel disks, wheel spokes, 1926–37*

Year	1926		1927		1928		1929		1930		1931	
	q	000 Kč	q	000 Kč	q	000 Kč	q	000 Kč	q	000 Kč	q	000 Kč
						EXPORTS						
Total	15,597	3,878	26,632	6,158	38,851	8,316	20,246	5,503	28,970	8,296	22,675	5,422
British India	2,314	670	4,802	1,293	8,460	2,548	3,579	1,102	6,808	2,403	1,620	383
Yugoslavia	4,961	1,211	6,937	1,825	5,278	1,617	6,216	1,621	6,582	1,701	6,272	1,003
Union of S. Africa	—	—	—	—	—	—	—	—	—	—	—	—
China	5,718	1,420	3,654	912	123	33	349	97	959	429	—	—
Norway	—	—	—	—	—	—	124	29	—	—	569	122
British S. Africa	—	—	1,979	622	2,508	835	—	—	1,146	516	5,971	1,617
Switzerland	1,940	346	903	164	106	46	15	4	66	25	120	95
Argentine	—	—	—	—	—	—	79	19	255	85	—	—
Colombia	—	—	—	—	—	—	—	—	—	—	—	—
Netherlands	—	—	—	—	—	—	—	—	318	93	—	—
Great Britain	24	8	981	311	733	239	—	—	69	63	653	192
Romania	434	160	524	118	1,091	345	1,247	424	1,112	313	944	268
Egypt	—	—	—	—	—	—	—	—	1,678	425	3,527	977
British Malaya	—	—	—	—	—	—	—	—	—	—	—	—
Belgium	—	—	—	—	—	—	—	—	—	—	—	—
Bulgaria	—	—	37	15	—	—	61	30	—	—	—	—
Austria	131	43	54	18	—	—	248	67	374	94	31	9
Poland	42	11	40	9	45	13	17	14	—	—	21	7
Brazil	21	5	—	—	324	74	—	—	—	—	—	—
Hungary	11	3	102	58	352	132	8,043	2,003	202	39	—	—
Danzig	1	1	32	9	—	—	—	—	—	—	—	—
Estonia	—	—	3,159	635	—	—	71	19	—	—	—	—
Italy	—	—	327	115	—	—	—	—	105	64	363	130
Portugal	—	—	80	48	—	—	86	26	—	—	—	—
Germany	—	—	21	6	—	—	39	28	—	—	90	55
U.S.S.R.	—	—	—	—	11,807	2,425	—	—	8,191	1,590	—	—
Other states	—	—	—	—	24	9	—	—	15	9	7	2
Latvia	—	—	—	—	—	—	42	13	330	99	—	—
Sweden	—	—	—	—	—	—	30	7	20	17	56	49
Denmark	—	—	—	—	—	—	—	—	60	48	—	—
British W. Africa	—	—	—	—	—	—	—	—	132	51	—	—
Japan	—	—	—	—	—	—	—	—	220	66	748	209
British E. Africa	—	—	—	—	—	—	—	—	328	166	—	—
Lithuania	—	—	—	—	—	—	—	—	—	—	1,463	234
British colonies in Asia	—	—	—	—	—	—	—	—	—	—	203	56
Spain	—	—	—	—	—	—	—	—	—	—	17	14
Other S. American republics	—	—	—	—	—	—	—	—	—	—	—	—
Greece	—	—	—	—	—	—	—	—	—	—	—	—
Finland	—	—	—	—	—	—	—	—	—	—	—	—
Price	—	240	—	261	—	270	—	272	—	286	—	239
						IMPORTS (tariff rate: 1q 232 Kč)						
Total	34	30	272	159	—	—	138	87	78	67	—	—
Germany	—	—	201	131	68	53	57	51	55	60	7	8
France	—	—	50	15	—	—	—	—	—	—	—	—
Yugoslavia	—	—	21	13	—	—	—	—	—	—	—	—
Romania	—	—	—	—	—	—	78	34	—	—	—	—
Other states	—	—	—	—	—	—	3	2	8	3	—	—
Austria	—	—	—	—	—	—	—	—	15	4	—	—
Sweden	—	—	—	—	—	—	—	—	—	—	—	—
Price	—	882	—	585	—	779	—	630	—	859	—	—

Table 5 (*cont.*)

Year	1932		1933		1934		1935		1936		1937	
	q	000 Kč	q	000 Kč	q	000 Kč	q	000 Kč	q	000 Kč	q	000 Kč
						EXPORTS						
Total	2,833	701	6,882	2,144	16,607	3,696	57,292	7,595	16,437	2,979	12,532	3,725
British India	93	27	2,530	805	4,988	1,107	7,571	1,620	5,259	1,325	6,881	2,133
Yugoslavia	490	130	783	214	4,810	1,158	14,398	2,059	772	182	1,271	384
Union of S. Africa	—	—	—	—	2,825	590	888	183	1,482	458	1,259	374
China	418	97	1,746	521	2,583	505	52	10	58	35	934	237
Norway	—	—	—	—	—	—	—	—	—	—	437	70
British S. Africa	260	48	1,005	431	—	—	—	—	—	—	318	94
Switzerland	—	—	—	—	58	11	513	166	35	9	278	77
Argentine	—	—	—	—	350	80	199	49	337	92	235	105
Colombia	—	—	—	—	38	10	—	—	—	—	233	58
Netherlands	935	222	—	—	580	146	—	—	132	28	195	49
Great Britain	—	—	—	—	—	—	—	—	—	—	191	57
Romania	456	140	519	112	48	22	—	—	—	—	150	26
Egypt	150	27	48	25	104	19	1,450	303	—	—	88	29
British Malaya	—	—	—	—	—	—	—	—	—	—	28	19
Belgium	—	—	—	—	—	—	—	—	—	—	17	7
Bulgaria	—	—	177	22	—	—	135	39	—	—	17	6
Austria	—	—	—	—	—	—	—	—	—	—	—	—
Poland	—	—	—	—	—	—	—	—	—	—	—	—
Brazil	—	—	—	—	—	—	—	—	—	—	—	—
Hungary	—	—	—	—	—	—	—	—	—	—	—	—
Danzig	—	—	—	—	—	—	—	—	—	—	—	—
Estonia	—	—	74	14	—	—	—	—	177	30	—	—
Italy	—	—	—	—	—	—	—	—	—	—	—	—
Portugal	—	—	—	—	—	—	—	—	—	—	—	—
Germany	—	—	—	—	20	7	—	—	—	—	—	—
U.S.S.R.	—	—	—	—	—	—	32,086	3,166	8,170	809	—	—
Other states	—	—	—	—	—	—	—	—	15	11	—	—
Latvia	—	—	—	—	—	—	—	—	—	—	—	—
Sweden	—	—	—	—	—	—	—	—	—	—	—	—
Denmark	—	—	—	—	—	—	—	—	—	—	—	—
British W. Africa	—	—	—	—	—	—	—	—	—	—	—	—
Japan	—	—	—	—	—	—	—	—	—	—	—	—
British E. Africa	—	—	—	—	—	—	—	—	—	—	—	—
Lithuania	—	—	—	—	—	—	—	—	—	—	—	—
British colonies in Asia	—	—	—	—	—	—	—	—	—	—	—	—
Spain	—	—	—	—	—	—	—	—	—	—	—	—
Other S. American republics	31	10	—	—	—	—	—	—	—	—	—	—
Greece	—	—	—	—	118	18	—	—	—	—	—	—
Finland	—	—	—	—	105	23	—	—	—	—	—	—
Price	—	247	—	312	—	223	—	133	—	181	—	297
						IMPORTS (tariff rate: 1q 232 Kč)						
Total	—	—	—	—	19	19	—	—	—	—	6	8
Germany	13	14	—	—	—	—	—	—	—	—	—	—
France	—	—	—	—	—	—	—	—	—	—	—	—
Yugoslavia	—	—	—	—	—	—	—	—	—	—	—	—
Romania	—	—	—	—	—	—	—	—	—	—	—	—
Other states	—	—	—	—	—	—	—	—	—	—	—	—
Austria	—	—	—	—	3	1	—	—	9	3	—	—
Sweden	—	—	—	—	16	18	—	—	—	—	—	—
Price	—	1,077	—	—	—	—	—	—	—	—	—	—

summer of 1938.[1] Changes in the German–Czechoslovak–Austrian cartel structure of the immediate post-war years began to assert themselves in 1926, when all partners signed a renewal of the Kontinental-Abkommen concerning gearwheel sets and their components. The new agreement, valid from 16 September 1926 to 6 February 1930, covered all exports to European countries, including the whole Soviet territory. The Czechoslovak–Austrian quota was fixed as 3/13 of all the orders received by the cartel members, i.e. 23 %, and the Czechoslovak and Austrian works were given preference in the markets of Hungary, Romania, Bulgaria, Yugoslavia, Poland and European Turkey. In all other European markets the German suppliers had priority, and trade with the Soviet Union was to be handled by the cartel partners in whose country a Soviet trade delegation existed. In all cases, however, except for the respective domestic markets, the proportions of 7/13:3/13 of the total were to be adhered to.[2] In this way both groups in the international cartel apparently had the opportunity of expanding into all European countries; but the most conspicuous change in favour of the German participants consisted in waiving the previous condition that the markets of the former Habsburg Monarchy should be exclusively reserved for the Czechoslovak–Austrian Group. Theoretically this cut both ways, for the condition which kept the Czechoslovak–Austrian products out of the other European countries was also dropped and replaced by overall proportions of export quotas. A brief look at the relevant statistics of Czechoslovak exports to most European countries between 1926 and 1938 suffices to show their decline. Table 4, giving the figures for railway wheels and wheelsets,[3] and Tables 5 and 6 for components of wheels, tyres

[1] Members of the Deutscher Lokomotiv-Radsatz-Verband: Borsigwerk A.G., Borsigwerk; Fried. Krupp A.G., Essen; Mitteldeutsche Stahlwerke A.G., Riesa; 'Rheinmetall' Rheinische Metallwaren- und Maschinenfabrik, Düsseldorf–Derendorf; Ruhrstahl A.G., Witten-Ruhr; Vereinigte Stahlwerke A.G., Düsseldorf (SÚA–KR 170). The cartel for tyres for wagons, locomotives and tenders was also joined by works of the Deutsche Stahlgemeinschaft: Gutehoffnungshütte Oberhausen, A.G. zu Oberhausen; Klöckner-Werke A.G., Abteilung Georgs-Marienwerke zu Osnabrück; Vereinigte Oberschlesische Hüttenwerke A.G. zu Gleiwitz 2; Press- und Walzwerk A.G. zu Reisholz (SÚA–KR 181).

[2] Cf. PA–ŠZ–Praha – právní oddělení, unnumbered material.

[3] Compiled from SÚS, Praha, *Zahraniční obchod Republiky československé* (1926–37).

and railway axles,[1] show that largely as a result of the cartel conditions Czechoslovak exports managed to hold out significantly only in Yugoslavia and Romania. After 1931 Czechoslovak exports to other European countries became insignificant except for an impressive rise in exports to the Soviet Union in 1935 and 1936 (viz. column in Tables 4 and 5). This is not accidental and follows closely upon Czechoslovakia's entry into official diplomatic relations with the Soviet Union in 1934 and the signing of the French–Soviet–Czechoslovak Treaty of 1935.

At the end of 1931 the whole system of cartels between Czechoslovakia, Austria and Germany concerning railway products was extended, with some significant, if not basic, changes. In the renewed Territorial-Abkommen of 3 December 1931 the areas of Luxemburg and Danzig were no longer included in the definition of the German domestic market, but were replaced by the Saar.[2] When analysing the International Steel Cartel we noted that Danzig was shifted from the German to the Polish sphere of interest in the 1930s. In the light of Germany's territorial demands of 1938 and 1939 these transfers are not without interest. However, 50 % of the Polish market remained reserved for German suppliers of railway parts.[3] At that time the Kontinental-Abkommen between the Deutsche Lokomotiv-Radsatz-Verband and the Czechoslovak–Austrian concerns was also renewed with the basic quotas unchanged. However, the position of the Škoda-Works within the cartel was markedly strengthened. Firstly, they joined the very few members of the international cartel whose export quota did not include production for indirect exports in their own locomotive shops,[4] and could thus produce greater quantities than the other cartel members whose indirect exports were included in their quotas. Secondly, as a departure from the practice before 1931, when the Škoda-Works were always part of the Czechoslovak–Austrian Group and shared in the quota of the

[1] Ibid.

[2] Cf. SÚA–KR 170, 181, 216; also PA–ŠZ, Praha – právní oddělení, unnumbered material.

[3] Cf. SÚA–KR 214, 215; also PA–ŠZ, Praha – právní oddělení, unnumbered material.

[4] Cf. Abkommen für Lokomotiv- und Tender Radsätze, 31 December 1931; the following works: Borsig Lokomotiv-Werke G.m.b.H., Berlin-Tegel, Fried. Krupp A.G. Abt. Iowa, Essen, Henschel & Sohn A.G., Kassel and the Škoda-Works, Plzeň. PA–ŠZ, Praha – právní oddělení, unnumbered material.

Table 6. *Czechoslovak foreign trade in railway axles, 1926–37*

Year	1926		1927		1928		1929		1930		1931	
	q	000 Kč	q	000 Kč	q	000 Kč	q	000 Kč	q	000 Kč	q	000 Kč
					EXPORTS							
Total	11,479	3,957	1,484	427	88	29	2,556	1,006	3,332	1,199	132	205
British India	5,316	2,025	639	217	—	—	—	—	2,198	759	—	—
Egypt	—	—	33	12	—	—	—	—	—	—	24	21
Switzerland	706	162	477	103	—	—	—	—	—	—	—	—
Norway	—	—	—	—	—	—	—	—	—	—	—	—
Netherlands	—	—	—	—	—	—	—	—	—	—	—	—
China	3,774	1,124	—	—	—	—	—	—	—	—	—	—
Great Britain	—	—	—	—	—	—	41	13	—	—	—	—
Union of South Africa	—	—	—	—	—	—	—	—	—	—	—	—
Argentine	—	—	—	—	—	—	—	—	—	—	—	—
Romania	1,387	555	—	—	—	—	108	86	—	—	—	—
Yugoslavia	126	35	128	37	79	25	2,357	861	167	40	—	—
U.S.A.	112	39	—	—	—	—	—	—	—	—	—	—
Denmark	29	7	94	22	—	—	—	—	—	—	—	—
Austria	26	9	47	17	—	—	—	—	—	—	—	—
Germany	3	1	—	—	—	—	—	—	—	—	—	—
Lithuania	—	—	66	19	—	—	—	—	—	—	—	—
Other states	—	—	—	—	9	4	10	10	—	—	2	3
Spain	—	—	—	—	—	—	40	36	—	—	—	—
British possessions in South Africa	—	—	—	—	—	—	—	—	775	269	—	—
British possessions in East Africa	—	—	—	—	—	—	—	—	163	82	—	—
France	—	—	—	—	—	—	—	—	29	49	—	—
Poland	—	—	—	—	—	—	—	—	—	—	59	111
Hungary	—	—	—	—	—	—	—	—	—	—	47	70
Belgium	—	—	—	—	—	—	—	—	—	—	—	—
Price		345		288		330		394		360		1553
Total	8	9	—	—	—	—	18	16	99	40	—	—
			IMPORTS (Tariff rate: 1q 232 Kč)									
Germany	4	6	—	—	94	46	16	14	—	—	9	3
France	4	3	—	—	—	—	2	2	—	—	—	—
Austria	—	—	6	5	—	—	—	—	—	—	—	—
Other states	—	—	—	—	—	—	—	—	9	12	—	—
Hungary	—	—	—	—	—	—	—	—	75	18	—	—
Sweden	—	—	—	—	—	—	—	—	15	10	—	—
Belgium	—	—	—	—	—	—	—	—	—	—	—	—
Price		1,125		833		489		889		404	—	—

Year	1932		1933		1934		1935		1936		1937	
	q	000 Kč	q	000 Kč	q	000 Kč	q	000 Kč	q	000 Kč	q	000 Kč
					EXPORTS							
Total	460	581	904	573	1,066	445	618	207	1,374	557	1,579	830
British India	38	62	—	—	813	263	—	—	864	345	915	416
Egypt	—	—	—	—	—	—	—	—	—	—	173	104
Switzerland	—	—	137	63	—	—	273	74	41	26	120	41
Norway	—	—	—	—	—	—	—	—	—	—	103	30
Netherlands	—	—	—	—	—	—	163	65	11	5	95	95
China	—	—	530	203	—	—	—	—	—	—	79	44
Great Britain	—	—	—	—	—	—	—	—	—	—	52	76
Union of South Africa	—	—	—	—	—	—	—	—	456	180	32	19
Argentine	—	—	—	—	—	—	150	40	—	—	10	5
Romania	—	—	—	—	11	17	—	—	—	—	—	—
Yugoslavia	10	3	—	—	163	91	32	28	2	1	—	—
U.S.A.	—	—	—	—	—	—	—	—	—	—	—	—
Denmark	—	—	—	—	—	—	—	—	—	—	—	—
Austria	1	1	—	—	—	—	—	—	—	—	—	—
Germany	—	—	—	—	—	—	—	—	—	—	—	—
Lithuania	—	—	—	—	—	—	—	—	—	—	—	—
Other states	—	—	—	—	—	—	—	—	—	—	—	—
Spain	—	—	—	—	—	—	—	—	—	—	—	—
British possessions in South Africa	—	—	—	—	—	—	—	—	—	—	—	—
British possessions in East Africa	—	—	—	—	—	—	—	—	—	—	—	—
France	—	—	—	—	—	—	—	—	—	—	—	—
Poland	—	—	34	72	—	—	—	—	—	—	—	—
Hungary	—	—	—	—	—	—	—	—	—	—	—	—
Belgium	411	515	203	235	45	37	—	—	—	—	—	—
Price		1,263		634		417		335		405		232
Total	—	—	—	—	—	—	—	—	—	—	—	—
					IMPORTS (Tariff rate: 1q 232 Kč)							
Germany	—	—	—	—	4	7	—	—	—	—	—	—
France	—	—	—	—	—	—	—	—	—	—	—	—
Austria	—	—	—	—	—	—	—	—	—	—	—	—
Other states	—	—	—	—	—	—	—	—	—	—	—	—
Hungary	—	—	—	—	—	—	—	—	—	—	—	—
Sweden	—	—	—	—	—	—	—	—	—	—	—	—
Belgium	—	—	—	—	—	—	—	—	8	3	—	—
Price	—	—	—	—	—	—	—	—	—	—	—	—

whole group, they participated in the agreement of 1931 as a completely independent partner with their own quota of 10 % of the cartel's total exports. The Vítkovice Mining and Foundry Works in Czechoslovakia and the Schoeller Works in Austria also formed an independent grouping in the cartel, with a quota of 13 % in European markets.[1] In 1933 the Škoda-Works enlarged their quota again by persuading Schoeller to transfer half of its export quota to them.[2] Table 3 (p. 233) clearly shows the growing share of the Škoda-Works' exports in comparison with the other members of the Czechoslovak–Austrian Group, especially with the firm of Schoeller. After the *Anschluss* of Austria to Germany the Schoeller-Bleckmann Stahlwerke were incorporated into the German Group and their quota was transferred to the cartel of the Deutscher Lokomotiv-Radsatz-Verband. The Austrian market thus passed completely into the sphere of German suppliers.[3]

After the mid-twenties only the Škoda-Works of the Czechoslovak–Austrian Group became a really serious competitor in the world trade of wheelsets, tyres and axles for railways. As a supplier for the Chinese Eastern Railway the Škoda-Works were not subject to the controls of the international cartel[4] and Tables 4 and 5 show relatively large and regular exports from Czechoslovakia to China. The Škoda-Works also supplied railway parts to the African possessions of Great Britain and to India and they became the only Central European engineering enterprise which gained a quota in the international agreements on India and South Africa along with the powerful British and German concerns.

The British and German combines negotiated from 1924 onwards in attempts to modify the fierce competition in railway construction in the British colonies. They tried to come to terms on quotas and prices for supplying tyres, axles and wheelsets for the Indian and African railways. The Škoda-Works were kept informed about these negotiations by the German concerns, Krupp and Bochumer Verein, who promised to let them have a third of their own share in deliveries to India should a

[1] Ibid.

[2] Addition to renewed cartel agreement, 16 October 1933, SÚA–KR 215.

[3] Cf. SÚA–KR 170, 216, 215.

[4] Orders for the Chinese Eastern Railway did not form part of the cartel agreement. SÚA–KR 215 (1926–38).

cartel agreement eventually be reached.[1] Although the Škoda-Works did not actually get a third of the German quota, when agreement was reached a stable 7½ % share of the African and Indian market for railway components was allocated to them alongside the large British and German suppliers. This also appears clearly in the export statistics of Czechoslovakia after 1926 (Tables 4 and 5).

In 1926 the British and German Groups and the Škoda-Works concluded cartel agreements concerning tyres, axles and wheel-sets for tenders, wagons and locomotives in India, the so-called Indian Pool, and for the Union of South Africa, the so-called South African Pool. The central office of the cartels was, as is usually the case, in the country of the strongest partner, i.e. in Sheffield,[2] where prices were fixed, orders distributed and profits divided according to an agreed quota system. Each cartel partner had to contribute £3 to the pool for each ton of tyres and axles and £2 for each ton of wheels etc. delivered to India or South Africa. The following quota system was agreed: The British Group – 67½ %, the German Group – 25 %, the Škoda-Works – 7½ %.[3] On the Indian market the cartel undercut by 2½ % the prices of domestic producers, who were unable to compete and had difficulties in getting industrial development on its feet under colonial conditions. In 1933 both pools were renewed. While the quota for the Škoda-Works remained unchanged at 7½ %, the British Group met the German demands for an increased share of exports to India and South Africa (in the South African Pool the British Group's quota fell to 57½ % and the German Group's quota rose to 35 %; in the Indian Pool the British share was reduced to 62½ % and that of the German Group increased to 30 %).[4] Thus the German concerns gained 10 % in Africa and 5 % in India from the British quota, compared with 1926. This relationship remained unchanged up to the outbreak of war in 1939, in spite of the increasing competitive pressure of the tightly concentrated and centrally controlled German industry. The only fairly substantial increase in the German quota before September 1939 came about by the

1 PA–ŠZ, Praha – právní oddělení, unnumbered material – letter of Bochumer Verein to Škoda-Works, 4 August 1924.

2 Messrs Peat, Marwick Mitchell & Co., Norris Deakin Buildings, Sheffield.

3 PA–ŠZ, Praha – právní oddělení, unnumbered material.

4 Ibid. and PA–ZVIL, Plzeň–GŘ, Kartely.

occupation of the Czech Lands and by the incorporation of the Škoda-Works into the German cartel system.

Our analysis of the changing cartel structure from 1921 to 1938 in the production of railway components shows how competition within the cartels led to the strengthening or weakening of national industrial groups or large concerns in international cartels, or to the complete extinction of individual enterprises. It becomes evident that Austrian output gradually declined during the competitive struggle with Czechoslovak and German producers. Czechoslovak output in this important field of railway parts, however, consolidated itself and expanded, especially in the Škoda-Works, and gained ground in Central and Southeastern European markets as against Austria. At the same time, it was forced to accept cartel conditions in agreements concluded with the concentrated German industry after 1926 which gave the German concerns greater access to the traditional and hitherto cartel-protected markets of the Czechoslovak–Austrian producers. It cannot be doubted that the Czechoslovak engineering works, which were moreover closely connected with British and French combines, also formed a serious obstacle to the expansive endeavours of the powerful German engineering industry in the important field of railway construction.

The participation of Czechoslovak works in international cartels of mechanical engineering products

The iron and steel and engineering works in Czechoslovakia, Austria and Germany which were members of the international cartel for railway products began to negotiate in September 1932 – at the height of the crisis – about establishing a cartel concerning forged pieces, the Schmiedestück-Vereinigung für den europäischen Kontinent, mainly in order to remove mutual competition from their own domestic markets.[1] The spokesmen for the individual concerns held that exports to their domestic markets should be permitted only exceptionally and in no case

[1] Minutes of meeting of 14 September 1932 in Berlin between representatives of the Deutsche Stahlgemeinschaft in Essen, the Vítkovice Mining and Foundry Works in Ostrava, the Škoda-Works in Plzeň and Schoeller-Bleckmann Stahlwerke A.G. in Vienna. PA–ŠZ, Praha – právní oddělení, unnumbered material.

should more than half the quantities of forged pieces which had previously been exported by them to their respective partners be allowed to enter their mutual trade.[1] A period of concentrated bargaining ensued about the precise definition of forged pieces to be covered by the cartel and, in particular, about each minute fraction of the percentages to be allocated as export quotas to the individual members. In the first phase the cartel agreement concluded on 24 October 1932 was concerned with all processed and moulded forged pieces weighing over 4,000 kg, and only with those forged pieces over 2,000 kg with a diameter of at least 500 mm.[2] These products constituted essential parts in the construction of turbines, excavators, cranes, rotaries and other large machines. In 1934 unprocessed, crude forged pieces were also included in the agreement.[3] As a result of the international cartel the large Czechoslovak producers of forged pieces strengthened their domination of the domestic market, as this was recognized to be the exclusive sphere of interest of the Vítkovice and Škoda Works. They in turn protected their interests by setting up a cartel association, the Evidenční kancelář pro výkovy (Evidence Bureau for Forged Pieces) in Prague, and divided the home market exclusively between themselves in the proportions Škoda 40: Vítkovice 60.[4]

Negotiations about fixing export quotas between partners in the international cartel took a whole year, because there was opposition to the demand of the Deutsche Stahlgemeinschaft for an increased German share. In the final agreement the German quota was raised by 0.05 % and the Austrian by 0.01 %, while the Czechoslovak share was reduced by a corresponding amount, as is shown in Table 7.

The division of export quotas leaves no doubt about the preponderance of the German groups, even after 1934, when the associated English group of producers joined the cartel. Here, as in other cartels, the central office, situated with the Deutsche Stahlgemeinschaft, i.e. the Schmiedestück-Vereinigung G.m.b.H. in Essen, assembled incoming orders for all European countries, including England, Scotland and Ireland (but excluding the Soviet Union) and allocated them to its members

[1] Ibid. [2] Cf. SÚA–KR 169, 24 October 1932–31 December 1934.
[3] Ibid., 169/2, addition of 3 February 1934.
[4] Cf. PA–ZVIL, Plzeň–Kartely–GŘ.

Table 7. *Export quotas in the cartel for forged pieces (1932)**

Cartel partners	Shares in the export of forged pieces according to agreement of 14 September 1932 (%)	26 September 1933 (%)
1. Deutsche Stahlgemeinschaft, Essen	75.86	75.91
2. Škoda-Works, Plzeň	12.20	12.18
3. Vítkovice Mining and Foundry Works, Ostrava	11.44	11.40
4. Schoeller-Bleckmann Stahlwerke, Vienna	0.50	0.51
Total	100	100

* Compiled from correspondence and minutes in PA–ŠZ, Praha-Commercial and Legal Department (not numbered).

according to their agreed quota system. At the same time, it determined the price to be quoted by the chosen supplier for each order (so-called Ernstoffert), whereas other works had to quote substantially higher prices (so-called Schutzpreise). At the annual rendering of accounts fines were imposed on members who had exceeded their quotas, and compensation was paid to those who had not fulfilled theirs; at the central office in Essen a confidential trustee was employed who had access to all member factories to supervise the fulfilment of cartel conditions.[1] After the *Anschluss* the Austrian share of exports to European countries was incorporated into the German quota,[2] a practice also followed by other steel and engineering cartels.

On the whole the cartel controlling the European market for forged pieces reflects the increasing influence of German industry in the 1930s.

Iron and steel products like connecting links, cocks, plugs, screws, bolts, rivets, nails and other fittings are indispensable to engineering construction. The capital required for starting up

[1] Cf. Abkommen über Schmiedestücke für die Ausfuhr, PA–ŠZ, Praha, unnumbered material.

[2] This cartel agreement was still valid in January 1939, except that Schoeller-Bleckmann Stahlwerke in Vienna had been transferred into the German Group. SÚA–KR 169.

production and the costs of maintaining it are comparatively low and production can be carried on in relatively small enterprises. In pre-Munich Czechoslovakia a number of scattered independent factories existed, as well as large concerns with their subsidiaries. During the years of the economic crisis these were either swallowed up by the large steel and engineering works, or they survived by associating voluntarily in cartels, submitting to government-decreed syndicalization. As foreign competition on the home market increased, domestic producers only had a reasonable chance of standing up to it if they took the initiative in negotiating an international understanding where none existed, or if they joined an already established international cartel which allotted exports according to the economic strength of the individual member firms. In most cases such a course protected at least the domestic market of the Czechoslovak producers.

Only in isolated instances were foreign cartel members successful in gaining guaranteed access to the Czechoslovak home market. This applied to an international cartel agreement about the marketing of cast-iron fittings between the Czechoslovak sales syndicate which had dominated the home market from its foundation in 1932,[1] and the German cartel, Fittingsverband in Düsseldorf, together with its Swiss partner the A.-G. der Eisen- und Stahlwerke vorm. Georg Fischer, Schaffhausen. The German and Swiss works obtained from 1 June 1935 a guaranteed 15 % of the annual total Czechoslovak consumption of all fittings and plugs for tubes conducting water, liquids of all kinds, steam, air, gas, etc. The German Fittingsverband obtained not only a fixed share of the Czechoslovak market, but also a seat on the Czechoslovak syndicate and corresponding voting rights.[2] This agreement constituted

[1] The Czechoslovak factories formed a domestic cartel, the 'Sdružení československých výrobců rourových spojek z kujné litiny a průchodních a výtokových kohoutů ze šedé litiny' (Association of Czechoslovak Producers of Malleable Tube Fittings and Grey Cast Iron Straight-way and Discharge Cocks) in 1932. No outsiders remained. The syndicate's sales were handled by Petzold & Co. in Prague, according to strict quotas on the domestic market. The German Fittingsverband intervened in this arrangement, competing strongly with the domestic cartel members until it forced them to agree to an import quota. SÚA–KR 275 and 929.

[2] Cf. SÚA–KR 929/1; the agreement ran from 1 June 1935 to 31 December 1936, and was later extended to the end of 1938.

part of a far-reaching international cartel, the International Malleable Fittings Association, in which the Czechoslovak market obviously came under the German sphere of influence.[1]

The economic crisis significantly altered the structure of the screw-producing industry in Czechoslovakia. It particularly affected the medium and small-scale factories, which felt the increasing pressure of the monopolistic iron and steel combines which supplied them with raw materials at cartel prices, and of their customers, the large engineering works and wholesalers, whose demand fell severely. In this way, the competitive struggle became unusually fierce and was, moreover, heightened by the competition of foreign makes on the Czechoslovak market.

An earlier chapter (Chapter 3 (1), pp. 115–117) discussed the progressive concentration in the production of wire goods (nails, wires, chains, etc.), where the motive force was the expansion of the Mining and Metallurgic Company's combine from the 1920s onwards. In the case of the Czechoslovak screw mills it was the economic crisis that abruptly accelerated cartelization. At the same time the strongest combines, the Prague Iron Co. and the Vítkovice Mining and Foundry Works, also manœuvred the other works into a cartel in February 1931, when nine screw mills founded a cartel registered as a commercial company 'Helika'.[2] Its activity involved rationalization and standardization of production, the working out of production programmes for member factories and the allocation of quotas and orders. At the same time, on 12 February 1931, a specialized price cartel and pool of four Czechoslovak producers of polished screws and bolts was formed, which coordinated sales in the Evidenční kancelář továren na lesklé šroubové zboží (Evidence Bureau of Screw Mills for Polished Products).[3] When the cartel closed the factory of its member, Winkler & Co. in Chomutov, it transferred Winkler's output quota to the Škoda-

[1] Ibid.: 'Die Originalausfertigung des Abkommens mit den Unterschriften, welches bisher bei uns lag (i.e. at the Sdružení výrobců kujných spojek etc. in Prague–A.T.), ist der International Malleable Tube Fittings Association, Düsseldorf, zuständigkeitshalber übergeben worden und wird auf dieser Stelle für die internationalen Vertragsparteien aufbewahrt.'

[2] Cf. SÚA–KR 110 – Basic Agreement.

[3] Cf. SÚA–KR 125 – Basic Agreement.

Works,[1] which in turn gained considerable influence in this cartelized area of production.

Both cartels, Helika and the Evidence Bureau of Screw Mills for Polished Products, represented their industries after 1932 in international cartel agreements about mutual territorial protection and obtained full protection of their home markets against competition from Yugoslavia, Hungary, Poland and Austria.[2] The most serious competitor of the Czechoslovak works, especially the Prague Iron Co. and the Vítkovice Mining and Foundry Works, was the Austrian concern Brevillier & Co. und A. Urban & Söhne, with their main company in Vienna and subsidiary works in Hungary and Yugoslavia. The territory of Yugoslavia became the most disputed market, because according to the cartel agreement of 2 January 1932 the Czechoslovak iron works were not to have the right to deliver connecting links, like screws, rivets, bolts and nuts, either with their railway material or with their other engineering constructions to Yugoslavia, and were to persuade their customers there to order these products from Brevillier & Urban's Yugoslav screw mill in Novi Sad.[3] In the following years complaints grew from the Czechoslovak works that the agreement prevented them from getting orders which in the end were obtained by West-European firms. Under pressure from the Czechoslovak cartel members the agreement was adjusted in 1936, entitling the Czechoslovak suppliers of engineering constructions to Yugoslavia to deliver them complete with screws and rivets and free of customs duties, but Brevillier & Urban had to be consulted in every case.[4]

The Viennese firm Brevillier & Co. und A. Urban und Söhne was also the biggest competitor of the Czechoslovak producers of wood screws, especially in their own domestic market. Until 1933 Czechoslovak wood screw production was fairly scattered and the first attempt at cartelization resulted only in firms

[1] Cf. J. Kašpar and R. Šimáček, *Československé kartely* (Czechoslovak Cartels) (Praha, 1934), p. 73.

[2] Cf. SÚA–KR 109 – the cartel agreement ran from 2 January 1932 to 31 December 1935, and was then extended until 1940; and SÚA–KR 27 – this agreement ran from 1 April 1932 to 31 December 1935, and was extended until 1941.

[3] Cf. SÚA–KR 109, VIII.

[4] Ibid., 109/2.

associating on 24 October 1933[1] in a cartel company 'VRUT, prodejna šroubů do dřeva s.s r.o.' (VRUT Selling Agency for Wood Screws Ltd). However, the Czechoslovak market only became the scene of fiercer competition between domestic enterprises: competition also increased greatly between them and the international cartel, the Wood Screw Syndicate, whose policy in the crisis years was either to drive competitors out of production by undercutting or to force them to join the cartel and to follow this up with a rise in prices. The Wood Screw Syndicate had been formed by the largest European producers in Belgium, Germany, Great Britain, France and Italy[2] and was naturally interested in penetrating the markets of South-east Europe, where Czechoslovak and Austrian suppliers already competed strongly.

Reacting to this foreign trade situation and urged on by representations from the most interested Czechoslovak cartel organization, VRUT, the Czechoslovak Ministry of Commerce enforced the syndicalization of domestic wood screw production. At the same time it imposed a *numerus clausus*, so that from 11 October 1935 VRUT was to represent selected Czechoslovak firms exclusively for the production of wood screws.[3] Others, not so selected, had to go out of production. In this case international cartelization influenced the process of concentration in Czechoslovakia, which took place with the help of state intervention. Thus fortified VRUT entered into a number of international cartel agreements about the mutual protection of members' home markets. Most importantly, the Czechoslovak cartel adjusted its relations with the Viennese concern Brevillier & Urban in a cartel agreement of 16 October 1935 (only a few days after the government had decreed carteliza-

[1] *Československé kartely*, p. 72 (the two firms were Bechert & Co., továrna na drátěnky, šrouby a ocelárna, a.s. [Bechert & Co., Wire Nail and Screw Factory & Steelworks, Ltd.] in Žatec, and Marek & Jasanský, továrna na šrouby do dřeva, drát, drátěné hřebíky a pletiva [Marek & Jasanský, Woodscrew, Wire Nail and Netting Factory] in Hvězdonice p. Chocerady).

[2] Cf. H. Friedlaender, *Examples of international cartels and other industrial understandings*, TNEC – Hearings – Part 25, pp. 13,368–9.

[3] SÚA–KR 867. Protocol of 11 October 1935 at the Ministry of Commerce, Rč 89318/35 (The member firms of VRUT were: Bechert & Co. a.s., Žatec; Fr. Konvyka, Velký Osek; Marek & Jasanský, Hvězdonice; Tatra-Závod, a.s., Praha-Kopřivnice; Josef Uher a spol., Brno-Židenice; Vichr a spol. Praha – Duchcov).

tion), allowing the Austrian firm to supply a fixed annual amount of wood screws to the Czechoslovak market. All other deliveries were covered by export quotas and price agreements between the partners. VRUT reserved for itself the right to keep accounts and to exercise controls.[1] This is the only agreement in this branch of production in which the Czechoslovak side conceded to a foreign firm a certain strictly defined access to the domestic market. In all other cartel agreements it vigorously protected its home market, although it did have to forego its exports to the other cartel partners' territories and in the agreement with the British wood screw cartel British India was specified as a prohibited area. VRUT signed such agreements with the Austrian cartel, Evidenzbureau der österreichischen Schraubenfabriken in Vienna (28 October 1935),[2] with the British concern Guest, Keen & Nettlefolds Ltd. in Birmingham and its Swedish subsidiary companies (25 February and 11 May 1936),[3] with the Polish cartel Zjednoczone polskie fabryki śrub spółka z ogr. odp. in Bielsko (18 July 1936),[4] with the German cartel Holzschraubenverband G.m.b.H. in Düsseldorf (4 December 1936),[5] and with three Hungarian works (15 October 1937).[6] The Czechoslovak producers did not become members of the International Wood Screw Syndicate, but by concluding agreements with the individual members of this powerful cartel they succeeded in preventing imports of wood screws to their home market. Of course they had to pay a price for this protection in fewer opportunities for exports. This cartel structure was comparatively short-lived, because in March 1938 all Austrian factories were incorporated into the German Holzschraubenverband in Düsseldorf, and after the Munich Agreement most of the Czechoslovak works went the same way, as they were situated in the territory ceded to Germany.[7]

In the 1930s the Swedish steel combine Aktiebolaget O. Mustad & Son, Gotheburg, intervened in the production and marketing of horseshoe nails in Czechoslovakia through its subsidiary enterprise Žatecká továrna na podkováky Mustad & syn in Žatec (Žatec Horseshoe Nail Factory Mustad & Son), which succeeded in subordinating the two remaining inde-

[1] SÚA-KR 867. [2] SÚA-KR 869. [3] SÚA-KR 930. [4] SÚA-KR 949.
[5] SÚA-KR 1005. [6] SÚA-KR 1088. [7] SÚA-KR 1005/1.

pendent factories in Czechoslovakia by a cartel agreement of 15 April 1934. The result of the agreement provides an almost classical example of the activities of cartels in the 1930s. Firstly, production was discontinued in the Schwedische Patent-Hufnägelfabrik Hugo Tauber G.m.b.H. at Nové Mesto nad Váhom (Slovakia). Then the second factory, Považsko-novomestoer Draht, Drahtstiften, Stahlgabel und Hufnägelwerke Adolf Reiss & Söhne, obtained permission to produce a fixed quantity, i.e. about 20 million horseshoe nails a year, exclusively for sale in Slovakia. In addition it could produce 180 tons of horseshoe nails annually for export, but it was not allowed to handle the exports itself; 100 tons were to be sold by the Swedish company in Gotheburg and the remaining 80 tons were not to be produced at all, in return for a compensation payment of 80,000 Kč. All other demands for horseshoe nails within the customs frontiers of Czechoslovakia had to be met by the Žatec Horseshoe Nail Factory Mustad & Son. The cartel strictly forbade the construction of new factories as well as the introduction of new production units and further investment in Czechoslovakia. A fine of Kč 100,000 was to be imposed for an infringement of the cartel conditions and at a further violation of the terms of the agreement the fine, payable within 8 days, was to be doubled.[1] This explicitly restrictive cartel was concluded for 10 years, but was terminated on the day of the outbreak of the Second World War. In this field of production, which still had a large market in the comparatively backward agricultural areas of Southeast Europe, the Swedish concern sought to gain complete control of the Czechoslovak market, using its substantial capital participation in the Czechoslovak iron and engineering industry to enforce the conditions of an international cartel.

All the international cartels concerning metal fittings and couplings in which Czechoslovak works participated had some common features: they divided markets according to the economic strength of their members; they fixed the highest prices which the markets effectively controlled by them could bear; they allocated output and export quotas; they forbade any expansion of production as well as the establishment of new factories; and national cartels, as members of international

[1] SÚA–KR 809.

agreements, tried to protect their own domestic markets as effectively as they could by the clause of mutual territorial protection. However, the reasons for Czechoslovak producers joining international cartels in this branch of mechanical engineering and the conditions under which they did so differed greatly according to the economic situation in the respective areas of production. As a rule, the establishment of an international cartel was preceded by domestic cartelization, either under pressure from and on the initiative of the big concerns, or by syndicalization forced with the help of the state. Conversely, tighter cartelization on a national scale occurred as a result of competitive pressure by international cartels on the home market, which compelled Czechoslovak enterprises to reorganize, rationalize and concentrate production. Finally, it is clear that Czechoslovak enterprises were not strong enough economically, even when they joined forces in national cartels, to ensure a complete monopoly on their home market and that they had to concede certain agreed quantities of imports to their foreign cartel partners.

Zinc, brass, tombac and aluminium products in the engineering industry

Zinc

International cartels attempting to regulate the world market for zinc began to intervene on the Czechoslovak market at the beginning of 1929. Crude zinc and rolled zinc products were especially important to the world's biggest producers and they became the subject of attempts to form a world-wide cartel, because the demand for zinc had risen steadily with the increased knowledge of its many uses in the engineering and electrical industry in the first decades of the twentieth century.

In the inter-war period Germany and Poland produced the largest amounts of zinc in Europe. This was mined mainly from the rich Upper Silesian lead and zinc deposits. The first cartel organization for the sale of rolled zinc products, the Zinkwalzwerksverband G.m.b.H. in Berlin, originated in Germany at the end of the nineteenth century, and as early as 1907 it was joined by the Polish producers. It was not until March 1928 that the Polish works established their own cartel company,

Table 8. *Export quotas of rolled zinc products according to cartel agreement of 19 January 1929**

Cartel partners	Quota (%)
Zinkwalzwerksverband G. m.b.H., Berlin and associates	63.75
Polish Works	21.25
Metal Rolling Mills, Přívoz and Horganyhengermü, Vác	15.00

* Compiled from SÚA–KR 561.

Biuro Rozdzielcze Zjednoczonych Polskich Walcowni Cynku in Katowice, in order to protect and monopolize their domestic market, but they retained an association with the German syndicate which had exclusive selling rights for the export quotas of its German and Polish members.[1] One of the main tasks of the Zinkwalzwerksverband was to coordinate action against foreign competitors with the aim either of crushing them or of subordinating them to the cartel. In pursuing this activity the Zinkwalzwerksverband encountered Czechoslovak competition on its own domestic markets and in Central and Southeastern Europe. At the beginning of 1929 it drew the biggest Czechoslovak competitor, the Válcovny Kovů in Přívoz (Metal Rolling Mills in Přívoz), into the cartel.[2] Together with the Czechoslovak works their Hungarian subsidiary, the Horganyhengermü r.t. in Vác, also joined up and shared in the export quota of the Czechoslovak cartel partner. The export quotas allocated by the cartel agreement of 1929 in rolled zinc products to all countries except each member's home market are shown in Table 8.

The domestic markets of each cartel partner consisted of Germany, Poland and Danzig for the Zinkwalzwerksverband and Czechoslovakia, Hungary and Austria for the Metal Rolling Mills in Přívoz. Thus the members of the Zinkwalzwerksverband recognized the fact that the Přívoz Metal Rolling Mills had connections with Austrian capital (p. 135). However, within the sphere of Czechoslovak–Austrian relations no special agreement about the division of their respective domestic

[1] For official data see *Statistyka karteli w Polsce, Główny urząd statystyczny Rzeczypospolitej Polskiej, Statystyka Polski, seria C, zeszyt 28* (Warszawa, 1935), p. 84.

[2] SÚA–KR 561, 19 January 1929–31 December 1933.

markets existed until the crisis year of 1931.[1] Even when a formal understanding did come into force a number of outsiders remained,[2] so that the cartel could impose neither an effective price policy nor a strict quota system in this area.

Very soon after the cartel convention of 1929 was concluded, competitive pressures against Czechoslovak zinc products increased within the German–Polish and Czechoslovak–Hungarian cartel. Even greater disruptive influences were at work with the growing crisis, and as early as 5 September 1930 the original Czechoslovak–Hungarian export quota was reduced from 15 % to 11.79 % (cf. Table 8),[3] but there it stayed through the further vicissitudes of the international cartel. While conditions for the Czechoslovak–Hungarian Group in the cartel also remained unchanged with regard to the understanding that the Zinkwalzwerksverband in Berlin continued to administer their exports, the Polish Group surprisingly managed remarkably to extricate itself from German dominance. After the disintegration of the original association between 1931 and 1933, they joined the newly formed cartel as an independent group with a significantly increased share of the export quota and with their own syndicate, the Blacha Cynkowa, Katowice, which administered sales in the home market as well as Polish export sales.[4] Table 9 shows the revised quotas of the German, Polish and Czechoslovak–Hungarian partners in the Export Convention of Rolled Zinc Products, concluded on 1 January 1934 and valid until 31 December 1936.

The renewed cartel agreement did not however secure for its members domination of the Central and Southeastern European markets, and even less so of European markets generally, where they encountered serious competition from significantly stronger British, Belgian and Dutch combines, which could draw on rich raw material supplies in their colonies. When the German–

[1] SÚA–KR 562, agreement between the Metal Rolling Mills, Přívoz, and the Österreichische Metallwerke Verkaufsgesellschaft m. b. H., Wien, of 1.–4. May 1931. At the *Anschluss* the cartel became irrelevant, as the Austrian zinc rolling mills were incorporated into the Zinkwalzverband G.m.b.H. in Berlin.

[2] Outsiders according to data in SÚA–KR 561 were: České závody kovů (Czech Metal Works) Robert Zinn, Engels & Co. Ltd., Varnsdorf; Brothers Dudek Ltd., Řetenice; Weimann-Werke in Teplice; and Manfred Weiss in Budapest-Czepel, and a Yugoslav factory in Cilli.

[3] SÚA–KR 561.

[4] Ibid., also *Statystyka karteli w Polsce.*

Table 9. *Export quotas of rolled zinc products according to cartel agreement of 1 January 1934**

Cartel partners	Quota (%)
Zinkwalzwerksverband G. m.b.H., Berlin	40.393
Blacha Cynkowa, Katowice	47.817
Metal Rolling Mills, Přívoz and Horganyhengermü, Vác	11.790
Total	100

* Compiled from SÚA–KR 561.

Polish–Czechoslovak–Hungarian Export Convention expired it was therefore not renewed.

A final attempt at international cartelization before the Second World War concerned a basic product (i.e. the control of exports and prices of zinc sheets) and took place in February 1938, when the most influential European producers established the Entente internationale des lamineurs de zinc with its seat in Liège. A control organ was formed, the Comité de Surveillance, with a Belgian chairman and secretary, in order to enforce the complicated cartel conditions laid down in the *Convention générale* and in a number of specialized agreements with individual national cartels or groups of companies.[1] Among them the Belgian group, the Union des lamineurs Belge de zinc in Liège, took a leading position. At the same time, it also dominated Italian production through its controlling capital participation in the Italian zinc rolling mills.[2] In the same way as the Belgians, the German and Polish partners joined as separate national cartels, i.e. the Zinkwalzwerksverband G. m.b.H. in Berlin and the Blacha Cynkowa sp. z o. odpow. in Katowice; the English, Dutch and Hungarian cartel members were represented by one concern in each case. The Czechoslovak group alone consisted of four separate works, because the former outsiders,[3] as well as the Metal Rolling Mills Ltd of Přívoz, joined the Entente internationale des lamineurs de zinc by a special agreement of 31 March

[1] SÚA–KR 1142.

[2] Cf. E. Hexner, *International Cartels*, p. 251.

[3] I.e.: Brothers Dudek Ltd, Řetenice, Franke & Scholz Metalworking Factories in Řymařov, and the Czech Metal Works Robert Zinn, Engels & Co. Ltd, Varnsdorf. SÚA–KR 1142, 31 March 1938–31 December 1938.

1938. It is interesting to note that barely a fortnight after the *Anschluss* the Austrian works already figured as part of the German Group in the Entente.[1] Although after the events of Munich, and particularly after the outbreak of war, the Entente des lamineurs de zinc lost its significance, some facts emerge from the cartel's terms and conditions which are relevant in assessing the relations of the various national engineering industries in this field of production, on the European and especially on the Czechoslovak market, on the eve of the Second World War. One of the foremost aims of the cartel was to try and limit world exports to the quantities exported in 1936. For each ton exported in excess of this quota the Comité de Surveillance was to impose a fine of £2. 10*s*. 0*d*. By limiting production for export at a time of rising demand the cartel hoped to create favourable conditions for a high price policy. From the division of markets and allocation of quotas it clearly emerges that the largest competitor of the English and Belgian suppliers to the European continent was the German Zinkwalzwerksverband. In many instances the German cartel partner had unwillingly to accept the terms of the stronger Anglo-Belgian Groups, as for instance the ruling that the former German colonies in Africa belonged exclusively to the Anglo-Belgian sphere of interest, and that German export quotas in the cartel were generally to be about one to two-thirds smaller than the Belgian. In relation to Czechoslovakia the Zinkwalzwerksverband had to retreat in face of Belgian competition. While the Zinkwalzwerksverband had taken over all export sales activity from the Czechoslovak works (see p. 255) up to the end of 1936, about 75 % of the total Czechoslovak exports of zinc sheets thereafter went through the hands of the Union des lamineurs de zinc in Liège and the German–Polish cartel was able to handle only the remaining amount. In a special agreement with the Czechoslovak works the Belgian Group also gained a guaranteed annual import quota of 75 tons of zinc sheet to Czechoslovakia. As the annual export quota from the ČSR was fixed at 289 tons by the Entente, this Belgian quota was certainly not insignificant. At the same time a special German–Czechoslovak–Hungarian agreement on mutual

[1] I.e. The firm of Friedr. von Neumann, Marktl, which was until the *Anschluss* a partner of the Metal Rolling Mills in Přívoz under the Czechoslovak–Austrian agreement of 1931. Cf. SÚA–KR 562 and 1142; also footnote 1, p. 255.

territorial protection within the Entente barred all the Zinkwalzwerksverband's rolled zinc products from entering the domestic markets of Czechoslovakia and Hungary.[1] Doubtless, the Czechoslovak production of rolled zinc materials was not very significant in relation to the powerful European cartels. Nevertheless, in the increasing competition for markets in Central and Southeastern Europe we can observe a shifting of Czechoslovak cartel relations from the German to the Belgian sphere of influence.

Similar tendencies are evident in the efforts of Polish and Czechoslovak entrepreneurs to extricate themselves from the dominant influence of their German cartel partners in the area of crude zinc exports. Between 1928 and 1931 two attempts were made to establish an International Zinc Cartel involving all zinc foundries except for those in North America and Japan, but it invariably disintegrated when prices began to fall.[2] At the height of the crisis in 1932–3 the International Zinc Cartel was resuscitated[3] in an effort to reduce crude zinc output for export by at least 45 %. However, output of cartel members for their own domestic consumption was not to be included in this quota system. For this purpose an international pool was founded and as an integral part of it the regional Polish–Upper Silesian–Czech Zinc Pool came into being from 1 January 1933. The driving force behind this pool was the German cartel centre, the Bergwerksprodukte G.m.b.H. in Berlin, which made decisions about prices, output and export quotas of crude zinc in the framework of this regional agreement. Sales on the Czechoslovak market were divided 50:50 between the Czech and Upper Silesian cartel members.[4] According to the calculations of the International Zinc Pool the Czech Group's share of total world exports amounted to 2–2½ %; however, German and Polish suppliers directed their attention to Czechoslovakia primarily as an importer of crude zinc for its large engineering

[1] SÚA–KR 1142. The agreement of 31 March 1928 consisted of a general convention and special bilateral and multilateral undertakings.

[2] Cf. *Statystyka karteli v Polsce.*

[3] According to TNEC – Hearings – Part 25 the European cartelized industries of Belgium, France, Germany, Great Britain, Holland, Hungary, Italy, Spain, Poland and Czechoslovakia united to form the International Zinc Cartel.

[4] Czechoslovak members of the Polish–Upper Silesian–Czech Zinc Pool were the Brothers Dudek, Řetenice, and the Weinmann-Werke, Teplice-Šanov, together with 2 Polish and 3 German works. SÚA–KR 525.

and electrical industry. As demand continued to shrink on all markets, competition for exports increased considerably and in the struggle the Polish–Upper Silesian–Czech Zinc Pool fell apart in 1935. In January 1936 Polish and Czechoslovak producers concluded separate cartels with the new centre in Katowice and without German participation. The agreement allowed Polish exports to cover 50 % of Czechoslovak crude zinc consumption, but 10 % of this quota was transferred back to the Czechoslovak works at a compensatory payment to the Polish Group of 1 gold shilling per ton supplied. The Polish–Czechoslovak agreement became an independent part of the International Zinc Cartel. The German Group also remained a member but from 1936 it ceased to be the spokesman for the Polish and Czechoslovak works and no longer represented them in the export syndicate. It is significant that the Danzig area, which had till that time belonged to the German zone of deliveries, in the Polish–Czechoslovak agreement of 1936 – just as in the international steel cartel agreements – became part of the Polish domestic market.[1] On 30 September 1938,[2] the day the Munich Agreement was signed, probably in expectation of a greater share in the trade of a politically weakened Czechoslovakia, the Polish cartel partners cancelled their bilateral agreement with the Czech firms.

In practice the International Zinc Cartel was able to influence the division of markets and export quotas amongst its members, but its endeavours to stabilize prices at a higher level were only successful in a negative way, i.e. prices of crude zinc would certainly have fallen more if no cartel had existed. For purposes of comparison Table 10 shows the movement of prices in the ČSR of crude iron, a highly cartelized product, and of crude zinc, a product less effectively cartelized, between 1926 and 1938. It illustrates how the iron and steel cartel kept prices of crude iron at a fairly stable level and prevented too sharp a fall during the economic crisis, even though the lowest price level in 1934 was 36 % below the stable annual level of 1926–32. In the movement of crude zinc prices the effects of the crisis were reflected in a consistent and substantially larger fall in prices from 1929 onwards. The lowest point was reached in 1932, when average prices were 64 % lower than in 1926. But even

[1] SÚA–KR 525/4. [2] Ibid.

Table 10. *Wholesale prices in the Czechoslovak Republic**

Year	Annual average (prices in Kč/100 kg) Crude iron	Crude zinc
1926	65	655.775
1927	65	563.55
1928	65	504.22
1929	65	499.53
1930	65	352.32
1931	65	266.77
1932	65	237.00
1933	63.15	258.75
1934	41.30	249.60
1935	42.05	243.00
1936	42.20	278.40
1937	56.20	418.45
1938	66.10	322.30

* Compiled from SÚS in Prague *Velkoobchodní ceny a indexy v Československé Republice*, 1926–38 (Wholesale prices and indices in the Czechoslovak Republic).

in the following years of partial recovery, and especially in 1937 and 1938, prices of crude zinc did not rise enough to reach the level of 1926–8, while, as a result of the activities of the iron and steel cartel, prices of crude iron rose steadily until in 1938 they exceeded the average level between 1926–32.

During the decade 1928–38 changes in the structure of international zinc cartels can be observed, especially in relations between the German, Polish and Czech industries. The influence of the German cartels was curbed and the importance of Belgian and Polish cartels in the Central European area increased. The disintegration of the original cartels during the economic crisis and the content of the entirely new cartel agreements concerning the Czechoslovak market provide evidence of this development. At the same time, the renewed and often short-lived attempts at international cartelization of crude zinc and zinc products demonstrate the force of competition, which in this case prevented an effective stabilization of prices.

Brass and tombac products

The uses of copper, brass and tombac semi-finished materials in the mechanical and electrical engineering industry are at least as many as those of zinc products. For this reason the large concerns in Czechoslovakia attempted to control all domestic copper and brass works. The Mining and Metallurgic Company, Křížík-Chaudoir, Copper, Cable and Electrotechnical Works in Prague, and the Czechoslovak Armaments Works in Brno, headed the drive towards cartelization. Under their leadership a national cartel of producers of semi-finished materials from copper and its alloys was formed in the 1920s, the Association of Copper and Brass Works in Czechoslovakia, which represented this entire branch of industry; later an export syndicate was established as part of it.[1] The Association of Copper and Brass Works in Czechoslovakia was connected by three separate bilateral international cartel agreements with producers' cartels in Germany (September/October 1928), in Hungary (October 1934) and Austria (November 1934).[2] In essence they were all price cartels to eliminate undercutting of domestic products, especially by German suppliers of the Czechoslovak market. Some German firms insisted on registering a written protest against the terms of the Czechoslovak–German cartel agreement of 4 October 1928, maintaining that the conditions concerning sales in the ČSR were severely damaging to their business interests; however, the differences were settled and the original terms of the cartel remained valid until the end of the pre-Munich Republic.[3]

The Czechoslovak cartel could only get the German firms to agree to abide by its prices; it could not prevent them from selling on its home market. However, it succeeded in getting the Austrian firms to abstain from offering their products on the Czechoslovak market for a monthly payment of Kč 20,000, to compensate them for the loss of potential export opportunities

[1] Hospodářský svaz mědáren a mosazáren v Československu, cf. *Compass, Čechoslovakei* (Praha, 1938), 774.

[2] SÚA–KR 291, 700 and 717.

[3] The German cartel, Zentralverband der deutschen Metallwalzwerks- und Hüttenindustrie, Berlin, undertook to offer and to sell in the ČSR according to a price-list provided for the German firms by the Czechoslovak cartel partners. SÚA–KR 291.

and for the costs of finding alternative markets.[1] These bilateral agreements also formed a protective system for all cartel partners against foreign outsiders on the markets of Central and Southeast Europe and established a certain balance of forces in their mutual competition.

Aluminium foils

The violent and extensive battle for control of the aluminium market[2] raged primarily between the American, West European and German producers and affected Czechoslovakia only peripherally. The engineering, electrical and chemical industries in Czechoslovakia were particularly dependent on imports for their aluminium supplies, and theoretically they could place their orders with any supplier they chose. This was because the International Aluminium Cartel directed its activity above all towards limiting total world output and fixing high monopoly prices for all markets, but did not – like other international cartels – allocate specific markets to individual cartel members.[3] Czechoslovak industrial companies preferred to have their demand satisfied by West European rather than by German suppliers.[4] However, on the European mainland German and Swiss concerns wielded an extraordinarily strong influence and gradually forced the Czechoslovak metal-working industry to accept a fixed guaranteed import quota. By signing a cartel agreement with the Aluminium Exportverband in Berlin on 1 April 1937, the Czech enterprises contracted to purchase 5.5 tons of aluminium foil annually from Germany and 1.5 tons annually from 3 Swiss firms. At the same time they undertook to remove the obstacles in the way of German and Swiss imports to Czechoslovakia.[5]

Although the aluminium foil cartel was not of great economic importance, it nevertheless pinpoints the sharpening competitive

[1] Cf. SÚA–KR 717. In 1939 the agreement of 10 November 1934 was incorporated into the Czechoslovak–German cartel No. 291.

[2] Cf. e.g. J. Borkin and Ch. A. Welsh, *Germany's Master Plan* (London/New York/Melbourne), chap. xv; E. Hexner, p. 216. Much has been published on American–German relations in the production and marketing of aluminium, and on the International Aluminium Cartel.

[3] Cf. Borkin and Welsh, p. 102.

[4] See e.g. Rochette's instructions to all subsidiary companies of the Škoda-Works. Agenda Rochette, PA–ZVIL, Plzeň, GŘ.

[5] SÚA–KR 1060.

struggles in Central Europe, which run like a thread through most cartel agreements.

The Czechoslovak–French automobile cartel

After the second half of the 1920s the Czechoslovak automobile industry grew considerably, especially after the concentration, modernization and expansion of motor-car manufacture in the Škoda combine.[1] Škoda products captured a leading position in the domestic market and the automobiles of ČKD lagged behind. Although Czechoslovakia remained an export market for foreign large-scale producers of automobiles, Czechoslovak cars began to compete with them in Eastern and Southeastern European countries, as well as in some overseas markets.

In its attempts to dominate the world market the American car industry promulgated the economic doctrine of 'adequate export quotas', which were to be allocated in proportion to the existing manufacturing and marketing capacity of individual national automobile industries.[2] It is not difficult to deduce that this doctrine was aimed at securing the largest export quotas for the American industry in any international cartel agreement. With regard to imports into Czechoslovakia the American car manufacturers also applied their doctrine in an international trade and customs contract with Czechoslovakia which was very like a cartel[3] and which allowed the French, American, Austrian, German, Italian, British and Belgian automobile industries to import a maximum of 750 cars each annually into Czechoslovakia on the basis of existing international trade treaties and respecting the most-favoured nation clauses in them. Only the U.S.A. exceeded its quota for imports into the ČSR – none of the other states reached their maximum import allowance, even in the boom of 1929.[4] At the same time a cartel agreement was in force between the Czechoslovak car manufacturers and the French syndicate Fédération Nationale de

[1] Cf. V. Jíša and A. Vaněk, p. 216.

[2] PA–ŠZ, Praha – obchodní oddělení, unnumbered material.

[3] Material on the automobile cartel is very fragmentary and no thorough analysis can therefore be attempted.

[4] Car imports to ČSR from the contracting countries in 1929 (annual maximum 750 cars) were as follows: France, 253; U.S.A., 1,031; Austria, 200; Germany, 514; Italy, 453. In the same year Czechoslovakia exported 1,406 cars. (*Source:* Data on cars cleared by customs in ČSR. PA–ŠZ, Praha – obchodní oddělení, unnumbered material.)

l'Automobile, du Cycle, de l'Aéronautique et des Industries qui s'y rattachent, containing guarantees of especially favourable customs duties in order to facilitate French imports into Czechoslovakia, chiefly against American competition.

From 1930 onwards international trade treaties disintegrated and with them the trade relations with the Czechoslovak automobile industry. The Italian government was the first to break without warning the mutual customs agreement, increasing import duties on cars substantially in June 1930. The Austrian government followed in October 1930, by officially terminating the secret Austro-Czechoslovak understanding on motor-car duties, and at the end of 1930 Czechoslovakia imposed a so-called autonomous tariff on the import of automobiles, which was markedly higher than the hitherto existing rate.

The conditions of the Franco-Czechoslovak automobile cartel came into conflict with the Czechoslovak state's new tariff policy. However, the cartel remained intact and the state adjusted itself to its terms in a roundabout way. According to an additional Franco-Czechoslovak agreement concluded in Paris at the time when the Czechoslovak authorities decided to increase tariffs, the French partners agreed to pay the higher rate to the Czechoslovak customs authorities only if they were to be reimbursed by the Czechoslovak car industry for the difference between the old and the new tariff, up to a maximum of 750 cars imported. According to a draft calculation drawn up by the Škoda-Works Commercial Department for the Czechoslovak Ministry of Finance this refund to the French car industry would be Kč 10,240,500 annually at the most. Eventually, the Ministry of Finance undertook to return payments by French car importers over and above the previous tariff rate to the Czechoslovak automobile industry, which then in turn would transfer the overcharges back to their French cartel partners. At the same time the Czechoslovak car manufacturers applied to their government for export premiums out of the expected increase in tariff revenue for car imports, in order to strengthen their competitive ability at least on some European markets against American, Italian and German dumping.[1]

When demand continued to fall, particularly in 1933 and 1934 at the height of the crisis in France and Czechoslovakia,

[1] Ibid.

competition broke out between Czechoslovak and French car manufacturers on their respective home markets, as well as on the markets of other countries. As a result the Czechoslovak automobile industry brought the cartel agreement with the French syndicate to an end in 1935, in the hope of ridding themselves of the irksome tariff refund payments and also of eventually negotiating an agreement with more favourable terms for its own car manufacturers.

In 1936 a new cartel was formed between the Czechoslovak producers (the Škoda-Works, ČKD and Ringhoffer-Tatra) and the French producers organized in the Chambre Syndicale des Constructions d'Automobiles, Paris.[1] The Czechoslovak Group got their French partners to accept the prevailing Czechoslovak tariffs on automobiles and in addition to pay the Czechoslovak motor-car industry Frs. 4. – for each kg of automobile that was imported from France to Czechoslovakia. In return the Czechoslovak partners had to pay the Chambre Syndicale des Constructions d'Automobiles 75 Heller for each kg of automobile sold in Czechoslovakia, i.e. on their own home market, or exported to France, and 20 Hellers for each kg of automobile exported from Czechoslovakia to markets where both industries competed. These Czechoslovak payments to the French syndicate were obviously also tied up with agreements on technical collaboration and they were limited to not less than Kč 3,000,000 and not more than Kč 4,000,000 annually. The French car manufacturers demanded these payments to compensate them for the consequent shrinkage of the Czechoslovak market; at the same time they agreed to reduce their exports to the ČSR to 200 automobiles annually, while Czechoslovak exports to France were not to exceed 30 cars annually.[2]

The Czechoslovak automobile industry gained by this agreement somewhat greater freedom of movement on its domestic market and also on markets where it competed with French products. It is, however, quite apparent that the Czechoslovak automobile works, an integral part of the engineering industry, remained strongly influenced by French capital investment and French cartels.

[1] SÚA–KR 904.
[2] PA–ŠZ, Praha – obchodní oddělení, unnumbered material.

International cartels in the Czechoslovak electrical industry

Before the Second World War industrial associations in the electrical industry for the control of prices, exports, sales and output were among the most effective cartels with the widest spheres of influence. The most tightly organized and relatively most durable were those concerning cables and bulbs. Within the framework of these cartels, and also outside it, there existed a highly complicated network of licence and patent agreements and of capital ties, especially with German and American monopolistic combines, which increased the effectiveness and relative stability of these cartels. The main Czechoslovak electro-technical companies became members of the principal international cartels soon after they were founded in the 1920s.

By 1928 the world market for *high voltage and low-voltage cables* had been brought under the control of the International Cable Development Corporation. From its headquarters in Vaduz in Lichtenstein it conducted the business of the cartel in accordance with a general convention signed by all members and many additional bilateral agreements between the various national cartels of the member countries.[1] Each national group was represented in the cartel centre in proportion to the number and financial strength of enterprises associated in it. The British, French and German Groups wielded the greatest influence and under the terms of the general convention the cartel would be dissolved if one of these national groups was to resign or itself disintegrated. An idea of the cartel partners' relative strength can be gained by comparing the numbers of delegates with voting powers at general meetings in Vaduz (see Table 11). Judging from the voting strength of the various national delegations it would seem that the Czechoslovak industry occupied a place of medium importance. However, in the decisive commission of the cartel which supervised the export agreement the

[1] The Czechoslovak cartel members signed 21 agreements altogether (14 concerning high-voltage cables valid from 17 September 1930 to 31 March 1933): SÚA–KR 192 – Czechoslovak–Swiss agreement, 193 with Sweden, 194 with Spain, 195 with Austria, 196 with Poland, 197 with Norway, 198 with Germany on Finland, 324 with Germany, 325 with Hungary, 326 with Italy, 327 with France, 328 with Holland, 329 with Denmark, 330 with Belgium (7 agreements concerning low-voltage cables): SÚA–KR 133 – General Agreement and Anglo-Czechoslovak Agreement, 186 with Germany, 187 with Austria, 188 with Norway, 189 with Hungary, 190 with France, 191 with Belgium.

Table 11. *Representation of member groups in the International Cable Development Corporation, Vaduz**

Group	Number of companies	Number of delegates
Germany	21	5
Great Britain	17	5
France	10	4
Italy	6	2
Belgium	4	2
Austria	4	2
Czechoslovakia	3	2
Sweden	2	2
Poland	4	1
Switzerland	3	1
Hungary	2	1
Spain	2	1
Holland	1	1
Denmark	1	1
Norway	1	1

* Compiled from SÚA–KR 133.

Czechoslovak Group could not assert any significant influence, as it shared its representative with the Austrian, Hungarian and Polish Groups. In the same commission the North-European countries (Denmark, Norway, Sweden and Holland) had one delegate between them, and the South European countries (Italy, Spain and Switzerland) had another, while Belgium, Great Britain, France and Germany sent one delegate each.[1] Thus the four main countries with their four delegates could outvote the three delegates representing the other eleven countries. The influence of the groups from the economically and politically more powerful countries was, of course, much greater than their mere supremacy in voting, for they actually owned many subsidiary electrical companies which were themselves members of the other national groups in the same cartel.

Most of the national groups, including Czechoslovakia, joined the international cartel to protect their domestic markets, as the general convention laid down that cartel products were

[1] SÚA–KR 133 – Addition III to Agreement.

not to be delivered to the territory of another member. Each national group had exclusive powers in its own territory to fix prices and divide the quota allocated to it by the International Cable Development Corporation. At the same time, however, cartel members were not permitted to erect new factories or to gain a directly or indirectly controlling influence in factories on the territory of other members. A pool was founded to which the member countries contributed in proportion to their quotas and into which they also paid fines amounting to 10 % of the excess output if they exceeded their allotted quotas. On the other hand, they received compensation payments from the pool if they did not fulfil their quotas. In 1933 all member countries had to deposit a fixed amount of gold into the pool – for the Czechoslovak Group the amount was 3,577,045 g – to guarantee the financial transactions of the cartel.

Driven by crisis conditions in the 1930s, the British and German monopoly groups drew the other European countries even closer into their orbit and organized united action against so-called enemy countries, i.e. those outside the cartel. Special measures and market manipulations financed by the pool were undertaken, particularly against American and Japanese infiltration into the areas dominated by the cartel.

The terms and activities of this international cartel implied tight cartelization in the individual member countries. Czechoslovak membership in the International Cable Development Corporation also accelerated cartelization of the domestic industry. The Czechoslovak Group consisted of the three largest works of Kablo, Cable and Wire Rope Factory in Prague which was a subsidiary of the Škoda-Works, the combine Křižík-Chaudoir, a copper, cable and electrotechnical works in Prague, and the Slovak Cable Factory in Bratislava. They set up a domestic cartel, the Evidence Bureau for Cables in Prague, which had the task of allotting $33\frac{1}{3}$ % of all orders to each of the three members and thus of administering the quotas allotted to Czechoslovakia by the international cartel.[1] Parallel with their efforts to unite in a national cartel they disposed of two weaker competitors, either by allowing them a certain quota on the domestic market in the first place, or later by compensating them for agreeing to discontinue production of the cartelized

[1] SÚA–KR 135 – domestic agreement of 15 August 1933.

commodities.[1] By forming a domestic cable cartel and by membership of the international cartel, the three largest enterprises secured a monopoly in the Czechoslovak market.

However, export possibilities for the Czechoslovak cable industry were severely curtailed by the terms of the general convention and bilateral agreements (as a rule containing mutual market protection), although the Czechoslovak engineering and electrical industry strove tirelessly for export orders. The 1926–37 foreign trade statistics show that the only regular export markets for Czechoslovak cables were Romania, Yugoslavia and Bulgaria.[2] Other markets were widely scattered all over the world, without any pattern, either in time, place or significant quantities, except for those national groups in the International Cable Corporation which allowed their Czechoslovak partners limited access to their domestic markets. Thus Czechoslovak works could make offers in Britain, but had to inform the British Group of the prices they quoted;[3] Germany and Austria also allowed strictly controlled amounts into their countries from Czechoslovak cartel members, who had to compensate the German or Austrian groups by passing on to them 10 % of their net profits on those deliveries.[4]

As was the case with other cartelized commodities in pre-Munich Czechoslovakia, we find an exact reflection of the international cartel's terms in the foreign trade statistics concerning cables.[5]

The *International Bulb Cartel* was far more complete and highly effective in the inter-war period. From 1924 to 1939 at the height of its monopolistic activity, it brought together 36 large concerns from 18 states, each of which was itself a mother company with numerous subsidiary enterprises. Thus the cartel controlled 90–95 % of the world's output of electric bulbs.[6] The cartel members founded a joint-stock company 'Phoebus, Industrial Company for the Development of Lighting', with an

[1] SÚA–KR 136, agreement with the Pražská továrna na káble spol. s r.o., Praha (Prague Cable Factory) on 15 June 1930; and 134, agreement with the firm Clement Zahn jr., Vejprty.

[2] *Zahraniční obchod Republiky československé* (1926–37).

[3] SÚA–KR 133.

[4] SÚA–KR 186, 187, 324.

[5] See footnote 2 above

[6] SÚA–KR 164; also *Československé kartely*, p. 100. Annual output reached 1 milliard bulbs in the 1930s.

initial capital of 500,000 Swiss Francs, to look after their extensive administration and financial transactions, especially the numerous and costly litigations about patents. They chose Geneva as the company's headquarters, as Swiss laws provided favourable legal conditions and secured for cartel members 'independence from varying legal systems in different countries'.[1]

The history and activity of the International Bulb Cartel seemed to provide such a good example of a perfect monopoly that it inspired a large number of economic publications on its development.[2] However, it also provoked many economic and political disputes and induced the governments in Great Britain and the U.S.A. to set up commissions of enquiry into unfair practices.[3] This industrial combination was fairly successful in dominating the world market within the framework of one of the earliest multinational cartels, which had emerged in the electrical industry in 1907 when the German monopoly company Allgemeine Elektrizitätsgesellschaft (AEG), and the Trust, General Electric Company (GEC), agreed to divide the world's markets between them. As late as 1938 an integral part of the general cartel agreement between the International General Electric Company (IGE) concerned terms and conditions relating to electric bulbs between IGE and Osram.[4] Under the prevailing circumstances in the electrical industry, when the most powerful combines of the U.S.A., Great Britain, Germany and Holland had shares in each other's capital, it was not too difficult for two or three of them to join in patent and other technical or commercial agreements and thereby to achieve almost complete cartelization under their own control.

The international cartelization of electric bulbs was achieved, above all, in order to advance the interests of three large

[1] A. S. Benni *et al.*, *General Report on Economic Aspects of Industrial Agreements* (Geneva, 1931), p. 55.

[2] E.g. Wilhelm Meinhardt, *Entwicklung und Aufbau der Glühlampenindustrie* (Berlin, 1932). The development of the electric bulb cartel is almost always included in comprehensive analyses of cartels and trusts, e.g. Robert Liefmann, Alfred Plummer, Ervin Hexner, Wendell Berge, and others.

[3] Cf. *Parliamentary Papers* XXIII, 120 – Profiteering Act, 1919, Findings and Decisions of a Sub-Committee appointed by Standing Committee on Trusts, to Enquire into the Existence of any Trusts or Trade Combination in the Electric Lamp Industry, Cmd. 622; U.S. Tariff Commission, *Incandescent Electric Lamps*, Report No. 133, Second Series, 1939; TNEC, Monograph 21.

[4] General agreement between IGE and AEG of 7 October 1938 quoted by Bone Committee, *Patent Hearings*, Part I, p. 233; also E. Hexner, p. 358.

companies which headed a pyramid of subsidiaries spread all over the world: the American General Electric Company, whose international operations were conducted by the International General Electric Company and the International Standard Electric Corporation; the concern Brüder Siemens and Osram G.m.b.H. in Berlin; and N.V. Philips in Eindhoven. These companies had mutual capital ties but American predominance, of course, remained undisputed, not only because of its capital strength but also because of its established priority in a long list of inventions and patents and the complicated system of licences emanating from this.

Before the First World War a cartel organization, the Convention for the Development and Progress of the International Incandescent Electric Lamp Industry, already controlled the output and marketing of electric light bulbs, and even the war did not seriously disrupt its activity. The great commercial success of electric light bulbs fitted with tungsten filaments (patented by GEC in New York) and filled with argon (the patent for which was held by Philips in Eindhoven) led to further research in the laboratories of other electrical companies between 1913 and 1919, and also to the patenting of the new results, which the American–Dutch partners regarded as an intrusion into its own patent rights. In order to avoid costly law suits, the British, German and Austrian manufacturers agreed to cartel conditions for the exchange of technical information and research results, as well as accepting output quotas, price lists and arrangements for a common sales policy. Thus in 1919 the bulb cartel emerged considerably strengthened by comparison with other international cartels.

The British Government Enquiry of 1920 ascertained that after only one year's activity of the reorganized cartel the British member, the Electric Lamps Manufacturers' Association of Great Britain Ltd, had succeeded in raising the prices of the raw material required for the production of electric light bulbs by 100 % and deliveries of raw materials were entirely denied to outsiders. In its report the Commission of Enquiry concluded that international and national monopolization through capital participation and cartels imposed oppressive conditions on British firms and, by means of licences, restricted their production. It further stated that the Anglo-American Trust GEC and British Thomson–Houston Co., together with the German concern of Siemens, insisted explicitly on the absolute validity of their patents. Because American combines had a majority interest in the three largest electrical companies in Britain and also had a decisive voice in the international cartel, the British Commission of Enquiry recommended public control of the British electric bulb industry to prevent its complete subordination to American interests.[1] Further developments confirmed the Commission's fears, when in 1924 the international cartel tightened its grip by establishing its central company 'Phoebus' in Switzerland and gathered all important manufacturers in the world around it under the leadership of the American electrical industry.

The results and recommendations of the official British enquiry sank into oblivion. However, its findings were very similar to the situation which existed in electric bulb manufacture in Czechoslovakia, except that the production and marketing of bulbs and radio equipment in the Czechoslovak area was allocated in the international cartel to the Philips sphere of interest.[2] Only two leading factories in Czechoslovakia were members of the International Bulb Cartel and were thus represented in 'Phoebus'. One of them, Osram a.s., Prague, was a subsidiary of Osram in Berlin which owned 95.3% of the Prague company's capital,[3] and the second firm, Elektra, Light Bulb Factory in Prague, belonged to the group Živnostenská Bank–Philips. Both companies either participated in the capital of other light-bulb factories in Czechoslovakia or dominated them by licence agreements. In this way they spread German and Dutch influence, as well as the international cartel system, throughout the domestic industry before the Second World War.

The effect on the Czechoslovak economy did not differ essentially from that on the economies of other countries where the International Bulb Cartel was influential. Its activity became the subject of another official enquiry in connection with the comprehensive investigation of the Temporary National

[1] Cf. *Parliamentary Papers* XXIII, 1920, Cmd. 622.

[2] Cf. U.S. Senate, Committee on Military Affairs, Subcommittee on War Mobilization, Monograph No. 1, Corwin D. Edwards, *Economic and Political Aspects of International Cartels* (Washington, 1944), pp. 8–20.

[3] ASÚS – Cizí účasti.

Economic Committee on the Concentration of Economic Power appointed by the United States government in 1938. It emerged from this enquiry, too, that American monopoly and patent rights in the manufacture of electric light bulbs led to restrictions of production both domestically and internationally, to disproportionately high prices in comparison with costs and thus to excessive profits.[1] The International Bulb Cartel also provides a classical example of member manufacturers deliberately reducing the quality of products to increase their profits. The GEC and the Westinghouse Electric Co. reduced the durability of electric light bulbs by one-quarter to one-third between 1932 and 1939, in order to increase turnover.[2] By means of patents and their monopoly position on the world market the cartel prevented the introduction of newly invented, cheaper and more durable electric lighting, in order to maintain its dominant role. This does not mean that technical progress was always hindered by the cartel. The American GEC, for instance, in 1928 introduced an important innovation in the manufacture of glass bulbs, the Corning bulb machine, and the inside frosting of the bulb, for which it again took out patents which further increased its influence. In countries where cartelization had reached a high level there existed undertakings between members of the bulb cartel and electric power works to the effect that bulb manufacturers would refrain from selling electric light bulbs with low power consumption and that in return electric power stations would help by selling cartelized electric bulbs.[3] Such agreements were not unknown in Czechoslovakia.

The international cartel agreement administered by Phoebus contained terms similar to those of other cartels of this type concerning quotas, prices, markets, voting rights etc. It differed from others, however, in that it paid more attention to the technological and manufacturing aspects of its activities and was particularly concerned with patents and licence agreements. Soon the Arbitration Tribunal of Phoebus became its most

[1] Profits of the GEC in the U.S.A. from 1935 to 1938 reached 88 % of total costs, and expenditure varied between 33 and 47% of the net value of investments in bulb manufacturre. Cf. Corwin D. Edwards, p. 13.

[2] E.g. the durability of a 110-volt bulb of 200 watts was lowered from 1,000 to 750 hours, and that of stronger bulbs from 300 to 200 hours. Ibid.

[3] Ibid., p. 17.

important organ. This tribunal attempted to settle the differences which frequently arose among cartel members and proceeded with claims against those who infringed the cartel's patent rights. It consisted of three Swiss experts: a university professor as chairman, a judge of the Swiss Federal administration and an expert on international cartels. Phoebus also established a special laboratory to control technological development in members' factories. All of them were contractually committed to exchange their technical expertise and make patents available in return, of course, for appropriate licence fees. A number of committees and sales syndicates were set up all over the world; perhaps of special interest is the fact that this influential cartel instituted a Committee for Standardization in Geneva, which directed scientific, technical and economic research employing five scientists and five economists permanently.

On the whole, the International Bulb Cartel had contradictory aspects, although most authors evaluate its activity, from the point of view of the consumer and of technical progress, as entirely negative. It is true that, on the one hand, whole national industries, as for instance in Czechoslovakia, became completely subordinated to the cartel, but on the other hand, member factories in Czechoslovakia were able to make use of the results of research at a level which they could not have achieved by themselves and thus the most recent technology and patents were made available to them within the framework of the cartel's licensing agreements. However, agreements of this kind were not favourable for Czechoslovakia's foreign trade, as they confined the sale of products made in Czechoslovakia almost exclusively to the domestic market, and even these domestic enterprises had difficulties in defending their territory against competition from more powerful cartel members.

A number of other international cartels, mainly bilateral, were joined by Czechoslovak electrical and engineering works. They affected output, prices and foreign trade of the cartelized products, on the whole adversely. An example is the Czechoslovak–German cartel agreement of 1934 concerning the sale of radiators, which the Czechoslovak firm, Auer Co. Ltd, had resisted since the early 1920s. In order to protect its home market against German competition the Auer company had entered into an agreement with the German factories in 1928 and had to submit to the commercial and technical control of the Convention's headquarters in Berlin in order to receive deliveries of the raw material needed for its manufacture. According to the Convention's ruling, the Czechoslovak firm could sell its products only on its domestic market, but at the same time Czechoslovakia became a protected territory which the German firms were not allowed to enter.[1] However, a later cartel agreement, signed on 2 November 1934 by the Auer Co. and the Berliner Gasglühlichtwerke, Richard Goetschke A.G. Berlin, broke through this protective barrier. It demanded from the Czechoslovak cartel partner 'that all obstacles and difficulties should be removed in order to facilitate the import of radiators from Germany to Czechoslovakia'.[2] The Berliner Gasglühlichtwerke got an assurance from the Czechoslovak works that they would 'in no way impede their imports into the territory of the ČSR' and 'should this undertaking be broken a fine of Kč 10,000 was to be imposed'. The Czechoslovak partners also pledged themselves to obtain orders from the Czechoslovak State Railways for the Berlin company.[3] The terms of the agreement were submitted to the Minister of Trade, Crafts and Industry for approval. The agreement remained in force until 1940, when the Goetschke Werke took possession of firms in occupied Czechoslovakia.[4]

The nature of the international cartels in the electrical industry in which Czechoslovak enterprises participated gives evidence of strong pressures from the powerful foreign monopolistic combines, especially those of the U.S.A., Holland and Germany. Quite logically, the weaker Czechoslovak industry had to subordinate its activities to the main forces in the cartels. It is, however, significant that in the area of Central and Southeast Europe, except Poland, only Czechoslovakia had an electrical industry which was sufficiently strong that international cartels

[1] SÚA–KR 702/1. Duration of the agreement 13 December 1928–30 June 1940 between the Auerova spol. s r.o., Praha and the Auslandstelle der Konvention der deutschen Glühstrumpf-Fabrikanten, Berlin (18 firms in Germany and 1 firm in Stockholm).

[2] SÚA–KR 705/1.

[3] AÚLSMHD – unnumbered material.

[4] ASÚS – Koncernové šetření (Enquiry into Combines).

could neither push it out of competition altogether nor completely disregard it, but had to take or force it into partnership. Of course, the conditions agreed upon secretly in international cartels often ran counter to the publicly announced goals of economic policy, especially where exports from Czechoslovakia were concerned.

5

The chemical industry

Because practically any processing of raw materials or semi-finished products involves a chemical operation and change, it is not easy to define the term 'chemical industry'.

The growth of chemical manufacture in the second half of the nineteenth century was the result of a rapidly increasing demand from textile, metal and other industries for acids (sulphuric, hydrochloric and nitric acids) and alkalis (soda and potash). This also applied to the dyestuffs industry, which was greatly affected by advances in organic chemistry. In general the technological practice of modern chemical manufacture benefited from scientific knowledge, as shown in the manufacture of synthetic drugs, itself a younger branch of the synthetic dyestuffs industry. Early this century physical chemistry played a major role in the discovery of the synthesis of ammonia, which had far-reaching consequences for the fertilizer and explosives industries and was 'perhaps the most important aspect of industrial chemistry in the inter-war years'.[1] Researches in the hydrogenation of oils and coal were applied in the margarine and motor fuel industries. The development of the petroleum and plastics industries, which owed much to chemical research, foreshadowed the great changes in chemical industrial fields which became more apparent after the Second World War.

As a result of scientific-technological advance large-scale enterprises became typical of the chemical industry. Before long the industry took the lead in cartelization and the formation of international trusts. As a rule, tendencies towards monopoly formation in the chemical industry emanated from technological processes or from interests in marketing certain specialized

[1] F. L. Haber, *The Chemical Industry 1900–1930* (Oxford, 1971), p. 91.

products. To put it in a rather simplified way, the rise to world domination in the chemical market of Solvay et Cie was essentially based on alkalis, of the predecessors of I.G. Farbenindustrie on dyestuffs, and of Nobel's on explosives. Although the output of these large concerns was originally fairly specialized, they expanded their manufacturing programmes and branched out into each other's fields, thus causing increased competition. This, in turn, reinforced tendencies towards concentration, combination and cartelization, and towards a limitation of spheres of interest among the most powerful chemical enterprises. The result was a tight network of capital links and a great variety of contractual ties.

The contribution of the chemical industry to economic growth in Czechoslovakia was second only to that of the leading sectors of metallurgy and engineering. Its index of industrial production increased from 100 in 1924 to 173 in 1937 while metallurgy and engineering rose to 178 over the same period.[1] My calculations are based on data concerning the whole chemical industry as defined in the Statistical Yearbook of Czechoslovakia,[2] so as to make possible comparisons with data of the 1930s. For practical reasons I deal with mineral and plant oils separately, excluding them from the calculations in the first part of this chapter, although in official Czechoslovak statistics these products are included under the general heading 'chemical industry'.

By 31 December 1937 foreign capital formed one-third of the total basic capital (33 %) of the chemical industry (without plant and mineral oils). The proportion of foreign to domestic capital was 46:54 in thirty-eight Czechoslovak companies where direct foreign investment was found. While these enterprises represented 16 % of the total number of chemical companies, their combined capital amounted to 67 % of the total employed in the industry.[3] These figures suggest considerable concentration; they also show that most of the industry's capital was tied up with international business. Table 1 gives an indication of the source of foreign investment in chemical products.

[1] Calculated from *Statistická ročenka*, 1941, p. 185.

[2] *Statistická ročenka*, 1941, p. 176.

[3] Calculated from *Statistická ročenka*, 1941, *Compass*, *Čechoslovakei*, 1939, p. 939, and tables in chapter 2 (1).

Table 1. *Territorial distribution of direct foreign investment in the chemical industry of Czechoslovakia (excluding mineral and vegetable oils), 31 December 1937*

Country of origin of investment	Nominal value in 1,000 Kč	Percentage of total foreign investment
Belgium	83,743	27.1
France	78,409	25.3
Great Britain	76,615	24.8
Austria	25,575	8.3
Germany	25,475	8.2
U.S.A.	11,000	3.6
Italy	5,080	1.6
Switzerland	2,413	0.8
Sweden	750	0.3
Total	309,060	100.0

1 Chemical products, mineral and vegetable oils

In Table 1 the first place is taken by Belgium, whose connection with Czech chemical production can be traced back to the beginning of the 1880s, when Solvay established close cooperation with Spolek pro chemickou a hutní výrobu (Association for Chemical and Metallurgical Production, henceforth referred to as Spolek) in Ústí nad Labem for the manufacture of ammonia soda.[1] Agreements on patents, licences and marketing intensified their relationship, which lasted throughout the pre-Munich Republic.

Under the Habsburgs Spolek was directed and controlled financially by the powerful Viennese bank Österreichische Boden-Credit-Anstalt, which, after the establishment of the new state, retained an influence in the Czechoslovak enterprise until the big Austrian bank crash in 1929–30. After October 1918 Czech capital appeared in Spolek, represented by the Živnostenská Bank, which, together with Solvay, became a

[1] On the history of Spolek see *Sto let Spolku pro chemickou a hutní výrobu v Ústí nad Labem* (One Hundred Years of the Association for Chemical and Metallurgical Production in Ústí nad Labem) (Ústí n.L., 1956); M. Novák, *Vysoká hra* (High Stakes) (Ústí n.L., 1966).

Table 2. *Association for Chemical and Metallurgical*

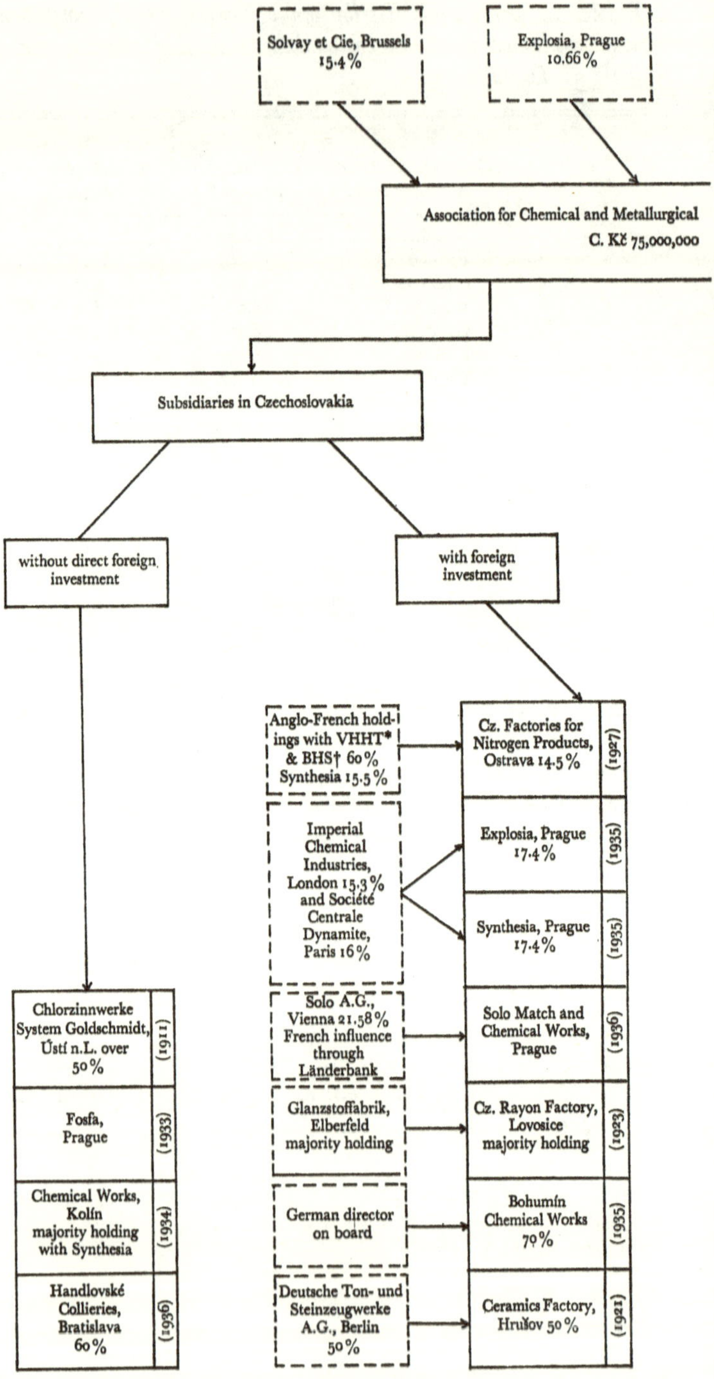

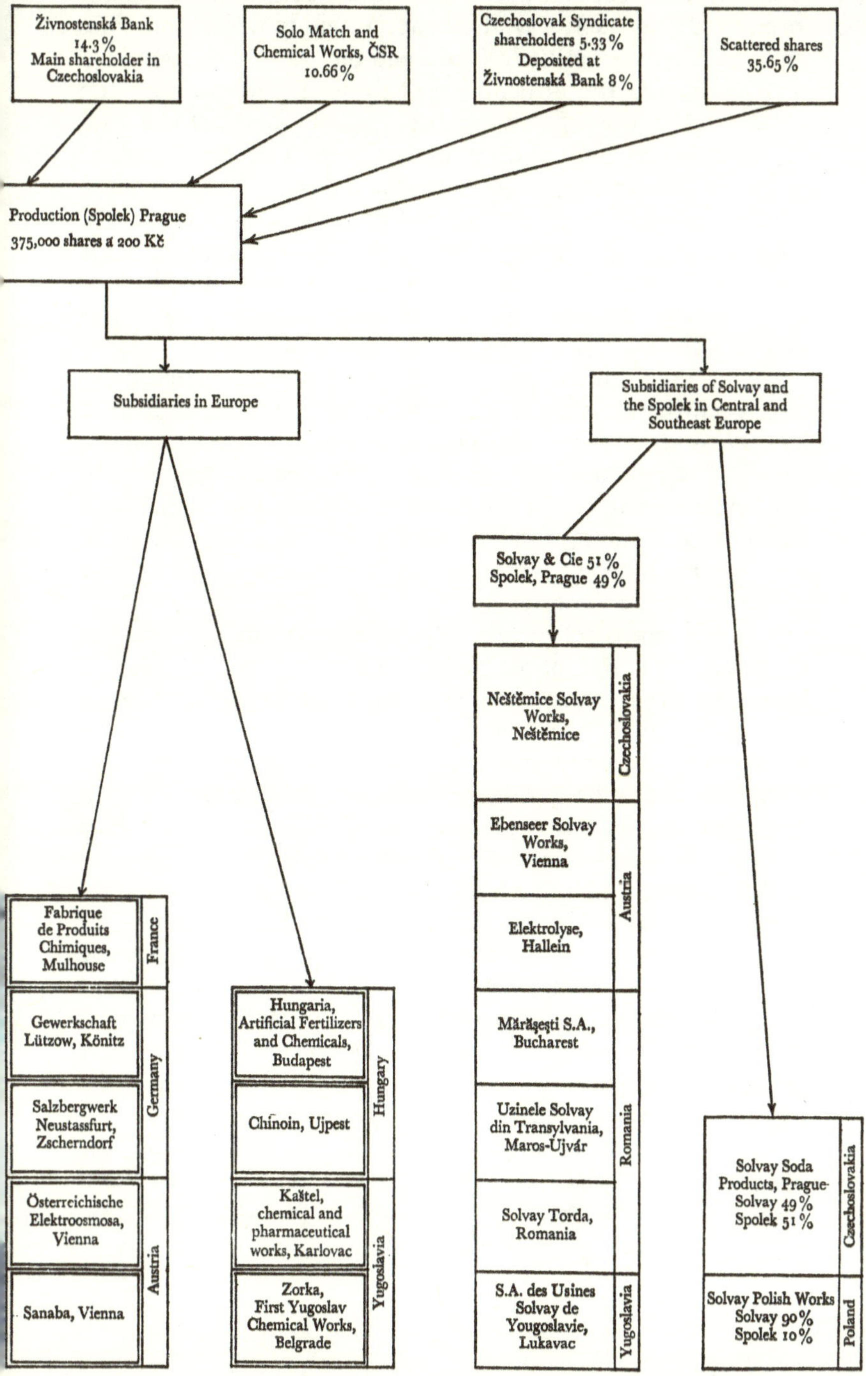
Živnostenská Bank 14.3% Main shareholder in Czechoslovakia
Solo Match and Chemical Works, ČSR 10.66%
Czechoslovak Syndicate shareholders 5.33% Deposited at Živnostenská Bank 8%
Scattered shares 35.65%
Production (Spolek) Prague
375,000 shares á 200 Kč
Subsidiaries in Europe
Subsidiaries of Solvay and the Spolek in Central and Southeast Europe
Solvay & Cie 51% Spolek, Prague 49%
Fabrique de Produits Chimiques, Mulhouse
France
Gewerkschaft Lützow, Könitz
Salzbergwerk Neustassfurt, Zscherndorf
Germany
Österreichische Elektroosmosa, Vienna
Sanaba, Vienna
Austria
Hungaria, Artificial Fertilizers and Chemicals, Budapest
Chinoin, Ujpest
Hungary
Kaštel, chemical and pharmaceutical works, Karlovac
Zorka, First Yugoslav Chemical Works, Belgrade
Yugoslavia
Nештěmice Solvay Works, Neštěmice
Czechoslovakia
Ebenseer Solvay Works, Vienna
Elektrolyse, Hallein
Austria
Mărăşeşti S.A., Bucharest
Uzinele Solvay din Transylvania, Maros-Ujvár
Solvay Torda, Romania
Romania
S.A. des Usines Solvay de Yougoslavie, Lukavac
Yugoslavia
Solvay Soda Products, Prague Solvay 49% Spolek 51%
Czechoslovakia
Solvay Polish Works Solvay 90% Spolek 10%
Poland

substantial shareholder in the Ústí works. Their alignment was formalized in 1929 by a syndicate agreement in which both sides undertook not to sell their shares without mutual consent.[1]

According to the distribution of shares in the company on 31 December 1937, Solvay et Cie. owned 15.4 % of the total capital and was thus the main foreign investor in this important sector of the Czechoslovak chemical industry. Solvay's share even exceeded that of the Živnostenská Bank, which was the main domestic shareholder, by 1.1 % (Table 2). In 1929 Dr Jaroslav Preiss of the Živnostenská Bank replaced Dr Sieghart of the Austrian bank as chairman of Spolek's board of directors and E. Tournay-Solvay became its vice-chairman.

Solvay's manufacturing, technological and commercial interests centred on alkalis. Its international position, supported by extensive agreements with the world's most powerful chemical combines on technical development, prices and markets, determined the relationship between the Belgian and Czechoslovak partners. Solvay was able to retain its influence over Spolek and thus indirectly over the most vital part of the chemical industry in inter-war Czechoslovakia. This cannot be adequately expressed merely by measuring statistically the size of Solvay's capital participation. Solvay's predominance in alkalis spread over the whole of Central and Southeast Europe, and although Solvay's and Spolek's joint ownership of a number of important enterprises in this region gave the Ústí company a considerable share in the profits of these works, it remained in a subordinate position. In all joint enterprises Solvay held a majority, ranging from 51 to 90 % of the capital against Spolek's 49 to 10 % (Table 2).

Solvay's head office for Central and Southeast Europe was in Vienna. From there the Southeast European Solvay combine was strictly controlled. Wherever Solvay's capital was involved a unified accounting system was applied to facilitate financial control from Brussels and great care was taken to ensure that production programmes and chemical-technological processes conformed with the Solvay–Spolek agreements.

It has been maintained that cooperation between Solvay, Spolek and Imperial Chemical Industries (ICI) increased as a result of a cartel agreement entered into in the 1930s concerning

[1] V. Král, II, p. 242.

the division of markets and the exchange of technical information, patents and licences.[1] However, this view is contradicted by the report of Spolek's executive committee, which met on 27 October 1932 to hear E. Lefèvre, Solvay's representative at the Vienna office, give his interpretation of the new agreements between Solvay and ICI. The Belgian and British companies had decided not to give detailed technical information of soda manufacture to all their subsidiaries, and in October 1932 Solvay informed Spolek that ICI had declined to let the Ústí works benefit from ICI's technical expertise which was to be made available to other Solvay factories. Thus only Spolek's delegation at the Viennese head office of the Central and Southeast European soda works could obtain information on manufacturing processes: Spolek was to be limited to information of a commercial nature.[2] Thus the agreement of 1923 on the manufacture and marketing of soda and its associated products between Solvay and Spolek and their joint factories in Czechoslovakia, Austria, Romania and Yugoslavia had to be revised.[3] Eventually they reached a secret agreement on 17 February 1936, taking into account potential mutual benefits from technical developments in electro-chemical production methods.[4]

It is significant that all Spolek's painstaking efforts to gain a more influential position in the joint soda-factories in the Successor States remained unrewarded. According to the 1923 agreement a delegation of three representatives from Solvay and Spolek assumed control of all joint enterprises from the Viennese central office, which was to be headed alternately by a director from Solvay and one from Spolek. However, in spite of repeated attempts, Spolek did not succeed in delegating a Czech representative to run the head office in Vienna in place of the Belgian, nor did the Czechs succeed in transferring the centre of the organization from Vienna to Prague. Similarly unsuccessful were efforts by representatives of Spolek to gain a majority on the board of the Czechoslovak Neštěmice–Solvay–Works, where Belgian directors retained their decisive voice and where the Belgian plenipotentiary Lefèvre never alternated with a Czech director, as had been expected by the Czech partners

[1] George W. Stocking and Myron W. Watkins, p. 432.
[2] SÚA–AI–SY–25. [3] Ibid., 55.
[4] Ibid., 20.

in Ústí.[1] Solvay's predominance was thus safeguarded: capital ties, patent, licensing and cartel agreements regulated the manufacture, output and marketing of soda and its products in the region of the former Habsburg Monarchy, so as to maintain virtual monopoly conditions, to prevent the emergence of new soda factories and to counter any kind of competition.[2]

ICI's reluctance to share technical secrets with Spolek probably resulted from its participation in the manufacture of explosives and fertilizers in Czechoslovak companies which directly competed with Spolek. The largest foreign influence in Czechoslovakia's chemical industry after Belgium was that of France and Britain: they were involved with the firm of Explosia, founded in 1921 for the manufacture of explosives. This company obtained from the Czechoslovak state the sole right to produce explosives for industrial and military purposes, in Semtín (about 50 miles northeast of Prague). Its capital was provided on the domestic side by the Živnostenská Bank and Agrarian Bank along with a group of other Czechoslovak commercial banks, and on the foreign side by Nobel Industries Ltd, London (after 1926 ICI), by the Société Centrale de Dynamite, Paris and by the Dynamit Nobel A.G., Vienna, which in 1923 became the Dynamit Nobel Company in Bratislava.[3] Foreign involvement was at the express wish of the Czechoslovak government and with the support of the British and French governments.[4] Before the First World War the British Nobel Industries Ltd. (before 1918 Nobel's Explosives Company [Glasgow]), and the German Dynamit Nobel A.G. with its associate in Austria–Hungary, the Dynamit Nobel A.G. (Vienna), had been part of the same international combine: the Nobel–Dynamit Trust Company Ltd, founded by Alfred Nobel in 1886. As a result of the war the Anglo-German trust fell apart. Dynamit A.G. (DAG) survived as an independent company in Germany until it was integrated into I.G. Farbenindustrie A.G. in 1925. In France the Société Centrale de Dynamite, which in the pre-1918 Nobel Trust had been known as the Latin Group, remained an influential force in the industry.[5]

[1] Ibid., 25, 'Geschäftsordnung für die Leitung der gemeinsamen Sodafabriken'.

[2] SÚA–KR 228, 223.

[3] *Compass, Čechoslovakei*, 1929, p. 937.

[4] PA–VCHZ–Ex–SII–54 and Správní rady (Board meetings), IV.

[5] For the history of the Nobel Trust see W. J. Reader, *Imperial Chemical Industries: A History*, I (London, New York, Toronto, 1970).

After the war the British Nobel Industries captured as much as possible of their former German associates' overseas trade and were assured of a free hand in Europe by market agreements with their American allies, the duPonts. The latter agreed to stay out of Europe if the British company stayed out of the U.S. The pre-war relationship between the American and British partners remained intact and even became closer, while the Germans were excluded. In spite of the U.S. anti-trust legislation, this cooperation was formalized in 1920 by a new Patents and Process Agreement, which was in fact a full-blown and extremely effective international cartel, dividing up world markets and giving scope to far-reaching collaboration, especially in face of threats from the German chemical industry.

In the early 1920s DAG again became a competitor to be reckoned with in markets which Nobel Industries and duPont had considered their own, especially in Europe and South America. In order to restrain DAG's expansion the Anglo-American combines began negotiations with the German company, which in the summer of 1925 produced a settlement comprising (in addition to market-sharing agreements and restoration of an exchange of technical information) a joint 20 % participation in DAG's capital by Nobel Industries and duPont.[1] When this settlement was reached DAG was drawn into the largest amalgamation in the history of concentration up to 1926, when virtually the whole German chemical industry merged into the I.G. Farbenindustrie A.G. However, the British and Americans remained shareholders of DAG even after it became a subsidiary of I.G. Farben. It seems that duPont still held 8 % and ICI (with which Nobel Industries had merged in 1926) 12.5 % of DAG's capital during the 1930s.[2] Although in relation to the enormous capital of I.G. Farben the Anglo-American participation was apparently insignificant,[3] it is reasonable to assume that the German chemical industry saw advantages in a closer financial connection with their British and American business partners in the mid-twenties. On the other hand, I.G. Farben's consent to Anglo-American–German capital ties may have been influenced by the ban on exports of military explosives imposed on

[1] Ibid., p. 411.

[2] G. W. Stocking and M. W. Watkins, p. 438.

[3] Cf. W. J. Reader, p. 413.

Germany in the Versailles Treaty and by the fact that Nobel and duPont were aware of the Germans' disregard of this restriction.

A tangible outcome of this settlement – mentioned by the influential chairman of Nobel Industries, Sir Harry Duncan McGowan – was the German undertaking to refrain for five years from any action which might threaten British interests in Southeast Europe.[1]

After 1918 Nobel Industries had clearly found an entirely new field of expansion in Central and Southeast Europe through their participation with the French Nobel Company (originally of 16 % each) in the joint-stock capital of the Czechoslovak Explosia.[2] Both the British and French companies received encouragement from their governments and their business interests were safeguarded by a thirty-year monopoly concession to produce explosives for military and civilian use, granted and guaranteed by the Czechoslovak government. Even the location of the factory – Semtín, in the heart of Bohemia – was chosen by the Czechoslovak General Staff as far away as possible from the German and particularly the Hungarian frontiers,[3] as fears of a Habsburg restoration from these quarters were greater than of possible aggression by Germany. The technical know-how in setting up the Semtín works was supplied by Adam Wilson, Nobel Industries' chief engineer, who came from the Ardeer plants to Czechoslovakia as technical director.[4] Initially, the necessary loans on current and capital accounts were also provided by the domestic and foreign shareholders in proportion to the amount of their investment.[5]

Although the Czechoslovak government granted the newly established company a concession for the exclusive manufacture of explosives, it took some time and effort to enforce complete monopoly on Czechoslovak territory. Dynamit Nobel's Austrian subsidiary in Bratislava continued to exist after 1918. Despite international cartel agreements and the closure of its Slovak factory by the Czechoslovak government, which enforced

[1] Cf. G. W. Stocking and M. W. Watkins, p. 438.

[2] PA–VCHZ–Synthesia–Pardubice, Řed. Expl. 9.

[3] Ibid., Ex–SII–54.

[4] Ibid., Správní rady II.

[5] Ibid., Řed. Expl. 9. The agreed proportions for credit supplies were one-third from the Anglo-French group and two-thirds from the Czech group.

Explosia's monopoly, it did not stop manufacturing chemicals, including explosives and safety fuses.[1] Moreover, the extension of monopoly rights to other Successor States envisaged by British Nobel Industries did not succeed, as monopoly concessions for the manufacture and sale of explosives in Romania and Hungary had been obtained by the Austrian Dynamit Nobel company, which obviously had not severed its connections with the German DAG.

The Austrian Nobel company had thus put itself in a stronger bargaining position for the inevitable negotiations with the Czechoslovak Explosia and its Anglo-French investors. After almost a year of three-cornered (German–Austrian, Anglo-French and Czechoslovak) bargaining, in which not only the companies but also their governments were involved, it was agreed in the summer of 1922 to end the manufacture of explosives in the Bratislava factory and to transfer its machinery to the Semtín works. This was in return for a 16 % participation by Dynamit Nobel in the capital of Explosia, which the Czechoslovak Ministry of Finance reluctantly accepted only after the Defence Ministry had insisted on a reduction from the 25 % originally demanded. The board of Explosia gave an assurance that no representative of Dynamit Nobel would sit on any executive body. Shares were to be held by the Slovak Nobel company, which had to transfer its headquarters from Vienna to Bratislava and register as a Czechoslovak firm.[2] For reasons of national defence as well as nationalistic reasons, Czechoslovak business and government circles were not very happy with this arrangement. Neither were the British and French companies particularly keen on partnership with a company which had actually merged with I.G. Farben in an area which since 1925 had become their own domain. Thus in 1931, at the expiry of their ten-year-agreement, ICI took over Dynamit Nobel's shares in Explosia, thereby increasing its investment to 32 % and becoming the strongest foreign investor. With the approval of the Czechoslovak government and Anglo-French diplomatic circles, I.G. Farben's indirect foothold in Czechoslovakia's explosives industry thus disappeared.

Anglo-Czechoslovak cooperation in the chemical industry was not merely financial. ICI had technical staff and advisers

[1] Ibid., Ex–SII–54.

[2] Ibid., Řed. Expl. 9.

in Semtín, regular technical reports were sent from Prague to their London office, research for the Czech factories was carried out in England, and four representatives of ICI held places on Explosia's board of directors, as against two from the Société Centrale de Dynamite. At the same time ICI had come to a working agreement with DAG in Southeast Europe protecting their Czech interests and had entrusted business in the whole region to their director L. W. Bickford-Smith,[1] who kept in constant touch with Prague from his Vienna office.

The syndicate of Czechoslovak–Anglo-French shareholders which was formed for Explosia extended its activities to the production of liquid ammonia in Czechoslovakia in order to ensure sufficient domestic supplies for the manufacture of nitric acid and nitrates. For this purpose Synthesia, an additional joint-stock company, was founded in Prague in 1928. The syndicate held 150,000 shares, proportionately distributed as in Explosia.[2] By the autumn of the same year Synthesia's plants in Moravská Ostrava–Mariánské Hory began to produce ammonia and nitrogenous compounds by the most advanced methods available and extended their production programme year by year. Soon the company turned its attention to the manufacture of artificial fertilizers, one of the main products of the nitrogen industry. ICI supplied the know-how for producing the required quantities of ammonia according to the methods used at Billingham[3] and the newly-built plant went into operation in the spring of 1934. Soon an impressive variety of artificial fertilizers came off the production lines, constituting a threat to Spolek in Ústí, which had previously been the main suppliers. This in fact precipitated a confrontation in Czechoslovakia, between the subsidiaries of ICI on the one hand and of Solvay on the other, about their respective shares in the market for the strictly cartelized nitrogen products, especially fertilizers.

[1] L. W. Bickford-Smith was a descendant of William Bickford, the inventor of the safety fuse. The family business, Bickford Smith & Co. Ltd of Tuckingmill, Cornwall, became part of the British Nobel concern during the big Explosives Trades merger in 1918. L. W. Bickford-Smith supervised all Nobel Industries' Central European affairs from his former family firm Bickford & Co. in Vienna. Cf. W. J. Reader, pp. 313, 381 and 406.

[2] PA–VCHZ–Synthesia–Pardubice, Řed. Expl. 9.

[3] Ibid., Semtín–Ex 147.

The ensuing competitive struggle fought in 1934 and 1935, mostly at the conference table, ended in a compromise which forced Synthesia to drop its ambitious plans for nitrogenous fertilizers in Mariánské Hory until 1940[1] and led to a much wider settlement, which improved the very strained relations between Spolek and Explosia. In a legalized contract approved by their foreign shareholders the Czechoslovak companies meticulously defined which chemical products each side was to manufacture and which compounds both of them could produce; they also stipulated that any new chemical manufactures could be introduced only by mutual consent and with a 50:50 participation of Ústí and Semtín. The same consent was required and the same proportions were to be applied for any newly acquired subsidiaries or extension of plant.

Finally, and most significantly, the partners exchanged shares in each other's companies in 1935. Explosia and Synthesia obtained 40,000 shares, i.e. 10.66 % of Spolek's capital, and three places on its board of directors; Spolek acquired 11.6 % of Explosia's and Synthesia's capital.[2] At the express demand of the Czechoslovak Ministry of Defence, which always had a representative on Explosia's board, an additional 500 Spolek shares had to be transferred to Explosia to equalize the proportions exchanged.[3] In all negotiations and agreements ICI's exclusive interest in the manufacture and sales of military and civilian explosives in Southeast Europe, traditionally Nobel's sphere, and in particular their monopoly position in Czechoslovakia, were unquestioningly respected by all sides. This attitude was maintained by the large chemical combines even after 1936, when the Anglo-American (and probably the German) understanding about Czechoslovakia had formally expired.[4]

The news towards the end of 1936 that ICI was offering its shares in Explosia for sale to the Živnostenská Bank was therefore received with surprise by contemporary participants and with consternation by Czechoslovak industrial, agrarian and government circles. In recent Czechoslovak historiography this

[1] Cf. p. 111.

[2] Ibid., Gen. řed. Expl. Kr. 25 and 32; Řed. Expl. 9.

[3] Ibid., Expl. 6.

[4] This was the case with a special agreement on Czechoslovakia between ICI, duPont and IG Farben. See also E. Hexner, *International Cartels*, p. 351.

step has been said to prove that 'British finance capital had become reconciled to a situation in which Central and Southeast Europe would constitute the exclusive sphere of interest of German monopolies', and that 'British capital began to withdraw from this area even before the well-known Munich settlement, thus *ex post* reflecting the changed relations between French, British and German monopolists which in turn crystallized as a result of the uneven development of capitalism in Western Europe in the preceding years'.[1] Much of the background to ICI's action remains obscure and this statement cannot therefore be easily accepted. In this particular case ICI did not, in the end, sell off all its Czech shares. After the rise of National Socialist Germany and her leaders' aggressive public postures Central and Southeastern Europe had undoubtedly become a less attractive region for international investment. Czechoslovakia herself was no longer financially as safe as in the 1920s, although in comparison with the economic and political vicissitudes of her neighbours her economy was generally recognized as sound. Thus Nobel's original positive assessment[2] was still valid in the 1930s when ICI decided to double its holding in Czechoslovakia and, even though military products remained the most important and most steadily expanding part of Explosia's turnover,[3] branched out from explosives into increased civilian production.

Almost certainly, the immediate cause of ICI's attempt to pull out of Explosia was disagreement over Czechoslovak strategic and economic policy. This was felt by the British as well as the French shareholders of Explosia to be commercially

[1] V. Král, II, p. 112.

[2] Cf. W. J. Reader, p. 405.

[3] Turnover of Explosia on the home market between 1932 and 1935 in Czechoslovak Crowns (Kč).

Year	Eruptiva*	Ministry of National Defence	Others	Total
1932	44,749,000	18,221,000	6,684,000	69,654,000
1933	34,765,000	31,876,000	19,916,000	86,557,000
1934	34,997,000	87,902,000	18,178,000	141,077,000
1935	35,379,000	146,608,000	16,108,000	198,095,000

* The firm 'Eruptiva' had exclusive rights to the sales of explosives to civilian users in Czechoslovakia.

PA–VCHZ–Synthesia–Pardubice, Řed. Expl. 9.

and politically unsound. Early in the autumn of 1936 the Czechoslovak Ministry of National Defence became increasingly concerned about the now vulnerable geographic location of the country's explosives industry. Explosia was asked by the army administration to construct additional plants in Slovakia to produce ammonia, nitric acid, ammonium nitrate and related chemicals for military and civilian use. To bring this about a new joint-stock company was to be founded by the army administration. Explosia was to take 25 % of the shares and the firm was to function as a mixed (state and private) enterprise until Explosia's monopoly expired, when the factory would become state property. At the same time the Czechoslovak army demanded two seats on Explosia's board of directors and one representative on the firm's executive committee, to replace the Government Commissary who had so far acted as liaison. In addition the Czechoslovak government wished to have a say in pricing policy and to have a third of any future increase in profits above the level of 1935–6.[1] The French and British shareholders instantly repudiated these demands as constituting a unilateral infringement of the concession granted to them until 1953. Discussions, correspondence and negotiations dragged on through the rest of 1936 and throughout 1937 under constant pressures not only from business but also from government. The French Société acted in close consultation with their Ministry of Defence, the Czechs did the same, and ICI's standpoint was occasionally impressed upon the Czechoslovak government through diplomatic channels.[2]

The foreign companies objected most strongly to an investment which they considered unprofitable, and particularly to the precedent of nationalization which would be created by the Slovakian project. While ICI's representatives, ranging from the Central European director, L. W. Bickford-Smith, to the president, H. J. Mitchell, and the chairman, Sir Harry McGowan, threatened to sever their connection completely, they did in fact intend to keep some shares in the Czechoslovak chemical industry. The Société Centrale de Dynamite did not want to accept the Czechoslovak army's financial demands, but expressed understanding of the defence needs of the country, especially after representations had been made to the company

[1] Ibid., Ex–SII–54; Řed. Expl. 6.

[2] Ibid.

by the French military attaché in Prague, General Boucherie, and public figures like Paul Clémenceau. Impressed by the attitude of his Ministry of Defence and of M. Lacroix, France's Ambassador in Prague, the Société's director, LePlay, assured his Czech counterpart, General O. Husák, that the French government was anxious to see the Société retain its interest in Explosia and Synthesia and would even favour an increase in French participation.[1] On the other hand, French willingness to step into the vacuum created by a British withdrawal and the possibility of a French interest purchasing ICI's shares in Explosia did not come to fruition, as a great deal of hesitation in Paris attended such an enterprise. An intense interest in ICI's shares was also shown by Spolek, with Solvay hovering in the background. French–Czechoslovak discussions were very soon superseded by a Czechoslovak–British settlement.

In the spring of 1937 ICI sold half its holding in Explosia and Synthesia to the Czech Agrarian group, Kooperativa, which paid for the shares by means of wheat exports from Czechoslovakia to Britain. Thus Kooperativa, a powerful agrarian monopoly organization, obtained a stake not only in the armament industry, in which the very influential Agrarian Party was strongly involved, but also in the manufacture of fertilizers. This gave it a much stronger bargaining position in dealing with the nitrogen cartel.[2] The British company retained 16 % of both Explosia's and Synthesia's capital, so reverting to the position it had held before purchasing Austrian Dynamit Nobel's shares, and to parity with the French partners in Czechoslovakia.[3] The demands of the Czechoslovak Ministry of National Defence were not pressed, probably so that a compromise between the domestic and foreign participants in this branch of the chemical industry could be reached quickly.

The extensive negotiations conducted on business, political and diplomatic levels in connection with the British group's proposal to transfer its shares to the Živnostenská Bank, which eventually resulted in ICI retaining a substantial proportion of them nevertheless, reflect the complicated political and

[1] Ibid., Gen. řed. Expl. 14 (Correspondence LePlay–Husák).

[2] Ibid. (Dividends 1925–35 amounted to £155,109, ICI received £292,000 for 50,000 shares and 48,000 shares were left in their possession.)

[3] Ibid., Gen. řed. Expl. 6.

economic aspects of this business transaction in a period of heightened international and domestic tension. Czechoslovak government circles around Eduard Beneš, whose Western orientation was well known, did not relish the prospect of a British withdrawal and could not contemplate severing the economic relations with Britain which they had actively sought after the foundation of the republic. The politically and economically powerful Czechoslovak Agrarian Party was not enthusiastic about a take-over which would increase the Živnostenská Bank's influence in Explosia to the detriment of its own interests. The Ministry of National Defence – traditionally controlled by the Agrarian Party – therefore voiced its opposition to the proposed transaction, especially if it was to mean an exchange of British for Belgian (Solvay) capital, as was clearly intended by the Živnostenská Bank.[1] This would undoubtedly have strengthened the position of Spolek against Explosia and Synthesia. In addition, the Czechoslovak government was vitally interested in retaining foreign shareholders from allied countries in the armament industry. This was especially true of France, and Agrarian businessmen and politicians would have been delighted if the Société Centrale de Dynamite had bought the British shares.

When negotiations at the highest government levels nevertheless failed to produce the desired result, Josef Beran, chairman of the Agrarian Party and a deputy of the Czechoslovak Parliament, intervened with Dr Ladislav Feierabend, the influential general director of Kooperativa. In February 1937 they persuaded ICI to sell only to them and to keep part of its shares. By this move the Agrarian Bank and the Kooperativa obtained parity with the Živnostenská Bank and Spolek in both Explosia and Synthesia.[2] In mid-July 1937 Dr Dvořáček, the managing director of the Živnostenská Bank, returned from London where he had held talks with ICI's president, H. J. Mitchell. He is reported as saying that 'the English have finally decided to maintain their participation and there will, perhaps, be a period of calm with regard to the proportions of holdings and time to settle outstanding questions'.[3] The problems Dvořáček referred to were almost certainly connected

[1] Ibid., Gen. řed. Expl. 14. [2] Ibid., Řed. Expl. 6.
[3] Cited by V. Král, II, pp. 116, 239.

with Anglo-French opposition to the Slovak project, which broke out again at the end of 1937. ICI threatened to dispose of its remaining shares and both the French and the British protested.[1] Solvay decided to act as mediator and tried to dissuade ICI.[2] After the Czechoslovak government's assurances that it would not pursue its plans in Slovakia and that nationalization was not intended the storm blew itself out.

Solvay's role in persuading ICI to remain in Explosia throws light on the cross-currents of international interests in the chemical industry of pre-Munich Czechoslovakia, when at the end of 1937 the Belgians joined with the British and French to counteract German infiltration. During the period of uncertainty about British shares in Explosia, I.G. Farben took steps to penetrate Spolek through their Bratislava Dynamit Nobel company. However, neither the Živnostenská Bank nor Solvay were prepared to agree to the capital link between Spolek and the Bratislava I.G. Farben subsidiary, which I.G. Farben repeatedly proposed before Munich.[3] On the contrary, they wanted to preserve their Anglo-French connections in the Czechoslovak chemical industry.

It has generally been believed that I.G. Farben held shares in Spolek before Munich.[4] But this is not true, although German technological influence in Spolek was considerable. I.G. Farben had invested its capital in a number of Czechoslovak chemical companies,[5] but investment in Spolek, the country's largest chemical combine, remained impossible. Although Solvay and ICI did have business dealings with I.G. Farben before Munich, the history of the Czechoslovak chemical industry does not confirm that they voluntarily retreated from Central and Southeast Europe in favour of the German trust. In this area both the large West European combines carefully protected their traditional interests in alkalis and explosives.

[1] PA–VCHZ–Synthesia–Pardubice. Správní rady IV.

[2] SÚA–AI–SY–20.

[3] Cf. correspondence between J. Preiss (Živnostenská Bank) and A. Basch (Spolek) cited by V. Král, II, pp. 248–50.

[4] Cf. e.g. G. W. Stocking and M. W. Watkins, p. 431.

[5] Akciová společnost pro zpracování draselnatých louhů v Kolíně (Co. for the Processing of Caustic Potash in Kolín); Bentlin Chemical Factories, Perečín near Užhorod; Hydroxygen formerly Dr Allers and Heller, Prosetice.

Mineral and vegetable oils

The processing of mineral and vegetable oils is closely integrated with the chemical industry. I examine it separately here in order to determine the precise proportions of foreign and domestic capital. All major enterprises in this branch of Czechoslovak industry were in the hands of international business. The overwhelming predominance of foreign investment is shown in the statistical analysis of chapter 2 (1), in which I estimated foreign participation as 97 % of the total nominal capital of all companies in the mineral and vegetable oil industry of Czechoslovakia. The territorial division of the investment according to countries of origin is presented in Table 3. In this table Britain's position is considerably underrated, as British capital formed an important part of the Dutch investment. However, even an approximate estimate of the respective shares of British or Dutch companies cannot be made without exploring Dutch and British business archives.

The extraordinarily large and controlling share of foreign capital in this field was basically the result of Czechoslovakia's complete dependence on imports of raw materials and semi-finished products.

Table 3. *Territorial distribution of direct foreign investment in the mineral oil and vegetable fat industries in Czechoslovakia, 31 December 1937*

Country of origin of investment	Nominal value in 1,000 Kč	Percentage of total foreign investment
Holland	256,719	62.1
U.S.A.	69,662	16.4
France	42,950	10.5
Switzerland	39,552	9.6
Great Britain	5,638	1.4
Total	414,521	100.0

The mineral-oil industry

The industrial refining of mineral oil in Czechoslovakia was mainly concerned with purifying and distributing imported oil. Before 1938 domestic annual output of oil amounted to only

25,000 tons, while total home fuel consumption amounted to 300,000 tons and consumption of lubricants to 45–48,000 tons. At no time did the refineries process the whole of the country's needs and semi-finished products had to be imported from Romania (40.6 %), Poland (21.7 %), the USSR (5.4 %) and the U.S.A. (32.3 %).[1] To some extent this situation indicates the direction of capital flows into the Czechoslovak mineral-oil industry. Three powerful Western monopoly groups were prominent: the American, French and Anglo-Dutch trusts. They turned to Southeast Europe in the inter-war period mainly because of the substantial losses which they suffered as a result of Russia's confiscation of foreign capital after 1917.

In the first place two companies of the Rockefeller Empire penetrated into Czechoslovakia – the Socony Vacuum Oil Co. Inc., New York, and the Standard Oil Co., New Jersey,[2] which wholly owned the Vacuum Oil Co., Prague, as well as the Naftaspol and the Standard mineral oil companies in Czechoslovakia, with a total capital of Kč 69 million. They were part of Rockefeller's Southeast European network of subsidiaries,[3] controlled and directed by Vacuum Oil's representative Reginald Henry Evans, who as president of all companies in this region (Vienna, Budapest, Prague, Czechowice, Bucharest) operated from an office in Vienna.[4]

French companies formed another group of investors. The capital of the Société française des pétroles de Tchécoslovaquie completely controlled the oil refinery Apollo in Bratislava and its trading firm Apollo-Nafta in Prague. The Société Franco-Polonaise owned the South Carpathian Oil Refinery in Mukačevo. These shareholdings formed part of a network of French oil interests stretching over most Central and Southeast European countries and all holdings were apparently concentrated in the financial house of the Société financière de Paris.[5]

[1] Cf. J. Tichý in *Hospodářství ČSR na jaře 1946* (The Economy of ČSR in Spring 1946), p. 67.

[2] The Standard Oil Trust was dissolved after an American High Court decision of 1911 resulting from a prosecution under the anti-trust legislation. However, the majority of the 20 main oil companies reregistered in the U.S.A. as separate companies but were part of the Rockefeller oil concern. Cf. TNEC, Roy C. Cook, *Control of the Petroleum Industry by Major Oil Companies*, Monograph 39, p. 3.

[3] ASÚS – Cizí účasti.

[4] *Compass, Personenverzeichnis.*

[5] AMZV, IV. Sekce (not numbered). Note au sujet de la Société française des pétroles de Tchécoslovaquie, 30 January 1932.

The main areas of investment were Poland, Romania, Czechoslovakia, Hungary and Austria, where the French shareholders maintained close contact through their representatives in the management of all subsidiaries and on their boards of directors. In Apollo, the Czechoslovak refineries and the South Carpathian company seats were held by Marcel Boucherie, Pierre Flipo and Alexandre Palliez from the French Central Office, by Viktor Hlasko of the Polish Grupy Francuskich Koncernow Naftowych 'Małopolski', and by Norbert Feith from Vienna. On the other hand, connections with leading business people and politicians of the host country were maintained by giving seats on the oil company's board to influential Czechoslovaks, like O. Husák, the director of Explosia, Dr V. Vaněk, the director of the Anglo-Czechoslovak bank, Kornel Stodola and Dr Edmund Bačinský,[1] senators and Slovak Agrarian politicians. Ultimate power, however, rested with the French oil companies.

In the 1930s French interests encountered strong competition in this region, particularly from Germany, and France concentrated on keeping intact her controlling influence in the Société française des pétroles Tchécoslovaquie. The controlling interest was held by the Société financière de Paris, which was so severely hit by the economic crisis that the Ministries of Finance in Paris and Prague feared German or Austrian capital would take over the oil business. Both governments averted this undesirable turn of events by financial aid, provided in connection with the Czechoslovak government loan in France at the beginning of 1932. Thus they secured the Société des pétroles de Tchécoslovaquie's control of its share in the Czechoslovak oil industry.[2]

The Dutch–Swiss group had a very similar structure of capital investment in Central and Southeast Europe. The Fanto Works and the Přívoz Works provide a significant example, with their respective subsidiaries in Czechoslovakia.[3]

[1] *Compass, Personenverzeichnis*; *Compass, Čechoslovakei*, 1929–39.

[2] AMZV, IV. Sekce. Petrolejové akcie (oil shares) – correspondence between the Ministry of Finance and the Ministry of Foreign Affairs 1930–2 (not numbered). See p. 376.

[3] The subsidiaries of the Fanto Works were: Ostia, Chemical and Oil Industry, Prague; Vesta, Slovak Oil Industry, Prague. Those of the Přívoz Works of Mineral Oil Products, Prague, were: Ostranaft, Moravská Ostrava; Company for the Production of Mineral Oils, Prague.

In both cases the influence of foreign capital was decisive, especially that of the N.V. Nederlandsche Petroleum Maatschappij,[1] which itself was among the numerous subsidiary companies of the world-wide Anglo-Dutch oil trust, the Royal Dutch Shell Co.[2] Its investment in Czechoslovakia was part of a chain of similar holdings in refineries, chemical works and oil trading companies in Germany, Austria, Danzig and Hungary. This becomes clear from an examination of Fanto's board of directors, which plainly personified the union of industrial, commercial and banking interests in the combine.[3] In the Czechoslovak economy Fanto was connected with the industrial interests of the Živnostenská Bank, which had only a 0.43 % share in its capital.[4]

Dutch oil interests also included the Prague companies of Shell-Products Ltd and Lubricant Sales Ltd. Their capital was owned by the N.V. Bataafsche Petroleum Maatschappij in The Hague, a company founded in 1907 by the Royal Dutch Petroleum Co. and the British Shell Union Oil Corporation, in which the Dutch and the British held 60 % and 40 % shares respectively.[5] These proportions were maintained in all joint enterprises until the Second World War.

There can be little doubt that French policy after the First World War aimed at complete control of oil resources and processing in Central and Southeast Europe. In my examination of foreign investment in the mineral-oil industry I have shown that this policy was not entirely successful in the case

[1] The capital of the Fanto Works, Prague, was divided between the N.V. Nederlandsche Petroleum Maatschappij, Amsterdam (22.6 %) and the Swiss holding company Continentale Gesellschaft für Bank und Industriewerke, Basel (76.8 %). The total share capital of the Přívoz Works was owned by the N.V. Nederlandsche Petroleum Maatschappij. Cf. ASÚS - Cizí účastí.

[2] Cf. *The Royal Dutch Petroleum Company 1890–1950* (The Hague, 1950), p. 15.

[3] Charles Francis Jacottet, the London representative in the Fanto Works, also represented the interests of the Österreichische Credit-Anstalt-Wiener Bankverein, as the deputy general director of the holding company, Société Continentale de Gestion, Monaco. The directorships of Robert Fanto illustrate the ramified capital structure of the Swiss–Dutch concern: Gallia, Mineralölprodukte Vertriebs-Gesellschaft A.G., Vaduz; Österreichische Fanto A.G., Vienna; Fanto Works, Prague; Vesta, Prague; Austria, Petroleumindustrie A.G., Vienna; Danubia, Mineralindustrie, Vienna; Alldemin, Allgemeine Industrie A.G., Vienna; Ungarische Öl- und chemische Industrie, Budapest; Hungarian Fanto Works, Ujpest; Continentale Motorschiffahrtsgesellschaft, Amsterdam–Vienna. Cf. *Compass, Čechoslovakei*, 1929–39.

[4] ASÚS - Koncernové šetření.

[5] Cf. *The Royal Dutch Petroleum Company*, p. 16.

of Czechoslovakia: French interests were strongly opposed and deflected by Anglo-Dutch, Swiss–Dutch, and particularly American oil combines.[1]

The vegetable-oil industry

Between 1918 and 1938 the entire Czechoslovak vegetable oil and fats industry was gradually subordinated to the Anglo-Dutch trust of Unilever, with its headquarters in London and Rotterdam. By 1938 Unilever produced 70 % of the world's output of vegetable oils and fats, controlled the soap and margarine industry, held first place in trade with West Africa and owned shares in at least 300 subsidiary companies in the British Empire, Europe and other parts of the world.[2] The way in which this Anglo-Dutch combine achieved supremacy in Central and Southeast Europe by penetrating the Czechoslovak economy provides an almost classic example of capital expansion in this region.

In the 1930s the vegetable oil and fats industry in Czechoslovakia employed about one-fifth of all employees[3] and one-fourth of the total nominal capital[4] of the chemical industry. The most important part of this branch of industry was concentrated in Georg Schicht Ltd with its centre in Ústí nad Labem. The Schicht Works had gradually gained a virtual monopoly in Czechoslovakia and also controlled the production and market of soap and edible fats in Southeast Europe. Table 4 traces the extent of the combine and its foreign links at the end of 1937.[5] By that time the Schicht concern already constituted an

[1] P. Eisler held that the French oil companies were themselves controlled by American oil trusts. That may have been so, for the international relationships of the oil industry were extremely complicated. Cf. P. Eisler, *Monopoly v hornictví kapitalistického Československa* (Monopolies in the Mining Industry of Capitalist Czechoslovakia), p. 32.

[2] PA–STZ, Ústí n/L. – Agreement–Koncern Unilever; also Stock Exchange Year Book, London, 1938.

[3] Calculated from basic data on individual industries in 1935 given in *Statistická ročenka*, 1941.

[4] Calculated from Ibid., p. 175 and *Compass, Čechoslovakei*, 1939.

[5] Table 4 'Lever Bros. & Unilever Combine in Central and Southeast Europe' is compiled from material in PA–STZ, Ústí n/L. The Schichts were Sudeten Germans, that is Germans living in Bohemia. Whereas in Czechoslovakia the firm was registered as Jiří Schicht, abroad it went under the name of Georg Schicht.

Table 4. *Lever Bros. & Unilever combine in Central and*

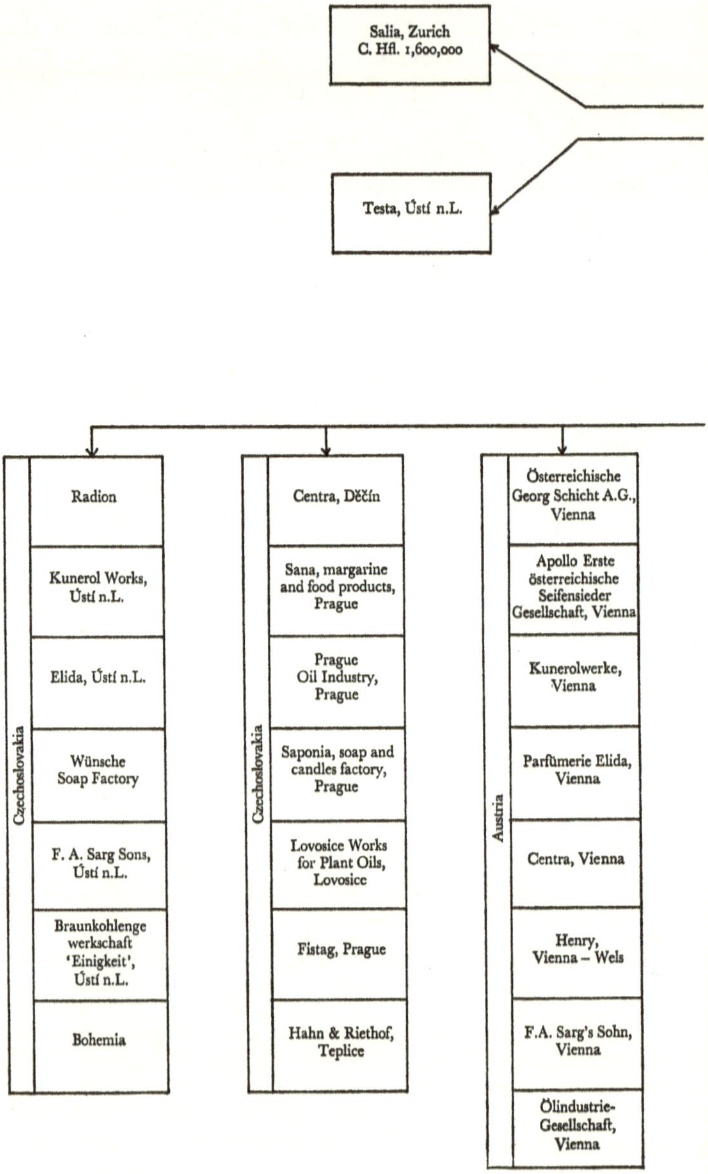

Southeast Europe, 31 December 1937

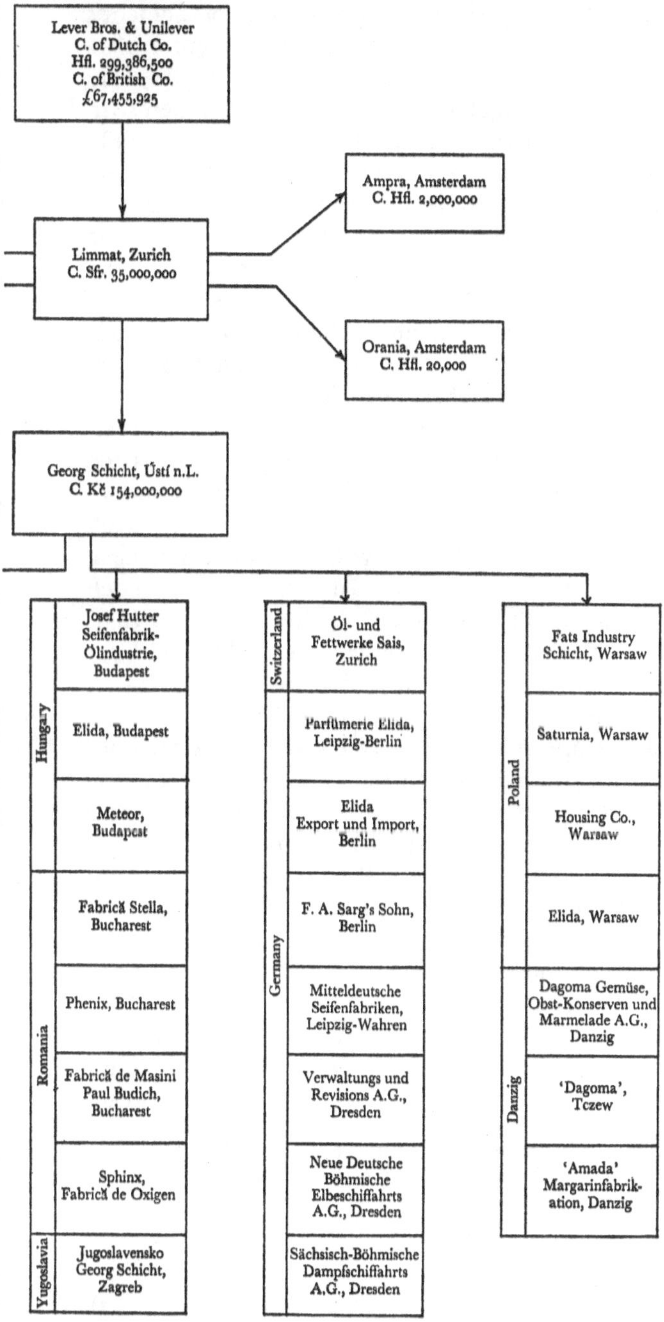

integral part of the world-wide trust of Lever Bros. and Unilever, London–Rotterdam.

Long before 1914 a considerable proportion of Schicht's undertakings had grown into successful business enterprises within the Austro-Hungarian Monarchy. From their early beginnings the Schicht factories encountered problems in securing a steady flow of raw materials from overseas, mainly from Dutch and British colonies, to keep production going. The sources of necessary raw materials, such as tropical oil seeds and copra, were controlled by Dutch and British companies. As one of the largest European buyers the Schichts had even before the First World War joined the international pool of purchasers of raw materials, and members of the Schicht family met their English and Dutch business partners at conferences to reach agreement on a common purchasing policy. While the Dutch companies, Anton Jurgens Vereenigde Fabrieken N.V., Oss, and Van den Bergh's Fabrieken N.V., Rotterdam, as well as the British companies, mainly Lever Brothers Ltd, London, developed their own plantations in Africa and Asia, no such enterprise could be contemplated by the Schicht brothers, because they would have needed at least forty times as much capital as they had at their disposal.[1] Quite part from that, Austria–Hungary did not possess the colonies, which without doubt were advantageous to Dutch and British entrepreneurs in obtaining the raw material they required.

The Western European countries, which were therefore both economically stronger and in control of the supply of raw materials, could thus apply pressure in their efforts to gain influence in the Schicht combine and hence on the Southeast European markets. As early as 1914 William Lever, the most important British soap manufacturer, came to Ústí with a proposal that he should acquire 50 % of Schicht's capital.[2] In the resulting negotiations the Schichts displayed little enthusiasm to sell. No doubt they hoped that the impending war might help to solve their raw material problems. Be that as it may, the war put an end to any plans for amalgamation[3] and Lever's first attempt to penetrate Central and Southeast Europe via Schicht failed.

[1] Cf. Ch. Wilson, *The History of Unilever*, II (London, 1954), p. 225.
[2] PA–STZ, Ústí n./L., Verhandlungen Unie-Lever 984.
[3] Cf. Ch. Wilson, II, p. 224.

If in the first years of the First World War the Schichts had harboured any hopes of victory for the Central Powers and consequently of acquiring access to raw materials in future colonies, then they were very soon disappointed. Realistically and without any patriotic misgivings, they assessed the economic situation of the Habsburg Monarchy, in which inflation and imminent collapse threatened their commercial interests and profits. Heinrich and Georg Schicht, the leading figures in the company, prepared therefore to transfer part of their financial reserves and all their shares to the safety of neutral Switzerland. The profit and loss accounts of the Schicht Works testify that they had been unfavourably affected, although not disastrously so, by the falling value of the Austrian Crown, by high taxation and lack of raw materials resulting from the Entente's blockade and above all by the disintegration of the Austro-Hungarian Monarchy, which had hitherto provided a secure market for their products. Faced with these difficulties and uncertainties, Georg, the Schicht family's expert in international commerce and finance, began to put his transfer plans into action. In 1917 he founded a holding company, Limmat Industrie- und Handels A.G., in Zurich with a nominal capital of Sfrc. 8,000,000. By 1921 all the Schichts' Czechoslovak shares had been exchanged for shares in their Swiss company (see Table 5A) and Limmat became the financial centre of the Schicht concern. Its basic capital increased until it reached Sfrs. 35,000,000 in 1937.[1] The brothers Schicht had succeeded in getting large sums of money out of the country before the complete break-up of the Habsburg Monarchy and before the currency was devalued. Limmat served a similar purpose during the pre-Munich Republic, when Schicht was able to conduct large financial transactions through Limmat and to transfer profits to it without having to pay taxes.

In the last stages of the war the Schicht brothers also took great care to amass large stores of scarce raw materials in neutral countries or in states which were certain to come out on the victorious side.[2] For this purpose they founded Heima, a

[1] PA–STZ, Ústí n./L. – Koncern.

[2] At the beginning of 1918 the Schichts accumulated considerable stocks of raw materials by purchases through neutrals, as quoted by Charles Wilson: '38,000 tons of copra in Java, 30,000 tons of linseed in the Argentine, 12,000 tons of resin and tallow in the United States, as well as large stocks of various oils in Spain'. Ch. Wilson, II, p. 226.

(A) 31 December 1918

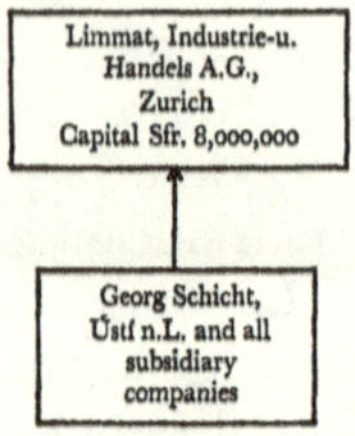

Dividends paid to Limmat in Zurich.

(B) 1 January 1921–29 November 1928

(a) 'The Great Entente' concluded between Schicht, Jurgens and Van den Bergh.

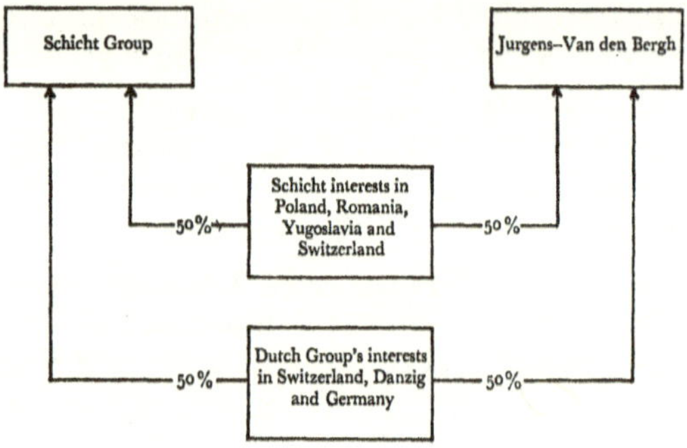

(b) 'The Little Entente' concluded between Schicht, Jurgens, Van den Bergh and Centra.

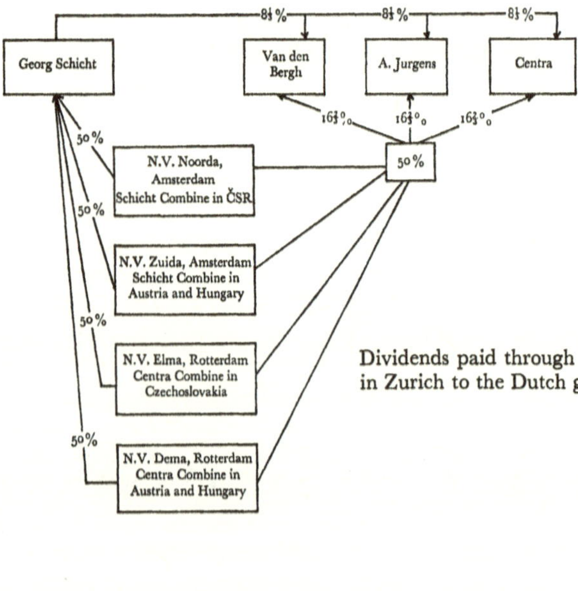

Dividends paid through Limmat in Zurich to the Dutch groups.

(c) 29 November 1928 (Preliminary Agreement) to 1 January 1930

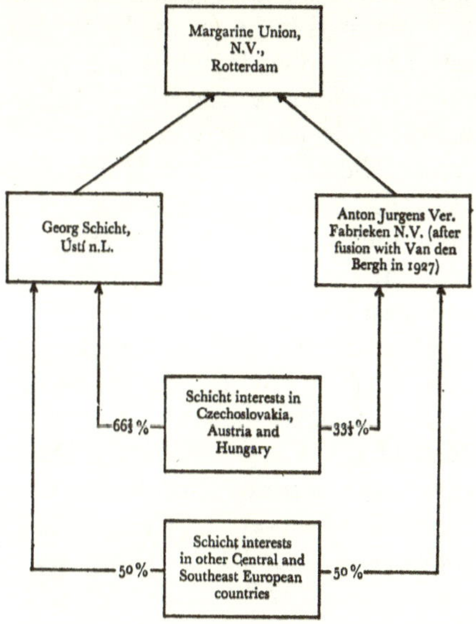

Dividends paid through Limmat in Zurich to Margarine Union N.V. in Rotterdam.

(d) 1 January 1930 (fusion with Unilever) to 1937

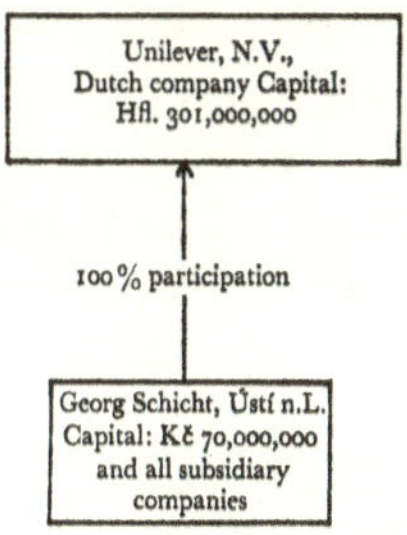

Dividends paid through Limmat in Zurich to the Dutch company of Unilever.

From 1937 the Dutch and British companies merged into Lever Bros. and Unilever later to become Unilever of London and Rotterdam. Dividends were paid from the Central and Southeastern European combine through Limmat in Zurich to Lever Bros. and Unilever in London.

trading company in Amsterdam. After the war the Schicht business therefore amassed large profits by processing accumulated raw material in its own factories and by selling at very high prices products and raw materials, which remained in short supply in Europe in the early post-war years.

Other companies followed Heima in Holland and in Switzerland (Ampra, Orania, Salia – viz. Table 4). As Schicht's subsidiaries in Europe they supplied it with raw material, and also became a convenient instrument for transferring profits from Central and Southeast Europe to the West. Within the Schicht combine this mechanism worked as follows: the Dutch and Swiss subsidiaries supplied raw material to Schicht factories in Czechoslovakia, Austria, Hungary and Romania at very high prices, added considerable supplementary charges, and thus increased their own rate of profit and lowered that of the enterprises producing finished goods in Central and Southeastern Europe. The capacity of these factories to pay taxes was therefore reduced and they further became indebted to their foreign suppliers and had to pay interest to them. Another channel for the transfer of earnings within the combine had therefore been created.[1] These and similar accounting operations were practised throughout the European Schicht concern, whether the main shareholders were the Czechoslovak Schichts, or later the Dutch Jurgens and Van den Berghs, or finally the British Levers.

Until 1919 neither of the two main Dutch soap and fats manufacturers, Jurgens or Van den Bergh, participated in the vegetable-oil industry of Czechoslovakia or of any other Southeastern European country. Their interests were in West European and Scandinavian countries and Germany. The break-up of the Austro-Hungarian market into smaller units resulted in greater competitive opportunities for the Western companies in a region which had so far been effectively monopolized by Schicht. The danger of growing competition multiplied Schicht's difficulties. In the new Czechoslovak state it had a market of 13 million inhabitants, but its productive capacity for soap was geared to the 60 million in its former

[1] PA–STZ, Ústí n/L. – Složení Koncernu průmyslu olejového, tukového, mydlářského v Československu, v Rakousku a Maďarsku (Structure of the concern of oils, fats, soaps in Czechoslovakia, in Austria and Hungary).

traditional home market.[1] Its largest competitors were the Dutch companies, especially the Rotterdam firm of Van den Bergh, which penetrated into Czechoslovakia. In December 1919 Van den Bergh invested directly in the group concentrated around Centra in Křešice, which constituted Schicht's domestic competitors.[2]

After a fierce competitive struggle between the Dutch groups Jurgens and Van den Bergh, and the Czechoslovak Schicht group, a corporation was formed, reflecting the European political alliances of the times: the Great Entente and the Little Entente of 1921 (see Table 5B a and b). Both Dutch companies gained a financial interest in Schicht and hence access to Southeast Europe. In the Great Entente the Schicht brothers ceded 50 % of their capital in Poland, Romania, Yugoslavia and Switzerland to the Dutch group in return for a 50 % share in Jurgens' and Van den Bergh's companies in Switzerland, Danzig and Germany (see Table 5B a). This, however, was worth less than the Schicht property.[3] The Little Entente divided the capital of the Schicht Works and of the Centra group in Czechoslovakia, Austria and Hungary in such a way as to leave 50 % in the hands of Schicht. The other half was shared out in three equal parts of 16⅔ % between Jurgens, Van den Bergh and Centra.[4] A complicated capital structure was created (as shown in Table 5B b), which was somewhat simplified in 1927 by the fusion of Jurgens and Van den Bergh;[5] their combined participation in the Schicht business became administratively linked to Schicht's Swiss holding company Limmat.[6]

The whole settlement was enmeshed in complex terms and conditions which imposed limitations on the freedom of decision-making in the Schicht combine. Most irksome to the Schicht brothers was the fact that they had been manœuvred into a permanent undertaking to refrain from independent production of edible fats, oils and soaps or any related product outside their combine: they were not to participate in any enterprises without the consent of the Dutch partners.[7] This led

[1] Ibid., Elaborát o historii odbytu (Memorandum on the history of marketing) (not numbered).
[2] Ibid., 049, 860. [3] Ibid., 049. [4] Ibid.
[5] For the story of the Dutch merger see Ch. Wilson, II, chapters XV and XVI.
[6] PA–STZ, 860. [7] Ibid., 2765.

to continuous and costly litigation between the Dutch and the Schicht groups.

On the one hand, the Dutch vegetable oil and edible fats companies exploited the post-war situation to force an entry for themselves into the markets of Central and Southeast Europe, where German–Austrian capital had previously been dominant. On the other hand, the newly established Czechoslovak–Dutch group formed a mutually protective partnership against its much-feared competitor, Lever Brothers of Great Britain. This was expressed in article 10 of the Great Entente: 'None of the contracting parties shall be permitted to participate in the capital of or to conclude an agreement with the company of Lever Bros. nor with any of its subsidiary companies without the consent of all contracting partners.'[1]

The agreements of 1921 clearly show that Schicht, with its headquarters in Czechoslovakia and possessing the largest productive capacity in Central and Southeast Europe, occupied a key position in the area.

Although a new set of relationships had been established and mutual agreements had been signed, fierce competition continued almost unabated.[2] This resulted in the amalgamation of the two Dutch companies in 1928 and the tighter international monopoly structure of the newly established Margarine Union N.V. in Rotterdam (see Table 5c). The Schicht group lost its independence by exchanging its shares for those of the Margarine Union. However, the Schicht brothers, Heinrich, Georg and Franz, obtained seats on the board of directors of the Margarine Union as shareholders and became salaried executive directors of this international concern.[3] This arrangement reflected the changes which had supervened in this international business, where the parties were as much involved in fighting each other as in promoting a combination of interests.

At the end of the twenties and the beginning of the thirties two giant concerns confronted each other in Europe. Of the two, the British trust, Lever Brothers Ltd., was financially the stronger and its world-wide connections were more extensive than those of the Margarine Union. The British Levers advanced steadily in the European markets, especially with

[1] Ibid., 860.
[2] Cf. Ch. Wilson, II, p. 272.
[3] PA–STZ – Bilance, and H.Sch., 723.

their soap products. However, despite all their efforts, they were unable to capture the Southeast European market until 1929. The Schichts became so worried that they asked their Dutch partner for protection against the unrelieved pressure from Levers.[1] Costly advertising campaigns were mounted by both sides in Austria, Hungary and Yugoslavia, where the sales agencies of both groups tried to oust one another. The outcome was yet another agreement: in May 1930 the sales apparatus of both companies in these countries was merged.[2] This understanding in turn reflects a much wider settlement concluded on 4 April 1930 between the Margarine Union and Lever Brothers, when they merged into a new company, Unilever Ltd London & Unilever N.V. Rotterdam (Table 5D).[3]

The 1929–30 merger which gave birth to the powerful trust of Unilever was according to *The Economist* '...one of the biggest industrial amalgamations in European history'.[4] The whole complex Schicht undertaking of Central and Southeast Europe, centred in Ústí, disappeared into Unilever. The Schichts exchanged their holding in Margarine Union again for Unilever shares and Heinrich, Georg and Franz Schicht advanced onto the board of directors of Unilever which was identical for the British and the Dutch company. From a practical point of view the two companies were really one single enterprise and the division was undertaken formally to avoid double taxation in Holland and in Britain,[5] a device learnt from the experience of the British and Dutch Margarine Union. In 1929–30, however, there was still a division of interests. The British group's interests ranged all over the world, while the Dutch group and the Schichts retained a two-thirds involvement in Europe.[6]

With the agreement of 31 December 1937 between Lever Bros. of London and Unilever of Rotterdam any such distinctions were abandoned. All capital investment and all interests were completely merged into a single monopoly organization

[1] Ibid., 861.

[2] Ibid., Zusammenlegung des Schicht–Lever–Verkaufs–Apparates–Österreich: Österr. Georg Schicht–Lever A.G.; Ungarn: Hutter–Lever r.t.; Yugoslavien: Jugoslavenska d.d. Schicht–Sunlight, Zagreb. 28. and 29. May 1930.

[3] Ibid., 861.

[4] Cited by Ch. Wilson, I, p. xvii.

[5] PA–STZ, 859; cf. also Ch. Wilson, II, p. 281.

[6] PA–STZ, 861.

of identical companies in Holland and in Britain, Lever Bros. & Unilever.[1] It had a total capital of £67,445,925. All decisions on production, financial and commercial policy were taken in London and Rotterdam, but most decision-making bodies had their headquarters in London. Central and Southeast Europe, formerly the Schicht domain, was thus firmly integrated into the Unilever Empire.

The history of these transactions proves beyond doubt that Anglo-Dutch capital consolidated its position and gained supremacy in the vegetable-oil industry, not only in Czechoslovakia, but through Czechoslovakia in the whole Southeast European region. The management of Lever Bros. & Unilever made a favourable assessment of their investment in the 1930s in Czechoslovakia and the Southeast European countries, where wages were substantially lower than in Western Europe. This is shown in Table 6, prepared by Schicht for negotiations preceding the fusion of 1929–30.

The leading personalities in Lever Brothers continued to press for expansion into this area at a time when Germany's demands for revision became more aggressive. This by no means brought an end to Anglo-Dutch interest in the region. On the contrary, the Chairman of Lever Bros. & Unilever, Francis d'Arcy Cooper, saw advantages in the creation of a 'Greater Germany' as a large number of Unilever companies would then be situated in a homogeneous customs territory. In his speech at the annual general meeting on 13 May 1938 he tried to convince the shareholders that there was no cause for concern and that in spite of the *Anschluss* production and transfers of profit in the usual manner could continue as before, especially as with the *Anschluss* the probability of European war decreased.[2] In common with some other prominent British commercial and political figures, D'Arcy Cooper did not assess future developments correctly. In 1940, not very long after his hopeful forecast, the German management of the Schicht concern in Ústí, where some of the Schicht brothers had stayed,[3]

[1] Ibid., Translations of the agreement of 31 December 1937 (not numbered).

[2] Ibid., 859, Chairman's Speech at the Annual General Meeting of Lever Brothers and Unilever Ltd. London, 13 May 1938.

[3] Georg Schicht became a British subject in 1938 and a high-ranking executive in Unilever (governor); thus he was able to protect the family property in the Western world.

Table 6. *Average earnings in several European factories of the Schicht combine, 1928*

Country	Average weekly wages in Dutch currency (hfl.)							Average monthly earnings of master-workers
				Unskilled workers				
	Master-workers	Foremen	Skilled workers	without piecework	with piecework	Fore-women	Women workers	
Czechoslovakia	18.30–25.80	16.80–23.30	11.20–19.00	14.20–17.30	15.00–23.50	11.30–12.70	6.30–10.00	80–228
Germany								
Leipzig	—	27.00–29.00	25.30–29.60	24.20	27.60	19.40	16.10	140.00
Hamburg	—	38.30	32.00	14.50–30.00	35.00	19.30	9.40–19.20	154.00–228.00
Austria								
Schicht	—	—	19.20–23.70	16.50	19.20	11.00	10.10	—
Kunerol	—	21.50	21.20	16.80–18.50	23.50–28.00	—	11.30	118.00
Warsaw	19.90–26.90	14.10–22.00	12.80–21.80	9.00–12.80	—	9.20–12.80	5.10–7.60	199–273
Budapest	17.80–24.00	13.60–15.60	10.70–14.40	8.00–13.30	17.10–19.40	12.10–13.00	5.00–6.40	130–152
Romania								
Stella	—	11.40	22.80	9.10	—	18.20	5.20	113–183
Phenix	—	19.80–27.00	19.80–28.50	10.30–14.70	—	—	7.90–10.60	106–274
Esseg	17.50	15.70	12.60–20.10	10.50–13.50	16.40	8.40–10.50	5.20–7.30	57–188
Sais*	63.20	38.40	34.50	26.90	32.30	31.00	13.70	—

Source: PA–STZ – Koncern. * *Switzerland.*

announced that the Anglo-Dutch concern had become a German–Dutch company.[1]

Thus Belgian, British and French investors clearly influenced the chemical industry in Czechoslovakia, although they did not acquire majority holdings. The mineral- and vegetable-oil industries, however, were under the complete control of American, French, Dutch and British capital.[2]

2 The influence of international cartels on the Czechoslovak chemical industry

Our enquiry into the international cartels in which Czechoslovakia participated during the inter-war period has demonstrated the existence of connections of varying degrees of intensity between direct investment and cartels, mainly in highly concentrated branches of industry. This is particularly the case in the chemical industry, where capital and cartel connections are extremely complicated and are intertwined in such a way as to make it very difficult to see through them. By attempting to disentangle part of these relationships it is hoped to contribute towards clarifying a certain section of pre-war economic history.

In all leading industrial countries a very small number of concerns, often only one, predominated in the chemical industry.[3] As a rule, the large concerns operating on an international scale had shares in each other's capital. Some idea of the enormous structure and the wide ramifications of the world's largest producers can be gained from the graphical representation of I.G. Farben and Imperial Chemical Industries in the second half of the 1920s which was put before the fact-finding commission of the U.S. government during the TNEC enquiry.[4] Besides holding shares in each other's capital these

[1] PA–STZ, 2765.

[2] The financial strength of Unilever made itself felt in the Czechoslovak economy in the 1930s in other ways as well. Through Schicht's participation in the Anglo-Czechoslovak and Prague Credit Bank, of which Heinrich Schicht was a director, Unilever provided a couple of loans: in 1935 to the Škoda-Works, and in 1936 through Martin's Bank to the textile factory of Schiel Brothers, Prague, to finance purchases of raw materials from the United Africa Co., a subsidiary of Unilever (PA–STZ, 01140).

[3] This was also the case in the Czechoslovak chemical industry (see preceding section).

[4] TNEC, Hearings, Part 25, Exhibit No. 2083 and 2086.

multinational combines achieved a high degree of control over the world's chemical production by concluding cartel agreements affecting whole groups of chemical products. Thus a very few alliances, sometimes bilateral, cartelized the main areas of chemical production internationally. In the context of this study only those phenomena can be dealt with which provide the international framework for Czechoslovak cartels. However, such an analysis, besides showing the place of Czechoslovakia in the international structure of chemical cartels, also reveals some general features of this historical development.

On the basis of their traditional cooperation in the field of patents, know-how and trade, but also as a result of the continuous competition between them, the American E.I. duPont de Nemours Co. and the British ICI agreed in 1929 to divide between them the world markets for all their chemical products. At the same time both partners recognized the validity of the similar far-reaching agreements between ICI and the German I.G. Farben, and ICI and the Belgian Solvay concern. These agreements included obligations to exchange technical information and patents and also to develop common research for the dissemination of their patents. In the activities of these cartels an interesting contradiction appeared: on the one hand, they supported and financed scientific research, emphasizing that their aim was to extend the uses of known chemicals and to discover new products and introduce them into their common production programmes; and on the other hand, however, they strove to prevent the production of newly developed or invented chemicals when there was a danger to prices and profits. At the same time, i.e., in the decade before the Second World War, comprehensive agreements existed in the chemical industry between duPont, ICI and I.G. Farben, as well as between I.G. Farben and the Standard Oil Company of the U.S.A. about patents, technology and the precise delimitation and restriction of production. Such cartels have been sharply criticized, especially by American economists in the 1940s, and I.G. Farben in particular was accused of deliberately misusing cartels in order to support Germany's preparation for aggression and war.[1]

Linked with these powerful world-wide cartels, covering

[1] Cf. especially the monographs of the investigators and experts of the TNEC: C. D. Edwards, Wendell Berge, J. Borkin and C. A. Welsh.

almost all basic chemicals and their numerous related products, further innumerable cartel agreements were concluded with chemical works which were less influential internationally but powerful in their own national economies. Many special understandings were also entered into by leading producers of dyes, plastics, explosives, pharmaceutical and other chemical products. Thus international and national cartels of varying degrees of effectiveness spread their influence by means ranging from monopolies over basic products to loose understandings or conventions about subsidiary products, creating a net of hierarchical relations which bear some resemblance to feudal vassal linkages and are difficult to unravel. There can, however, be no doubt that international cartelization in the chemical industry increasingly impeded the development of those enterprises wanting to pursue an independent policy. Also it became progressively more difficult for governments to make their influence effectively felt on their own chemical industries, as these were firmly linked to international cartels. Against the background of this worldwide cartel structure and its complicated economic and political relationships we shall evaluate the involvement of the Czechoslovak chemical industry with international cartels.

Most of the international cartel agreements involving Czechoslovakia were concluded in the chemical industry. According to my calculations based on the Czechoslovak Cartel Register, 74 international agreements were registered between 1926 and 1938 involving 56 groups of chemical products. The most frequently occurring cartel partner on the Czechoslovak side was the Spolek pro chemickou a hutní výrobu (Association for Chemical and Metallurgical Production), which signed 80 % of all international cartels affecting the chemical industry of Czechoslovakia. As was shown in the preceding section, Spolek could without exaggeration be regarded as the spokesman for the whole Czechoslovak chemical industry, standing at the head of an extensive holding company and competing in Central and Southeast Europe with other great chemical combines, so that it was drawn into their sphere of interest and also into their cartel system. The most frequent foreign partners of Czechoslovak chemical cartels were German companies, which were signatories to 60 % of all such agreements.[1]

[1] Compiled from the Cartel Register in SÚA; cf. also Jan Plhal, p. 90.

While Belgian, British and French capital was directly invested in Czechoslovak chemical companies, German cartels intervened perceptibly in Czechoslovak manufacture of most of the important chemicals and our further analysis is primarily concerned with them.

Nitrogen compounds take an extremely significant place among basic chemicals because of their importance in agriculture (artificial fertilizers) and in the manufacture of explosives. Originally, in the nineteenth century, Chile dominated the world market, with her natural deposits of sodium nitrate exploited by British and American capital investment. At the beginning of the twentieth century a method was invented of using atmospheric nitrogen for the manufacture of ammonia. Industrial production began in 1913 in Germany in the Badische Anilin A.G. (later I.G. Farben), using the method known as the Haber–Bosch process. After 1927, when the original patents expired, this process became indispensable for the heavy chemical industry in all countries,[1] and a competitive struggle ensued between the large chemical corporations. At the same time competition continued from Chile's natural sodium nitrate products. The first attempt at international cartelization of nitrogen products was made in 1929, with the foundation of the Convention Internationale de l'Industrie de l'Azote, which Chilean producers joined. After a number of unsuccessful agreements a more stable nucleus emerged in Europe, consisting of Imperial Chemical Industries for the British manufacture of nitrogen products, the Stickstoff-Syndikat, a subsidiary of I.G. Farben, for Germany and the Norsk Hydro Elektrisk Kvaelstofaktieselskab for Norway, known as the DEN-Gruppe (Deutschland, England, Norwegen). These three powerful combines entered into a basic cartel agreement in 1930 and also drew other European countries in, thus establishing the International Nitrogen Cartel.[2] As early as 1930 the Czechoslovak Spolek was drawn into the international cartel by an agreement with the Stickstoff-Syndikat concerning nitrogen products for technical purposes.[3] In this agreement, valid till 1938, Czechoslovak enterprises undertook to forego direct

[1] Cf. Alwin Mittasch, *Geschichte der Ammoniaksynthese* (Weinheim, 1951).

[2] Cf. E. Hexner, p. 326; also W. Berge, p. 241.

[3] SÚA–KR 385/1, 1 August 1930–1 October 1938.

exports from Czechoslovak territory in exchange for permission to manufacture annually nitrogen products with a nitrogen content of 1,150 tons over and above requirements on the domestic market, although – as stated explicitly in the agreement – their capacity to produce for export after deducting domestic needs amounted to 1,400 tons of nitrogen content. Of the output allocated for export Spolek was allowed to sell nitrogen compounds not exceeding 190 tons of nitrogen content to Hungary, Romania and Yugoslavia and a maximum of 8 tons of nitrogen content to Austria. The remainder had to be supplied to the Stickstoff-Syndikat; orders from the Successor States in excess of the allocation also had to be handed over to be executed by the Stickstoff-Syndikat. In addition to this, firms in Czechoslovak territory not wishing to buy from Czechoslovak manufacturers could obtain the requirements of nitrogen products from the Stickstoff-Syndikat. At the same time, a special provision gave I.G. Farben the right to sell sodium nitrite – mainly needed for the manufacture of dyes – directly and freely in Czechoslovakia. Thus was organised one of the most effective means by which the German chemical concern penetrated the markets of Southeast Europe and the Czechoslovak domestic market.

However, the intervention of this international cartel into the Czechoslovak chemical industry went even further. It stipulated that all manufacture of nitrogen products for technical purposes in the Czechoslovak works Československé továrny na dusíkaté látky akc. spol. (Czechoslovak Factories for Nitrogen Products Ltd) in Moravská Ostrava should be suspended for the duration of the cartel, except for the manufacture of ammonia for delivery to the firm of Synthesia in Semtín and liquefied anhydrous ammonia for the manufacture of ammonium carbonate and ammonium chloride in the Moravian Ostrava works. A trustee was appointed by the Stickstoff-Syndikat to ensure strict observance of the agreement and was given access to all documents. The final clause strongly emphasised the confidential character of the agreement.

In the field of nitrogen fertilizers the Czechoslovak chemical industry resisted pressure from the International Nitrogen Cartel for a period which was inevitably brief. The fact that Spolek entered into an agreement with the Polish, Austrian and

Hungarian chemical industries about the marketing of calcium cyanamide can be seen as a defensive measure.[1] Spolek undertook to purchase 2,600 tons annually from Poland for the Czechoslovak market, while the Polish works had to undertake not to deliver calcium cyanamide to Czechoslovakia, Hungary, Yugoslavia, Austria and Romania. In return, the Austrian and Romanian cartel partners had to forego their exports to Czechoslovakia and Poland. This agreement seems to suggest that the Czechoslovak chemical industry still influenced the market for calcium cyanamide in the former Austro-Hungarian Monarchy at the beginning of the 1930s. However, in June 1932 the Czechoslovak manufacturers of nitrogenous fertilizers, who had concentrated their forces in the cartel organization Sdružení pro prodej dusíkatých látek, s.s r.o., Praha (Sales Association for Nitrogen Products), were attached to the DEN-Gruppe of the International Nitrogen Cartel.[2] In Table 1 the position of the Czechoslovak manufacture of nitrogen fertilizers in relation to all other cartel members is shown graphically. With a quota of 0.62 % of European exports the Czechoslovak group was at the bottom of the list of cartel partners. A letter dated 25 October 1933 from the Stickstoff-Syndikat G.m.b.H. representing the German, English and Norwegian groups addressed to the Sales Association for Nitrogen Products sums up the content of the agreement very clearly when confirming the export position: 'This export [i.e., from Czechoslovakia] is to be conducted exclusively by us or by our partners; you undertook not to contravene the agreement and neither yourself nor through any other person to offer, sell or deliver nitrogen fertilizers outside the customs barriers of Czechoslovakia.'[3] Should the Sales Association be unable to satisfy the demand on the Czechoslovak market with its own output it was committed to meeting domestic needs exclusively with products from the Stickstoff-Syndikat. For this purpose the Czechoslovak partners were to attempt to get exemption from tariffs for the Syndikat's imports. Here we meet an open demand concerning the public revenue of the Czechoslovak state in an international agreement by private enterprise, which was

[1] SÚA-KR 219/1, 1 July 1930.
[2] SÚA-KR 246/1, 2, 6 June 1932–3 October 1939.
[3] SÚA-KR 246/1, 6 June 1932–30 March 1934.

Table 1. *The International*

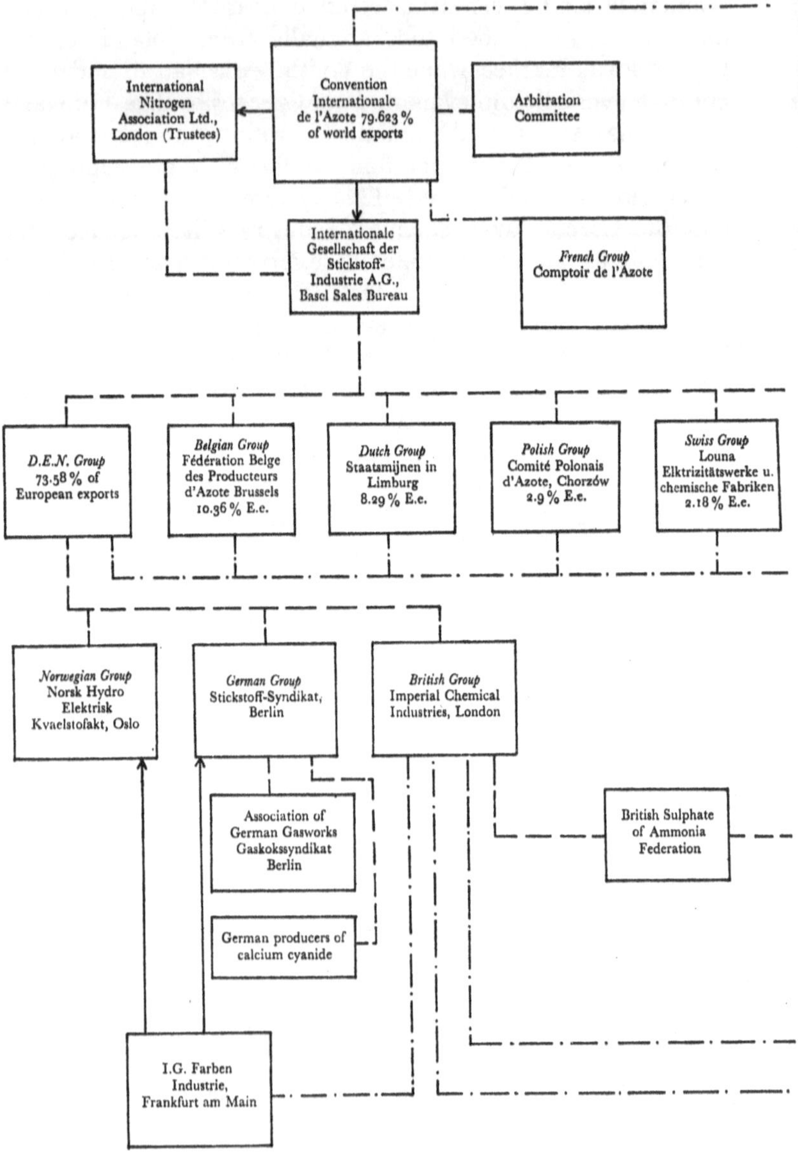

Source: compiled from Cartel Agreements SÚA-KR, 246/5 and 689/4 – 15 July 1938

Signs and abbreviations: ———→ controlling influence of shareholding

— — — — membership or sales bureau of cartel members

—· —· — cartel agreements concerning division of markets

E.e. = European export

D.E.N. = Deutschland, England, Norwegen

Nitrogen Cartel

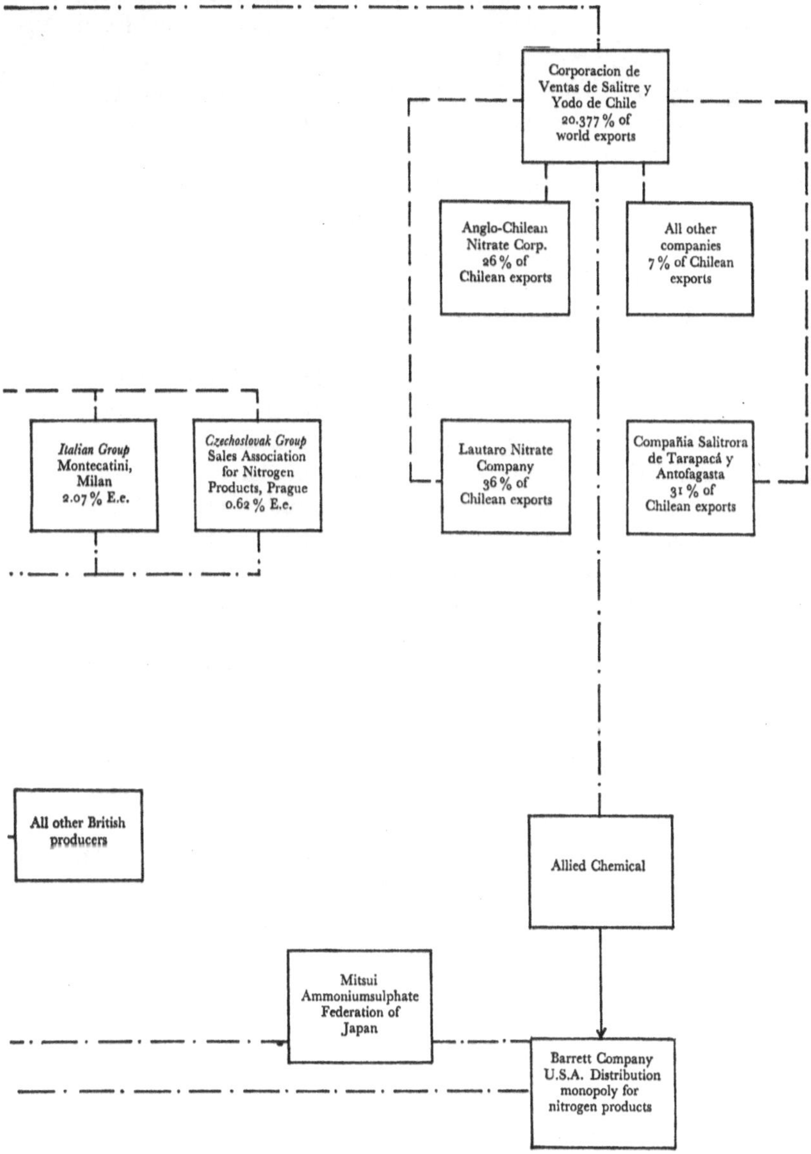

actually put into force. The agreement was extended in 1934.[1] In 1935 the Dutch and Belgian groups joined and, together with the DEN-Group, divided up the world market and fixed smaller export quotas, with a complicated system of fines for 'infringements'.[2] The Czechoslovak export trade in nitrogen fertilizers practically ceased and the domestic market was to all intents and purposes controlled by the Stickstoff-Syndikat of Berlin. The International Nitrogen Cartel had obviously linked this branch of the Czechoslovak chemical industry to the Stickstoff-Syndikat's interests – which, at the same time, meant to I.G. Farben's. This is also borne out by the fact that all dealings of the Czechoslovak Group with the international cartel were through Berlin.

In 1935 the Stickstoff-Syndikat G.m.b.H., Berlin, concluded a cartel agreement in which it ceded to the Czechoslovak factory of Blumberg & Rindskopf in Cukmantl its interest in the Czechoslovak domestic market for finely crystallized ammonium chloride.[3] In return the Czechoslovak firm undertook to abstain from exporting this product itself, to transfer to the Syndikat its annual export quota of 360 tons, and to deliver not more than 30 tons annually to Austria. When the agreement was extended in 1936 the Czechoslovak quota was reduced to 240 tons. Although a year later the quota regained its previous level, the Czechoslovak partner was given the option of foregoing its export quota and receiving compensation from the Syndikat's funds for 20 % of the average amount of lost profits. At every renewal of the agreement the cartel partners raised the price of their product.

Another highly cartelized chemical was hydrogen peroxide, which is used in industry for bleaching and in medicine as a disinfectant. In the inter-war period the Internationale Wasserstoffsuperoxyd-Konvention attempted to capture the world market for hydrogen peroxide. Corwin Edwards, the Head of the American Anti-Trust Department, charged the Internationale Wasserstoffsuperoxyd-Konvention with using patents to prevent new enterprises from starting production.[4]

[1] SÚA–KR 246/2, 30 March 1934–1 July 1935.
[2] SÚA–KR 246/3, 1 July 1935, terminated by telegram from the Norwegian Group on 3 October 1939.
[3] SÚA–KR 749/1, 1 January 1935–11 September 1939.
[4] C. D. Edwards, Military Affairs Committee, Monograph No. 1, pp. 38 and 322.

The agreement of the Czechoslovak Spolek with the Konvention clearly illustrates the activities of this cartel.[1] When the Czechoslovak chemical industry joined the Internationale Wasserstoffsuperoxyd-Konvention in 1935, a three-cornered agreement was signed between the Deutsche Gold- und Silberscheideanstalt, Frankfurt a.M. – a subsidiary of I.G. Farben and also the head office of the cartel – Spolek, Ústí n.L., and the Moravsko-ostravské chemické závody (Moravian–Ostrava Chemical Works). The latter undertook to cease construction of their new hydrogen peroxide plant and to abstain for the following fifteen years from any direct or indirect participation in the production of hydrogen peroxide. In compensation for the loss of profits incurred the Moravian–Ostrava Works received one million Czechoslovak Crowns.[2] At the same time Spolek restricted its output for 1934 and completely stopped exports of hydrogen peroxide products in 1935 and 1936. In addition, Spolek and the Deutsche Gold- und Silberscheideanstalt divided the Czechoslovak domestic market 50:50 between themselves with the prospect of a change to 75:25 in favour of Spolek for the year 1936. In the understanding Spolek also engaged not to make any licences for its production techniques available at home or abroad and to prevent the production of hydrogen peroxide in its subsidiaries and in firms in which it could make its influence felt, in order to ensure that no competition with the Konvention arose. This agreement remained valid until the end of 1939.[3]

Czechoslovak–German cartels included a number of agreements on far-reaching exchanges of manufacturing secrets,[4] and giving German trustees full access to confidential documents and commercial books and papers of their Czechoslovak partners.[5] The potential political impact of these cartel conditions at a time when Nazi Germany was preparing her aggression against the Czechoslovak Republic cannot be discounted.

In the same way as the International Nitrogen Cartel, other international cartels drew Czechoslovakia into the German

[1] SÚA–KR 776/1, 7 March 1935–31 December 1939.

[2] SÚA–KR 788/1, 17 January 1935; also letter enclosed with the text of the agreement from the Deutsche Gold- und Silberscheideanstalt, A.G., Frankfurt, of 13 February 1935.

[3] SÚA–KR 776/1.

[4] SÚA–KR e.g. 386/1, 568/1 and others.

[5] SÚA–KR 385/1, 246/1 and many others.

sphere of influence.[1] For example, the world-wide titanium cartel left the whole Czechoslovak market to be drawn into its system by the Titangesellschaft.[2] In the agreement of 1933 with Spolek, valid until 1945, the Titangesellschaft G.m.b.H., Leverkusen, was apportioned 72–5 % of the annual consumption in Czechoslovakia.[3] It was also stipulated that technical information and expertise on production methods would be exchanged between the Titangesellschaft, I.G. Farben and Spolek. At the same time a trustee was appointed by the German side to control the observance of contractual obligations.[4] Similarly, the International Bismuth Convention, in which the German, English, French and Dutch industries participated, regarded the Czechoslovak works as part of the German group.[5]

The above-mentioned content of some of the most effective international cartels in the chemical industry shows the means by which they intervened in the Czechoslovak chemical industry, and also the leading part played by the German chemical combines, especially I.G. Farben. The effect of these powerful cartels on the economic policy of their states, and even on the relations between states, cannot be doubted, although it is difficult to measure.

In pre-Munich Czechoslovakia the decisive strength of the chemical industry doubtless lay with the combine of Spolek where cartels were concerned. In the production and marketing of chemical products which were not wholly controlled by Spolek on the home market individual enterprises were tied to it through bilateral or multilateral undertakings about technical cooperation and patents, or by selling syndicates. Therefore most domestic agreements which were entered in the Cartel Register centred round Spolek, just as was the case with international agreements.[6] For this reason a smaller number of cartel companies existed in the chemical industry

[1] Ibid.

[2] Titangesellschaft m.b.H., Leverkusen, belonged to the sphere of interests of I. G. Farbenindustrie and E.I. duPont de Nemours Co. The American–German combination was predominant on the market for this valuable product. Titanium is important in the production of paints, artificial rubber, glass, paper and enamel. Cf. W. Berge, pp. 124–41.

[3] SÚA–KR 568/1, 2 November 1933–17 August 1945.

[4] Ibid.

[5] Ibid.

[6] *Československé kartely*, part V.

than in other comparatively less concentrated branches of industry, for instance the engineering industry (viz. chapter 4 (2), Table 1). Thus only three cartel organizations can be regarded as relatively representative and effective on the domestic market, their central offices undertaking marketing, exports and accounting for their members and concluding international agreements on their behalf: Sdružení pro prodej dusíkatých látek, s.s r.o., Praha (Sales Association for Nitrogen Products); Fosfa, společnost pro obchod výrobky chemického průmyslu, spol. s r.o., Praha (Superphosphate Syndicate of the Czechoslovak Works); and Acetic, spol. s r.o. Praha (Tarboard Cartel). However, the economic supremacy of Spolek overshadowed them and they too were in one way or another tied to it either by cartels or by other relationships.

The mutual intertwining of many domestic and international cartels is as characteristic for the Czechoslovak chemical industry as it is for the chemical industry generally. For a clearer view Table 2 lists in alphabetical order those chemical products which were the subject of international cartel agreements with Czechoslovak participation, together with the countries of origin of the foreign cartel partners and the duration of the agreements. Thus an overview is obtained of Czechoslovak chemical cartel associations with foreign firms on the eve of the Second World War.

It is apparent from Table 2 that essentially all basic chemicals were drawn into the international cartel system. About 25 % of the cartelized products manufactured in Czechoslovak chemical works became the subject of multilateral conventions, syndicates and other cartel associations; however, the large majority of cartelized chemical products manufactured in Czechoslovakia belonged – mainly by contractual consent among the strongest international cartel partners – to the sphere of influence of the German members of international cartels. This is also borne out by the content of the Czechoslovak–German agreements, which we discussed previously.

From the point of view of cartel policy the situation in the chemical industry of Czechoslovakia was less favourable than in the iron and steel industry. While the Czechoslovak iron and steel works could join forces with the large iron and steel combines of Western Europe against their main competitors in

Table 2. *Chemical products in international cartels with Czechoslovak participation**

Product	Cartel partners outside Czechoslovakia	Duration of cartel agreement
Acid-resistant stoneware	Germany	1933–41
Ammonia	Germany	1935–8
Ammonia–soda and by-products	Belgium, Austria, Romania, Yugoslavia,	1933–7
Ammonium carbonate	Germany	1930–40
Anthraquinone	Germany	1933–41
Artificial sweeteners	International Saccharine Cartel	1930–8
Bismuth	International Bismuth Cartel	1933–9
Bismuth products	International Bismuth Cartel	1933–8
Bone-glue and industrial bone by-products	EPIDOS – International Bone-Glue Cartel	1926–40
Calcium carbide, calcium cyanamide	Italy	1928–38
Calcium cyanamide	Poland, Austria, Hungary	1930–8
'Calgon'	Germany	1936–8
Chemical products except for soda and soda products	Belgium	1908 for an undetermined period
Chemicals (phosphorus products and artificial fertilizers)	Austria	1936–45
Cocaine	International Cocaine Convention	1932–43
Codeine, opium alkaloids	International Morphine and Codeine Convention	1933 – unlimited validity
Cyanous salts (cyanides, prussiates of potash, blues, etc.) from calcium cyanamide	Germany	1925–35
Earthenware for chemical purposes	Germany	1921–37
Ferrosilicon	International Ferro-Silicon Syndicate	1933–8
Fire-resistant magnesite products	Austria, Germany, Great Britain	1929–46
Fluorine products	Germany	1933–8
Formic acid	Germany	1933–8
Hydrochloric acid, sodium sulphate, sodium sulphide	Austria, France	1925–35

* Compiled from data in SÚA–KR and TNEC, Hearings, Part 25.

Table 2 (*cont.*)

Product	Cartel partners outside Czechoslovakia	Duration of cartel agreement
Hydrogen peroxide	International Wasserstoff-superoxyd Konvention	1933–8 1935–9 1935–46
Hydrogen peroxide, technical and medicinal	Austria, Germany	1930–9
Nitrogenous fertilizers	European Nitrate Fertilizer Cartel	1932–9 1934–9
Nitrogen products for technical purposes	Germany	1930–8
Oxalic acid	Oxalsäurekonvention (Germany)	1937–9
Potassium dichromate and sodium dichromate	Germany	1934–9
Potassium hypochlorite, sodium hypochlorite, 'Neamocan', 'Veloxiol', 'Flavol', 'Trifirmin'	Germany	1933–7
Potassium permanganate, sodium permanganate, calcium permanganate	Germany	1933–8
Sodium chlorate	International Sodium Chlorate Convention	1937–8
Sodium perborate	Germany	1933–9
Sodium peroxide	Germany	1933–43
Stannic chloride	Germany	1911–39
Sulphates	Germany	1933–7
Sulphuric acid	France	1928–35
Sulphuric acid	Poland	1933–8
Sulphuric acid, aluminium hydroxide, aluminium oxide and aluminium salts	Germany	1934, 1935–9
Superphosphate	Italy	1934–5
Synthetic horn	International Artificial Horn Cartel	1929–37
Synthetic resin	Austria, Germany	1938 for 1 year
Titanium dioxide	Germany	1933–9
Titanium paints, zirconium, monazite sand	France	1926 for 20 years
Trichloroethylene	Austria	1933–42
White lead	International White Lead Convention	1934–9

Germany, the Czechoslovak chemical industry was in many instances by the international cartels themselves subordinated to its German cartel partners and thus at the same time exposed to the pressure of one of the most expansive forces of German big business. In a limited sense the capital ties of the leading Czechoslovak chemical works with the great chemical combines of Britain, France and Belgium acted as a corrective in Czechoslovak–German competition which found expression in the cartel conditions. Table 2 also shows that almost half of the cartelized products were the subject of bilateral German–Czechoslovak agreements, most frequently between Spolek and I.G. Farben and their respective subsidiaries. Usually understandings were reached only after sharp price wars or tenaciously pursued litigation concerning patents. This is reflected in the content of many agreements on the cessation of production, the adaptation of production programmes, or the amount and direction of exports of Czechoslovak products. The drive of German cartels into Czechoslovakia became especially concentrated between 1933 and 1938.

Because of the large number of different chemicals and chemical products in international cartels and because of their uncommonly complicated interconnections it is difficult to measure the amount of damage or benefit from their activities in the economy of Czechoslovakia. However, it seems obvious that discontinuing the manufacture of certain products, prohibiting the expansion of output or the erection of new plant, and limiting exports cannot be considered as entirely beneficial to the growth of the Czechoslovak chemical industry. On the other hand, the Czechoslovak chemical works applied exactly the same methods in cartel agreements with their weaker partners in the Southeast European countries as the large chemical combines enforced on the Czechoslovak industry, for the main criterion in cartel systems, as in competition, is the balance of economic forces.

In my efforts to obtain some measure of the effectiveness of international cartels in Czechoslovakia I enquired more closely into their effect on foreign trade. I examined the foreign trade statistics for all chemical products which figured in international cartels and occurred in the official statistics of the Republic of Czechoslovakia between 1925 and 1937. This was

Table 3. *Foreign trade of the Czechoslovak Republic in hydrogen peroxide, 1925–37: cartel no. KR 180 concluded in 1930*

Destination or country of origin	1925 Amount q	1925 1,000 Kč	1926 Amount q	1926 1,000 Kč	1927 Amount q	1927 1,000 Kč	1928 Amount q	1928 1,000 Kč	1929 Amount q	1929 1,000 Kč	1930 Amount q	1930 1,000 Kč	1931 Amount q	1931 1,000 Kč
Export total	—	—	6	11	—	—	12	12	5	5	10	2	—	—
Germany	—	—	6	11	—	—	—	—	—	—	—	—	—	—
Austria	—	—	—	—	—	—	—	—	5	5	—	—	—	—
Price	—	—	—	—	—	—	1q	Kč 1,000	—	—	—	—	—	—
Import total	1,339	1,897	1,135	1,264	1,129	1,181	1,486	1,565	1,369	1,664	1,752	1,983	2,066	2,156
Austria	889	1,314	815	965	1,039	1,070	1,001	1,021	789	948	898	975	899	925
Germany	450	583	295	376	86	105	462	518	446	554	841	992	993	1,009
Japan	—	—	—	—	—	—	—	—	—	—	—	—	—	—
Great Britain	—	—	16	20	4	6	—	—	—	—	—	—	—	—
France	—	—	9	3	—	—	3	2	—	—	—	—	—	—
Italy	—	—	—	—	—	—	20	24	125	151	13	16	174	222
Switzerland	—	—	—	—	—	—	—	—	—	—	—	—	—	—
Price	1q	Kč 1,417	1q	Kč 1,202	1q	Kč 1,046	1q	Kč 1,097	1q	Kč 1,215	1q	Kč 1,132	1q	Kč 1,044

Destination or country or origin	1932 Amount q	1932 1,000 Kč	1933 Amount q	1933 1,000 Kč	1934 Amount q	1934 1,000 Kč	1935 Amount q	1935 1,000 Kč	1936 Amount q	1936 1,000 Kč	1937 Amount q	1937 1,000 Kč
Export total	—	—	—	—	2	2	—	—	—	—	—	—
Germany	—	—	—	—	—	—	—	—	—	—	—	—
Austria	—	—	—	—	—	—	—	—	—	—	—	—
Price	—	—	—	—	—	—	—	—	—	—	—	—
Import total	1,840	1,917	1,795	2,002	3,204	2,932	241	265	201	224	288	319
Austria	833	916	1,042	1,146	1,960	1,808	194	208	101	110	148	156
Germany	1,007	1,001	708	803	1,155	1,044	47	57	100	114	100	117
Japan	—	—	—	—	—	—	—	—	—	—	40	46
Great Britain	—	—	—	—	—	—	—	—	—	—	—	—
France	—	—	—	—	—	—	—	—	—	—	—	—
Italy	—	—	—	—	—	—	—	—	—	—	—	—
Switzerland	—	—	45	53	89	80	—	—	—	—	—	—
Price	1q	Kč 1,042	1q	Kč 1,115	1q	Kč 915	1q	Kč 1,100	1q	Kč 1,114	1q	Kč 1,108

Since 1928 customs duty 360 Kč per 1q, contractually 180 Kč per 1q.

Table 4. *Foreign trade of the Czechoslovak Republic in ammonium sulphate, 1925–37: cartel no. KR 246 concluded in 1932*

Destination and country of origin	1925 Amount q	1925 1,000 Kč	1926 Amount q	1926 1,000 Kč	1927 Amount q	1927 1,000 Kč	1928 Amount q	1928 1,000 Kč	1929 Amount q	1929 1,000 Kč	1930 Amount q	1930 1,000 Kč	1931 Amount q	1931 1,000 Kč
Export total	21	6	77,535	13,005	3,244	530	28,657	5,025	233,401	35,887	163,586	23,009	38,707	5,025
Spain	—	—	—	—	—	—	—	—	148,469	22,435	25,370	3,676	9,000	1,184
Lithuania	—	—	—	—	—	—	—	—	—	—	—	—	—	—
Germany	—	—	43,737	7,212	2,190	326	25,805	4,489	9,861	1,783	281	39	5,969	795
British India	—	—	—	—	—	—	—	—	29,994	5,144	11,010	1,684	—	—
Switzerland	—	—	—	—	—	—	—	—	—	—	—	—	2,271	307
Hamburg	—	—	28,066	4,807	—	—	2,182	420	—	—	52,751	6,900	16,331	2,094
Great Britain	—	—	—	—	—	—	—	—	21,612	3,026	9,260	1,130	—	—
Romania	—	—	—	—	—	—	—	—	67	16	473	64	450	49
Italy	—	—	4,101	760	650	133	—	—	—	—	46,347	7,164	100	8
Japan	—	—	—	—	—	—	—	—	6,638	981	—	—	—	—
Sweden	—	—	—	—	—	—	—	—	—	—	13,420	1,731	1,500	225
Hungary	—	—	1,329	184	—	—	—	—	54	14	1,400	178	—	—
Dutch colonies in Asia	—	—	—	—	—	—	—	—	3,706	624	—	—	—	—
Austria	—	—	295	37	400	70	500	86	402	62	2,161	298	2,100	249
Bulgaria	—	—	6	5	—	—	166	29	—	—	—	—	—	—
Mexico	—	—	—	—	—	—	—	—	—	—	—	—	—	—
Poland	—	—	1	—	4	1	4	1	8,050	1,043	—	—	—	—
Irish Free State	—	—	—	—	—	—	—	—	1,524	293	—	—	—	—
Yugoslavia	—	—	—	—	—	—	—	—	—	—	1,100	141	986	114
British colonies in Asia	—	—	—	—	—	—	—	—	1,524	216	—	—	—	—
U.S.A.	—	—	—	—	—	—	—	—	1,500	250	—	—	—	—
Turkey	—	—	—	—	—	—	—	—	—	—	—	—	—	—
Greece	—	—	—	—	—	—	—	—	—	—	—	—	—	—
Other states	—	—	—	—	—	—	—	—	—	—	13	4	—	—
Price	1q	Kč 260	1q	Kč 168	1q	Kč 163	1q	Kč 175	1q	Kč 154	1q	Kč 141	1q	Kč 130
Import total	165,227	30,044	80,420	13,519	26,681	4,200	11,080	1,702	13,354	1,556	1,211	219	40	19
Germany	137,109	25,278	53,868	9,033	19,955	3,253	7,340	1,217	5,978	947	1,211	219	37	19
Poland	26,025	4,405	25,639	4,319	6,625	928	3,430	438	5,366	607	—	—	—	—
Romania	895	146	—	—	—	—	—	—	—	—	—	—	—	—
Austria	606	105	760	143	101	19	—	—	—	—	—	—	—	—
Hungary	493	94	—	—	—	—	—	—	—	—	—	—	—	—
France	100	17	—	—	—	—	10	1	10	2	—	—	—	—
Great Britain	—	—	3	1	—	—	300	46	—	—	—	—	—	—
U.S.A.	—	—	150	23	—	—	—	—	—	—	—	—	—	—
Other states	—	—	—	—	—	—	—	—	—	—	—	—	3	—
Price	1q	Kč 182	1q	Kč 168	1q	Kč 157	1q	Kč 153	1q	Kč 137	1q	Kč 181	1q	Kč 475

Destination and country of origin	1932 Amount q	1932 1,000 Kč	1933 Amount q	1933 1,000 Kč	1934 Amount q	1934 1,000 Kč	1935 Amount q	1935 1,000 Kč	1936 Amount q	1936 1,000 Kč	1937 Amount q	1937 1,000 Kč
Export total	18,069	2,633	2,946	291	4,053	339	2,010	165	1,320	115	41,871	3,379
Spain	13,027	2,160	—	—	—	—	—	—	—	—	—	—
Lithuania	—	—	5	—	—	—	10	1	—	—	—	—
Germany	3,047	279	—	—	—	—	—	—	—	—	—	—
British India	—	—	—	—	—	—	50	8	—	—	—	—
Switzerland	—	—	—	—	—	—	—	—	—	—	1	—
Hamburg	—	—	—	—	—	—	—	—	—	—	—	—
Great Britain	—	—	—	—	—	—	—	—	—	—	—	—
Romania	1,150	106	1,499	125	2,889	207	1,050	74	450	46	800	76
Italy	—	—	—	—	—	—	—	—	—	—	40,000	3,206
Japan	—	—	—	—	—	—	—	—	—	—	—	—
Sweden	—	—	—	—	—	—	—	—	—	—	—	—
Hungary	—	—	—	—	—	—	—	—	—	—	—	—
Dutch colonies in Asia	—	—	—	—	—	—	—	—	—	—	—	—
Austria	—	—	1,082	124	417	56	100	12	—	—	300	36
Bulgaria	—	—	—	—	—	—	—	—	—	—	—	—
Mexico	—	—	60	10	10	—	—	—	—	—	—	—
Poland	—	—	—	—	—	—	—	—	—	—	—	—
Irish Free State	—	—	—	—	—	—	—	—	—	—	—	—
Yugoslavia	845	78	300	32	619	57	800	70	870	69	770	61
British colonies in Asia	—	—	—	—	—	—	—	—	—	—	—	—
U.S.A.	—	—	—	—	—	—	—	—	—	—	—	—
Turkey	—	—	—	—	75	11	—	—	—	—	—	—
Greece	—	—	—	—	19	3	—	—	—	—	—	—
Other states	—	—	—	—	24	5	—	—	—	—	—	—
Price	1q	Kč 145	1q	Kč 99	1q	Kč 84	—	—	—	—	—	—
Import total	90	33	56	34	12	11*	4	3	6	5*	3	3
Germany	88	33	56	34	—	—	4	3	—	—	3	3
Poland	—	—	—	—	—	—	—	—	—	—	—	—
Romania	—	—	—	—	—	—	—	—	—	—	—	—
Austria	—	—	—	—	—	—	—	—	—	—	—	—
Hungary	—	—	—	—	—	—	—	—	—	—	—	—
France	2	—	—	—	—	—	—	—	—	—	—	—
Great Britain	—	—	—	—	—	—	—	—	—	—	—	—
U.S.A.	—	—	—	—	—	—	—	—	—	—	—	—
Other states	—	—	—	—	—	—	—	—	—	—	—	—
Price	1q	Kč 367	1q	Kč 607	—	—	—	—	—	—	—	—

* Country of origin not known.
Customs duty 1q = 21.60 Kč. Since 1930 raised to 1q = 71 Kč; 15 July 1933 reduced to 1q = 60 Kč.

Table 5. *Foreign trade of the Czechoslovak Republic in potassium hydrogen sulphate, 1925–37: cartel no. KR 349 concluded in 1933*

Destination and country of origin	1925 Amount q	1925 1,000 Kč	1926 Amount q	1926 1,000 Kč	1927 Amount q	1927 1,000 Kč	1928 Amount q	1928 1,000 Kč	1929 Amount q	1929 1,000 Kč	1930 Amount q	1930 1,000 Kč	1931 Amount q	1931 1,000 Kč
Export total	601	99	451	76	454	80	5	1	409	50	156	24	—	—
Poland	150	27	150	27	150	27	—	—	150	26	150	23	—	—
Switzerland	150	27	300	49	300	52	—	—	—	—	—	—	—	—
Yugoslavia	—	—	—	—	—	—	—	—	—	—	—	—	—	—
Germany	—	—	—	—	—	—	—	—	253	23	—	—	—	—
Austria	—	—	1	—	4	1	5	1	6	1	—	—	—	—
Great Britain	300	45	—	—	—	—	—	—	—	—	—	—	—	—
Other states	—	—	—	—	—	—	—	—	—	—	6	1	—	—
Price	1q	Kč 164	1q	Kč 168	1q	Kč 176	—	—	1q	Kč 122	1q	Kč 154	—	—
Import total	1	1	8	2	5	4	1	1	6	4	5	7	30	7
Germany	—	—	8	2	5	4	1	1	6	4	5	7	30	7
Switzerland	—	—	—	—	—	—	—	—	—	—	—	—	—	—
Other states	—	—	—	—	—	—	—	—	—	—	—	—	—	—
Price	1q	Kč 645	1q	Kč 250	1q	Kč 800	—	—	—	—	—	—	—	—

Destination and country of origin	1932 Amount q	1932 1,000 Kč	1933 Amount q	1933 1,000 Kč	1934 Amount q	1934 1,000 Kč	1935 Amount q	1935 1,000 Kč	1936 Amount q	1936 1,000 Kč	1937 Amount q	1937 1,000 Kč
Export total	150	27	—	—	151	26	1	—	—	—	—	—
Poland	—	—	—	—	—	—	1	—	—	—	—	—
Switzerland	149	27	—	—	148	25	—	—	—	—	—	—
Yugoslavia	—	—	—	—	3	1	—	—	—	—	—	—
Germany	1	—	—	—	—	—	—	—	—	—	—	—
Austria	—	—	—	—	—	—	—	—	—	—	—	—
Great Britain	—	—	—	—	—	—	—	—	—	—	—	—
Other states	—	—	—	—	—	—	—	—	—	—	—	—
Price	1q	Kč 180	—	—	1q	Kč 172	—	—	—	—	—	—
Import total	3	1*	100	10	56	13	7	6	19	13	14	9
Germany	—	—	—	—	51	8	7	6	19	13	11	7
Switzerland	—	—	—	—	5	5	—	—	—	—	—	—
Other states	—	—	—	—	—	—	—	—	—	—	3	2
Price	—	—	—	—	1q	Kč 232	—	—	1q	Kč 684	—	—

* Country of origin not given. Customs duty 1q = 57 Kč.

the case with 35 groups of chemicals. By comparing the conditions of the cartel agreements and the dates of their conclusion on the one hand, and the direction, amount and price movements of foreign trade in each product before the conclusion of the cartel agreement and during its existence on the other, a definite and effective relationship between movements in foreign trade and the conditions of the international cartels in chemical products can be established. The movement of foreign trade in those chemical products proves to be an almost exact reflection on the conditions contained in the cartels. This relationship exists for all cartelized products and I therefore present only a few illustrations, which are typical of the products investigated.

In the first place, one part of the international cartel system in the chemical industry caused a complete, or almost complete, cessation of exports of cartelized products from Czechoslovakia. This situation is shown in Table 3; after the conclusion of the cartel on hydrogen peroxide with the Internationale Wasserstoffsuperoxyd-Konvention in 1930 Czechoslovak exports were cut off. Even before that exports of hydrogen peroxide from Czechoslovakia were very small but the cartel intervened just at the point when Czechoslovak manufacturers wanted to increase them. At the same time, Austrian and German imports of hydrogen peroxide into Czechoslovakia were also maintained, in accordance with the conditions of the cartel agreement.[1]

Exports of a whole range of nitrogenous products from Czechoslovakia were almost wholly discontinued as a result of the Czechoslovak manufacturers becoming members of the International Nitrogen Cartel under the control of the DEN-Gruppe, i.e. I.G. Farben for practical purposes. Table 4 shows the effect of this cartel on foreign trade in one of the nitrogenous products, ammonium sulphate, after 1932 when the agreement was signed. The amount exported fell substantially and the number of countries to which Czechoslovakia exported was reduced to two, Yugoslavia and Romania.[2] Similar developments occurred with the other nitrogen products.

Another part of the international cartel system intervened to direct and limit Czechoslovak exports. In Tables 5, 6 and 7 the

[1] SÚA–KR 180 and *Zahraniční obchod Republiky československé.*
[2] SÚA–KR 246 and *Zahraniční obchod Republiky československé.*

Table 6. *Foreign trade of the Czechoslovak Republic in potassium sulphate (fertilizer), 1925–37: cartel no. KR 349 concluded in 1933*

Destination or country of origin	1925		1926		1927		1928		1929		1930		1931	
	Amount q	1,000 Kč	Amount q	1,000 Kč	Amount q	1,000 Kč	Amount q	1,000 Kč	Amount q	1,000 Kč	Amount q	1,000 Kč	Amount q	1,000 Kč
Export total	3,438	494	2,429	355	3,611	590	6,907	1,146	4,831	762	8,169	1,310	7,293	1,127
Netherlands	—	—	—	—	1,770	286	1,699	269	—	—	3,001	495	—	—
Poland	450	81	600	98	450	74	750	136	450	77	450	77	600	99
Germany	—	—	—	—	150	17	150	28	505	63	—	—	1,019	133
Austria	266	14	2	—	1	1	602	87	1,875	278	1,174	172	935	120
Switzerland	800	127	600	100	900	159	1,200	220	1,500	274	1,350	251	1,600	289
Japan	—	—	153	28	100	15	—	—	—	—	—	—	—	—
Yugoslavia	—	—	—	—	—	—	5	1	—	—	2	1	—	—
Greece	—	—	—	—	150	27	—	—	—	—	—	—	—	—
Italy	—	—	—	—	—	—	—	—	—	—	350	64	1,200	225
Hamburg	1,042	154	802	95	—	—	2,501	405	400	56	1,725	234	1,175	170
Hungary	479	68	167	23	90	11	—	—	—	—	16	3	5	1
U.S.A.	400	50	102	10	—	—	—	—	101	14	101	13	759	90
Romania	—	—	3	1	—	—	—	—	—	—	—	—	—	—
Other states	—	—	—	—	—	—	—	—	—	—	—	—	—	—
Price	1q	Kč 143	1q	Kč 146	1q	Kč 163	1q	Kč 166	1q	Kč 158	1q	Kč 155	1q	Kč 160
Import total	277	46	164	25	166	26	101	25	182	37	174	44	203	37
Germany	277	46	164	25	166	26	101	25	182	37	174	44	203	37
Great Britain	—	—	—	—	—	—	—	—	—	—	—	—	—	—
Switzerland	—	—	—	—	—	—	—	—	—	—	—	—	—	—
(Fertilizer) Poland	—	—	—	—	—	—	—	—	—	—	—	—	—	—
Fertilizer price Price	1q	Kč 165	1q	Kč 152	1q	Kč 157	1q	Kč 248	1q	Kč 204	1q	Kč 253	1q	Kč 182

Destination or country of origin	1932 Amount q	1932 1,000 Kč	1933 Amount q	1933 1,000 Kč	1934 Amount q	1934 1,000 Kč	1935 Amount q	1935 1,000 Kč	1936 Amount q	1936 1,000 Kč	1937 Amount q	1937 1,000 Kč
Export total	6,452	1,008	3,203	550	2,412	427	3,370	452	5,250	631	5,701	873
Netherlands	—	—	—	—	—	—	—	—	—	—	—	—
Poland	596	101	148	26	502	94	1,081	122	3,931	459	3,797	597
Germany	—	—	—	—	—	—	—	—	—	—	—	—
Austria	800	112	300	41	307	42	253	33	870	110	560	98
Switzerland	1,040	186	1,487	266	1,193	211	1,935	282	449	62	1,344	178
Japan	—	—	—	—	—	—	—	—	—	—	—	—
Yugoslavia	—	—	—	—	101	16	101	15	—	—	—	—
Greece	—	—	—	—	—	—	—	—	—	—	—	—
Italy	747	134	900	157	297	59	—	—	—	—	—	—
Hamburg	247	35	—	—	—	—	—	—	—	—	—	—
Hungary	—	—	—	—	—	—	—	—	—	—	—	—
U.S.A.	3,022	440	368	60	—	—	—	—	—	—	—	—
Romania	—	—	—	—	—	—	—	—	—	—	—	—
Other states	—	—	—	—	12	5	—	—	—	—	—	—
Price	1q	Kč 155	1q	Kč 172	1q	Kč 177	1q	Kč 134	1q	Kč 120	1q	Kč 153
(Fertilizer)	—	—	200	27	2,921	319	5,027	569	3,821	467	6,365	622
Import total	289	49	67	12	111	19	20	11	135	25	179	35
(Fertilizer)	—	—	200	27	2,821	312	5,027	569	3,821	467	6,365	622
Germany	289	49	67	12	111	19	13	6	125	19	163	26
Great Britain	—	—	—	—	—	—	3	2	10	6	16	9
Switzerland	—	—	—	—	—	—	4	3	—	—	—	—
(Fertilizer)	—	—	—	—	100	7	—	—	—	—	—	—
Poland	—	—	—	—	—	—	—	—	—	—	—	—
Fertilizer price	—	—	1q	Kč 135	1q	Kč 109	1q	Kč 113	1q	Kč 122	1q	Kč 98
Price	1q	Kč 170	1q	Kč 179	1q	Kč 171	—	—	1q	Kč 185	1q	Kč 196

Customs duty 1q = 57 Kč; no customs duty on fertilizer.

Table 7. *Foreign trade of the Czechoslovak Republic in sodium hydrogen sulphate, 1925–37: cartel no. KR 349 concluded in 1933*

Destination or country of origin	1925 Amount q	1925 1,000 Kč	1926 Amount q	1926 1,000 Kč	1927 Amount q	1927 1,000 Kč	1928 Amount q	1928 1,000 Kč	1929 Amount q	1929 1,000 Kč	1930 Amount q	1930 1,000 Kč	1931 Amount q	1931 1,000 Kč
Export total	9,156	522	20,768	877	17,783	824	15,859	731	5,314	236	5,860	238	732	31
Yugoslavia	—	—	—	—	9	4	—	—	—	—	—	—	—	—
Bulgaria	—	—	—	—	—	—	—	—	—	—	—	—	—	—
Austria	6,514	398	8,058	394	7,158	329	6,276	288	3,011	125	2,478	108	454	19
Romania	—	—	—	—	2	1	221	12	1,147	60	366	16	—	—
Germany	2,584	121	12,554	475	10,456	480	8,456	382	406	18	1,896	70	—	—
Hungary	57	3	156	8	—	—	—	—	104	4	456	19	278	12
Poland	—	—	—	—	155	10	800	43	646	29	664	25	—	—
Persia and Afghanistan	—	—	—	—	—	—	—	—	—	—	—	—	—	—
Other states	—	—	—	—	—	—	106	6	—	—	—	—	—	—
Price	1q	Kč 57	1q	Kč 42	1q	Kč 46.35	1q	Kč 46.10	1q	Kč 44.40	1q	Kč 40.60	1q	Kč 42.35
Import total	—	—	1	1	9	3	14	8	4	2	176	7	330	15
Germany	—	—	1	1	9	3	14	8	4	2	176	7	3	2
Poland	—	—	—	—	—	—	—	—	—	—	—	—	327	13
Price	—	—	—	—	—	—	—	—	—	—	1q	Kč 39.75	1q	Kč 45.45

Destination or country of origin	1932 Amount q	1932 1,000 Kč	1933 Amount q	1933 1,000 Kč	1934 Amount q	1934 1,000 Kč	1935 Amount q	1935 1,000 Kč	1936 Amount q	1936 1,000 Kč	1937 Amount q	1937 1,000 Kč
Export total	1,571	64	4,556	190	5,235	213	2,210	106	1,702	82	1,032	42
Yugoslavia	—	—	—	—	—	—	—	—	—	—	—	—
Bulgaria	—	—	1,180	68	129	9	714	45	932	62	476	27
Austria	1,027	38	513	14	707	19	611	17	770	20	457	12
Romania	440	21	274	15	1,173	55	1,724	37	—	—	99	3
Germany	—	—	2,588	91	3,217	129	152	6	—	—	—	—
Hungary	103	5	—	—	—	—	—	—	—	—	—	—
Poland	1	—	—	—	9	1	9	1	—	—	—	—
Persia and Afghanistan	—	—	1	2	—	—	—	—	—	—	—	—
Other states	—	—	—	—	—	—	—	—	—	—	—	—
Price	1q	Kč 40.75	1q	Kč 41.70	1q	Kč 40.70	1q	Kč 47.95	1q	Kč 48.15	1q	Kč 40.70
Import total	2	1	1	1	1	1	3	2*	1	1	1	1
Germany	2	1	1	1	1	1	—	—	1	1	1	1
Poland	—	—	—	—	—	—	—	—	—	—	—	—
Price	—	—	—	—	—	—	—	—	—	—	—	—

* Country of origin not given. Customs duty 1q = 19 Kč.

effect of the agreements on sulphates between Spolek and the German cartel centre in Berlin in 1933 is shown. The restriction of exports is clear from Table 5, which concerns potassium hydrogen sulphate. The limitation of exports to a certain area is reflected in Table 6 concerning potassium sulphate, and Table 7 concerning sodium hydrogen sulphate between 1933 and 1937.[1]

Finally, from an examination of the price movements of cartelized chemical products a marked stability emerges during the years of crisis and depression. This illustrates the general effect of cartels on the stability of prices, achieved by restrictions on production, price fixing and allocation of markets. The prices of cartelized products in the chemical industry fluctuated less than prices of non-cartelized products; in the cartel agreements which I investigated there were no clauses about price reductions, but agreement to increase prices was very frequent.

There can be little doubt that international, especially German, cartels directly influenced production and foreign trade in the Czechoslovak chemical industry.

[1] SÚA–KR 349 and *Zahraniční obchod Republiky československé*. This cartel agreement is connected with a number of other undertakings about the division of the Czechoslovak home market among the cartel partners, exports to Southeast Europe, and the Czechoslovak partners' obligation to pay a high percentage of realized profits if the Czechoslovak works exceed their quotas or deliver to 'forbidden territories'. This applies to the following group of sulphates: potassium sulphate, potassium hydrogen sulphate, artificial calcium sulphate, sodium hydrogen sulphate, magnesium sulphate, aluminium sulphate, nickel sulphate, nickel ammonium sulphate, lead sulphate.

6

Banking and longterm foreign loans

1 Foreign investment in Czechoslovak banking before Munich

The history of direct foreign investment in the joint-stock banks of Czechoslovakia between the two world wars deserves a thorough analysis. A competent financier with inside information on the problem, the former director of the Živnostenská Bank, Ing. Dvořáček, repeatedly mentioned the extraordinarily strong influence of foreign capital on Czechoslovak banking and industry in his evidence as a witness at the Nuremberg Trials.[1] It was precisely in the area of Czechoslovak banking that leading representatives of German finance attempted to make a break-through, clandestinely before Munich, openly after 30 September 1938 and even more so after the occupation of the Czech Lands, in order to gain a controlling interest in the large joint-stock banks and thereby in the subsidiary industrial and commercial companies belonging to their extensive concerns.[2] The present situation in Czechoslovakia, when there is almost no access to the banks' archives, does not favour a thorough examination of the question of foreign investment in Czechoslovak banks and this chapter must necessarily remain somewhat fragmentary. I therefore base the following discussion on material from the economic trials at the International Military Tribunal at Nuremberg, on sources in the Prague Central State Archives and in Czechoslovak business archives and German archives, as well as on commercial directories and on monographs, but not on systematically arranged bank archives.

[1] DZAP-IMT, Nr. IV, Fall XI, pp. 8155, 8282, especially p. 8532.
[2] DZAP-IMT-B 185-998PS-USA Exh. 91. Cf. V. Král, II, p. 135.

During the inter-war period the process of concentration in Czechoslovak banking[1] reached a similarly high level to that in other advanced capitalist countries, where a few leading banks concentrated a substantial amount of the national industrial and banking capital in their own concerns. In Czechoslovakia joint-stock banks participated to a very large extent in industrial enterprises and in transport and trading companies.[2] Numerous industrial companies clustered around the big banks, tied to them either by credits or by direct investments.[3] In this way the large joint-stock banks threw a net of relationships of various degrees of dependency over almost all branches of production in the country. As a result the financial groups dominant in the central banks also gained commensurate influence in the banks' subsidiaries. It follows from these interrelations that direct foreign participation in the capital of any one of the big banks brought in its wake a whole system of indirect holdings in the bank's concerns, through which foreign investors could influence economic life in Czechoslovakia to a far greater extent than by merely holding an isolated direct share in a joint-stock company.

The active interest of the joint-stock banks in industrial enterprises was an effect of the fusion of banking and industrial capital which had begun in Czechoslovakia during the time of the Austro-Hungarian Monarchy. In accordance with the balance of forces in those days between Czech and Austrian businessmen and bankers, the great Viennese banks headed large and ramified concerns. The only exception was the Živnostenská Bank in Prague, which built up its business by accumulating only Czech capital. With the disintegration of Austria–Hungary and the rise of an independent Czechoslovak state the Czech business community tried to sever its financial and capital ties with Vienna as quickly as possible and to gain possession of the maximum number of direct shares in banks and industrial enterprises within the new boundaries, mainly from Viennese banks. I have already discussed these attempts by

[1] R. Olšovský *et al.*, *Přehled hospodářského vývoje Československa v letech 1918–1945*, especially chapter v, part II.

[2] In the United States, and also to some extent in England, this activity was mainly the concern of investment banks or specialized financial houses.

[3] Cf. A. Pimper, *Hospodářská krise a banky* (Economic crisis and the banks) (Praha, 1934), p. 44; M. Weirich, p. 265, R. Wagner, p. 71.

Table 1. *Czechoslovak joint-stock banks with nominal capital exceeding Kč 100 million, 31 December 1927*

No.	Bank	Capital (million Kč)	Foreign participant	Amount of investment held by participant and means of obtaining it
1	Czech Industrial Bank	210		
2	Živnostenská Bank	200		
3	Czech Escompte Bank and Credit Institute	200	(*a*) Niederösterreichische Eskompte Gesellschaft – 3 members on the board of directors	In 1918 45 % remained in Austrian bank and 55 % was taken over by the Živnostenská Bank.
			(*b*) Banque de Bruxelles – 1 member on board of directors	50,000 shares in issue of 1920
			(*c*) Kleinwort & Sons, London – 1 member on board of directors	Larger parcel of shares, in 1923
			(*d*) International Acceptance Bank, New York and Harriman & Co. Inc.	
4	Czech Bank Union	200	(*a*) Banca Commerciale Italiana, Milano and Lazard Frères et Cie, Paris	120,000 shares at 360 Kč obtained in 1920 of issue of 200,000 shares
			(*b*) Prudential Assurance Ltd, London	Larger parcel of shares, in 1926
5	Bank for Commerce and Industry, formerly Länderbank	120	Founded by the Czech Agrarian Bank, the French Banque de Paris et de Pays Bas and the Austrian Länderbank (later Banque des Pays de l'Europe Centrale). In 1926 the Agrarian Bank ceded its shares to the French, leaving the bank entirely in the hands of Vienna, London and Paris	Decisive majority

Table 1. (*cont.*)

No.	Bank	Capital (million Kč)	Foreign participant	Amount of investment held by participant and means of obtaining it
6	Moravian Bank	120	Dutch and French bank group	Kč 45 million from issue of 1920
7	Anglo-Czechoslovak Bank	120	Founded by Anglo-International Bank to take over Austrian branches in the ČSR after 1918. On 30 June 1927 part of shares ceded to Czech holders: 25 % to the Czechoslovak state, rest to group of industrialists (Škoda-Works, Kooperativa, Schicht-Works, Ignaz Petschek and Prince Liechtenstein). Anglo-International Bank, Samuel & Co., London, Harriman & Co., New York	100 % until 1927 16.6 % 6.25 % 6.25 %
8	Prague Credit Bank	100	French Bank Syndicate; Société Générale, Banque de Paris et des Pays Bas, Rotterdamsche Bankvereinigung	66 %

Czech bankers and industrialists in connection with the history of foreign investment in the basic industries after 1918; in banking, too, they led to a significant shift in property relations. Here Czech financial circles could purposefully apply their new state's legislation on monetary reform, nostrification and nationalization.[1] Both activities, nostrification and nationalization, continued for the duration of the First Czechoslovak

[1] Cf. A. Pimper, pp. 138, 488; M. Ubiria–R. Kadlec–J. Matas, *Peněžní a úvěrová soustava ČSR za kapitalismu* (Monetary and credit system of the ČSR under capitalism) (Praha, 1958), p. 78.

Republic, although the most active years were 1919–21, nostrification being virtually completed by 1930.[1] The nationalization drive brought shares previously held by Viennese banks in industrial and commercial companies into the vaults of Czechoslovak banks. Transactions of this kind continued well into the 1930s.

As a result of post-war changes in the distribution of spheres of influence significant changes also occurred in the capital structure of the great European banks. The Czechoslovak banks, in fact, reflected these objective transfers in the balance of economic forces among the chief groups of international finance at that time. Investment by banking houses from the countries of the Entente replaced Austrian, German and Hungarian participation in the capital structure of the Czechoslovak joint-stock banks, at the same time as Czech domestic capital took a firmer hold. Together with Czech bankers and industrialists, representatives of financial groups from Great Britain, France, the United States, Belgium, Holland and Italy moved on to the boards of directors of the large Czech banks. Table 1 shows foreign investment in banks with a nominal joint-stock capital of more than Kč 100 million. Up to 31 December 1927 eight banks had each registered more than Kč 100 million capital; while their number amounted to only 6.15 % of all joint-stock banks in the country, their combined capital came to 58.5 % of the total.[2] In six of these leading banks West European and American financial groups owned substantial shares and before 1918 all of them had belonged to Viennese central banks.

The Czechoslovak government facilitated investment by West European countries in Czechoslovak banking through her nostrification and nationalization laws. At the same time Czech financial circles, especially the Živnostenská Bank, consolidated their position against Austrian and German financial influence,[3] depending for support in their efforts on foreign financial partners and becoming subordinated to them in the process. This was the inevitable result of the far greater financial power

[1] At the end of 1930 235 firms with a total capital of about 2 milliard Kč had transferred their head offices to Czechoslovakia as required by nostrification. Cf. *Statistický zpravodaj* (Statistical Reporter), 1, 1938, 212.

[2] Calculated from data in *Compass, Čechoslovakei* (1929).

[3] M. Ubiria and others, p. 124.

of foreign banks and industrial combines in the West, compared with that of the Czech banks.[1]

Essentially, both foreign and domestic financial groups attempted to expand their profit basis. The Živnostenská Bank joined forces in this endeavour in the first place with Solvay et Cie and the Brussels banks controlled by them, then with Schneider's bank, L'Union Européenne in Paris, and with the electrical combine Philips in Eindhoven and the financial institutions in Holland connected with them.[2] In the post-war years the Czech Agrarian Bank aligned its interests closely with French capital in the Prague Länderbank.[3] Although neither the Živnostenská Bank nor the Agrarian Bank harboured any foreign participation in their joint-stock capital, many of their subsidiary industrial companies were controlled by foreign investment (see Table 8), which was also an effective form of infiltration of foreign investment into the banks.

Without doubt the pressure of foreign on domestic capital was considerable and in many significant areas of Czechoslovak economic life decisive. This meant that bankers and industrialists in Czechoslovakia had to share their profitable opportunities with foreign partners, who were at the same time their competitors. On the one hand, foreign investment supported Czech efforts towards greater economic independence, and also towards increasing the profitability of the domestic economy. On the other hand, the Czech business community strove to increase its own share in the profits, which to a large extent flowed out of the country to foreign investors. From this contradictory situation competition between foreign and domestic interests quite logically developed in industry and banking, with the domestic side trying to gain at least partial independence from

[1] S. I. Prasolov expresses a similar opinion on the relationship between foreign and domestic capital in inter-war Czechoslovakia in his book *Československo v době ohrožení fašismen a hitlerovskou agresí* (Czechoslovakia in the period of Fascist and Hitler aggression), p. 31.

[2] DZAP–IMT–Q9 Rasche–Dok. Nr. 171. Karel Nowotny, a former director of the Czech Escompte Bank and Credit Institute, testified that these foreign concerns operated in Czechoslovakia through the Živnostenská Bank.

[3] The Agrarian Bank is not included in my tables of the big joint-stock banks because its nominal joint-stock capital was under Kč 100 million. Its influence on the economic and political life of the ČSR, especially in conjunction with other agrarian groups, was very great indeed. Cf. e.g. Olšovský *et al.*, *Přehled hospodářského vývoje*, p. 249.

international capital. The question is how far the domestic Czechoslovak industrialists and bankers succeeded. In the branches of industry which have been the subject of our analysis (mining and metallurgy, engineering, electrical and chemical industries) no striking changes occurred in the relationships between foreign and domestic capital investment between 1929 and 1937. However, there is evidence – although this could not be verified in banks' archives – for the belief that, especially in the years of the Great Depression, domestic capital increased its share in the banks in which it participated together with foreign shareholders. The most powerful banking circles in Czechoslovakia carried through important amalgamations of the large banks, which were supported and subsidized by the Czechoslovak state. I believe that these transactions led not only to a greater concentration of bank capital but also to a relative strengthening of domestic as against foreign capital in the large joint-stock banks. In the process of merging Czechoslovak banks took over a considerable number of investments from Viennese banks, in the first place from the Österreichische Boden-Credit-Anstalt and the Österreichische Credit-Anstalt für Handel and Gewerbe, which went bankrupt in 1929–30 and dragged the whole Austrian economy down with them.[1] On the whole, however, Czechoslovakia's leading joint-stock banks were not able to free themselves from foreign capital: foreign investment remained relatively large until the end of the pre-Munich Republic.

Up to 31 December 1937 about 15 % of the total capital of all joint-stock banks was foreign-owned. In the seven banks in which foreign investment was ascertained, the relation between foreign and domestic participation was 42:58. The territorial origin of foreign investments in banking is shown in Table 2.[2]

The most significant foreign investments were those in the big Czechoslovak joint-stock banks which were also the centres of large concerns. At the end of 1937 only six banks had a nominal basic capital of over Kč 100 million. They made up only 7.6 %

[1] J. Pátek tried to assess the changes in capital relations between Austria and Czechoslovakia in the crisis years in his article 'Poznámky k některým problémům v československo-rakouských vztazích na počátku světové hospodářské krize' (Comments on some problems in Czechoslovak–Austrian relations at the beginning of the world economic crisis), p. 44.

[2] Excerpt of Table IV, Chapter 2 (1).

Table 2. *Territorial distribution of direct foreign investment in Czechoslovak joint-stock banks, 31 December 1937*

Country of origin of investment	Nominal value in 1,000 Kč	Percentage of total foreign investment
France	100,068	44.5
Great Britain	54,425	24.2
Belgium	38,320	17.1
Italy	24,000	10.6
U.S.A.	8,004	3.6
Total	224,817	100

of all joint-stock banks in the country, but they controlled 57 % of the total joint-stock capital of all Czechoslovak banks.[1] Table 3 shows the structure of foreign capital investment in the large joint-stock banks.[2] Comparing the data in Table 3 with those in Table 1, the result of concentration between 1927 and 1937 is clearly visible, as is the absolute and relative growth of the Živnostenská Bank. Foreign capital penetrated into four large banks, but the only foreign majority holding was the French participation in the Länderbank. In all other banks foreign shareholders were in a minority but, as can be seen from Table 3, they were represented on the boards of directors.

The tables also show that only Western capital participated in Czechoslovak joint-stock banks. I could not find one investment by a German bank. This fact was a constant irritation, especially to the Deutsche Bank and the Dresdner Bank, which closely observed the development of Czechoslovak banks and untiringly sought to draw them into their sphere of influence. Their repeated efforts to buy Czechoslovak shares remained unsuccessful.[3]

During the economic crisis Austrian investment disappeared from Czechoslovak banks; however, the traditional connections with Vienna were not completely severed, because a number of

[1] Calculated from data in *Compass, Čechoslovakei* (1939).

[2] Table 3 is compiled from data about foreign investments contained in the material of the Nuremberg Trials and *Compass, Čechoslovakei* (1938, 1939).

[3] Cf. H. Radandt, in Kdo zavinil Mnichov (Who is responsible for Munich), p. 312. In the material of the German Economic Ministry there are regular reports on the development of Czechoslovak banks. DZAP–RWiM–2890.

Table 3. *Czechoslovak joint-stock banks with nominal capital exceeding Kč 100 million, 31 December 1937*

No.	Bank	Capital (million Kč)	Foreign participant	Amount of investment held by participant (%)
1	Živnostenská Bank	240		
2	Czech Bank Union	150	(*a*) Banca Commerciale Italiana, Milano	16
			(*b*) British Overseas Bank, London	13·33
			(*c*) Société Générale de Belgique, Bruxelles (3 representatives of foreign investors on board of directors)	9·33
3	Czech Escompte Bank and Credit Institute	130	(*a*) Banque de Bruxelles	18.15
			(*b*) Kleinwort Sons & Co., London (4 representatives of foreign investors on board of directors)	2.5
4	Bank for Commerce and Industry, formerly Länderbank	120	Banque des Pays de l'Europe Centrale, Paris (8 members on the board of directors)	77.87
5	Anglo-Czechoslovak and Prague Credit Bank	120	(*a*) Anglo-International Bank, London	16.6
			(*b*) Samuel & Co., London (4 representatives of British investors on board of directors)	6.25
			(*c*) A. W. Harriman & Co., New York	6.26
			(*d*) Schneider et Cie., Paris (indirectly through Škoda-Works, 10.5 %)	
			(*e*) Unilever (indirectly through holding in Schicht-Works *c*. 3 %)	
6	Czech Industrial Bank	100.1		

West European financial groups controlled their investments not only in Czechoslovakia but also in Southeastern Europe through centres established in Vienna. Such was the structure of the direct investments of the Banque des Pays de l'Europe Centrale in Paris, which owned a controlling share in the Bank for Commerce and Industry, formerly Länderbank in Prague,[1] and controlled its investments in Czechoslovakia, Poland and Yugoslavia mainly through its Viennese branch, the Zentraleuropäische Länderbank, Niederlassung Wien.[2] The Belgian group Société Générale de Belgique, Bruxelles, linked its holding in the Czech Bank Union[3] with a whole network of investments which reached from the Wiener Bank-Verein in Vienna to similar banks in Poland, Romania and Yugoslavia.[4] The Czech Escompte Bank also maintained its ties with the Viennese Niederösterreichische Escompte Gesellschaft, even though the Austrian participation gradually disappeared and only the main Anglo-Belgian investor remained.[5] The Viennese bankers who held seats on the boards of directors of Czechoslovak banks were as a rule themselves representatives of British, French, Belgian or American banks.

The significance of direct foreign investment in the central banks of Czechoslovakia was greatly enhanced by the ramified concerns of these banks. These relationships were extraordinarily complex, but I have tried to present the capital and credit interests of the four joint-stock banks graphically in Tables 4–7, together with their connections with foreign shareholders. Direct foreign investments in the banks and the subsidiary enterprises directly or indirectly tied to them are given, according to my findings as on 31 December 1937, in Table 4 for the Bank for Commerce and Industry, formerly Länderbank; Table 5 for the Anglo-Czechoslovak and Prague Credit

[1] DZAP–IMT–Q9 Rasche–Nr. 171. For the precise structure of investment, see Table 4.

[2] DZAP–IMT–Q9 Rasche–Nr. 224.

[3] ASÚS – Cizí účasti – Dobrozdání Nos. 1 and 9.

[4] The representatives of the Belgian financial group in the Czech Bank Union, the director of the Société Générale de Belgique, Auguste Callens, and the commercial director of the Banque Belge pour l'Etranger Paul Ramlot, had seats on the boards of directors of all banks in Central and Southeast Europe in which their capital was invested. Cf. *Compass*, *Personenverzeichnis*.

[5] DZAP–IMT–V 186–NID 13 405. The precise structure of shares is given in Table 7.

Table 4. *Bank for Commerce and Industry,*

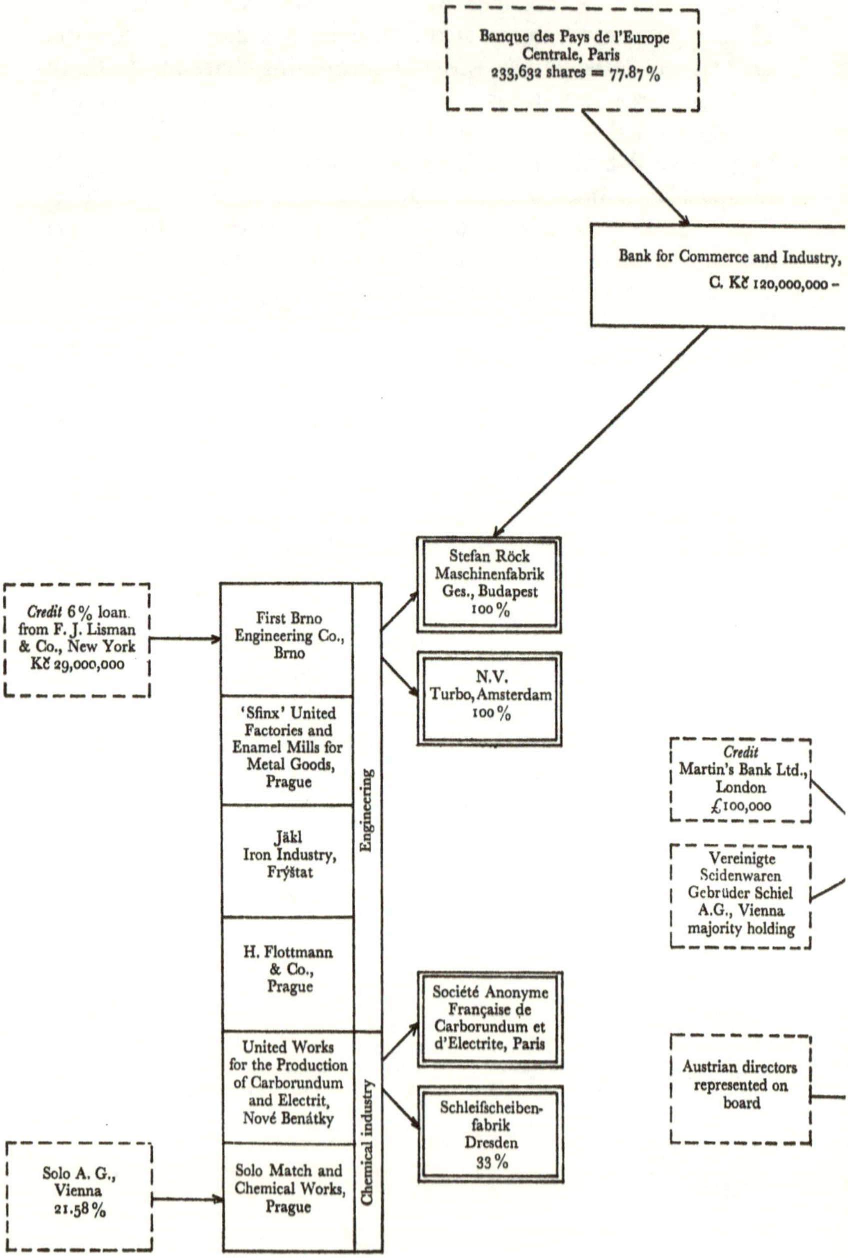

formerly Länderbank, 31 December 1937

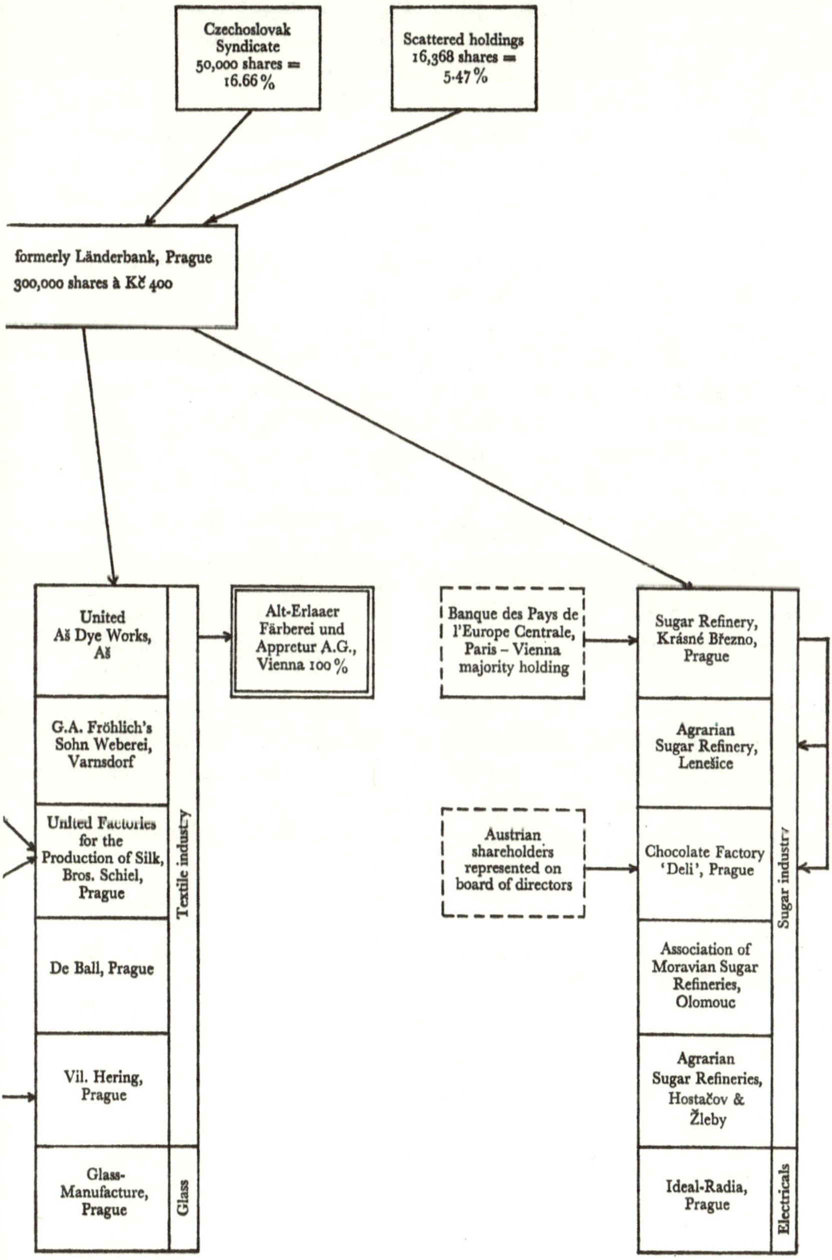

Bank; Table 6 for the Czech Bank Union, and Table 7 for the Czech Escompte Bank and Credit Institute. For comparison I have added, in Table 8, a plan of the complicated structure of the Živnostenská Bank concern, where there was found to be no direct foreign investment in the joint-stock capital, although foreign capital was strongly represented in the most important subsidiary or related companies. These enterprises were themselves often important centres of businesses and in a way formed concerns within the bank's concern. The tables show a wide range of mutual relationships between the banks and industrial, trading and other companies, ranging from capital and credit participation to indirect financial ties.[1]

The Bank for Commerce and Industry, formerly Länderbank in Prague (see Table 4), performed the role of a branch of the large Paris bank, Banque des Pays de l'Europe Centrale, in Czechoslovakia. Its activities were controlled from the Paris central office and coordinated with the Viennese branch.[2] It was not concerned only with purely banking transactions for its clients, but also with the financing of industrial enterprises within its own concern. The most valuable direct investments of the Länderbank were in the engineering industry, with a majority share in the Spojené továrny a smaltovny na kovové zboží a.s. v Praze 'Sfinx' (United Factories and Enamel Mills for Metal Goods in Prague 'Sfinx');[3] in the chemical industry, with a controlling share in the Spojené závody pro výrobu karborunda a elektritu (United Works for the Production of Carborundum and Electrit) in Nové Benátky;[4] in the textile

1 The data in Tables 4–8 were gathered from archives (see list of archives, pp. 383–385) and from a wide range of commercial directories and publications. Explanatory notes to the tables are given on p. xiii.

2 'Sie kennen die Bedeutung unserer österreichischen Niederlassung, sie ist einerseits eine Folge des bedeutenden Umfanges ihrer Geschäfte in Österreich selbst, sowohl was die Geschäfte der Kundschaft betrifft, als auch ihre Teilnahme an den Geschäften des Landes, andrerseits rührt sie von der Tatsache her, daß unsere Interessen an den anderen Nachfolgestaaten, wie Tschechoslowakei, Polen und Jugoslavien teilweise in ihrer Niederlassung zusammenliefen und tatsächlich durch ihre Dienste unter der Autorität von Paris gelenkt wurden.' Excerpt of the authorized translation of the speech by the President of the Banque des Pays de l'Europe Centrale, M. André Luquet, at the general meeting 18 July 1938 in Paris, when he explained the situation surrounding the sale of the Viennese Länderbank to the Dresdner Bank after the *Anschluss* of Austria. DZAP-IMT-D III-Q6-Fall XI, Dok. Nr. 224.

3 ASÚS - Cizí účasti.

4 DZAP-IMT-Q9-Fall XI, Dok. Nr. 171.

industry, in particular, with participation in the joint-stock capital of the Spojené Ašské barvírny (United Aš Dye-Works) and of the Prague and Viennese Spojené továrny pro výrobu hedvábí bratří Schielové (United Factories for the Production of Silk, Bros. Schiel); and especially in the food industry, with a majority share in the Rafinerie cukru (Sugar Refinery) in Krásné Březno.[1] The Länderbank in Prague was not very large but a number of its enterprises played an important part in the economy of Czechoslovakia, especially as a result of their export capacity. In the sugar industry the Länderbank held some investments alongside domestic agrarian capital (see Table 4 – sugar industry). The investments of the Länderbank in Czechoslovak industrial companies automatically became those of the Paris central bank which owned 77.87 % of the joint-stock capital of the Bank for Commerce and Industry, formerly Länderbank.[2]

The Banque des Pays de l'Europe Centrale followed up its majority share in the Czechoslovak bank with representation on the board of directors, by sending four directors from the Paris centre and three from the branch in Vienna and by appointing Charles Rist, the well-known French financier and economist, to the presidency in Prague.[3] In the 1930s the Czechoslovak vice-president of the Länderbank, Dr Bohumil Vlasák, who before 1929 had been Minister of Finance, personified the link between the French investment and Czechoslovakia. His connections with the Ministry of Finance, and also the fact that he was an associate of Dr Engliš and was said to be close to the National Democratic Party, provided the French with a certain guarantee of cooperation with the Czechoslovak state apparatus.

With the *Anschluss* of Austria by Germany in mid-March 1938 the Banque des Pays de l'Europe Centrale decided, after urgent and repeated representations from German banks, to sell its branch in Vienna to the Dresdner Bank. This decision was made after consultation with the director of the Bank of England, Otto Niemeyer.[4] At the same time, however, the French financiers in the Paris bank were not prepared to

[1] ASÚS – Cizí účasti. [2] DZAP-IMT-Q9-Fall XI, Dok. Nr. 171.

[3] Charles Rist held many influential posts in his country. After the First World War he was also for a time Vice-Governor of the Banque de France and member of the board of directors of the Suez Company.

[4] DZAP-IMT-D III-Q6-Fall XII, Dok. Nr. 224.

vacate Czechoslovakia for the German banks. On the contrary, they strove to preserve their spheres of influence outside Germany.[1] The reality of the changed situation meant, of course, that significant ties with the French capital investment in Vienna were disrupted and as a result the French position in Southeastern Europe as a whole was weakened.

Just as French financial interests were centred on the Länderbank in Prague, British investment strongly influenced the Anglo-Czechoslovak and Prague Credit Bank. From Table 1 it is evident that up to 1927 the then Anglo-Czechoslovak Bank was entirely in the hands of the Anglo-International Bank, a subsidiary of the Bank of England. At a meeting of the board of directors of the Anglo-Czechoslovak Bank on 30 June 1927 it was decided that the majority of its shares were to be transferred to the Czechoslovak state and the remainder were to be divided up between influential financial groups in Czechoslovakia (the Škoda-Works, Kooperativa, the Schicht-Works and the firm of Petschek in Ústí) and Prince Liechtenstein.[2] The British bank remained the largest shareholder after the Czechoslovak state. In addition, comparatively smaller shares were held by the banking house of Samuel & Co. in London and by the investment bank Harriman & Co. in New York.

The economic and political power of the Anglo-Czechoslovak Bank grew noticeably in 1930 when the then Minister of Finance, Dr Engliš, organized a merger with the Prague Credit Institute in a general move towards state-aided concentration of banks. Thus a financial centre arose in the ČSR in which British capital played an important role and which, in a sense, formed a counterbalance to the Živnostenská Bank. In addition it enjoyed the support of the 'Castle' (the seat of the

[1] 'Auf diese Weise kamen wir schließlich zu dem Ergebnis, daß wir unseren Nachfolgern (Dresdner Bank – A.T.) nur die spezifisch oesterreichischen Geschaefte kredidierten, mit Ausschluß aller unserer Interessen und Beziehungen in den anderen Staaten Mittel-Europas, ausserhalb Deutschland. Unsere Einflussphaere bleibt damit intakt.' From the speech of the President of the Banque des Pays de l'Europe Centrale, André Luquet, cited above. In the light of this material it is difficult to agree with the one-sided verdict on the whole transaction between the Paris and Dresden banks of V. Král, who deduced that 'the action of the Paris Länderbank is further proof of the fact that Western capital evacuated Czechoslovakia for German monopolies before Munich'. V. Král, II, p. 152.

[2] *Compass, Čechoslovakei* (1929), 289.

Czechoslovak President).[1] The capital structure of the merged banks, under the new name of Anglo-Czechoslovak and Prague Credit Bank, remained essentially unaltered until the end of the pre-Munich Republic. This is shown in Table 5.[2]

The Bank of England's interests were represented on the board of directors of the Anglo-Czechoslovak and Prague Credit Bank by four British members, whose widespread capital connections in Britain were reflected in their seats on the boards of numerous investment banks, and especially in the case of H. E. Carter on boards of companies in the food industry.[3] It is more than likely that his interest in the British sugar industry was linked with the investments of the Anglo-Czechoslovak and Prague Credit Bank in the sugar industry of Central and Southeast Europe (see the Bank's concern in Table 5).

The British shareholders' policy in the Prague bank was directed by the London Committee of the Anglo-Czechoslovak and Prague Credit Bank, which in turn was subordinated to the Bank of England. A. G. M. Dickson, one of the British members of the board of directors in Prague, was at the same time chairman of the London Committee, thus embodying the

[1] Cf. *Za chleb, práci, půdu a svobodu* (Bread, work, land and freedom), p. 444.

[2] The structure of the joint-stock capital is taken from data in the archives of the Deutsche Bank, part of which is in the Deutsche-Wirtschafts-Institut in Berlin. DWI-DO6.

[3] Arthur George Mitton Dickson: Director of the Anglo-International Bank, London; Chairman of the London Committee of the Anglo-Czechoslovak and Prague Credit Bank, London; British and Polish Trade Bank, London, Ionian Bank Ltd; Trade Indemnity Co. Ltd; Anglo-Czechoslovak and Prague Credit Bank, Prague.

Harold Edward Carter: Chairman of Carters (Merchants) Ltd, London; Chairman of Crymsdyke, Princes Risborough, Bucks. Corp.; Chairman of British Sugar Corp. Ltd; Director of Allen Wack & Shepherd Ltd; Chairman British Overseas Stores Ltd; Chairman of Dominions and Overseas Trust Ltd; Director of Fletcher & Cartwrights Ltd; Member of London Committee of Imperial Cold Storage and Supply Co. Ltd; Chairman of Filling Stevens Ltd; Anglo-Czechoslovak and Prague Credit Bank, Prague.

Donald Swinton Campbell: Director of the banks Grindley & Co. Ltd and Forbes, Campbell & Co. Ltd, London; Director of London Committee of the Anglo-Czechoslovak and Prague Credit Bank, London; Vice-President of London Produce Clearing House Ltd; Director of United City Property Trust Ltd, Anglo-Czechoslovak and Prague Credit Bank, Prague.

Walter Sidmore Draper: Director of Charterhouse Investment Trust Ltd, London; Anglo-Czechoslovak and Prague Credit Bank, Prague.

Data from the *Directory of Directors* (London, 1937–40), *Stock Exchange Year Book* (London, 1938), *Compass*, *Personenverzeichnis*.

Table 5. *Anglo-Czechoslovak*

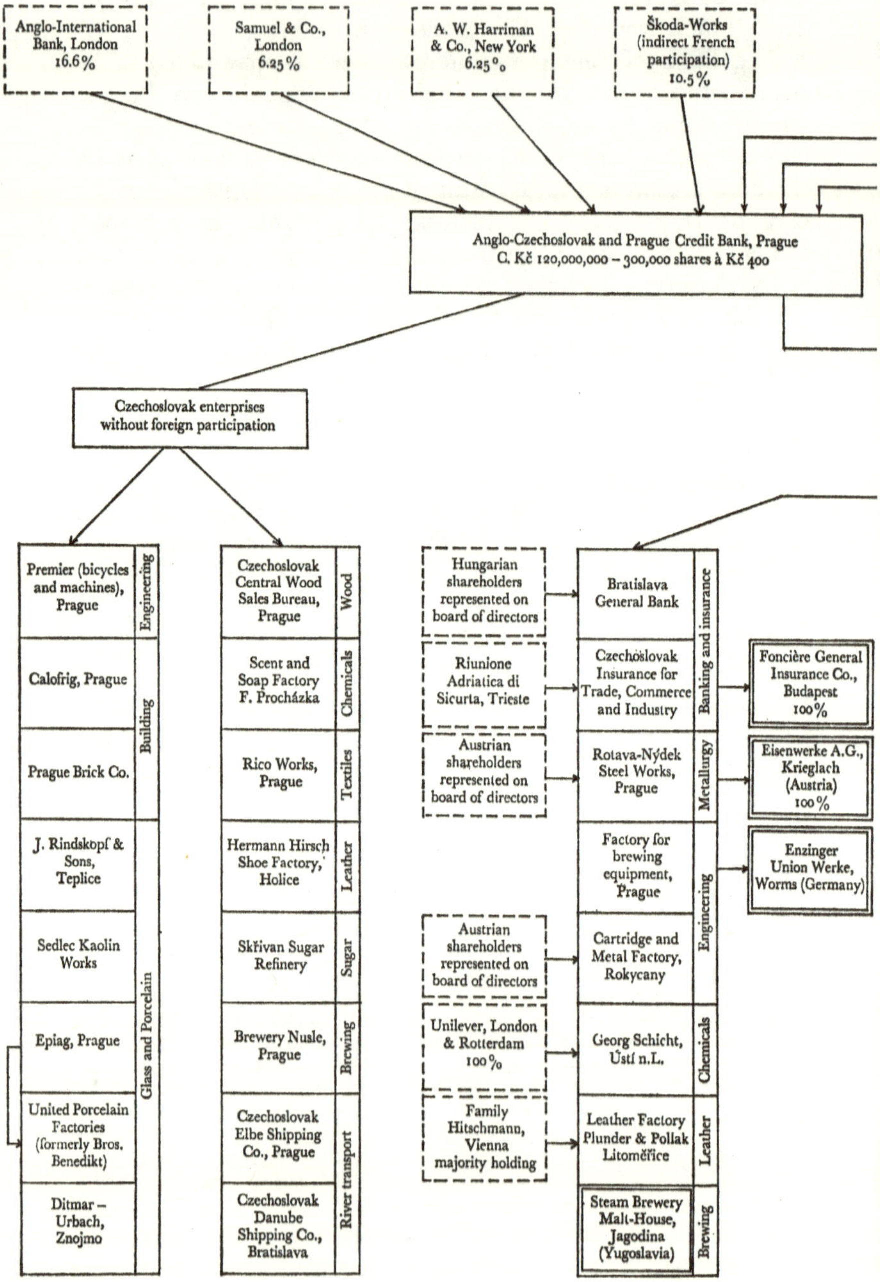

nd Prague Credit Bank, 31 December 1937

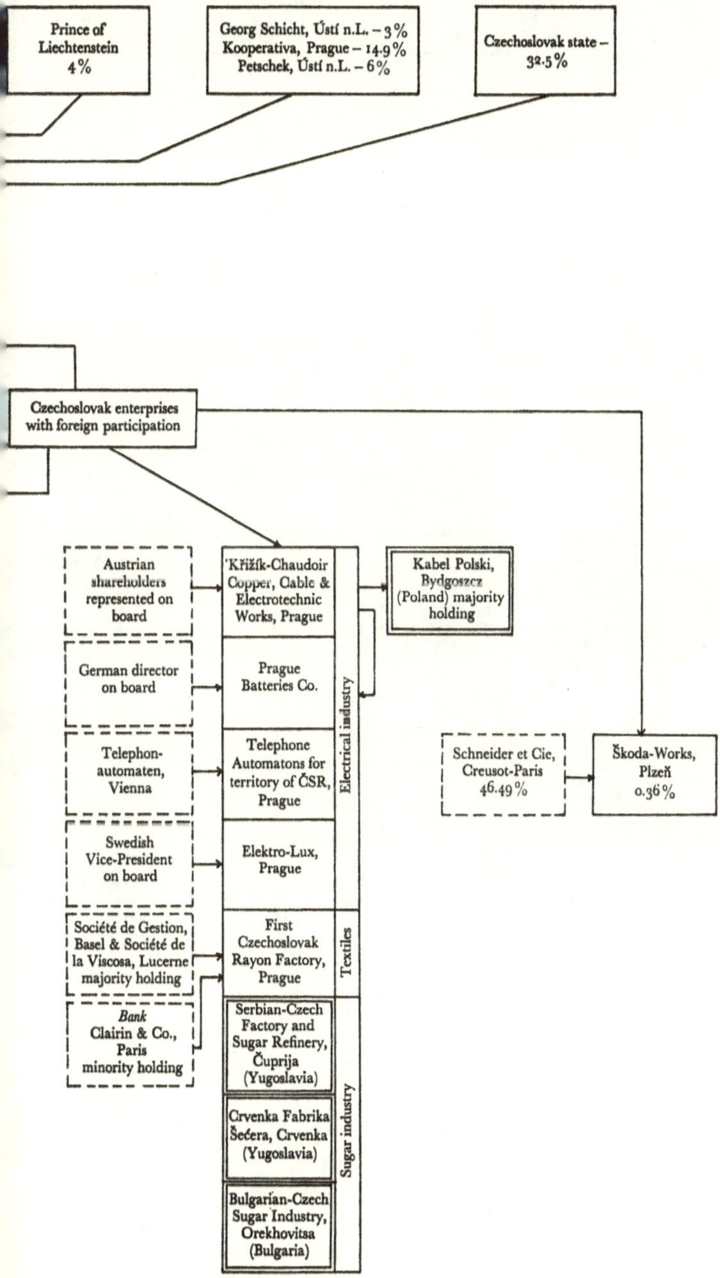

Table 6. *The Czech Bank*

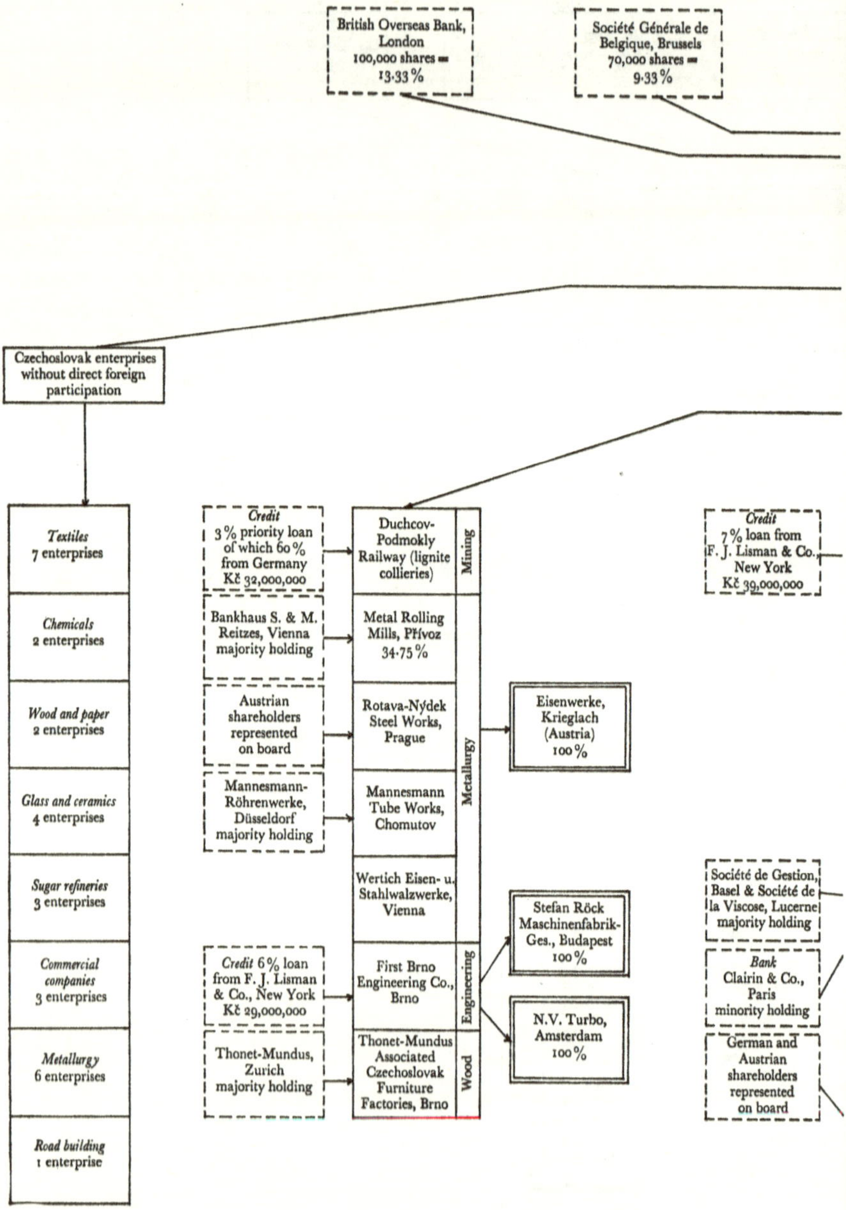

Union, 31 December 1937

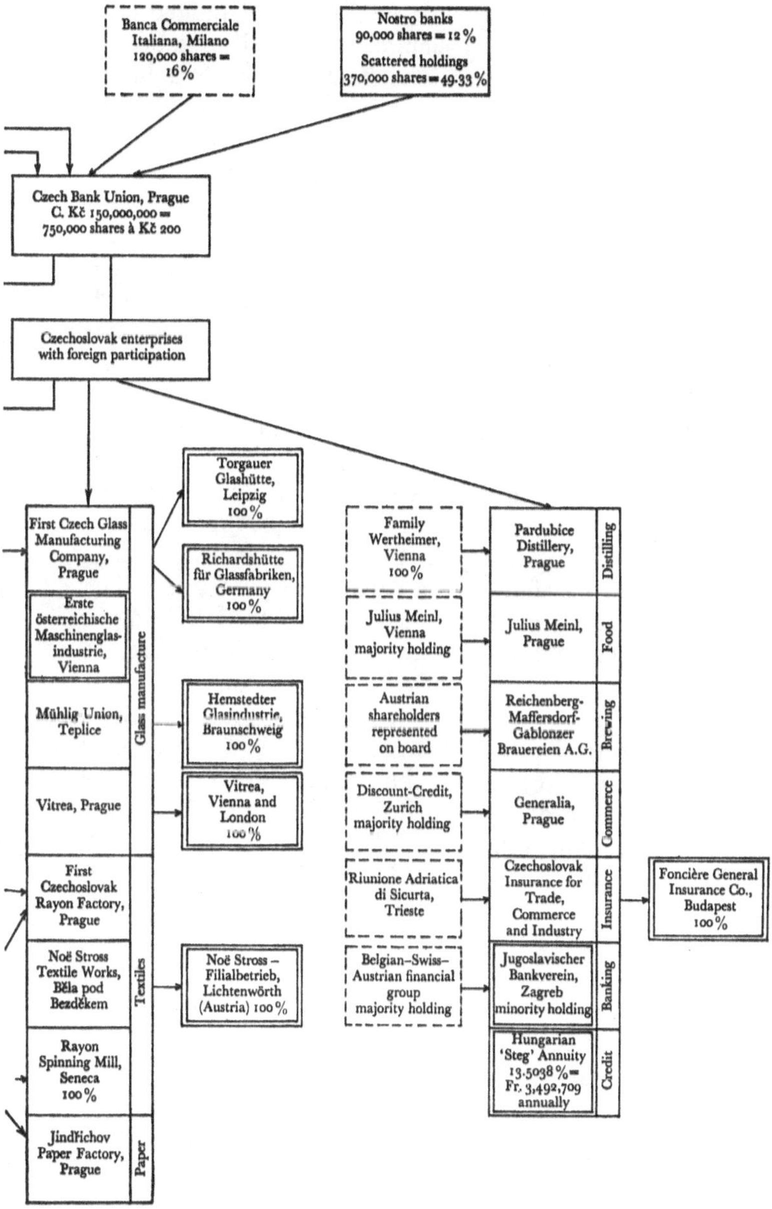

connection between London and Prague. There can be little doubt of the effectiveness of British influence on the financial policy of the Anglo-Czechoslovak Bank, even if judged only from the great capital strength behind the British members of the Prague board of directors. The bank formed a point of intersection for Czechoslovak and international, mainly British, capital, in which the Škoda-Works (belonging to the French but being greatly indebted to the British) and the Schicht-Works (which belonged to the sphere of interests of the Anglo-Dutch combine of Unilever) also participated. Another shareholder in the bank, the financial and commercial house of the Petscheks, was closely associated with British capital through business transactions.[1] Thus the Anglo-Czechoslovak and Prague Credit Bank can be regarded as a centre of British capital in Czechoslovak banking.

British capital also participated together with Belgian in the Czech Bank Union in Prague. The British Overseas Bank in London owned 13.33 % and the Société Générale de Belgique in Brussels 9.33 % of the joint-stock capital of the Prague bank.[2] In *Compass* an Italian participation is also mentioned, which is entered in the schema of the Czech Bank Union in Table 6. The domestic shareholders succeeded in enlarging their holding in 1935, when 113,520 shares were transferred to them from the Österreichische Credit-Anstalt-Wiener-Bankverein.[3]

In this case Belgian capital seems to have been the most active. Towards the end of the 1930s the two directors of the Brussels central bank who held seats on the board of directors of the Czech Bank Union also represented their Belgian bank in other Southeast European countries.

In the case of the Czech Bank Union the traditional connection with Vienna is very evident, as is a wide range of relationships with other foreign companies and banks. These, for the most part, held a majority share in the enterprises belonging to the sphere of interest of the Czech Bank Union, which suggests that their ties with the bank were more through credits than through direct investments (see Table 6). When,

1 This became particularly apparent during the continued efforts of the Goering Concern to take over Petschek's possessions, first in Germany and after Munich in Czechoslovakia. DZAP–IMT–Flick Concern, especially B 181.

2 ASÚS – Cizí účasti, Dobrozdání Nos. 1 and 9.

3 *Compass, Čechoslovakei* (1938), 260.

before Munich, Sudeten German industrialists and bankers held secret negotiations with representatives of the Dresdner Bank, in which they tried to ascertain which was the Czechoslovak bank best suited for the penetration of German capital into the Czechoslovak economy, they considered the Czech Bank Union to be financially safer and stronger than the large and widespread concern of the Czech Escompte Bank and Credit Institute.[1] In spite of this they selected the Czech Escompte Bank,[2] among other reasons evidently because they would thus get an immediate opportunity to acquaint themselves with the affairs of the Živnostenská Bank, which was closely linked with the Czech Escompte Bank through direct investment and credits, and decisively influenced a number of subsidiary companies.[3]

Belgian capital aligned through the Banque de Bruxelles with Solvay et Cie. and the Belgian Monarchy,[4] was the main foreign shareholder in the Czech Escompte Bank and Credit Institute, the other being the London financial house of Kleinwort Sons & Co. The Banque de Bruxelles held a share of 18.15 % in the joint-stock capital of the Czechoslovak bank.[5] The other shares were held by subsidiary enterprises of the bank and by outside firms, and more than a third were scattered among a large number of shareholders (see Table 7). The holding of the Živnostenská Bank fell from 55 % in 1920 to 16 % in 1937–8 (see Tables 1 and 7). However, the Živnostenská Bank maintained a close association with the Czech Escompte Bank via the numerous industrial companies which belonged to the sphere of interest of both banks, and also by providing the Czech Escompte Bank and Credit Institute with substantial credits.[6]

While foreign capital participated directly in the Czech Escompte Bank, this was not the case with the Živnostenská Bank. However, considerable foreign investment was present in the industrial, transport and commercial companies belonging to both banks (see Tables 7 and 8). In previous chapters I have analysed the amount and the significance of these investments

1 DZAP-B 185-NID-13399. Bericht über die Zusammenkunft in Unter-Polaun, 25 July 1938.

2 Ibid., B 186, 13400, 13405.

3 Ibid., B 185-NI 11870.

4 Ibid., B 186-NID-13400.

5 ASÚS-Cizí účasti, Dobrozdání No. 8.

6 DZAP-IMT-Nr. IV, Fall XI, pp. 8306, 8322.

Table 7. *Czech Escompte Bank and*

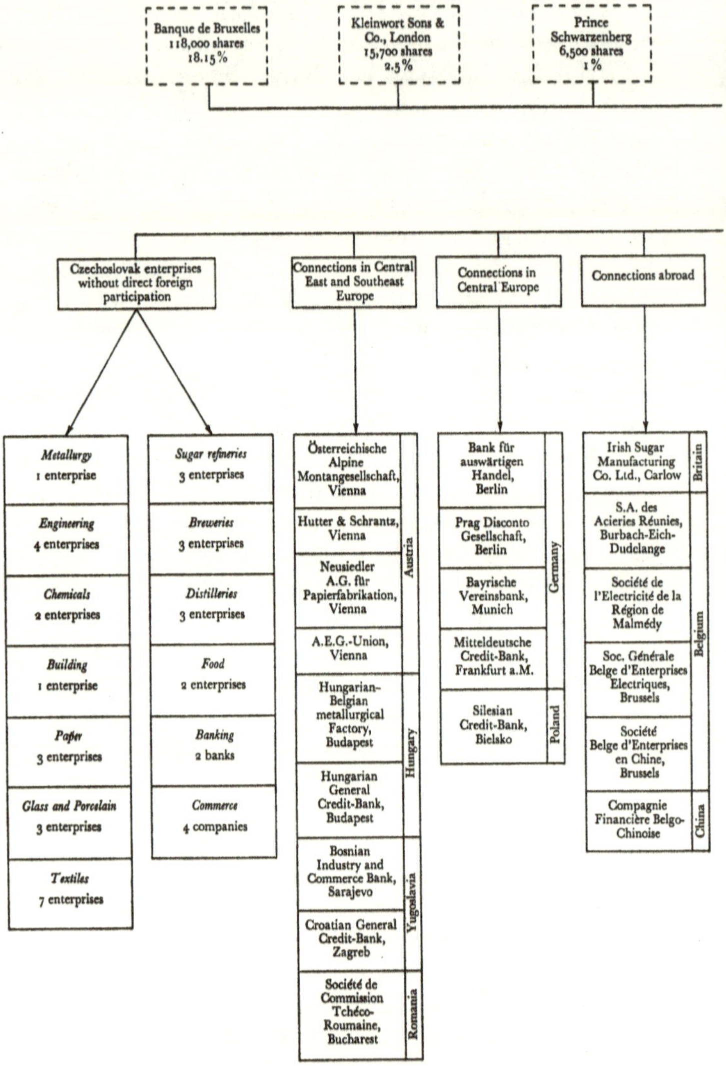

Credit Institute, 31 December 1937

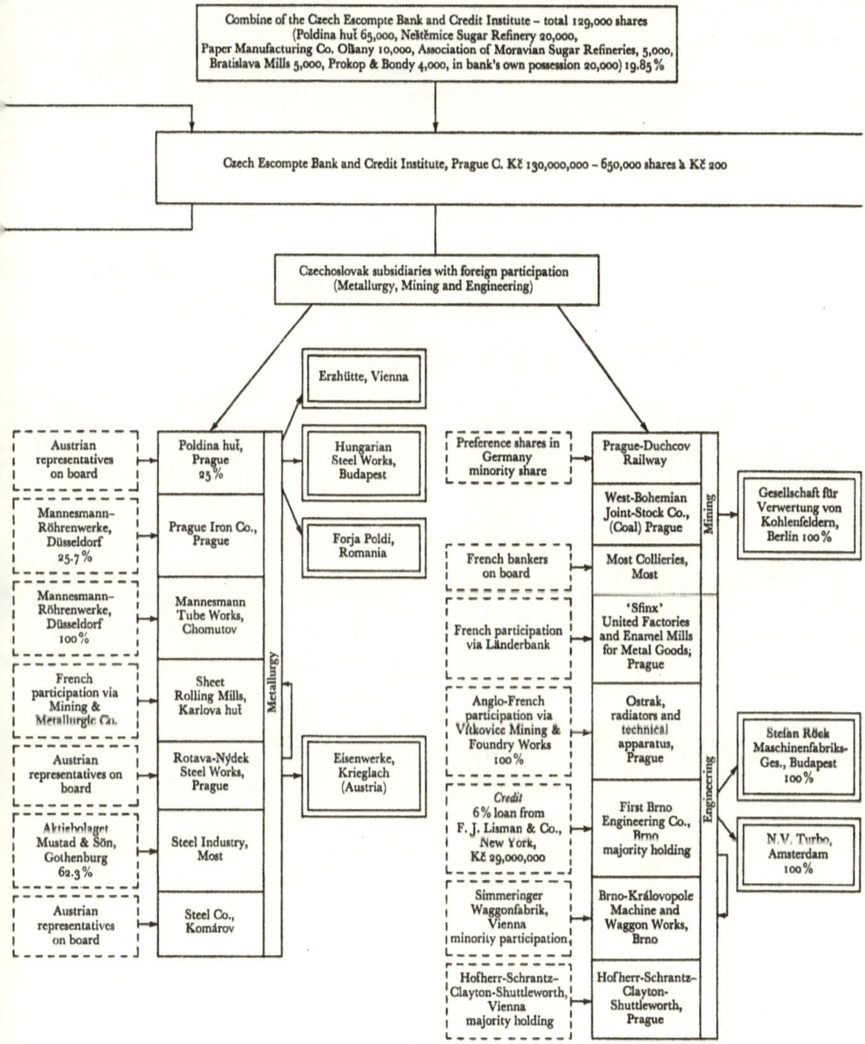

Table 7 (*contd*)

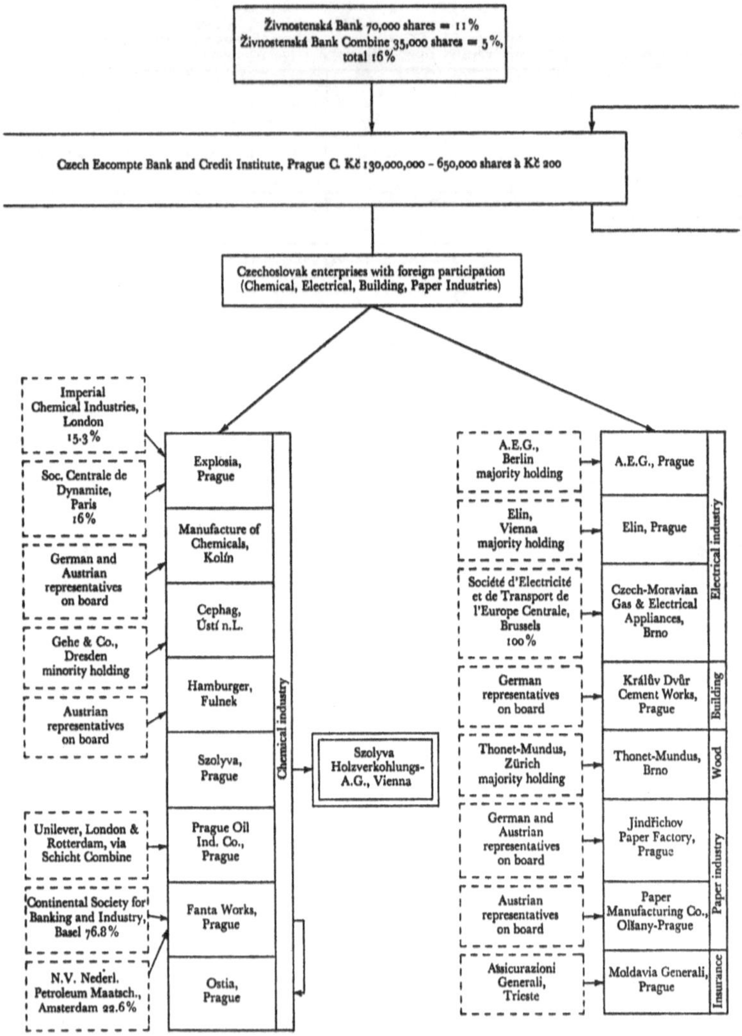

Table 7 (*contd*)

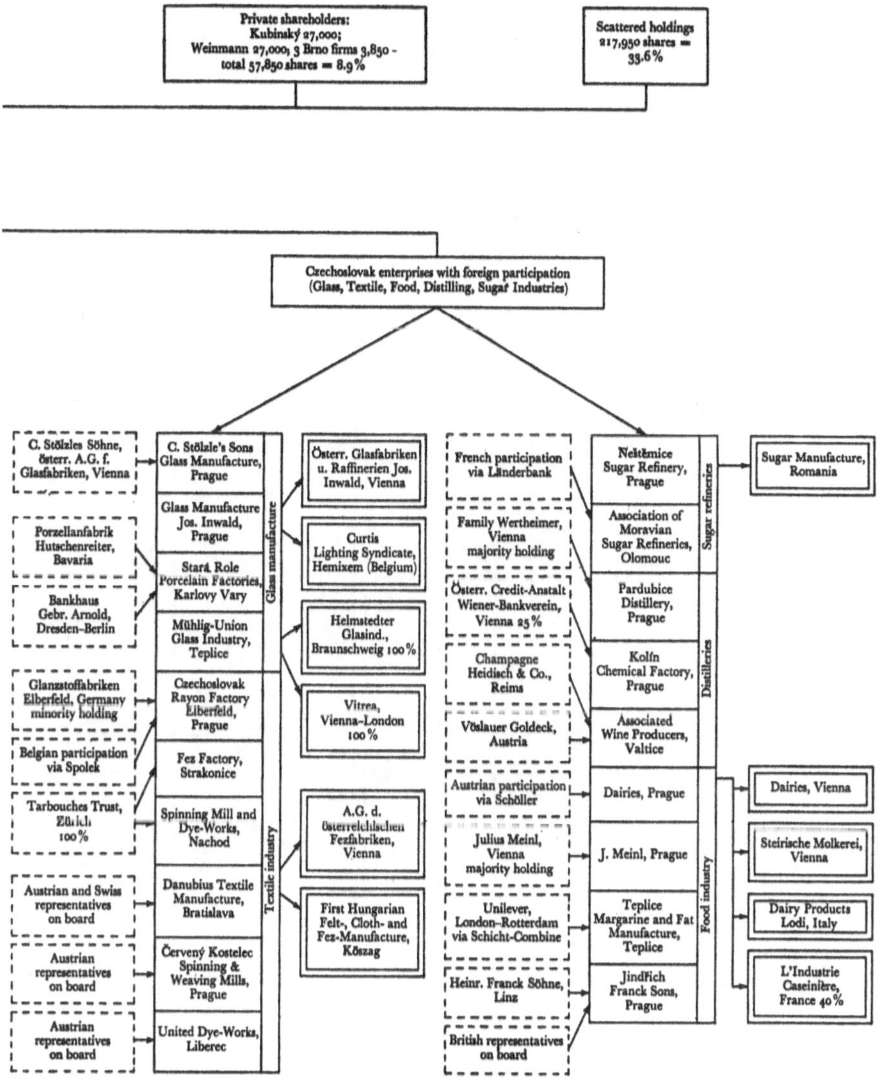

Table 8. *Živnostenská*

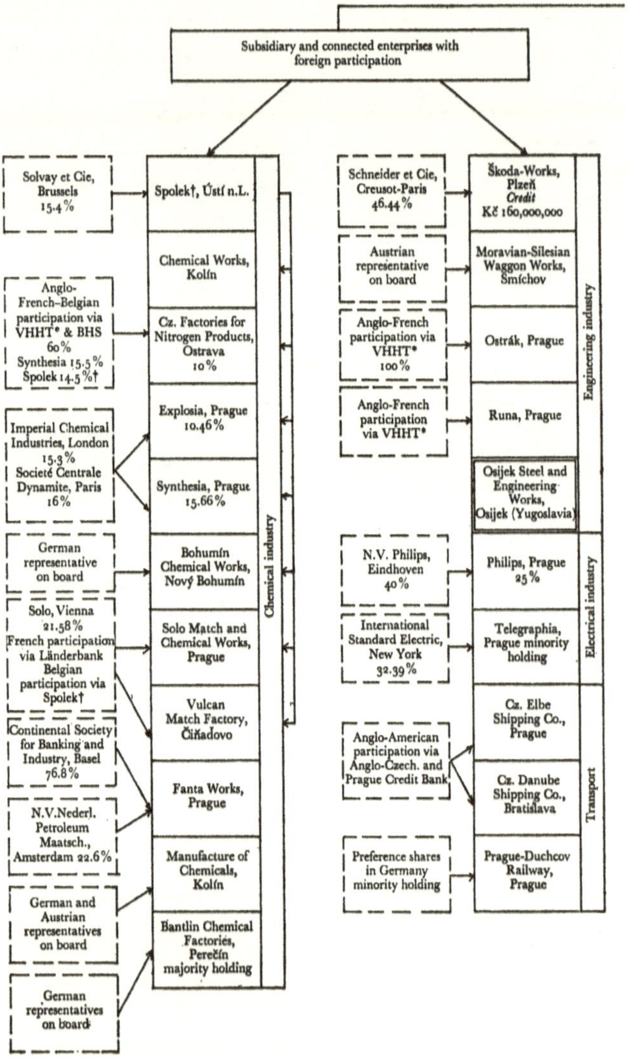

* VHHT = Vítkovice Mining and Foundry Works, BHS = Mining and Metallurgy Co.
† Spolek = Association for Chemical and Metallurgical Production, Ústí n.L.

Bank, 31 December 1937

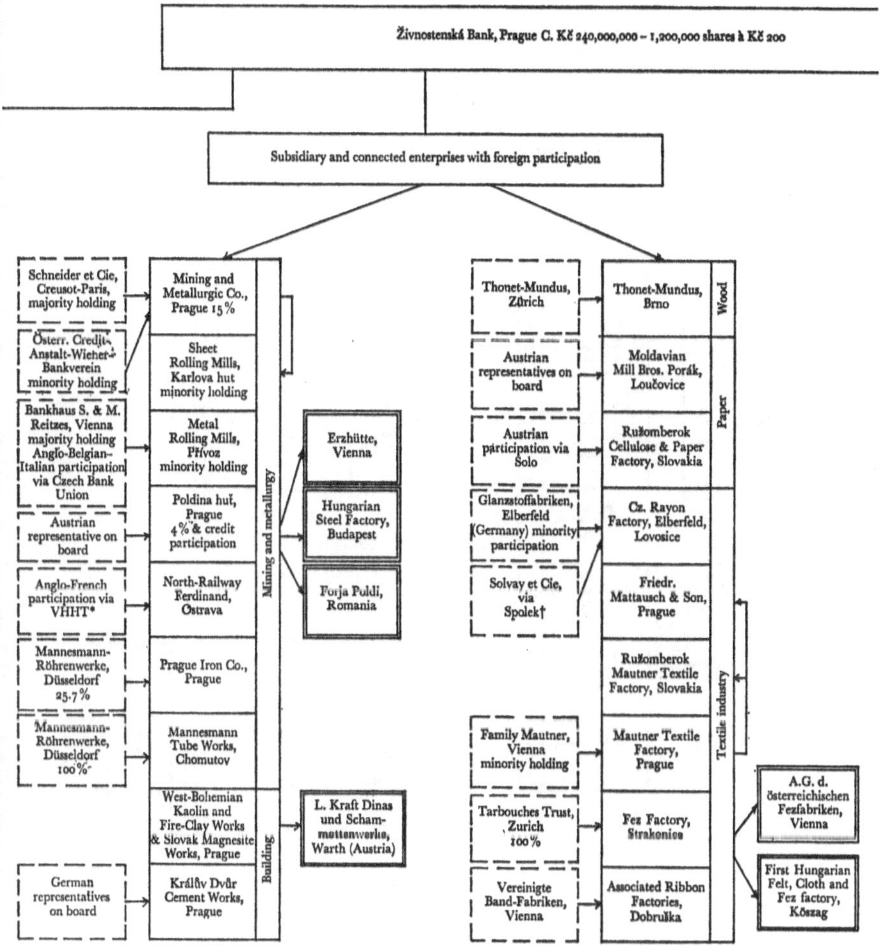

Table 8 (*contd.*)

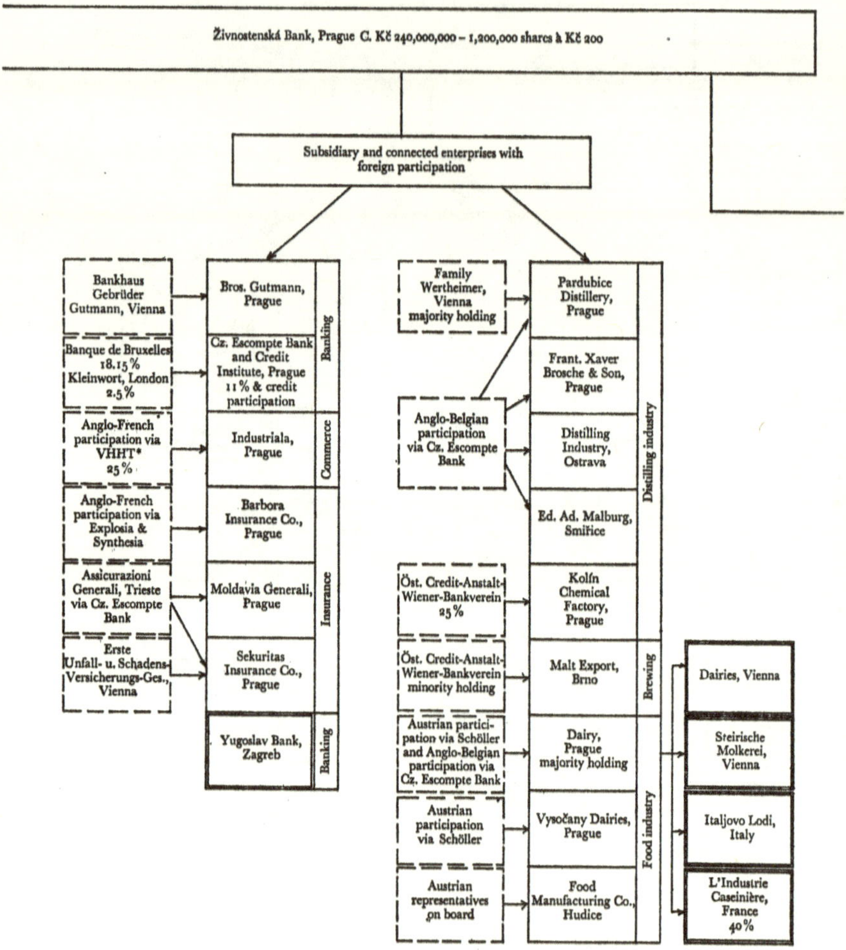

Table 8 (*contd.*)

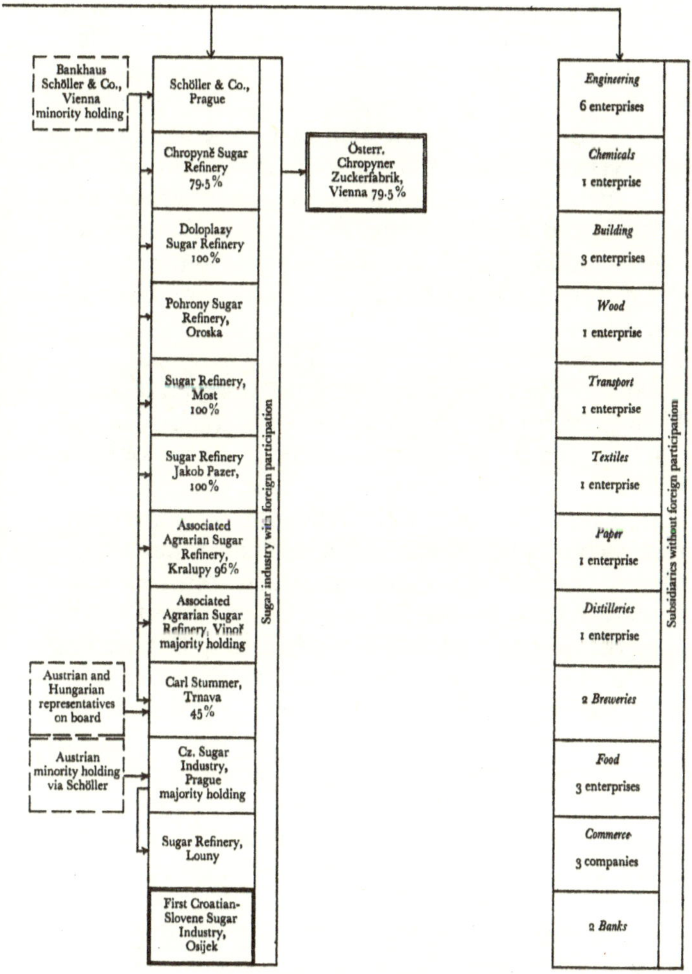

in the mining, metallurgic, engineering, electrical and chemical industries and I have shown that wherever a disproportionately stronger foreign combine or bank held a majority or a large minority share in a Czechoslovak enterprise, the relatively small minority share held by a Czechoslovak bank in the same enterprise cannot be considered as playing a decisive role, especially where the rest of the shares were scattered among numerous unknown holders. In Tables 7 and 8 the powerful presence of foreign investment (French, British, Swiss, Austrian and German) can be observed in the textile, glass, food, distilling and sugar industries. On the other hand, the tables show investments of Czechoslovak banks and companies abroad, mainly in Central and Southeast Europe, which often took the form of an indirect investment by a foreign shareholder through his Czechoslovak subsidiary. In such cases the Czechoslovak Escompte Bank and Credit Institute and the Živnostenská bank, as well as other large Czechoslovak joint-stock banks, appear as cooperators, mediators and agents of foreign financial and industrial groups.

In their financial and business operations the Czechoslovak Banks naturally pursued their own interests. However, it would be unrealistic to ignore the strong influence on their policy of their foreign investors. In this sense even the Živnostenská Bank could not have been free of all foreign influence, considering the extraordinarily large foreign participation in the enterprises which were closely associated with it. One cannot assume a completely independent field of decision for the Živnostenská Bank where it met with partners like Solvay, I.C.I., Société Central de Dynamite, Schneider, Philips, Mannesmann and Rothschild.

From this outline of foreign direct capital investment in Czechoslovak banking before Munich it can be deduced that West European and to a smaller extent American capital participated. Through direct investment in the large joint-stock banks, i.e. penetrating from 'above' into the centre of the banks' concern, foreign participants also gained influence in the subsidiary companies of those banks. At the same time linkages arose from 'below', i.e. by direct foreign investment in the individual industrial and other companies belonging to the banks, which in turn affected the banks' policy. In the inter-war period the leading French, Belgian and British banks established their main bases in Czechoslovakia in the Länderbank, the Anglo-Czechoslovak and Prague Credit Bank, the Czech Bank Union and the Czech Escompte Bank and Credit Institute in Prague.

2 Foreign longterm loans in Czechoslovakia before Munich

From the very beginning of the Czechoslovak Republic and throughout its existence the government, the town councils, large industrial enterprises and banks contracted longterm loans from abroad and frequently political as well as economic considerations played a significant role.

During the waves of revolution in Europe following the October Revolution in Russia and the First World War the British government provided the Czechoslovak state with a longterm credit for the purchase of food (see Table 1, item 1), which was to allay the unrest increased by lack of food supplies. Even German banks seeking credits abroad themselves provided short-term loans to enable the Czechoslovak government to buy food, such as the RM 360 million credit of the united German banks, or the RM 78 million loan from the Deutsche Bank in Berlin for the purchase of flour from the firm of Klein in Dresden.[1] These were soon repaid by the Czechoslovak government with sugar exports. However, the Czechoslovak government was not prepared to accept longterm loans from Germany, as on the one hand its political orientation was towards the Western Powers and on the other hand Germany was not, at that time, in a strong enough position to provide large longterm credits.

The ruling circles of both Czechoslovakia and the Western democracies were interested in building a strong army in Central Europe, for a variety of military tasks within and beyond the frontiers of Czechoslovakia. The French military command in particular saw in the Czechoslovak army an ally not only against the Soviet Union but also against France's potential enemy, a revived Germany. France therefore extended a government loan to Czechoslovakia for military purposes (see

[1] Cf. *Deset let Republiky Československé*, Vol. 2 (Praha, 1928) (A Decade of the Republic of Czechoslovakia), p. 101.

Table 1. *Statement of government debts of the Czechoslovak Republic, 31 December 1927*

Item	Specification of loan	Interest (%)	Amount on 31 December 1927 (Kč)	Note
1	*British government loan* for purchase of food, goods and transport of American flour Original position £445,083. 11*s*. 9*d*. Present position £243,072. 5*s*. 7*d*.	5	44,910,531.45	Payments on 1 October 1926, 1927, 1928 to the amount of £130,775. 9*s*. 4*d*. including interest from 1 January 1925
2	*British government loan* for repatriation of Czech legions Original position £826,520 Present position £692,199	5	113,728,295.70	Half-yearly payments for 10 years from 1925 of £53,000 including interest
3	*French government loan* Original position Frs. 99,679,517.92 Frs. 33,916,626.35 Frs. 1,149,210.60 for military purposes Present position Frs. 99,679,517.92 Frs. 33,916,626.35 Frs. 700,000.00	5	299,038,553.76 101,749,879.05 15,050,000.00	Method of repayment not agreed upon, interest not paid up Interest always antedated on 16 August. Part of debt repaid in 1927
4	*Italian government loan* Original position Lir. 169,984,605.68 Present position Lir. 169,984,605.68		69,637,508.64	Payments and interest not yet agreed
5	*U.S. government loan* Original position shown in government budget $2,873.238, $89,006,433 Actual position $115,000,000		143,661,912.50 1,860,773,041.42	According to agreement in Washington 13 October 1920 repayment from 1943 to 1987 Interest to 1943 3⅛% and after 1943 3%

Table 1 (*cont.*)

Item	Specification of loan		Interest (%)	Amount on 31 December 1927 (Kč)	Note
6	*Gold loan of ČSR abroad in 1922*				
	First and second issue	Present position			
	$14,000,000	13,245,214	8	504,106,974.00	Call for repayment from 1951 to 1952
	£3,300,000	3,122,684	8	571,548,349.80	
	$9,250,000	8,942,006	8	305,096,888.83	
	£2,050,000	1,981,740	8	294,766,789.14	
7	*Gold loan of ČSR abroad in 1926*				
	Original position $25,000,000				Debt repaid in 1928
	Present position $21,768,834		7.5	759,207,450.00	
	Total foreign loans			5,083,276,174.29	

Debts arising out of the peace treaties not included

Recapitulation

A. Internal government debt	22,650,462,901.44
B. Foreign debt (22.4% of total indebtedness)	5,083,276,174.29
Total Czechoslovak debt	27,733,739,075.73

Source: Deset let Republiky, vol. 2 (Praha, 1928), pp. 104–5.

Table 1, item 3) and at the same time intervened directly with military and political support. According to the Franco-Czechoslovak Treaty of 1918, signed by the Czechoslovak Foreign Minister Dr Beneš, the Czechoslovak army became an integral part of the French army. The French General Staff was represented in Czechoslovakia by high-ranking officers, whose presence on the territory of the new state was officially sanctioned in a series of agreements between 1919 and 1920. The Head of the French Military Mission in Czechoslovakia, General Pellé, was appointed Chief of the General Staff of the Czechoslovak Army in 1920; he was later replaced by General Mittelhausser, who held the post until 1925.[1] Further loans for

[1] Cf. *Přehled československých dějin* (Survey of Czechoslovak History), III, p. 71; also V. Soják, in *O československé zahraniční politice 1918–1939* (Czechoslovak Foreign Policy) (Praha, 1956), p. 44. Changes in the Czechoslovak General Staff were made after the conclusion of the Czechoslovak–French Treaty of 1924. Ibid., p. 120.

military purposes were provided by the United States of America and by Great Britain, in connection with the upkeep and the repatriation of the Czechoslovak Legionaries in Siberia (see Table 1, items 2 and 5).

Although the credits granted to the Czechoslovak government had political motives, the economic interests of the lenders were not neglected. As well as enabling them to sell off their stocks of redundant war material, a 5 % rate of interest was agreed on the loans for the purchase both of food and of armaments. For example the British food loan, amounting to £445,008. 11*s*. 9*d*., was repaid in four instalments of £130,725. 9*s*. 4*d*. each, the last being remitted on 17 October 1929. The interest alone came to £77,813. 5*s*. 3*d*.[1]

As a result of the Peace Treaty of Versailles the new Czechoslovak state was burdened with the greater part of the indebtedness of the former Austro-Hungarian Monarchy.[2] It was also decided that Czechoslovakia should pay into the reparation account the value of the former Austrian Emperor's family property taken over by the new state. In addition, the Successor States were charged with a 'liberation tribute' of 1.5 milliard gold francs, of which Czechoslovakia in spite of her protests was to pay half, i.e. 750 million gold francs.[3] The whole question of Czechoslovakia's financial commitments to the Entente Powers came under review during the Reparation Conference at the Hague in January 1930. There representatives of the Czechoslovak government entered into a new agreement to pay regular instalments of 10 million gold marks annually for 37 years.[4] The rate of interest for the debts resulting from the Peace Treaties was fixed at 6 % and by 1937 this indebtedness, together with the 'liberation tribute', was still Kč 1,672,300,899.[5]

As early as 1918–20 Czechoslovakia became an attractive

[1] Calculated from data in AMZV, IVth Section, fasse 'anglické půjčky' (fascicle 'English loan').

[2] Czechoslovakia was burdened with 41.7 % of the Austrian and 15.9 % of the Hungarian debt. Cf. R. Wagner, p. 78.

[3] Cf. *Deset let zahraniční politiky* (A Decade of Foreign Policy) (Praha, 1928), p. 31.

[4] Cf. APSNSRČ–ZV, Zpráva výboru 466 k vládnímu návrhu 441 (Committee's Report 466 on Government Proposal 441), 21 May 1930.

[5] Cf. AMZV–Státní rozpočet Republiky Československé na rok 1938, Správa státního dluhu (Budget of the Republic of Czechoslovakia 1938, Administration of the Public Debt).

area for foreign investment. With the greater stability of the new state the interest grew stronger. In 1922 the Czechoslovak government issued an investment loan in Britain and in the United States (see Table 1, items 6 and 7), which had a good reception in London and New York in spite of strong German competition.[1] In many respects the situation in Germany and Czechoslovakia was similar in the 1920s, with disrupted industry and relatively low wages attracting foreign investment. The Czechoslovak state pledged as securities for their loans the income from customs and taxes and from the state monopolies of tobacco and saccharine. Thus the financial policy of the state was significantly influenced by its foreign indebtedness and was tied to that of the creditor states.

The most powerful foreign creditor of the Czechoslovak state was the U.S.A., providing 70 % of the total public foreign loans in Czechoslovakia.[2] The pre-Munich Republic of Czechoslovakia was among those debtors of the United States which had to pay the highest rate of interest. Table 2 shows Czechoslovakia among the states paying 8¾ % interest or more annually for their loans issued in the United States.[3]

A number of investment banks in New York specialized in issuing loans in the United States for foreign governments or concerns between 1925 and 1930.[4] Before the First World War such issues had been handled mainly in Paris and London. However, they became a characteristic feature of the American financial scene – an unmistakable sign that the world's financial centre was moving to New York. The world economic crisis depressed this activity of American banks in the 1930s.

The Czechoslovak government loan in the United States was negotiated by one of the leading investment banks of New York, Kidder, Peabody and Co., which was associated with the powerful National City Bank.[5] The Czechoslovak government received 90 % of the nominal value of the loan – as shown in

[1] Baring Brothers Ltd in London and Kidder, Peabody & Co. in New York were entrusted with the sale of Czechoslovak bonds in Britain and the U.S.A. respectively, while the National City Bank held Czechoslovakia's loan account in the United States. AMZV, IVth Section, fasse 'anglické půjčky' and 'americké půjčky' (fascicles 'English Loans' and 'American loans').

[2] Calculated from balance of accounts for 31 December 1927, see Table 1.

[3] Cleona Lewis, *America's Stake in International Investments*, p. 408.

[4] Cf. *The Problem of International Investment*, p. 168.

[5] Cf. AMZV, IVth Section, fasse 'americké půjčky'.

Table 2. *U.S. foreign loans at interest of 8¾ per cent or more annually,* in terms of the rate to maturity*

(Based on nominal rate, price to bankers, and length of life of each issue) (in $1,000)

Borrower	Term	Face	Price to public	Price to banker	Interest rate Nominal	Interest rate Maturity
Austria:						
Lower Austria Hydro-electric	1924–44	3,000	85	68.7	6½	10.2
Province of Lower Austria	1926–50	2,000	98½	87	7½	8.8
Tyrol Hydroelectric	1925–55	3,000	96½	81½	7½	9.3
Colombia:						
Antioquia (Dept.)	1925–45	3,000	90	83	7	8.8
Barranquilla (City)	1925–35	500	99	86	8	10.3
Barranquilla (City)	1925–40	500	100	86	8	9.8
Barranquilla (City)	1926–46	500	101	88	8	9.3
Barranquilla (City)	1928–48	500	102	89	8	9.2
Bogota (City)	1924–45	6,000	98	89	8	9.2
Caldas (Dept.)	1926–46	6,000	95½	83½	7½	9.3
Caldas (Dept.)	1926–46	4,000	98	85	7½	9.1
Cauca Valley (Dept.)	1926–46	2,500	96½	83½	7½	9.3
Medellin (City)	1923–48	3,000	98	90	8	9.0
Czechoslovakia:						
Brunner Turbine & Equipment Co.	1925–55	3,500	95¾	82¼	7½	9.2
Czechoslovak Government	1922–51	14,000	96½	90	8	9.0
Czechoslovak Government	1924–52	9,250	96½	91	8	8.9
Greater Prague	1922–52	7,500	92½	86½	7½	8.8
Germany:						
City of Munich	1925–35	8,700	96¾	88¼	7	8.8
Good Hope Steel and Iron Works	1925–45	7,500	91	83	7	8.8
Good Hope Steel and Iron Works	1925–45	2,500	92	83	7	8.8
Hamburg Electric Co.	1925–35	4,000	95½	87.8	7	8.9
Leonhard Tietz	1926–46	3,000	97	83	7½	9.4
Oberpfalz Electric Power Corp.	1925–45	1,250	97½	82.3	7	8.9
Greece:						
Greek Government	1925–52	11,000	—	85	8	9.6
Hungary:						
Consolidated Cities	1925–45	10,000	89	81½	7½	9.6
Kingdom of Hungary	1924–44	7,500	87½	80	7½	9.8
Japan:						
Great Consolidated Electric Power	1924–44	15,000	91½	80	7	9.2

* Prices received by borrowers were a point or two below the prices paid by borrowers, and interest rates to borrowers were roughly 0.25 per cent higher than those shown in the table.

Source: Cleona Lewis, *America's Stake in International Investments*, p. 408.

Table 2 – but was, of course, required to pay back the full 100 %; the investment bank charged 3½ % at issue and the buyers of bonds were allowed 6½ % besides interest. Further, Table 2 shows that the actual rate of interest was in all cases higher than the nominal rate. This difference is even more pronounced in the case of loans to towns and private enterprises (see column 'Czechoslovakia' in Table 2). The town of Prague received 86½ % outright, whilst the rest went to the New York investment bank of Kuhn, Loeb and Co.,[1] which negotiated the loan.[2] When issuing a loan for the První brněnská strojírenská společnost (First Brno Engineering Co.), the American investment bank of F. J. Lisman and Co. received 13½ % on issue and a further 4¼ % went to the buyers of the bonds. The First Brno Engineering Co. obtained 82¼ % of the total amount of the loan – a total which it had to repay at an annual rate of 9.2 % (see Table 2). These examples demonstrate the stringent conditions attached to foreign longterm loans to public and private bodies in the Successor States.[3]

The relative importance of the main creditor countries which provided the Czechoslovak government with longterm loans remained essentially unchanged until 1938, as is shown in Table 3 'Statement of government debts of the Republic of Czechoslovakia, 1 January 1938'.[4]

In the 1930s investment slackened as a result of the general development of the international economy (see chapter 1). Between 1929 and 1939 the U.S.A. limited its longterm credits primarily to its own domestic market and directed its foreign investment mainly to Canada and the Argentine.[5] British investments flowed almost exclusively into the British Empire, and France also gave preference to her own colonies, although trying to retain her credit relations with European countries.[6] Czechoslovakia was considered the most solvent country in

[1] The banking house of Kuhn, Loeb and Co., New York, belonged to the eight leading investment banks in the United States. Cf. TNEC, *Investment Banking*, Hearings, Part 24, pp. 13,001 ff.

[2] AMZV, IVth Section, fasse 'americké půjčky'.

[3] L. Grosfeld in his book *Pánstvo przedwrześniowe w słuzbie monopoli kapitalistyeznych* (Warszawa, 1951), p. 107 describes a similar course of action by the American investment bank with regard to Poland.

[4] Compiled from data in AMZV, IVth Section, fasse 'anglické půjčky'.

[5] Cf. TNEC, *Investment Banking*, p. 12290.

[6] Cf. *The Problem of International Investments*, p. 220.

Table 3. *Statement of government debts of the Czechoslovak Republic, 1 January 1938 (from the Budget for 1938)*

Item	Specification of loan	Interest (%)	1 January 1938	Total in Kč
1	*Political debts:*			
	Arising out of the First World War and immediately after it. On the one hand credits from:			
	U.S.A.	3½	$115,000,000	
	Britain	5	£401,491	
	France	3	Kč 254,688,056	
	Italy.	5	Kč 472,258,351	
	On the other hand the Liberation Debt	6	Kč 335,401,315	5,720,547,313
2	*Commitments to the Caisse Commune in Paris:*			
	Part of the debt of the former Austro-Hungarian Monarchy which the Czechoslovak state took over according to the peace treaties	6		1,336,899,584
3	*Actual foreign debt:*			
	Loans negotiated by the Czechoslovak government abroad: gold loan of ČSR in U.S.A. and Britain in 1922	8	Kč 466,454,520	
	Loan of ČSR in France of 1937 (conversion loan of Frs. 600 million of 1932)	5	Kč 697,674,000	1,164,128,520
	Czechoslovak foreign debt total			8,251,575,417
	Foreign debt amounts to 17.5% of total Czechoslovak debt			47,094,386,474

Central and Southeastern Europe. In spite of this, however, particularly after Hitler's rise to power in Germany, investors preferred to provide her with short-term loans and tried to avoid entering into new longterm engagements.[1]

This situation is reflected in Table 3, where the only longterm loan to the Czechoslovak state is a French credit of 600 million frs. in 1932, which was converted to 697,674,000 Kč

[1] Cf. AMZV, IVth Section, fasse 'zahraniční půjčky' (fascicle 'foreign loans').

Table 4. *Longterm foreign loans in Czechoslovakia, 31 December 1937*

Specification of loan	Position at the end of 1937 in Kč	Total in Kč
Foreign debt of the government		8,251,575,417
Foreign debt of municipalities:		
Prague (1923)	—	—
Britain £1,081,550	—	—
U.S.A. $5,401,000	307,507,250	
Karlovy Vary (1923)	—	
U.S.A. $1,002,500	28,771,750	336,279,000
Main loans to industry:		
Škoda-Works		
British Loan (1930)	229,724,250	
French Loan (1930)	192,940,170	
Unilever (1935)	29,000,000	
Martin's Bank (1935)	30,000,000	
První čs.a.s.pro výrobu*		
F. J. Lisman and Co., New York	39,000,000	
Lánderbanka and Agrární banka†		
Martin's Bank (1935)	14,100,000	
První brněnská strojírenská spol.‡		
F. J. Lisman and Co., New York	29,000,000	563,764,420
Total		9,151,618,837

Sources: Government and municipal debts are taken from data in AMZV, section IV; loans to industry were compiled from data in works archives. The list may be incomplete.

* First Czechoslovak Company for Manufacture.

† Bank for Commerce and Industry, formerly Länderbank, and Agrarian Bank.

‡ First Brno Engineering Company.

in 1937 with an issue of 92 % and a rate of interest of 5 %.[1] The French loan of the 1930s is notable because of the conditions attached to it, providing evidence of pressure exerted by the creditor on the debtor country. From the negotiations surrounding the loan between the representatives of the French Ministries of Foreign Affairs and Finance and the Schneiders on the one side, and the diplomats of Czechoslovakia on the other, it emerges that the loan was primarily designed to save the Škoda-Works.[2] Further, France demanded an assurance

[1] AMZV, IVth Section, correspondence between the Ministry of Finance and the Ministry of Foreign Affairs, unnumbered.

[2] AMZV, Political Reports, Paris, No. 449, 11 December 1931 and Nos. 454, 455, 16 December 1931; ibid., handwritten note of Dr Beneš of 17 December 1931. See p. 207.

from the Czechoslovak government to the bond-holders' organization L'Association nationale des porteurs français de valeurs mobilières in France that the claims of the French owners of old Austro-Hungarian bonds would be satisfied.[1] Finally, before signing the loan agreement, the French Foreign Minister Flandin wanted a guarantee from the Czechoslovak government in the interest of the French shareholders of the Société française des pétroles de Tchécoslovaquie that neither Germans nor Austrians would gain significant interests in Czechoslovak oil.[2] Doubtless the loan of 1932 and its conversion in 1937 were designed to strengthen French influence in Czechoslovakia and point directly to French–Czechoslovak and German–Austrian competition.[3]

Besides the French government loan, some longterm loans were granted to Czechoslovak private enterprise by British creditors in the 1930s. At the end of 1937 the Czechoslovak government negotiated the conversion and increase of the 8 % loan of 1922 with the London bankers Baring Brothers.[4] This never materialized because of the *Anschluss* of Austria to Germany and the Munich events of 1938. The main longterm loans contracted by Czechoslovakia abroad up to 31 December 1937 are given in Table 4. In comparison with the preceding period, lending from governments and private sources in the United States, Great Britain and France decreased although it never ceased entirely. In this field of economic relations also, Czechoslovakia remained in the sphere of Anglo-American–French interest.

1 AMZV, IVth Section, correspondence between the Ministry of Finance and the Ministry of Foreign Affairs, unnumbered.

2 Ibid., confidential letters No. 167221/30-IV, No. 156.180/30-IV, No. 10.575/32-II B/4b, No. 55/32. See p. 297.

3 In this connection it is interesting that the French government provided Poland with a loan of 2,600 million French Francs in January 1937. Cf. L. Wellisz, p. 59.

4 AMZV, IVth Section, fasse 'anglické půjčky'.

Conclusion

This study has attempted to evaluate the role and influence of foreign capital in Czechoslovakia (and indirectly in Central and Southeastern Europe) in the inter-war period, not only quantitatively but particularly in its many-sided economic and historical aspects. Starting from a statistical analysis of quantifiable factors, it has investigated the evidence behind the figures on the degree of power exerted by international direct investment, foreign credit and international cartels over control and decision-making in business enterprises and banks, their effects on the development of fundamental branches of industry and thus the structure of the economy, and the role they played in relations between the investing countries and the host country. Let us summarize the main findings in the light of these questions and in their appropriate historical context.

The First World War resulted in a redistribution of spheres of influence between the Great Powers. Accordingly, after the victory of the Entente a transfer of foreign capital holdings in Czechoslovakia took place, to the disadvantage of Austrian and German capital and in favour of domestic Czech capital and financially very powerful groups from Great Britain, France, Belgium and the United States of America.

The prominence of West European capital in Czechoslovakia after the First World War was moreover connected with the loss of the Russian market for capital exports. All political, economic and military decisions, especially in Central and Southeastern Europe, were significantly affected by the results of the October Revolution.

There can be little doubt that Central and Southeast Europe became, after the British Empire and South America, the third most important area for investment by the victorious Entente

Powers in the post-war world. The U.S.A. found it a profitable outlet for her capital. For British and French capital it could compensate at least in part for the loss of Russian investments. Although the Great Powers accepted the political reality of the existence of the new states in Central and Southeastern Europe, they often used them as instruments in international power politics. It is also not insignificant that transnational combines like Schneider–Creusot, Imperial Chemical Industries, Solvay, Unilever and others regarded the territory of Central and Southeastern Europe as a single unit with relation to their economic interests.

Among the countries of Central and Southeastern Europe Czechoslovakia attracted foreign capital investment not so much because she was less developed but because of the relatively high degree of concentration in her industries and banking, the comparatively low level of wages and the fairly stable political conditions of her democratic, republican system of government. The strong tendencies towards combination enabled foreign investment to penetrate deeply into basic industries in the Czechoslovak economy. I have estimated that up to 31 December 1937 almost 25 % of the capital of industry, commerce, transport, banking and insurance in Czechoslovakia consisted of direct foreign investment. Foreign investment was particularly large in the economically strongest enterprises. Only just over 10 % of the total number of companies were connected with foreign capital, but in them was concentrated more than 48 % of the total capital of the Czechoslovak economy.

The share of direct foreign investment in Czechoslovak joint-stock companies amounted to nearly one-third (32 %) of the total capital of industrial enterprises, somewhat more than one-seventh (15 %) of the total nominal capital of banks and about one-fourth (26 %) of the total nominal capital of insurance companies. The exceptional importance of foreign investment in the Czechoslovak economy is documented by the fact that it owned the majority or a significant part of the joint-stock capital of those companies in which foreign holdings were found: in the mining and metallurgical industry 64 %, in the mechanical engineering industry 40 %, in the electrical industry 52 %, in the chemical industry 66 %, in the mineral- and vegetable-oil industry 97 %.

British and French business enterprises and banks, followed by German and Austrian, were among the leading foreign investors in the mining and metallurgical industry; in the mechanical engineering industry the order of importance was French, Austrian and then British; in the electrical industry German, Swiss, Belgian and British; in the chemical industry Belgian, French and British; in the mineral- and vegetable-oil industry American and French, Dutch and British. West European investment was strikingly prominent and according to the estimates calculated in this study British, French, Dutch and Belgian direct longterm investment amounted to 68.1 % of total foreign direct longterm investment in Czechoslovak industrial enterprises and banks. The share of American direct capital investment was relatively small. However in the field of longterm loans it was substantially greater and American creditors in public and private Czechoslovak institutions in fact led the British and French.

German capital investment was weak in comparison with British and French. The relatively high share of Austrian investment is somewhat surprising, even though the historical roots of Austrian economic influence cannot be overlooked. A more precise evaluation of the character of Austrian capital investment in Czechoslovakia will only be possible after more thorough study of the role of foreign capital in Austria between 1918 and 1938. It is possible that this investment in Czechoslovakia was hardly Austrian at all or only partly of Austrian origin. In the case of the Dutch share its composition is clearly Anglo-Dutch, but to make an exact territorial distinction would be extremely difficult. Similarly there existed interlocking interests in the electrical industry, where American capital stood behind the German investment.

A merely quantitative evaluation of foreign capital investment – apart from marginal errors and omissions contained in statistics of this kind – cannot give a sufficiently accurate picture of its influence on production, and on domestic and foreign trade, nor can it directly measure the impact on the domestic and foreign policy of Czechoslovakia. Neither can the profits, dividends, interest payments and other outflows resulting from foreign investments, or the benefits accruing to the Czechoslovak economy, be exactly measured. However, the outflow of earnings from foreign investment did form a considerable proportion of the national income and affected the balance of payments of Czechoslovakia constantly and usually adversely. As a result of the interlocking of Czechoslovak capital with that of international business and financial groups, another economic factor arises concerning the export of capital from Czechoslovakia. In addition to purely Czechoslovak capital exports, some capital was exported from Czechoslovakia which belonged, in the last analysis, to one or other of the powerful foreign combines or banks operating in the country. In this sense not all foreign investments appearing to originate in Czechoslovakia can be truly regarded as Czechoslovak capital exports.

Between the domestic groups of industrialists and bankers a continuous competitive conflict existed. Their representatives in the economy, in politics or in government sought to strengthen their own positions through alignments with groups of foreign investors. On the other hand, the powerful foreign financial groups also competed fiercely with each other, in spite of agreements between them on the division of markets and spheres of interests. The Czechoslovak combines and banks were necessarily drawn into these intricate and conflicting financial, technical and market relations, but in the role of a weaker partner.

Czechoslovakia became an area of complicated competitive struggles between international business and financial groups, especially those of Western Europe and Germany. The continuously sharpening competitive struggle between Czechoslovak and German groups took place within the framework of West European and German competition. German capital endeavoured to capture economic positions in Czechoslovakia and tried to sever the economic and political ties between Czechoslovakia and the Western Powers and between the states of the Little Entente.

In its drive for expansion German capital was forced to penetrate the Czechoslovak economy in ways other than direct capital investment. In the first place German big business tried to tie important Czechoslovak industrial combines to their own by way of cartel agreements. The most numerous and most influential German cartels gained a hold on the Czechoslovak chemical, mining, metallurgical, engineering and electrical industries, i.e. in those industries in which West European direct foreign investment was strongly present. It seems clear that German business groups attempted through cartels to obtain greater influence in the economic life of Czechoslovakia before Munich and thus to weaken the position of its competitors, mainly Anglo-French capital.

In an analysis of the economic background of this period of political struggle and increasing economic competition it is essential to consider the effect of cartel policies as a whole, especially of German cartel tactics. In this connection the important question arises, whether long before the Munich Agreement a voluntary withdrawal of West European capital investment from Central and Southeastern Europe in favour of German interests had been taking place. Certainly until the annexation of Austria to Germany, and essentially up to Munich, no convincing evidence can be found to support the hypothesis that direct foreign investment was withdrawn from Czechoslovakia by West European investors. It is almost generally accepted in historical interpretations that the Munich Agreement was an attempt at bridging the differences between the West European Powers and the German Reich, above all between Great Britain and Germany, on the basis of the sacrifice of Czechoslovak independence and the prospect of an anti-Soviet, and possibly also anti-American, alignment.

Far-reaching economic adjustments between Great Britain and Hitler's Germany were to take place after Munich. This is documented by the public and secret negotiations that were conducted between representatives of Germany and Great Britain in the period following the Munich Agreement and lasted until the very outbreak of the Second World War. However London and Berlin were not able to overcome their differences. These did not affect only the problem of colonies, which is often quoted as the crucial question.

The question of the division of capital investment and foreign trade in Central and Southeastern Europe also loomed large in the intensive negotiations. In the spirit of the Munich policy the representatives of Great Britain did not object to a certain strengthening of German economic, political and military influence in this area. Great Britain had comparatively less interest there than in the areas of her main concern, the British Empire and Latin America. Britain's readiness to make concessions to Germany was, however, accompanied by a demand for safeguards for her own share of economic influence in the Central and Southeast European countries; on this a satisfactory agreement could not be reached. Britain was not prepared to withdraw from her economic positions to the extent demanded by Hitler's Germany; but she was not able to protect and retain them without war against her biggest competitor.

We lay no claim to have presented an exhaustive analysis of the intricate international economic and political problems in the inter-war period. It is, however, important to point out that the activities of foreign capital in Czechoslovakia were part of the process of capital movement in the pre-war world, which contributed to the prominence of large economic units and their growth across national barriers.

The history of direct foreign investment and cartels in Central and Southeastern Europe shows a territorial expansion of the activities of influential business or banking concerns, their movement towards horizontal and vertical monopoly and their efforts to control and regulate the market. Changes in the economic structure in the inter-war period appear to have foreshadowed the post-war economic predominance of the powerful multinational companies.

Sources consulted

I. LIST OF ABBREVIATIONS FOR ARCHIVES USED IN THIS WORK

Archives are listed in order of central state institutions, ministerial and parliamentary archives, business archives and archives in Germany.

SÚA Státní ústřední archiv v Praze (State Central Archives in Prague)

SÚA–KR Kartelový rejstřík (Cartel-Register)

SÚA–SÚ Spolek pro chemickou a hutní výrobu v Ústí n.L. (Association for Chemical and Metallurgical Production in Ústí n.L.)
Solvay

AMZV Archiv ministerstva zaharaničních věcí v Praze (Archives of the Foreign Ministry in Prague)

AMZV–IV. sekce Fourth Section

AMZV Zprávy Paříž, Vídeň, Londýn, Berlín (Reports of Embassies in Paris, Vienna, London, Berlin)

APSNSRČ Archiv poslanecké sněmovny Národního shromáždění Republiky Československé (Archives of the Parliament of the Czechoslovak Republic)

APSNSRČ–ZV Zahraniční výbor (Foreign Affairs Committee)

APSNSRČ–IC Incompatibility Committee

ASÚS Archiv státního úřadu statistického (Archives of the State Statistical Office)

ASÚS Koncernové šetření (Enquiry into Combines)

ASÚS Cizí účasti–Šetření Státního úřadu statistického o cizích účastech (Enquiry of the State Statistical Office into Foreign Participation)

ASÚS Dobrozdáni (Reports on Combines)

ANTM Archiv Narodního technického musea (Archives of the National Technical Museum)

ANTM–SDS Prodejna sdružených československých železáren (Selling Agency of the United Czechoslovak Ironworks)

ANTM–MK Mezinárodní kartely (International Cartels)

ANTM Vzpomínky–Memoirs

AMCHP Archiv ministerstva chemického průmyslu (Archives of the Ministry of the Chemical Industry)
AÚLSMHD Archiv Ústřední likvidační správy ministerstva hutí a dolů (Archives of the Central Liquidating Office of the Ministry of Foundries and Mines)
AÚLSMHD–MKS Mezinárodní kartelové smlouvy (International Cartel Agreements)
AÚLSMHD–BH Báňská a hutní společnost (The Mining and Metallurgic Company)
AÚLSMHD–PŽ Pražská železářská společnost (The Prague Iron Company)
PA–ZVIL, Plzeň Podnikový archiv závodů V.I. Lenina, Plzeň (Works Archives of the V.I. Lenin Works, Plzeň)
PA–ZVIL, Plzeň–GŘ generální ředitelství (General Management)
PA–ZVIL, Plzeň agenda Rochette (Files of Rochette)
PA–ŠZ, Praha Podnikový archiv Škodových závodů (Works Archives of the Škoda-Works, Prague)
obchodní a právní oddělení (commercial and legal department)
PA–VŽKG, Ostrava Podnikový archiv Vítkovických železáren Klementa Gottwalda, Ostrava (Works Archives of the Klement Gottwald Vítkovice Ironworks, Ostrava)
PA–VŽKG–gen. řed. generální ředitelství (General Management)
PA–VŽKG–VHHT Vítkovické horní a hutní těžířstvo (The Vítkovice Mining and Foundry Works)
PA–STZ Podnikový archiv Severočeských tukových závodů Ústí n.L. (Works Archives of North Bohemian Fats Industry Ústí n.L.)
PA–TŽ–BH, Třinec Podnikový archiv třineckých železáren Báňská a hutní společnost, Třinec (Works Archives of the Třinec Ironworks, The Mining and Metallurgic Company, Třinec)
PA–VCHZ–Pardubice Semtín Podnikový archiv Vychodočeských chemických závodů, Pardubice, Semtín (Works Archives of the East Bohemian Chemical Works)
AÚOŽK Archiv ústřední obchodní a živnostenské komory (Archives of the Central Chamber of Commerce and Trades)
AOŽK–P Archiv obchodní a živnostenské komory (Archives of the Chamber of Commerce and Trades in Plzeň)
DZAP–AA Deutsches Zentralarchiv Potsdam
Auswärtiges Amt
DZAP–RWiM Reichwirtschaftsministerium
DZAP–RMdI Reichsministerium des Innern
DZAP–RWA Reichswirtschaftsamt
DZAP–St.RA Statistisches Reichsamt

DZAP–DSt Deutsche Stiftung
DZAP–VdRRM Vertretung der Reichsregierung München
DZAP–Akten Tschechoslowakei
DZAP–IMT Deutsches Zentralarchiv Potsdam–Internationales Militärtribunal
DZAP–IMT–NID Nachfolgeprozesse (Subsequent Trials) Protokolle, Dokumentenbücher
SLHAD Sächsisches Landeshauptarchiv, Dresden
SLHAD–AA Auswärtiges Amt
ADWI Archiv des Deutschen Wirtschafts-Instituts in Berlin
AIGP Archiv für die Geschichte der Partei, Berlin
AIZG Archiv des Instituts für Zeitgeschichte, München

II. LIST OF OFFICIAL PUBLICATIONS

Anuarul Statistic al României
Bilans Płaticzny Polski
Committee on Finance and Industry Report, Cmd. 3897, HMSO (London, 1931)
Committee on Trusts:
(*a*) Cmd. 622, HMSO (London, 1920)
(*b*) Cmd. 4825, HMSO (London, 1935)
(*c*) Cmd. 5461, HMSO (London, 1937)
(*d*) Cmd. 5201, Parliamentary Papers XX (1935–6)
(*e*) Cmd. 5292, Parliamentary Papers VII (1935–6)
(*f*) Cmd. 5507, Parliamentary Papers XII (1936–7)
(*g*) Cmd. 3601, HMSO (London, 1930)
(*h*) Cmd. 633, Parliamentary Papers XXIII (1920)
(*i*) Cmd. 832, ibid.
(*j*) Cmd. 563, ibid.
(*k*) Cmd. 930, ibid.
Concise Statistical Yearbook of Poland
Czechoslovakia No. 1 (1959), Cmd. 720 (London, 1959)
Documents on German Foreign Policy 1918–1945, Series D (DGFP), (London, 1956)
Documents on British Foreign Policy 1919–1939, Third Series (London, 1951–5)
Dokumente und Materialien aus der Vorgeschichte des zweiten Weltkrieges, I, II (Moskau, 1948, 1949)
Enqueteausschuss – Ausschuss zur Untersuchung der Erzeugungs- und Absatzbedingungen der deutschen Wirtschaft (Berlin, 1928–31)
Final Report of the Committee on Industry and Trade, Cmd. 3282, HMSO (London, 1929)

Internationales Militär Tribunal, Fall XI, Grüne Serie
Investigation of Concentration of Economic Power, Temporary National Economic Committee (TNEC), Descriptions of Hearings and Monographs of the Temporary National Economics Committee, 31 Vols. + 6 supplementary Vols, 42 Monographs (Washington D.C., 1941)
Royal Institute of International Affairs, The Problem of International Investment (London, New York, Toronto, 1937)
Sbírka zákonů a nařízení státu Československého (Sb.z. a n.) (Collection of Laws and Regulations of the Czechoslovak State)
Statistical Society Annual
Statistical Yearbook of the League of Nations
Statistická ročenka ČSR (Statistical Yearbook of the ČSR)
Statistická ročenka Protektorátu Čechy a Morava 1941 (Statistical Yearbook of the Protectorate of Bohemia and Moravia 1941) (Praha, 1941)
Statistisches Jahrbuch für das Deutsche Reich
Statystyka karteli w Polsce, Głowny urzad statystyczny rzeczypospolitej polskiej, Statystyka polski, serya C, zeszyt 28 (Statistics of Cartels in Poland, Main Statistical Office of the Polish State) (Warszawa, 1935)
Těsnopisecké zprávy poslanecké sněmovny Národního shromáždění Republiky Československé (Stenographic Reports of the Czechoslovak Parliament)
Treaty Series No. 32 (1959), Cmd. 720 (London, 1959)
Trial of the Major War Criminals, Secretariat of the Tribunal (42 Vols.) (Nuremberg, 1947)
United Nations Balances of Payments (Geneva, 1948)
Velkoobchodní ceny a indexy v Československé Republice 1926–38 (Wholesale Prices and Indices in the Czechoslovak Republic 1926–38)
Zahraniční obchod Republiky Československé (Foreign Trade of the Czechoslovak Republic)
Zprávy Státního úřadu statistického Republiky Československé (Reports of the State Statistical Office of the Czechoslovak Republic)

III. LIST OF PERIODICALS

Acta Universitatis Carolinae, Philosophica et historica
Berliner Börsen-Zeitung
Československý časopis historický (Czechoslovak Journal of History)
Československý průmysl (Czechoslovak Industry)
Economic Development and Cultural Change
Economic Journal

Economic Record
Ekonomický časopis Slovenské akademie vied (Economic Journal of the Slovak Academy of Sciences)
Financial News
Frankfurter Zeitung
Geschichte in der Schule
Hamburger Studien zur neueren Geschichte
Historica
Historický časopis
Hospodářská politika (Economic Policy)
Hospodářské hovory (Economic Conversations)
Hospodářský rozhled (Economic View)
Jahrbuch für Wirtschaftsgeschichte
Journal of Central European Affairs
Journal of Contemporary History
Komrevue
Labour Monthly
Labour Research
Leipziger Vierteljahresschriften für Südosteuropa
Národní listy (National Letters)
Nové obzory (New Horizons)
Obzor národohospodářský (Economic Horizon)
Prager Presse
Přítomnost (The Present)
Rudé právo (The Red Right)
Sborník Vysoké školy pedagogické (Collected Studies of the University of Education) Filosofie-Historie I, Historie II
Schriften des Vereins für Sozialpolitik, Gesellschaft für Wirtschafts- und Sozialwissenschaften
Slezský sborník (Silesian Collection)
Statistický obzor (Statistical Horizon)
Statistický zpravodaj (Statistical Reporter)
Statistisches Taschenbuch von Rumänien
The Economist
The Slavonic and East European Review
Tradition: Zeitschrift für Firmengeschichte und Unternehmerbiographie
Tvorba (Creation)
Venkov (The Countryside)
Völkischer Beobachter
Wirtschaftskurve
Wissenschaftliche Zeitschrift der Friedrich-Schiller Universität Jena
Zahraniční politika (Foreign Policy)
Zeitschrift für die gesamte Staatswissenschaft
Zeitschrift für Geschichtswissenschaft

IV. LIST OF DIRECTORIES AND BUSINESS PUBLICATIONS

Československé bursovní papíry, J. Kašpar, Praha (Czechoslovak Stock-Exchange Papers)

Československé kartely, J. Kašpar a R. Šimáček, Praha (Czechoslovak Cartels)

Compass, Čechoslovakei, Praha

Compass, Österreich, Wien

Compass, Personenverzeichnis, Wien

Directory of Directors, London

Moody's Manual of Investments, New York

The Bank and Insurance Shares Year Book, London

The Stock Exchange Official Intelligence, London

The Stock Exchange Year Book, London

Wer ist wer, Berlin

Who's Who, London

Bibliography

Adams, W. (ed.) *The Structure of American Industry, Some Case Studies* (New York, 1954).

Adams, W. and Gray, M. H. *Monopoly in America* (New York, 1955).

Adler, J. H. (ed.) *Capital Movement and Economic Development. Proceedings of a Conference held by the International Economic Association* (London, New York, 1967).

Alexander, W. and Street, A. *Metals in the Service of Man* (Harmondsworth, New York, 1944).

Allen, G. C. *British Industries and their Organisation* (London, 1939).

Arndt, H. (ed.) *Die Konzentration in der Wirtschaft; Schriften des Vereins für Sozialpolitik*, Vol. 20 (Berlin, 1960), Vol. 22 (Berlin, 1961).

Arnold, E. *Trusts – eine Lebensgefahr* (Zürich, 1947).

Arnold, T. *Anti-Trust Law Enforcement, Past and Future* (Durham, Winter 1940).

Bandera, V. N. *Foreign Capital as an Instrument of National Economic Policy: A Study based on the Experience of East European Countries between the World Wars* (The Hague, 1964).

Bareš, G. *Proti Mnichovu* (Against Munich) (Praha, 1958).

Basch, A. *The Danube Basin and the German Economic Sphere* (London, 1944).

Baumann, G. *Eine handvoll Konzernherren* (Berlin, 1953).

Benni, A. S., Lammers, C., Marlio, L. and Meyer, A. *General report on economic aspects of international industrial agreements*, League of Nations (Geneva, 1931).

Berge, W. *Cartels – Challenge to a Free World* (Washington, 1946).

Bernal, J. D. *Science in History* (London, 1965).

Bernášek, V. and Bernášek, V. V. *Bez slávy a bez ilusí* (Without Glory and without Illusions) (Praha, 1956).

Berov, L. 'Le capital financier occidental et les pays balkaniques dans les années vingt', *Études balkaniques*, T. II–III (separatum) (Sofia, 1965).

Borkin, J. and Welsh, Ch., with an introduction by Arnold, T. *Germany's Master Plan* (London, New York, Melbourne, n.d.).

Brandt, K., Müller, J. H. and Krelle, W. 'Beiträge zur Theorie der Produktion und der Einkommensverteilung' in Schneider, E. (ed.) *Schriften des Vereins für Sozialpolitik*, Gesellschaft für Wirtschafts- und Sozialwissenschaften, N.F.B. 12 (Berlin, 1956).

Braslavsky, I. M. *Vneshnyaya torgovlya kapitalisticheskikh stran na pervom etape obshchego krizisa kapitalizma* (Kiev, 1957).

Brogan, D. W. *The Development of Modern France (1870–1939)* (London, 1945).

Cassel, G. *Recent monopolistic tendencies in industry and trade, being an analysis of the nature and causes of the poverty of nations*, League of Nations (Geneva, 1927).

Černý, B. 'K otázce zřízení obilního monopolu' (The Problems of the Establishment of the Grain Monopoly), *ČSČH*, III/3 (1955).

César, J. and Černý, B. *Od sudetoněmeckého separatismu k plánům odvety* (From Sudeten German Separatism to Plans for Revenge) (Praha, 1960). *Politika německých buržoasních stran v Československu v letech 1918–1938* (The Policy of the German Bourgeois Parties in Czechoslovakia between 1918 and 1938), Vol. I (Praha, 1961), Vol. II (Praha, 1962).

'The Nazi Fifth Column in Czechoslovakia', *Historica*, IV (1962).

Chamberlain, E. H. (ed.) *Monopoly and Competition and their Regulation, Papers and Proceedings of a Conference held by the International Economics Association* (London, 1954).

Charques, R. D. and Ewen, A. H. *Profits and Politics in the Post-War World* (London, 1934).

Chmela, L. *Hospodářská okupace Československa, její metody a důsledky* (The Economic Occupation of Czechoslovakia, its Methods and Results) (Praha, 1946).

Chylík, J. *Vývoj zahraničního obchodu v našich zemích* (The Development of Foreign Trade in our Country) (Praha, 1947).

Coleman, D. C. *Courtaulds*, Vols. I and II (London, 1969).

Conditions of private foreign investment: report by special joint committee, League of Nations (Princeton, 1946).

Corey, L. *Decline of American Capitalism* (London, 1935).

The House of Morgan (New York, 1930).

DeCugis, H., Olds, R. E. and Tschierschky, S. *Review of legal aspects of industrial agreements prepared for the Economic Committee*, League of Nations (Geneva, 1930).

Dějiny diplomacie (History of Diplomacy), 3 (Praha, 1949).

Denny, L. *America Conquers Britain* (London, New York, 1930).

'Der Aufstieg einer Grossindustrie' – Čs. moravská Kolben-Daněk A.G., *Prager Presse* (Sonderbeilage) 29 January 1928.

Deset let Národní banky československé (A Decade of the National Bank of Czechoslovakia) (Praha, 1937).

Deset let Republiky československé (A Decade of the Czechoslovak Republic) (Praha, 1928)

Deset let zahraniční politiky Republiky československé (A Decade o Foreign Policy of the Czechoslovak Republic) (Praha, 1928).

'Die Agrikultur der Tschechoslowakischen Republik', *Prager Presse* (Sonderbeilage), 13 May 1928.

Die Milliarden Truste in Frankreich (Translation from the original *Les trusts milliardaires en France*, Numéro special des *Notes et Études Économiques*, Paris, 1952) (Berlin, 1953).

Die Monopole der USA (Berlin, 1952).

Dimitrijević, S. *Das ausländische Kapital in Jugoslawien* (Berlin, 1963).

Dobb, M. *Studies in the Development of Capitalism* (London, 1947).

Dobrý, A. *Hospodářská krise československého průmyslu ve vztahu k Mnichovu* (Economic Crisis in Czechoslovak Industry in relation to Munich) (Praha, 1959).

Kdo vládl v předmnichovské republice (Who ruled the pre-Munich Republic) (Praha, 1948).

Dobrý, A. 'Základní směry vývoje československého průmyslu v letech 1913–1938 a některé otázky sociálně politické' (Basic Trends of Development of Czechoslovak Industry 1913–1938 and some Social and Political Questions), *ČSČH*, XII (1964).

Dokumenty o protilidové a protinárodní politice T. G. Masaryka (Documents on the anti-popular and anti-national policy of T. G. Masaryk) (Praha, 1953).

DuBois, J. E. *The devil's chemists, 24 Conspirators of the International Farben Cartel who Manufactured Wars* (Boston, 1952).

Duisberg, C. *Abhandlungen, Vorträge und Reden aus den Jahren 1922–1933* (Berlin, 1933).

Dunning, J. H. *American Investment in British Manufacturing Industry* (London, 1958).

Studies in International Investment (London, 1970).

DuPont, B. G. *E. I. duPont de Nemours and Company: A History, 1902–1920* (Boston, 1920).

Dutt, R. Palme *Fascism and Social Revolution* (London, 1934).

World Politics 1918–1936 (London, 1936).

The Crisis of Britain and the British Empire (London, 1953).

Dutton, W. S. *DuPont – One Hundred and Forty Years* (New York, 1949).

Edwards, C. D. *Economic and Political Aspects of International Cartels*, Senate Committee Print – 78th Congress 2nd Session – Monograph No. 1, Committee on Military Affairs, Subcommittee on War Mobilization (Washington, 1944).

A Cartel Policy for the United Nations (Washington, 1946).

Control of Cartels and Monopolies (New York, 1967).
Cartelisation in Western Europe (U.S. Department of State, June 1968).
Einzig, P. *World Finance 1935–1937* (London, 1937).
Appeasement (London, 1941).
Eisler, P. *Monopoly v hutnictví kapitalistického Československa* (Monopoly in the Metallurgical Industry of Capitalist Czechoslovakia) (Praha, 1955).
Monopoly v hornictví kapitalistického Československa (Monopoly in the Mining Industry of Capitalist Czechoslovakia) (Praha, 1956).
Monopoly v chemickém průmyslu kapitalistického Československa (Monopoly in the Chemical Industry of Capitalist Czechoslovakia) (Praha, 1959).
Europe's Trade: A study of the Trade of European countries with Each Other and the Rest of the World, League of Nations (Geneva, 1941).
Feinstein, Ch. H. (ed.). *Socialism, Capitalism and Economic Growth* (Cambridge, 1967).
Fiez, R. *Die Veränderugen in der Wirtschaftsstruktur und das Problem der internationalen Kapitalanlagen* (Berlin, 1946).
Fomin, V. I. *Agressiya fashistskoí Germanii v Evrope, 1933–1939gg.* (Moscow, 1963).
Friedländer, N. *The legal position of Cartels and Concerns in Europe* (Zürich, 1938).
Fuchs, G. *Gegen Hitler und Henlein* (Berlin, 1961).
Gajan, K. *Německý imperialismus a československo-německé vztahy v letech 1918–1921* (German Imperialism and Czechoslovak–German Relations 1918–1921) (Praha, 1962).
Gajanová, A. 'Příspěvek k objasnění příčin roztržky v táboře české buržoasie v roce 1934' (The Reasons for Discord in the Camp of the Czech Bourgeoisie in 1934), *ČSČH*, IV (1956).
'K některým otázkám mezinárodního postavení předmnichovské ČSR' (Some Problems of the International Situation of Pre-Munich Czechoslovakia), *ČSČH*, IX (1961).
Dvojí tvář (Two Faces) (Praha, 1962).
ČSR a středoevropská politika velmocí 1918–1938 (Czechoslovakia and Central European Policy of the Great Powers) (Praha, 1967).
Gedye, G. E. R. *Fallen Bastions* (London, 1939).
Gollan, J. *The British Political System* (London, 1954).
Gottwald, K. *Spisy* (Works), I–VIII (Praha, 1951–3).
Grosfeld, L. *Panstwo przedwrzesniowe w sluzbie monopoli kapitalistycznych* (The Pre-September Government in the Service of Capitalist Monopolies) (Warsaw, 1951).
Gross, Hermann. 'Die Wirtschaftskräfte Südosteuropas und Deutschlands', *Leipziger Vierteljahresschriften für Südosteuropa*, 1, 4 (1931).
Südosteuropa. Bau und Entwicklung der Wirtschaft (Leipzig, 1937).

Günther, G. *Lebenserinnerungen* (Wien, 1936).
Haber, L. F. *The Chemical Industry 1900–1930* (Oxford, 1971).
Hájek, J. S. *Mnichov* (Munich) (Praha, 1958).
Hausmann, F. *Der Wandel des internationalen Kartellbegriffs* (Bern, 1947).
Haxey, S. *Tory M.P.* (London, 1939).
Heinemann, M. *Britain's Coal* (London, 1944).
Heinig, K. *Geschichte der I. G. Farben* (Berlin, 1958).
Hejda, J. 'Komu patří československý průmysl' (Who owns Czechoslovak industry), *Přítomnost*, v (1927).
Hertz, F. O. *The Economic Problems of Danubian States* (London, 1947).
Hexner, E. *The International Steel Cartel* (Chapel Hill, 1943).
International Cartels (Chapel Hill, 1946).
Hobson, J. A. *Imperialism: A Study* (London, 1948).
Hoffmann, W. G. 'Die unverteilten Gewinne der Kapitalgesellschaften in Deutschland', *Zeitschrift für die gesamte Staatswissenschaft*, 115 (1959).
Hospodářská politika čs. průmyslu v letech 1918–1928 (Economic Policy of Czechoslovak Industry 1918–1928) (Praha, 1928).
Hospodářská politika čs. průmyslu v letech 1918–1938 (Economic Policy of Czechoslovak Industry 1918–1938) (Praha, 1938).
Hospodářství ČSR na jaře 1946 (The Economy of the Czechoslovak Republic in the Spring of 1946) (Praha, 1946).
I.C.I.: The History of Nobel's Explosives Co. Ltd. (London, 1939).
Imperial Chemical Industries. Compiled from a Survey by *The Times* (London, 1962).
Industrialization and Foreign Trade, League of Nations (Geneva, 1945).
International Capital Movements during the Inter-War Period, United Nations (Lake Success, 1949).
Iverson, C. *Aspects of the Theory of International Capital Movements* (Copenhagen, 1935).
Jindra, Z. *Germany and the Slavs in Central Europe* (Praha, 1961).
'Průmyslové monopoly v Rakousku-Uhersku' (Industrial Monopolies in Austria–Hungary), *ČSČH*, IV (1956).
'K otázce pronikání německého imperialismu na jihovýchod v období před r. 1918' (The Problem of the Penetration of German Imperialism into the Southeast in the Period before 1918) *Acta Universitatis Carolinae*, Philosophica et historica 2 (Praha, 1961).
Jindra, Z. and Křížek, J. *Beiträge zur neuesten Geschichte der mitteleuropäischen Völker* (Praha, 1960).
Jíša, V. and Vaněk, A. *Škodovy závody 1918–1938* (The Škoda-Works 1918–1938) (Praha, 1962).
Jones, W. R. *Minerals in Industry* (Harmondsworth, New York, 1943).

Jurković, B. *Das ausländische Kapital in Jugoslawien* (Berlin, 1941).
K dějinám závodu V. I. Lenina Plzeň (History of the V. I. Lenin Works in Plzeň) (Plzeň, 1962).
Kdo zavinil Mnichov (Who is Responsible for Munich) (Praha, 1959).
Kemp, M. C. 'Foreign Investment and the National Advantage', *Economic Record*, XXXVIII (March, 1962).
Kenwood, A. G. and Lougheed, A. L. *The Growth of the International Economy* (London, Sydney, 1971).
Keynes, J. M. *The Economic Consequences of the Peace* (London, 1920).
Kindersley, R. M. 'British Overseas Investments 1937', *Economic Journal* (1938).
Kindleberger, Ch. P. *International Short-term Capital Movements* (New York, 1937).
Foreign Trade and the National Economy (New Haven, 1963).
Kleinwächter, F. *Die Kartelle* (Innsbruck, 1883).
Klepetar, H. *Seit 1918...* (M. Ostrau, 1937).
Klimecký, V. *Strukturní změny v hospodářství světovém a československém* (Structural Changes in World Economy and the Czechoslovak Economy) (Praha, 1936).
König, H. 'Konzentration und Wachstum', *Zeitschrift für die gesamte Staatswissenschaft*, 115 (1959).
Kramer, J. *K dejinám priemyslu na Slovensku za prvej ČSR* (History of Industry in Slovakia during the First ČSR) (Bratislava, 1955).
Král, V. *O Masarykově a Benešově kontrarevoluční protisovětské politice* (Masaryk's and Beneš' Counter-revolutionary and Anti-Soviet Policy) (Praha, 1953).
Otázky hospodářského a soiálního vývoje v českých zemích v letech 1938–1945 (Questions of the Economic and Social Development of the Czech Lands 1938–1945), Vol. I (Praha, 1957), Vol. II (Praha, 1958).
'Recenze A. Teichové, Příspěvek k poznání zahraničních spojů finančního kapitálu v Československu' (Review of A. Teichová's Contribution on Foreign Links of Finance Capital in Czechoslovakia), *ČSČH*, 3, VI (1958).
'Monopoly v přípravě a uskutečnění Mnichova' (Monopolies prepare and realize Munich) in *Kdo zavinil Mnichov* (Praha, 1959).
'K úloze zahraničního kapitálu v Československu před r. 1938' (The Role of Foreign Capital in Czechoslovakia before 1938), *ČSČH*, 3, VII (1959).
'Československo a Mnichov' (Czechoslovakia and Munich), *ČSČH*, 3, VII (1959).
Politické strany a Mnichov (Political Parties and Munich) (Praha, 1961).

Kratochvil, K. *Bankéři* (Bankers) (Praha, 1962).
Kreibich, K. *Jak došlo v Německu k fašismu* (How Fascism Arose in Germany) (Praha, 1957).
Křen, J. *Mnichovská zrada* (The Munich Betrayal) (Praha, 1958).
Československo v období dočasné a relativní stabilisace kapitalismu (1924–29) (Czechoslovakia in the Period of Temporary and Relative Stabilisation of Capitalism (1924–29)) (Praha, 1957).
Krofta, K. *E. Beneš a československá zahraniční politika 1924–1933* (E. Beneš and Czechoslovak Foreign Policy 1924–1933) (Praha, 1934).
Kruliš-Randa, I. 'Situace železářského průmyslu' (The Situation of the Iron Industry), *Hospodářský rozhled* (Economic Review) (24 May 1928).
Kuczynski, J. *Die Geschichte und Lage der Arbeiter unter Kapitalismus*, Vol. 16: *Studien zur Geschichte des staatsmonopolistischen Kapitalismus in Deutschland 1918–1945* (Berlin, 1963).
Kuznets, S. 'Quantitative Aspects of the Economic Growth of Nations: VI. Long-Term Trends in Capital Formation Proportions', *Economic Development and Cultural Change*, IX, 4/2 (July 1961).
Economic Growth and Structure (London, 1966).
Modern Economic Growth, Rate, Structure and Spread (New Haven, 1966).
Kvaček, R. *Osudná mise* (Fateful Mission) (Praha, 1958).
Nad Evropou zataženo (Clouds over Europe) (Praha, 1966).
Lamer, M. *Weltwirtschaftliche Verflechtungen Südslaviens* (Zagreb, 1933).
Lammers, C. *Review of legislation on cartels and trusts*, League of Nations (Geneva, 1927).
Landau, Z. and Tomaszewski, J. *Kapitaly obce w Polsce 1918–1939* (Foreign Capital in Poland 1918–1939) (Warsaw, 1964).
Lehár, B. *Dějiny Baťova koncernu (1894–1945)* (The History of the Baťa Works) (Praha, 1960).
Lenin, V. I. *The Development of Capitalism in Russia*, Collected Works, 3 (London, 1960).
Imperialism, the Highest Stage of Capitalism. A Popular Outline, Collected Works, 22 (London, 1964).
Lewinsohn, R. *Das Geld in der Politik* (Berlin, 1931).
Die Umschichtung der europäischen Vermögen (Berlin, 1925).
Lewis, C. *The International Accounts* (New York, 1927).
America's Stake in International Investments (Washington, 1938).
Nazi Europe and World Trade (New York, 1941).
United States and Foreign Investment Problems (New York, 1948).
Liefmann, R. *Cartels, Concerns and Trusts* (London, 1932).

Lipták, L. 'Podrobenie slovenského priemyslu německým kapitálom v čase fašistického panstva' (The Subjugation of Slovak Industry by German Capital during the Fascist Rule), *Historický časopis* (Historical Journal), III/1 (1955).

Lund, P. J. and Holden, K. *An Economic Study of Private Sector Gross Fixed Capital Formation in the U.K., 1923–1938* (Oxford Economic Papers n.s. XX, 1).

Lutz, F. A. and Hague, D. C. (eds.). *The Theory of Capital* (New York, 1961).

MacGregor, D. H. *International Cartels*, League of Nations (Geneva, 1927).

Maiwald, K. 'Pokus o provisorní sestavení indexu průmyslové výroby v ČSR' (An Attempt to Compile a Provisional Index of Industrial Production in the ČSR), *Statistický obzor* (Statistical Horizon), XII/9–10.

Maleček, K. *Hospodářská diktatura koncernů* (The Economic Dictate of Concerns) (Praha, 1948).

Mantoux, E. *The Carthaginian Peace or the Economic Consequences of Mr Keynes* (1952).

Marx, K. *Das Kapital*, I–III (Berlin, 1947, 1948, 1949).

Zur Kritik der politischen Ökonomie, K. Marx, F. Engels, Werke 13 (Berlin, 1964).

Grundrisse der Kritik der politischen Ökonomie (Berlin, 1953).

Theorien über den Mehrwert (Berlin, 1956).

Die Klassenkämpfe in Frankreich 1848 bis 1850, K. Marx, F. Engels, Werke 7 (Berlin, 1964).

Matveev, V. A. *Proval myunkhenskoĭ politiki, 1938–1939 gg.* (Moscow, 1955).

Mayall, L. K. *International Cartels* (Tokyo, 1951).

Meinhardt, W. *Entwicklung und Aufbau der Glühlampenindustrie* (Berlin, 1932).

Mills, D. C. *Price, Quantity Interactions in Business Cycles* (New York, 1946).

Mitrany, D. *The Effect of the War in Southeast Europe* (New Haven, 1936).

Mittasch, A. *Geschichte der Ammoniaksynthese* (Weinheim, 1951).

Moltke, K. *Krämer der Kriege. Die 5. Kolonne der Monopole* (Berlin, 1953).

Morton, F. *Die Rothschilds. Porträt einer Familie* (München, 1962).

Moulton, H. G. and Pasvolsky, L. *War Debts and World Prosperity* (Washington, 1932).

Mowat, C. L. *Britain between the Wars 1918–1940* (London, 1955).

Müller, K. *Der Kapitalimport* (St Gallen, 1947).

Myrdal, G. *An International Economy, Problems and Prospects* (New York, 1956).

Na obranu republiky proti fašismu a válce (Defence of the Republic against Fascism and War) (Praha, 1955).

Nekrich, A. M. *Politika angliiskogo imperializma v Evrope, oktyabr' 1938–sentyabr' 1939* (Moscow, 1955).

Němec, Zd. 'Zápas o využitie slovenských medených rúd v rokoch 1918–1938' (The Struggle for the Utilisation of Slovakian Copper 1918–1938), *Nové obzory* (New Horizons) (1966/8).

'Výskum vývoja slovenského železnorudného banictva v rokoch 1918–1938' (Research on the Development of Slovakian Iron Ore Mining), *Ekonomický časopis Slovenské akademie vied* (Economic Journal of the Slovak Academy of Sciences) (Bratislava, 1967).

'Poznámky k problematice sestrojení indexu československé průmyslové výroby v letech 1918–1938' (The Problem of Compiling an Index of Czechoslovak Industrial Production), *ČSČH*, XIV (1966).

Němci proti Hitlerovi (The Germans against Hitler) (Praha, 1961).

Německý imperialismus proti ČSR (1918–1939) (German Imperialism against the ČSR (1918–1939)) (Praha, 1962).

Nicolson, H. *Peacemaking 1919* (London, 1933).

Norden, A. *Zákulisí německého imperialismu* (The Background of German Imperialism) (Brno, 1950).

Novák, M. *Vysoká hra* (High Stakes) (Ústí n.L., 1966).

Nurkse, R. *Internationale Kapitalbewegungen* (Vienna, 1935).

Problems of Capital Formation in Underdeveloped Countries (Oxford, 1953).

Obermann, K. *Die Beziehungen des amerikanischen Imperialismus zum deutschen Imperialismus in der Zeit der Weimarer Republik (1918–1925)* (Berlin, 1952).

Obradović, S. D. *La politique commerciale de la Yougoslavie* (Belgrade, 1939).

O československé zahraniční politice 1918–1939 (Czechoslovak Foreign Policy 1918–1939) (Praha, 1956).

Olivová, V. *Československo-sovětské vztahy v letech 1918–1922* (Czechoslovak–Soviet Relations in 1918–1922) (Praha, 1957).

Olšovský, R., Průcha, V., Gebauerová, H., Dobrý, A. and Pražský, A. *Přehled hospodářského vývoje Československa v letech 1918–1945* (Survey of Economic Development in Czechoslovakia) (Praha, 1961).

Olšovský, R., Průcha, V., Gebauerová, H., Pražský, A., Dobrý, A. and Faltus, J. *Přehled hospodářského vývoje Československa v letech 1918–1945*, Second revised edition (Praha, 1963).

Olšovský, R. *Světový obchod a Československo 1918–1938* (World Trade and Czechoslovakia) (Praha, 1961).

Pronikání německého imperialismu do jihovýchodní Evropy (*období 1890–1940*) (The Penetration of German Imperialism into Southeast Europe (Period 1890–1940)) (Praha, 1963).

Otáhal, M. *Dělnické hnutí na Ostravsku v letech 1917–1921* (The Working Class Movement in Ostrava in 1917–1921) (Ostrava, 1955).

Palmer, A. *The Lands Between: A History of East-Central Europe since the Congress of Vienna* (London, 1960).

Pátek, J. 'Poznámky k některým problémům v československo-rakouských vztazích na počátku světové hospodářské krize' (Comments on some Problems in Czechoslovak–Austrian Relations at the Beginning of the World Economic Crisis), *Sborník Vysoké školy pedagogické* (Collected Studies of the University of Education), Historie II (Praha, 1959).

PEP, *Economic Development in South-East Europe* (London, 1945).

Petráň, J. and Fuchs, V. *90 let práce a bojů* (90 Years of Work and Struggle) (Praha, 1961).

Pimper, A. *České obchodní banky za války a po válce* (*1914–1928*) (Czech Commercial Banks during the War and after the War) (Praha, 1929).

Hospodářská krise a banky (Economic Crisis and Banks) (Praha, 1934).

Piper, W. *Grundprobleme des wirtschaftlichen Wachstums in einigen Suedosteuropaeischen Laendern in der Zwischenkriegszeit* (Berlin, 1961).

Píšek, Fr. and Jeníček, L. *Nauka o materiálu* (Science of Materials), III, 2 (Praha, 1962).

Plhal, J. 'Kartelové spojení československého finančního kapitálu s mezinárodními monopoly v letech 1926–září 1938' (Cartel Connections of Czechoslovak Finance Capital with International Monopolies from 1926 to September 1938), *Sborník Vysoké školy pedagogické* (Collected Studies of the University of Education), Historie II (Praha, 1959).

Plummer, A. *International Combines in Modern Industry* (London, 1949).

Raw Materials or War Materials? (London, 1937).

Postavení ČSR ve světovém hospodářství (Position of the ČSR in the World Economy) (Praha, 1956).

Prasolov, S. I. *Československo v době ohrožení fašismem a hitlerovskou agresí* (*1933–1937*) (Czechoslovakia in the Period of Fascist and Hitlerite Aggression) (Praha, 1956).

'Chekhoslovakiya v g. ekonomicheskogo krizisa (1930–1933)', *Ucheniye zapiski instituta slaviyanovyedeniya*, XII (1956).

Přehled československých dějin (Survey of Czechoslovak History), III (Praha, 1960).

Přehled nejnovějších dějin (Survey of Recent History), I, II (Praha, 1962, 1963).

Pribram, K. *Cartel Problems* (Washington, 1935).

Purš, J. 'Použití parních strojů v průmyslu v českých zemích v období nástupu imperialismu' (The Employment of Steam-engineIs in ndustry in the Czech Lands in the Period before the Rise of Imperialism), *ČSČH*, III, 3 (1955).

Radandt, H. 'Die IG Farbenindustrie A.G. und Südosteuropa bis 1938', *Jahrbuch für Wirtschaftsgeschichte*, Teil III (1966).

Radandt, H., Zumpe, L. and Puchert, B. 'Zur Rolle des deutschen Monopolkapitals bei der Okkupation im zweiten Weltkrieg', *Bulletin des Arbeitskreises 'Zweiter Weltkrieg'*, 3 (1963).

Rašín, A. *Finanční a hospodářská politika Československa do konce roku 1921* (Financial and Economic Policy of Czechoslovakia to the End of 1921) (Praha, 1922).

Raupach, H. *Wirtschaft und Politik in Ost-Europa* (Berlin, 1968).

'The Impact of the Great Depression in Eastern Europe', *Journal of Contemporary History*, 4, 4 (1969).

Read, J. *Explosives* (London, 1932).

Reader, W. J. *Imperial Chemical Industries: A History* (London, 1971).

Reimann, G. *Patents for Hitler* (London, 1945).

Richardson, J. H. *British Economic Foreign Policy* (London, 1937).

Richta, R. (ed.). *Civilizace na rozcestí* (Civilization at the Crossroads). Third revised edition (Praha, 1969).

Rieker, K. 'Die Konzentrationsentwicklung in der gewerblichen Wirtschaft', *Tradition*, 5, 3 (1960).

Říha, O. *Hospodářský a sociálně-politický vývoj Československa 1790–1945* (Economic and Socio-Political Development of Czechoslovakia 1790–1945) (Praha, 1945).

Ohlas Říjnové revoluce v ČSR (Repercussions of the October Revolution in the ČSR) (Praha, 1957).

Rochester, A. *Rulers of America* (London, n.d.).

Roller, M. *Dějiny Rumunska* (History of Romania) (Praha, 1957).

Rosenstein-Rodan, P. N. 'Problems of Industrialization of Eastern and Southeastern Europe', *The Economic Journal* (1943).

Rothschild, K. W. *Austria's Economic Development between the Two Wars* (London, 1947).

Rothstein, A. *The Munich Conspiracy* (London, 1938).

Sasuly, R. *I. G. Farben* (New York, 1947).

Šauer, L. *Co nám říkají data o průmyslové výrobě* (What do Facts about Industrial Production tell us) (Praha, 1940).

Sborník Luděk Pik 1876–1936 (Luděk Pik *Festschrift*) (Plzeň, 1926).

Schmidt, P. *Statist auf diplomatischer Bühne* 1923–1925 (Wien, 1953).

Scott, J. D. *Vickers* (London, 1962).

Seton-Watson, R. W. *A History of the Czechs and Slovaks* (London, 1943).

Slánský, R. *Stati a projevy* (Articles and Speeches), I (Praha, 1951).

Šnejdárek, A. *Německý imperialismus proti ČSR* (German Imperialism against the ČSR) (Praha, 1958).

Solodnikov, V. *Vyvoz kapitala* (Moscow, 1957).

Sonnemann, R. 'Über die Duisberg-Denkschrift aus dem Jahre 1915', *Jahrbuch für Wirtschaftsgeschichte*, Part III (1966).

Spiru, B. *Freiheit, die sie meinen* (Berlin, 1957).

Stalin, J. V. *Leninism* (London, 1940).

Štamberger, W. *Kolonie proti imperialismu* (Colonies against Imperialism) (Praha, 1951).

Stambrook, F. G. 'The German–Austrian Customs Union Project of 1931', *Journal of Central European Affairs*, XXI (1961).

'A British Proposal for the Danubian States: the Customs Union Project of 1932', *The Slavonic and East European Review*, XLII, 98 (December, 1963).

Stočes, B. *Dvacetpět let Báňské a hutní společnosti* (Twenty-five Years of the Mining and Metallurgic Company) (Praha, 1931).

Stočes, F. *Postavení zemědělské malovýroby za kapitalistické ČSR* (Agricultural Small Scale Production in Capitalist Czechoslovakia) (Praha, 1958).

Stocking, G. W. *Workable Competition and Antitrust Policy* (Nashville, 1961).

Stocking, G. W. and Watkins, M. W. *Cartels in Action* (New York, 1947).

Cartels or Competition (New York, 1947).

Monopoly and Free Enterprise (New York, 1951).

Sto let kladenských železáren (One Hundred Years of the Kladno Iron Works) (Praha, 1959).

Sto let Spolku pro chemickou a hutní výrobu v Ústí nad Labem 1856–1956 (One Hundred Years of the Association for Chemical and Metallurgical Production in Ústí nad Labem 1856–1956) (Ústí nad Labem, 1956).

Strhan, M. *Kríza priemyslu na Slovensku v rokoch 1921–1923, počiatky odbúravania slovenského priemyslu* (The Crisis of Industry in Slovakia 1921–1923, the Beginnings of the Dismantlement of Slovak Industry) (Bratislava, 1960).

'Odbúravanie banského a železárského priemyslu na Slovensku v rokoch 1921–1923' (The Dismantlement of the Mining and Iron Industry in Slovakia 1921–1923), *Historický časopis* (Historical Journal), IV (1954).

Svennilson, I. *Growth and Stagnation in the European Economy* (Geneva, 1954).

Teich, M. 'Zu einigen Fragen der historischen Entwicklung der wissenschaftlich-technischen Revolution', *Jahrbuch für Wirtschaftsgeschichte*, Teil II (1966).

Teichová, A. 'Hospodářské kořeny prohitlerovské politiky britské buržoasie v předvečer druhé světové války' (The Economic Roots of the Pro-Hitlerite Policy of the British Bourgeoisie on the Eve of the Second World War), *ČSČH* (1954).

'O výdělečné činnosti členů poslanecké sněmovny ve volebním období 1929–1935' (Deputies in the Czechoslovak Parliament and their Business Interests in the Electoral Period 1929–1935), *ČSČH*, I (1955).

'Příspěvek k poznání zahraničních spojů finančního kapitálu v Československu' (Foreign Links of Finance Capital in Czechoslovakia), *Sborník Vysoké školy pedagogické* (Collected Studies of the University of Education), Filosofie-historie (Philosophy-History), I (Praha, 1957).

'Über das Eindringen des deutschen Finanzkapitals in das Wirtschaftsleben der Tschechoslowakei vor dem Münchener Diktat', *Zeitschrift für Geschichtswissenschaft*, v, 6 (1957).

'K úloze zahraničního kapitálu v československém hospodářství před Mnichovem' (The Role of Foreign Capital in the Czechoslovak Economy before Munich), *ČSČH*, I (1959).

'Die bürgerliche Tschechoslowakei im System des Imperialismus (1928–1938)', *Geschichte in der Schule*, Heft 6 (1959).

'K otázce kartelové politiky německých monopolů v Československu před Mnichovem' (The Problems of the Cartel Policy of German Monopolies in Czechoslovakia before Munich) *Kdo zavinil Mnichov* (Praha, 1959) – also in German, English and Russian.

'Die geheimen britisch–deutschen Ausgleichsversuche am Vorabend des zweiten Weltkrieges', *Zeitschrift für Geschichtswissenschaft*, VII, 4 (1959).

'Britská zahraniční politika a anglo-francouszká sovětská jednání v roce 1939' (British Foreign Policy and the Anglo-French–Soviet Negotiations in 1939), *Sborník Vysoké školy pedagogické* (Collected Studies of the University of Education), Historie II (Praha, 1959).

'Great Britain in European Affairs', *Historica* III (Praha, 1961).

'Zur Aussenpolitik Grossbritanniens am Vorabend des zweiten Weltkrieges', *Zeitschrift für Geschichtswissenschaft*, IX, 6 (1961).

'Über die Beziehungen des deutschen Imperialismus zur deutschen Minderheit in der Tschechoslowakei (1918–1933)', *Wissenschaftliche Zeitschrift der Friedrich-Schiller-Universität*, Jena, Gesellschafts- und Sprachwissenschaftliche Reihe, Heft 2 (1965).

'Zur Verflechtung der monopolkapitalistischen innen- und aussenpolitischen Interessen in der vormünchener Tschechoslowakischen Republik' in *Monopole und Staat in Deutschland 1917–1945* (Berlin, 1966).

'Die Rolle des Auslandskapitals in der Berg- und Hüttenwerks-Gesellschaft AG in der Tschechoslowakei 1918–1938', *Tradition*, 3 (1967).

'Poznámky k působení československého železářského kartelu na Slovensku mezi oběma světovými válkami k vývoji průmyslových oblastí' (The Effects of the Czechoslovak Steel Cartel on the Development of Industrial Areas in Slovakia between the Two World Wars), *Colloquium on Problems of Eastern Slovakia's Industrial Areas 1900–1950* (Košice, 1967).

'Die Rolle des Auslandskapitals in der Stahl- und Eisenindustrie der vormünchener Tschechoslowakei', *Historica* XVII (Praha, 1969).

The Royal Dutch Petroleum Co. 1890–1950 (The Hague, 1950).

Thorez, M. *France To-day and the People's Front* (London, 1936).

Toms, M. and Hájek, M. *Teorie stádií ekonomického růstu* (Theory of the Stages of Economic Growth), publication of the Economic Institute of the Czechoslovak Academy of Sciences No. 16: Studie z teorie ekonomického růstu (Studies in the Theory of Economic Growth) (Praha, 1966).

Tschierschky, S. *Review of the legislation concerning economic agreements*, League of Nations (Geneva, 1932).

Ubiria, M., Kadlec, V. and Matas, J. *Peněžní a úvěrová soustava Československa za kapitalismu* (Monetary and Credit System of Czechoslovakia under Capitalism) (Praha, 1958).

Urban, Z. *Příručka k dějinám Československa v letech 1919–1948* (Handbook of the History of Czechoslovakia 1918–1948) (Praha, 1959).

Ústřední svaz československých průmyslníků v roce 1934 (Central Association of Czechoslovak Industrialists in 1934) (Praha).

Valenta, J. 'K počátkům internacionalistického směru v dělnickém hnutí na Ostravsku a Těšínsku v letech 1918–1920' (The Beginnings of Internationalism in the Working Class Movement of Ostrava and Těšín in 1918–1920), *Slezský sborník* (Silesian Collection) (Opava, 1961).

'Plány německé buržoasie na neutralizaci Ostravska a Těšínska v letech 1918–1920' (Plans for the Neutralization of Ostrava and Těšín by the German Bourgeoisie in 1918–1920), *Slezský sborník* (Silesian Collection) (Opava, 1960).

Varga, E. S. *Kapitalismus dvacátého století* (Capitalism of the Twentieth Century) (Praha, 1962).

Veselý, J. *Vznik a charakter předmnichovského Československa* (Origin and Character of the Pre-Munich Czechoslovakia) (Praha, 1958).
Vogel, G. *Agrarpolitik der Monopole* (Berlin, 1957).
Wagner, R. *Panství kapitalistických monopolů v ČSR* (The Rule of Capitalist Monopolies in ČSR) (Praha, 1958).
Weirich, M. *Staré a nové Československo* (Old and New Czechoslovakia) (Praha, 1938–9).
Wellisz, L. *Foreign Capital in Poland* (London, 1938).
Wendt, B.-J. *Appeasement 1938: Wirtschaftliche Rezession und Mitteleuropa*, Hamburger Studien zur neueren Geschichte, Vol. 5 (1966).
München 1938: England zwischen Hitler und Preussen, Hamburger Studien zur neueren Geschichte, Vol. 3 (1965).
Werth, A. *France and Munich* (London, 1939).
The Destiny of France (London, 1937).
Whittleslay, Ch. R. *National Interest and International Cartels* (New York, 1946).
Whitney, S. N. *Antitrust Policies*, 2 Vols. (New York, 1958).
Wiedenfeld, K. *Cartels and Combines*, League of Nations (Geneva, 1927).
Wille, H. H. *Nafta* (Oil) (Praha, 1962).
Wilson, Ch. *The History of Unilever*, I, II (London, 1954), III (New York, 1968).
Young, E. P. *Czechoslovakia: Keystone of Peace and Democracy* (London, 1938).
Za chléb, práci, půdu a svobodu (Bread, Work, Land and Freedom) (Praha, 1954).
'Zehn Jahre Friedensarbeit der Škodawerke', *Prager Presse* (Sonderbeilage, 13 May 1928).

Index

NOTES

(1) The index includes, as fully as possible, business organizations in Czechoslovakia mentioned in the book with cross-references to their English names. In some entries the Czech and Slovak title or its corresponding English term is inserted in brackets, e.g. Agrarian Bank (Agrární banka), Poldina huť (Poldi Works).

In the case of the largest chemical combine, Association for Chemical and Metallurgical Production, the abbreviated name of Spolek (pro chemickou a hutní výrobu) is adopted.

(2) Abbreviations used in the text and the index refer to:

joint-stock company

A.G.	Aktiengesellschaft	(German)
a.s. akc. spol.	akciová společnost	(Czech)
r.t.	részvénytársaság	(Hungarian)
úč. spol.	účastinná spoločnosť	(Slovak)

limited liability company

G.m.b.H.	Gesellschaft mit beschränkter Haftung	(German)
N.V.	Naamloose Venootschap	(Dutch)
S.A.	Société Anonyme	(French)
s. s r.o. spol. s r.o.	společnost s ručením omezeným	(Czech)
sp. z o. odp(ow).	spółka z ograniczoną odpowiedzialnością	(Polish)

others

bří.	bratří (Czech) brothers
dř.	dříve (Czech) formerly

(3) Entries beginning with č (read cz), š (read sh) and ž (read zh) follow the Czech method of alphabetization.

A.G. der Eisen- und Stahlwerke vorm. Georg Fischer 247
A.s. Červenokostelecké a erlašské přádelny a tkalcovny, *see* Červený Kostelec Spinning and Weaving Mills
A.s. dř. Coburg horní a hutní závody v Bratislavě, *see* Coburg Mining and Metallurgic Works
A.s. dříve Škodovy závody, *see* Škoda-Works
Acetic spol. s r.o., *see* Tarboard Cartel

INDEX

Accounting Office for Tyres, Axles and Gear Wheelsets 231–2
Agrarian Bank (Agrární banka) 219–20
  Bank for Commerce and Industry, formerly Länderbank 341
  Explosia 284
  French capital, links to 341
Akciová společnost pro zpracování draselnatých louhů v Kolíně, *see* Company for the Processing of Caustic Potash in Kolín
Akciové železárny v Hrádku u Rokycan, *see* Hrádek-Rokycany Iron Works
Albania, *see* Czechoslovakia and Albania
Allgemeine Credit Bank 136
Allgemeine Elektrizitätsgesellschaft (AEG) 218, 270
Alliance Assurance Co. Ltd 82–3, 87
Alpine, *see* Österreichische Alpine Montangesellschaft
Als Thom Company 218
Aluminium Export Verband 262
Anglo-Czechoslovak Bank (Anglo-československá banka) 113
  Anglo-International Bank 350
  Harriman & Co. 350
  Kooperativa 350
  Liechtenstein, Prince 350
  Petscheks 350
  Prague Credit Institute, merger with 350
  Samuel & Co. 350
  Schichts 350
  Škoda-Works 350
  see also Anglo-Czechoslovak and Prague Credit Bank
Anglo-Czechoslovak and Prague Credit Bank (Anglo-československá a Pražská úvěrní banka) 301–2, 366–7
  Bank of England 350–1, 356
  British capital, links to 350–6 *passim*
  Škoda-Works 203, 206–10, 356
  West European banks, links to 367
Anglo-German Naval Treaty 187
Anglo-International Bank
  Anglo-Czechoslovak Bank 350
  Bank of England 350
Apollo 296–7
Apollo-Nafta 296–7
Arciéries Réunies de Burbach-Eich Dudelange (ARBED) 140
armaments 193, 196, 198
Association for Chemical and Metallurgical Production, *see under* Spolek (pro chemickou a hutní výrobu)
Association of Copper and Brass Works 261
Association of Czechoslovak Producers of Malleable Tube Fittings, etc. 247n, 248n
L'Association nationale des porteurs français de valeurs mobilières 376
Aubrun, J., industrialist 100, 211–12
Auer Company (Auerova spol. s r.o.) 274–5
Austria 15
  Anglo-American capital 121
  Anschluss 31, 36, 47, 91, 159, 187, 242, 246, 310, 349, 376
  banking system 105
  see Czechoslovakia and Austria
Austrian Syndicate of Wholesalers 164
Austro-Hungarian Empire, *see* Austro-Hungarian Monarchy
Austro-Hungarian Monarchy 20, 24, 71, 79, 93, 100, 119, 138, 225–6, 238, 284, 302–3, 337, 370
  iron and steel cartel 71, 93, 110, 119
  railway materials cartel 224–5

BHS, *see* Mining and Metallurgic Company
Bablik Brothers, Firm of (Vienna) 166
Bačinský, E., politician 297
Badische Anilin A.G. 315
balance of payments 7, 9, 12–13, 19, 23, 28
Bank for Commerce and Industry, formerly Länderbank
  Agrarian Bank 341
  Banque des Pays de l'Europe Centrale 345, 348–9
  French capital, links to 341, 343, 348–50
  industrial financing 348–9
  West European banks, links to 367
Bank of England
  Anglo-International Bank 350
  Anglo-Czechoslovak and Prague Credit Bank 351
  Škoda-Works, loan to 215
Banka pro obchod a průmysl, dř. Länderbanka, *see* Bank for Commerce and Industry, formerly Länderbank

banking, foreign investment in
American 350, 366
Belgian 121, 345, 356–7
British 350–7 *passim*
French 341–50 *passim*
Italian 356
Banque de Bruxelles: Czech Escompte Bank and Credit Institute 121, 357
Banque de France 204
Banque des Pays de l'Europe Centrale
Bank for Commerce and Industry, formerly Länderbank 345, 348–9
Zentraleuropäische Länderbank, Niederlassung Wien 345, 348
Báňská a hutní společnost, *see* Mining and Metallurgic Company
Baring Brothers: Czechoslovak government, loan to 376
Bataafsche Petroleum Maatschappij 298
Bechert & Co., Wire Nail and Screw Factory and Steelworkers (továrna na drátěnky, šrouby a ocelárna a.s.) 116n, 250n
Bělohříbek, J., banker 122
Beneš, E., statesman 195, 196, 197, 293, 369
Bentlin Chemical Factories (Bentlinovy chemické továrny a.s.) 294n
Beran, J., politician 293
Bergwerksprodukte G.m.b.H. 258
Berliner Gasglühlichtwerke Richard Goetschke A.G. 275
Berliner Handelsgesellschaft 120, 123, 127, 132
Bickford-Smith, L.W., industrialist 288, 291
Bierwes, H., industrialist and banker 125, 131
Biuro Rozdzielcze Zjednoczonych Polskich Walcowni Cynku 254
Blacha Cynkowa sp. z o. odpow. 255–6
Blumberg & Rindskopf 320
Bohemia, *see* Czech Lands
Boschan, Firm of (Vienna) 166
Boucherie, general 292
Branka Iron Works (Branecké železárny a.s.) 135
Brenner, V., industrialist 146
Brevillier & Co. und A. Urban und Söhne 249–50
British Empire as an investment area 3, 377, 382
British Iron and Steel Federation 187
see International Steel Cartel, British Group
British Overseas Bank: Czech Bank Union 356
British Shell Union Oil Corporation 298
Brown Boveri et Cie. 220
Budějovice Screw Factory (Budějovická továrna na šrouby) 117n
Bulgaria 15, 29
see Czechoslovakia and Bulgaria
Bulín, H., banker 106

Cable Factory 268
capital export(s), motive of 7–8
cartel and foreign investment 61
Carter, H. E., banker 351
Centra 307
see Van den Bergh, Schichts
Central and Southeast(ern) Europe
as investment area 1–3, 15–16, 290, 377
capital interests
American 296
Belgian 294, 356
British 86–7, 91–2, 294, 310 (*see also* Dutch)
Dutch 297–8, 310
French 118, 137, 202, 294, 296–9, 350
Swiss 297–8 (*see also* Dutch)
German sphere of influence 2–3, 35, 54–7, 132, 182–3, 217, 323
international competition, area of xix–xx, 54, 91, 118, 137, 153, 173, 197, 214, 294, 350, 381–2
Viennese banks, role of 345
West European capital, withdrawal of 35–6, 91–2, 117–18, 216–17, 288–94, 381
Central Bureau of Czechoslovak Wire and Wire Nail Manufacturers 116, 133, 156
Central Powers 1, 93, 225, 303
Chambre Syndicale des Constructions d'Automobiles 265
Champigneul, V., industrialist 196, 212
Chanove, J., industrialist 100

Chanzy, J., industrialist 212
chemical industry, foreign investment in 44, 45, 50, 278–94
  and cartel ties 326
  Belgian 279–84, 294
  British 284, 286–94
  French 284, 286–8, 290–4
  German 287, 294
chemicals
  alkalis 278, 282–4, 294
  ammonia 111, 288, 315–16
  ammonium carbonate 316
  ammonium chloride 316, 320
  ammonium sulphate 331, 335
  calcium cyanamide 317
  dyestuffs 278, 314, 316
  explosives 278, 284–94 *passim*, 314–15
  fertilizers 284, 315–17
  hydrogen peroxide 320–1, 331
  pharmaceutical products 314
  potassium hydrogen sulphate 335
  sodium hydrogen sulphate 335
Clémenceau, P., politician 292
Coburg Mining and Metallurgic Works 110, 114–15
combines
  cooperation-competition 110
  multinational 9
Comité des Forges 102, 140
Compagnie Internationale pour l'Exportation des Products Tréfilés, Société Cooperative, *see* International Wire Export Company (IWECO)
Company for the Production of Mineral Oils 297n
Company for the Processing of Caustic Potash in Kolín 294n
Comptoir de Vente de la Sidérurgie Belge 'Cosibel' 141, 160
  see European Steel Cartel (ESC), Founder Groups
Comptoir Sidérurgie de France 141, 160
  see European Steel Cartel (ESC), Founder Groups
concentration 9
Continental Society for the Iron Trade Kern & Co. 88, 90, 110, 112–13
Convention Internationale de l'Industrie de l'Azote 315
Cooper, F. d'Arcy, industrialist 310
Crédit Lyonnais 81, 103
Crossé-Brissac, P., industrialist 212
Czech Bank Union 113, 367
  Belgian capital, links to 345, 356
  British capital, links to 356
  British Overseas Bank 356
  Central and Southeast(ern) Europe 356
  Dresdner Bank, interest of 357
  Italian capital, links to 356
  Österreichische Credit-Anstalt-Wiener-Bankverein 356
  Société Générale de Belgique 345, 356
  West European banks, links to 367
Czech Escompte Bank and Credit Institute 113, 341n, 366–7
  Banque de Bruxelles 121, 357
  Belgian capital, links to 220, 357
  Central and Southeast(ern) Europe 366
  Dresdner Bank, interest of 357
  Kleinwort Sons & Co. 121, 357
  Niederösterreichische Escompte Gesellschaft 120–1, 134, 345
  Poldina huť 134
  Prague Iron Company 120–3
  West European banks, links to 367
  Živnostenská Bank 121–3, 131, 357
Czech Lands (i.e. Bohemia, Moravia, Silesia) 25, 92, 135, 244, 336
Czech Metal Works Robert Zinn, Engels & Co. 255n, 256n
Czech-Moravian-Kolben-Daněk Company 190, 194, 218–19
  motor-car manufacture 263, 265
  see also Škoda-Works and Czech-Moravian-Kolben-Daněk Company, Westinghouse Electric
Czechoslovak Armaments Works 216
  copper and brass materials 261
  Czechoslovak state as shareholder 199
  Škoda-Works as shareholder 199
Czechoslovak Factories for Nitrogen Products 111, 316
Czechoslovak-French automobile cartel 263–5
Czechoslovak Oder Shipping Company 89, 111

Czechoslovak state, shareholder
Anglo-Czechoslovak Bank 350
Czechoslovak Armaments Works 199
Škoda-Works 203
Czechoslovakia
Bohemia, *see* Czech Lands
capital competition, Anglo-French and German 128, 380–1
capital import-export, balance of 27, 380
Cartel Act 57
cartel policy, problems of 57–61 *passim*
Cartel Register 58, 314, 322
Currency Separation Act 98
foreign enterprises 51–3
foreign policy 54
foreign trade 171, 175, 186, 206, 274, 326–35
French-Soviet-Czechoslovak Treaty 239
industries, concentration of 25, 40, 378
joint-stock companies, law on 98
Mining Law 82
Nostrification Act 98, 103, 122, 339–40
Silesia, *see* Czech Lands
Slovakia, *see under separate heading*
world economy, position in 24–9
Czechoslovakia, banks in
concentration of 25, 40, 337, 342, 378
foreign and domestic capital 342
Germans banks, relations with 343
largest joint-stock banks 338–41
Viennese banks, relations with 98, 105, 337, 340, 342 3
West European capital, participation of 340–67 *passim*
see also banking, foreign investment in; *also under individual banks*
Czechoslovakia, foreign investment in
estimation 36–53, 378
opportunities for 25–6, 378
sources of study of 30–4
territorial distribution, order of 379
territorial origin, problem of, 46–7, 379
withdrawal of 35–6, 91–2, 117–18, 216–17, 289–94, 381
see individual industries and banks, also under Czechoslovakia, banks in; banking, foreign investment in; Czechoslovakia, foreign longterm loans in
Czechoslovakia, foreign longterm loans in
American 370–1, 373
British 367, 371, 376
French 367, 374–6
Czechoslovakia, political parties in
Agrarian Party 209, 292–3
National Democratic Party 209, 349
Social Democratic Party 205, 209
Czechoslovakia and
Albania
cartel relations, steel 167
Austria
capital relations 120, 132
cartel relations, railway materials 226–32, 238–9, 242; steel 164–6, 168
Viennese banks, position of 98, 105, 337, 340, 342–3, 356–7
Bulgaria
cartel relations, steel 167, 170
Central and Southeast(ern) Europe
alkalis 282–4, 294
capital expansion 133
chemical cartels 326
explosives 284–94 *passim*
horseshoe nails 252
large joint-stock banks 256, 366
mineral oil 295–9
motor-cars 263
nitrogen products 316
railway materials 226, 228–32, 242–4
soap and edible fats 299–310 *passim*
steel 148–9, 162–3, 167–8, 171–3, 182–7
zinc products 253–5, 258, 260
West European capital, withdrawal of 35–6, 91–2, 117–18, 216–17, 289–94, 381
France
alliance 146
Czechoslovak-Polish frontier dispute 97
French capital, withdrawal of 117–18, 216–17

Czechoslovakia and France (*cont.*)
French Military Mission 97, 205, 369
Treaty of 1918 369
Germany
border regions, annexation of 135
capital relations 55, 132
cartel relations 57–9, 380–1; chemicals 314–35 *passim*; railway materials 227–32, 238–9; steel 148–52, 323, 326
Czech Lands, occupation of xix, 135
economic competition 55, 326
German banks, penetration efforts of 343, 357
German banks, short-term loans by 367
German property, liquidation of 102, 122
Nazi aggression, preparation of 321
Great Britain
British capital, withdrawal of 91–2, 289–94
Hungary
cartel relations, railway materials 228, 230
cartel relations, steel 168–71
Poland
cartel relations, railway materials 228, 230
cartel relations, steel 173–5
frontier dispute 93–101 *passim*
Romania
cartel relations, railway materials 229
cartel relations, steel 146, 167, 170
Yugoslavia
cartel relations; railway materials 228, 230
cartel relations, steel 147–8, 167, 170
ČKD, *see under* Czech-Moravian-Kolben-Daněk Company
Červený Kostelec Spinning and Weaving Mills 121n
Česká banka Union, *see* Czech Bank Union
Česká eskomptní banka a úvěrní ústav, *see* Czech Escompte Bank and Credit Institute
České závody kovů Robert Zinn, Engels a spol. a.s., *see* Czech Metal Works Robert Zinn Engels & Co. Ltd.
Českomoravská Kolben-Daněk a.s., *see* Czech-Moravian-Kolben-Daněk Company
Československá plavební a.s. oderská, *see* Czechoslovak Oder Shipping Company
Československá zbrojovka a.s. Brno, *see* Czechoslovak Armaments Works
Československé továrny na dusíkaté látky akc. spol., *see* Czechoslovak Factories for Nitrogen Products

DEN-Gruppe 315, 317, 320, 331
see also International Nitrogen Cartel
Deutsche Bank 118, 125, 127, 134–5, 343, 367
Deutsche Drahtwalzwerke A.G. 159
Deutsche Gold- und Silberscheideanstalt 321
Deutsche Stahlgemeinschaft 228–30, 245
Deutscher Lokomotiv-Radsatz Verband 231–2, 239, 242
Drahtverband G.m.b.H. 156
Dickson, A. G. M., banker 351
Dresdner Bank 33, 92, 343, 349, 357
Dubský, Albrecht, firm of 117n
Dudek, Brothers (Dudkové, Bří. a.s.) 255n, 256n, 258n
Duisberg, C., industrialist 54
Dvořáček, J., banker 293, 336
Dynamit A.G. (DAG) 284–5
Dynamit Nobel (Bratislava), connections with 287, 294
I.G. Farben(industrie), integration into 284–5
Dynamit Nobel (Bratislava)
Dynamit A.G. (DAG), connections with 287, 294
Explosia, participation in 287; shares take-over by ICI in 287

Eisner & Levit, firm of 116n
Electric Lamps Manufacturers' Association of Great Britain 271
electrical industry 193
foreign investment in 44, 45, 50, 217–21
Elektra Light Bulb Factory (akciová továrna na žárovky) 272

Elektrotechna Company for Low-tension Techniques (a.s. pro slaboproudou techniku) 218
engineering industry
diversity of products 221
metallurgy 192–3
see also electrical industry; mechanical engineering, foreign investment in
Engliš, K., banker and politician 106, 205, 349
Entente internationale de l'Acier (EIA) 256–7
see European Steel Cartel (ESC)
Entente Powers, *see* Great Powers (of the Entente)
Eruptiva a.s. 290n
European Steel Cartel (ESC) 137–63 *passim*, 172
Austrian Group 151, 166, 170, 172, 175
Belgian Group 140, 150
Central and Southeast(ern) Europe 148–9, 162–3, 167–8, 172–3, 182–3, 187
Central European Group (ZEG) 142–54 *passim*, 162–3, 168–9, 171–3, 175, 183; *see also* Selling Agency
Czechoslovak Group 141–83 *passim*; *see also* Selling Agency
Founder Groups 139–41, 144, 148, 153, 159–60, 176, 178–9
French Group 140, 150
German Group 151–2
home markets 141
Hungarian Group 170, 172, 175
Luxemburg Group 140, 150
National Groups 141–3, 152–3
patents and technology 141
Polish Group 175, 179
Saar Group 139
see also Österreichische Alpine Montangesellschaft, Rimamurány Iron Works (RIMA), Selling Agency (of the United Czechoslovak Iron Works), national cartel
Evans, R. H., industrialist 296
Evidence Bureau for Cables (Evidenční kancelář kabeloven v Praze) 268
Evidence Bureau for Forged Pieces (Evidenční kancelář pro výkovy) 245
Evidence Bureau of Screw Mills for Polished Products (Evidenční kancelář továren na lesklé šroubové zboží) 248–9
Evidenzbureau der österreichischen Schraubenfabriken 251
Explosia, a.s. pro průmysl výbušnin (Explosives Industry)
Dynamit Nobel (Bratislava), links with 287
foundation 284
ICI, relations with 287–94
Société Centrale de Dynamite, relations with 286–8, 290–4
Spolek, shares exchange with 289
Export Convention of Rolled Zinc Products 255

Fajfrlík, K., banker 106
Fanto Works (Fantovy závody a.s.) 297–8
Féderation Nationale de l'Automobile, du Cycle, de l'Aéronautique et des Industries qui s'y rattachent 263–4
Feierabend, L., businessman and politician 293
Feith, N., industrialist 297
Ferra (metal trading company) 112
First Brno Engineering Co. 373, 375
First World War, after
international investment, importance of 9–29 *passim*
revolutionary waves 367
Successor States 67, 93, 96–7, 226, 283, 316, 370, 373
First World War, before
Austrian iron cartel, *see* Austro-Hungarian Monarchy
bulb cartel 271
Central and Southeast(ern) Europe 2–3
Czech capital, export of 20
German capital, export of 20
international steel cartels 138; *see also* International Railmakers Association (IRMA)
Fischer, Karel, firm of 117n
Fittingsverband 247
Flandin, P. E., politician 376
Flipo, P., industrialist 297
food industry, foreign investment in 45, 50, 349, 351, 366

Fosfa, společnost pro obchod výrobky chemického průmyslu, spol. s r.o. (Superphosphate Syndicate of the Czechoslovak Works) 323
Fournier, industrialist 99, 106
France
  creditor 1
  debtor 1
  foreign investment of 1–6 *passim*
France and
  Czechoslovakia, *see* Czechoslovakia and France
  Germany, *see* Germany and France
Franke & Scholz Metalworking Factories (kovodělné závody v Rýmařově) 256n
Freja Bergwerks Aktiebolaget 88
Fürstenberg, J., banker 120

Germany 15, 31
  cartel policy 58–9, 61, 380–1
  creditor 1
  debtor 1
  foreign investment in 2
  foreign investment of 1
  Nazi Party (NSDAP) 125
  Reichsgruppe Industrie 127
Germany and
  Czechoslovakia, *see* Czechoslovakia and Germany
  France: Ruhr, occupation of 139, 214
  Great Britain: differences between 380–1
  Western Europe 186, 380–1
glass, porcelain and ceramics industry, foreign investment in 45, 50, 366
Great Britain
  Central and Southeast(ern) Europe 381–2
  creditor 1
  debtor 1
  foreign investment of 1–5, 9–11
Great Britain and
  Czechoslovakia, *see* Czechoslovakia and Great Britain
  Germany, *see* Germany and Great Britain
Great Depression, *see* world economic crisis
Great Powers (of the Entente) 3, 14–15, 96–7, 370, 377–8
Grupy Francuskich Koncernow Naftowych 'Małopolski' 297
Günther, G., industrialist 93, 99, 106, 112, 128, 146
Guest, Keen & Nettlefolds Ltd 251
Gutmanns, bankers
  Gutmann, W. 79
  Rothschilds 77–82
  Vítkovice Mining and Foundry Works 77–80, 82
Gutmanns, coal traders, Živnostenská Bank 82

Habsburg, F. von, archduke 93, 100
Habsburg Empire, *see* Austro-Hungarian Monarchy
Habsburg Monarchy, *see* Austro-Hungarian Monarchy
Hague Reparation Conference 370
Hajts, industrialist 146
Harriman & Co., bankers, Anglo-Czechoslovak Bank 350
Helika 248–9
Hirsch, Richard, firm of 116n
Hitler, A. 58, 91
Hlasko, V., industrialist 297
Hoffmann, F., industrialist 194
Holland, foreign investment of 2
Holzschraubenverband G.m.b.H. 251
Hoover, H., mining engineer and politician 96
Horganyhengermü r.t. 254
Hornád Iron Works (Krompachy) 75, 110
Hořovský, industrialist 146, 158
Hospodářský svaz mědáren a mosazáren v Československu, *see* Association of Copper and Brass Works
Hrádek-Rokycany Iron Works 72n, 199
Huet, R., industrialist 100
Hungarian State Iron Works 'Diosgyör' 168
Hungary 15, 31
  see Czechoslovakia and Hungary
Husák, O., general 292, 297
Huty Bankowé 100
Hydroxygen, formerly Dr Allers and Heller 294n

I.G. Farben(industrie) 54n, 278, 284–5, 312, 315, 322, 331

I.G. Farben (industrie) (*cont.*)
Central and Southeast(ern) Europe 316
Dynamit Nobel (Bratislava), indirect links to 287, 294
Spolek, attempts at penetration of 294
Imperial Chemical Industries (ICI) 315
Central and Southeast(ern) Europe xx, 288–94 *passim*, 378
Explosia-ICI settlement, Solvay's meditation in 294
Explosia, relations with 287–94
Spolek 284, 292
Synthesia, participation in 288, 292
Živnostenská Bank 292–3
industrial unrest 96
insurance companies, foreign investment in 43
International Aluminium Cartel, Czechoslovakia, impact on 262
International Bismuth Convention 322
International Bulb Cartel 269–70, 272–4
International Cable Development Corporation 266, 268–9
International Cartel for the Protection and Sale of Wire Products 156
international cartels in electric industry
British Government Enquiry 271–2
Central and Southeast(ern) Europe 275–6
Czechoslovakia, participation of 266–76 *passim*
Temporary National Economic Committee (U.S.A.) investigation 272–3
international cartels of copper and brass products, Czechoslovak participation in 261–2
international cartels of engineering products
Czechoslovakia participation of 244–53 *passim*
fittings and plugs 248, 252–3
horseshoe nails 252
screws and bolts 248
wire goods 248
wood screws 249–51
international cartels of railway materials
Central and Southeast(ern) Europe 226, 228–32, 238, 244
Czechoslovakia, participation of 224–44 *passim*
international chemical cartels
Czechoslovak foreign trade 326, 331, 335
Czechoslovakia, participation of 314–35 *passim*
nitrogen products 315–17, 320, 331; *see* International Nitrogen Cartel
Nobel industries and duPont Patents and Process Agreement 285
world-wide structure 313–14
international chemical cartels and foreign capital in Czechoslovak chemical industry 326
International General Electric Company (IGE) 270–1
International Malleable Fittings Association 248
International Nitrogen Cartel 112, 315–17, 320–1, 331
International Railmakers Association (IRMA) 138, 162, 224
Central European Group (ZEG) 154–5
Polish Group 154
International Standard Electric Corporation 220, 271
International Steel Cartel (ISC) 90, 140, 159, 160, 172, 175–87, 239
American Group 160, 187
British Group 160, 179, 187
Czechoslovak steel industry 176–88
Internationaler Walzdrahtverband (IWV) 159
Munich Agreement 188
see also European Steel Cartel (ESC)
International Tube Cartel 162
International Wire Export Company (IWECO) 156, 162
International Wire Rod Association, *see* Internationaler Walzdrahtverband (IWV)
International Wood Screw Syndicate 250–1
International Zinc Cartel 258–9
international zinc cartels
Central and Southeast(ern) Europe 254–5, 258, 260
Czechoslovakia, participation of 253–60 *passim*

Internationale Wasserstoffsuperoxyd-Konvention 320–1
Internationaler Walzdrahtverband (IWV) 157–8, 162
  Austrian Group 158–9
  Central and Southeast(ern) Europe 158
  Central European Group (ZEG) 157–9
  Czechoslovak Group 158
  German Group 158–9
  Hungarian Group 158
  Polish Group 158
investment, international
  longterm, importance of 9–29 *passim*
  short-term 2
Iron and Iron Sheet Company Union 75, 110
iron and steel
  blast-furnaces in Slovakia 110
  combines, competition between 71, 76, 81, 128–31, 134–5; cooperation between 75–6, 89–90
  high-quality steel 134
  monopoly structure 70–5
Iron Works Rotava-Nýdek 113–14, *see* Schneider et Cie. and Petzold, C. T. & Co.; Mining and Metallurgic Company

Jahn, J., banker 106
Jihokarpatská rafinerie minerálních olejů a obchodní a.s., *see* South Carpathian Oil Refinery
Jouza (iron works) 72n
Jurgens Vereenigde Fabrieken N.V., Anton 302, 306
  Schichts, settlement with 307
  Van den Bergh, fusion with 307-8
  see also Margarine Union N.V.

Kablo, Cable and Wire Rope Factory (akciová továrna na káble a drátěná lana) 268
Keitel, W., general 91
Kidder, Peabody and Co., Czechoslovak government loan 371
Kleinwort Sons & Co., Czech Escompte Bank and Credit Institute 121
Koninklijke Nederlandsche Hoogovense Staalfabrieken N.V. (Ijmuiden) 151
Kontinentale Eisenhandelsgesellschaft Kern & Co. 164, 166; *see also* Continental Society for the Iron Trade Kern & Co.
Kontinentální společnost pro obchod železem Kern a spol. v Praze, *see* Continental Society for the Iron Trade Kern & Co.
Konvyka, Fr., firm of 250n
Kooperativa 292–3
  Anglo-Czechoslovak Bank 350
Koula, V., industrialist 194
Kovařík, Fr., politician 205
Králodvorská cementárna (cement plant at Králův Dvůr) 125, 130–1
Kratochvil, firm of 117n
Kruliš-Randa, O., industrialist 107, 109, 116, 156, 158
Krupp, Friedrich A. G. 194, 214
Křížík-Chaudoir, mědárna, kabelovna a elektrotechnické závody (Copper, Cable and Electrotechnical Works) a.s.
  copper and brass materials 261
  domestic cable cartel 268
  international ties 218–19
Kuhn, Loeb and Co., Prague loan 373
Kux, W., banker and industrialist 121, 134

Lacroix, diplomat 292
Latin America, *see* South America
Laurin and Klement (car works) 199
Le Groupement des Industries Sidérurgiques Luxembourgeoises, *see* International Steel Cartel (ISC), Founder Groups
Le Play, industrialist 292
League of Nations 7, 30, 139
Lefèvre, E., industrialist 283
Lepercq, A., industrialist and banker 107, 109–10, 136, 158, 211–12
Lever Brothers Ltd 302, 306, 308
  Lever, W. 302
  Margarine Union N.V., merger with 309
  see Unilever Ltd London and Unilever N.V. Rotterdam
Lever Bros. and Unilever 302
  Central and Southeast(ern) Europe xx, 299, 302, 309–10, 378
  establishment of 309–10

Lever Bros. and Unilever (*cont.*)
Schichts, take-over of 309–10
Škoda-Works, loan to 215
Liechtenstein, Prince, Anglo-Czechoslovak Bank 350
Lisman, F. J. and Co., First Brno Machine Company, loan to 373
Little Entente xx, 14–25 *passim*, 34–5, 153
Czechoslovakia 55, 146
loans
government 2, 7
interest on 9, 11, 123
longterm 7–8
war 4
Locarno Treaty 139
Loevenstein, K., industrialist 202, 209
Lubricant Sales Ltd 298

McGowan, H. (Sir Harry), industrialist 286, 291
magnesite 135–6
Magnezitový priemysel (Magnesite Industry) úč. spol. (Bratislava) 136
Mannesmann-Röhrenwerke (Chomutov) 124, 132
Mannesmann-Röhrenwerke A.G. 115, 134, 166
Nazi Party (NSDAP) 125
Prague Iron Company 119, 123–7, 130–2
Marek & Jasanský (woodscrew manufacturers) 250n
Margarine Union N.V. 308
Lever Brothers, merger with 309, *see also* Unilever Ltd London and Unilever N.V. Rotterdam
Schichts, arrangement with 308
Martin's Bank, Škoda-Works, loan to 215
Masaryk, T. G., statesman 197
Mátyás, industrialist 159
Mayrisch, E., industrialist 140
mechanical engineering, foreign investment in 44, 45, 50
British 215–16
French 193–217 *passim*, *see also* Škoda-Works
Mědárny Čechy (Copper Works Bohemia) 72n
Metal Rolling Mills 135, 254–6
Meyer, A., industrialist 140
mineral oil industry, foreign investment in 45, 50
American 296
British 298
Dutch 297–8
French 296–7
Swiss 297–8
Mining and Metallurgic Company 71–2, 76, 81, 89–90, 92–118 *passim*, 156–7, 177
Austrian capital, decline of 103–5
board of directors, composition of 106; reorganization of 100
copper and brass materials 261
French capital, links to 100–1, 109, 117–18
Iron Works Rotava-Nýdek, merger with 113–14
magnesite products 136
Prague Iron Company 119, 128–31
Schneider et Cie. 99–118 *passim*, 190–1, 197, 212
Škoda-Works, connection with 190–1
Vítkovice Mining and Foundry Works 71–2, 75–6, 81, 89–90
Živnostenská Bank 99, 100, 102–3, 106, 109, 118
mining and metallurgy, foreign investment in 44, 45, 50
American 134
Anglo-American 121
Austrian 114
Belgian 134
British 118, 134, 136
French 117–18, 128, 133, 136
German 125, 128
Swedish 116, 133
Mitchell, H. J., industrialist 290, 293
Mittelhausser, E. D. A., general 369
Moravia, *see* Czech Lands
Moravian-Ostrava Chemical Works (Moravsko-ostravské chemické závody) 321
Moravian-Silesian Electricity Power Plant (Moravsko-slezské elektrárny a.s. Moravská Ostrava) 111
Müller-Tele (iron works) 72n
Munich Agreement
balance of power, changes in 217, 381–2
economic roots 36
significance of xix, 381–2

Munich Agreement and
  International Steel Cartel (ISC) 188
  West European capital, withdrawal of 35–6, 91–2, 117–18, 216–17, 289–94
Mustad, O. and Son 133, 251

Naftaspol 296
National City Bank 371
  see also Kidder, Peabody and Co.
National Provincial Bank, Škoda-Works, loan to 215
N.V. Nederlandsche Petroleum Ind. Maatschappij 298
Neštěmice Solvay Works 283
  see Solvay et Cie., *also* Spolek
Neurath, L., banker 105
Niederösterreichische Escompte Gesellschaft
  Czech Escompte Bank and Credit Institute 120–1, 134, 345
  Poldina huť 134
  Prague Iron Company 119–21, 123, 127, 132
Niemeyer, O., banker 349
Nobels
  Nobel, A. 284
  Central and Southeast(ern) Europe 286
  Dynamit Nobel (Bratislava) *see under separate heading*
  Dynamit Nobel A.G. (Germany) 284; *see also* Dynamit A.G. (DAG)
  Dynamit Nobel A.G. (Vienna) 284, 286–7; *see also* Dynamit Nobel (Bratislava)
  Latin Group 284; *see also* Société Centrale de Dynamite
  Nobel Industries Ltd 284–6; *see also* Imperial Chemical Industries (ICI)
  Nobel's Explosives Company 284
  duPont de Nemours, E.I. & Co. 285–6
Norsk Hydro Elektrisk Kvaelstofaktieselskab 315
North Bohemian Electric Power Works 220
Novák, L., politician and industrialist 205
Nuremberg Trials 33, 91, 336

Ocelářský průmysl a.s. (Most) *see* Steel Industry (Most)
October Revolution 14, 367, 376
Österreichische Alpine Montangesellschaft 93, 119–20, 145, 148–51, 158–9, 164, 166–8, 170
Österreichische Berg- und Hüttenwerks-Gesellschaft A.G. 93
Österreichische Boden-Credit-Anstalt 93, 89–100, 279, 342
Österreichische Credit-Anstalt für Handel und Gewerbe 80, 342
Österreichische Credit-Anstalt-Wiener-Bankverein 105
  Czech Bank Union 356
  Société Générale de Belgique 345
Omnipol 202
Osram a.s. (Prague) 272
Osram G.m.b.H. (Berlin) 220, 270, 272
Ostia (chemical works) 297n
Ostranaft 297n

PŽS, *see* Prague Iron Company
Pánek (wire factory) Praha-Vysočany 117n
paper industry, foreign investment in 45
Paris Peace Conference 96
Pellé, M., general 369
Palliez, A., industrialist 297
Petscheks, bankers
  Anglo-Czechoslovak and Prague Credit Bank 350
  British capital, links to 356
Philips 220–1, 271–2
Phoebus, Industrial Company for the Development of Lighting 269, 272–4
Pik, L., politician 205
Plants for the Manufacture of Galvanized Metals – Bablík Brothers (Chomutov) 114
Poland xx, 5, 15, 27, 118
  foreign investment in 16–20
Poland and Czechoslovakia, *see* Czechoslovakia and Poland
Poldina huť (Poldi Works) 72n, 121, 133, 224n, 227, 230n, 231
  Czech Escompte Bank and Credit Institute 134
  Deutsche Bank, interest of 134–5
  Niederösterreichische Escompte Gesellschaft 134
  Prague Iron Company 134

Polish-Soviet War 96
duPont de Nemours, E.I. & Co., Nobel Industries 285–6
Pospíšil, V., banker 106, 122
Považsko-novomestoer Draht, Drahtstiften, Stahlgabel und Hufnägelwerke Adolf Reiss & Söhne 117n, 252
Prague Cable Factory 269n
Prague Credit Institute
  Anglo-Czechoslovak Bank, merger with 350
  see also Anglo-Czechoslovak and Prague Credit Bank
Prague Iron Company 71–2, 76, 93, 116, 119–37 *passim*, 157–8, 177
  Berliner Handelsgesellschaft 120, 123, 127
  controlling group 123
  Czech Escompte Bank and Credit Institute 120–2
  First World War, before 119
  Králodvorská cementárna 130–1
  Mannesmann-Röhrenwerke 119, 123–7, 130–2
  Mining and Metallurgic Company 119, 128–31
  Niederösterreichische Escompte Gesellschaft 119–21, 123, 127, 132
  ownership, after First World War 122, 128, 132
  Poldina huť 134
  screws, domestic cartel of 248–9
  Vítkovice Mining and Foundry Works 119, 128–31
  Živnostenská Bank 121–3, 131–2, 134
Pražská továrna na káble spol. s r.o., *see* Prague Cable Factory
Pražská železářská společnost, *see under* Prague Iron Company
Pražský úvěrní ústav, *see* Prague Credit Institute
Preiss, J., banker and industrialist 77, 103, 106, 122, 210, 282
Prodejna sdružených československých železáren a.s. Praha, *see* Selling Agency (of the United Czechoslovak Iron Works)
Prodejní kancelář sdružených ostravsko-karvínských kamenouhelných dolů s. s r.o., *see* Sales Bureau of the United Ostrava Karviná Collieries
Prodejní společnost mazacích olejů s r.o., *see* Lubricant Sales Ltd
Prodejní společnost pro řetězy a drátěné výrobky, *see* Sales Association for Chains and Wire Products
První brněnská strojírenská společnost, *see* First Brno Engineering Company, *see also* Lisman, F. J. and Co.
Přívoz Works of Mineral Oil Products (Přívozské závody minerálnćh olejů a.s.) 297, 298n

Rafinerie cukru v Krásném Březně, *see* Sugar Refinery in Krásné Březno
Rasche, K., banker 33, 92
rationalization 113, 133, 205–6
Reitzes, bankers (Vienna) 135
Reşita 146
Rimamurány Iron Works (RIMA) 110, 148–9, 158, 168–70
Ringhoffer, F., industrialist 106
Ringhoffer-Tatra Works 265
Rist, Ch., economist and financier 349
Rochette, Christophe, industrialist 211–12
Roheisenverband 149–52
Rohstahlgemeinschaft, *see* European Steel Cartel (ESC)
Romania 15, 20, 27, 29
  foreign investment in 23–4
  Škoda-Works 206
  see Czechoslovakia and Romania
Rothschilds, bankers 80, 83
  Alliance Assurance Co. Ltd 82–3, 87
  Czechoslovak investments abroad 87
  Gutmanns, bankers 77 82
  London branch 77, 79
  Paris branch 77, 79
  Rothschild, E. 79, 92
  Rothschild, L. 79
  Vickers Ltd 86
  Vienna branch 77, 79–80, 91, 166
  Vítkovice Mining and Foundry Works 76–87, 90–2
Royal Dutch Petroleum Company 298
Royal Dutch Shell Company 298
Royal Institute of International Affairs 7
  foreign investment, survey of 7–8
Rütgers, Julius (Ostrava) 111

Russia
  foreign investment in Tsarist 14
  losses of investment in Soviet 14, 79, 378

Saint-Sauveur, industrialist 212
Sales Association for Chains and Wire Products 117, 133
Sales Association for Nitrogen Products Ltd. 111, 317, 323
Sales Bureau of the United Ostrava-Karviná Collieries 112, 131
Samuel & Co., bankers, Anglo-Czechoslovak Bank 350
Schauer, A., banker 208
Schicht, Jiří a.s. Ústí n.L., *see* Schichts
Schichts, soap and edible fats producers 299–312 *passim*
  Ampra 306
  Anglo-Czechoslovak Bank 350
  before First World War 302
  Centra as domestic competitor 307
  Central and Southeast(ern) Europe 299, 306, 308, 310
  Heima 303, 306
  Jurgens, settlement with 307
  Lever Bros. and Unilever, integration into 310
  Limmat Industrie- und Handels A.G. 303
  Margarine Union, arrangement with 308
  Orania 306
  Salia 306
  Schicht, F. 308–9
  Schicht, G. 303, 308–9
  Schicht, H. 303, 308–9
  Van den Bergh, settlement with 307
Schmiedestück-Vereinigung für den europäischen Kontinent G.m.b.H. 244–5
Schneider et Cie
  Central and Southeast(ern) Europe xx, 197, 378
  International Steel Cartel (ISC) 140
  Mining and Metallurgic Co. 99–118 *passim*, 190–1, 197, 212
  Petzold, C. T. & Co. (Paris Agreement) 113–14
  Rothschild groups 112–13
  Schneider, E. 102, 140, 196, 211–12
  Škoda-Works 190–216 *passim*
  L'Union Européenne Industrielle et Financière 100, 107, 109, 136, 199, 207–8, 211, 217, 341
Schoeller-Bleckmann Stahlwerke 166, 231–2, 242
Schwedische Patent-Hufnägelfabrik Hugo Tauber Nové Mesto nad Váhom G.m.b.H. 252
Schweizerische Gesellschaft für elektrische Industrie 220
Sdružení československých výrobců rourových spojek z kujné litiny a průchodních kohoutů ze šedé litiny v Praze, *see* Association of Czechoslovak Producers of Malleable Tube Fittings, etc.
Sdružení pro prodej dusíkatých látek s. s r.o., *see* Sales Association for Nitrogen Products
Second World War xix, 16–17, 21, 36, 87, 127, 175–6, 252, 256–7, 266, 323, 381
Selling Agency (of the United Czechoslovak Iron Works) 34, 66n, 71–5, 112, 116, 124–5, 129–30, 133
  foundation and composition 71–2
  national cartel 72, 137–76 *passim*
Semler, Simon (wire manufacturer) 116n
Severočeské elekrárny Podmokly, *see* North Bohemian Electric Power Works
Sheet Rolling Mill Ltd 114
Shell Products Ltd (Shell produkty minerálnch olejů a.s.) 298
Sieghart, R., banker and industrialist 103, 282
Siemens Company for the Production of Electrical Equipment (Siemens a.s. pro výrobu elektrických zařízení) 218
Siemens, Technical Industry Company (Siemens, technický průmysl a.s.) 218
Siemens and Halske 218, 220
Slovakia
  chemical plant, project of 291, 294
  iron industry, dismantlement of 110–11
  magnesite industry 136

Société Centrale de Dynamite 284
  Central and Southeast(ern) Europe 288–94 *passim*
  Explosia, role in 286–8, 290–4
  Synthesia, participation in 288
Société Electricité de Transporte de l'Europe Centrale S.A. 220
Société financière de Paris 296–7
Société française des pétroles de Tchécoslovaquie 296–7, 376
Société Franco-Polonaise 296
Société Générale de Belgique
  Czech Bank Union 345, 356
  Österreichische Credit-Anstalt-Wiener-Bankverein 345
Socony Vacuum Oil Company 296
Solvay et Cie. 111, 278–84, 292–4
  Central and Southeast(ern) Europe xx, 282–4, 294, 378
  Explosia-ICI settlement, mediation in 294
  I.G. Farben's infiltration of Spolek, opposition to 294
  Imperial Chemical Industries (ICI) 282–3, 288
  Spolek 279–84
Sonnenschein, A., industrialist 99, 128, 146–7
South America as investment area 3, 377, 381
South Carpathian Oil Refinery 296–7
Soviet Union 16, 159, 172, 238–9, 367
sphere(s) of influence 1, 93, 96, 127, 135, 340, 377
sphere(s) of interest, *see* sphere(s) of influence
Spojené Ašské barvírny, *see* United Aš Dye-Works
Spojené strojírny, *see* United Machine Factories
Spojené barvírny a smaltovny na kovové zboží a.s. v Praze 'Sfinx', *see* United Factories and Enamel Mills for Metal Goods in Prague 'Sfinx'
Spojené továrny pro výrobu hedvábí bratří Schielové, *see* United Factories for the Production of Silk Bros. Schiel
Spojené závody pro výroby karborunda a elektritu Nové Benátky, *see* United Works for the Production of Carborundum and Electrit
Společnost pro výrobu minerálních olejů s r.o., *see* Company for the Production of Mineral Oils
Spolek (pro chemickou a hutní výrobu) 111, 279–84, 288–9, 292, 294
  Explosia, shares exchange with 289
  I.G. Farben, attempts at penetration by 294
  Imperial Chemical Industries (ICI) 284, 292
  international cartels, 314, 316–17, 321–3, 326, 335
  largest chemical combine 294
  ownership, after First World War 279–82; before First World War 279
  Solvay et Cie 279–84
  Synthesia, shares exchange with 289
  Živnostenská Bank 279–84
Stahlwerks-Verband 139, 141, 144, 149, 160
  see European Steel Cartel (ESC), Founder Groups
Standard Elektrizitäts-Gesellschaft A.G. 220
Standard Oil Company 296
Steel Industry (Most) 116–17, 133–4, 157–8
Steinhal, Max, banker and industrialist 125
Stickstoff-Syndikat G.m.b.H. 315–17, 320
Stodola, K., politician 297
Successor States, *see* First World War, after
Súčtovací kancelář pro obruče, nápravy a soukolí, *see* Accounting Office for Tyres, Axles and Gear Wheelsets
Sugar Refinery in Krásné Březno 349
sugar refining, foreign investment in 45, 50, 351, 366
Sweden, foreign investment of 2
Switzerland, foreign investment of 2
Syndikat Polskich Hut Żelaznych 173
Synthesia, a.s. chemická továrna (Chemical Factory)
  foundation 288
  nitrogen products, cartelization of 288–9, 316
  Spolek, shares exchange with 289
  see also Explosia

ŠZ, *see* Škoda-Works
Šimonek, J., industrialist 209
Škoda-Works 100–1, 103, 190–1, 193–245 *passim*
  Anglo-Czechoslovak Bank 350
  Anglo-Czechoslovak Bank and Prague Credit Bank 203, 206–9, 356
  Bank of England 215
  British capital, links to 203, 206–9, 215–16, 350, 356
  British loans 215
  Central and Southeast(ern) Europe 202
  Czechoslovak Armaments Works, shareholder in 199
  Czechoslovak state, connections with 195–209 *passim*
  domestic cable cartel 268
  dominating engineering combine 194
  French capital, role of 216–17
  French loans 215, 375
  horizontal monopoly 202
  Lever Bros. and Unilever, loan by 215
  Martin's Bank, loan by 215
  Mining and Metallurgic Co., connections with 190–1
  motor-car manufacture 263–5
  National Provincial Bank, loan by 215
  ownership after First World War 196
  railway products 226, 231, 239, 242–4
  Romania 206
  Schneider et Cie 190–216 *passim*
  Syndicate Agreement 207–8
  Škoda, K. 196
Škoda-Works and Czech-Moravian-Kolben-Daněk Company
  electrical industry, competition in 218–19
  engineering cartel agreement 195, 202, 211, 219, 222
  fusion, question of 210
Šrobár, V., politician 205

Tarboard Cartel 323
Tatra-Závod a.s. (Tatra-Works) Praha-Kopřivnice 250n
technology 90
  role in chemical cartels 313
  sheet rolling mill 113–14
  wire mill 115
Telatko, Leopold, firm of 116n
Telegrafia, Telegraph- and Telephone Factory (továrna na telegrafy a telefony) 220
textile industry, foreign investment in 45, 50, 348–9, 366
'The Big Three' 71–6, 92, 110–16 *passim*, 128–37 *passim*, 146, 176–7, 181
  'Agreement' 73, 129–30, 137
  'Brno Agreement' 129
Thomson-Houston Company 272
Thyssen, F., industrialist 139
Tille, A., banker 106
Titangesellschaft G.m.b.H. 322
titanium cartel 322
Tournay-Solvay, E., industrialist 282
Továrna na káble a.s. Bratislava, *see* Cable Factory
Továrny na železo a plech a.s. Union Bratislava, *see* Iron and Iron Sheet Company Union

U.S.A., *see* United States of America
Uher, Josef a spol. 250n
Unilever Ltd London and Unilever N.V. Rotterdam 309
  see also Lever Bros. and Unilever
Union des lamineurs Belge de zinc 256–7
L'Union Européenne Industrielle et Financière, *see* Schneider et Cie.
United Aš Dye-Works 349
United Czechoslovak Iron Works 74–5, 128
  see also Selling Agency
United Factories and Enamel Mills for Metal Goods in Prague 'Sfinx' 348
United Factories for the Production of Silk Bros. Schiel 312n, 349
United Machine Factories 199
United States of America
  creditor 1, 4
  debtor 1, 4
  foreign investment of 2–4, 150
United Works for the Production of Carborundum and Electrit 348

Ústřední kancelář československých továren na drát a drátěné hřebíky akc. spol., *see* Central Bureau of Czechoslovak Wire and Wire Nail Manufacturers

VHHT, *see* Vítkovice Mining and Foundry Works
Vacuum Oil Company Ltd. (Prague) 296
Valečka, Fanny, firm of 117n
Válcovna plechů a.s., *see* Sheet Rolling Mill
Válcovny kovů a.s. Přívoz, *see* Metal Rolling Mills
Van den Bergh Fabrieken N.V. 302, 306
  Centra 307
  Jurgens, fusion with 307–8; *see also* Margarine Union N.V.
  Schichts, settlement with 307
Vaněk, V., banker 208, 297
vegetable oil industry, foreign investment in
  British 310
  Dutch 310
Veitscher Magnesitwerke 136
Vereinigte Stahlwerke 120, 139, 150, 162
Vereinigung der Magnesitwerke 136
Versailles Peace Treaty 102, 138, 153, 195–6, 286, 370
Vesta (Slovak oil industry) Ltd Prague 297n, 298n
Vicaire, A., industrialist 100
Vichr a spol. Praha-Duchcov 250n
Vickers Ltd 86, 194
Viškovský, K., politician 205
Vítkovice Mining and Foundry Works 37, 71–2, 76–92 *passim*, 110–12, 177
  British capital, links to 82–7
  Central and Southeast(ern) Europe 86–7, 91
  engineering products, domestic market of 245
  European economic relations 86, 91–2
  largest industrial combine 87
  Mining and Metallurgic Company 71–2, 75–6, 81, 89–90
  ownership, after First World War 77
  Prague Iron Company 119, 128–31
  railway products 226–8, 231, 242
  Rothschilds 76–87, 90–2
  screws, domestic cartel of 248–9
  Standstill Agreement 80
  Transfer Agreement 82–3
  vertical monopoly 88
  Živnostenská Bank 76–7, 81–2
Vítkovické horní a hutní těžířstvo, *see* Vítkovice Mining and Foundry Works
Vlasák, B., banker and politician 349
Voigtmann-Janovice, firm of 72n
VRUT Selling Agency for Wood Screws (prodejna šroubů do dřeva s. s r.o.) 250–1

Weinmann-Werke, Teplice-Šanov 255n, 258n
Wendel, G., industrialist 136
West-Bohemian Kaolin and Fire-Brick Manufacture and Slovak Magnesite Works 136
Westinghouse Electric Company 219, 273
Weyl, E., banker 100, 211
Wilson, A., industrialist 286
Winkler & Co., Chomutov 248
wood industry, foreign investment in 45, 50
working-class movement 96
World Economic Conference 186
world economic crisis 6, 11, 58, 61, 105, 118, 121, 150, 152–3, 247–8, 259–60, 342

Yugoslavia
  foreign investment in 21–3
  see Czechoslovakia and Yugoslavia

Zahn, Clement jr., firm of 269n
Zangen, W., banker and industrialist 127, 132
Západočeské závody kaolinové-šamotové a slovenské magnesitové, *see* West-Bohemian Kaolin and Fire-Brick Manufacture and Slovak Magnesite Works
Závody pro pozinkování kovů a.s. v Chomutově – Bří. Bablíkové, *see* Plants for the Manufacture of Galvanized Metals – Bablík Brothers

Zentraleuropäische Länderbank, Niederlassung Wien 345, 348
Zinkwalzwerkverband G.m.b.H. 253–8
Zjednoczone polskie fabryki śrub spółka z ogr. odp. 251
Žatec Horseshoe Nail Factory Mustad & Son (Žatecká továrna na podkováky Mustad & syn) 251–2
Železárny Rotava-Nýdek a.s., *see* Iron Works Rotava-Nýdek
Živnostenská Bank (Trade Bank)
  Central and Southeast(ern) Europe 366
  Czech Escompte Bank and Credit Institute 121–2, 131, 357
  Czech-Moravian-Kolben-Daněk Company 210–11, 219
  early history 337
  Explosia 284
  foreign influence 357, 366
  growth 343
  Gutmann brothers, coal traders 82
  I.G. Farben's infiltration of Spolek, opposition to 294
  Imperial Chemical Industries (ICI) 292–3, 366
  Mining and Metallurgic Company 99–100, 102–3, 106–7, 109, 118
  Philips 220, 272, 341, 366
  Poldina huť 134
  policy, two lines of 137
  Prague Iron Company 121–3, 131–2, 134
  Solvay et Cie 279–84, 341, 366
  Spolek 279, 284
  Škoda-Works 210–11
  Vítkovice Mining and Foundry Works 76–7, 81–2, 98

For EU product safety concerns, contact us at Calle de José Abascal, 56–1°,
28003 Madrid, Spain or eugpsr@cambridge.org.

www.ingramcontent.com/pod-product-compliance
Lightning Source LLC
LaVergne TN
LVHW090259210926
848480LV00001B/72
9780521073967